WITHDRAWN

HANDBOOK OF
COUNSELLING
PSYCHOLOGY

PRAISE FOR THE BOOK

'*The Handbook of Counselling Psychology* continues to be a key resource for people considering undertaking a career as a counselling psychologist, current students, and more experienced practitioners. It has continued to develop its focus over time and has justly earned a reputation as a classic text. It has consistently provided an excellent overview of the majority of topics which form the basis of counselling psychology. The latest edition has considered the major developments within counselling psychology and the writers have incorporated these into the book. Many of the chapters are thought-provoking and challenging. It is also well organized and very readable. This book deserves a place on the bookshelf of every counselling psychologist.'
Professor Rachel Tribe, Director of Professional Doctorate in Counselling Psychology and related programmes at the University of East London

'The profession of counselling psychology has matured greatly over recent years and the publication of the third edition of the *Handbook of Counselling Psychology* provides evidence of this. The contents of the *Handbook* cover key areas of theory and practice and I particularly welcome the inclusion of the theme of personal development and the key issue of reflexivity that is a particular philosophy and signifier of this profession. There is also a more coherent formulation of the strands of integration in relation to the range of theoretical ideas and practice based concerns in the profession. The articulation of future opportunities highlights some leading edge ideas of benefit to the field.'
Professor Vanja Orlans, Metanoia Institute and Middlesex University

'This book has done the almost impossible – improve on what was an informative and worthwhile second edition. It has achieved this by building on one of its strengths, which include the return of established and respected authors. This winning ingredient is mixed with experienced practitioners who have not previously written for the *Handbook*, making it a volume to savour and frequently return to because of its richness and substance. Sections such as "What is Counselling Psychology?" revisit a much answered question, not simply with one chapter, but with a multidimensional theme that considers this question from many angles. Indeed, a noticeable feature of this handbook is that each section, (whether it deals with a range of therapeutic approaches, aspects of difference or the future of counselling psychology) is imbued with chapters that engage the reader in an interaction with each author's practice and experience whilst also providing an in-depth critical approach of the domain.

'Similarly to the previous editions, I have enjoyed reading this third edition, especially the manner in which the writers link theory with practice. The consideration of forward-looking topical issues and debates critical to the survival and shape of our profession, such as the HPC and IAPT, contribute to making this edition a contemporary resource that will be consulted and referenced for some time to come.

'I recommend this well-structured and thought-provoking text that has a wide-ranging appeal, not just for those in the profession, but also for those who are interested in knowing more about the profession. In this way, it is not just educational but also an advert for our profession.'
Dr Gella Richards, Roehampton University, London

HANDBOOK OF
COUNSELLING
PSYCHOLOGY

Edited by
RAY WOOLFE, SHEELAGH STRAWBRIDGE,
BARBARA DOUGLAS AND WINDY DRYDEN

THIRD EDITION

Los Angeles | London | New Delhi
Singapore | Washington DC

First edition published 1996. Reprinted 1997, 1998, 2001
Second edition published 2003. Reprinted 2006, 2007
Third edition published 2010

SAGE Publications Ltd
1 Oliver's Yard
55 City Road
London EC1Y 1SP

SAGE Publications Inc.
2455 Teller Road
Thousand Oaks, California 91320

SAGE Publications India Pvt Ltd
B 1/I 1 Mohan Cooperative Industrial Area
Mathura Road
New Delhi 110 044

SAGE Publications Asia-Pacific Pte Ltd
33 Pekin Street #02-01
Far East Square
Singapore 048763

Library of Congress Control Number: 2009924450

British Library Cataloguing in Publication data

A catalogue record for this book is available from the British Library

ISBN 978-1-84787-078-0
ISBN 978-1-84787-079-7 (pbk)

Typeset by C&M Digitals (P) Ltd, Chennai, India
Printed in Great Britain by TJ International Ltd, Padstow, Cornwall
Printed on paper from sustainable resources

CONTENTS

LIST OF FIGURES

LIST OF TABLES

NOTES ON THE CONTRIBUTORS

Katrina Alilovic (Registered Counselling Psychologist (HPC); Chartered Psychologist (BPS)) has 15 years' experience working with individuals, couples, children and families and specializes in bereavement and post-trauma counselling. She trained in Australia as a Counselling Psychologist in the early 1990s and since then has worked in a variety of clinical settings, including employee assistance, policing, university counselling and private practice. Katrina now combines academic work with clinical practice in both the NHS and private practice. Among Katrina's previous writing is a chapter on the impact of suicide on children and families included in *Then, Now and Always* (Stokes, 2004), and articles focusing on children's bereavement experiences and personal therapy issues in the training of counselling psychologists.

Alan Bellamy chaired the Division of Counselling Psychology in 2004 and 2005 and was the editor of *Counselling Psychology Review* between 2002 and 2004. He served as the NHS Lead National Assessor for Counselling Psychology from 2004 to 2008 and represented the profession on a number of British Psychological Society and governmental committees and bodies during that time. He was also a senior member and an assessor for the BPS Register of Psychologists Specialising in Psychotherapy. Alan was a Consultant Counselling Psychologist working in NHS Adult Mental Health Services until leaving the NHS in 2008.

Simon Biggs is Professor of Social Gerontology and Director of the Institute of Gerontology at King's College London. His main interests include social theory, social policy and the study of adult identity, with a particular emphasis on midlife and late-life transitions. He has, with others, edited two special editions of the *Journal of Social Work Practice* on counselling and later life. His book *The Mature Imagination* (1999) examines therapeutic approaches to adult ageing. Prior to working in universities, he was a community psychologist, undertook Jungian psychotherapy, trained as a counsellor and in psychodrama. He is a member of the Division of Counselling Psychology of the British Psychological Society. He has links with Heidelberg and Helsinki Universities and is a fellow of the World Demographic Association.

Cassie Cooper is a practising Kleinian trained Psychoanalytic Psychotherapist and Counselling Psychologist with strong leaning towards Attachment Theory. A founder member and Fellow of The British Association for Counselling and Psychotherapy and an active member of The United Kingdom Council for Psychotherapy, she is the author of many papers on psychotherapy and counselling published in learned journals and has contributed chapters in text books on these subjects. The former Head of a University Diploma Course on Counselling, she continues to work full time as a psychotherapist and supervisor in the Greater London area and acts as a consultant to Carlton Television and the Metropolitan Police on counselling issues.

Sarah Corrie is a Chartered Psychologist (British Psychological Society) and Registered Clinical Psychologist (Health Professions Council) who has extensive experience in both public and private sector services. She runs her own practice as well as working as a freelance writer, trainer and lecturer. Sarah is Deputy Programme Director of the Postgraduate Diploma in Cognitive Behavioural Psychotherapy run by Central and North West London Mental Health NHS Foundation Trust in conjunction with Royal Holloway, University of London and is also a faculty member of the Professional Development Foundation. She received her undergraduate degree in Psychology and Counselling Psychology from the University of Surrey, her doctorate in Clinical Psychology from Canterbury Christchurch College and undertook her post-doctoral training in cognitive behaviour therapy at the University of Oxford. Before embarking on a career in psychology, Sarah worked in the performing arts and continues to be a member of Equity and the Imperial Society of Teachers of Dancing.

Dee Danchev is Pastoral Advisor at Nuffield College, Oxford and has worked as a university counsellor for over 15 years, first at Keele University and then later as Head of Service at the University of the Arts, London. She has had a parallel career in counsellor training, teaching on the Masters Degree in Counselling at Keele University and then on the Doctorate in Counselling Psychology programme at City University, London. She is currently an Examinations Moderator and Co-ordinator of Training for the British Psychological Society's Qualification in Counselling Psychology, a practice supervisor for the Metropolitan Police Service counsellors and has a small private practice in Oxford.

John Davy is a Registered Counselling, Educational and Health Psychologist (HPC) and a UKCP Registered Psychotherapist. He is a Chartered Psychologist and Associate Fellow of the British Psychological Society, and a founding member with Senior Practitioner Status of the BPS Register of Psychologists Specialising in Psychotherapy. John works in a child and adolescent mental health service with Cambridgeshire and Peterborough NHS Foundation Trust, and as a Partner with the Health Professions Council. His interests include psychotherapy integration and interplay, parental and infant mental health, domestic abuse and clinical supervision. John writes fiction and enjoys exploring fruitful connections between narrative, therapy, film and creative writing.

Barbara Douglas is a Chartered Psychologist, Registered Counselling Psychologist and Medical Historian. She currently works as Registrar for the British Psychological Society's Qualification in Counselling Psychology and in private practice. She is Chair of the Division of Counselling Psychology (2009–2011) and an Honorary Fellow of the University of Exeter. Barbara was formerly Senior Lecturer in Counselling Psychology at the University of the West of England and prior to that was Director of the North West Centre for Eating Disorders, in Association with Stockport Primary Care Trust. She completed her PhD in Medical History at the University of Exeter and has particular interest in the histories of both psychology and psychiatry.

Windy Dryden is Professor of Psychotherapeutic Studies, Professional and Community Education (PACE) at Goldsmiths College, University of London. Windy has authored or edited more than 140 books and edited 13 book series on counselling. His current professional interests lie in the area of using humour in counselling to promote client reflection, learning and change.

Zack Eleftheriadou has completed a BA in Psychology, MSc in Child Development, MA in the Psychology of Therapy and Counselling, has Diplomas in Infant Mental Health (Parent-Infant Clinic) and Eating Disorders (NCfED), is a BPS Chartered Psychologist, HPC Registered Psychologist and a Chartered Scientist, and a UKCP Reg. Integrative and Psychoanalytic Psychotherapist. She has written extensively in the area of cross-cultural work, including the book *Transcultural Counselling* (1994). She lectures widely in the field of cross-cultural therapy and child development. She is currently an infant observation and clinical supervisor for IATE, a Thesis Reader for various counselling psychology and psychotherapy courses and has a private clinical practice in North London. She is also staff psychotherapsit for the School of Life, London.

Ralph Goldstein pursued academic research into emotional learning theories and hormonal influences on animal brain and behaviour, funded by the UK Medical Research Council, and then took up a lecturing post at University College of Worcester. But the motivation for all this study was really to do clinical work with a Jungian orientation. He has also been chair of the Division of Counselling Psychology (2006–2007) and a member of the psychotherapy implementation group, which devised the Society's post-qualifying Register of Psychologists Specialising in Psychotherapy. Current research interests are mainly directed to the somewhat neglected field of emotions in psychology and psychotherapy.

Fiona Goudie is a Registered Clinical Psychologist (HPC) and Chartered Psychologist (BPS) and Associate Fellow of the British Psychological Society. She has been a clinical psychologist working with older people since 1986. She is the co-author, with Graham Stokes of *Working with Dementia* (1990) and the *Essential Dementia Care Handbook*

(2002). Since 1992 she has been Head of Older Adult Psychology, Psychological Health Sheffield. She became clinical director of the Older People's Functional Mental Illness and Community Directorate in Sheffield Health and Social Care Foundation Trust in 2005. Her research and clinical interests include reminiscence, depression in later life and the adaptation of psychological approaches to chronic ill health. Her longstanding involvement in lifespan and cohort approaches has been enhanced outside work through sporting, internet and cookery pursuits with her daughter Ailsa, aged 9.

Kristina Gyllensten is a Registered Counselling Psychologist, a Chartered Psychologist, a licensed CBT psychotherapist and a coach. She currently works as a psychologist, lecturer and researcher at a Centre for Cognitive Therapy in Gothenburg, Sweden and is also involved in a cognitive coaching centre providing coaching and training courses. Kristina completed her Doctorate in counselling psychology at City University, London focusing on the experiences of coaching and stress in the workplace. Her particular interests are workplace stress, stress management, gender and stress, and cognitive therapy and coaching, on which she has co-authored a number of articles and book chapters.

Diane Hammersley is a Chartered Counselling Psychologist, practicing as a psychotherapist, supervisor, co-ordinator of training and trainer. Having worked in a clinical and research team concerned with dependence on prescribed medication, she ran workshops around the UK. Later her research explored therapists' experience of clients who had been taking medication and how that impacted on the therapeutic process and how medication might be viewed more realistically and metaphorically. More recently she has developed a qualitative approach to assessments in child care proceedings as an independent expert witness, using creative approaches as well as interviews and observations with children, parents and carers. She has served on a number of BPS Boards and Committees and is a former Chair of the Division of Counselling Psychology.

Mary Brownesombe Heller is a Consultant Clinical Psychologist and Fellow of the British Psychoanalytic Society. She worked in the Health Service for over 25 years and is now in private practice, while retaining some NHS involvement. Having begun her professional life as a primary school teacher, she had thought to become an educational psychologist but found her clinical studies so interesting that she trained as a Clinical Psychologist instead, her Relate Counsellor background forming an invaluable adjunct to academic theory. Initially an eclectic clinician, she became increasingly interested in dynamics and the unconscious motivations underlying behaviour. She trained in psychoanalytic psychotherapy at the Tavistock Clinic, then with the Institute of Psychoanalysis. Before retiring from full-time work in the NHS, she managed a Psychoanalytic Psychotherapy Service in Teesside for ten years. Her particular interests concern the effects on the mind and brain of early trauma and the ways in which this impacts on adult life, attachment relationships, feelings and behaviour.

Sam Heywood is a Chartered Counselling Psychologist currently based in North Staffordshire. She has worked as part of a community psychology service for children and families for 7 years and has a particular interest in women's mental health and attachment. Prior to this, she worked in a Child and Adolescent Mental Health Service. She also works at Staffordshire University as a part-time lecturer on the Doctorate of Clinical Psychology course, facilitating reflective groups and contributing to teaching in supervision and personal and professional development.

Colin Hicks is a Chartered Counselling Psychologist and a Member of the British Association for Counselling and Psychotherapy. Colin completed his doctorate at the University of Surrey and went on to complete the diploma in cognitive therapy for complex mental health problems at the University of Southampton. Colin currently works in an NHS specialist secondary care service for university students with moderate to severe mental health problems within Hampshire Partnership Trust. He also runs a small private counselling and psychotherapy practice. Colin's research interests include student mental health and non-discriminatory therapeutic practice with clients of different sexualities.

Pamela E. James graduated with a BSc(Hon) in Psychology; she then carried out research in the psychology of learning in which she attained her doctorate. After teaching science in secondary schools, she returned to psychology as a lecturer in higher education in 1987. Her interest turned to training as a counsellor, and subsequently she became a chartered counselling psychologist via the independent route. During the last 15 years she has held management positions at Liverpool John Moores University where she is currently Professor of Counselling Psychology. She has been Chair of the Division of Counselling Psychology and is now Chair of the Board of Assessors for the Qualification. For the last 8 years she has been seconded to work sessionally in adult mental health in Mersey Care NHS Trust. She believes strongly in the philosophy of counselling psychology and has Senior Practitioner Status on the Register of Psychologists specialising in Psychotherapy.

Lynne Jordan is Registered Counselling Psychologist (HPC), Chartered Psychologist (BPS) and a Senior Accredited Counsellor with British Association of Counselling and Psychotherapy. She has worked with complex trauma for over two decades and has developed expertise in working with survivors of relational trauma. She established and coordinated a countywide specialist service in adult mental health for adults sexually abused in childhood for several years. This service also won local and national awards for Demonstrating Excellence and for Making a Difference within the mental health services. She has academic links with numerous universities as visiting lecturer and external examiner, mostly on DPsych programmes in Counselling Psychology and is an Associate Lecturer with the Open University, developing expertise in working therapeutically and educationally online. She is an examiner and moderator of the BPS

Qualification in Counselling Psychology, the independent route to chartership with BPS and registration as a Practitioner Psychologist with HPC. She is also Clinical Director of Jordan Consultancy Ltd, an independent psychological therapy, supervision and training consultancy based in South East England and central London, with local and worldwide practice due to the developing online service alongside the face-to-face work.

Carolyn Kagan is Professor of Community Social Psychology at Manchester Metropolitan University where she is the Director of the Research Institute for Health and Social Change. She combines qualifications in social work and counselling psychology in her community practice. Her work includes prefigurative action research with those marginalized by the social system (in the UK and other places) and she has worked for many years supporting public and voluntary service developments as well as citizen advocacy projects. She teaches on undergraduate and Masters' programmes in community psychology and psychology and counselling, combining the two groups of students to examine social justice and community action approaches to change.

Peter Martin is Principal Lecturer in Counselling Psychology at Roehampton University. His research interests are in the self of the therapist, intersubjectivity, and in the critique of Heuristic methodologies. He is active in the organization of the yearly Division of Counselling Psychology Conference, and was until recently a member of the BPS Admissions Committee. He has a keen interest in celebrating the complementary elements of the psychological institutions and Counselling Psychology training in Ireland and the United Kingdom and has taken part in several joint endeavours to this end. He is a Foundation Member of the Register of Psychologists Specialising in Psychotherapy with Senior Status. He is in Private Practice in Southampton and is also a Management Consultant.

Martin Milton is a chartered counselling psychologist, a foundation member of the BPS Register of Psychologists Specialising in Psychotherapy with senior practitioner status and a UKCP registered psychotherapist. He is an Associate Fellow of the BPS and a Chartered Scientist. Martin is Senior Lecturer in the department of psychology at the University of Surrey and he also runs an independent practice in psychology, psychotherapy and supervision <www.swlondonpsychology.co.uk>. Martin's specialist interests include lesbian and gay psychology and psychotherapy, existential psychotherapy and the therapeutic aspects of the natural world. In this regard Martin is on the editorial boards of several journals including *Counselling Psychology Review*, *Psychology and Sexuality*, *Lesbian and Gay Psychology Review* and *Ecopsychology*. Martin is also consultant editor to BPS/Blackwell for counselling psychology.

   Martin has been active in the BPS, having served on the committee of the Lesbian and Gay Psychology Section as well as being a former Chair of the Division of Counselling Psychology.

Maja O'Brien is a Visiting Professor at Middlesex University and a Principal Lecturer at Metanoia Institute London. She works working on the Post-Qualification Doctorate in Psychotherapy by Professional Studies and by Public Works, both joint programmes with the Institute of Work-based Learning at Middlesex University. Her clinical experience of over 30 years includes working as a clinical and counselling Psychologist in the NHS and as a psychotherapist and supervisor in private practice, currently in Oxford. The second edition of her book *Integrative Therapy: A Practitioner's Guide* written in collaboration with Gaie Houston was published by Sage in 2007. The first edition has been translated in Greek.

Stephen Palmer is Director of the Centre for Stress Management and the Centre for Coaching. He is an Honorary Professor of Psychology at City University and Founder Director of the Coaching Psychology Unit. He is a Visiting Professor of Work-Based Learning and Stress Management at the Institute for Work Based Learning, Middlesex University. He has authored or edited 35 books on a variety of subjects including counselling, psychotherapy, management, coaching and coaching psychology. He received from the British Psychological Society, Division of Counselling Psychology, the Annual Counselling Psychology Award for 'Outstanding Professional and Scientific Contribution to Counselling Psychology in Britain for 2000' and in 2004 he received an Achievement Award from the Association for Rational Emotive Behaviour Therapy. In 2008 the British Psychological Society, Special Group in Coaching Psychology gave him the 'Lifetime Achievement Award in Recognition of Distinguished Contribution to Coaching Psychology', awarded at the First European Coaching Psychology Conference, 2008.

Simon du Plock is a Registered Counselling Psychologist and Psychotherapist (HPC), a Chartered Psychologist (BPS), a Foundation Member with Senior Practitioner Status, BPS Register of Psychologists Specialising in Psychotherapy, and Visiting Professor at Middlesex University. Simon is Head of the Post-Qualification Doctoral Department at the Metanoia Institute in London, and Programme Leader of the Doctorate in Psychotherapy by Professional Studies, and the Doctorate in Psychotherapy by Public Works, both joint programmes with Middlesex University. He lectures internationally on existential therapy, and has edited *Existential Analysis*, the journal of the Society for Existential Analysis, since 1993. He is a co-founder and the Director of the Centre for Practice-Based Research at the Metanoia Institute, and maintains a private practice as an existential psychotherapist and clinical supervisor.

Jacqui Porter is a Registered Counselling Psychologist (HPC) and Chartered Psychologist (BPS) and she runs a busy private practice in Bristol. Specializing in cognitive behaviour therapy, she recently completed a post-graduate diploma at Oxford for supervisors and trainers of CBT. In her practice she works with clients across a wide range of adult mental health issues; she provides clinical supervision for therapists working in many different settings; and she runs introductory training courses in CBT for psychologists, counsellors and other health workers. When she first set up her own business, Jacqui provided consultancy services and executive coaching to organizations, but for the past ten years she has focused exclusively on the provision of therapeutic services.

Rosemary Rizq is a Registered Counselling Psychologist (HPC), a Chartered Psychologist (BPS) and Senior Practitioner member of the BPS Register of Psychologists Specialising in Psychotherapy. She is Principal Lecturer in Counselling Psychology at the Research Centre for Therapeutic Education, Roehampton University, and is Specialist Lead for Research and Development for Ealing PCT's Mental Health and Wellbeing Service where she also has a clinical and supervisory role. Rosemary is currently completing PhD research at University College London's Psychoanalysis Unit, where she is exploring the role of attachment in how counselling psychologists describe the meaning of personal therapy in training and clinical practice. She was awarded the Excellence in Research prize 2008 by the BPS Division of Counselling Psychology. Rosemary is Submissions Editor for *Psychodynamic Practice* and is on the editorial board of *Counselling Psychology Review*.

Julia Robinson is a Senior Lecturer in Psychology at Manchester Metropolitan University where she teaches on undergraduate and Masters' degree programmes. After studying psychology at university she trained and taught in primary education and as special educational needs co-ordinator, she developed an interest in working alongside children and the families of children who were classed as having special educational needs. She decided to train as a counselling psychologist through the independent route and in addition to teaching psychology at Bolton Community College, worked as a school counsellor in secondary schools. She has also held honorary positions in a specialist adult psychotherapy service and in an adult primary care service.

Diana Sanders is a counselling psychologist in Psychological Medicine in Oxford, and a BABCP accredited CBT psychotherapist. She specializes in applications of CBT for physical health problems, including chronic fatigue syndrome, cardiac rehabilitation, medically unexplained symptoms and health anxiety. She is particularly interested in new developments integrating mindfulness based traditions with CBT, and is currently training to run MBCT groups with medical patients. She has written extensively in the area of CBT and physical health, and co-authored *Cognitive Therapy: Transforming the Image* (1997) and *Cognitive Therapy: An Introduction* (2005) which promote cognitive approaches in counselling and psychotherapy. Her interest in physical health partly arose from a long-term cardiac condition and eventual heart-lung transplant, and she actively campaigns in favour of organ donation. As she gets older, the work side of life diminishes in favour of family, singing, walking and watching the world go by.

Carol Shillito-Clarke was one of the first people to be chartered as a Counselling Psychologist. She was also a Foundation Member of the Register of Psychologists Specialising in Psychotherapy with Senior Practitioner status and received the Division's 'Award for Outstanding Contribution to Counselling Psychology' in 2007. She is a Fellow of the British Association for Counselling and Psychotherapy and was, before retiring from her work as a therapist, accredited by them as a counsellor and supervisor. Throughout her time as a therapist, supervisor, trainer and consultant, her concern has been to promote high standards in training and practice. She has worked in education and the National Health Service as well as running a private practice.

Clive Sims has wide-ranging experience as an applied psychologist and is professionally chartered in five areas of psychology: counselling, forensic, clinical, health and neuropsychology. He also holds professional qualifications in business administration and in information technology. He is currently Lead Consultant Forensic Psychologist with the Suffolk Mental Health Partnerships NHS Trust. Clive's professional interests lie in existential psychotherapy, dual diagnosis and the inter-relationship between criminal behaviour and mental illness. He is also interested in the legal process as a therapeutic tool. Clive is committed to an integrated approach to therapy and considers that improvements in psychological health and well-being can only come about through concerted effort by the society in which we live and through major public health initiatives. He has recently been elected Fellow of the Royal Society of Public Health.

Sheelagh Strawbridge is a freelance Chartered Psychologist and Registered Counselling Psychologist with experience in university teaching, professional training and examining and was, untill recently, the Lead Assessor for the British Psychological Society's Register of Psychologists Specialising in Psychotherapy. She has been actively involved in the BPS Division of Counselling Psychology for many years, is a Fellow of the British Association for Counselling and Psychotherapy and an Associate of The Northern Trust for Dramatherapy. Her publications include *Exploring Self and Society* (with Rosamund Billington and Jenny Hockey, Macmillan, 1998), book chapters and journal articles and she was an editor of *The Handbook of Counselling Psychology*, 2nd edition.

Léonie Sugarman is a Registered Psychologist (HPC), Chartered Psychologist (BPS) and Reader in Applied Psychology at the University of Cumbria. She is author of *Life-Span Development: Frameworks, Accounts and Strategies* (Psychology Press, 2001) and *Counselling and the Life Course* (Sage, 2004); and co-author with R. Wright of *Occupational Therapy and Life Course Development* (Wiley, 2009). She is a member of the Editorial Board of the *British Journal of Guidance and Counselling,* and is an Honorary Fellow and former Vice President of the British Association for Counselling and Psychotherapy.

Margaret Tholstrup, C. Psychol., has had a long and varied career in independent practice, psychiatric inpatient and outpatient departments, primary care and student counselling. She tutored on the PsychD at the University of Surrey and assessed and examined for the Diploma and Qualification in Counselling Psychology. Very active in the BPS Division of Counselling Psychology and its Committee, she served for three years as Honorary Secretary and was a member of the Board of Examiners and a Coordinator of Training. With Michael Carroll she co-edited *Integrative Approaches to Supervision* (2001) as well as other chapters and articles on supervision. Most recently she co-authored the Division of Counselling Psychology 'Guidelines on Supervision' with Carol Shillito-Clarke and was awarded the Outstanding Contribution to

Counselling Psychology 2008 prize. Margaret is an Associate Fellow of BPS, and when actively practising, was also a UKCP-registered Integrative Psychotherapist and BACP-registered Group and Individual Supervisor. She is now retiring from the profession.

Carol Tindall is Director of the MSc in Psychology and Counselling at Manchester Metropolitan University and involved in teaching psychology and counselling on both undergraduate and postgraduate programmes. She has also been employed as an external examiner for both BSc and MSc Psychology and Counselling programmes. She has many years' experience of supervising the applied qualitative counselling psychology research of BSc, MSc and PhD students. Since completing initial counselling training in 1988 she has worked as a part-time practitioner in a variety of settings. Her practice, working with both women and men, is firmly grounded in feminist principles.

Susan van Scoyoc is a Chartered Psychologist and a founding member of the Register of Psychologists Specialising in Psychotherapy. She is a Registered Counselling Psychologist and Registered Health Psychologist. Susan has a long-term interest in the use of psychometric assessment and gained the BPS level A and B occupational certificates in psychometric testing. She is Past Chair of the Society's Division of Counselling Psychology and has published papers exploring the use of psychometric tests by counselling psychologists. Susan is also a UK Registered Expert Witness working in areas such as human rights, family law and cognitive testing. Susan presently divides her time between training and independent practice.

Ray Woolfe is a Registered Counselling Psychologist (HPC), Chartered Psychologist (BPS), Psychoanalytic Psychotherapist and Accredited Counsellor. A career as a university teacher involved jobs as Staff Tutor in Educational Studies and Senior Lecturer in Health and Social Welfare at the Open University and then Senior Lecturer in Counselling Studies at Keele University. He now operates a private practice in psychology and psychotherapy in Manchester and Cheshire. He is a Fellow of BACP and an Associate Fellow of BPS. He was Chair of the Special Group in Counselling Psychology at the time it achieved divisional status within BPS and was the first Registrar of the Examination Board for the then Diploma in Counselling Psychology. He is a foundation member on the Register of Psychologists Specialising in Psychotherapy with Senior Practitioner Status. In 2001 received a Special Centenary Award from the Division for the Development of Counselling Psychology within the Society.

Sarah Yassine is a Psychologist with over seven years' experience. She specializes in working with children, young people and their families. Sarah trained as a Psychologist in Queensland, Australia and there she worked with children and families in a range of different settings including foster care, community counselling, domestic violence and parental divorce and/or separation. In 2005 she moved to the UK where she worked for a leading childhood bereavement service for three and a half years. Sarah currently works for a local authority on a project aimed at improving mental health in schools.

PREFACE

This is the third edition of the *Handbook of Counselling Psychology* and it reflects the changes which have taken place since the second edition was published. However, in thinking about these changes, it is useful to remind ourselves about the first edition. In retrospect, this focused somewhat inwardly around the question of self-identity, representing the attempt of a newly established discipline to justify its existence. By the time the second edition was published, the discipline had developed a greater ability to look outside itself and to explore its boundaries with the outside world. This third edition expresses the confidence of a more mature enterprise which is now well established within the family of psychology, but nevertheless facing a number of crucial challenges. It is a key intention of this text to provoke debate in relation to these challenges as well as to provide an up-to-date overview of the field.

This book is significantly different in a number of ways from the previous edition. We have placed less emphasis on traditional therapeutic modalities. Instead we have taken a broader view, introducing new developments such as neuroscience and narrative approaches and examining contemporary issues such as evidence based practice, difference and discrimination, relational trauma, testing and diagnosis and the interface between psychopharmacological and psychotherapeutic approaches. New chapters have been included on the nature of evidence, disorder and its discontents, interpreting case material, legal frameworks, community psychology and testing and measurement.

There is one point of regret about the individual chapters. In the section on difference and discrimination we had hoped to include a chapter on disability but unfortunately were not able to secure one that met our editorial requirements. Despite this we believe that the book has a contemporary relevance and a radical edge expressed particularly in this section by the chapter on relational trauma.

In addition to major changes in content from the previous edition, there is also a contrast in pedagogy. The earlier edition had sought to constrain writers within a tight framework. This reflected traditional understandings of what constituted a Handbook. However, it seemed to us that this was a somewhat narrow interpretation of what constituted such a text. Our view is that the most essential features of this kind of publication are that it should be comprehensive in its coverage of the whole field and authoritative in its treatment of specific subjects within the field. Standardization without these characteristics would mean little, and in any case does not have to mean a rigid formulaic approach to chapter structure.

We were also influenced in our thinking by the humanistic philosophy that underlies counselling psychology which values diversity and a respect for individual difference. We feel that this is in tune with the postmodern zeitgeist. Therefore, for this edition we made a deliberate editorial decision to loosen the fetters and encouraged authors to follow their own preferences with regard to the balance between theory, research and practice. At the same time, we did not lose sight of the principle of standardization and authors were asked to pay attention to a number of specified topics covering the research evidence, current issues and debates, theoretical and philosophical underpinnings and political and resource issues.

The result of this process is that some authors chose a traditional, academic style of writing in the third person and emphasizing research and scholarship while the voice of others is much more personal and presented in the first person. Some might argue that the latter approach is neither critical nor impartial, but our view is that this by inference elevates academic science to a position which is at best arguable. In any event, the essence of counselling psychology is its belief in the value of subjective accounts of experience.

Almost every chapter is characterized by illustrative case study material. Our intention was to ensure that the book as a whole carries the traditional values of counselling psychology. These include a focus on the internal subjective world both of psychologist and client, an emphasis on the importance of the therapeutic relationship and a social model of distress in which problems are understood in a developmental framework. The result is a rich and multi-textured product which in our opinion gives the book a lively and topical feel in addition to being comprehensive and authoritative in its coverage of the discipline.

Psychology does not stand still. At the time of writing this preface in 2009, the project entitled IAPT (Increasing Access to Psychological Therapies) is having a major impact on policy and practice. In addition, psychology is about to become regulated by the Health Professions Council and this will no doubt have a significant impact upon the profession. It may be that, in time, the present divisional boundaries will move towards a more general training for applied psychologists, especially those working in the area of health. Our belief is that our discipline has much to offer discussions about such key issues and our hope is that this book will stimulate counselling psychologists to make a vigorous contribution to the debates.

ACKNOWLEDGEMENTS

Planning and executing a project of such magnitude as represented by this book involves the participation of many people, not least the individual contributors. There are many more counselling psychologists whom we would like to have asked to write a chapter but inevitably there has to be a limit on size. However, the discipline could not have flourished without their contribution.

We want to thank Alice Oven and Rachel Burrows at Sage for their support and encouragement in helping to bring the process to a successful conclusion.

When case study material has been used, all identifiable material has been removed and pseudonyms have been used in order to protect client anonymity.

PART I

WHAT IS COUNSELLING PSYCHOLOGY?

This part of the book sets the scene by exploring the nature of counselling psychology. As a discipline it arose as a particular approach to helping people, which proposed an alternative that challenged prevailing approaches. As counselling psychology has developed, it has not only influenced the mainstream but also encountered pressures to align itself with what continue to be more traditional approaches. This is perhaps most strongly experienced in its relation to clinical psychology, which is more established in the National Health Service, also a key employer of counselling psychologists. Within this context, at a time when the professional practice of psychology as a whole is about to be regulated by the Health Professions Council, and when the efficacy of differing methods of dealing with mental health issues is featuring highly on the political agenda, engaging in debate about the nature of our discipline seems particularly appropriate.

The text as a whole seeks to highlight issues and invites you, our readers, to join the debate at what we see as a watershed in our history. In pedagogical terms it takes a stand against reducing education to the provision of information. A key premise is that engaging in the process of debate is crucial both to understanding and to the vitality of a discipline. As trainees or qualified practitioners, you will be actively or passively involved in decisions that, made now, will shape counselling psychology for a significant period of its future. This part of the book enters the debate by focusing on some of the areas that are fundamental in defining the identity of our discipline.

Chapter 1 paints with a broad brush in attempting to locate counselling psychology professionally and intellectually. In reflecting on philosophical, theoretical, political and organizational themes and issues, it links comparatively recent developments within the context of British psychology to broader philosophical, social and political debates. Along with other chapters in the book it presents a particular perspective and argues its case.

Working with people experiencing psychological distress is a central focus of practice. Identifying the nature and causes of such distress has always been a matter of controversy and linked to the development of those professions charged with its alleviation. In recent years, the notion of 'disorders' of the mind has pre-dominated and psychological distress, of varying kinds, has increasingly been located within the field of mental health. Chapter 2 considers evolving narratives, which have constructed our changing understandings and approaches to distress and its 'treatment', and this social and historical perspective situates current approaches to categorization in a context that provokes questioning.

Counselling psychology has positioned itself between the science of psychology and the therapeutic practices of counselling and psychotherapy. It has constructed an identity that espouses the complementary aspects of 'scientist practitioner' and 'reflective practitioner'. These aspects are explored in differing ways throughout the book. In this section, Chapter 3 focuses on the importance of evidence in relation to the scientific basis of effective practice. It considers the nature of evidence and, in doing so it offers a timely reminder of its complexity in the face of a current tendency, which, though stressing the need for 'evidence-based practice', can lead to a narrowly conceived and over-simple conception of evidence. Chapter 4 addresses an equivalent complexity in reflective practice and considers ways of writing, reading, interpreting and learning from case material such as that presented in subsequent chapters.

1

COUNSELLING PSYCHOLOGY: ORIGINS, DEVELOPMENTS AND CHALLENGES

Sheelagh Strawbridge and Ray Woolfe

COUNSELLING PSYCHOLOGY IN BRITAIN

The task of locating counselling psychology, professionally and intellectually, is complex. As a professional field of activity it developed rapidly in Britain. Within the space of 12 years, between 1982 and 1994, counselling psychology evolved from a section within the British Psychological Society (BPS) to a division, thus gaining full professional status for the first time. It now has a network of accredited courses and maintains a significant independent route to a Society qualification. As a discipline within psychology it proposed an alternative to prevailing approaches. As such it had a critical edge and is rooted in intellectual traditions tangential to what was, and to some extent still is, the mainstream of psychological theory and practice. Our focus in this chapter is on the development of what we see as counselling psychology's distinctive identity as a discipline and some of the challenges it currently faces. Others will see things somewhat differently, and engaging in discussion about the nature of our discipline seems particularly appropriate at a time when mental health issues are high on the political agenda.

To understand what we now refer to as counselling psychology, we need to recognize its links with a tradition dating back at least 150 years. For example, in the 1850s, Wundt argued that psychology is the science of consciousness whilst William James suggested that the 'self' is the product of the multiplicity of relationships that the person has with others. This early interest in consciousness, subjective experience and inter-relationship was also developed in Continental Europe within the framework of phenomenology and existential-phenomenology. However, until recently this was largely neglected in the UK and the USA, although it was pursued by symbolic-interactionists such as G.H. Mead who emphasized the social context in which the self is constructed, as well as its capacity for self-reflection or to be, in Cooley's metaphor, a 'looking-glass' self.

Counselling psychology springs from, and is inspired by, the work of these thinkers and others like them who see understanding the subjective worlds of self and other to be central in psychology. It also owes much to more recent North-American humanistic and existential thinkers such as Maslow, Rogers and May who argued the need to ground the practice of psychology in humanistic values. Indeed, counselling as a practice has its origin in this American perspective, and the term was reputedly coined by Rogers. In Britain, counselling and psychotherapy largely developed separately, outside the profession of psychology, and counselling psychology represents a return to psychology initiated by psychologists trained in those disciplines, particularly in humanistic approaches. It has, nevertheless, evolved into a broad church, committed to exploring a range of approaches to inquiry and recognizing the contribution of differing traditions in psychology, including: the phenomenological (existential and humanistic); the psychoanalytic/psychodynamic; the cognitive-behavioural; and the strongly emerging and related constructionist, narrative and systemic traditions.

In attempting to characterize counselling psychology, a question that is still asked is: How does it differ, if at all, from other psychological disciplines, particularly clinical psychology? Given the complexities of both histories and forms of practice, this is not easy to answer. However, Woolfe (1990) identified factors favourable to the growth of the discipline in Britain that highlighted some of its priorities and therapeutic focus:

- An increasing awareness among many psychologists of the significance of the helping relationship.
- A growing questioning of the 'medical model' of professional–client relationships and a move towards a more humanistic value base.
- A developing interest in facilitating well-being as opposed to responding to sickness and pathology.

It is perhaps the focus on the relationship that is particularly significant, as research supports a growing awareness that helping involves more than the application of specific treatment regimes in a standardized fashion. Evidence confirms that specific techniques contribute less to therapeutic effectiveness than the quality of the relationship (see, for example, Roth and Fonagy, 1996; Hubble et al., 1999; Cooper, 2008). Rogers (1951) described this quality in terms of the personal dispositions of empathy, acceptance and congruence. The construct 'empathy' represents a particularly well-researched domain, for example, Barkham (1988) charted its continuing influence on psychologists over three decades.

However, as counselling psychology has become more established, particularly within mental health work and more specifically the National Health Service (NHS), a countervailing tendency has gained in strength. In these contexts, the pressure on resources, coupled with a justifiable demand for accountability, emphasizes evidenced-based practice and encourages short-term problem or solution-focused work and standardized, packaged or manualized treatments linked to a medically oriented focus on 'disorders', defined psychiatrically. This tendency is also influencing other arenas of practice, such as employee assistance programmes (EAPs).

This creates a tension that will also be explored in later chapters. Here we characterize it as between 'being-in-relation' and 'technical expertise'. We link the pressure towards technical expertise with a wider social process associated with the growth of industrial capitalism, and termed 'rationalization' by Weber in the early twentieth century. The tension affects how we define science, the relationship between science and values and how we position ourselves in respect to long-standing questions about human free-will and the extent to which human behaviour is determined by internal and external causes. We can only outline some of the issues as we see them.

We have acknowledged that attempting to locate counselling psychology is a complex task. It includes a consideration of historical processes, social and political forces, philosophical and psychological theories and changing contexts of employment. As therapists we know that mining aspects of history to make sense of current issues is a messy business, and no doubt in what follows there will be confusion and over-simplification. Our views will likely run counter to some expressed in this book but will resonate with others and be explored further. Our chapter, in common with all the others, offers a contribution to ongoing debates in which we invite you, the reader, to participate.

SCIENTIST-PRACTITIONERS

We have noted that counselling psychology in Britain originated as a return of counselling to psychology. The former is rooted in humanistic and existential-phenomenological psychology in which the search for understanding and meaning is central and the focus is upon an engagement with subjective experience, values and beliefs. The latter (in the UK and USA) has traditionally characterized itself as a behavioural science. Bringing the two together requires a creative synthesis and much depends on what we mean by science and how we understand its relation to practice. Far from being dismissive of the demand to justify practice on the basis of evidence, counselling psychology recognizes the importance of clear conceptual frameworks within which we can research, evaluate and develop practice. Nevertheless, it is in acknowledging the contribution of different traditions that the relationships between science and practice and science and values and the nature of science itself, have all become critical issues in the evolving identity of counselling psychologists. Much discussion has focused on the notion of the 'scientist-practitioner' (for example, Lane and Corrie, 2006).

Before reading further we suggest that you reflect on your own position. Do you think of yourself as a scientist-practitioner? If so how do you define and justify this? How do your colleagues or members of your supervision group see it?

Whilst the emphasis on psychological theory and research highlights differences between the training of counselling psychologists and that of many counsellors and psychotherapists, it suggests a kinship with clinical psychologists further encouraged by increasing employment in clinical situations defined in medical terms. In these contexts the powerful, natural-science based, biomedical tradition of psychiatry, with its discourse of 'psychopathology', 'disorders' and 'mental illness', has held sway since the nineteenth century (see, for example, Chapter 2). In such settings the effectiveness of the struggle to establish and maintain a distinctly psychological approach has been enhanced by the bias towards behavioural science, and this adds attraction to identifying ourselves as scientist-practitioners. The term suggests an engagement in research and the role of the practitioner as producer, as well as user, of knowledge and understanding. Nevertheless, practitioners often display a resistance to research. A variety of reasons may account for this (Pelling, 2000; Woolfe, 1996), but a significant factor must be its perceived limitations from the point of view of practice.

Indeed, Schön, writing generally about professional practice, famously described the predominant or 'technical rationality' model of science as painting a picture of:

> a high, hard ground overlooking a swamp. On the high ground, manageable problems lend themselves to solution through the application of research based theory and technique. In the swampy lowland, messy, confusing problems defy technical solution. ... [But] ... in the swamp lie the problems of greatest human concern. (1987: 3)

In the swampy lowlands, which are the 'indeterminate zones of practice' characterized by uncertainty, uniqueness and value conflict, the canons of technical rationality do not apply. Moreover, by focusing on problem solving, it detracts from the crucial task of problem setting, for example, there are issues arising from accepting rather than questioning the widespread diagnosis of depression, which are discussed below.

Schön finds that, rather than applying formal theory and research, successful practitioners learn from experience. Reflection-on-action, often with colleagues, and reflection-in-action, the monitoring of practice in process, are central to this learning and keep practitioners alive to the uniqueness and uncertainty of practice situations. The stress on supervision in counselling psychology acknowledges this reflective activity as key to good practice. It is perhaps given insufficient consideration as a process within which knowledge is actively produced, and this is something that could be more explicitly recognized in the way practice experience is written up for publication (see, for example, Chapter 4).

Nevertheless, effective reflective practice is not haphazard. Patches of higher ground can offer perspective, and useful maps to aid navigation through the swamps can be drawn. Over-simple though the technical rationality model may be, such maps can be provided, in part, by psychological theories linked to a sound research base, and this requires a more adequate understanding of the nature of science in relation to practice, and a range of approaches to more formal research that can comprehend the realities of practice (for example, Lane and Corrie, 2006). Moreover, many practice decisions involve ethical dilemmas and are guided by ethical codes underpinned by ethical theories (see Chapter 26) and a broader understanding of social, political and organizational contexts and dimensions of practice can be very significant. Understanding this complexity is crucial in transcending the gulf that has existed between the prevailing view of science, as objective and value-free, and practice that engages with subjectivity and meaning and is characterized by uncertainty and value conflict.

This is becoming more urgent as psychologists are increasingly called upon to justify their practice on the basis of evidence and to demonstrate technical expertise in treating definable conditions and disorders. In clinical contexts it is difficult to resist the biomedical model, and this is extending outwards to other organizations (such as EAPs) offering therapeutic interventions in human distress. All this highlights the tension between a model of science that favours medical and behavioural models of practice, and the humanistic-values based practice stressed in counselling psychology. Economic forces, used for example by Layard to justify the Increasing Access to Psychological Therapies (IAPT) programme discussed later, coupled with the demand to be scientific and deliver evidence-based practice, bring pressure to conform to the criteria of this limited model of science and by extension of evidence. The bias towards behavioural science, notwithstanding the 'cognitive revolution', leads to research constrained by notions of good design often inappropriate to complex life situations and an unbalanced emphasis on cognitive-behavioural therapy (CBT).

Nonetheless, in the absence of strong and well-defined alternatives, the pressure is difficult to resist. So, if 'scientific' and 'evidence-based' are key terms in the claim of counselling psychologists to professional competence, it is imperative that we examine and refine our own conceptions of science, research and evidence in order to avoid an uncritical acceptance of medicalized forms of practice and research which are limited in their application. Corrie's chapter in this book examines the nature of evidence in some depth, and in this chapter we re-visit the prevailing model of science and reflect on newer perspectives that can offer ways forward.

SCIENCE AND COUNSELLING PSYCHOLOGY

The technical rationality view of scientific psychology can be traced back to the Enlightenment, a complex notion concerning a framework of ideas about nature, human beings and society usually seen as originating in eighteenth-century France. It marks the beginning of the modern period, or 'modernity', and has been characterized by its challenge to an overarching European world-view defined by Christianity and the Church's authority. Reason and rationality were promoted as the basis of knowledge and a view of science born in the 'scientific revolution' of the seventeenth-century was increasingly seen as the key to the expansion of human knowledge. This belief in the power of science was coupled with equally strong beliefs in technological and social progress, which would itself be enhanced by the scientific understanding of human beings and the workings of human societies (see, for example, Porter, 2001, for an analysis of the Enlightenment).

The model of science that emerged was linked to the philosophies of empiricism and positivism. It stressed that knowledge claims must be based on objectively observable 'facts' verifiable against sense-experience. This was important as it proposed a rational, empirically based method for creating knowledge free from religious dogma, and one legacy of the Enlightenment project is our continuing faith in science as the yardstick for judging claims to rational knowledge. Of course, the power of science is clear when we consider its enormous influence in our lives. It is, therefore, not surprising that what was seen as the natural science method was pre-eminent in the development of modern psychology, which had its origins in the second half of the nineteenth century, as one of the disciplines aiming to apply scientific methods to the study of human beings. The emphasis on objectivity and observability favoured a focus on behaviour, rather than subjective experience, and it was assumed that there are discoverable laws that could constitute a body of knowledge allowing the prediction and control of human behaviour. Once discovered, these laws could be applied to the treatment of criminality and mental illness, the assessment of abilities and aptitudes, the education of children, the organization of the workplace and so on.

This natural science perspective is inherently deterministic and conformist, it locates control outside those being controlled and its thrust is towards an adjustment to, rather than a critique of, social conditions. Nonetheless, knowledge is not static and the early emphasis on behavioural psychology and behaviour modification shifted significantly through the 1980s. Bergin and Garfield (1994: 824) note the dramatic influence of research evidence, of the efficacy of cognitive interventions, on its re-conceptualization as cognitive-behavioural psychology and therapy. Although the picture has become increasingly complex, as practitioners of differing approaches continue to learn from each other, cognitive-behavioural psychology and CBT still incline towards a natural science perspective and research based in this tradition, with randomized control trials (RCTs) taken to be the 'gold standard'.

However, notwithstanding the power of natural science, from the earliest conceptions of social science and psychology, people have questioned the appropriateness of using the same methods to study both the natural and the human world. Such questioning characterized the humanistic psychology, originating in the USA around 1940 in which Rogers and Maslow were key figures. This claimed to be a 'third force', challenging the perceived determinism of behaviourism and psychoanalysis, as well as the biomedical model in psychiatry. Its emphasis on free-will and human potential became significant in the context of emerging protest movements (Herman, 1992) and counselling was just one of a range of democratizing practices in humanistic psychology.

Whilst the ideas of humanistic psychology are peculiarly American, Rogers, Maslow and others recognized their roots in, for example, the European phenomenological tradition (for example, Rogers, 1964) dating back at least to the nineteenth century. By this time history, psychology, sociology, economics and social anthropology had emerged as empirical disciplines and claims were already being made that their subject matter is significantly different from that of the natural sciences and requires differing methods of study. In Britain, J.S. Mill coined the term 'moral sciences' to distinguish this group of disciplines, and their distinctiveness was similarly argued by the German philosopher Dilthey. He linked the notion of 'human science' to a theory of understanding and influenced the development of research into human consciousness, subjective experience, meaning and culture.

In Britain and the USA, although more complex conceptualizations of natural science were developing, a positivist-empiricist philosophy predominated throughout the social sciences and psychology, at least until the 1960s. However, by then the phenomenological tradition was enjoying a period of revitalization in the climate of political and intellectual upheaval in Europe, where it was posing a vigorous challenge to over-deterministic conceptions of history, social structure, social processes and human behaviour. Consciousness and human agency were re-emphasized and methods appropriate to the study of self-conscious, reflective and self-determining beings were sought. The range of rigorous, qualitative research methods now available owes much to this fruitful period. Initially these were more eagerly embraced in sociology, anthropology and cultural studies than in psychology, although there are notable exceptions. Bruner, for instance, made his important distinction between 'paradigmatic' and 'narrative' knowing in the 1980s and drew attention to the significance of stories in human experience (Bruner, 1986). It is worthy of note that the BPS now has Sections devoted to the scientific study of consciousness and experience and the development of qualitative methods.

Whilst we argue below that psychology, as such, best fits a human science model, this is not to say that it cannot be informed by disciplines located more firmly within natural science or, for that matter, in the arts. For instance, an understanding of narrative that owes much to literature and linguistics has proved very fruitful in the development of narrative approaches within psychology and therapy (see Chapter 8). Equally, developments in neuroscience offer new insights and an enhanced understanding of brain function that it would be folly to disregard (see Chapter 33).

HUMANISTIC VALUES AND HUMAN POTENTIAL

The more we emphasize humanistic values, the more we connect counselling psychology to a human science as opposed to a natural science model. Values are inseparable from a view of human beings as self-conscious and reflective, with the capacity for choice and personal responsibility, rather than being entirely determined by internal and external causes (for example, Patterson, 2000: 235–325). However, we do not see this as being at odds with developments in cognitive-behavioural, or, for that matter psychodynamic, approaches (see Chapters 5 and 6). Indeed, the increasing cross-fertilization between therapeutic approaches has only strengthened our view that a human science model offers a sound scientific approach, which acknowledges the significance of philosophical and moral questions and values artistry in professional work (see Strawbridge, 2003). It recognizes the centrality of relationship and the intersubjective nature of therapeutic processes.

Also central to a humanistic perspective is a positive view of human beings as 'in the process of becoming', guided by what Maslow described as a 'self-actualizing' tendency understood both as the potential driving development and as a valued developmental goal. Rogers' (1961) similar notion of a 'fully functioning person' is of someone who is open to experience and is not defensive, who lives existentially (constantly in process, flexible and adaptable) and whose locus of evaluation and control is internal. At the heart of this perspective is a belief that the intention of therapy is to enhance the self-determination and fulfilment of potential of the person in the client role. This remains valid whatever the nature of the problems or distress presented, and an attitude emphasizing becoming what one is capable of becoming is adopted. This involves a holistic and developmental view of an individual's life. Duffy (1990) stresses the importance of the helper's mind-set so that problems and crises are perceived not as evidence of pathology but in the context of coping with ordinary human experiences. So, difficulties and distress are seen as part and parcel of the human condition and there is always potential for creative change and enhanced well-being even in the face of death.

This emphasis on ordinary experience, well-being and potential can also be seen in the wider and more recent resurgence of interest in 'positive psychology' (for example, Joseph and Worsley, 2007). It is in contrast with both the biomedical and older behavioural models. In these the focus is on 'illness', 'pathology', 'disorder' or 'maladaptive behaviour' and helpers are seen as emotionally distanced, employing standardized assessment and clinical techniques from a perspective external to clients' subjective worlds. Counselling psychology advocates an interactive alternative. Rather than expecting clients to submit compliantly to treatment prescribed by professionals, it emphasizes the subjective experience of clients and the need for helpers to engage with them as collaborators, seeking to understand their inner worlds and constructions of reality. The notion of *doing something to* clients is replaced by that of *being with* them and the core conditions of empathy, acceptance and authenticity are paramount whatever the therapeutic modality.

The centrality of this humanistic value system offers one answer to the question of how counselling psychology differs from medical and other psychological approaches. As Duffy (1990) points out, the difference lies not in the methods employed or type of problem worked with but in the philosophical position from which they do it. As the focus shifts away from the application of specific treatments, what we do *to* clients, to how we are *with* clients, the emphasis becomes one of *being-in-relation* rather than *doing*. It follows from this that the self of the helper is acknowledged as an active ingredient in the helping process. So it is neither a specific range of skills and techniques nor its client groups that distinguishes counselling psychology, but its approach, the attitude or intentionality brought to the helping relationship. This emphasis on the person of the therapist is not just a theoretical proposition. It involves understanding therapy as a shared exploration into which the helper brings his or her own emotional history and baggage. Like our clients we are people, with issues and difficulties in our lives, and understanding how this impacts upon relationships with clients demands a willingness to explore our own histories, attitudes and emotional defences. Hence, there is a stress in training and practice on personal therapy as well as supervision (see Chapters 29 and 30).

Seeing counselling psychology as rooted in humanistic values and adopting a human science perspective does not, however, imply an uncritical attitude towards humanistic psychology. We noted earlier that counselling psychology is committed to exploring and evaluating the strengths and limitations of all major traditions in psychology. The intention to increase the capacity for self-determination can involve offering insights and techniques from a range of traditions for clients to explore and utilize for themselves. This, however, raises theoretical and technical issues about integration that are a matter of ongoing debate (for example, O'Brien in this book and with Houston, 2007; Palmer and Woolfe, 2000; Lapworth et al., 2001).

STRUCTURALISM, POST-STRUCTURALISM, AND POSTMODERNISM

Theoretical developments in the human sciences have a complex history and we cannot here unpack the interweaving threads in any detail. However, it can be useful to think in terms of a broadly dialectical movement of thesis, antithesis and synthesis. An understanding of the processes and conditions that determine behaviour is difficult to reconcile with the human capacity for free-will. This results in crucial shifts in emphasis between historical processes, social structure and behaviour on the one hand and subjectivity and action on the other.

The humanistic psychology of the early 1960s championed free-will and subjectivity but it courted utopian ideas of democracy and human perfectibility. From a more existential viewpoint, May challenged Rogers about the neglect of the human capacity for evil (see Kirschenbaum and Henderson, 1990) and Spinelli notes its over-optimistic view of human nature and human freedom (2005: 179–180). Moreover, though linked with protest movements, it lacked critical purchase. The individual's capacity for self-actualization was over-emphasized, and the tools of social theory needed to analyse oppressive social conditions were neglected. Significant attempts to understand the impact of historical processes and social conditions on the human psyche were being made, however, by thinkers of the Frankfurt School. Their 'critical theory' drew on both Freud and Marx, and the synthesis developed contributed to a revitalization of interest in these theorists that is still bearing fruit. From this perspective humanistic psychology was as conformist as the behaviourism it opposed. Jacoby (1977) provides an account of this challenge to conformist psychology that seems particularly relevant to current conditions favouring medicalization.

Although the stress on subjective experience and self-determination was criticized for over-accentuating the responsibility of individuals for their own circumstances and life-chances, as an interest in the role of historical processes and social structures in shaping human identities was re-kindled, the focus on meaning remained. This was manifest in the Frankfurt School's return to Freud and structuralist theory in linguistics also became increasingly important. 'Structuralism' defined languages as structured symbolic systems. Subjective consciousness, dependent upon language, could now be seen as fundamentally social and more obviously available for scientific study. Human action could be understood as generated within symbolic meaning systems in which socio-political power is legitimated in ideologies. Marxist and feminist studies were particularly important in showing how power relations are reproduced through the construction of personal identities (see, for example, Billington et al., 1998: 52–57). As the structures of language and ideology operate below the level of consciousness, interest in psychoanalytic studies was enhanced, particularly through the work of Lacan who claimed that 'the unconscious is structured like a language' (1977: 20). Language thus provided a key, unlocking possibilities for studying both conscious and unconscious meanings and motivations and linking individual psychology with social structures.

Structuralism, though resulting in both exciting insights and new methods of research, was in turn criticized. Its stress on social structures swung the pendulum too far in the direction of determinism. 'Post-structuralism' emerged and was related to a broader movement of ideas termed 'postmodernism'. We can here only sketch the significance of these complex and debatable ideas for the development of counselling psychology. Post-structuralism was first associated with a number of French thinkers, including Foucault and Deleuze, who were critical of all overarching conceptions of reason and truth, declaring them to be repressive. They argued that the world cannot be grasped within a single unified theoretical system. Life is inherently multifarious and contradictory and all thinking and evaluation limited within perspectives. They maintained a similar view, of the centrality of language, to the structuralists but rejected the conception of languages as large unified systems in favour of smaller systems or 'discourses' located in specific forms of social relationship.

A central concern of postmodern thinkers is the way grand theories and overarching systems of thought tend towards totalitarianism and terror (see Gray, 2007, for one account of this consequence of the Enlightenment). The opposite danger, however, lies in an extreme relativism of standards of truth and value in which anything goes, 'might' comes to mean 'right' and consensus becomes a dangerously totalizing force. Influential thinkers such as Foucault and Lyotard recognized this and struggled, in their later works, to move beyond the tendency to equate truth with power (for example, Lyotard, 1979; Lyotard and Thebaud, 1979; Foucault, 1988). Lyotard, nonetheless, maintains a stance against overarching belief systems, which he calls the great 'meta-narratives' of the modern period, and seeks to identify the liberating potential in postmodernism. He sees social life as governed by a multiplicity of 'little narratives' inherently open to challenge and cancellation and postmodernism as having the potential of liberating us from the terror consequent on the search for a totalizing meta-narrative.

Polkinghorne (1992) has drawn attention to the relevance of postmodern thinking for a practice-led model of psychology. He argues that practice emerged under the shadow of academic psychology and that, whilst the latter focused on the discovery of general laws of human behaviour, the former focused on pragmatic action in the service of mental health and personal development. Finding academic psychology's model of knowledge of limited relevance in responding to clients, practice was informed by a developing a body of knowledge that consisted of a 'fragmented collection of discordant theories and techniques', based on actual interactions between practitioners and clients. Underlying the generation of knowledge through practice is an implicit epistemology that is postmodern in character. It assumes that: there is no firm foundation for establishing indubitable truth; bodies of knowledge consist of fragments of understanding, little narratives rather than large logically integrated systems; these fragments are constructed in cultures; and knowledge is tested pragmatically, by its usefulness. This sits easily alongside Schön's reflective-practitioner model and Polkinghorne too links his 'postmodern epistemology of practice' to a range of studies of the ways in which professionals in a variety of disciplines actually develop and apply knowledge.

This brief account can only indicate the broad tendency of postmodern thinking and we can simply note its relationship with a range of approaches to the study of human beings gaining influence in psychology, including social constructionism, discourse and narrative analysis, deconstruction and critical psychology (see, for example, Fox and Prilleltensky, 1997; Smith et al., 1995). These approaches put values and political critique back on psychology's agenda and, alongside developments in phenomenological research and psychoanalysis, they are also contributing much to the study of social relationships, culture and ideology, subjectivity and meaning and conscious and unconscious processes, by rigorous qualitative methods.

When we consider counselling psychology's approach to practice and inquiry we can find some strikingly postmodern characteristics. Its recognition of competing therapeutic theories and refusal to align itself with a single model indicates a resistance to a meta-narrative, particularly that of the prevailing model of scientific rationality. In its respect for the subjective truths expressed in the little narratives of our individual lives, in its celebrating and valuing of difference, whilst recognizing the power of ideologies, and in its espoused intent to empower, it has the potential to contribute to challenging oppression. More specifically, the interest in narrative approaches to therapy and the significance of stories in human lives is developing rapidly and, as we can see, this emphasis on narrative is central in postmodern thinking.

TECHNICAL EXPERTISE AND BEING-IN-RELATION IN THE EMPLOYMENT CONTEXT

In this context the technical rationality model of science can be seen as limited in its application and, with the rapid development of qualitative and more politically conscious forms of research, we are in a position to espouse methods more adequate to the study of what we do in practice. There is no shortage of evidence of the significance of common factors across models of therapeutic practice, and amongst these the quality of the therapeutic relationship is emphasized as central to therapeutic success (for example, Hubble et al., 1999). Therapy depends more on our capacity for being-in-relation than on our tool bags of techniques for diagnosing and treating specific problems. We now have research methods appropriate to exploring and describing more systematically and in depth the nature of such human meeting and we should not forget that psychotherapy is, *in its very nature*, research or, as Mair (1999) prefers, 'inquiry'.

If, in this way, we can see our way into enriching our view of the identity of scientist-practitioner it is, nevertheless, only part of the story. We noted how the natural science model, which claimed value-freedom, became the yardstick of rationality in general. This led to the neglect of other forms of reason, such as those appropriate to ethical and political thought and action (for example, Shotter, 1993). In contrast, we have seen that the more modest postmodern emphasis, on little narratives, the context-bound nature of knowledge and on pragmatism or usefulness rather than truth, carries the danger of relativism and the association of truth with power. In the context of practice we have noted Schön's stress on how the limited applicability of technical rational knowledge brings into focus value conflicts and the unavoidable responsibility that we have to others. Many situations are vague and uncertain, decisions must be made, actions taken and accounted for. Social life is, in a real sense, radically open and social and moral concepts 'essentially contestable' (Gallie, 1956). Under these conditions values provide the guiding principles, hence the importance of our humanistic values, and an adequate scientist-practitioner identity must embrace forms of ethical and political reason within its compass.

So what are the obstacles to moving forward in the manner we have suggested? Currently policies such as IAPT draw us back towards the technical rationality model of science and the medical model of practice. We have already linked this model of science with the coming of modernity that can be seen as part of a more general process conceptualized by Weber as rationalization (see, for example, Brubacker, 1984; Whimster and Lash, 1987). Rationalization involves the application of criteria of rational decision making, tied to calculable economic efficiency, into increasing areas of social life and is closely associated with the rise of industrial capitalism. Its effect is to construct a complex system geared only to increasing productivity. This, coupled with scientific and technological progress, becomes an end in itself, the rationale of the whole system and, as such, beyond question, as opposed to a means whereby human needs may be satisfied. So, for example, at present it seems only possible to conceive of the way out of global financial crisis in terms of growth.

George Ritzer (1993) argues that the process of rationalization continues to intensify. He coined the term 'McDonaldization' to characterize the highly controlled, bureaucratic and dehumanized nature of contemporary, particularly American, social life. The fast-food restaurant, built on principles of efficiency, calculability, predictability and control, where quantity and standardization replace quality and variety as the indicators of value, serves as a metaphor for the general mania for efficiency. Increasing areas of social life are subject to McDonaldization through, for example, shopping malls, packaged holidays, hotel chains and digital television. Perhaps more seriously, areas such as education and medicine are subject to this process. The stress on grades and league tables in education focus attention on what is quantifiable in the end product, rather than the quality of the experience, and health care is increasingly impersonal and technological.

Ritzer (1998: 59–70) has also considered the organization and experience of work and linked his perspective to Braverman's (1974) analysis of the labour process. He recognizes that the deskilling and degradation of labour is characteristic of rationalization. Work is highly routinized, thinking is reduced to a minimum and even social interactions (for example with customers) are scripted (Hochschild, 1983). Higher-level skills (such as planning), creativity, critique and genuine human contact, are effectively excluded so both producers and, in the service industries, consumers are systematically disempowered.

Even this brief outline suggests insights into the labour market, dominated by medicine, in which counselling psychologists are increasingly employed. The deskilling of work in general has broad political implications, to which we cannot here do justice, but it is of particular concern to a profession that defines its practice in terms of human relationships. For now we can only note some of the means whereby, in therapy, complexity is minimized, process routinized and thinking and human contact reduced: for example by the strong emphasis on training in techniques (despite the significance of the therapeutic relationship); attempts to operationalize competences; the demand for quantification in efficacy studies (without due regard to the adequacy of the measures or the quality of the experience); the consequent stress on diagnosis and problem specification (as opposed to the subjective experience of distress); attempts to package delivery through therapy manuals; and the use of computers to deliver some such packages (see Strawbridge, 2002).

MEDICAL SETTINGS

Gaining recognition and employment in medical settings and in particular in the NHS is a measure of the success of our discipline. However, it brings into focus a number of issues. The size and power of the NHS is such that it has an enormous influence on how our work is understood and counselling psychology, alongside psychotherapy and counselling, is increasingly defined as 'health care'. Together with other branches of psychology, such as occupational and educational psychology, which are clearly not health professions, and in the face of strenuous opposition from the BPS, it will be regulated under the Health Professions' Council. There is considerable debate about the implications of all this (see Chapter 20), and here we can only contribute briefly by highlighting some of our concerns that most clearly relate to the themes of this chapter.

The current government policy of IAPT offers a useful focus, and it mirrors other changes in the health service that display aspects of McDonaldization. Layard, an economist who has written about happiness and observed that a record of 'mental illness' contributes significantly to unhappiness, has heavily influenced this policy (Layard, 2004). The targeted mental illnesses are anxiety and depression, which, predicted to affect between 25 and 45 per cent of the population by 2010, are of considerable economic significance. According to the guidelines of National Institute of Clinical Excellence (NICE) the strongest evidence, based on RCTs, points to CBT as the treatment of choice. It is, therefore, proposed, under the IAPT policy, to fund CBT training and a programme of 'stepped care', which is already being piloted.

Whilst, given resource constraints, stepped care may be a reasonable way of widening access and we might welcome the increased funding and commitment to training, the implementation of the policy could prove problematic for the integrity of our work in that: a) plans for stepped care lean towards packages, which, particularly at the 'low intensity' end of the spectrum of treatments, are manualized and may involve computer programs; and, b) funded training will be relatively short and focused on the technical skills and competencies of CBT. The above discussions about technical rationality and

McDonaldization alert us to the implications of all this. Skills and competencies are essential but, just as good driving requires road-sense, which is harder to define than the skills of vehicle control, good therapy requires a depth of thinking and human response that is not reducible to formulaic prescriptions. We can only reiterate the importance of a capacity to form therapeutic relationships, a broader understanding of psychological theory, ethical and socio-political awareness, and a commitment to inquiry and reflective practice.

Defining our work as health care also reinforces the tendency to medicalize psychological distress. It is linked to the expansion of psychiatry, beyond extreme forms of distress and 'psychosis' or 'madness' into areas that were, for instance, previously of moral and social concern by defining, for example, 'alcohol use disorders', 'anti-social personality disorder' and 'adjustment disorders'. So the language of symptomatology, disease and disorder replaces that of social conditions, interpersonal relations, subjective experience and moral responsibility. These categories of 'illness' and 'disorder', devised and articulated, for example, in the Diagnostic and Statistical Manuals (DSM) have been extensively criticized (for example, Kutchins and Kirk, 1999; Pilgrim and Bentall, 1999; Bentall, 2003; Cromby et al., 2007) and other articles in this Special Issue of *The Psychologist*; Appignanesi, 2008; and Chapter 2). They conform to technical rationality in suggesting the existence of objective states that are value-free and which require specific treatments, though, unlike categories of physical disorders, they are rarely linked to theories of aetiology, consisting only of descriptions of 'symptoms', and this renders them more arbitrary. Such diagnoses may well have some beneficial effects in de-stigmatizing sufferers. However, they also perform a political function, for example, in defining 'homosexuality' as a disorder in DSM 3 and in focusing on the internal state of an individual as illustrated by the category of 'depression'.

Remembering Schön's warning about a focus on problem solving rather than problem setting, we note that depression is unquestioned as a clinical diagnosis in relation to IAPT policy. However, it is something of a catch-all category and can be linked to the development and marketing of antidepressant drugs (Leader, 2008: 13–17). Appignanesi too notes that the use of antidepressants rose by 234 per cent between 1992 and 2002 and remarks, 'There is nothing like a much publicized set of pills to invoke a mirroring illness' (2008: 3). Moreover, seen as an individual problem, depression deflects attention from wider social and political concerns. It is certainly worth asking *why* psychological distress, manifest, for example, in issues around eating, alcohol consumption and drug use, as well as in depression and suicide, seems to be so widespread and increasing. All of these can be indicators of social problems and classic research such as Durkheim's study of suicide (2006, first published 1897), which linked suicide rates to social cohesion, and Brown and Harris' study of 'depression' in women (1978) still offer insights as do more recent studies (for example, Kinderman, 2005; Black 2008). Pilgrim and Rogers (2002) provide a useful sociological perspective.

In the longer term, claiming too much may cast doubt on the real value of psychological therapies. Antidepressants were over-sold and are now under fire (Kirsch et al., 2008) and in due course the IAPT programme, as currently conceived, is itself likely to be found limited. We are reminded of notions of compensatory education, the high hopes resting on the Educational Priority Areas, implemented following the Plowden Report, and the subsequent realization that education alone cannot solve problems of social deprivation (see, for example, Halsey and Sylva, 1987; Winkley, 1987). More generally, Lasch warned of a 'retreat from politics' where collective grievances are transformed into personal problems amenable to therapeutic intervention (1979: 5–14). So accepting an over-emphasis on psychological treatments for what are, at least in part, socio-political problems risks acquiescing to what Furedi (2004) has called 'therapy culture'. For example, we may question the ethics of providing therapy through EAPs and IAPT if a focus on individuals, and the intention of getting them back to work, contributes to the avoidance of the organizational issues that caused the problems.

In relation to the philosophy and values of counselling psychology we have noted its emphasis on enhancing self-determination. This contrasts with powerful cultural assumptions that go along with being diagnosed as ill, identified by Parsons (1951) as the 'sick role'. This removes responsibility from sufferers, who can't help being ill, and re-defines them as patients with limited personal resources and in need of specialized help (see Johnstone, 2000: 40). It also includes disregarding patients' views and distancing them from their experience through increasingly technical language (for example, Pilgrim and Rogers, 2002). The picture is of passive victims who must put themselves in the hands of professional rescuers. It excludes any account of their social, economic or political contexts and variables such as gender, class and race are ignored. Interestingly, CBT, the treatment recommended by NICE for most disorders, is itself at odds with this picture in requiring patients to work hard and take considerable responsibility for their distorted cognitions.

None of this seeks to question the reality or minimize the experience of psychological distress. What it does do is question the adequacy of the disease model and the psychopathological classifications this entails. As Hacking argues, classifications in human science are interactive. People classified are treated differently by others and, crucially, they may understand how they are classified and 'rethink themselves accordingly' (Hacking, 2001: 108). Acknowledging that medical categorizations of mental illness are permeated by socio-cultural values and processes (see Chapter 2) emphasizes the significance of alternative discourses about psychological well-being and distress which encourage a recognition of the validity of sufferers' own experiences and perceptions. The individual can be seen as existing at the centre of a matrix in which biology, social structure and life events combine with developmental processes to present each person, at any one time, with a unique set of challenges. This fits the collaborative stance of counselling psychology where a formulation about the nature of the distress and an approach to its amelioration is shared with the client. It also fits the alternative discourses of user movements that challenge the medical model by supporting self-advocacy and regarding users of services as consumers or survivors, both of which are seen as more empowering positions; the former by acknowledging that people can make positive choices, the latter by rendering professional services problematic (see, for example, Pilgrim and Rogers, 2002).

CONCLUSION

We have sought, in this chapter, to explore and contextualize the developing identity of counselling psychology as a dynamic socio-historical process. We are ourselves involved in this process and the chapter is itself an intervention. In practice, we regularly confront the tension between being-in-relation and technical expertise and find ourselves re-asserting the centrality of values and counselling psychology's emphasis on *being*, not *doing* (Woolfe, 2001).

Irrespective of the approach, research supports the stress on relationship in therapy, and Rogers noted that therapeutic relationships are not substantially different *in kind* from those in our everyday lives (Strawbridge, 2000). Writing from a psychoanalytic perspective, Lomas (1999) has expressed concerns, similar to our own, about the pull away from relationship into technical expertise and the 'retreat from the ordinary'. This seems particularly pertinent in a climate of McDonaldization in which what is crucial in therapy is threatened by the same process that undermines the quality of ordinary human relationships and increases psychological distress.

Finally, we have emphasized counselling psychology's recognition of significantly different traditions in psychology. This acknowledges the impossibility of theorizing reality within a single meta-narrative. It does not mean that anything goes, and we would not wish to minimize issues of integration. However, we believe it does carry the injunction to resist closure and dogmatism and to maintain open and inquiring minds, and a degree of humility in the face of complexity, that is in the spirit of genuine science.

We are well aware that the issues addressed here and in other chapters will continue to be debated and invite you, the reader, to engage in the debates and participate in shaping the future of our discipline.

REFERENCES

Appignanesi, L. (2008) *Mad, Bad and Sad: A History of Women and the Mind Doctors from 1800 to the Present*. London: Virago.

Barkham, M. (1988) 'Empathy in counselling and psychotherapy: Present status and future directions', *Counselling Psychology Quarterly*, 6 (1): 24–28.

Bentall, R.P. (2003) *Madness Explained: Psychosis and Human Nature.* London: Allen Lane, Penguin Books.

Bergin, A.E. and Garfield, S.L. (1994) *Handbook of Psychotherapy and Behaviour Change,* 4th edn. Chichester: Wiley.

Billington, R., Hockey, J. and Strawbridge, S. (1998) *Exploring Self and Society.* London: Macmillan.

Black, Dame C. (2008) *Working for a Healthier Tomorrow: Review of the Health of Britain's Working Age Population.* London: The Stationery Office.

Braverman, H. (1974) *Labour and Monopoly Capitalism: The Degradation of Work in the Twentieth Century.* London: Monthly Review Press.

Brown, G.W. and Harris, T.O. (1978) *The Social Origins of Depression.* London: Tavistock.

Brubaker, R. (1984) *The Limits of Rationality: An Essay on the Social and Moral Thought of Max Weber.* London: Allen and Unwin.

Bruner, J. (1986) *Actual Minds, Possible Worlds.* London: Harvard University Press.

Cooper, M. (2008) *Essential Research Findings: The Facts are Friendly.* London: Sage.

Cromby, J., Harper, D. and Reavey, P. (2007) 'Moving beyond diagnosis: Practising what we preach', *The Psychologist,* Special Issue: Practising what we preach, 20 (5).

Duffy, M. (1990) 'Counselling psychology USA: Patterns of continuity and change', *Counselling Psychology Review,* 5 (3): 9–18.

Durkheim, E. (2006) trans. R. Buss. *On Suicide.* London: Penguin.

Foucault, M. (1988) (ed.) L.D. Kritzman. *Politics, Philosophy, Culture: Interviews and Other Writings 1977–1984.* London and New York: Routledge.

Fox, D. and Prilleltensky, I. (eds) (1997) *Critical Psychology: An Introduction.* London: Sage.

Furedi, F. (2004) *Therapy Culture: Cultivating Vulnerability in an Uncertain Age.* London: Routledge.

Gallie, W.B. (1956) 'Essentially contested concepts' in *Proceedings of the Aristotelian Society,* 56, reprinted in M. Black (ed.), (1962) *The Importance of Language,* Englewood Cliffs, NJ: Prentice-Hall.

Gray, J. (2007) *Black Mass: Apocalyptic Religion and the Death of Utopia.* London: Allen Lane, Penguin.

Hacking, I. (2001) *The Social Construction of What?* Cambridge, MA: Harvard University Press.

Halsey, A.H. and Sylva, K. (1987) 'Plowden, history and prospect', *Oxford Review of Education,* 13 (1).

Herman, E. (1992) 'Being and doing: Humanistic psychology and the spirit of the 1960s', in B.L. Tischler (ed.), *Sights on the Sixties.* New Brunswick, NJ: Rutgers University Press.

Hochschild, H.R. (1983) *The Managed Heart: Commercialization of Human Feeling.* London: University of California Press.

Hubble, M.A., Duncan, B.L. and Miller, S.D. (1999) *The Heart and Soul of Change.* Washington, DC: American Psychological Association.

Jacoby, R. (1977) *Social Amnesia: A Critique of Conformist Psychology from Adler to Laing.* Hassocks: Harvester Press.

Johnstone, L. (2000) *Users and Abusers of Psychiatry: A Critical Look at Psychiatric Practice,* 2nd edn. London and Philadelphia: Routledge.

Joseph, S. and Worsley, R. (eds) (2007) *Person-centred Psychopathology: A Positive Psychology of Mental Health.* Ross-on-Wye: PCCS Books.

Kinderman, P. (2005) 'A psychological model of mental disorder', *Harvard Review of Psychiatry,* 13: 206–217.

Kirsch, I., Deacon, B.J., Huedo-Medina, T.B., Scoboria, A., Moore, T.J. and Johnson, B.T. (2008) 'Initial severity and antidepressant benefits: A meta-analysis of data submitted to the food and drug administration' *PLoS Med,* 5 (2).

Kirschenbaum, H. and Henderson, V.L. (eds) (1990) *Carl Rogers: Dialogues*. London: Constable.
Kutchins, H. and Kirk, S.A. (1999) *Making Us Crazy: DSM – The Psychiatric Bible and the Creation of Mental Disorders*. London: Constable.
Lacan, J. (1977) *The Four Fundamental Concepts of Psycho-Analysis*. London: Hogarth Press.
Lane, D.A. and Corrie, S. (2006) *The Modern Scientist Practitioner: A Guide to Practice in Psychology*. London and New York: Routledge.
Lapworth, P., Sills, C. and Fish, S. (2001) *Integration in Counselling and Psychotherapy: Developing a Personal Approach*. London: Sage.
Lasch, C. (1979) *The Culture of Narcissism*. New York: Norton.
Layard, R. (2004) *Mental Health: Britain's Biggest Social Problem*. London: Department of Health.
Leader, D. (2008) *The New Black: Mourning, Melancholia and Depression*. London: Hamish Hamilton.
Lomas, P. (1999) *Doing Good: Psychotherapy Out of its Depth*. Oxford: Oxford University Press.
Lyotard, J.-F. (1979, trans. 1984) *The Postmodern Condition: A Report on Knowledge*. Manchester: Manchester University Press.
Lyotard, J.-F. and Thebaud, J.L. (1979, trans. 1985) *Just Gaming*. Manchester: Manchester University Press.
Mair, M. (1999) 'Inquiry in conversation – questions, quests, search and research', *Psychotherapy Section Newsletter*, 25 June: 2–15. Leicester: The British Psychological Society.
O'Brien, M. and Houston, G. (2007) *Integrative Therapy: A Practitioner's Guide*, 2nd edn. London: Sage.
Palmer, S. and Woolfe, R. (eds) (2000) *Integrative and Eclectic Counselling and Psychotherapy*. London: Sage.
Parsons, T. (1951) 'Illness and the role of the physician: a sociological perspective', *American Journal of Orthopsychiatry*, 21: 452–460.
Patterson, C.H. (2000) *Understanding Psychotherapy: Fifty Years of Client-centred Practice*. Ross on Wye: PCCS Books.
Pelling, N. (2000) 'Scientists versus practitioners: A growing dichotomy in need of integration', *Counselling Psychology Review*, 15 (4): 3–7.
Pilgrim, D. and Bentall, R.P. (1999) 'The medicalisation of misery: a critical realist analysis of the concept of depression', *Journal of Mental Health*, 8 (3): 261–274.
Pilgrim, D. and Rogers, R. (2002) *A Sociology of Mental Health and Illness*, 2nd edn. Buckingham: Open University Press.
Polkinghorne, D.E. (1992) 'Postmodern epistemology of practice', in S. Kvale (ed.), *Psychology and Postmodernism*. London: Sage.
Porter, R. (2001) *Enlightenment: Britain and the Creation of the Modern World*. London: Penguin.
Ritzer, G. (1993) *The McDonaldization of Society*. London: Pine Forge.
Ritzer, G. (1998) *The McDonaldization Thesis*. London: Sage.
Rogers, C. (1951) *Client-centred Therapy*. London: Constable.
Rogers, C. (1961) *On Becoming a Person: A Therapist's View of Psychotherapy*. London: Constable.
Rogers, C. (1964) 'Towards a science of the person', in T.W. Wann (ed.), *Behaviourism and Phenomenology: Contrasting Bases for Modern Psychology*. Chicago, IL: Chicago University Press.
Roth, A. and Fonagy, P. (1996) *What Works for Whom?* London and New York: Guildford Press.
Schön, D.A. (1987) *Educating the Reflective Practitioner*. London: Jossey-Bass.
Shotter, J. (1993) 'Rhetoric and the roots of the homeless mind', *Theory Culture and Society*, 10 (4).
Smith, J.A., Harré, R. and Langenhove, L. van (eds) (1995) *Rethinking Psychology*. London: Sage.
Spinelli, E. (2005) *The Interpreted World*, 2nd edn. London: Sage.

Strawbridge, S. (2000) 'Carl Rogers: A personal reflection', *The Psychologist*, 14 (4): 185.

Strawbridge, S. (2002) 'McDonaldization or fast-food therapy', *Counselling Psychology Review*, 17 (4): 20–24.

Strawbridge, S. (2003) 'Ethics, psychology and therapeutic practice', in C. Jones and D. Hill (eds), *Forms of Ethical Thinking in Therapeutic Practice*. Maidenhead: Open University.

Whimster, S. and Lash, S. (eds) (1987) *Max Weber, Rationality and Modernity*. London: Allen and Unwin.

Winkley, D. (1987) 'From condescension to complexity: Post-Plowden schooling in the inner city', *Oxford Review of Education,* 13 (1).

Woolfe, R. (1990) 'Counselling psychology in Britain: An idea whose time has come', *The Psychologist*, 3 (12): 531–535.

Woolfe, R. (1996) 'The nature of counselling psychology', in R. Woolfe and W. Dryden (eds), *Handbook of Counselling Psychology*. London: Sage.

Woolfe, R. (2001) 'The helping process', *The Psychologist*, 14 (7): 347.

2

DISORDER AND ITS DISCONTENTS

Barbara Douglas

Counselling psychologists work in a variety of contexts, including statutory and voluntary services, all of which have their own ethos and organizational understandings. For many colleagues, this involves therapeutic relationships with those who are experiencing mental health problems. Such problems have, historically, given rise to a variety of discourses that frame attempts to understand such experiences. These include the religious, supernatural, moral, medical and psychological. Such discourses frame the way we attempt to make sense of difference and each gives rise to its own classificatory systems as the means of imposing order and understanding on the unfamiliar, the different, the frightening and the distressing. While we acknowledge that the situated contexts of practice play an integral part in the development of our therapeutic work, we may be less aware of how the historical context too has played an important part in the way we view the world and, in the context of this chapter, the notion of disorder.

Much of our current classification of mental disorders, debatably referred to as Neo-Kraepelinian (Bentall, 2004; Horwitz and Wakefield, 2007), can be argued to have arisen from turn of the twentieth-century biological psychiatry and the Kraepelinian twin axes of dementia praecox and manic depressive psychosis (Berrios, 1996). Psychology too grew from the soil of this modern period, with its positivist discourse of scientific endeavour framing the accepted means of furthering knowledge (Gergen and Graumann, 1996), and offering a world-view which separates out, and prioritizes, scientific knowing over narrative knowing. As Ellenberger suggests, 'the science of a certain period is always unconsciously determined by its 'Weltanschauung' (world-view)' (1970: 201). This concept is a useful one here in that it delineates 'a specific way of perceiving the world particular to a nation, a historical period, or an individual' (1970: 201). One manifestation of a modernist world-view is evident in the medicalization of distress and its expression in our institutions and practices. Ahistoricism, oblivious to a notion of world-view, can give rise to acceptance of concepts such as disorder and diagnosis as statements of truth rather than culturally contextualized constructs. In this chapter, therefore, I invite you to consider evaluating the concept of disorder as a construct situated within a particular historical and cultural framework and to explore the implications this has for your practice. With this in mind I will discuss the contested nature of the concept of disorder before examining historical constructions of the concept, as illustrated by the notions of borderline personality and self-harm. Suggested topics for reflection and debate are interspersed in the text to facilitate further discussion, perhaps with colleagues or in training groups.

THE CONTESTED SITE OF DISORDER

What are mental disorders?

Historically the locations of counselling psychology practice have changed. Many more of our colleagues than in the 1990s now work in statutory organizations and indeed mental health services have increasingly taken on psychological therapy as their own (see Chapter 20 on working in the NHS). One of the fundamental implications of this movement is how to retain a humanistic value base within a framework dominated by a medical model of distress in which treatment guidelines focus on disorder, in which the burgeoning industry of manualized, protocol-based therapy for specific disorder is promulgated, and in which therapy could be argued to be an adjunct to the politics of employment. Within such a framework therapies, and their research bases, are premised on the notion of disorder and its classification. Yet these constructs, as I will illustrate, are themselves contested sites which represent the conflation of many stakeholder agendas, past and present.

DISCUSSION POINT
How do you maintain a relational stance within a framework that emphasizes the treatment of disorder?

The *Diagnostic and Statistical Manual of Mental Disorders* (DSM-IV-TR) defines mental disorder as follows:

> Each of the mental disorders is conceptualized as a clinically significant behavioural or psychological syndrome or pattern that occurs in an individual and that is associated with present distress or disability or with a significant risk of suffering death, pain, disability, or an important loss of freedom. In addition this syndrome or pattern must not be merely an expectable and culturally sanctioned response to a particular event, for example the death of a loved one. Whatever its original cause it must currently be considered a manifestation of a behavioural, psychological or biological dysfunction in the individual. Neither deviant behaviour nor conflicts that are primarily between the individual and society are mental disorders unless the deviance or conflict is a symptom of a dysfunction in the individual as described above. (APA, 2000: xxxi)

Thus, in a philosophical defence of a medical model of mental disorder, Resnek (1991) argued that a descriptive approach, as is evidenced above, is sufficient to account for mental illness. Theories, he suggested, may come and go but descriptions remain the same. Yet, the statement 'in the individual' is made three times within the DSM definition and is clear evidence of an epistemological, rather than descriptive, stance. Disorder, it tells us, almost without our noticing, is located firmly within the person, that is, within the brain, mind, personality or neuronal pathways of the individual. Social theorist and semiotician Barthes argued that in popular culture silent sign systems act to reinforce and normalize ideological presuppositions (Brown, 2005). In light of this, perhaps we can view the DSM and it's near silent epistemological stance as just such an example, one in which we are encouraged to accept such a classificatory system of distress as the norm.

In addition, and contrary to Resnek's (1991) view, descriptions do change considerably over time. Depression, for example, can only be categorized as a 'mood disorder' when underpinned by a culturally sanctioned construct of affectivity. As Berrios (1996) argued, this was not the case in nineteenth-century understandings of melancholia which focused on hypochondrias and delusion. Thus, Vassilev and Pilgrim argue, disorders such as depression or schizophrenia 'actually refer to a set of complex psychosocial relationships which are closed off by the very act of psychiatric diagnosis' and that 'this closure is complete when the inherent social nature of diagnosis (its transactional and evaluative character) is not recognised' (2007: 349). Finally, the apparently descriptive stance of the DSM belies that the research bases of classification are determined by statistical analytical processes that in themselves require decisions and choices. Thus, Cooper (2004) argues, classification of disorder is theory-driven despite its claims to the contrary.

> **DISCUSSION POINT**
> The statement that 'disorders are a set of complex psychosocial relationships' suggests that we cannot simply diagnose and treat them. What might this mean for your practice?

Can disorders be classified?

Classification is a means of making sense of the world. Haslam (2000) argues that empirical evidence suggests we are cognitively predisposed to essentialist thinking, something which makes evolutionary sense as a fundamental survival need to distinguish friend from foe. However, that we make sense of distress specifically through a medicalized classification of disorder, rather than, for example, via notions of demonic possession, humoral balance or witchcraft, is framed by our own historically located cultural world-view, and accordingly we are predisposed to classify and intervene in this manner. To illustrate, Lane (2007: 149), for example, argues that while 'there is no evidential correlation between anxiety or depression with low levels of serotonin', this association is part of modern neuromythology. Often readily accepted phrases such as 'chemical imbalance' have little evidential substance but act as placeholders for essentialist thinking (Haslam, 2000) containing within them the less visible, but equally powerful, unsubstantiated implication that 'there is a normal ideal neurochemical state that can be achieved by rectifying individual brain chemistry' (Mulder, 2008: 244).

Classification of mental disorder took a powerful turn at the beginning of the twentieth century with the work of German psychiatrist Emil Kraepelin (1856–1926). Kraepelin developed a nosology of psychiatric illness underpinned by a medical model that stressed aetiology and disease process and which was based upon the twin axes of manic depression and dementia praecox (Greene, 2007). Emphasis on the physical substrata of mental disease process was given further weight by the discovery of syphilis as the cause of general paralysis of the insane (GPI). GPI was a devastating, terminal condition and a major contributor to asylum admissions and deaths. The discovery of the syphilitic spirochete in the brain as its cause, and the drug salvarsan, as the first effective treatment, offered psychiatry both the opportunity to raise its previously poor medical collegial standing as well as optimism that similar physical causation of mental illness would be found in other conditions.

Yet it was psychoanalytic constructs that influenced the emergence of the early DSM, and psychiatrist and president of the APA, Adolf Meyer (1866–1950), was particularly influential. Initially immersed in Kraeplinian psychiatry, Meyer later argued for, and led the development of, a more socially based view of mental illness in which individual experiences were described as reactions, or responses to, individual circumstances rather than biological-based disease entities. It was this framework of individual response, continuum of experience and behaviours as manifestations of unconscious conflict that underpinned the original DSM-I and its successor DSM-II. Only with the DSM-III was there a paradigmatic shift to the catagorical classification of mental disorder, sometimes referred to as the rise of the second biological psychiatry (Shorter, 1997: 239) or neo-Kraepelinian in its epistemology (Mayes and Horwitz, 2005).

In its wake, this paradigm shift in DSM classification of mental disorder has brought about much debate. Mayes and Horwitz (2005), for example, have argued that it was based not on scientific endeavour but rather emerged from conflated professional, political, pharmaceutical and financial agendas. Discussion, as shown below, has also emerged on the nature of the categories. Whether, for example, mental disorders can be considered natural kinds is a much debated topic within the philosophy of psychiatry (Haslam, 2000; Zachar, 2000; Kendell, 2003; Cooper, 2004; Pilgrim, 2007).

DISCUSSION POINT
By what process have you and your clients become familiar with the belief that a chemical imbalance in the brain is the cause of depression? Can you identify any research evidence that supports this belief?

Are mental disorders natural kinds?

Perhaps the concept of 'natural kind' can best be outlined via a metaphor of a British pound coin. While the meaning of the coin and its transactions exist only through socially constructed agreement, the metals of which it is composed exist with specific and stable properties as discrete bounded entities, regardless of meaning systems. If mental disorders are natural kinds then, as Adriaens suggests, they need to be demonstrably 'indifferent to changing conventions in psychiatric diagnostics, to differ categorically from each other, as well as from normality, and to be grounded in discrete biological causes' (2007: 514). The debate as to whether mental disorders are natural kinds has focused largely on schizophrenia (Crow, 2000; Haslam, 2000; Bentall, 2004; Cooper, 2004; Read et al., 2004; Pilgrim, 2007). Following on from Kraepelin's finding of the condition world wide, a universality thesis argues that schizophrenia is an integral part of an evolutionary function. Empirical evidence, Crow suggests, shows it to be a 'language-based disorder that is connected with the adaptive functions of hemispheric lateralisation, whereby equi-balanced handedness appears to be linked to schizophrenia' (2000: 123).

Other work, however, has suggested that the cluster of behaviours and symptoms we refer to as schizophrenia have only been in existence for around 200 years and that it is of viral origin, emerging as a consequence of urbanization in industrialized society.

(Ledgerwood, et al., 2003). By contrast, a heterogeneity hypothesis suggests that not only is schizophrenia not a natural kind, but it is 'a reified umbrella concept constructed by psychiatry to cover a heterogeneous group of problems' (Adriaens, 2007: 524) and that neither research or practice evidence supports the existence of such a unitary concept (Boyle, 1990).

As this very bald outline suggests, varied and conflicting theories of schizophrenia and its existence illustrate the importance of critical appraisal of the concept of disorder as discrete entity. As Richards suggests, 'Naming endows the named with discrete status, raises it to consciousness, changes how it is experienced and managed – changes, in short, its entire psychological character' (2002: 24). As therapists and clients, we are active participants in this process which can powerfully and subtly alter the fundamental nature of the therapeutic relationship from that of I–thou to I–it (Buber, 1971).

DISCUSSION POINT
How might naming a disorder change the nature and focus of your therapeutic relationships?

Is disorder a useful notion?

Mental disorders may or may not be natural kinds but they are arguably 'practical kinds' (Kendell, 2003). Haslam (2000: 1003), for example, argues that classification is either about a need to develop a taxonomy which comes ever nearer to the 'truth of biomedical causes of disorder' or that we need to see it simply as a useful way to group people in terms of similarities of behaviour. Similarly, Mulder (2008) suggests that even if diagnostic categories are not discrete groups they may have clinical utility, and Sadler suggests of the DSM-III that it 'improved reliability and facilitated communication between clinicians and researchers' (2002: 12). But what assumptions underpin the notions of reliability, usefulness, utility and communication?

Kendell suggested of classification that 'if it is the art of carving nature at its joints, it should indeed imply that there is a joint there, that one is not sawing through bone', (1975: 65) High levels of dual diagnoses suggest that, rather than moving ever nearer to scientifically accurate diagnoses, what we are seeing may be a fundamental problem in the essentialist and reductionist notion of classification. If the concept of disorder does indeed cut through bone, then we need to question the usefulness of a group of people honing their mutual communication *about* it, developing expertise *in* it and coming ever closer in their shared understandings *of* it. Indeed, the notion of classificatory systems as a means of facilitating intra- and inter-professional communication could itself be argued to be the rhetoric of a hegemonic process. In such a process, the badge of expert is displayed in the use of acronyms such as BPD (borderline personality disorder) or DSH (deliberate self-harm), and acts to close off the complexity of lived experience to empathic understanding.

We might also ask whether the notion of disorder is useful to the practitioner. Research into mental disorders seeks to exclude potential participants who do not meet clearly defined criteria for specific disorders, or who are considered to have a dual diagnosis. Practitioners, on the other hand, usually work within a somewhat different framework in which the client has been rather more broadly identified as experiencing emotional or psychological distress. While researchers may use DSM to facilitate inclusion/exclusion criteria for randomized controlled trials, in practice clients come context-bound and rarely so neatly packaged as the DSM would have us believe. How useful to practitioners are the results of the researchers' work if it is based on highly selective populations created in artificial settings where real-life problems are separated out into a framework of dual diagnosis? Would best practice not be supported by greater value being placed on, and resources provided for, practice-based research evidence? (See Chapter 3 on the nature of evidence.)

Similarly, we can ask whether the notion of disorder is useful to the client. A client with anorexia, for example, may see the diagnosis of a disorder as the beginning of a process of externalizing a problem, facilitating the client and therapist in working collaboratively to find a more comfortable way of living. For others, being given a diagnostic label may be experienced as welcome evidence that perhaps their distress is not self-induced and thus paves the way for development of a less punitive self-concept. Yet for others, a diagnosis may represent a compromised identity which is both stigmatizing and socially detrimental. How the client makes narrative sense of the classification, however, is an oft-forgotten variable in the separation of scientific discourse from narrative understanding.

DISCUSSION POINT
How might the development of practice-based evidence best support your work with clients experiencing mental health issues?

Disorder as personhood

Appignanesi (2008: 447) suggests that diagnoses have the hypnotic power of master words, and certainly terms such as bipolar disorder, depression or schizophrenia can very easily slip into descriptions of personhood. Consider, for example, the word 'lunatic', which you would probably think of as a stigmatizing, global attribution of personhood and one which we would not now consider attaching to a human being. Yet are our current terminological '-ics' (including anorexic, schizophrenic or psychotic) any less stigmatized attributions of personhood or do we only hear them as acceptable because they are a part of today's common parlance? If there are few stops on the therapist's journey from seeing their client as 'meeting the criteria for anorexia' to 'being anorexic' to 'being an anorexic', we might wonder how the client with anorexia is to find a wider identity for themselves than the empty one they so often see as lying beyond the anorexia?

Essentialism has been defined as 'the attachment of inherent qualities to individuals through structural belonging' (Brown, 2005: 79) and attribution of disorder as embodied within the individual also overlooks the relational space between person and social environment. Vassilev and Pilgrim point to the importance of acknowledging lay relationships as the initial place in which attributions of mental illness are developed and that 'psychiatric diagnosis can consequently be accused of being a form of vacuous scientific reification or of simply rubber stamping and codifying decisions made already by others' (2007: 349). The value and outcome of therapy, however, perhaps lies less in curing the disorders it treats than in its provision of a relationship within which the client can build a coherent narrative, an experientially meaningful autobiographical account of their distress, that is constructed in the presence of another, shared and validated by the other. It is perhaps paradoxical that the very moment when postmodern views of the world facilitate multiple meaning systems and multivocality of voices, is simultaneously the moment when these very tenets of counselling psychology are in danger of being subsumed into the vast machinery of disorders' institutions and practices?

DISCUSSION POINT
Why are some essentialist notions considered prejudicial, for example around disability, while others, such as diagnostic classifications, are culturally sanctioned and reified?

Visibility of disorder

Professional gaze settles variably on the problematization of particular clusters of behaviours that threaten contemporaneous cultural ideologies. At the turn of the nineteenth and twentieth centuries, for example, social concern about apparent declining physical health of the population was reflected in discourses of mental decline of nation and empire. This latter was given a powerful platform by the hereditarian psychiatry of Benedict-Auguste Morel (1809–1873) and Henry Maudsley (1835–1918) in France and Britain respectively. Psychiatric and educational focus settled on the emergence of a perceived growth in the numbers of the weak-minded, that is, those on 'the borderlands of imbecility' (Jackson, 2000). The social construction of the feeble-minded as a group was both mirrored in, and developed by, the emergence of the eugenics movement and legitimated a discourse of necessary containment and segregation. Such individuals, however, needed first to be identified and made visible, and as Jackson suggests, 'mental defectives were arranged on an axis of visibility in which the least visible were construed as the most menacing, a process which placed a premium on the precise recognition of the physical signs of deficiency' (2000: 96). It was within this world-view of evidencing and making visible the signs of weak-mindedness that tests of intellectual functioning emerged. However we consider their use today, their origins are inseparable from the socio-political context in which a discourse of protection of society from invisible menace was privileged (see Chapter 5 on psychometric testing).

Thus, disorders are not simply located within the individual, but rather are socially and historically constructed in partnership with provision. With the de-institutionalization of psychiatry, Vassilev and Pilgrim suggest that 'forms of mental disorder, once locked away out of sight and out of mind, now appear in public spaces' (2007: 351). Consequently, dangerousness, in those deemed personality disordered, has become defined as an important construct, one which has taken central place in recent reviews of mental health legislation. Borderline personality disorder too is currently a highly visible, and somewhat feared, diagnostic category. The client who struggles to contain their emotions is not contained and held within current service provision structures and so becomes a highly visible 'problem' upon whom the gaze of the psychologist is turned. I will now turn to the concept of borderline personality and its history in more detail in order to illustrate this process.

DISCUSSION POINT
It has been suggested that we are in the middle of an epidemic of depression. Might this be alternatively constructed as the interplay of the politics of employment and the power of the pharmaceutical industry?

THE HISTORICAL CONSTRUCTIONS OF DISORDER

Borderline personality disorder

In *An Age of Anxiety*, W.H. Auden (1948) sparked the notion of human behaviour as a reflection of cultural experience and that mid-twentieth-century Western society, immersed as it was in war, Cold War and nuclear threat, was one dominated particularly by anxiety. Reisman et al. (1950) developed this theme, suggesting that social character types may be 'formed at the knee of society' (1950: v). On this basis, the emergence of the borderline personality could be argued to represent a mirror to a Western society characterized by meaninglessness and emptiness, one which finds vacuous attempts at relationship in its impulsive need for shopping, work, substance misuse or other relationship substitutes (Lunbeck, 2006: 151). Certainly there is ample evidence of this in the vast, domed, marble-floored shopping malls where attempts at meeting others are played out in fear of abandonment and isolation but which, missing the mark, find only quasi-fulfilment in the substitute of the purchase. Are these not characteristics similarly identified in those labelled as having borderline personality disorder? The impulsive, often self-destructive, behaviour that gives temporary release only to be followed by emptiness, fear of abandonment and ongoing need for relationship? Thus, Rose argues, scientific psychologization may be 'a kind of shadow play, in which the vicissitudes of knowledge claims are merely the ghostly projection of outside forces' (1996: 104).

By contrast, DSM-IV-TR locates borderline personality disorder firmly within the individual, who displays:

> A pervasive pattern of instability in interpersonal relationships, self image and affects, and marked impulsivity beginning by early adulthood and present in a variety of contexts. (APA, 2000: 710)

Nine criteria are outlined as indicative of the disorder: fear of abandonment, unstable relationships, identity disturbance, impulsivity, recurrent suicidal behaviour, affective instability, chronic feelings of emptiness, anger management problems and transient paranoid ideation or dissociative symptoms. Diagnosis requires the presence of five of these (APA, 2000: 710). Additionally, borderline personality disorder is organized as an Axis 2 diagnosis, but often associated with co-morbidity on Axis 1. The National Institute of Health and Clinical Excellence (NICE) offers evidence of the prevalence of borderline personality disorder as between 0.7 per cent and 2 per cent in the general population; about 20 per cent of in-patients in psychiatric wards; 10–30 per cent of psychiatric out-patients; and suggests that 75 per cent of those diagnosed are women. Within the prison population it suggests estimates of 23 per cent prevalence among male remand prisoners, 14 per cent among sentenced male prisoners and 20 per cent among female prisoners (NICE, 2007: 2).

While the above discourse implicitly conveys a knowledge-based understanding of a disorder, the following statement from NICE regarding causation suggests otherwise:

> Specific causes of borderline personality disorder have not been identified. Although the processes that lead to its development remain a matter of debate, it appears likely that borderline personality disorder develops through the accumulation and interaction of multiple factors, including temperament, childhood and adolescent experiences and other environmental factors. (2007)

Could the human condition itself not be attributed to these same causes? Such a generalized portrait, Masterson (1988) suggests, has developed as a waste-basket notion, a view supported by NICE that the 'diagnostic label tends to divert attention from helping the person to overcome their problems and can even lead to the person being denied help' (2004: 21). Equally, concepts such as co-morbidity and axes are themselves problematic. Co-morbidity, it could be argued, is nothing more than a reified discursive mechanism that acts to separate the non-separable. The notion of axes also has difficulties. Axis 1 is designed for the reporting of clinical conditions, and Axis 2 for the reporting of personality disorders or mental retardation. Yet these are separated on a questionable assumption of Axis 2 personality disorder presentations as enduring characteristics of an individual, a notion, not only empirically unsupported but one which also requires underpinning by what is a debated conceptual understanding of the 'normal' personality as individualized, autonomous and enduring.

Evidence for the embryonic emergence of notions of a borderline personality disorder can be found in the late 1890s as, for example, in the work of Rosse, professor of nervous diseases at Georgetown University who wrote of 'a class of persons standing in the twilight of right reason and despair' (1890: 32). The concept of borderline personality disorder, however, is a twentieth-century construction, one that gradually uncoupled itself from the concepts of neurosis and psychosis within psychoanalysis and psychiatry.

The formal history of the concept of the borderline personality is usually credited as beginning with a seminal paper in 1938 by New York psychoanalyst Adolph Stern (1879–1958). Stern's paper was representative of contemporary analytic discussions concerning the emergence of the 'new patient', that was, the apparently increasing numbers of clients who did not fit conventional patterns of neuroses but exhibited a broad range of problems that found expression in problematic transferences:

> There is a degree of immaturity and insecurity that is not present in the ordinary transference neurosis with which we are familiar. (1938: 63) … so intense an affective involvement can this attachment become that attention to this aspect of the transference takes up an inordinate amount of time. (1938: 66)

Thus the rationale for conceptualization of the borderline patient was located firmly within psychodynamic theory and the transference relationship. This relational conceptualization of the borderline was furthered by Main (1957), whose influential object relations research paper 'The ailment' focused less on characteristics of the individual deemed 'borderline' and more on the interaction between client and therapist. This intersubjective space was, he suggested, the location where relational complexities evolved and 'sentimental appeal' from the patient enmeshed with 'arousal of omnipotence' in the nurse (1957: 136).

While psychoanalytic approaches were evolving an understanding of the borderline patient based on transferential relationships, within psychiatry the focus was on psychopathological features of such patients. Here the borderline concept was detaching from schizophrenia. Hoch and Polatin (1949), for example, argued that the borderline patient evidenced a form of schizophrenia which they termed 'pseudoneurotic schizophrenia', based on a differential analysis of the features of psychoneuroses and schizophrenia. Similarly, Rapaport et al. (1946) conceptualized the borderline as one of 'preschizophrenic personality structure', in which patients' structured thinking (as measured by the Wechsler adult intelligence scale) was normal while unstructured thinking (as evidenced by Rorschach tests) was disordered.

However, this idea of the borderline as a vacillating position between neurosis and psychosis was transformed fundamentally by an emerging notion, introduced by Schmideberg (1959) and Kernberg (1967), of the stability of such a personality structure. While Schmideberg (1959) introduced the idea of the patient as 'stably unstable', Kernberg, argued of such patients that 'their personality organization is not a transitory state fluctuating between neurosis and psychosis' (1967: 279). He introduced the term 'borderline personality organization' as more accurately describing the specific, stable, pathological personality organization that he evidenced. This developing notion of an enduring personality structure was firmly consolidated by neo-Kraepelinian descriptive psychiatry, which, although with a different underpinning epistemology, similarly described borderline personality as 'characteristic of most of adult life' (APA, 1980: 306).

But this clinical history of the borderline personality did not develop in a social vacuum and there are two other threads to consider. These involve the changing nature of institutional provision for the mentally ill and the necessary development of a meta-theory of the normal personality from which to hang the notion of the disordered personality. Of the first, in the early twentieth century, internationally asylums were increasingly unlocking their doors in attempts to reduce the stigma of admission which, it was argued, prevented patients and families seeking the benefits of early treatment. In England and Wales, the 1930 Mental Treatment Act enabled admission to a mental hospital without certification. Consequently, institutional psychiatry's engagement with the neuroses began in earnest.

Of the second, notions of personality emerged only as part of a wider psychological world-view in which the rather different Victorian notion of 'character' as moral, and trainable, gave way to twentieth-century conceptualizations of personality as autonomous, individualistic and stable. Within this framework contemporaneous psychological study focused on the enduring traits of 'normal' personality. Thus, historically located conceptualizations which define 'normal' similarly define the different or unusual and act to produce and confirm that deemed 'abnormal'.

Currently, this modernist world-view of personality as individualized, stable and autonomous is giving way to postmodernist views of personality as more fluid, inter-subjective and embedded in relationship. Within this evolving framework, Fonagy concludes that 'the behaviours and experiences clustered around the notion of borderline personality disorder do not comprise an intractable, stable organisation but rather they remit in relatively short periods' (2007: 3). Links et al. (1998), for example, found that 53 per cent no longer met criteria for borderline personality disorder at seven years follow-up; Zanarini et al. (2003) found that at two years follow-up 34.5 per cent no longer met criteria, a figure which rose to 49.4 per cent at four years and at six years was 68.6 per cent, and Paris et al. (1987) found that 75 per cent no longer met criteria for borderline personality disorder 15 years after first admission. Thus, given the very uncertainties surrounding borderline personality disorder it might, as Pilgrim (2001) suggests, itself be considered a 'disordered concept'.

Borderline personality disorder may also be seen as a disordered concept in its power to invite anxiety in health care professionals. Paradoxically, although optimism and therapeutic persistence are important in working with clients deemed to have borderline personality disorder (Linehan, 1993), optimism is lower for borderline personality disorder than either depression or schizophrenia (Markham, 2003: 607). Thus, a catch-22 situation arises whereby the very labelling of someone as having this 'disorder' may in itself become a predictor of likely poorer outcome for the client. If this is an experiential cluster that develops from difficult childhood experiences, which remits over a period of time and is negatively connoted with good outcome, the adoption of a descriptive psychiatric model of disorder within which to locate such experiences appears to be destructive. Perhaps twentieth-century conceptualizations of the 'borderline' replaced nineteenth-century conceptualizations of 'lunatic' whose process similarly implied a trajectory of hopeless chronicity.

Recent psychological approaches are instead adopting a life-course perspective in which such clusters are understood as problems of psychological development (Winston, 2000) with markers in abuse, neglect or otherwise traumatic childhood events that trigger disturbances of identity and selfhood. Such a conceptualization sits comfortably with postmodernism's shift of emphasis from personality as a fixed individualized structure to a much more intersubjective relational experience and is entirely consistent with the philosophy of counselling psychology in which 'there is a particular focus on the wide range of human psychological functioning across the life span, which leads to a consideration of ways of addressing developmental obstacles and promoting developmental change' (BPS, 2008: 5). Fongay argues that in adopting a developmental framework 'we are likely to see behavioural organizations that we currently term personality disorders as age specific adaptations to biopsychosocial pressures, which are best treated by developmentally specific interventions' (2007: 3) Such psychological therapies currently include mentalization, cognitive analytical therapy, interpersonal therapies; schema-focused cognitive therapy and dialectical behaviour therapy.

In conclusion, borderline personality disorder can be argued to be a historically constructed disorder that is currently in the process of being psychologically reconstructed. By contrast, in self-harm we see distress that is currently viewed as evidence of disorder rather than disorder itself, although there are concerted efforts to have it considered as a disorder in its own right. In the next section I will use self-harm to illustrate a process by which a disorder may come to be constructed.

DISCUSSION POINT
The nature of service provision co-creates problematic behaviours. To what extent do you think this statement reflects the position with regard to clients experiencing behaviour clusters labelled as borderline personality disorder?

Self-harm

The Nice Guideline CG16 (2004) defines self-harm as 'self-poisoning or self-injury, irrespective of the apparent purpose of the act'. Although it can occur at any age, self-harm is predominantly found in adolescents and young adults (Meltzer et al., 2002a). Estimates of its occurrence range between 4.6 per cent and 6.6 per cent (Meltzer et al., 2002a) to 13 per cent of young people aged between 15 and 16 (Hawton et al., 2002), with incidents in adolescence girls three times as many as in boys (Meltzer et al., 2002b).

Self-harm is currently viewed not as a disorder, but as a criteria of several DSM disorders; that is, borderline personality disorder, dissociative disorder and bulimia nervosa (APA, 2000). Most regularly it is seen as a part of borderline personality disorder, and approximately half of those attending casualty departments are deemed to meet the criteria for borderline personality disorder (Haw et al., 2001). Yet conceptualization of self-harm within a framework of disorder is only one cultural interpretation of many historical world-views that encompass, for example, blood-letting as communication with the gods, or later as a treatment for the insane. Uncritical acceptance of terminologies can have a tendency to be played out on the person of the client who subsequently carries the burden of that social belief for society, in this instance the client who self-harms, and in this section I will focus particularly on cutting, the most commonly used means of self-harming (Hawton et al., 2002).

Jenny had a history of anorexia in her teenage years, which subsequently developed into bulimia. She experiences this latter as a dreadful burden and is self-deprecating about being unable to restrict her eating anymore, something on which she had placed a high personal value. In addition to making herself sick, Jenny cuts herself on a regular basis, along her arms, her stomach and the tops of her legs. She is clear that this is not about suicide, or attention seeking – although the latter is something she has been told by others – but about the sense of relief that she gets when she cuts herself, an effect which she describes as emotionally anaesthetizing.

It seems therefore that both professional and lay perceptions are framed by a medical model. The former view cutting as likely evidence of disorder while the latter, as evidenced by Jenny's understanding, is articulated as anaesthesia. It is within this interplay of lay and professional discourses that cultural ideologies develop and are mutually reinforced. Historically, however, cutting has been framed within discourses of communication, religiosity and treatment. Blood-letting has been in existence as long as recorded information has been available and evidence for the use of phlebotomy by the ancient Egyptians, for example, has been found in the 65-foot long Ebers Papyrus (Ventura and Mandeep, 2005). While detailed explanation for its use by the ancient Egyptians is unavailable, argument has been made that the importance the river Nile, and its annual flooding, to the survival of the people was mirrored by bodily notions of channels and tributaries and their management through the use of phlebotomy (Thorwald, 1962).

Crossing the ocean to the ancient Mesoamerican civilization of the Mayans, the process of blood-letting was again central to cultural belief, this time in the form of communication between the people and their gods. An understanding of Mayan beliefs and their gods is enormously complex and well beyond the scope of this chapter; communication with the gods, however, was central to a belief system in which the survival of the people depended on relationship and communication with their gods. Kings, nobles and priests were ritually bled, their blood mixed with bark paper, the mixture burnt and the smoke 'nourished the gods with the divine forces they had implanted in the human body so aligning the earthly world with the supernatural realm' (Sokolow, 2002: 25).

Ancient Greek society, on the other hand, framed blood-letting within a structure of humoral medicine. The fundamental theoretical constructs of the Hippocatatic school stressed the need for balance and complimentarity between the four world elements of fire, earth, water and air, and the four body humors of blood, phlegm, bile and black bile. Health within this understanding became a matter of balance both within the body and between body and environment. Good health depended on a balance of the humors. Intervention, with the aim of rebalancing, was the remit of the physician and could be achieved by the prescription of diet, rest, exercise or, in a case of plethora (excess of humors), by blood-letting or purging of the digestive system. Thus, for the Greeks, the concept of blood-letting was very firmly conceptualized as a treatment for illness within a framework of humoral medicine.

Humoral medicine long remained the mainstay of medical understanding within Western cultures and, in the medieval period, became intertwined with Christian constructs. The notion of priest physician was integrated with understandings of illness and pain as representations of the suffering of Christ. In consequence, between the ninth and sixteenth century, periodic blood-letting was part of the regimen of religious communities where men and women were bled at regular intervals throughout the year for spiritual prophylaxis, their blood representative of the blood of Christ.

Humeral notions of blood-letting were also influenced by astrological notions during the medieval period and prophylactic blood-letting, as a form of heath promotion, was also part of a way of life for those outside the religious communities who were susceptible to plethoric ailments, that is, ones of excess and imbalance of particular humours which threatened the maintenance of a healthy balance in the body. Timings of bleedings were specified in the many medieval health regimes, and such advice is evidenced in the excerpt below from the most well-known of these documents, the Regimen Sanitatis Salernitanum:

> These are the good months for phlebotomy – May, September, April –
> Which are lunar months just as are the Hydra days.
> Neither on the first day of May nor the last day of September or April
> Should blood be drawn or goose be eaten.
> In the old man or in the young man whose veins are full of blood
> Phlebotomy may be practiced in every month.
> These are the three months – May, September, April –
> In which you should draw blood in order to live a long time. (Harington, 1920: 149)

Subsequently, in the development of modern medicine humoral notions of excesses and blood-letting conflated with understandings of madness. Voltaire (1764), for example, described the treatment of madness as 'baths, blood-letting and diet' and Pinel (1806) argued that 'It is a well established fact, that paroxysms of madness are in many instances prevented by a copious bleeding' (both cited in Morgan and Lacey, 1998: 484). Blood-letting, therefore, far from being considered a manifestation of disorder, was variously framed by notions of communication with the gods as treatment within classical and medieval humoral medicine and as a means of managing madness.

As humoral medicine declined, however, so the process of phlebotomy became increasingly distrusted and marginalized, although this was by no means synonymous with the development of notions of self-harm as we currently understand it. Although French psychiatrist Esquirol (1772–1840) alluded to 'suicide simule' (Berrios, 1996: 445), self-harm in the nineteenth and early twentieth centuries was generally undifferentiated as a concept, remaining encapsulated within legal and religious understandings of suicide as a criminal and moral offence. The conceptual uncoupling of self-harm from suicide began in the second half of the twentieth century (Stengel and Cook, 1958), influenced by the incorporation of the neuroses into psychiatry and by the decriminal-ization of suicide in 1961. Conceptual separation of attempted suicide was given a polit-ical platform in the Ministry of Health Circular (1961) which highlighted that for every one completed suicide there were an estimated six attempted suicides. The latter, it sug-gested, should be treated as a medical and social problem, with all cases presenting to hospital being offered psychiatric assessment. Revised legal and health service frame-works therefore legitimated delineation of attempted suicide, which began to attract terms such as deliberate self-injury or self-poisoning (Kessel, 1965), parasuicide (Kreitman et al., 1969) and deliberate self-harm (Morgan, 1979).

Potter et al. (1999) suggest that 'truth, certainty and evidence may be seen as situ-ated practices', and with discursive legitimation of self-harm came empirical research. This supported the construction of a differentiated parasuicide population, whose pre-dominant age range was 20–29, closely followed by the under-20s. Consequently, an embryonic concept of self-harm emerged that was delineated around the notion of intent (Kessel, 1965), and interest rose in why this newly perceived group was increasing in incidence while simultaneously completed suicide rates were falling.

Conceptual construction continued apace with the hegemonic abbreviation of deliberate self-harm to its initials DSH as the badge of common medical understanding. In addition, the shifting status of blood-letting towards accepted discourse of disorder was concurrently evidenced in DSM-III-R (APA, 1987: 347) where as 'recurrent suicidal threats, gestures, or behaviour, or self mutilating behaviour' it became one of eight criteria of borderline personality disorder, although interestingly the status of intent has been removed.

A further reframing of blood-letting from communication with the gods through its conceptualization as a treatment to one of disorder is currently underway in arguments that these behaviours should be considered a DSM disorder in themselves. American psychotherapist Steven Levenkron, for example, argues that 'in the most severely pathological forms, self-mutilation can be classified using the following diagnostic criteria':

- Recurrent cutting or burning of one's skin.
- A sense of tension present immediately before the act is committed.
- Relaxation, gratification, pleasant feelings and numbness experienced concomitant with the physical pain.
- A sense of shame and fear of social stigma, causing the individual to attempt to hide scars, blood or other evidence of the acts of self-harm.

(1998: 25)

Self-harm is not (yet) a diagnostic category, although the above classification clearly attempts to define it as such. Yet if loss of blood engenders a sensation that is variously interpreted according to religious experience, treatment effects, or as self-induced anaesthesia, then apparent decontextualization of the notion of disorder is meaningless. Disorder is itself a cultural interpretation.

This is not to detract from the very real suffering associated with the need to let blood in this way, nor the need to offer help to alleviate such distress. History, however, suggests we loosen the discursive armour of expert treating disorder and, as the *National Inquiry into Self-Harm among Young People* invites us, 'remain rooted in the core professional skills and values of empathy, understanding, non-judgemental listening, and respect for individuals' (Brophy, 2006).

DISCUSSION POINT
What does self-harm mean to you, and how does this understanding impact on your perceptions of your clients?

CONCLUSION

Categorization is a psychological process that has long since engaged humanity in its attempts to impose sense on the environment in which it found itself (Haslam, 2000). However, that we make sense of distress through a medicalized classification of disorder is framed by our own 'Weltanschaung', and mental disorder is a conceptual framework and not a natural kind. By the end of his career, Kraepelin himself suggested that in categorically distinguishing manic depressive psychosis from dementia praecox 'the suspicion remains that we are asking the wrong questions' (Kraepelin and Beer, 1992: 527). Perhaps we too are asking the wrong questions. Paul Tillich (1988: 118) coined the term 'thingification' to describe how a culture may objectify its people, alienating them from humanness. In considering therapy as the treatment of mental disorders, are we not 'thingifying' counselling psychology?

I have attempted to offer some arguments for the constructed nature of the concept of disorder, its subdivisions into reified packages of experience and the implications of this for therapeutic process. Vassilev and Pilgrim suggests that 'there is no single theory that can tell us everything about a phenomenon; the best we can hope for is to zoom in and out and change the angles of our observation to improve our understanding' (2007: 350). In this chapter I have attempted to zoom in on a historical perspective in order to invite you to critically evaluate and debate the conceptual phenomenon of disorder and its impact on the nature of therapeutic process.

REFERENCES

Adriaens, Pieter (2007) 'Evolutionary psychiatry and the schizophrenia paradox: A critique', *Biology and Philosophy*, 22: 513–528.

American Psychiatric Association (1980) *Diagnostic and Statistical Manual of Mental Disorders*, 3rd edn. Washington, DC: American Psychiatric Association.

American Psychiatric Association (1987) *Diagnostic and Statistical Manual of Mental Disorders*, 3rd edn, Text Revision. Washington, DC: American Psychiatric Association.

American Psychological Association (2000) *Diagnostic and Statistical Manual of Mental Disorders*, 4th edn, Text Revision. Washington, DC: APA.

Appignanesi, Lisa (2008) *Mad, Bad and Sad: A History of Women and the Mad Doctors from 1800*. London: Virago.

Auden, W.H. (1948) *The Age of Anxiety: A Baroque Eclogue*. London: Faber and Faber.

Bentall, Richard (2004) *Madness Explained: Psychosis and Human Nature*. London: Penguin.

Berrios, German (1996) *The History of Mental Symptoms: Descriptive Psychopathology since the Nineteenth Century*. Cambridge: Cambridge University Press.

Boyle, M. (1990) *Schizophrenia: A Scientific Delusion*. London: Routledge.

British Psychological Society Board of Assessors in Counselling Psychology (2008) *Candidate Handbook for the Qualification in Counselling Psychology*. Leicester: British Psychological Society.

Brophy, Marcia (2006) *Truth Hurts: Report of the National Inquiry into Self-harm among Young People*. London: Mental Health Foundation.

Brown, Callum (2005) *Postmodernism for Historians*. Harlow: Pearson Longman.

Buber, Martin (1971) *I and Thou*. London: Simon and Schuster.

Cooper, Rachel (2004) 'What is wrong with the DSM', *History of Psychiatry*, 15 (1): 1–25.

Crow, T. (2000) 'Schizophrenia as the price to pay that homo sapiens pay for language: A resolution of the central paradox in the origin of the species', *Brain Research Reviews*, 31: 118–129.

Ellenberger, Henri F. (1970) *The Discovery of the Unconscious: The Evolution of Dynamic Psychiatry*. New York: Basic Books.

Fonagy, Peter (2007) 'Editorial: Personality disorder', *Journal of Mental Health*, 16 (1): 1–4.

Gergen, K. and Graumann, C. (1996) 'Psychological discourse in historical context: An introduction', in C. Graumann and K. Gergen (eds), *Historical Dimensions of Psychological Discourse*. Cambridge: Cambridge University.

Greene, Talya (2007) 'The Kraepelinian dichotomy: The twin pillars crumbling?', *History of Psychiatry*, 18 (3): 361–379.

Harington, John (1920) *The School of Salernum. Regimen Sanitatis Salernitanum. The English Version*. New York: Paul B. Hoeber.

Haslam, Nick (2000) 'Psychiatric categories as natural kinds: Essentialist thinking about mental disorders', *Social Research*, 67 (4): 1031–1058.

Haw, C., Hawton, K., Houston, K. and Townsend, E. (2001) 'Psychiatric and personality disorders in deliberate self-harm patients', *British Journal of Psychiatry*, 178 (1): 48–54.

Hawton, K., Rodham, K. and Evans, E. (2002) 'Deliberate self-harm in adolescents: self report survey in schools in England', *British Medical Journal*, 325 (7374): 1207–1211.

Hoch, P. and Polatin, P. (1949) 'Pseudoneurotic forms of schizophrenia', in M. Stone (ed.), (1986) *Essential Papers on Borderline Disorders: One Hundred Years at the Border*. New York: New York University Press. pp. 119–147.

Horwitz, A. and Wakefield, J. (2007) *The Loss of Sadness: How Psychiatry Transformed Normal Sorrow into Depressive Disorder*. Oxford: Oxford University Press.

Jackson, M. (2000) *The Borderland of Imbecility: Medicine, Society and the Fabrication of the Feeble Mind in Late Victorian and Edwardian Britain*. Manchester: Manchester University Press.

Kendell, Robert (1975) *The Role of Diagnosis in Psychiatry*. London: Blackwell.

Kendell, Robert (2003) 'Distinguishing between the validity and utility of psychiatric diagnoses', *American Journal of Psychiatry*, 160 (1): 4–12.

Kernberg, Otto (1967) 'Borderline personality organisation', in M. Stone (ed.), (1986) *Essential Papers on Borderline Disorders: One Hundred Years at the Border*. New York: New York University Press. pp. 279–319.

Kessel, N. (1965) 'Self-poisoning', Part I, *British Medical Journal*, 2: 1265–1270.

Kraepelin, Emil and Beer, Dominic (1992) 'The manifestations of insanity', *History of Psychiatry*, 3 (12): 509–529.

Krietman, P., Greer, S. and Bagley, C. (1969) 'Parasuicide', *British Journal of Psychiatry*, 115: 746.

Lane, C. (2007) *Shyness: How a Normal Behaviour Became a Sickness*. New Haven, CT: Yale University Press.

Ledgerwood, L., Ewald, P. and Cochran, G. (2003) 'Genes, germs and schizophrenia: An evolutionary perspective', *Perspectives in Biology and Medicine*, 46 (3): 317–348.

Levenkron, S. (1998) *Cutting: Understanding and Overcoming Self-Mutilation*. London: Norton.

Linehan, M. (1993) *Cognitive Behavioural Treatment for Borderline Personality Disorder*. New York: Guilford Press.

Links, P., Heslegrave, R. and van Reekum, R. (1998) 'Prospective follow-up study of borderline personality disorder: Prognosis, prediction of outcome and Axis 11 co-morbidity', *Canadian Journal of Psychiatry*, 43: 265–270.

Lunbeck, E. (2006) 'Borderline histories: Psychoanalysis inside out', *Science in Context*, 19 (1): 151–173.

Main, T.F. (1957) 'The ailment', *British Journal of Medical Psychology*, 30: 129–145.

Markham, Dominick (2003) 'Attitudes towards patients with a diagnosis of "borderline personality disorder": Social rejection and dangerousness', *Journal of Mental Health*, 12 (6): 595–612.

Masterson, J. (1988) *The Search for the Real Self: Unmasking the Personality Disorders of our Age*. New York: The Free Press.

Mayes, Rick and Horwitz, Allan (2005) 'DSM-111 and the revolution in the classification of mental illness', *Journal of the History of the Behavioural Sciences*, 41 (3): 249–267.

Meltzer, H., Lader, D. and Corbin, T. (2002a) *Non-Fatal Suicidal Behaviour Among Adults Aged 16 to 74 in Great Britain*. London: The Stationery Office.

Meltzer, H., Harrington, R. and Goodman, R. (2002b) *Children and Adolescents Who Try to Harm, Hurt or Kill Themselves. A Report of Further Analysis from the National Survey of the Mental Health of Children and Adolescents in Great Britain in 1999*. London: Office for National Statistics.

Ministry of Health (1961) *Attempted Suicide*. Circular HM (61) 94. London: Ministry of Health.

Morgan, H. (1979) *Death Wishes? The Understanding and Management of Deliberate Self Harm*. Chichester: Wiley.

Morgan, J. and Lacey, H. (1998) 'Blood letting in anorexia nervosa: A case study', *International Journal of Eating Disorders*, 27 (4): 483–485.

Mulder, Roger (2008) 'An epidemic of depression or the medicalisation of distress?', *Perspectives in Biology and Medicine*, 51 (2): 238–50.

National Institute for Health and Clinical Excellence (2004) *Self-harm: The Short-term Physical and Psychological Management and Secondary Prevention of Self-harm in Primary and Secondary Care*. London: NICE. Available at www.nice.org.uk/guidance/CG16.

National Institute for Health and Clinical Excellence (2007) *Final Scope: Borderline Personality Disorder: Treatment and Management*. London: NICE. Available at www.nice.org.uk/nicemedia/pdf/BPD_Final_scope.pdf.

Paris, J., Brown, R. and Nowlis, D. (1987) 'Long-term follow-up of borderline patients in a general hospital', *Comprehensive Psychiatry*, 28: 530–536.

Pilgrim, D. (2001) 'Disordered personalities and disordered concepts', *Journal of Mental Health*, 10 (3): 253–265.

Pilgrim, D. (2007) 'The survival of psychiatric diagnosis', *Social Science and Medicine*, 65 (3): 536–547.

Potter, J., Edwards, D. and Ashmore, M. (1999) 'Regulating criticism: Some comments on an argumentative complex', *History of the Human Sciences*, 12 (4): 79–88.

Rapaport, D., Gill, M. and Shafer, R. (1946) *The Thematic Apperception Test in Diagnostic Psychological Testing*, Vol 2. Chicago, IL: Year Book Publishers. pp. 395–459.

Read, J., Mosher, L. and Bental, R. (2004) *Models of Madness: Psychological, Social and Biological Approaches to Schizophrenia*. London: Routledge.

Reisman, David in collaboration with Denny, Reuel and Glazer, Nathan (1950) *The Lonely Crowd*. New Haven, CT: Yale University Press.

Resnek, Lawrie (1991) *Philosophical Defence of Psychiatry*. London: Routledge.

Richards, Graham (2002) 'The psychology of Psychology: A historically grounded sketch', *Theory and Psychology*, 12 (1): 7–36.

Rose, Nikolas (1996) 'Power and subjectivity: Critical history and psychology', in C. Graumann and K. Gergen (eds), *Historical Dimensions of Psychological Discourse*. Cambridge: Cambridge University Press. pp. 103–124.

Rosse, Irving (1890) 'Clinical evidences of borderland insanity', in M. Stone (ed.) (1986) *Essential Papers on Borderline Disorders: One Hundred Years at the Border*. New York: New York University Press.

Sadler, J. (2002) *Descriptions and Prescriptions: Values, Mental Disorders and the DSMs*. Baltimore, MD: Johns Hopkins University Press.

Schmideberg, M. (1959) in Marvin W. Acklin (1993) 'Psychodiagnosis of personality structure 11: Borderline personality organization', *Journal of Personality Assessment*, 61 (2): 329–341.

Shorter, Edward (1997) *A History of Psychiatry: From the Era of the Asylum to the Age of Prozac*. New York: Wiley.

Sokolow, Jayme (2002) *The Great Encounter: Native Peoples and European Settlers in the Americas, 1492–1800*. New York: Sharpe.

Stengel, E. and Cook, N. (1958) *Attempted Suicide: Its Social Significance and Effects*. London: Oxford University Press.

Stern, Adolph (1938) 'Psychoanalytic psychotherapy in the borderline neuroses', *Psychoanalytic Quarterly,* 14: 190–198.

Thorwald, Jurgen (1962) *Science and Secrets of Early Medicine: Egypt, Babylonia, India, China, Mexico, Peru*. London: Thames and Hudson.

Tillich, Paul (1988) *The Spiritual Situation in our Technical Society*. Atlanta, GA: Mercer University Press.

Vassilev, I. and Pilgrim, D. (2007) 'Risk, trust and the myth of mental health services', *Journal of Mental Health,* 16 (3): 347–357.

Ventura, H. and Mandeep, R. (2005) 'Bloodletting as a cure for dropsy: Heart failure down the ages', *Journal of Cardiac Failure*, 11 (4): 247–252.

Winston, Antony (2000) 'Recent developments in borderline personality disorder', *Advances in Psychiatric Treatment,* 6: 211–218.

Zachar, Peter (2000) 'Psychiatric disorders are not natural kinds', *Philosophy, Psychiatry and Psychology,* 7 (3): 167–182.

Zanarini, M., Frankenburg, F., Hennen, J. and Silk, K. (2003) 'The longitudinal course of borderline psychopathology: 6-year prospective follow-up of the phenomenology of borderline personality disorder', *American Journal of Psychiatry*, 160: 274–283.

3

WHAT IS EVIDENCE?

Sarah Corrie

The ever-pressing need to advance psychological practice has, in recent years, led to the privileging of evidence and the use of that evidence to guide professional decision making. Enshrined in the concept of evidence-based practice, a framework which elevates research findings to the heart of the therapeutic endeavour, evidence has been proposed as a means of ensuring that our clients receive the best of what psychology has to offer and that service planning is informed by sound, scientific findings.

The use of evidence to develop practice affords many opportunities to enhance the quality of our services. However, it also poses many challenges. In particular, the notion of evidence-based practice raises critical issues of a methodological, epistemological and professional nature which require our individual and collective attention if we are to respond effectively to the political, economic and social pressures of our time.

This chapter aims to explore these opportunities and challenges by considering the nature of the evidence with which counselling psychologists need to be familiar, debates about its 'rightful' place in our work and how to navigate these debates in a way that encourages informed reflection on the services we offer our clients. Specifically, the chapter considers the following questions:

- What exactly is evidence?
- What types of information, produced by whom and in what contexts, represent 'legitimate' forms of evidence?
- In what ways should the available evidence shape our practice, and at what point are we obliged to alter our work in light of it?

The debates which follow are both complex and emotive. In reading this chapter you will bring your own assumptions about the nature of evidence and its appropriate place in psychology practice – your own, as well as the practice of others. As these assumptions will inevitably affect how you engage with the ideas presented, I invite you to reflect on your own experiences of accessing, critiquing, using, discarding and contributing to the evidence-base of counselling psychology and to reflect on the implications of your choices for your work with clients.

THE ROLE OF EVIDENCE IN A COMPLEX CLIMATE

Recent decades have witnessed an escalating demand for psychological interventions, and this trend looks set to continue. The growing interest in, and market for, our services attests in part to heightened public awareness of what psychology can offer. This is a very positive development. As Bor (2006) observes, counselling psychology in the UK has achieved a great deal in its young life and counselling psychologists now provide their services to a highly diverse range of clients in an equally diverse range of settings.

However, with this growing demand comes responsibility. The call for increased access to psychological interventions requires us to apply the knowledge of our discipline to areas that are sometimes far removed from those in which that same knowledge was developed. In such circumstances, how do we apply psychology in ways that are effective, yet respect the limits of what we can offer? Responding to client need is part of ethical practice, but so too is the need to avoid over-optimistic claims for the effectiveness of psychological approaches.

Questions about effectiveness and responsibility are also confronting us from outside the profession. In recent years, clinical practice itself has come under increased scrutiny and the decision-making prowess of the practitioner is no longer assumed. In the public sector in the UK, this has resulted in greater monitoring of the professions through systems of audit and evaluation. Specifically, concerns about the accountability of clinicians, variability in standards of health care and escalating costs have led the government to prioritize quality assurance initiatives aimed at establishing clear national standards for practice.

In consequence, it is now the responsibility of all National Health Service Trusts to incorporate systems of monitoring that are informed by clinical governance frameworks. Clinical governance is a system through which public health care services are accountable for ongoing improvement. By implementing procedures for audit and life-long learning, as well as using the results of research to inform treatment planning, the intention is to address the developmental needs of both the organization and its practitioners, thus achieving standards of excellence and ensuring that the NHS remains cost-efficient (Department of Health, 1997, 1999).

Concerns about clinical effectiveness and cost containment are, of course, shared by other purchasers of psychological services. Third-party payers such as private health insurers increasingly impose limits on the type of treatment they will reimburse and expect that measurable outcomes will be achieved during specific timeframes. In consequence, certain ways of working (largely time-limited, goal-focused and empirically-supported approaches) are gradually becoming prized over others.

These changing expectations, combined with advances in technology, emphasis on consumer rights and the need to revise our theories of human experience in the light of social and cultural diversity, have required us to re-examine what we offer the public and how we offer it. Psychology, alongside other health care professions, needs to appeal to something more robust than its own publicly declared expertise.

Against this backdrop of evaluation and justification, evidence-based practice has emerged as a framework for guiding service provision. Broadly speaking, the notion of evidence-based practice reflects the principle that the delivery of treatment, including psychological interventions, should reflect decisions informed by the best available evidence of effectiveness (Department of Health, 1996, 1997; Evidence-Based Medicine Working Group, 1992). Put simply, if there is evidence to suggest that a particular therapy is effective in addressing a specific clinical problem, then that therapy should be the approach of choice (Department of Health, 2001). In this way, research evidence has been given a principal role in the government's agenda for informing policy development, service commissioning and increasingly, choice of therapeutic approach at the level of service delivery.

Evidence-based practice has critical implications for counselling psychology training, practice and professional identity. A defining contribution of counselling psychology is its humanistic vision, whereby respect for the personal, subjective experience of the client is prized over and above notions of diagnosis and treatment (Division of Counselling Psychology, 2001). Underpinned by these values, counselling psychology 'pays particular attention to the meanings, beliefs, context and processes that are constructed both within and between people' (British Psychological Society, 2003: 3.7.3: 4).

However, this idiographic and relational world-view is not wholly consistent with the concept of evidence-based practice which prioritizes questions about what works best for which clinical populations. Thus, we must consider the extent to which these two world-views might be compatible and the implications for our clients, ourselves and our profession of operating within this culture of evaluation. These concerns are not merely academic. As Drabick and Goldfried (2000) observe, psychology is at a critical point in its history. Our response to these issues is vital to ensuring that the future direction of counselling psychology is one of our choosing.

EVIDENCE AND EFFECTIVENESS: THE CASE FOR A RESEARCH–PRACTICE PARTNERSHIP

The phenomenon of evidence-based practice has been identified as an important innovation (see Sackett et al., 1996). Some have gone as far as proposing that it has the potential to revolutionize the care that our clients receive (Salkovskis, 2002). In principle, the notion that our practice should be informed by evidence of effectiveness would seem to be a sound, if not optimum, philosophy. Indeed, the idea is not new. From the earliest days of applied psychology, psychologists have been committed to an integrated relationship between science and practice (American Psychological Association, 2006). Obtaining evidence through observation, analysis and evaluation continues to be of critical importance to all branches of psychology and the British Psychological Society emphasizes knowledge of a wide range of research designs as vital for counselling psychologists (British Psychological Society, 2003).

A thorough understanding of the available evidence is vital for counselling psychologists because if there is no robust knowledge base, we cannot progress our understanding of human experience in any systematic way (Owen, 1996). Moreover, psychology has made impressive advances in understanding and working with a wide range of specific disorders through accumulating and applying its evidence. There is an extensive and impressive literature on the effectiveness of various psychotherapeutic approaches (Roth and Fonagy, 2005) and client concerns that were once deemed to be beyond the reaches of psychology are now recognized as amenable to intervention, partly due to the careful collection of research data (two obvious examples of this would be treatment for obsessive-compulsive disorder and psychological interventions for schizophrenia).

Arguably, there are a number of ways in which evidence-based practice may advance our work. The first, and most critical, is that it promises a means of achieving more consistently effective results for our clients. By developing sound knowledge about what works best for which type of presenting problem, and basing our practice firmly on this knowledge, we can feel confident that we are providing our clients with the best of what psychology has to offer.

Second, working judiciously to apply evidence has the potential to improve the consistency of our therapeutic decision-making. Over time, the pressures of routine practice may cause our responses to become habitual. Basing our decisions on state-of-the-art knowledge can ensure that our clients are protected against the uncritical application of theory or technique, or practices that are simply out of date. In this way, awareness of the evidence provides a benchmark against which to evaluate our professional judgement.

A third potential benefit is that of creating closer links between academic and professional psychology, permitting a rich exchange of ideas and expertise. Just as clinical practice provides a source of inspiration for identifying and refining research questions (Salkovskis, 2002), so academic psychology has produced many theories of cognition and behaviour that have been productively applied to mental health problems (Thomas et al., 2002). Certainly, research has the potential to develop our understanding of our clients' dilemmas, highlighting gaps in our knowledge whilst also providing a route through which effective practices might be disseminated.

As noted by Corrie (2003), behind the arguments in favour of evidence-based practice lies a certain moral imperative. Within the broader framework of clinical governance, evidence-based practice challenges us to reflect on what we offer our clients in a systematized way so we can be sure that we are relying on something more robust than clinical judgement, with all its biases and errors (Meehl, 1954). As Salkovskis observes:

> It is encouraging that those who worked solely on the basis of clinical judgement and personal prejudices are now being encouraged to take a more systematic approach, and to base the choice of treatment on what is defined as 'gold standard' outcome evidence. (2002: 3)

This sentiment echoes the critique of Dawes (1994), who argued that traditionally practitioners have failed to pay sufficient attention to the scientific literature, relying instead on poorly validated technical procedures based on clinical reasoning. In doing so, he makes the case that psychologists have fallen short of their obligations to society, thus elevating the use of evidence to the realms of responsibility and ethics.

On the surface at least, it is difficult to oppose the concept of evidence-based practice. Surely no self-respecting counselling psychologist would disagree with the need to ensure that our clients are offered only effective interventions. Moreover, who would honestly claim to have no interest in information that could consistently improve the services they offer their clients? It is also easy to appreciate the appeal of evidence-based practice to those who have the responsibility of deciding how to spend limited funds on their local populations. Basing service planning on evidence lends an air of credibility to the decision-making process, promising a means of simplifying a complex set of factors into something more definite and prescriptive.

However, such a position belies certain assumptions that require further scrutiny: namely that evidence is a straightforward and incontrovertible entity; that it can provide clear answers about what works best for whom; that our clients are harmed by ineffective practices which occur through a lack of evidence; and that evidence provides a direct route to effective practice. On closer inspection, these assumptions become problematic, particularly when we appreciate that in many respects the evidence may not be influencing practice in the way that was originally envisaged.

EVIDENCE-BASED PRACTICE: MIND THE GAP BETWEEN RHETORIC AND REALITY

Despite wide official endorsement, evidence-based practice has proved controversial and as a framework for guiding decision-making and service planning, may not have had the impact that its supporters would have wished. Salkovskis highlights that despite the value of empirical studies there has been a 'co-existing uneasiness that something was missing, and that [evidence-based medicine] promised more than it was able to deliver' (2002: 1).

Of course, it is not the first time that the relationship between research and practice has been called into question (see Lane and Corrie, 2006, for a detailed review).

Perhaps, however, one of the most damning criticisms was that of Matarazzo who, in a survey of practitioners, claimed that:

> even after 15 years, few of my research findings affect my practice. Psychological science per se doesn't guide me one bit … My clinical practice is the only thing that has helped me in my practice to date. (cited in Bergin and Strupp, 1972: 340)

Marzillier (2004) has similarly challenged the relevance of evidence when he states that, in over 30 years of professional practice, he is unable to identify any outcome studies that have had an impact on his work. The views of Matarazzo and Marzillier would appear to be supported by the fact that many psychologists are unlikely to engage in research once qualified (Nathan, 2000), and that they may not even feel compelled to read research or keep up to date with the empirical literature (Nathan, 2000; Parry, 1992).

Although it would perhaps be difficult to argue convincingly that psychologists ignore research, particularly in the current climate, there is undoubtedly a hiatus. Therapists do not feel compelled to alter their practice merely because the evidence appears to point in one particular direction. Nor will they necessarily deem guidelines derived from research evidence to be worthy of implementation. In reflecting on your own practice, for example, to what extent is your practice determined by research evidence, or guidelines derived from this? If you were to conduct an audit of your use of time, what percentage would be devoted to accessing and implementing the research literature in relation to other activities such as accessing theory, reading case studies, learning about technique, receiving supervision or engaging in personal reflection and other forms of learning? What assumptions – explicit and implicit – might have guided your choices?

While those who champion evidence-based practice might regard a lack of attention to research evidence as unprofessional or even unethical behaviour, to do so would be to miss a crucial point: namely that, for many practitioners, it is not a framework that feels meaningful to their work. So what is missing? If, as a profession, we believe our science provides a secure basis for developing knowledge, why should evidence-based practice have proved so problematic?

If the reality has failed to live up to the rhetoric, perhaps the answer lies partly in the need to differentiate knowledge from evidence. Current priorities in health services research tend towards investigating treatment effectiveness and cost-efficiency rather than identifying psychological processes through experimental research – the traditional core of psychological science (Turpin, 1994). Whereas evidence was once accumulated, applied and effectively owned by those who sought to enhance their knowledge, it is now the property of multiple stakeholders: service managers, funding bodies, the state and (at least in principle) our clients. In this context, evidence-based practice is not a science, but a social phenomenon (American Psychological Association, 2006). In order to understand the implications of this social phenomenon for ourselves and our clients, we must consider carefully what is meant by 'evidence' and whose evidence 'counts'.

WHAT EXACTLY *IS* EVIDENCE? NAVIGATING THE TERRAIN

It is one thing to advocate grounding professional practice within the available evidence, but quite another to be able to define exactly what we mean by this. What sources of information constitute evidence? With which types of evidence should we be concerned when reflecting on our individual approach?

It is important to note that the concept has not been defined as any one type of data. It can be gathered from a wide range of sources that span clinical observation, qualitative research, case studies, randomized controlled trials and meta-analyses, where data from individual studies are aggregated so that they might be considered collectively. It also includes data relating to treatment effectiveness, cost-effectiveness, cost-benefit and epidemiology.

To take account of this variety, a number of frameworks have been devised to organize and categorize sources of knowledge according to their origins and status. The Department of Health (1999), for example, has identified five types of evidence where Type I refers to at least one good systematic review, including a minimum of one randomized controlled trial; Type II evidence, a minimum of one good randomized controlled trial; Type III, at least one well-designed study without randomization; Type IV, a minimum of one well-designed observational study; and Type V, the opinion of experts, service users and carers.

Roth and Fonagy (2005) emphasize that hierarchical positioning should not be confused with clinical usefulness. As they explain, there can be no optimum research design; the 'ideal' approach will depend on multiple factors, with each methodology designed to answer only a limited range of questions. However, in the quest for scientific respectability, there is a clear preference for the rigorously objective over the relative and subjective. In the pursuit of evidence-based practice, the randomized controlled trial is undoubtedly the 'gold standard' (Department of Health, 1996; 2001).

For those who carry the responsibility of funding or planning services, the hierarchy may be an intuitively appealing framework, promising clear guidance about which kind of information to prioritize when making complex decisions about service development. This was illustrated all too clearly in my recent conversation with a member of a local funding body who described the sense of relief that came from 'finally knowing which forms of psychology really worked'. The comment, whilst light-hearted in tone, revealed a more serious underlying message: namely that the nature of the work called 'therapy' had felt somewhat amorphous until the arrival of 'gold standard' evidence which offered clarity, security and therefore peace of mind.

In a professional world where there is growing demand for transparency we might feel some sympathy for this colleague for whom the individually-tailored approach of much of what psychologists do contrasted markedly with his own medically-informed understanding of mental health problems. However, hierarchies are deceptively simple. Evidence does not present itself as neatly organized packages that can be readily assigned to categories of varying scientific respectability. Rather, it has to be extracted, interpreted – even crafted – from a diverse range of sometimes contradictory findings (Newnes, 2001).

Moreover, there are substantial difficulties with translating 'gold standard' evidence into local therapeutic practice. Although a detailed consideration of these issues is beyond the scope of this chapter (for a detailed review, see Roth and Fonagy, 2005), a major challenge is that the priorities and methods of researchers are very different from those of practitioners. While researchers aim for 'pure' findings that can uncover the causal relationship between therapeutic approach and clinical change (and will, therefore, aim to deliver an intervention in ways that minimize the interference of extraneous influences), practitioners are concerned with enhancing the well-being of their individual clients and use evidence in ways that reflect context, relationship and the need for moment-to-moment decision making. In this sense, gold standard evidence is essentially 'product focused', whereas practitioners are 'person focused', less concerned with global statements about effectiveness than how information can inform the subtleties of what they do.

There is, of course, a danger in polarizing researchers and practitioners in ways that are inaccurate and unhelpful. However, the critical point is that the effects of an intervention in a research trial tell us little about its effectiveness in routine practice. Randomized controlled trials and systematic reviews provide important information about populations and the effectiveness of specific approaches under controlled conditions, but they cannot eliminate the need for individualized assessment, formulation and treatment planning which are based as much on professional judgement as they are on empirically-derived data.

Seen in this light, it becomes apparent that the relationship between research and practice must be bi-directional; clinical practice has a vital role to play in informing research just as much as the other way round. In order to be of substantive benefit, evidence-based practice must be complemented by its counterpart, practice-based evidence.

EASING THE TENSION BETWEEN RHETORIC AND REALITY: THE CASE FOR PRACTICE-BASED EVIDENCE

It is reasonable to propose that in the main, psychological interventions are effective (Carter, 2006). However, despite the growth in knowledge about specific diagnostic profiles and clinical presentations, there remain many client concerns about which relatively little is known. In such circumstances, how do we balance the need to intervene with the lack of established guidelines about what works best?

Haarbosch and Newey (2006) highlight this dilemma in their work with young people who sexually offend. They explain how, when they established their service in the late 1980s, there was no evidence on how to work safely and effectively with the sexually offending behaviour of adolescents. The only available models of practice were based on adult offenders, which were not fit for purpose. Haarbosch and Newey explain how they responded to this challenge by adopting an alternative approach: one that combined critically appraising the existing research with their own professional expertise in order to develop a framework that could be refined in the light of subsequent experience. The needs of their clients (and their clients' communities) dictated the need to intervene in the absence of adequate knowledge.

Arguably, this is the reality of professional practice for much of the time. In order to respond to their clients' needs, therapists will always be in a position where they have to devise innovative methods. Whilst Dawes (1994) argues that psychologists should restrict their work to areas where knowledge (particularly actuarial data) already exists, this fails to account for the fact that practitioners are ethically bound to provide the best service that they can in the light of client context, risk management issues and service constraints.

Furthermore, many therapists innovate very effectively (Barlow, 1981). In consequence, there may be good reasons for remaining true to the wisdom of one's professional experience, which might explain why few psychologists are prepared to change the style or content of their practice in the light of the research literature.

Consider, for example, the case of a newly qualified counselling psychologist working with a client whose particular constellation of difficulties has been extensively empirically researched. If the 'gold standard' evidence demonstrates the benefits of one approach over another for addressing this client's needs, the practitioner would do well to consider this. However, what if their supervisor recommends an alternative approach, based on years of experience of working with this type of difficulty, knowledge of the client's circumstances and coping style, and a sensitivity to their supervisee's strengths and needs relative to their stage of career? How should practitioners respond if so called 'Type I' evidence exists which contradicts 'Type V' evidence? It would be the rare practitioner who is prepared to over-ride their own local evidence in favour of more global findings. Indeed, Sternberg (2006) argues that in such circumstances it would be unethical to ignore or actively contravene the lessons of one's professional experience. It is only through experience that we learn how to combine theoretical constructs, models and techniques in ways that are unique to each individual client.

It is regrettable, therefore, that to date relatively little attention has been given to developing an evidence-base that might shed light upon the impact of different methods of engagement, assessment, approaches to formulation and use of creativity that could equip practitioners with information that is immediately relevant to their day-to-day work. Along these lines Corrie (2003) has identified a number of questions that, if investigated, might resonate with the needs of practitioners more directly whilst simultaneously benefiting our clients. These questions include:

- What are the personal qualities, skills and types of knowledge needed to achieve best practice?
- What skills do we need to innovate successfully?
- What skills do we need to be effective knowledge-gatherers in our work with clients?
- What skills are involved in asking incisive and facilitative questions that might create new possibilities for functioning in the world?
- What are the skills needed to decide which methodology (that is, approach to enquiry, measurement tool) is most helpful for investigating a particular kind of question?
- What skills are needed for effective decision making?

Such contextually informed enquires would not directly address questions about comparative outcomes. However, they would be consistent with an approach that acknowledges a brand of expertise more fully informed by the realities of the therapeutic setting. Moreover, through elevating the decision-making and creative processes of the practitioner to the heart of the research endeavour, questions such as these would guide us towards a knowledge-base of the components of mastery that could improve training and inform continuing professional development.

A number of practitioners (for example, Barkham and Mellor-Clark, 2000) have considered how a more genuine partnership between research and practice might be achieved through developing practice-based evidence. Practice-based evidence is concerned with how research might be tailored to meet the needs of those delivering psychological and psychotherapeutic interventions. As a framework of enquiry, it prizes the local, contextual knowledge produced by therapists in their daily practice, yet also supports practitioners and managers in evaluating the impact of the services provided. Substantive guidelines are yet to be developed and the specific forms that practice-based evidence might take, as well as its relationship to evidence-based practice, still need to be established. However, it offers one framework for thinking creatively about how to bridge the gap between research and practice and would certainly engage therapists by investigating questions that have direct implications for how they work.

Nonetheless, practice-based evidence is a very different type of enquiry from evidence-based practice, particularly when we consider the latter as a social phenomenon. Where evidence is used in the service of evaluation and justification, it has been identified as a potential threat to professional autonomy as well as to the practitioner–client relationship (Hampton, 2002). This leads us to consider another facet of evidence; namely, its use as a political tool.

THE POLITICS OF EVIDENCE

Science is a marketable product and has an investment value to those who produce and use it. Sturdee (2001) argues that we would do well to consider carefully the issue of who decides what counts as evidence, the best way to use the data obtained, the likely impact of the knowledge gained and who will benefit most and least from it. We are no longer dealing with neutral questions about best practice but winners and losers, depending on how evidence is defined and who gets to define it (Lane and Corrie, 2006).

This is illustrated in the therapeutic professions quite clearly. For example, few of us are likely to take issue with the sizeable body of evidence that demonstrates the effectiveness of a wide range of psychological and psychotherapeutic approaches. Here we are winners. However, depending on our own theoretical persuasion and relationship to the research literature, we might be more inclined to challenge the literature which asserts the apparent superiority of one approach over another – we could become losers. In this context, as Marzillier (2004) wryly notes, appealing to the evidence-base (when we perceive ourselves to be winners) enables us to justify our position in a competitive market and to feel more secure about our professional credibility.

Evidence as a marketable product takes on a particular meaning when we consider how changes in employment patterns in the 1990s have resulted in the end of the job-for-life culture. Specifically, the move away from employment towards employability has generated the need for individuals to take more responsibility for their own development and marketability (Lane et al., 2000).

Lane and Corrie (2006) highlight the uncomfortable reality that with the expansion of the European Union specifically, and greater competitiveness generally, many now claim to offer psychology-based interventions. In such a climate, why would someone spend several years training to become a counselling psychologist when it is possible for them to offer their services to the public after a brief training in commercially packaged manuals derived from psychological evidence? This question may seem heretical but in the context of a knowledge-driven labour market, Lane and Corrie (2006) make the point that we need to be clear (and vociferous) about where the added value lies in employing a psychologist as opposed to any other professional, including those whose competence derives from minimal training.

Thus, we must think carefully about how the political contexts in which we are immersed are shaping our practice and the expectations of those who have an investment in our services. This includes our clients. Whilst the official discourse of evidence-based practice is one of enhancing client care, we have not necessarily given sufficient thought to their position as winners and losers in the politics of science. Two examples drawn from my own practice highlight how clients can be affected by the social phenomenon of evidence-based practice in ways that may not be to their advantage.

In a previous paper (Corrie, 2003) I described the challenge of working with a client diagnosed with depression who, in the opening moments of our initial meeting, pronounced that he needed 'either IPT (interpersonal therapy) or CBT (cognitive-behaviour therapy)'. This was based on a conscientious review of the literature in which the choice of approach seemed to him both obvious and unproblematic. However, his decision had been based on viewing his difficulties as a series of psychological symptoms that required a prescriptive, psychological response – much akin to being told to follow a regime of medication in order to alleviate specific biological symptoms. When he discovered that a psychological approach did not involve receiving instructions on how to 'get cured', he felt bewildered and quickly disengaged. The guidelines he had accessed and upon which he had based his expectations of therapy had not helped him consider how therapy might involve something other than objectifying his experience as 'symptoms' and that I, as his therapist, might not come equipped with pre-packaged solutions.

The second example concerns a critique of CBT written by a psychotherapist for the tabloid press. The article, which presented the case that CBT achieved change at a superficial level only, left another client of mine with significant concerns that she had somehow not 'dealt with the deeper issues' that had led to her original distress, despite having benefited significantly from that approach. The article had undoubtedly been intended as a challenge to the position of CBT in an evidence-focused culture and raised provocative questions that, as a practitioner, I found intellectually stimulating. For my client, however, the article felt undermining of the work she had put into improving her life and left her dwelling on what her 'deeper issues' might be. Unaware of the professional and political undercurrents shaping debates about evidence, the article eroded her faith in what had been a rewarding experience of therapy.

The issue here is not about the superiority of one approach over another, but rather about appreciating that clients are not passive recipients of evidence. They seek it out, interpret it and use it to make judgements about what they need. They are affected by the political face of evidence-based practice and the marketability of science, consuming evidence in ways we may be neither aware of nor intend. Although attempts have been made to produce guidelines that are accessible to the general public, such guidelines are open to misunderstanding, as at least one of the examples above implies. Moreover, official guidelines typically contain little in the way of advice on how members of the public should make sense of the broader issues involved. That evidence is used in the service of multiple agendas may not be immediately obvious to the distressed client who is seeking psychological support.

WORKING TOWARDS A MORE SOPHISTICATED INTERPRETATION OF EVIDENCE-BASED PRACTICE

The current political use of evidence is by-passing the practitioner's traditional role of interpreter of research into practice (Lane and Corrie, 2006). As a result, we must consider our position in relation to our science and clarify whether we see ourselves primarily as consumers or producers of research.

Monk (2003) argues for the importance of counselling psychologists having a place in their work for conducting research in order to have a voice in the evidence-based debate at a higher professional and political level. A similar argument has been made by Thomas et al. (2002), who express concern that unless psychologists reassert their research credentials, the evidence-base of the future may be constructed by other professions. If we are not proactive producers of research, then increasingly we may find others' research imposed upon us, regardless of whether or not it makes sense to the core values of our discipline.

However, we need to be clear about the activities and responsibilities that adopting the role of consumer or producer might entail. As producers we must consider carefully the kinds of knowledge we are developing. Do we have a responsibility to ask only certain types of question and police how our knowledge is used? If so, we may have a key role to play in challenging contemporary definitions of evidence, or commenting publicly if we believe that methodologies are being misapplied. As consumers we need to consider how we wish to position ourselves in relation to other people's evidence, how and when we should adjust our working practices in light of it and how much knowledge of research methods we need to have an informed dialogue with other stakeholders – including where, necessary, to challenge simplistic ideas about the scientific basis of practice.

If we are willing to accept the responsibilities that come with being producers of research, then we must consider how we define evidence and what represents 'legitimate' knowledge. Roth and Fonagy (2005) make the case that any adequate formulation of evidence-based practice must do justice to the complex relationship between practice, research and policy. (Given the position of science in our culture discussed previously, we might also add the politics of science.)

Certainly, more sophisticated definitions of evidence-based practice that include a recognition of clinical expertise, client characteristics and values and cultural factors are beginning to emerge (American Psychological Association, 2006). Gradually, ideas about the definition and nature of evidence are being expanded to include a greater focus on therapeutic process and context (McLaren and Ross, 2000). There is also a new outlook on the research protocol which argues for the importance of including idiographic assessment and treatment within a case formulation approach (Persons, 1991; Tarrier and Calam, 2002) as well as those who have made explicit their model of working so that colleagues and clients can follow and critique the basis of their judgement (see Lane, 1998).

In an effort to address the complexity that an adequate interpretation of evidence entails, Roth and Fonagy (2005) have also devised a model that takes account of a wide range of potential sources of evidence, including work derived from individual practice, professional consensus, systems of service delivery and training and research. In their model, practitioners can devise new ways of working, derived from existing theories and knowledge acquired from their own practice. Ways of working which appear effective are then formally tested for efficacy and effectiveness. Knowledge derived from research evidence and clinical consensus contributes to the development of formal guidelines and is used to determine the extent to which findings can and cannot be generalized. Standards for practice are then established, with auditing procedures used to determine whether these standards are achieved and any shortfalls identified becoming the basis for staff training. What is significant here is that research is just one part of a much larger and more complex process. The 'gold standard' evidence, even when appropriate to pursue, can only ever be one stage in a larger process.

The search for knowledge must always begin with a desire to understand our clients' stories: it is the phenomenology of our clients' difficulties that enables us to identify meaningful hypotheses about specific psychological problems and to use the results of our investigations to inform subsequent theoretical and practice-based interventions (Salkovskis, 2002). Thus, moving towards an evidence base that is phenomenologically (rather than methodologically) driven may hold the key to a more fruitful partnership between research and practice in the longer-term. However, if we elevate the search for phenomenological understanding to the heart of our enquires, it may become necessary to embrace a very wide range of methodologies and epistemologies.

Consistent with this broader vision, a number of writers (Newnes, 2001; Milton and Corrie, 2002) encourage us to draw upon a much wider range of evidence than was traditionally conceived. Newnes, for example, challenges us to consider a qualitatively different range of evidence which might come from 'literature, our senses and personal experience' (2001: 6). This would be considered controversial by many. Nonetheless, it is interesting that a number of therapists are looking towards non-academic sources, such as fiction, to address aspects of their work which our official evidence-based discourse does not seem able to illuminate (see Symington, 1993).

Embracing a more liberal interpretation of evidence will require a willingness to sacrifice the comforting respectability that a scientific approach seems to offer. However, this may be a positive development in its own right. Van Deurzen-Smith (1990) has argued that for too long, psychology has organized itself around discovering objective facts rather than exploring what it means to be human, with all the dilemmas and choices that this entails. For her, psychology needs to embrace more fully its artistic and dialogic dimensions over and above its preoccupation with what she sees as overly narrow scientific principles. A more inclusive definition would encourage us to look towards a much wider range of 'evidences' and perhaps to help others see the benefits of doing the same.

However, for the foreseeable future, there is still a need for caution. Definitions of evidence and how to gather it are being elaborated, but the emphasis on evidence as outcomes will remain alluring for those who have to make concrete decisions about how to organize and fund services. We have a long way to go before we can be certain that the rhetoric and the reality finally coincide.

SO WHERE ARE WE NOW? QUESTIONS FOR THE FUTURE

As we grapple with definitions of evidence and ponder its rightful role in shaping our practice, we would perhaps do well to remember the words of Bertrand Russell, who is quoted as saying that 'even when all the experts agree, they may well be mistaken' (http://home.att.net/~quotations/bertrandrussell.html, accessed 25 May 2009).

Evidence is situated in a particular historical, social and cultural context. What is 'true' in one context is not necessarily generalizable to others. We must concede that in the past, science has been used to justify practices that today we would consider ethically dubious or even morally unacceptable. To acknowledge this is not an attempt to undermine the science of our discipline, but rather a call for respectful caution in how much faith we place in our research and a willingness to abandon apparent certainties when this knowledge proves to be outdated or unworkable. This, of course, applies just as much to our models of practice as it does to our research data.

To the extent that the gathering of evidence is genuinely concerned with improving the services we offer our clients, the philosophy is a laudable one. Unquestionably, we need sound frameworks for evaluating our practice. At its best, evidence-based practice is a reminder of how much we don't yet know and a requirement that we recognize the limits of our knowledge. At the same time our evidence, drawn from the science of our discipline, has benefited practice in important ways and will continue to do so, providing that it remains grounded in reflective clinical thinking. When viewed as a context for discovery rather than a context for justification (Carter, 2006), evidence-based practice does indeed have a great deal to offer.

However, given its status as a social phenomenon it is interesting that there is no evidence for the effectiveness of evidence-based practice, a fact that has not escaped those who have attempted to think creatively about the issues involved (see Weisz and Addis, 2006). This leaves us with many unanswered questions. For example, to what extent does a judicious use of the evidence actually improve practice? What kinds of evidence are most likely to improve practice? How many studies does it take before a particular way of working can be said to be 'empirically supported'?

The fact that we are not yet asking these types of questions may be significant in its own right. We live in a world that exalts science and privileges its data over other forms of knowing. Subjecting the phenomenon of evidence-based practice to empirical scrutiny may, therefore, seem too challenging to contemplate at the present time, running the risk of shaking a foundational belief about the power of science to provide us with the answers we seek.

In the absence of a knowledge-base that enables us to predict what type of approach will make most sense to an individual client, it is reasonably safe to assume that we need access to a broad range of models, theories and methods, and to avoid imposing restrictions based on empirical evidence – gold standard or otherwise – until such time as specific practices are demonstrated to be ineffective or even damaging.

When it comes to navigating the debates about evidence perhaps, then, the most helpful position is one of walking the line between unquestioning acceptance and dismissive cynicism; what our experience tells us to be true and how the available evidence might challenge us to refine our habitual ways of working; what we know about general theoretical principles and the need to be passionately engaged with the client's self-told story.

In the spirit of walking the line between unquestioning acceptance and dismissive cynicism, a useful starting point might be to personalize the debates to your own practice by engaging with the following questions:

- How do you investigate the effectiveness of your own practice? What methods do you use and why?
- When investigating a client's presenting concerns, on what sources of evidence do you tend to rely? What sources do you discard? What do you and your client gain and lose from your choices?
- As a consumer of other people's research, at what point would you be prepared to radically alter your approach based on what the evidence says? How much evidence, and of what type, would it take?
- What do you need in terms of knowledge, research skills or supervision to use the evidence to best advantage – for your clients and your own professional development?
- Do you see yourself primarily as a producer or a consumer of research evidence? What are the implications of your choice?
- What would a local version of evidence-based practice mean for your own work at this stage in your career?

As Roth and Fonagy (2005) remind us, our science cannot be all things to all people. There are many questions for which we have no evidence and as a global community, we are having to grapple with dilemmas which our expertise cannot answer. However, as psychologists we are also scientists and must not allow the current social preoccupation with justification and cost-effectiveness to blight our appreciation of the value of analysis and evaluation, in its myriad forms.

As we attempt to work out what exactly we mean by evidence, how we should use it and how precisely it might make a difference to our work, we would do well to remember that research is only one part of a broader process of enquiry. The questions outlined above are offered in the hope that they might stimulate reflection and debate as part of that broader process. If we keep asking them of ourselves and our colleagues, and discussing them with all those who have an investment in the future of counselling psychology, then a more equal partnership between research and practice might ultimately emerge – one that can truly inform the needs of everyone who is genuinely concerned with improving their clients' lives.

REFERENCES

American Psychological Association Presidential Task Force on Evidence-Based Practice (2006) 'Evidence-Based Practice in Psychology', *American Psychologist*, 61 (4): 271–85.

Barkham, M. and Mellor-Clark, J. (2000) 'Rigour and relevance: the role of practice-based evidence in the psychological therapies', in N. Rowland and S. Goss (eds), *Evidence-Based Counselling and Psychological Therapies: Research and Applications*. London: Routledge. pp. 127–42.

Barlow, D.H. (1981) 'On the relation of clinical research to clinical practice: Current issues, new directions', *Journal of Consulting and Clinical Psychology*, 49: 147–55.

Bergin, A. and Strupp, H. (1972) *Changing Frontiers in the Science of Psychotherapy*. Chicago, IL: Aldine.

Bor, R. (2006) 'A brief reflection on counselling psychology', *Counselling Psychology Review*, 21 (1): 25–6.

British Psychological Society Training Committee in Counselling Psychology (2003) *Criteria for the Accreditation of Postgraduate Training Programmes in Counselling Psychology*. Leicester: British Psychological Society.

Carter, J.A. (2006) 'Theoretical pluralism and technical eclecticism', in C.D. Goodheart, A.E. Kazdin and R.J. Sternberg (eds), *Evidence-Based Psychotherapy. Where Practice and Research Meet*. Washington, DC: American Psychological Association. pp. 63–79.

Corrie, S. (2003) Keynote paper. 'Information, innovation and the quest for legitimate knowledge', *Counselling Psychology Review*, 18 (3): 5–13.

Dawes, R.M. (1994) *House of Cards: Psychology and Psychotherapy Built on Myth*. New York: The Free Press.

Department of Health (1996) *NHS Psychotherapy Services in England Review of Strategic Policy*. London: Department of Health.

Department of Health (1997) *The New NHS: Modern, Dependable*. London: Department of Health.

Department of Health (1999) *National Service Frameworks for Mental Health: Modern Standards and Service Models*. London: Department of Health.

Department of Health (2001) *Treatment Choice in Psychological Therapies and Counselling: Evidence-Based Clinical Practice Guidelines*. London: Department of Health.

Division of Counselling Psychology (2001) *Professional Practice Guidelines*. Leicester: British Psychological Society.

Drabick, D.A.G. and Goldfried, M.R. (2000) 'Training the scientist-practitioner for the 21st century. Putting the bloom back on the rose', *Journal of Clinical Psychology*, 56 (3): 327–40.

Evidence-Based Medicine Working Group (1992) 'Evidence-based medicine: a new approach to teaching the practice of medicine', *Journal of the American Medical Association*, 268 (17): 2420–25.

Haarbosch, V. and Newey, I. (2006) 'Feeling one's way in the dark: Applying the scientist-practitioner model with young people who sexually offend', in D.A. Lane and S. Corrie (eds), *The Modern Scientist-Practitioner: A Guide to Practice in Psychology*. London: Routledge. pp. 130–45.

Hampton, J.R. (2002) 'Evidence-based medicine, opinion-based medicine and real-world medicine', *Perspectives in Biology and Medicine*, 45 (4): 549–68.

Lane, D.A. (1998) 'Context focused analysis: An experimentally derived model for working with complex problems with children, adolescents and systems', in M. Bruch and F.W. Bond (eds), *Beyond Diagnosis: Case Formulation Approaches in CBT*. Chichester: Wiley. pp. 103–39.

Lane, D.A. and Corrie, S. (eds) (2006) *The Modern Scientist-Practitioner: A Guide to Practice in Psychology*. London: Routledge.

Lane, D.A., Puri, A., Cleverly, P., Wylie, R. and Rajan, A. (2000) *Employability: Bridging the Gap Between Rhetoric and Reality: Second Report: Employees' Perspective*. Tonbridge: Create/PDF/CIPD.

Marzillier, J. (2004) 'The myth of evidence-based psychotherapy', *The Psychologist*, 17 (7): 392–5.

McLaren, S.M.G. and Ross, F. (2000) 'Implementation of evidence in practice settings: Some methodological issues arising form the South Thames Evidence Based Practice Project', *Clinical Effectiveness in Nursing*, 4 (2): 99–108.

Meehl, P. (1954) *Clinical Versus Statistical Prediction: A Theoretical Analysis and Review of the Evidence*. Minneapolis, MN: University of Minnesota Press.

Milton, M. and Corrie, S. (2002) 'Exploring the place of technical and implicit knowledge in therapy', *The Journal of Critical Psychology, Counselling and Psychotherapy*, 2 (3): 188–95.

Monk, P. (2003) 'Information, innovation and the quest for legitimate knowledge – first response', *Counselling Psychology Review*, 18 (3): 14–20.

Nathan, P.E. (2000) 'The Boulder model: A dream deferred – or lost?', *American Psychologist*, 55: 250–2.

Newnes, C. (2001) 'On evidence', *Clinical Psychology*, 1: 6–12.

Owen, I. (1996) 'Are we before or after integration?', *Counselling Psychology Review*, 11 (3): 12–18.

Parry, G. (1992) 'Improving psychotherapy services: Applications of research, audit and evaluation', *British Journal of Clinical Psychology*, 31: 3–19.

Persons, J.B. (1991) 'Psychotherapy outcome studies do not accurately represent current models of psychotherapy: A proposed remedy', *American Psychologist*, 46: 99–106.

Roth, A. and Fonagy, P. (2005) *What Works for Whom? A Critical Review of Psychotherapy Research*. New York: Guilford Press.

Sackett, D.L., Rosenberg, W.M., Gray, J.A., Haynes, B. and Richardson, W.S. (1996) 'Evidence-based medicine: What it is and what it isn't', *British Medical Journal*, 312: 71–2.

Salkovskis, P.M. (2002) 'Empirically grounded clinical interventions: cognitive-behavioural therapy progresses through a multi-dimensional approach to clinical science', *Behavioural and Cognitive Psychotherapy*, 30: 3–9.

Sternberg, R.J. (2006) 'Evidence-based practice: Gold standard, gold plated or fool's gold?', in C.D. Goodheart, A.E. Kazdin and R.J. Sternberg (eds), *Evidence-Based Psychotherapy: Where Practice and Research Meet*. Washington, DC: American Psychological Association. pp. 261–71.

Sturdee, P. (2001) 'Evidence, influence or evaluation? Fact and value in clinical science', in C. Mace, S. Moorey and B. Roberts (eds), *Evidence in the Psychological Therapies: A Critical Guide for Practitioners*. Hove: Brunner-Routledge. pp. 61–79.

Symington, N. (1993) *Narcissism: A New Theory*. London: Karnac.

Tarrier, N. and Calam, R. (2002) 'New developments in cognitive-behavioural case formulation. Epidemiological, systemic and social context: an integrative approach', *Behavioural and Cognitive Psychotherapy*, 30: 311–28.

Thomas, G.V., Turpin, G. and Meyer, C. (2002) 'Clinical research under threat', *The Psychologist*, 15 (6): 286–9.

Turpin, G. (1994) 'Service evaluation within the NHS: The challenge to applied psychological research', *Clinical Psychology Forum*, 72: 16–19.

Van Deurzen-Smith, E. (1990) 'Philosophical underpinnings of counselling psychology', *Counselling Psychology Review*, 5 (2): 8–12.

Weisz and Addis, M.E. (2006) 'The research-practice tango and other choreographic challenges: Using and testing evidence-based psychotherapies in clinical care settings', in C.D. Goodheart, A.E. Kazdin and R.J. Sternberg (eds), *Evidence-Based Psychotherapy: Where Practice and Research Meet*. Washington, DC: American Psychological Association. pp. 179–206.

4

INTERPRETING CASE MATERIAL

John Davy

This chapter introduces some ideas from literary studies, narrative theory and constructionism to help conceptualize the tasks and possibilities involved in reading and responding to case material, considered here as 'text'. Much of the discussion relates to written text such as file notes, case studies or interview transcripts, but many of the arguments also apply to therapeutic interaction. Texts conjure worlds into being (one can become lost in a good book), but the world can also be read as text, as when we speak of 'reading' someone's face, or children study a clinic's reception area to see what kind of place it is.

The ideas presented share a basis that language is not an unproblematic, transparent medium through which the facts of clinical experiences can be neutrally conveyed from writer to reader. Writing and reading involve selective transformations and constructions of meaning. Written studies are not unproblematic representations of clinical work as it actually happens. From a deconstructionist perspective, interpreting case material may mean attending to textual lacunae – that which might have been written, but was not. One meaning of Derrida's (1976) dictum '*il n'y a pas de hors-texte*' (there is nothing but the text) is a reminder that the presence of text is surrounded by the nothingness of what remains unwritten, that absences signify. For example, traumatic experiences are often reflected in what cannot easily be named, expressed or recalled. A five-page letter referring an adolescent mentioned one parent only by: 'Her father committed suicide when she was a baby'. Clinically, therapists must be sensitive to that which is omitted or minimized, tracking both content and process, such as repeating patterns when subjects get changed or confusion arises.

NARRATIVE SMOOTHING

Spence (1989) argued that clinical case studies are poor representations of what actually happens in clinical practice because of tendencies towards 'narrative smoothing', a kind of censorship process. Authors tend to write more about some aspects of a therapeutic encounter than others, whilst also editing out material which does not fit with their preferred public story. Material may be marginalized if it is shameful, seen as clinically insignificant, or undermines solidarity with the chosen community of validation (cf. Rorty, 1989). To take an unsubtle example, it is extremely rare for therapists to write about times when they themselves have abused a client. 'Narrative smoothing' means that case material accounts often either omit or minimize major errors or moral failings, or use 'minor' errors as evidence of the positive capacity of the therapist to notice and respond to setbacks in therapeutic process (for example, Casement, 2002), linking the account of a minor lapse with a description of how harm was minimized, the relational rupture repaired and so on.

For example, in Box 4.1 under 'Second reflexive commentary' I wrote about a case study I had presented in counselling psychology training some years before (the 'Original commentary'), in which I presented a 'confessional' narrative (van Maanen, 1988) consistent with an image of myself as an improving professional.

BOX 4.1   EXAMPLE OF NARRATIVE SMOOTHING

Original commentary

A PROCESS OF SHAME AND FAILING WORDS …

Megan explained that she felt that her own upbringing and early adult life had been good until about ten years ago when her husband Peter had suffered a small stroke. She described Peter as becoming increasingly aggressive to her after this, both verbally and physically, taking drugs and becoming extremely sexually demanding.

Second reflexive commentary

My original case study continued with a further section here describing some of the abuse which Megan had experienced from Peter, including rape. I have omitted that passage because in hindsight I now feel that some of my account verged on the voyeuristic (although this was not something which my original assessors commented on). I think perhaps I included excessive detail in the original case study because I was still struggling to relate professionally to such extreme experiences and was using the study to process this secondary or vicarious traumatization. Although I had the client's permission to write about our work together in an anonymised case study, ethically such permission does not release the therapist from a duty to write sensitively and respectfully about their clients. (Davy, 2004: 28)

More pervasively, narrative smoothing also describes the tendency to render a messy, complex process, perhaps containing false starts, digressions, misunderstandings, avenues half-explored then abandoned, into a relatively coherent, logical sequential account. Most Western psychologists train and practice within a regime of truth (Foucault, 1980) which socializes professionals into developing an emphasis on clarity, coherence and the 'central meaning' of accounts (Potter and Wetherell, 1987: 168). However, we live in cultures which may be fragmented, contradictory and conflicted, with complex, multiple and shifting experiences of self and relationships (cf. Elliott, 2007).

Narrative smoothing does not simply result from self-censorship, but also reflects the activity of publishers and readers. Publishers are less likely to accept case studies which claim to represent mediocre, messy therapy experiences. They may encourage authors to trim material seen as tangential to the 'main theme' of the article or chapter, which in turn will reflect the constructs privileged by a journal or book. Similarly, editors and peer-reviewers usually prefer case material which seems to have a coherent story to tell about 'interesting' findings. Case material can be subject to publication bias against 'negative results' in a similar way to empirical reports.

In reflexive turn, the kinds of case material published in journals and other professional arenas then play a part in reproducing a certain kind of professional subjectivity (cf. van Langenhove and Harré, 1999). Psychologists may read such articles as apparent exemplars of what they should aspire to, promoting both overt and covert norms about being a proper professional. Readers who discipline and monitor themselves (for example, Foucault 1977, 1980, 1988) to read as 'good psychologists' may then tend to disregard or denigrate accounts of case material which do not comply with a dominant narrative of coherent, logical, articulate professional psychology. (Although secretly, they might simultaneously experience themselves as failing in their own practice if they find themselves working with clients in ways that don't appear valued in the literature; for example, Rogers, 1991; White, 2002.)

Narrative smoothing affects both what is written about and the manner in which it is written. MacMillan (1992), a clinical psychologist and poet, contrasts his psychological writing in public, professional domains with what he terms his 'writings in the margin' about clinical encounters:

> Many of these notes emerge in the form of free verse, which feels to me more able than the serial logic of prose to catch some of the immediacy of the imagery that is suggested, and to catch and reflect the sense of ambiguity, and the multiple meanings and readings that interpretations of behaviour and experience invite. These writings can be important ways of trying to inhabit the world of clients imaginatively. (MacMillan, 1992: 9)

Here is one example of his verse, 'written when working with a boy who had 11 changes of carer between the ages of five months and four years':

Reviewing the past,
the truth becomes a variable commodity.
Thin lines part right from wrong:
lines of words, words and more words,
struggling to ease former pains.
New words for the cruelties, the hurt,
the partings – always the partings.
Now ornately garbed in politic phrases,
a new life is seeded in the past,
The future pinned wriggling to the page.

(MacMillan, 1992: 11; reprinted with permission from Angus Macmillan)

THE DEATH OF THE AUTHOR/BIRTH OF THE READER

Who is the 'I' speaking to you from this text? One answer is obviously me, John Davy, the author. But as you sit (stand, lie in the bath, wherever works for you, don't mind me) and read, the relationship producing meaning or interpretations is a conversation between you and the text, not between you and Davy. (Ignore him anyway, he may have changed his mind, lost interest in psychology, died for all you know. But the chapter is here.) Within this metaphor, texts including written case material can be understood as devices designed to produce 'model' readers who will make certain kinds of interpretation (Eco, 1990: 58–59, 148). However, the designer of each textual machine cannot control the interpretations made or foresee all possible actual 'empirical' readers and readings once the text has been released into the wild to proliferate and associate.

Any text is a message in a bottle, adrift in the ocean of potential readers. Even a text aimed towards a single specific reader, such as an intimate love letter, may one day be found in the attic by grandchildren or pored over by historians investigating a bygone era. A parent may have hopes and plans for their child, but once they've left home, who knows what will happen? And although a parent may like to think the child is theirs, many things shape a child's development besides that parent. Texts originate not simply from authors' intentions, but also from the cultural and discursive milieu, including the connotations and history of the language in which they are written, and their relationships with other texts. We write more than we intend about ourselves and our cultural resources.

Our language can be seen as an ancient city: a maze of little streets and squares, of old and new houses, and of houses with additions from various periods; and this surrounded by a multitude of new boroughs with straight regular streets and uniform houses. (Wittgenstein, 1958: PI I 8e)

Does this matter? On the one hand this view of text can liberate you from the tyranny of the author, who loses their author-ity and becomes a mere 'scriptor' in Barthes' (1981) terms. Just because you're reading a case study by Freud doesn't mean you have to understand it as he wanted, or castigate yourself if you don't. But on the other hand you have a job of work to do. The 'death of the author' (Barthes, 1981) means 'the birth of the reader'. Since your reader response (Fish, 1976; Iser, 1978) constructs meaning from case material text, you will need to take responsibility for the different ways which you could choose to interpret, and their consequences. However, many of us tend to take the way we read for granted.

This might not matter if one is simply reading for the pleasure of unrestrained free interpretation, for the delight of conjuring as many different readings as possible from a text without regard to whether one is 'better' than another. Imagine a citizen on holiday on the beach, sipping a cool drink while flicking idly through the pages of Yalom's fictionalized case studies (1991). But counselling psychologists may want to read case material in order to influence their professional practices with clients and colleagues. (Is that you on the beach? If it is, are you a psychologists as you read Yalom, or performing one of your other identities?) Clearly, it does matter how you write and read referrals, clinical letters and case studies (for example, Steinberg, 2000; Cross et al., 2003), file notes, assess trainee case studies, read case material for continuing professional development, interpret research case studies in journals (cf. Mair, 1999; McLeod, 2002; Turpin, 2001) and so on.

TEXTS AS BOTH OPEN AND LIMITED

Following Eco, texts are open in the sense that they can be interpreted in an infinite number of ways (1962), but limited in the sense that not all interpretations are good ones or valid (1990, 1992).

An analogy between the words of a case study and the stars in the sky may help. As I lie back on the grass gazing up at a clear night sky, I will be able to see many patterns within the stars, constellations. These reflect my own construing, but are also co-determined by social processes. I will be able to 'read' some constellations because they are already known in my culture (consensual validity). I could point one of these out with relative ease to a friend from my community, and perhaps even give them directions for navigation drawing on these shared patterns (pragmatic validity).

I might also see a 'new' constellation connecting some stars and invent a name for it (although perhaps tending to identify a constellation consistent with familiar cultural templates, for example, gods, mythology, animals). I could not use this reading with others in my community until I persuaded and taught them how to see 'it' as well (persuasive validity). Eventually, I might construct a small interpretive community which shares that certain way of reading the sky, forming a community of validation

(Fish, 1976). If I had the charisma and energy of Freud, Rogers, Bateson or Beck, the community might eventually become very large.

The number of constellations formed by imagined lines intersecting stars visible from our point on the Earth is potentially infinite. However, if I tried to persuade others to recognize a new constellation formed by imagined lines which just did *not* actually intersect stars visible from our point on the Earth, they would probably object. Even if some agreed, the constellation could not help them navigate across an actual ocean since it lacks physical referents. A communally valid reading of stellar constellations is one that I can imagine (construction); that is shared with others (social construction); and corresponds with some material affordances offered by the distribution of the physical stars themselves (critical realism).

Given 1000 words of case material, one could playfully develop an infinite number of interpretations. (A feminist reading, a cognitive one, a Marxist reading, the case as tragedy, morality tale, religious allegory and so on.) However, these interpretations need to 'intersect' with the actual type and distribution of the words in order to form a reasonable reading which is loyal to the text. You could choose to read this chapter as a coded message about the location of the Holy Grail (and possibly even persuade a few like-minded fanatics to do likewise, cf. *Foucault's Pendulum*, Eco, 1989), but this reading is unlikely to help you find the Grail. The text simply lacks the relevant data.

HERMENEUTICS

My reference to the Holy Grail was not entirely frivolous. Much of the early impetus for the development of hermeneutics, the science of textual interpretation, came from attempts to understand the divine Word as reflected in holy scripture. Hermeneutic scholars wanted to understand the relationship between God's will and religious texts that had been recorded, and then repeatedly copied, altered and 'corrected' by mortal beings. Biblical hermeneutics aimed towards a decoding of the divine hidden beneath layers of human textual distortion. Taken to its structuralist extreme, gnostic hermeticism assumed that since the world itself was a divine creation, all things must in some way reflect the divine. Hence the world itself could in principle be 'read' by someone with the right means of interpretation and decoding to get beyond surface appearances and understand the deepest, hidden truth of God (cf. Eco, 1990: 8–22, 1992).

It is not difficult to see the parallels with expert technologies (for example, free association, counter-transference, Freud's 'royal road' of dream interpretation, repertory grids, genograms, behavioural analyses) deployed by experts of the psy-complex such as therapists and psychologists (Rose, 1989), attempting to reveal the truth of a person, an interaction or an account beyond the outward appearance. A framework of working assumptions for interpretation is described as a 'hermeneutic approach'. The various psychologies and psychotherapies can be viewed as hermeneutics.

There is, however, an important distinction to be drawn between gnostic hermeticism, which aims to reveal the secret whole beyond broken codes, versus a hermeneutics of suspicion, which accepts a legitimate plurality of interpretation (Ricouer, 1981; Kvale, 1996). The latter assumes that settled, final meaning cannot be achieved, that there will always be further meanings that can be constructed beyond any given interpretation, with no ultimate end point (Cecchin, 1987). Any interpretation you may reach about some case material must be expressed in language, yet more text, which imports new connotations, is subject to further interpretation, and so on. Hence another meaning for Derrida's claim that 'there is nothing but the text'; since any textual interpretation is made in further text, final meaning is infinitely postponed.

When reading case material, a gnostic reader aims towards a reduction of data and meaning, 'boiling down' the text until some core theme, process or underlying phenomenon is revealed (the kind of data reductive hermeneutics used in grounded theory, interpretative phenomenological analysis or conversation analysis, for instance). By contrast, a psychologist interpreting case material through a hermeneutics of suspicion multiplies and expands the data and meanings rather than reduce them, and must choose some pragmatic endpoint for the (always incomplete) interpretation. Later in this chapter I provide an example from a critical reading of clinical supervision in palliative care.

In one of my cases, two parents of two half-sisters were talking to me and a co-therapist about some problems they were experiencing regarding the children's behaviour at school. They explained that part of the difficulty stemmed from the children being taught by two part-time teachers. One was friendly but tended to minimize the problems, whereas the other took them seriously but tended to be authoritarian and harsh. Both parents had busy working lives. Each was biological parent to one girl but step-parent to the other.

How might their story be interpreted? (NB, here treating talk as text.) I could choose to hear the story as a concrete description of difficulties in home–school liaison associated with particular communication and teaching styles. But I could also understand the account as a displaced description of parental dilemmas balancing home with work, and trying to find a way to integrate and negotiate with each other different assumptions about good parenting practices brought in from their families of origin and prior families of creation (Byng-Hall, 1995). Additionally, drawing upon a hermeneutic technology from psychoanalysis termed 'abstraction of the frame' (Casement, 1985), I heard the parents as offering me and my co-therapist some indirect clinical supervision about their experience of our differing professional styles. Abstracting the themes of their story, they were talking about two part-time professionals who both had something positive to offer and wanted to help, but who sometimes made it worse by giving conflicting messages. I could also read them as suggesting that we were operating in a hierarchical, teaching relationship with them rather than something more collaborative. This interpretive choice to understand the case material as attempted supervision of us by the clients seemed the most useful in working out how to go on, and so was privileged by us. This was a pragmatic decision rather a decoding of truth.

THE HERMENEUTIC SPIRAL

Each of the three interpretations outlined above suggested different trajectories for therapeutic action, which would each provide a new context for the parents to act into (Shotter, 1984). These subsequent actions would then invite us to re-interpret what it might have meant when they first told us about the teachers.

For example, suppose on page 1 of some case notes I read something about a new patient. I interpret these notes in a certain way, based partly on the features of the text, but also depending on the knowledge, assumptions and tendencies I bring to this first reading. This includes, of course, my previous experiences with other cases. The meaning of the text is realized through an interaction of the reader's 'horizons of potential meaning' (Gadamer, 1975) with the potentialities of the text. These horizons are neither static nor unitary. If I am feeling tired and depressed I may 'see' different things in the notes than if I am refreshed. Or if the context for my reading has somehow incited me to read particularly from a male perspective, whether or not I am conscious of this (that is, interpellated me into that subject position; Althusser, 1971), I interact differently with the text than reading 'as' a child psychologist.

There is a parallel between this hermeneutic notion of the reader's horizon and Vygotsky's (1978) zone of proximal development (ZPD). Reader and text provide mutual scaffolding for each other to achieve new meanings which would not be possible alone. The scope for new meaning will be influenced dynamically by the properties of both reader and text, and the 'fit' between them. A child's ZPD will depend partly on the style of scaffolding offered by any particular teacher (for example, humorous/ serious) as well as on the child's state. A hungry, cold, frightened child will probably show a smaller ZPD with the same material and teacher than a relaxed, secure child.

Then I turn to page 2 of the case notes. The way that I interpret this page will now be a function of my current state, including the interpretation I developed on page 1, interacting with the material of page 2. And so to page 3, page 4 and so on until I then thumb the pages back to page 1. But now I will re-interpret this page in a new way, since I have become a different reader through my engagement with pages 1, 2, 3, 4 the first time round. I may have learnt something new. Perhaps also the text has successfully interpolated me to re-read from a different subject position, for example, with my own experience as someone with mental health problems more to the fore.

This recursive process of interpretation and re-interpretation is termed a 'hermeneutic spiral'. On each return to the text, I create a different text by my re-reading, while the text also changes me iteratively. Think how common it is that something a client says in one session puts something they said previously in a new light, or how differently you might approach a recurrent but apparently stale topic with a client just after you have attended a stimulating training day on that theme. In therapy, we support clients to expand the range of meanings they can develop about their own life, through repeated, spiralling return with changing attention and new sensitivities to their lived experience. If the therapist provides the attachment security of a 'safe base' (Holmes, 2001), the client's ZPD can encompass a wider horizon of potential meaning.

INTENTIONS OF AUTHORS, TEXTS AND READERS

Even if the text reaches one of the readers anticipated by an author, there is no guarantee that a reader will read it as the author envisaged. Each reader brings their own intentions to the text, and so will construct different meanings from it. But the meaning constructed is not the product of authorial intent interacting with the reader's intentions, since the reader is engaging with the written word, not with the author.

Texts deploy a variety of strategies and cultural resources to incite the reader to function as their model reader should – in Gadamer's (1975) hermeneutical terms, 'fore-structuring' the horizon of potential meaning. For example, a case study may be prefaced with remarks about the importance of evidence-based practice and a scientist-practitioner model of counselling psychology, attempting to interpellate readers into a position in which certain categories of information about the client and therapist are seen as more significant and credible than others. If text appears in a journal under a heading of 'Keynote paper', with two professors named as authors, this rhetorical effect may be redoubled. Conversely, a case study about the 'same' client could be couched in language that speaks of user-empowerment and Marxist critique, deconstructing contemporary evidence-based psychotherapy discourse as a tool of advanced capitalism and industrial productivity, attempting to position the reader as a critical psychologist.

In Box 4.2, I use a 'Second reflexive commentary' – an attempt at deconstructive reading – to reflect on my choice of title for a narrative therapy case study I'd written some years before in counselling psychology training (the 'original commentary'):

BOX 4.2   TEXT STRATEGIES

Original Commentary

CASE STUDY – 'MEGAN'

Introduction
This case study describes counselling work over a six-week period between me and Megan, a 42-year-old white Irish woman, at an urban GP practice where I was employed to provide brief counselling to individual adult clients.

The referral
A male doctor at the practice referred Megan to me for 'depression', adding that Megan wanted help in managing her daughter's behaviour. The doctor wrote that the daughter might be anorexic.

Initial contact with the referrer

I felt it was unclear from the referral letter what sort of intervention might be needed and what the GP's expectations were, so I discussed the referral with the GP. He explained that he had only met the daughter, Cary (17 years old), on one occasion when she had refused a full medical examination, but he suspected as did Megan that she might be anorexic. The GP said that Megan seemed very depressed about her own inability to change this or other aspects of Cary's behaviour, which was described as 'unco-operative', and he wanted someone (i.e. me) to help Megan 'come to terms with her helplessness'.

Second reflexive commentary

Within the first few lines of the study, I have already introduced four subjects (Megan, her daughter Cary, myself and the GP), yet the title names only one. The title does not simply summarize or 'represent' the case in any simple way, but also suggests certain readings of the text over others.

[...]

My decision to name the study 'Megan' could be read as a demonstration of a client-focused attitude compatible with the 'decentred practice' of narrative therapy (White, 1997) which positions the therapist's concerns as peripheral to the client's best interests. However, there is also a sense in which this 'client-centred'/'decentred therapist' stance is also a flight from context into text. The title implies that the focus for intervention is located clearly within the identified patient's belief systems and actions. Megan is constructed as the object for the critical gaze of therapist and reader, and as the necessary site for change. This is paradoxically both empowering and objectifying. The woman is positioned as an object of pathology in need of intervention by others (here, specifically male others such as me and her GP), but is accorded the responsibility for change.

By contrast, more contextually oriented cybernetic therapies would note that Megan has been offered as the 'identified patient', but foreground the wider system that has produced and responded to the referral as the unit for analysis and intervention (for example, Bor et al., 1996; Minuchin, 1974).

[...]

Some alternative titles may help clarify this. For example, I could have titled the study as 'Therapeutic responses to male violence against women', or 'Problematizing masculine accountability in relation to therapy with an abused female client'. Drawing on the referring doctor's request to me, the study might be titled 'Help her come to terms with her helplessness', drawing attention to the traditional role of mental health services in pacifying women's distress and reproducing gendered power relations (see, for example, Kitzinger, 1993; Kutchins and Kirk, 1997; Masson, 1989; Ussher, 1991). Such cybernetically informed titles might have seemed incompatible with

(Continued)

(Continued)

presenting the case as a narrative study. However, these titles also make sense when read as narrative 'externalizations' of problems (for example, Title: 'Megan and John protest against male violence'). My wish to show theoretical consistency in the case study cannot adequately account for the exclusive focus on Megan in the title. The title of the case study reproduces a patriarchal dynamic that deflects critical attention from masculinity.

These titles do not necessarily offer 'better' readings of the case. Rather, my analysis draws attention to the necessary partiality of any reading or representation of clinical practice, in the double sense that any single account (a) offers an incomplete view of therapy, which is always open to elaboration or revision (Scheflen, 1978), and (b) is partial in the sense that it supports a particular set of purposes and values. (Davy, 2004: 23–25)

The limits of a text are not the same as the explicit authorial intent. Shakespeare's plays may constrain modern readers differently than they did his contemporaries. It is possible to develop coherent, plausible and thought-provoking analyses of Freud's cases and letters to show Freud's fear of acknowledging the reality of widespread child abuse (Masson, 1984). It is unlikely that Freud consciously intended his studies to be read as a demonstration of his personal limitations.

READERLY AND WRITERLY TEXTS

Some texts seem designed to invite multiple interpretations, and require a very active engagement from the reader to 'make sense'. A common technique in literary fiction (cf. Mullan, 2006) to invite the reader's active involvement is the use of a preface or prologue in which important developments within the novel are foreshadowed but not explained in detail, or are obscured so that the reader does not know whether the prologue refers to an event in a fictional character's history or one which is yet to come. Similarly, a text may challenge readers with an ambiguous ending, or an ending that reveals new information to the reader which then invites re-interpretation of what has gone before, as in McEwan's *Atonement* (2001). In *The Curious Incident of the Dog in the Night-Time* (Haddon, 2004), the use of an autistic boy as narrator, who describes behaviour in detail but cannot interpret emotions, invites readers to work hard at making affective meaning to fill the narrative lacunae around disturbing events.

Texts which seem crafted to demand particularly active participation by the reader are termed 'writerly texts' by Barthes (1981). That is, the story is incomplete, so that the reader has to 'write' into the gaps, ambiguities and 'indeterminacies' (Iser, 1978) of the text as they read in order to make a satisfying story. Writerly texts contrast with readerly texts in which it seems that the events and meaning of the text are spelled out step by step in a clear and unambiguous way, so that the text seems to operate to produce a model reader who is a relatively passive consumer of the information provided. When writing a feedback letter to a GP and client, the aim may be partly to convey facts and formulations, but you may also want to stimulate both readers into further thinking and re-storying, therapeutically disrupting previously settled understandings to stimulate curiosity (cf. White and Epston, 1990: Ch. 3).

Importantly, Barthes (1981) noted that the distinction between readerly and writerly activity can be understood as a disposition of the reader, rather than a static and quantifiable property of the text. That is, two readers might read the same text (referral letter, case notes and so on) with different interests, sensitivities and interpretive resources. One might see the text as a relatively straightforward 'readerly' account to be unwrapped. ('Good, I wanted a good description of phobia treatment by exposure, here's a nice case study telling me how to do it.') The other reader might be more interested and/or able to think about gaps and inconsistencies, things that could have been written about but were not, about the connotations and cultural quotations used within the text, or the rhetorical strategies deployed within the text to make the account seem plausible, coherent and straightforward, lulling unwary readers into passive acquiescence to the values and world-view reproduced in and by the text.

It's probably reasonable to describe *Five On a Treasure Island* (Blyton, 1942) as a readerly text, but a determined writerly reader could work on it to render multiple readings, for example, as an exploration of boundaries between adult and child sexuality, as reflected in Uncle Quentin's dealings with the Five. Conversely, Calvino's postmodern work *If On a Winter's Night a Traveller* (1981) could be interpreted by a steadfastly readerly reader 'simply' as a lament about the difficulties of finding a decent bookshop.

A PRAGMATIC STANCE TO INTERPRETATION

A pragmatic stance to interpreting case material means having an understanding of the purposes which you value, and selecting an appropriate mode of interpretation to fit your purpose. Imagine that you are looking at a letter written by a psychologist in a case file. You are likely to read in different ways, for example:

1. You wrote the letter yourself some time ago, and you want to refresh your thinking before the next session.
2. The client of a colleague has committed suicide. You have been asked by the service manager to review the notes as part of an internal investigation.
3. The other psychologist was writing about their clinical work with you. You have asked to read the notes they have written about you after some sessions about embarrassing personal dilemmas.
4. You have been asked to take on a new client. Previous therapeutic work by another psychologist has failed.

Each of these scenarios is likely to involve different affective components. In case 1, you will probably be reading very carefully for concrete details, dates, facts and sequences, and in relation to your service's agreed policies on record-keeping. By contrast, in case 2 you are unlikely to be focusing on the same kind of themes, and may want to be more open to divergent thoughts, connotations and implications for your own action. A section of text which seems very useful and generative for the reader in context 1 might strike a reader in context 2 as excessively focused on relational issues and the client's lived experience rather than the written risk management plan. In the latter case, the reader would be very interested to see who were the intended recipients of the letter, while in the former case this might not seem so significant.

AN EXTENDED EXAMPLE OF CRITICAL READING

The extracts that follow come from my doctoral thesis (Davy, 2000), which examined some uses of deconstruction in counselling psychology. They illustrate an interpretation of interview transcripts informed by a hermeneutics of suspicion to produce a 'critical reading'. Deconstructive readings aim towards a destabilization and denaturalization of manifest meaning in favour of a proliferation of meanings, reading a text for unacknowledged silences and unspoken assumptions. Critical reading places an additional emphasis on power and privilege, asking what hidden functions are at work within a text and what interests these serve (Lather, 1991, 1995).

I was not trying to explore the individual psychologies and beliefs of Dawn (a children's hospice service manager), Anya (an adult hospice nursing auxiliary) or myself. Rather, my purpose was to develop understandings about the discursive construction of clinical supervision in palliative care, to assist thinking about the meanings and function of clinical supervision in counselling psychology.

The use of a textual metaphor in counselling psychology reminds us that any given construction of experience draws on, or quotes from, existing cultural and symbolic resources within a community, and is not simply a matter of individuals' skilled language use independent of ecological/historical meanings. Discourses can be seen as analogous to literary genres (horror stories, romances and so on, cf. Mullan, 2006: 105–126) and cultural story repertoires (for example, fairytales), which help constrain and inform the construction and reading of any given text (such as the body, the self or an interview transcript).

The construction and functions of clinical supervision are shaped by local discursive contexts. Discourse analysis offers a way to focus on 'organizational' and 'contextual' factors in a way that recognizes institutional contexts such as palliative care as dynamic and contested rather than unitary and static.

I adopted a Foucauldian approach to the critical reading. This focuses on the variability, construction and functions of text as recommended by Potter and Wetherell

(1987), but with a more politicized emphasis on the contested nature of subjectivity, and the relationships between power, knowledge and modern identity (Henriques et al., 1984). Selfhood and individual experience are viewed as socially constructed phenomena with complex relations of (re)production and resistance to wider cultural and societal structures, processes and changes.

1) Variability should be read dialectically in terms of conflict and competition. (What are the different ways in which it is possible to speak of supervision in palliative care? How can this be understood in terms of a conflict between different discursive practices?)

2) The construction of accounts should be interpreted in terms of the cultural resources involved, not just an individual's tactics. (What discourses or cultural resources are drawn on to construct conversations about clinical supervision in palliative care?)

3) Function should be examined in terms of power effects, not simply as power to prevent or repress, but also through creating 'conditions of possibility'. (What sustains the legitimacy of clinical supervision within palliative care?) (Davy, 2000: 140–141)

Space precludes detailed discussion of the heuristic guidelines I adopted for interpretative reading from discourse analysis. Interested readers are referred to Davy (2000: 158–168) and Parker (1994). Some key elements include:

- Attend carefully to what is not said, and to instances where something can only be half-said before confusion or oppositional positions creep in.
- Regard the way things are said as attempts to manage or solve some problem(s).
- Avoid the temptation to read for a general sense or overall theme. Foucauldian analysis assumes that the material does not 'add up to' a coherent whole, but rather points towards conflict between different meanings.
- Regard the meanings studied as *inter*subjective and situated in the community of palliative care professionals, rather than 'belonging' to particular individuals.
- Systematically itemize 'objects' and 'subjects' or categories of person invoked in the text, mapping the different identities available within this social world.

In the material that follows, references such as [Y: 19–30, C, B: 24–31, Z: 3–21] refer to line numbers in different interview extracts, Y, C, B, Z. Only extracts Y and BB are provided here, but I have retained the referencing to illustrate the style of the argument through close reading of multiple texts.

In extract [Y], Anya appears to suggest that concealment of negative emotions from patients and families is a positive part of the palliative care experience, but also criticizes management for failing to realize how difficult the work is for the staff.

[Y] *John:*   Which ones of these things, like supervision or debriefing, actually have an impact on patients or family?

Anya: Well, I think we're very good here, 'cos I always call it the Cheshire Cat syndrome. Walk through the door, and then my smiling face goes on.

5   Walk out that door, you can do what you like, kick the car, kick the wall, have a fag. But, when you're in here, you know, the patients tend to come first, and you've got it in the back of your mind, that the patients don't see what goes on, and if by any chance a patient will pick up and say 'well, so and so's in a bad mood today', or 'there is a bit of

10   undercurrent, I can sense it' (Mmm), then, you stand back and you think, because if a patient can pick it up – Many a time, we all know, the stress morale around here is very very low, and you can sometimes cut the atmosphere with a knife. And it's not nice, but we will carry on regardless, and once again the Cheshire Cat smile's on. But if a patient

15   or a relative remarks on it, then we know then that it really is bad and something is got to be done. And I think something positive then is done, we have a night out, not that that doesn't do anything, 'cos a night out is just for that evening, you've still got to come back to it the next day.

John: So, something else then?

20   *Anya:*   No, no, you just forget it that day. Perhaps, on a couple of occasions, we have gone to management and said, look, a, we need more staff, b, the dependency has got to come down, and then the doctors, or the management, will appreciate and see that, and we do see notes on the board saying 'no more cases except in dire emergency because of bed status'

25   (Mm), so that helps us a bit, so … and they do try and get bank, and once again we have the budget, and cut-backs, and they say, oh you can manage, but that doesn't help, because you're going to, it's a vicious circle, because then you're going to, you get the emotional side of the nurses, they're going to need supervision, they're going to need the

30   counselling, they're going to go off sick, the bank nurses won't turn up or they won't come because they sense the atmosphere that's going on. Where do you go? And if the management don't listen, I'm sorry.

Anya praises staff for their ability to appear to cope in the face of adversity [Y:3–4, Y:11–14], and identifies failure as those moments when the mask slips and problems show through [Y:14–15]. She suggests a strategy of distraction and forgetting may be helpful to staff in such circumstances, together with additional resourcing or reduction of workload [Y:20–32]. She suggests that clinical supervision arises from the failure of such measures, rather than offering a solution. This suggests that management faith in staff's coping ability may contribute to staff's difficulties in coping [H:20–29]. More broadly, Anya seems to relate workplace stress to issues of resourcing, control and management practices, rather than clinical experience with particular patients. This could be read as denial or displacement within a psychotherapeutic discourse [J:2–5], but also seems consistent with research into workplace stress in other settings … (Davy, 2000: 208–209)

In Extract [BB] Dawn suggests that supervision can provide a protected space in which to process some of the special problems of palliative care [BB:5–14], but indicates that the hospice team need to be protected from public misinterpretation of these precisely because of the lack of public knowledge about palliative care [BB:26–49]. The hospice seeks to manage life-shortening illness openly and compassionately, but is constrained by public conceptions of a 'good death'. In concealing other scenarios, the hospice then helps to reproduce this narrative while creating internal dissonance about the functions and success of the team's work [BB:16–39].

[BB] *Dawn:*   Well, in my day of course [laughs loudly], you grin and bore it, didn't you? You, you didn't actually go to anybody, you went to your peers and had a, a chat with them. The actual official supervision really didn't almost enter my … career, or thoughts, until after I was here
5   actually, interestingly enough (Mmm). We were very new then, only opened in [early 1990s], so we only had one or two children here. And there was, every time people came, because we were [one of the first] hospices, they'd ask, what sort of support do you get? And we'd all go, 'nothing, nothing'. So I think after about three years it was
10   decided that there should be something …

John: It was embarrassing to be asked …

Dawn: Precisely! Yeah, you're a pioneer and you're not supporting anybody. So in effect, a counsellor was appointed, to actually supervize the setting up of the supervision system that we still have.

15 *John:* This is the group?

Dawn: This is the group, which is multidisciplinary, which has caused hiccups over the years, because it is multidisciplinary, so at one point the nurses felt they couldn't sort of create and say, well that was a terrible death, I think they should have had more morphine or whatever,
20   because you wouldn't like to do that in front of one of the cooks, who … wouldn't really understand (Mmm) if you felt the death wasn't right, you know, if, if, that the nurses had failed. Do you get what I'm trying to say here? They felt a bit restricted that they couldn't say, as a nurse you can actually complain about something (OK), or comment about something.

25 *John:* But it would have been … I'm not sure if I do understand … It would, it might have been exposing themselves a bit much, might have been showing their vulnerabilities a bit too much?

Dawn: No, not from that point of view, in as much as, if you're debating … a clinical subject to a lay person, and saying, yes, I think we did that
30   wrong (Mm-hm), then, it was felt that perhaps that lay person would think that that child died badly.

John: Might that not have been partly what the nursing team was trying to say at that point?

Dawn: Well, yes and no. I get what you're saying, but then you would have
35   somebody else who would say, no, this happened, and it was right, do

you see what I mean? But that would still ... not necessarily be the right thing for telling (Hmm), or letting – there's nothing wrong with our cooks, but you know, they're fantastic (Sure), but who might go and ... tell someone, ooh crumbs, they were discussing the way that
40   that ... [*voice tails off*]

John: So there might be a concern that discussing difficulties, for example, management of nursing care, that, this might lead to some undermining of confidence (Yeah) in the way the hospice works, perhaps within the wider team as a whole, or worse within the community?

45   *Dawn:*   Yeah. Though, basically everybody is bound by confidentiality, but I mean the more people you have in any organization, and that's including the nurses as we all know [*laughs*] (Mmm), not immune to um, you know ... The conversations on the buses I've heard (Mm-hm) ... defy belief at times.

The relationship between the discourses of concealment, psychotherapy and management is complex. To the extent that a discourse of concealment emphasizes the importance of smooth running [Y:1–18] and maintaining 'normal' appearances despite problems, it clearly fits with a managerialist emphasis on maintaining product consistency and positive customer relations. However, psychotherapeutic discourse also provides a means by which resource conflict may be reinterpreted primarily in terms of worker inadequacy and poor emotional coping strategies (Hingley and Harris, 1986), [B:10–18, J, K], rather than labour relations and management/worker consultation [Y:20–32, C, B:24–31, Z:3–21].

[...]

Viewed psychotherapeutically as a confidential cathartic space primarily for emotional processing, clinical supervision may help reproduce concealment and smooth short-term organizational functioning. This may replicate the way in which the distress of death was pushed out of sight into side rooms within traditional medical wards, as clinical supervision formalizes, structures and 'tidies away' disturbing thoughts and feelings from the routine conversations and interactions of hospice life under the guise of acknowledgement. Although at one level psychotherapeutic discourse seems to privilege insight and openness, there is also a sense in which it privileges the private and concealed processing of distress which might otherwise be public and unsettling to others. (Davy, 2000: 211–213)

DISTURBING PLEASURES AND THE LIMITS OF PRAGMATISM

I have tended to emphasize that psychologists interpret case material in accordance with intended purpose(s), a pragmatic perspective in which texts are treated instrumentally with the reader response transforming the text. However, sometimes reading destabilizes purposes. We begin to ask new questions, act in unforeseen ways. Rorty (1992: 106) suggests a distinction 'between methodical and inspired readings of texts', '... knowing what you want to get out of a person or thing or text in advance and hoping that the person or thing or text will help you want something different – that he or she or it will help you to change your purposes, and thus to change your life.'

I remember stumbling across a book on the Nicaraguan literacy campaign (sadly, I can't remember the title) whilst mooching around a library where my partner was working. I was captivated by the ideas and vision described, and intrigued by the references to Freire's *Pedagogy of the Oppressed* (1972). All these were new to me. I became a nursery class teacher, a career I had not considered before. And thence I came, through zigs and zags, into counselling psychology and psychotherapy.

Game (1991) has suggested that texts should be evaluated for their 'disturbing pleasure', in which a reader comes to re-evaluate their own purposes and desire for knowledge, opening up new questions. Earlier, I introduced Barthes' distinction between readerly and writerly texts, the latter being encounters in which readers were active in writing further meaning into texts. Game's idea suggests that writerly texts can also write into the psychologist, transporting us (White's 'katharsis', 2007: 194–201) to different ways of understanding ourselves and the world. Counselling psychologists tend to think of helping others to change but case material transforms us too, within the limits of our potential horizons of being and despite a dominant narrative of instrumentality in Western psychology.

COUNSELLING PSYCHOLOGY AS A LIMINAL DISCIPLINE

This chapter has introduced several terms and ideas from domains such as literary theory that may seem alien to mainstream psychology. New concepts and language can facilitate defamiliarization (Shklovsky, 1917), making strange the taken-for-granted, assisting us to 'entertain and explore alternative possibilities, by extending [our] awareness and sensitivities' (MacMillan, 1992: 12). As a liminal discipline (Davy, 2000: 236–237), counselling psychology exists in between more established, orthodox psychologies and other domains such as psychotherapy, rhetoric, poetry, anthropology, literature and philosophy. This marginal position can be uncomfortable at times, but it allows counselling psychology to operate as a fertile meeting ground for diverse knowledges and practices.

REFERENCES

Althusser, L. (1971) *Lenin and Philosophy, and Other Essays*. London: New Left Books.
Barthes, R. (1981) 'The death of the author', in J. Caughie (ed.), *Theories of Authorship*. London: Routledge.

Blyton, E. (1942) *Five on a Treasure Island*. London: Hodder and Stoughton.

Bor, R., Legg, C. and Scher, I. (1996) 'The systems paradigm', in R. Woolfe and W. Dryden (eds.), *Handbook of Counselling Psychology,* 1st edn. London: Sage.

Byng-Hall, J. (1995) *Rewriting Family Scripts*. London: Guilford.

Calvino, I. (1981) *If On a Winter's Night a Traveller*. Trans. W. Weaver. London: Secker and Warburg.

Casement, P. (1985) *On Learning from the Patient*. London: Routledge.

Casement, P. (2002) *Learning from Our Mistakes*. Hove: Brunner-Routledge.

Cecchin, G. (1987) 'Hypothesising, circularity, and neutrality revisited: an invitation to curiosity', *Family Process*, 26 (4): 405–413.`

Cross, M., Papadopoulos, L. and Bor, R. (2003) *Reporting in Counselling and Psychotherapy*. London: Brunner-Routledge.

Davy, J. (2000) 'Text and context in counselling psychology: Some uses of deconstruction', DPsych thesis, City University, London.

Davy, J. (2004) 'The functions of case studies: Representation or persuasive construction?', *Counselling Psychology Review*, 19 (1): 22–38.

Derrida, J. (1976) *Of Grammatolog*. Trans. G. Spivak. Baltimore: Johns Hopkins University Press.

Eco, U. (1962) *Opera Aperta*. Milan: Bompiani. (Partial English translation: *The Open Work*. Cambridge, MA: Harvard University Press, 1989).

Eco, U. (1989) *Foucault's Pendulum*. Trans. W. Weaver. London: Secker and Warburg.

Eco, U. (1990) *The Limits of Interpretation*. Bloomington, CA and Indianapolis, IN: Indiana University Press.

Eco, U. (1992) 'Overinterpreting texts', in S. Collini (ed.), *Interpretation and Overinterpretation: Umberto Eco*. Cambridge: Cambridge University Press.

Elliott, A. (2007) *Concepts of the Self,* 2nd edn. Cambridge: Polity.

Fish, S. (1976) 'Interpreting the variorum', *Critical Inquiry*, 2 (Spring): 465–485.

Foucault, M. (1977) *Discipline and Punish: The Birth of the Prison*. London: Allen Lane.

Foucault, M. (1980) *Power/Knowledge: Selected Interviews and Other Writings 1972–1977*. Hemel Hempstead: Harvester Wheatsheaf.

Foucault, M. (1988) 'Technologies of the self', in L. Martin, H. Gutman and P. Hutton (eds), *Technologies of the Self*. Amherst, MA: University of Massachusetts Press.

Freire, P. (1972) *Pedagogy of the Oppressed*. Harmondsworth: Penguin.

Gadamer, H.G. (1975) *Truth and Method*. New York: Seabury Press.

Game, A. (1991) *Undoing the Social: Towards a Deconstructive Sociology*. Buckingham: Open University Press.

Haddon, M. (2004) *The Curious Incident of the Dog in the Night-Time*. London: Vintage.

Henriques, J., Hollway, W., Urwin, C., Venn, C. and Walkerdine, V. (1984) *Changing the Subject: Psychology, Social Regulation and Subjectivity*. London: Methuen.

Hingley, P. and Harris, P. (1986) 'Burnout at senior level', *Nursing Times*, 82 (31): 28–29 and 82 (32): 52–53.

Holmes, J. (2001) *The Search for the Secure Base: Attachment Theory and Psychotherapy*. Hove: Brunner-Routledge.

Iser, W. (1978) *The Act of Reading*. Baltimore, MD: Johns Hopkins University Press.

Kitzinger, C. (1993) 'Depoliticising the personal: A feminist slogan in feminist therapy', *Woman's Studies International Forum*, 16 (5): 487–496.

Kutchins, H. and Kirk, S.A. (1997) *Making Us Crazy*. London: Constable.

Kvale, S. (1996) *InterViews: An Introduction to Qualitative Research Interviewing*. London: Sage.

Lather, P. (1991) *Getting Smart: Feminist Research and Pedagogy with/in the Postmodern*. New York: Routledge and Kegan Paul.

Lather, P. (1995) 'The validity of angels: Interpretive and textual strategies in researching the lives of women with HIV/AIDS', *Qualitative Inquiry*, 1: 41–68.

MacMillan, A. (1992) 'Communicating about clients: Speaking for myself and others', *Clinical Psychology Forum*, 49: 8–12.

Mair, M. (1999) 'Inquiry in conversation: Questions, quests, search and research', *BPS Psychotherapy Section Newsletter*, 25: 2–15.

Masson, J.M. (1984) *The Assault on Truth: Freud's Suppression of the Seduction Theory*. Harmondsworth: Penguin.

Masson, J.M. (1989) *Against Therapy*. London: Collins.

McEwan, I. (2001) *Atonement*. London: Jonathan Cape.

McLeod, J. (2002) 'Case studies and practitioner research: Building knowledge through systematic inquiry into individual cases', *Counselling and Psychotherapy Research*, 2 (4): 265–268.

Minuchin, S. (1974) *Families and Family Therapy*. London: Tavistock.

Mullan, J. (2006) *How Novels Work*. Oxford: Oxford University Press.

Parker, I. (1994) 'Discourse analysis', in P. Banister, E. Burman, I. Parker, M. Taylor and C. Tindall (eds), *Qualitative Methods in Psychology: A Research Guide*. Buckingham: Open University Press.

Potter, J. and Wetherell, M. (1987) *Discourse and Social Psychology: Beyond Attitudes and Behaviour*. London: Sage.

Ricouer, P. (1981) *Hermeneutics and the Human Sciences*. Cambridge: Cambridge University Press.

Rogers, A.G. (1991) 'A feminist poetics of psychotherapy', in C. Gilligan, A.G. Rogers and D.L. Tolman (eds), *Women, Girls and Psychotherapy: Reframing Resistance*. London: Harrington Park Press.

Rorty, R. (1989) *Contingency, Irony and Solidarity*. Cambridge: Cambridge University Press.

Rorty, R. (1992) 'The pragmatist's progress', in S. Collini (ed.), *Interpretation and Overinterpretation: Umberto Eco*. Cambridge: Cambridge University Press.

Rose, N. (1989) *Governing the Soul: The Shaping of the Private Self*. London: Routledge.

Scheflen, A.E. (1978) 'Susan smiled: On explanations in family therapy', *Family Proceedings*, 17: 59–68.

Shklovsky, V. (1917/1988) 'Art as technique', Trans. L.T. Lemon and M.J. Reis (1965). Reprinted in D. Lodge (ed.), *Modern Criticism and Theory: A Reader*. London: Longmans.

Shotter, J. (1984) *Social Accountability and Selfhood*. Oxford: Basil Blackwell.

Spence, D.P. (1989) 'Rhetoric vs. evidence as a source of persuasion: A critique of the case study genre', in M.J. Packer and R.B. Addison (eds), *Entering the Circle: Hermeneutic Investigations in Psychology*. New York: Addison-Wesley.

Steinberg, D. (2000) *Letters from the Clinic*. London: Routledge.

Turpin, G. (2001) 'Single case methodology and psychotherapy evaluation: From research to practice', in C. Mace, S. Moorey and B. Roberts (eds), *Evidence in the Psychological Therapies*. Hove: Brunner-Routledge.

Ussher, J. (1991) *Women's Madness: Misogyny or Mental Illness?* Hemel Hempstead: Harvester Wheatsheaf.

Van Langenhove, L. and Harré, R. (1999) 'Positioning and the writing of science', in R. Harré and L. van Langenhove (eds), *Positioning Theory*. Oxford: Blackwell.

Van Maanen, J. (1988) *Tales of the Field*. Chicago, IL: University of Chicago Press.

Vygotsky, L.S. (1978) *Mind in Society: The Development of Higher Psychological Processes*. Cambridge: Cambridge University Press.

White, M. (1997) *Narratives of Therapists' Lives*. Adelaide: Dulwich Centre Publications.

White, M. (2002) 'Addressing personal failure', *International Journal of Narrative Therapy and Community Work*, 3: 33–76.

White, M. (2007) *Maps of Narrative Practice*. London: Norton.

White, M. and Epston, D. (1990) *Narrative Means to Therapeutic Ends*. London: Norton.

Wittgenstein, L. (1958) *Philosophical Investigations,* 2nd edn. Trans. G.E.M. Anscombe. Oxford: Blackwell.

Yalom, I.D. (1991) Love's *Executioner and Other Tales of Psychotherapy*. Harmondsworth: Penguin.

PART II

TRADITION, CHALLENGE AND CHANGE

Counselling psychology has developed out of a creative tension between the disciplines of psychology and counselling/psychotherapy. The latter has evolved as a range of approaches or models grounded in theoretical traditions whereas psychology has had less regard for theoretical concepts but has placed a strong emphasis on empirical research and evaluation. Nevertheless, psychology, in common with psychotherapy, can be thought of in relation to broad theoretical traditions which can also be seen as underpinning a wide range of models and approaches in psychotherapy. These traditions have differing foci and have developed as a result of challenges both within each tradition and from outside. In recent years we have seen efforts towards integration and the identification of common factors.

The chapters in this part of the book focus on three historically important and contrasting traditions: psychodynamic, cognitive-behavioural and humanistic, as well as a strongly emerging narrative tradition. The psychodynamic tradition focuses on the unconscious dynamics which shape experience and distress; the cognitive-behavioural tradition, on learned behaviour and the capacity for thinking about it; and the humanistic tradition on subjective experience, personal meaning and self-worth. The more recently emerging narrative tradition can be understood in relation to postmodernism. Its emphasis is on the social construction of identity and experience and it has some affinity with recent systemic thinking which, although not considered as a separate tradition here, informs other chapters in the book. The final chapter in the section grapples with issues of integration.

The author of each chapter has focused on key questions and has illustrated the approach with case material. The questions include:

What is the underlying theory of the person with its normative concepts of, for example, maturity and health?

What kind of knowledge is sought, for example, an understanding of unconscious/structural forces or of patterns of learning?

What constitutes distress, dysfunction, maladaptation or pathology?

What is the relation between the theoretical framework and the therapeutic practice?

What constitutes relevant evidence and research and what is the existing evidence?

5

PSYCHODYNAMIC APPROACHES

Rosemary Rizq

It is odd that psychoanalysis, a field that has consistently championed the disowned and marginalized aspects of the self has, ever since Freud's (1895) 'Project for a scientific psychology', continued resolutely to position itself within mainstream science. These days, such paradoxical territory appears to overlap to some extent with the concerns of counselling psychology, a field that embraces the science of psychology and evidence-based practice alongside the art of counselling and the phenomenology of subjectivity. In spite of, or perhaps because of, having to straddle not dissimilar epistemological con-tradictions, counselling psychology and psychoanalysis make for rather uneasy bedfel-lows. Compared with psychoanalysis, of course, counselling psychology can certainly be considered a psychotherapeutic newcomer. Eager to prove its professional, academic and scientific credentials in an age of evidence-based practice, it has within less than two decades had some success in establishing a public foothold within the regulation and professionalization of the talking therapies. Psychoanalysis, on the other hand, influen-tial in virtually every sphere of Western culture during the twentieth century, is cur-rently seen as an 'embattled profession' (Fonagy, 2003), undergoing intense public scrutiny and critical adjudication of its training methods, therapeutic practices and clinical outcomes. Perhaps it is not surprising, then, that therapeutic approaches derived from psychoanalysis – including psychodynamic counselling and psychoanalytic psychotherapy – are frequently regarded by counselling psychologists as fraught with the potential for antagonism, competition and disagreement.

But disagreements have histories. The bifurcation of academic psychology and psychoanalysis actually goes back over a century, indicative of a troubled and increasingly distant relationship that Whittle has characterized as 'a case study in incommensurability' (1999: 233). Academic psychology has generally been roundly dismissive of the psychoanalytic project. As early as 1930, Watson declared that 'Twenty years from now an analyst using Freudian concepts and Freudian terminology will be placed on the same plane as a phrenologist' (1930: 27).

In a similar vein, Eysenck was later trenchantly to claim of Freud:

> He was, without doubt, a genius, not of science, but of propaganda, not of rigorous proof, but of persuasion, not of the design of experiments, but of literary art. His place is not, as he claimed, with Copernicus and Darwin, but with Hans Christian Anderson and the Brothers Grimm, tellers of fairy tales. (1985: 208)

Psychoanalysis, on the other hand, has been equally dismissive of the claims of psychology and of the methods of modern social science. Brenman Pick, for example, has argued strongly that research fundamentally threatens the very fabric of psychoanalytic work:

> Overvaluation of 'Research' often goes together with an undervaluation or devaluation, of the research with which we engage in our psycho-analytic work. And if this Research (with a capital R) is privileged within psychoanalysis, we will, in order to placate and propitiate our enemies from without, succeed in destroying psychoanalysis from within. I believe this to be a 'real' (not just a fantasized) danger! (2000: 109).

Whittle characterizes the differences between these two disciplines as 'a fault line running down the centre of psychology' (1999: 234), a gap or gulf that is all the more surprising since both fields are clearly concerned with the study of the mind. He delineates the scale of the problem thus:

> The size of this split within what outsiders regard as a single subject is without parallel in any other academic discipline. Neither side reads the literature of the other. On the whole, they don't try to: it does not seem interesting or relevant. If they do try, they find it almost impossible. To each side, the literature of the other seems profoundly misconceived. Everything seems wrong ... It is a gap between different subcultures, encompassing different belief systems, practices and institutions, vocabularies and styles of thought. (1999: 236)

It is certainly interesting that both psychoanalysis and psychology originally derived from a common parental root. Freud initially trained as a neurologist within the school of Helmholtzian physiology, the backdrop against which modern experimental psychology was later to be developed by Wilhelm Wundt. Freud, however, subsequently turned his attention to unconscious internal structures and to the complex interplay of instinctual drives, identifications, defences and conflicts in the development of the individual's personality. Fonagy (2000) has pointed out that, during the Second World War, the need for briefer, more widely available models of clinical practice became acute; a demand that was largely met by the new profession of clinical psychology pioneering models of therapy derived from experimental findings rooted in a natural science model. Psychoanalysis, embroiled in various internal splits, most notably in the 'controversial discussions' of the 1940s, meant that psychoanalysts by and large remained sequestered within their private training institutions, unwilling to develop new techniques, to submit to academic critique, or to contribute to interdisciplinary debate and discussion. Against this troubled history, Fonagy bemoans psychoanalysis's 'forced separation' from psychology which:

> has not only contributed to the reduction of psychoanalysis to a state perilously close to intellectual bankruptcy, but more importantly, it has encouraged the development of alternative modes of clinical practice that have more hostility than affinity towards the psychoanalytic tradition and manifest every sign of being able to take over from it as the pre-eminent intellectual force behind the delivery of psychosocial mental health interventions. (2003: 229)

Counselling psychology only emerged as a distinct discipline in the 1990s, seeking from the outset to distinguish itself from both psychoanalysis and behaviourism. In contrast to clinical psychology, counselling psychology's roots are in humanism, a 'third force' in psychology that privileges a non-pathologizing account of psychological distress and which emphasizes the uniqueness of each person and his or her self-actualizing tendencies. The centrality of the therapeutic relationship and a commitment to understanding the client's subjective experience are considered central to counselling psychology practice. This is in contrast to what has been seen as the psychoanalytic preference for explaining behaviour in terms of unconscious processes rooted in traumatic early childhood experiences, or, as in the case of behaviourism, to stimulus-response contingencies.

I have elsewhere (Rizq, 2008) discussed how some in our own profession have continued to construct a 'straw man' vis-à-vis psychoanalysis, portraying it as old-fashioned, authoritarian and scientifically questionable. But if we are to consider such charges in any detail, we will certainly need to ask which kind of psychoanalysis we are referring to. Ryle (1949) has described psychology as 'a federation of enquiries and techniques'; but I suspect this portrayal is equally valid for psychoanalysis, which has evolved over the last few decades into a far more pluralistic and fragmented field than the one Freud originally envisioned. Indeed, Whittle (2000) has referred to the 'diaspora' of psychoanalysis, pointing to the many variants including psychoanalytic psychotherapy and psychodynamic counselling now taught in training institutions, and to the plethora of psychoanalytically oriented counsellors and therapists currently in clinical practice. Clearly, we can include psychodynamic approaches to counselling psychology amongst these variants. Whilst it is not possible – nor shall I attempt – in a single chapter to adduce the many different models and approaches encompassed within the psychoanalytic framework, what I do want to do is touch on some of the ways in which psychodynamic theory, research and practice has evolved over the last century, in search of those aspects that we might consider most congenial to the counselling psychology project.

WHICH PSYCHOANALYSIS?

Whilst Freud continued to doubt, revise and rework his ideas throughout his lifetime, his original drive-conflict theories, including the topographical and structural models of mind, can broadly be understood in terms of a distinctive metaphor, model and method: an archaeological metaphor, emphasizing unearthing the buried treasure of repressed memories within the patient's unconscious; a medical model of theory and practice that sought to cure the patient's symptoms; and a clinical method based on reconstructing the past and restoring to the patient an accurate awareness of his or her unconscious conflicts and childhood traumas via interpretation of resistance and reso-lution of the transference. Over the last century since Freud first outlined the role of the instincts in development and psychopathology, psychoanalysis has grown and evolved considerably. A number of refinements to Freud's structural model of the mind were advanced by theorists interested in the development and role of the ego, with writers such as Hartmann (1939), Spitz (1959) and later Anna Freud (1965) and Mahler (1968) outlining the ego's structure and function in what became known as 'ego psychology'.

However, it has been the rise of the object relations school that has largely come to dominate psychoanalytic theory and practice. Object relations theories all broadly cohere around a view of the individual as driven less by biological instincts than by an intrinsic need for relationship. Focusing primarily on the early mother–infant dyad and its significance for interpersonal relationships and their internal representation across the lifespan, these theories can be contrasted with the classical Freudian view of intrapsychic development taking place more or less independently of the individual's relational environment. Fonagy and Target admit that object relations theory is 'far too diverse to have a single, agreed definition' (2003: 107), but argues that such approaches all include several shared assumptions such as:

- The significance of the pre-oedipal period in the aetiology of severe pathology.
- The increasing complexity of object relationships over the lifespan.
- The existence of a maturational sequence of development that may be influenced by personal pathological experiences.
- The repetition of early patterns of object relating throughout life.
- The association of adult pathology with early disturbances in object-relating.
- The client's relationship to the therapist provides a vehicle for exploring early relation-ship patterns.

Object relations frameworks include those of theorists such as Klein (1935), Bion (1959) and other contemporary Kleinians such as Joseph (1985), Steiner (1994) and, in the US, Kernberg (1970). Other major theorists include Winnicott (1965), Balint (1937) and Guntrip (1961). These latter analysts, joined by others such as Fairbairn (1952), Khan (1963), Bollas (1987) and Casement (1985) epitomize what has become known as the 'independent' tradition in British psychoanalysis, an object relations school comprising the contributions of a wide variety of analysts and theorists that have subsequently made a major contribution to our understanding of early child development and the importance of the 'facilitating environment' in the child's progression to mature independence. The independent tradition is also characterized by an increasing interest in and articulation of the therapist's countertransference as indicative of the client's internal world, and the therapist's own contribution to therapeutic process and progress. A further strand is provided by Kohut's (for example, 1977) self-psychology, more prevalent in the US than in Britain, an approach that focuses on the therapist's empathic attunement and mirroring to repair the patient's early developmental deficits. These latter object relations approaches, together with the US interpersonal school of the 1940s and 1950s comprising writers such as Sullivan, Fromm–Reichmann and Fromm, have been extended and developed by contemporary relational psychoanalysis (for example, Mitchell, 1988) where the role of the therapist as active participant rather than merely observer within a shared therapeutic encounter is claimed as a distinctive feature of clinical work. Finally, we should note a significant alternative framework to the prevailing object relations paradigm: the European tradition of theorists such as Lacan, Green and Laplanche as well as feminist writers such as Kristeva, Irigaray and Cixous. These are major theorists whose work would require a separate chapter to review adequately and consider.

In view of the huge array and variety of theoretical approaches on offer, of which the above is only a sample, it is certainly interesting that psychology in general, and counselling psychology in particular, has in many cases had little positive to say about psychoanalysis, and has been notably reluctant to engage in discussion and debate about the role and contribution of psychodynamic approaches to practice and research. Much of this failure to engage on the part of our own profession is, I suspect, constitutive of Whittle's (1999) 'fault line', and indicative of a presupposition that psychoanalysis holds a world-view incompatible with that of the postmodern, constructivist agenda of counselling psychology. Indeed, Rustin (1999) has claimed psychoanalysis as the 'last modernism', drawing attention to its essentialist project of uncovering an ultimate, knowable 'truth' about an authentic 'self' via the lifting of repression. Freud, of course, linked self-knowledge to the notion of cure; and cure lay in the hands of the analyst, whose expert authority, neutrality and objectivity in decoding the patient's unconscious was considered crucial to the scientific legitimacy and probity of the psychoanalytic profession.

Postmodernism's stance of epistemological pluralism, holding that there is no one privileged way of knowing, has since thoroughly deconstructed the position of expert, introduced the notion of truth as necessarily local, provisional and contextual and highlighted the role of linguistic discourse in constructing, evaluating and experiencing the self. Social constructionism in particular has been an influential force in revealing the way underlying power dynamics obscure the values, principles and privileged status of dominant social groups. Counselling psychology has been the psychotherapeutic child of this post-modern turn, adopting a pluralist model of training and practice where no one single theoretical approach is considered pre-eminent. Rejecting the 'expert' stance, it situates the therapist as a guide or collaborator, privileging the therapeutic relationship and the role of the therapist's own subjectivity in influencing therapeutic process and progress; clinical practice is seen as embedded within and subject to a range of psychological, social, political, cultural and contextual factors. Perhaps it is hardly surprising, then, that many counselling psychologists consider the modernist enterprise of psychoanalysis to be obsolete, an anachronistic relic of a bygone epistemology.

However, over the past two decades the postmodern turn, evident across a wide range of fields, has resulted in what has generally been considered a 'sea change' in psychoanalytic thinking. One effect of this has been an increasing openness to alternative epistemologies and theories, some of which now appear to be closer to addressing the issues of interpersonal relationships, experience and subjectivity that counselling psychology adopts as its field of inquiry. A dominant and rapidly-evolving contemporary trend here is the relational approach to psychodynamic work, a field that looks set to become a future nexus for the integration of a number of interrelated contemporary concerns such as the relevance of a two-person psychology to clinical work and the contributions of developmental research, attachment theory and neuroscience to our understanding of intersubjectivity. Relational psychodynamic thinking thus spans a number of clinical and epistemological issues salient to counselling psychologists, and the next section focuses on this approach in more detail.

RELATIONAL PSYCHOANALYSIS

The replacement of drive-conflict models with developmental deficit models was part of the process that Winnicott (1965) and Bowlby (1969) started, with their emphasis on the significance of interpersonal processes and the external environment in organizing the individual's internal world. Relational psychoanalysis (for example, Greenberg and Mitchell, 1983) emerged from the middle ground between British object relations theory and American self-psychology, and provides a conceptual link between the intrapsychic and interpersonal models of mind. In this model, the therapist is an active participant within the therapeutic dyad who brings his or her own unique subjectivity to the therapeutic encounter in an effort to understand and experience the way early relational experiences have structured the client's internal world and how this impacts on his or her behaviour and interpersonal functioning. Clearly, this stance involves a radical re-examination of classical psychoanalytic assumptions privileging analytic neutrality and objectivity, assumptions that Stolorow and Atwood (1997) have characterized as the modernist 'myth of the neutral analyst'.

Relational psychoanalysis comprises a number of key elements outlined by Hargaden and Schwartz. These include:

- The centrality of relationship.
- Therapy as a two-way street involving a bi-directional process.
- Both the vulnerability of the therapist and client are involved.
- Countertransference is used not merely as information but in thoughtful disclosure and collaborative dialogue.
- The co-construction and multiplicity of meaning. (2007: 4)

These elements cohere around an overriding assumption of mutuality, where the therapist, as much as the client, brings his or her subjectivity to the consulting room, listening and responding from a position of willing emotional engagement.

Aron (2007) distinguishes between the classical stance where authority is located in the therapist's knowledge, and the relational stance where authority is located in the therapeutic dyad, awaiting construction between the two participants. This means that the classical ideal of the omnipotent, all-knowing analyst is replaced with the therapist who can tolerate uncertainty and not-knowing and whose technique is tailored to the unique subjectivity of the client, rather than attempting a 'one-size-fits-all' approach to interpretation (Orbach, 2007). This is clearly a far more egalitarian and interpersonal perspective of the therapeutic relationship – indeed, Orbach (2007) refers to it as a 'democratisation of psychoanalysis' – one in which the field of inquiry is constituted by the therapeutic dyad, now seen as mutually involved in a reciprocal cycle of interactional sequences.

Epistemologies, of course, have clinical consequences. As we have seen, a common assumption behind all psychodynamic approaches is that developmental factors underlie the evolution of psychological distress. From the classical perspective, however, this can all too easily imply that adult psychopathology is simply reducible to childhood difficulties, and that clinical work consists in the reconstruction of historical problems or unconscious 'fixation points' in the client. In this version of psychoanalysis, we might say that the future is simply the past dressed up in long trousers: the adult client is consigned to endless repetition of early feelings and behaviour enacted and interpreted within the transference.

Mitchell (1988) has robustly critiqued this rather dispiriting account of the patient-as-infant, trapped inside an adult body awaiting the necessary 'facilitating environment' (Winnicott, 1965) through which his or her 'true self' can emerge. A more relational, non-linear perspective suggests that early disturbance sets in train a complex series of relational experiences, reactions and interpersonal cycles, resulting in the creation of a unique interpersonal world. It is this interpersonal world that the client brings with him or her to the therapeutic relationship, a world that the therapist comes to inhabit, experience and respond to according to the vectors of his or her own subjectivity. The past is thus in constant dynamic interplay with the present, and the intersubjective climate is constituted by the therapist's own reactions and feelings which the client is unconsciously evoking and responding to. Importantly, this is a model in which the practitioner, rather than authoritatively deciding on, delimiting and interpreting the client's presumed repertoire of unconscious patterns and relationships, instead offers an opportunity for *new* ways of relating, where the re-organization of memory and meaning can emerge within the interpersonal context of the therapeutic relationship. I hope to illustrate something of this in the following clinical vignette.

VIGNETTE

Lucy, 35 years old, was referred for help with feelings of acute depression. An outstandingly attractive, intelligent woman, she told me at our first meeting that she had already had eight years of psychoanalysis with a 'useless woman', and now wanted help in dealing with her feelings of depression and loneliness. An alcoholic since she was 15, she had been 'dry' for five years, helped by ongoing attendance at AA, but her feelings of depression were such that she was worried she would relapse. Lucy had been abused between the ages of 9 and 13 by her stepfather, and her mother had failed to recognize or respond to her complaints. As an adult, she had a history of sexually abusive relationships, underpinned by an overwhelming need to please and placate. Her sense of helplessness and self-disgust had eventually led her to alcohol abuse and three serious suicide attempts, which she told me about in great and lurid detail. From the start, I had wanted her to accept a referral for long-term psychotherapy but she had refused, insisting that a shorter number of sessions was all she needed to 'get me back on track'.

Lucy was sustained by an active fantasy life, in which she saw herself working as a musician, financially solvent and in a successful relationship. In reality, she was living alone, unemployed and on benefits, with a substantial debt problem exacerbated by online shopping and an inability to deal with everyday financial demands and bills. Early on in the work, she told me she had always needed to lie to people: as a teenager, she had lied her way into university, but been unable to cope with the academic demands there; she lied to her various boyfriends about her earlier abusive relationships; and she was currently lying to social security about her financial situation. I was uneasy about these admissions of falsehood, and wondered what she might be hiding from me. I nonetheless liked her: there was something warm and eager about her, and we developed what felt like a strong working alliance. Lucy seemed to feel safe in the sessions, and regularly told me that I was a 'good therapist', in contrast to what she described as her earlier 'rather useless' analyst. Whilst initially I felt uneasy at these admiring comments, over the weeks I found myself pushing this disquiet aside in favour of simply enjoying work with an interesting, appreciative and articulate client who seemed to work hard during and between sessions to think about herself. Much of the early work revolved around trying to understand Lucy's relationships with abusive men, and her fury and disappointment at a mother whom she felt had failed to respond to her need for rescue from an abusive stepfather. While Lucy continued to visit this mother regularly, she always returned contemptuous, angry and depressed, feeling ignored, unwanted or simply not up to what she saw as her more successful (and loved) older sister. After these visits, Lucy preferred to stay in her house for several days on end, usually hiding in bed, refusing to answer the telephone or the door. After a couple of sessions missed in this way, when I had been extremely anxious at not hearing from Lucy at all, we came to an agreement that if she did not come in for her session, I would send her a note to maintain contact and keep her session open the following week.

Four or five months into the work Lucy's moods seemed to stabilize a little, and she even started to look for work. We were both pleased, and I was relieved, to see obvious signs of change that included Lucy's willingness to consider some of her responsibilities in the external world. At this time I was due to go on leave for two weeks, and had told Lucy about this well in advance; she had appeared to be unperturbed by, even rather dismissive of, the news despite my efforts to discuss how she might feel about my absence. In the session before the break, however, she arrived with a dream which she said had been 'bugging' her:

> *Lucy:* In the dream, I am out with my friends, happy and enjoying life, having a good time. Suddenly, I look down and see my hand. It is encased in a tight-fitting glove, so close and smooth that it can be mistaken for my hand itself; no-one knows I am wearing it. Underneath, I can move my hand independently, and I'm holding something sharp, perhaps a pin or a needle. Without anyone noticing, I regularly and agonizingly dig this into my hand. This is going on all the time I am gaily chatting and enjoying my friends' company. Nobody notices.

As we puzzled over this dream, I started to feel increasingly uncomfortable and anxious about what Lucy might be trying to tell me. In some ways, the dream seemed to throw into relief the way in which Lucy had always presented a kind of false front – a second skin – that fooled people into thinking that all was well. I became aware of a series of feelings washing over me: a feeling of shame that I had allowed myself to slip into a comfortable sense that all was well – indeed, that Lucy might actually be improving; anxiety that I was now going away; concern that Lucy might harm herself during the break; and an awareness that between us, we had managed to ensure that there was simply no place in the work for Lucy's depressed, angry feelings (she had merely remained in bed rather than coming to sessions) and I had allowed myself to be lulled into a false sense of security that all was well between us. This sense, I suspect, had evolved as part of an implicit and mutual 'way of being' with Lucy; one that had resulted in my cumulative failure – perhaps like her mother who had failed to notice the sexual abuse – to note and attend to a hidden quality of desperation, anxiety and fear that Lucy was unconsciously masking within an adaptive, placatory 'false self'. My sense of shame was partly professional pride, but also a kind of horrified awareness that I had somehow been unconsciously colluding (perhaps even been comfortably 'hand in glove?') with a mutually destructive way of relating and responding for which Lucy had wanted help.

With a great sense of personal failure I tried to share some of these thoughts with Lucy, and said how I felt that somewhere she had been aware of and desperate about a lack of proper care and attention from me. In response to these rather halting attempts, Lucy was at first reluctant to respond, but eventually admitted rather defensively to a sense of hopelessness and a feeling of futility about ever sharing and expressing any 'real feelings' with anybody: 'What's the point?' she laughed, rather grimly, 'nobody's ever been interested'. By now, even if rather late in the day, I was indeed interested, and we started to explore how the false atmosphere of optimism that we seemed to have jointly engineered and cultivated prevented either of us from noticing and commenting on Lucy's hidden feelings of despair and, as it turned out, contempt at my failure. Although Lucy rather sulkily rejected my efforts to take responsibility for a failure to properly comprehend her sense of internal distress, she eventually – and angrily – admitted that she had a stash of painkillers at home that she was thinking of taking during my absence 'if it all gets too much for me'. Although I felt alarmed at this admission (and the force of her latent fury behind it), I felt – and conveyed to Lucy – that it required a thoughtful consideration of why she had told me this; and of how, since we had clearly both been involved in the therapeutic difficulties we had been experiencing, perhaps we both needed to think, this time more constructively, about how we could ensure that she was taken care of during the break.

I am by no means suggesting that the foregoing is the only or best way of understanding Lucy's dream. From a relational perspective, what I am trying to convey is how I came to understand the unconscious intersubjective climate in the session to be, in part at least, constituted by my own rather narcissistic pleasure in working with someone whom I experienced as a rewarding client together with the defensive fantasy that I was doing a reasonable job as a 'good therapist'. (Perhaps this was a fantasy that mirrored Lucy's wishful vision of her own successful life as an musician; certainly, my own very acute sense of personal failure at being yet another contemptibly 'useless woman' in Lucy's life gave me clues as to how sensitive she might be feeling about her lack of success in life.) Unpicking and discussing my own contribution to the therapeutic mire in which we found ourselves enabled me and Lucy to discuss the possibility of my contacting her GP and the local psychotherapy service to arrange cover if she felt she needed it during my absence. This very concrete plan – which Lucy eventually agreed to and in fact made use of during the break – proved to be a turning point in the work where she could allow herself, at this point at least, to admit for the first time that she needed help; and to experience, if only temporarily, a new, more co-operative – rather than merely collusive – form of relating.

MODELS OF RELATIONAL PRACTICE AND RESEARCH

The model of practice that I have tried to illustrate above draws heavily on a two-person psychology which assumes that we are formed by and constituted in relation to one another. Much recent attachment-related and developmental research has, over the past few decades, provided a rich seam of information and ideas about how early relational experiences link with adult behaviour and functioning. I have reviewed some of this research in earlier papers (Rizq, 2007, 2008), highlighting the increasingly important distinction that has been made in cognitive science between implicit and explicit memory systems.

Implicit memory includes 'procedural' or 'how to' knowledge of processes and skills. In borrowing the term 'procedural knowledge' from cognitive psychology, relational psychoanalysis has started here to move away from Freudian notions of a dynamic unconscious, constituted by the repressed contents of a traumatic past, towards a 'relational' unconscious (Davies, 1996) that is made up of relational schemas that come to be enacted within affective-interpersonal cycles generated between therapist and client. For example, Stern et al.'s (1998) dynamical systems view of psychotherapeutic process, drawing on developmental research examining early, non-verbal interactions between infant and caregiver, proposes that therapeutic change is sponsored less by cognitive insight, established via traditional transference interpretations and more through the quality of interpersonal experiences in the shared implicit relationship between client and therapist. Stern has introduced the concept of 'now' moments, or 'moments of meeting' that carry the potential to alter the shared implicit relationship via a genuine rather than role-determined response from the therapist. Such non-interpretative mechanisms result in new 'ways of being with' or procedural routines that do not necessarily require conscious insight or explicit reflection to deliver their therapeutic benefits. Stern et al.'s (2003) notions of 'sloppiness' and 'co-creativity' further elaborate the dynamic, non-linear and emergent qualities of therapeutic interactions which are constantly in the process of creating new and unpredictable forms of shared implicit knowing. Lyons-Ruth (1999) has pointed out how more collaborative and intersubjective encounters with the therapist may offer the opportunity to destabilize the client's existing psychological and affective organization, established via developmental and attachment-related experiences. These models of practice anneal with theories of intersubjectivity such as those by Benjamin (1990), which suggest that psychological change occurs within a therapeutic relationship characterized by mutual 'recognition' between 'subjects' via a constantly shifting, non-linear process of self-organization, disorganization, mutual repair and joint re-organization.

ATTACHMENT AND MENTAL REPRESENTATION

Relational models of practice, then, are grounded in assumptions about the development of intersubjectivity and how we come to understand the existence of mental states in ourselves and others. For this reason, one of the more salient areas of research for counselling psychologists using psychodynamic approaches has been in the field of attachment and mental representation. Work over the last two decades suggests that the way in which we represent feeling states mediates self-organization, affect regulation and ultimately may determine the impact of the environment on the individual. Whilst a lot of contemporary psychoanalytic research has focused on the quality and status of early childhood attachments, particularly the detailed description of early non-verbal or proto-conversational mother–infant interactions (for example, Beebe et al., 1997), much of this assumes that the infant arrives with the innate capacity to perceive and infer subjective mental states in the caregiver (for example, Trevarthen, 2005). But the ability to conceive of others as having minds at all, suggest Fonagy and Target (1996), is not an inbuilt capacity, but rather one which is learned and built up during infancy, and which requires the evolution of a symbolic representational system permitting understanding of other's mental states. Fonagy and Target's (1996) developmental theory of mentalization suggests that the capacity to think of the self and others in psychological terms, to adopt the 'intentional stance' (Dennett, 1978) towards others seen as having beliefs, motives, desires and goals of their own, is rooted in the experience of secure attachment and contingent interactions with a sensitive caregiver. They draw on Gergely and Watson's (1996) social biofeedback model of parent–infant mirroring, which shows how contingent interactions and parental 'marking' of the infant's feelings states allows the infant to tolerate and attribute psychological states to himself and others. The representation of the infant's psychological states in the mind of the caregiver is what sponsors a 'second order' representation of affect in the infant that subsequently forms a platform for the developing child's understanding and regulation of his own psychological states. A further body of research, drawing on the significance of adult attachment narratives (Main et al., 1985) in the intergenerational transmission of attachment patterns (Fonagy et al., 1991) shows that a mother's ability to take a psychological perspective on her child, including demonstrating 'mind-mindedness' and 'reflective function' while describing their infant, is clearly associated with the evolution of secure attachment and a mentalzing capacity in the child. Of interest here, I think, to counselling psychologists is a basically constructivist model of mind, in which the quality, status and consistency of the caregiver's emotional attunement to, and psychological containment of, the infant's affective state is crucial to the evolution of the child's mature ability to understand and regulate his or her own feelings, and to recognize and empathize with others.

Neuroscience, a rapidly expanding, if controversial, field within psychotherapeutic and psychoanalytic research, is also beginning to add to our understanding here. The above research on mental representation is in line with Schore's (for example, 2001) work demonstrating that attachment theory is essentially a regulatory theory, where securely attached mothers continuously regulate their baby's variable arousal level and concomitant emotional states. Schore (2002) has further argued that the early social environment 'sculpts' or 'prunes' neurochemical structures in the infant's brain. Drawing on a comprehensive range of research from neurobiological, developmental psychopathology and behavioural neurology, he demonstrates how the early maturing right brain, the orbitofrontal cortex in particular, is influenced by dyadic interactions within the attachment relationship, impacting on the developing infant's capacity to regulate and process stress.

   In a different context, Gallese' et al.'s (2007) notion of 'embodied simulation' has been used to examine the neurobiological basis for an automatic awareness of others' emotions. Gallese et al. (2007) have examined how neural networks, or 'mirror neurons' activated by an individual performing an action, are similarly activated in the individual watching the action. Originally demonstrated in macaque monkeys (for example, Rizzolatti et al., 1996), the existence of a mirror neuron system matching action perception and execution has been located in humans, via brain-imaging techniques (for example, Buccioni et al., 2004). It now seems possible that an involuntary and intersubjectively evoked neural activation mechanism operating between observer and actor may underpin a basic experiential level of emotional appreciation of another's mental state. This is, of course, likely to become of interest to psychodynamic clinicians, particularly in the light of Freud's injunction for the practitioner to listen to the patient's unconscious with his own:

> To put it in a formula: he must turn his own unconscious like a receptive organ towards the transmitting unconscious of the patient. He must adjust himself to the patient as a telephone receiver to the transmitting microphone … (1912: 115)

One possibility being developed here is that the mirror neuron system may provide the neural basis for those disowned aspects of the client that are projected into the therapist and come to be experienced as his or her own. Whilst it is unlikely that such a system alone could mediate a fully aware and sophisticated grasp of countertransference, it does seem possible that there may be a two-level system underpinning our awareness of others' minds: an automatic neurobiological system underlying basic experiential understanding; and a frontal-cortical system sponsoring explicit, declarative awareness.

   The above can only provide a brief sample of the range and nature of current neuroscientific research that points to the inherent intersubjectivity of the developing brain and the ways in which we seem predisposed to relate, respond and neurobiologically adapt to our social, relational environment. However, the potential for traditional psychoanalytic concepts such as countertransference and projective identification to become subject to re-examination in the light of neuroscientific advances is, of course, not without controversy. Whilst there are considerable methodological issues raised by the use of neuroimaging techniques (cf. Beutel et al., 2003), it is the epistemological issues that are likely to continue to raise concerns. Anxieties about what Dennett (1995) has provocatively termed 'greedy reductionism' have resulted in the 'neurosceptic' response amongst many clinicians: a belief that the results of neuroscientific research will serve only to diminish the meaning and significance of psychotherapeutic work; and that, as clinicians, we will be seduced into treating brains rather than minds, synapses rather than subjectivities. Whilst beyond the scope of the current discussion, this is clearly a rich philosophical and epistemological seam to dig.

OUTCOME RESEARCH

Although the above research may arguably lend some weight to the theoretical basis for relational psychodynamic approaches, evidence supporting psychodynamic clinical *outcomes* has hitherto been considerably less convincing. In these days of evidence-based practice, cost-effectiveness and clinical guidelines, it is clear that the psychodynamically-oriented therapies have been slow to gain a foothold in the public services. Frosh (2006) points out that the question of whether or not psychoanalytically-oriented interventions work is one that inevitably provokes a degree of controversy, not the least because of lack of clarity over what constitutes a 'cure'. A related issue here, of course, is the continuing prevalence of the drug metaphor (Stiles and Shapiro, 1989) in outcome research, replete with assumptions about 'treatment' that is constituted by stable, active and inert 'ingredients', whose precise functions can be specified by the researcher in order to prescribe and, increasingly these days, manualize psychotherapeutic treatments deemed to be effective.

From a methodological perspective, Westen et al. (2004) have argued that there are a number of shortcomings in the research methods used to establish the status of evidence-based practice or empirically-supported treatments, methods which include the use of randomized-controlled trials (RCTs). By now, many of us will be familiar with the critique of RCTs as the 'gold standard' methodology for psychotherapeutic research. Leichsenring (2004), for example, has reviewed the uneasy relationship between RCTs and psychotherapy conducted under naturalistic conditions, and concludes that it is not possible simply to garner evidence from the former and apply it to the latter. Fonagy et al. (2005) has reviewed some of the main reasons why RCTs in public healthcare lack external validity, including:

- The unrepresentativeness of participating clinicians.
- The unrepresentative homogeneity of clients selected for inclusion in research studies.
- The use of atypical treatments designed for single disorders.
- Measuring outcome in terms of symptoms that are the focus of the study but of little meaningful relevance to participants.

In an exhaustive review of the literature, based on an updated version of the UK's Department of Health psychotherapy outcome review (Roth and Fonagy, 1995), Fonagy et al. (2005) examined recent evidence for both short- and long-term psychodynamic therapies. This is a substantial, wide-ranging paper that for reasons of space cannot be adequately summarized here, and interested readers should certainly consult the full version. Briefly, it includes a review of the evidence for short-term psychodynamic therapy for depression; studies contrasting psychoanalytic psychotherapies with other psychotherapies; and psychodynamic approaches to anxiety disorders including panic disorder, post-traumatic stress disorder and complex grief reaction. Eating disorders, substance misuse and personality disorder are amongst the other diagnostic categories included in this comprehensive review, as well as long-term psychotherapies.

Fonagy et al. claim only modest conclusions:

> Considerable evidence has accumulated for the evidence of psychoanalytic approaches for a range of diagnostic conditions … In no area is the evidence compelling, but in most areas where systematic investigation has been carried out, outcomes are comparable to those obtained by other therapeutic methods. There are disorders where the outcome of psychoanalytic therapy is in certain respects better than that of alternative treatment (e.g. borderline personality disorder). In other areas (e.g. depression) opportunities for the psychodynamic approach are created by the known limitations of rival orientations. (2005: 43–44).

However, a paper by Smith (2007) examining the development and adoption of clinical guidelines issued by the National Institute for Clinical Effectiveness (NICE) for mental health care within the National Health Service in the UK robustly questions the exclusion of psychodynamic therapies from the current recommendations (NICE, 2004) for the treatment of anxiety and depression. Examining more recent evidence for the efficacy of psychodynamic psychotherapy, Smith cites reviews by Abbass (2002) and Leichsenring et al. (2005) that support the efficacy of both short- and long-term psychodynamic psychotherapy across a range of conditions. Amongst current promising approaches included in Smith's discussion is Milrod et al.'s (2007) panic-focused psychoanalytic psychotherapy, which has recently been the subject of a rigorous RCT.

Outcome research of the above type, however, has been radically critiqued by Luborsky et al. (1999), who found that 70–80 per cent of the variance in clinical outcomes across a range of psychotherapy studies was predicted by the theoretical allegiance of the researchers. Partly for this reason, contemporary clinical outcome research is now branching out into the controversial field of neuroscience in search of non-biased, non-subjective measures of change. Kandel (1999), for example, has argued cogently for the place of psychiatry and psychotherapy within the context of modern neurobiology, and has pointed out, on the basis of animal research, that changes in long-term memory due to the impact of learning sponsors altered synaptic connections in the brain. This clearly has implications for the learning that takes place within psychotherapy. For instance, Schwartz et al.'s (1996) studies incorporating positon emission tomography (PET) scans have shown that successful treatment of obsessive compulsive disorder with cognitive behavioural therapy results in substantial changes to patterns of neural activity in the orbitofrontal cortex, the cingulate gyrus and the basal ganglia. Whilst psychodynamic theorists and practitioners are heavily divided in opinion about the relevance of such research for clinical practice, with Fonagy (2004), Solms (1998) and others willing to straddle interdisciplinary and epistemological divides, and others such as Green (2000) roundly condemning the attempt, it seems likely that neuro-imaging research is likely to form a significant part of future psychodynamic outcome research.

But all psychotherapy outcome research, as Smith (2007) above notes, is now taking place against the backdrop of a forceful political and economic agenda driving public purchasing decisions in relation to the 'talking therapies' in the NHS. The government's response to the Layard (2004) report on *Mental Health: Britain's Biggest Social Problem* has been to fund and implement the Improving Access to Psychological Therapies (IAPT) programme, which incorporates the stepped care model proposed within the NICE guidelines and which advocates the introduction of large numbers of mental health practitioners in the NHS delivering 'low-intensity' self-help interventions and 'high intensity' therapeutic work based on cognitive behavioural principles. At the time of writing, this programme is currently the focus of intense political and research investment, in the teeth of which many practitioners, researchers and academics are struggling to make a convincing case for the efficacy of psychodynamic models in working with psychological distress. It remains to be seen whether their endeavours will result in the future inclusion of psychodynamically oriented therapies within forthcoming versions of the NICE guidelines for depression, anxiety and other psychological problems.

CONCLUSION

This chapter has attempted to convey a flavour of the way in which psychodynamic theory and practice has evolved from early classical models to more recent relational approaches that are consistent with counselling psychology's emphasis on intersubjectivity, the self of the therapist and the therapeutic relationship. Despite the increasing pluralism and, some would say, fragmentation of the field, acknowledging the *significance of the unconscious* in the development of conflict and disturbance remains at the core of our theoretical and clinical understanding and is constitutive of the psychodynamic approach to counselling and psychotherapy in all its forms.

Readers may be aware at this point that there are many versions of the unconscious that we have not touched on. Among these are included Gellner's characterization of the unconscious as 'cunning' and 'totally polymorphous in its manifestations and daily behaviour' (1985: 152) and Rorty's view of the unconscious as 'conversational partner' (1991: 149) or intellectual equal of our conscious selves. These descriptions are, of course, just some of the possible alternatives to the rather more domesticated account of the unconscious available from developmental research, neuroscience and, alas, textbook chapters such as this one!

Perhaps we may regard these various and competing descriptions of the unconscious as symbolic of the enormous difficulties facing psychoanalysis and psychodynamic approaches today. The predominantly positivist research and outcome agenda (still) characteristic of twenty-first-century clinical science is radically at odds with the constructivist epistemology that is embedded in all relational forms of clinical theory and practice. The temptation we face is always to adjudicate between descriptions and epistemologies, thereby running the risk of locating ourselves on one or other side of Whittle's 'fault line'. Either way, what is at stake perhaps is less the status of psychodynamic theory, research and practice and more the status of science itself: as an endeavour characterized either by formal positivist–empiricist sets of practices, values and methods; or as a constructivist process entailing interpersonal understanding, contextual awareness, empathic identification and what Geertz (1983) has evocatively termed 'thick description'.

Rather than continue the attempt to arbitrate between these rival claims for 'truth', a future task for the psychodynamic counselling psychologist might include the search for a middle ground: a space in which to forge a compromise between the polarities of an extreme positivism on the one hand and a radical relativism on the other. Perhaps more than any other psychotherapeutic profession, counselling psychology is accustomed to, and indeed predicated on, sustaining and celebrating difference and dialectic; respecting and remaining open to differing perspectives, descriptions, theoretical models and research methodologies. I would go so far as to suggest that our willingness to cultivate and sustain a stance that acknowledges and celebrates a plurality of perspectives is profoundly sympathetic to, and indeed may exemplify, the wider relational project that lies at the heart of contemporary psychoanalysis.

REFERENCES

Abbass, A. (2002) 'Intensive short-term psychotherapy in a private practice: clinical and cost-effectiveness', *American Journal of Psychotherapy*, 56: 225–232.

Aron, L. (2007) 'Relational psychotherapy in Europe', *European Journal of Psychotherapy and Counselling*, 9 (1): 91–103.

Balint, M. (1937) 'Early developmental states of the ego, primary object of love', in M. Balint, *Primary Love and Psycho-analytic Technique*. London: Tavistock 1965. pp. 90–108.

Beebe, B., Lachmann, F. and Jaffe, J. (1997) 'Mother–infant interaction structures and presymbolic self and object representations', *Psychoanalytic Dialogues*, 7: 113–182.

Benjamin, J. (1990) 'Recognition and destruction: An outline of intersubjectivity', *Psychoanalytic Psychology*, 7 (suppl): 33–47.

Beutel, M., Stern, E. and Silberweig, D. (2003) 'The emerging dialogue between psychoanalysis and neuroscience: Neuroimaging perspectives', *Journal of the American Psychoanalytic Association*, 51: 773–801.

Bion, W. (1959) 'Attacks on linking', *International Journal of Psychoanalysis*, 40: 308–15.

Bollas, C. (1987) *The Shadow of the Object*. London: Free Association Books.

Bowlby, J. (1969) *Attachment and Loss, Vol. 1: Attachment*. New York: Basic Books.

Brenman Pick, I. (2000) 'Discussion III', in J. Sandler, A.M. Sandler and R. Davies (eds), *Clinical and Observational Psychoanalytic Research*. London: University College and Anna Freud Centre.

Buccioni, G., Vogt, S., Ritzl, A., Fink, G., Zilles, K., Freudn, H.-J. and Rizzolatti, G. (2004) 'Neural circuits underlying imitation learning of hand actions: An event-related fMRI study', *Neuron*, 42: 323–334.

Casement, P. (1985) *On Learning from the Patient*. London: Tavistock.

Davies, J. (1996) 'Linking the "pre-analytic" with the postclassical: Integration, dissociation and the multiplicity of unconscious process', *Contemporary Psychoanalysis,* 32: 553–576.

Dennett, D. (1978) *The Intentional Stance*. Cambridge, MA: MIT Press.

Dennett, D. (1995) *Darwin's Dangerous Idea: Evolution and the Meanings of Life*. London: Simon and Schuster.

Eysenck, H. (1985) *Decline and Fall of the Freudian Empire*. Harmondsworth: Viking.

Fairbairn, W. (1952) *An Object-Relations Theory of the Personality*. London: Tavistock.

Fonagy, P. (2000) 'Grasping the nettle: Or why psychoanalytic research is such an irritant'. Paper presented at the Annual Research Lecture of the British Psychoanalytical Society. London, March 1st.

Fonagy, P. (2003) 'Genetics, developmental psychopathology and psychoanalytic theory: The case for ending our (not so) splendid isolation', *Psychoanalytic Inquiry*, 23 (2): 218–248.

Fonagy, P. (2004) 'Psychotherapy meets neuroscience: A more focused future for psychotherapy research', *Psychiatric Bulletin*, 28: 357–359.

Fonagy, P. and Target, M. (1996) 'Playing with reality: 1. Theory of mind and the normal development of psychic reality', *International Journal of Psychoanalysis*, 77: 217–233.

Fonagy, P. and Target, M. (2003) *Psychoanalytic Theories: Perspectives from Developmental Psychopathology*. London and Philadelphia, PA: Whurr.

Fonagy, P., Roth, A. and Higgitt, A. (2005) 'Psychodyamic psychotherapies: Evidence-based practice and clinical wisdom', *Bulletin of the Menninger Clinic*, 69 (1): 1–58.

Fonagy, P., Steele, H., Moran, G., Steele, M. and Higgitt, A. (1991) 'The capacity for understanding mental states: The reflective self in parent and child and its significance for security of attachment', *Infant Mental Health Journal*, 13: 200–217.

Freud, A. (1965) *Normality and Pathology in Childhood*. Harmondsworth: Penguin.

Freud, S. (1895) 'Project for a scientific psychology', in J. Strachey (ed.), *The Standard Edition of the Complete Psychological Works of Sigmund Freud, Vol. 1*. London: Hogarth Press. pp. 295–387.

Freud, S. (1912) 'Recommendation to physicians practising psycho-analysis. Papers on Technique', in J. Strachey (ed.), *The Standard Edition of the Complete Psychological Works of Sigmund Freud, Vol. 12*. London: Hogarth Press.

Frosh, S. (2006) *For and Against Psychoanalysis*, 2nd edn. London: Routledge.

Gallese, V., Eagle, M. and Migone, P. (2007) 'Intentional attunement: Mirror neurons and the neural underpinnings of interpersonal relations', *Journal of the American Psychoanalytic Association*, 55: 131–176.

Gellner, E. (1985) *The Psychoanalytic Movement*. London: Paladin.

Geertz, C. (1983) 'The way we think now: Toward an ethnography of modern thought', in C. Geertz (2000), *Local Knowledge*. New York: Basic Books. pp. 147–166.

Gergely, G. and Watson, J. (1996) 'The social biofeedback model of parental affect-mirroring', *International Journal of Psychoanalysis*, 77: 1181–1212.

Green, A. (2000) 'Science and science fiction in infant research', in J. Sandler, A.-M. Sandler and R. Davies (eds), *Clinical and Observational Psychoanalytic Research*. London: Karnac. pp. 41–73.

Greenberg, J. and Mitchell, S. (1983) *Object Relations in Psychoanalytic Theory*. Cambridge, MA: Harvard University Press.

Guntrip, H. (1961) *Personality Structure and Human Interaction*. New York: International University Press.

Hargaden, H. and Schwartz, J. (2007) Editorial. *European Journal of Psychotherapy and Counselling*, 9 (1): 3–5.

Hartmann, H. (1939) *Ego Psychology and the Problem of Adaptation*. New York: International Universities Press.

Joseph, B. (1985) 'Transference: The total situation', *International Journal of Psychoanalysis*, 66: 447–54.

Kandel, E. (1999) 'Biology and the future of psychoanalysis: A new intellectual framework for psychiatry revisited', *American Journal of Psychiatry*, 156: 505–524.

Kernberg, O. (1970) 'A psychoanalytic classification of character pathology', *Journal of the American Psychoanalytic Association*, 18: 800–22.

Khan, M. (1963) 'The concept of cumulative trauma', *The Psychoanalytic Study of the Child*, 18: 283–306.

Klein, M. (1935) 'A contribution to the psychogenesis of manic-depressive states', in *Love, Guilt and Reparation: The Writings of Melanie Klein, Vol 1*. London: Hogarth Press. pp. 236–89.

Kohut, H. (1977) *The Restoration of the Self*. New York: International Universities Press.

Layard, R. (2004) *Mental Health: Britain's Biggest Social Problem*. Available at www.strategy.gov. uk/downloads/files/mh_layard.pdf

Leichsenring, F. (2004) 'Randomised-controlled vs. naturalistic studies: A new research agenda', *Bulletin of the Menninger Clinic*, 68: 137–51.

Leichsenring, F., Biskup, J., Kresihsece, R. and Staats, H. (2005) 'The Gottingen study of psychoanalytic psychotherapy: First results', *International Journal of Psychoanalysis*, 86: 433–455.

Luborsky, L., Diguer, L., Seligman, D.A., Rosenthal, R., Krause, E.D., Johnson, S., Halperiu, G., Bishop, M., Berman, J.S. and Schweiger, E. (1999) 'The researcher's own therapy allegiances: A wild card in comparison of treatment efficacy', *Clinical Psychology: Science and Practice*, 6: 95–106.

Lyons-Ruth, K. (1999) 'The two-person unconscious: Intersubjective dialogue, enactive relational representation and the emergence of new forms of relational organization', *Psychoanalytic Inquiry*, 19: 576–617.

Mahler, M. (1968) *On Human Symbiosis and the Vicissitudes of Individuation*. New York: International Universities Press.

Main, M., Kaplan, N. and Cassidy, J. (1985) 'Security in infancy, childhood and adulthood: A move to the level of representation', in I. Bretherton and E. Waters (eds), *Growing Points of Attachment Theory and Research. Monographs of the Society for Research in Child Development. Vol. 50*. Chicago, IL: Chicago University Press. pp. 66–104.

Milrod, B., Leon, A., Busch, F., Rudden, M., Schwalber, M., Clarkin, J., Aronson, A., Singer, M., Turchin, W., Klass, E., Graf, E., Teres, J. and Shear, M. (2007) 'A randomized controlled clinical trial of psychoanalytic psychotherapy for panic disorder', *American Journal of Psychiatry*, 164: 1–8.

Mitchell, S. (1988) *Relational Concepts in Psychoanalysis: An Integration*. Cambridge, MA: Harvard University Press.

National Institute for Clinical Excellence (NICE) (2004) *Depression: Management of Depression in Primary and Secondary Care*. Clinical guideline 23. London: NICE.

Orbach, S. (2007) 'Democratizing psychoanalysis', *European Journal of Psychotherapy and Counselling*, 9 (1): 7–21.

Rizq, R. (2007) 'Tread softly: Counselling psychology and neuroscience', *Counselling Psychology Review*, 22 (4): 5–18.

Rizq, R. (2008) 'Psychoanalysis revisited: A psychologist's view', *Counselling Psychology Review Special Issue: Psychologists Specialising in Psychotherapy*, 23 (1): 6–19.

Rizzolatti, G., Fadiga, L., Gallese, V. and Fogassi, L. (1996) 'Premotor cortex and the recognition of actions', *Cognitive Brain Research*, 3 (2): 131–141.

Rorty, R. (1991) *Contingency, Irony and Solidarity*. Cambridge: Cambridge University Press.

Roth, A. and Fonagy, P. (1995) *What works for Whom?* London: Department of Health.

Rustin, M. (1999) 'Psychoanalysis: The last modernism?', in D. Bell (ed.), *Psychoanalysis and Culture: A Kleinian Perspective*. Tavistock Clinic Series. London: Duckworth.

Ryle, G. (1949) *The Concept of Mind*. Chicago, IL: University of Chicago Press.

Schore, A. (2001) 'The effects of a secure attachment relationship on right brain development, affect regulation and infant mental health', *Infant Journal of Mental Health*, 22: 7–66.

Schore, A. (2002) 'Dysregulation of the right brain: A fundamental mechanism of traumatic attachment and psychopathogenesis of posttraumatic stress disorder', *Australian and New Zealand Journal of Psychiatry*, 36: 9–30.

Schwartz, J., Stoessel, P., Baxter, L., Martin, K. and Phelps, M. (1996) 'Systematic changes in cerebral glucose metabolic rate after successful behaviour modification treatment for obsessive compulsive disorder', *Archives of General Psychiatry*, 53: 109–117.

Smith, J. (2007) 'From base evidence through to evidence base: A consideration of the NICE guidelines', *Psychoanalytic Psychotherapy*, 21 (1): 40–60.

Solms, M. (1998) 'Preliminaries for an integration of psychoanalysis and neuroscience', paper presented at a meeting of the Contemporary Freudian Group of the British Psychoanalytical Society. London, 10th June.

Spitz, R. (1959) *A Genetic Field Theory of Ego Formation: Its Implications For Pathology*. New York: International University Press.

Steiner, J. (1994) 'Patient-centred and analyst-centred interpretations: Some implications of "containment" and "counter-transference"', *Psychoanalytic Inquiry*, 14: 406–422.

Stern, D., Sander, L., Nahum, J., Harrison, A., Lyons-Ruth, K., Morgan, A., Bruschwelier-Stern., N. and Tronick, E. (1998) 'Non-interpretative mechanisms in psychoanalytic therapy: The something more than interpretation', *International Journal of Psycho-analysis*, 79: 903–921.

Stern, D., Sander, L., Nahum, J., Harrison, A., Lyons-Ruth, K., Morgan, A., Bruschweiler-Stern, N. and Tronick, E. (2003) 'The "something more than interpretation" revisited: Sloppiness and co-creativity in the psychoanalytic encounter', *Journal of the American Psychoanalytic Association*, 53 (3): 694–727.

Stiles, W. and Shapiro, D. (1989) 'Abuse of the drug metaphor in psychotherapy process-outcome research', *Clinical Psychology Review*, 9: 521–543.

Stolorow, R. and Atwood, G. (1997) 'Deconstructing the myth of the neutral analyst: An alternative from intersubjective systems theory', *Psychoanalytic Quarterly*, LXVI: 431–449.

Trevarthen, C. (2005) 'Stepping away from the mirror: Pride and shame in adventures of companionship – reflections on the nature and emotional needs of infant intersubjectivity', in C.S. Carter, L. Ahnert, K.E. Grossman, S.B. Hrdy, M.E. Lamb, S.W. Porges and N. Sachser (eds), *Attachment and Bonding: A New Synthesis*, Dahlem Workshop Report 92. Cambridge, MA: MIT Press. pp. 55–84.

Watson, J. (1930) *Behaviourism*. New York: Norton.

Westen, D., Morrison, K. and Thompson-Brenner, H. (2004) 'The empirical status of empirically supported psychotherapies: Assumptions, findings and reporting in controlled clinical trials', *Psychological Bulletin*, 130: 631–663.

Whittle, P. (1999) 'Experimental psychology and psychoanalysis: What we can learn from a century of misunderstanding', *Neuro-psychoanalysis*, 1 (2): 233–245.

Whittle, P. (2000) 'Response to commentaries', *Neuro-Psychoanalysis*, 2 (2): 259–235.

Winnicott, D. (1965) *The Maturational Processes and the Facilitating Environment*. London: Hogarth Press.

6

COGNITIVE AND BEHAVIOURAL APPROACHES

Diana Sanders

Cognitive behavioural therapy (CBT) is currently receiving excellent press and occupies a central place in the move towards evidence-based practice. The National Institute for Clinical Excellence (NICE – http://guidance.nice.org.uk/) recommends CBT more often than other therapeutic approaches for many psychological problems and there is substantial evidence to show CBT is effective for people with anxiety and depression (Roth and Fonagy, 2005). CBT is now the primary model for clinicians, counsellors and therapists from many backgrounds, and the preferred mode of therapy in the Improving Access to Psychological Therapies (IAPT) programme (DOH, 2007). The Layard report (Layard, 2006) is encouraging CBT training for an army of mental health workers with minimal clinical experience. CBT fits well with 'stepped care' models of delivery, such as self-help and computerized packages, large group therapies and brief interventions, as well as traditional psychotherapeutic approaches of individual therapy.

CBT is no doubt riding on a wave of its own popularity; however, the approach is not without its problems. Although CBT helps a lot of people, it is not effective for everyone; although the method is well-developed for many clinical problems, from panic attacks to psychosis, it is still less developed in helping those with long-term, complex issues, bereavement or relationship problems; and despite its popularity and effectiveness, demand well outstrips supply, some NHS centres running waiting lists of over a year. The term 'cognitive behavioural psychotherapies' covers a number of approaches, including Beckian cognitive therapy, meta-cognitive and mindfulness-based cognitive therapy, dialectical behaviour therapy, rational-emotive behaviour therapy and multi-modal therapy (Nelson Jones, 2005; Feltham and Horton, 2006), adding confusion for consumers as to what CBT actually involves.

This chapter covers the basics of CBT: its history and development, the cognitive model, key ingredients of the approach and the main methods. I discuss some of the current issues in CBT, its applications to common psychological difficulties, and the new developments which take CBT a long way away from its historical routes in behaviourism, looking at how CBT meets the philosophy and standards of contemporary counselling psychology. I focus on Beckian cognitive therapy, my own training and practice model, illustrated with modified clinical examples.

ORIGINS OF COGNITIVE AND BEHAVIOURAL PSYCHOTHERAPIES

The cognitive therapies

The cognitive therapies began their development in the 1950s, when ego-analytic theorists who broke away from Freud began to focus on attitudes, beliefs and 'shoulds' which determine our emotions and behaviours. Kelly's (1955) human construct theories contained the central cognitive concept that how we feel relates to the sense or meaning we make of our experiences: examining and changing these constructs or meanings can lead to therapeutic change. Ellis (1962) developed his ideas that reason can be used to regulate psychological problems and emotion.

Aaron Beck was originally trained as an analyst, but noticed in his work that people's moods and emotions were far less influenced by unconscious conflicts than his analytic training had told him. Instead, he observed that emotions could be explained and understood in terms of current thoughts and interpretations of events. By developing awareness of thoughts and interpretations, and using methods to change these, people felt better. With his two major publications of the 1970s, *Cognitive Therapy and the Emotional Disorders* (Beck, 1976) and *Cognitive Therapy of Depression* (Beck et al., 1979), Beck and his colleagues established what many now regard as the original model of cognitive therapy. The model contained a theory of how people develop emotional problems, a model of how to alleviate and eliminate disturbance, and a model of how further problems might be prevented. The model was also supported by what was, for the psychotherapy field, an impressive range of research validation for both its processes and its outcomes. Beck's work began the development of constructs such as 'core beliefs', 'schema' and 'assumptions' which determined negative automatic thoughts (Kuyken et al., 2009). The work of Kelly, Ellis and Beck moved therapy from interpretation of unconscious material to education and enquiry, using Socratic questioning and evidence testing.

Behaviour therapy

Behaviour therapy has a longer history, starting with the Russian physiologist Pavlov and the work of Thorndike and Watson. The behaviour of rats, pigeons, salivating dogs and terrifying bunnies characterize much of early behaviorism, showing that many basic physiological systems could be *conditioned* via the association of stimuli – a truth noticed by all when the sight of a tasty meal produces salivation when hungry. Although human learning is much more complex, basic laws of learning are still good science for how animals, including humans, adapt to their environments – we learn to increase certain behaviours to produce rewards, and reduce them to avoid punishment. Behaviour therapy arose from these laws, with ideas of reward, punishment and 'token economies', in ways which can seem barbaric from our twenty-first-century perspective, such as aversion therapy for homosexuality. However, behavioural methods are widely used today – television programmes such as 'Dog Borstal' and those working with disturbed children illustrate how behavioural change, such as changing punishment to reward schedules, can influence emotion as well as behaviour.

Cognitive behavioural therapy

The marriage of cognitive and behavioural therapies in the 1970s was not initially happy, both holding strongly to their methods and principals. However, with time and evidence, and tolerance from both sides, CBT arose, combining the best of each world. The British Association of Behavioural Therapies (BABT), formed in 1972, changed to the British Association of Behavioural and Cognitive Psychotherapies (BABCP) reflecting the integration of both approaches in what we know as CBT today (www.babcp.com).

Most cognitive therapists use elements from behaviourism, such as exposure to feared and avoided situations and specific behavioural tasks in the form of behavioural experiments. Change in behaviour in itself does not lead automatically to emotional change, but the means by which cognitive change mediates between behaviour and emotion is better understood. For example, a person with agoraphobia may go through the motions of going out of the house, in a series of graded behavioural exposure tasks, but still believe at some level that the outside world is highly dangerous and therefore remain fearful. However, if she also learns 'I can go out because the world is much safer than I believed', and experiences feeling safe, long-term cognitive and behavioural change is possible.

CBT is closely informed by the evidence-based, scientific research of behaviour therapy, in its understanding of psychological processes such as cognition, attention, memory and decision making, linking theory, experimental research and outcome studies (Salkovskis, 2002). CBT has always aimed to develop demonstrably effective treatments, although the focus on randomized controlled trials (RCTs) to the neglect of qualitative and process research is not without controversy (for example, Chapters 3 and 4 in this volume). Therapy conducted in routine clinical practice, such as the NHS, tends to fare less well than the trials of carefully selected clients (Westbrook and Kirk, 2005).

CBT has not been readily embraced by the counselling world (Sanders and Wills, 2005). The structured and focused approach, and use of techniques to promote change, rested uncomfortably with counselling psychologists trained in client-centred and psychodynamic approaches, and cognitive therapy was felt to pay insufficient attention to the therapeutic relationship and to the influence of past events on current problems. However, the last few years have seen a major change in the way cognitive therapy is being adopted within counselling and counselling psychology, with greater integration of at least some CBT approaches. The attraction of CBT within counselling psychology is increasing, with more overt focus placed on the therapeutic relationship, long-term approaches and schema-focused work inherent in newer models.

CBT TODAY

Cognitive behavioural therapies today have many new forms. Second- and third-wave models of cognitive therapies are developing ways of working with people who have complex and long-standing problems, typically from abusive backgrounds and who have disturbed attachment systems, poor ability to self-soothe, and tend to come with labels such as 'personality disorder'. Such people have not done well with traditional cognitive therapy, being more likely to drop out of therapy or find standard methods impossible to implement. For example, compassion-focused therapy, developed by Paul Gilbert and others, has been developed for people with severe shame and self-attacking problems, who have few emotional memories of being self-soothed or validated (Gilbert, 2005). In this therapy, compassion is used as a specific therapeutic process and outcome. Schema therapies, dialectical behaviour therapy (DBT) (Linehan et al., 2007), mindfulness-based cognitive therapy (MBCT) (Segal et al., 2002) and acceptance and commitment therapy (ACT) (Hayes, 2004) all give a range of models and ways of working to enrich cognitive approaches, and offer therapies that help a wider range of people. Interestingly, such therapies are moving away from models of *change*, such as challenging thoughts or beliefs, but are focusing on how to begin to tolerate and *accept* strong feelings, images, memories or thoughts. Thus, in MBCT, all experience is to be welcomed, observed as it is, in the moment, in a non-judgemental manner, and left to go on its way (Segal et al., 2002).

The language of CBT is changing. Traditional labels of cognitive distortions, thinking errors, negative thinking, which can feel judgemental, implying 'I've got my thinking wrong', are being replaced by understandable but unhelpful ways of thinking; seeing anxiety as a useful but rather over-enthusiastic alarm system, conditioned early in life; depression is viewed less as an illness but more as an evolutionary adaptive way of coping when conditions outside are not safe, but no longer necessary for today.

THE COGNITIVE MODEL

At the heart of CBT there is a very simple yet effective working model: the way people think about situations influences the way they feel and behave. The following dialogue gives a rationale for CBT.

> *Therapist*: I'd like to explain how CBT works by telling a story. A large computer software company was facing financial difficulties, and had to make people redundant. Our two men in the story, A and B, were similar ages and did similar jobs. A, hearing about his redundancy, thought, 'Oh no, this is a disaster. I might never work again. What will my wife think of me? I won't be able to look after the family.' How do you think he felt?
>
> *Client*: Desperate, I'd guess. Very upset, low. Scared.
>
> *Therapist*: That's right. And what might he do?
>
> *Client*: He'd want to give up, I guess. He'd be sort-of paralyzed.
>
> *Therapist*: I'd guess that as well. Our other man, B, same age, same skills, had a different reaction. He thought, 'What a shock. This will be a huge change. But I've not been happy for a while. It might be a chance to get something better, more interesting.' How would he feel? And what might he do?
>
> *Client*: He'd feel quite shocked for a bit, but then might feel a bit excited, like getting on with the next stage of life.
> (Wills, 2008: 6)

We can see from the dialogue that two people have very different reactions to the same event depending on their interpretation of the event, or the meaning given to the situation. We can then think about why people have different interpretations, how their circumstances, background and experience determine their beliefs or rules about themselves, others or the world. We may speculate that A did not get enough support and encouragement in his early years, and was picked on and bullied at school. He never felt very confident in himself, but did well in his career by hard work and what he called 'luck'. His beliefs included: 'To be OK, I must do well at my work. If others criticize me, it means I'm a failure.' He interpreted the redundancy as a criticism. B, in contrast, was a more resilient soul, not putting a huge amount of importance on his job, feeling satisfied with his family and life beyond work. His beliefs might be along the lines of: 'Life can be tough but something else always turns up.'

The thought–emotion cycle

One of the aims in cognitive therapy is to look at the meaning the client gives to situations, emotions or biology, often expressed in the client's 'negative automatic thoughts'.

The essence of the model shows there is a reciprocal relationship between emotional difficulties and seeing events as exaggerated beyond the available evidence. These exaggerated ways of seeing things tend to exert further negative influences on our feelings and behaviour. Some have interpreted the model as causal: we feel emotions as a direct result of our thoughts. In practice, the emotion may well come first. For example, depression leads to a negative bias on our thoughts, emotions and behaviour, and therefore when depressed we think negative thoughts. When anxiety and fear levels are raised, the mind automatically becomes focused on danger, and we think fearful thoughts. Thoughts and feelings are often experienced as a unitary phenomenon, and our labelling of 'thought' and 'feeling' is more a useful heuristic device for therapy than a truly knowable reality.

Cognitive distortions: negative thoughts

Beck (1996) outlined a range of negative, distorted and biased ways in which we think that enabled people to begin to label thoughts and notice the effect on mood and behaviour, summarized in Sanders and Wills (2005). For example, the thought 'I'm stupid', a very common negative automatic thought in emotional disturbance, betrays 'all or nothing' or 'black and white' thinking because it usually refers to the actually narrower reality that the person may occasionally do some things which, with the benefit of hindsight, may be construed as 'stupid'. The depressed client, however, will often go on to conclude that this makes him a 'stupid person'. In this type of reasoning, there are only two possible conditions: doing everything right and being 'not stupid', or doing some things wrongly and being 'stupid'. Thus the negatively biased person begins to use self-blame, thereby depressing mood even further in a vicious cycle. Other common types of distorted thought include 'mind reading' (everyone is judging me; they must think I'm a real tosser) 'crystal-ball gazing' (my whole life is going to be this bad) or 'emotional reasoning' (I feel terrified therefore it must be dangerous; I feel stupid therefore I must be stupid).

From thoughts to beliefs and schema

Cognitive therapy has traditionally distinguished between 'core beliefs' or 'schema', 'unhelpful assumptions' and 'negative thoughts', which form layers of meaning which we unpeel during therapy. CBT usually starts with identifying and working with the layer of thoughts, which are easily accessible, then working downwards to uncover and examine unhelpful assumptions. In more complex people, perhaps with difficult or abusive backgrounds, work on core beliefs will be far more important and central in therapy compared to people with relatively helpful central beliefs.

> Eleanor came from an extremely difficult background. Her father was an alcoholic and showed very little interest in either of his two children. He was violent towards her mother, and at 11, Eleanor and her sister were removed from the family and lived with a succession of foster families. At 14, Eleanor was abused by one of her foster brothers, and always felt it was her fault. She began self-harming at 15, and took an overdose at 17, more as a cry for help than seriously wanting to end her life. Her first husband was much older than her, and appeared charming at first, 'someone reliable in my life', but was an alcoholic, and like her father, began to be abusive towards her. Eleanor had been treated for depression and had been in and out of the psychiatric services.

Eleanor's core beliefs related to safety:

- The world is not a safe place.
- People cannot be trusted; people are out to abuse me.
- I'm rubbish.

Such beliefs led to her rules of life or assumptions:

- If I say how I feel, people abuse me.
- If I get close to anyone, they'll find out how dirty I am.
- If I can keep busy all the time, I won't let the past get in and upset me.

Schema like these are not 'objects' but more 'schematic processes'. Although the autonomous existence of these processes is hard to prove, the concept remains a useful one.

The role of behaviour

What we do in response to our thoughts, feelings and beliefs links in the chain, locking the sequence of thought–feeling–behaviour into persistent, repetitive and unhelpful patterns. Some of these patterns are life-long, such as long-standing anxiety and low self-esteem leading to chronic avoidance, agoraphobia and other problems; others may be in response to short-term depression, such as a temporary withdrawal from normal life.

Mary was five when her mother died of cancer. When Mary was 29, the same age as her mother had been when she died, Mary became convinced she also was going to die, and became extremely anxious about her health. She started to avoid 'taking any risks', including driving and coming into contact with friends in case they had any infections, and focused so much on her body that she began to interpret any slight twinges as evidence of illness. She repeatedly visited her GP for reassurance. Her anxiety made her feel ill and exhausted most of the time, and she was off sick so much, she lost her job. She spent hours at home worrying about her health, lost contact with friends and became extremely low.

We can see from Mary's example that her belief, 'I am going to die young', led to a number of behaviours which maintain health anxiety: avoiding situations which might be dangerous (driving, seeing other people), focusing on her body and seeking reassurance. Her responses also maintain her low mood and depression: withdrawal from life, social isolation, spending time ruminating and so on. In other problems such as obsessive compulsive disorder, behaviours such as repeated hand washing, house cleaning and rituals to neutralize 'bad' thoughts, are flagrant manifestations of thoughts and beliefs (Sanders and Wills, 2003).

KEY FEATURES OF CBT

The basic principles of the cognitive-behavioural approach are:

- A collaborative relationship in which client and therapist work together to understand and resolve problems.
- Cognitive formulation of the individual client, based on a general understanding of the problems brought to therapy.
- The method is structured, educational and focused, using Socratic enquiry and experimentation to promote change.
- CBT is parsimonious, doing the least number of sessions for the maximum effect, and generally but not always a short-term therapy, initially focusing on present problems, based on an understanding of background issues.
- CBT uses a variety of techniques developed in cognitive and other disciplines.
- Homework is a central feature.

Collaborative therapeutic relationship

CBT has often been criticized for paying insufficient attention to the therapeutic relationship, a criticism which, whilst exaggerated, contains a grain of historical truth. Although cognitive therapy developed in parallel to Carl Rogers' work (Rogers, 1957), CBT prided itself on the effectiveness of its 'specific' factors, such as formulation and structure, as central to change. Early cognitive therapists were already trained therapists from other, mainly analytic, disciplines. The quality of the relationship was taken as read; the new cognitive approaches needed to highlight and sell the technical aspects, different as they were from the process of analysis. In fact, close reading of Beck's work shows he has always stressed the need for therapists to be genuinely warm, empathic and open, in order to foster a strong therapeutic relationship where they can collaboratively develop therapy goals, ways of working and homework tasks.

The therapeutic relationship came centre-stage with the seminal work of Safran and Segal (1990) and the development of ways of working with people with long-term problems and so-called 'personality disorders' (Layden et al., 1993). The importance of the interpersonal dimension to therapy is now firmly established in CBT theory and practice (Gilbert and Leahy, 2007; Wills, 2008). The last decade of work in CBT has focused far more on relationship factors, with compassion, empathy and ways of working with alliance ruptures as common subjects for research and practice (Gilbert, 2005; Gilbert and Leahy, 2007).

CBT has always stressed the importance of establishing a strong *collaborative* relationship between client and therapist, with the therapist playing an active role. Collaboration means therapists are open about their way of working, giving rationales to the client and being open to feedback from the client, which further strengthen the relationship. Collaboration is clear from the opening moments of a session, where the therapist might greet a new client with the following words:

> 'Today, we have about an hour, and I'd like to find out about what you see are you main difficulties. I'd like to ask you about your background, and then I can tell you about cognitive therapy and how it might help you. How does that sound? Are there specific issues or questions you'd like to spend time on?'

Therapeutic techniques are only as good as the therapeutic alliance in which they are used. For example, emotion-focused methods, such as imagery or role play, rely on a high level of trust. The relationship needs to be good enough for the client to allow himself to feel vulnerable and exposed and explore early memories, and trust the therapist to be able to deal with whatever she hears. When working with Eleanor, the quality of the relationship was central, and much of the early stages of therapy concentrated on building a strong-enough alliance for her to begin to look at her beliefs.

We now have many more ways of working with therapeutic ruptures. For example, a client who has particular concerns about being invalidated, believing that 'People don't believe me, people don't respect me and what I say', may experience the process of challenging negative thoughts as invalidating and painful. If the therapist continues along the route of challenging the client, she is likely to simply confirm the client's belief 'People don't respect me' (Katzow and Safran, 2007). The therapist needs to be aware of the very first signs of discomfort in the client – from a subtle drawing back to overt anger – and stop to explore what was going on between them at *that moment* in therapy. Early CBT might have encouraged the therapist to confront and challenge the accuracy of the client's beliefs, risking the client thinking 'If my therapist questions my thoughts, it means she doesn't believe me', which could well lead to a considerable rupture in the relationship. Instead, it is essential at this stage that the therapist unhooks from the interaction, stops further cognitive interventions and avoids becoming defensive or feeling criticized herself, but instead empathize with the client and explore his feelings. A way of using such methods can be summarized as:

- Awareness of therapist's subjective feelings and experience.
- Collaboration with the client in focusing together on relationship difficulties.
- Focus on the present, the here and now – right now, at this moment, what are you feeling?
- An emphasis on understanding and awareness rather than change.

Safran et al.'s model of working in cognitive therapy draws from Zen and the concept of the 'beginners mind', encouraging therapists to be intensely curious about one's inner experience as it unfolds – a method paralleled in Schon's (1983) concept of 'reflection-in-action' and counselling psychology's ethos of reflective practice. Mindfulness is a way of developing such awareness. Such work is much more in tune with counselling and psychotherapy in general, whereby the process of forming, and healing, the relationship with the therapist is in itself a valuable aspect of therapy. I may, for example, be aware of shutting off in therapy, my moment of 'empathy bypass', when a client is describing events or emotions in a manner devoid of actual emotion. Alternatively, I may feel extremely emotional listening to a client's story, whereas the client's description is devoid of emotion. Both reactions are interesting, suggesting the client is either avoiding or is unaware of the emotional impact of what they are saying.

Rob, who was referred by the cardiac rehabilitation team for depression, had survived a dramatic aortic dissection, where the aorta wall partially ruptured. The damage extended up his carotid arteries, and he was completely dissociated from any fear or emotion during the dissection, which occurred when he was abroad and unable to speak the language. It was a miracle that he had survived. He had told the story many times to many friends and medics, and had to him always been just a story.

By pointing out my reaction, of shock and sadness, Rob began to realize he had not really begun to believe what had happened to him. He felt as though all the emotion was trapped inside himself, stagnating, leading him to feel so heavy and low. He began, slowly, to express the shock of what had happened, and his mixed feelings of delight and terror that he had survived, by writing and talking about his experiences.

Formulation

A cognitive formulation (also known as 'conceptualization') is a means of making sense of the origins, development and maintenance of a person's difficulties. The formulation develops in collaboration with the client, and leads to a plan for intervention and therapy (Tarrier and Calam, 2002). The idea of formulating a person's difficulties as part of therapy is not unique to cognitive approaches, but has been developed within other therapeutic models. In cognitive analytic therapy, for example, case formulation is overtly used to build a shared understanding of the client's presenting issues, develop the therapeutic relationship and guide interventions (Ryle and Kerr, 2003).

Formulation is different from diagnosis, although the two are connected. CBT has relied, in its development, on diagnostic systems such as the *Diagnostic and Statistical Manual of Mental Disorders* (DSM-TR) (American Psychiatric Association, 2000) to categorize the problems people bring to therapy, and as a basis for research. As an aid to therapy, however, it is far more limited (Harvey et al., 2004) and generally unpopular within counselling psychology (Sequeira and Van Scoyoc, 2001). Using an individual formulation bypasses the need for diagnosis; however, a rough idea of the 'diagnosis' such as anxiety, depression, obsessive-compulsive disorder can be very helpful in guiding the therapist towards specific cognitive models and guidelines for therapy (see Sanders and Wills, 2005: 50–51).

There are many models of formulation in the cognitive therapy literature (Grant et al., 2008; Tarrier, 2006). At its simplest, formulation describes vicious cycles linking thoughts and emotions. It brings in behaviour and biology, and how these impact on and are affected by thoughts and emotions. As well as looking at the issues the client brings to therapy, a formulation enables an understanding of problems in terms of underlying psychological mechanisms, namely assumptions and beliefs the client holds about him/herself, others and the world (Kuyken et al., 2009; Grant et al., 2008).

David had worked for years in education, was well regarded by his colleagues and felt he had 'always done a good job'. He had been well for most of his life, had hardly taken any time off sick, but was knocked off his bicycle and suffered a nasty leg fracture

(Continued)

(Continued)

requiring several months off work. When he returned, he was shocked to find how anxious he had become: he had episodes of feeling like he was 'losing it', which 'wasn't like him' – his GP had diagnosed panic attacks. During our first meeting, we drew a vicious cycle based on the cognitive model of panic (Figure 6.1).We also discussed David's background, which he had 'not thought about for years'. Although, on the whole, David had a 'happy childhood' – 'no problems' – he was in intense competition with his older brother, and always felt slightly inferior. David had failed his 11 plus and gone to the local comprehensive, whereas his 'clever clogs' older brother had passed and as a result went to grammar school. David set out to 'prove himself', which he had certainly done through his job. He had not, however, realized that failure had a high price. One of his beliefs was 'I'm OK so long as I do well' and 'I must keep up my standards at all time'. The accident and subsequent problems had activated these beliefs, so going back into situations where he had to perform made him feel like 'an 11-year-old kid, not as good as my big brother'.

A good formulation must explain the individual's difficulties, and make sense to the client (Kuyken et al., 2009). It is a working model, and can be added to or revised at any time during therapy, even in some cases scrapped completely in the light of new information. Formulation provides a bridge between what we know about psychological difficulties in general – such as how particular thoughts and behaviours might maintain anxiety problems, or how patterns of negative thinking and rumination make depressed people feel even worse – and an understanding of the client as an individual. The danger of formulation based on general models is that we hear what we want to hear in order to fit the model, and perhaps do not look in other places for information which may later turn out to be crucial. A working knowledge of a range of formulations is very helpful, to hold in the back of our minds while we focus on the unique person in front of us.

Structure

One of the characteristic features of cognitive therapy is the structured, focused approach. Each session has a formal structure roughly covering the following areas:

- Identifying an agenda for the session – what are the most important thing to cover?
- Review of homework and learning from last session.
- Main issues for today with homework.
- Feedback on how the client has found the session today.

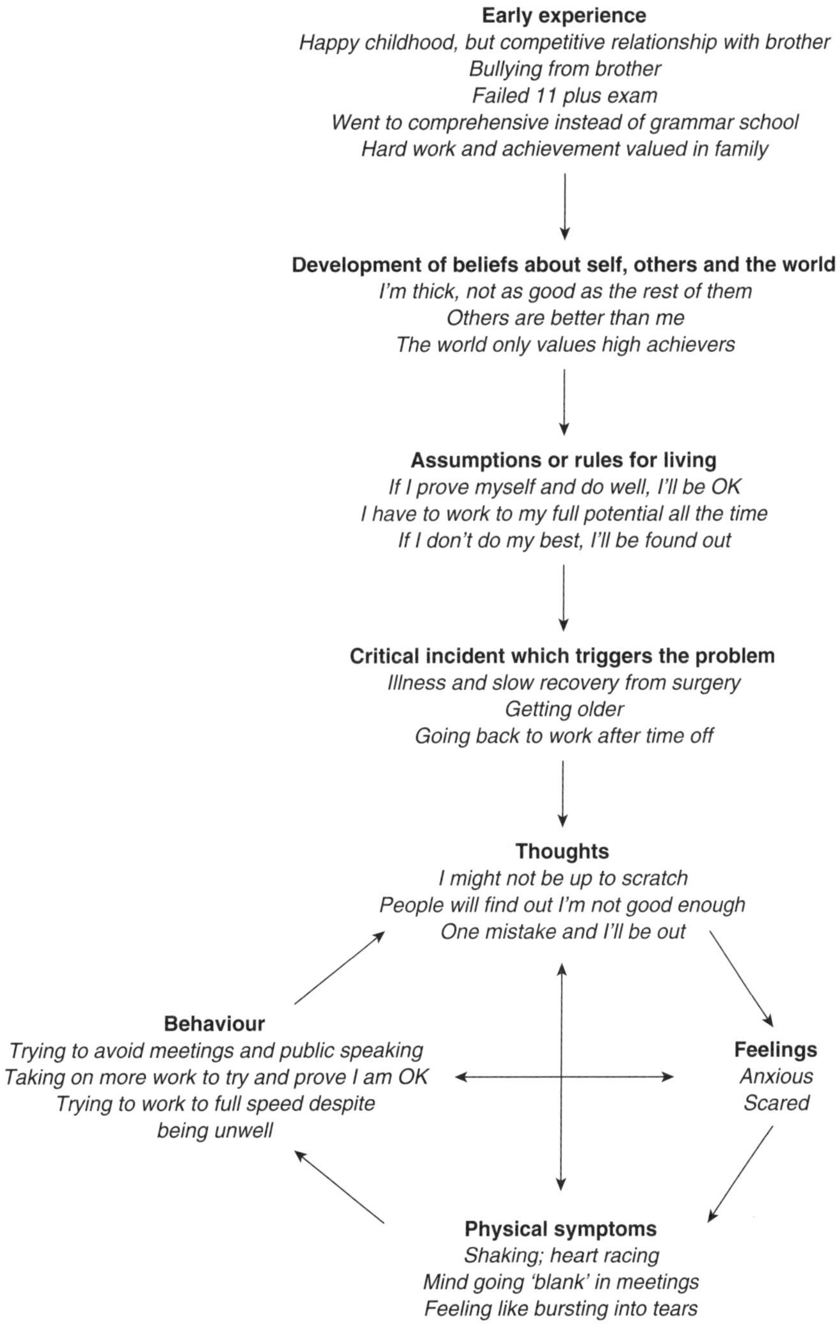

Early experience
Happy childhood, but competitive relationship with brother
Bullying from brother
Failed 11 plus exam
Went to comprehensive instead of grammar school
Hard work and achievement valued in family

Development of beliefs about self, others and the world
I'm thick, not as good as the rest of them
Others are better than me
The world only values high achievers

Assumptions or rules for living
If I prove myself and do well, I'll be OK
I have to work to my full potential all the time
If I don't do my best, I'll be found out

Critical incident which triggers the problem
Illness and slow recovery from surgery
Getting older
Going back to work after time off

Thoughts
I might not be up to scratch
People will find out I'm not good enough
One mistake and I'll be out

Behaviour
Trying to avoid meetings and public speaking
Taking on more work to try and prove I am OK
Trying to work to full speed despite
being unwell

Feelings
Anxious
Scared

Physical symptoms
Shaking; heart racing
Mind going 'blank' in meetings
Feeling like bursting into tears

FIGURE 6.1   FORMULATION FOR DAVID

TABLE 6.1   STRUCTURE OF COGNITIVE THERAPY ACROSS SESSIONS

Session number	Main focus
Assessment	Initial meeting
	Collect information about current problems, maintenance factors and background. Beginnings of simple formulation. Engaging client in cognitive approach, showing collaboration. Education about cognitive therapy. First 'homework' (for example, reading about CT, diary etc).
1	Formulation: building up a model. Engagement and socializing about how therapy works. Homework focusing on collecting information, for example, thought diaries, behavioural methods such as activity diary.
2–4	Continuing formulation, engagement and socialization. Working with information to start change, for example, identifying negative thoughts and how to change these; activity scheduling in depression.
5–7	Using cognitive and behavioural methods to produce changes, for example, thought challenging, beginning behavioural experiments.
8–9	As above, but beginning to identify and work with assumptions and rules. Testing out rules verbally and through behavioural experiments.
10–11	As above, introducing ideas of ending therapy. Looking at what client is learning and able to do outside sessions. Generalizing learning to other problems and client's life.
12	Ending – blueprint for ending. What client has learned and how to tackle future difficulties. Issues around endings.
6 month follow-up	Review progress, troubleshoot difficulties and problem solve future problems.
Yearly follow-up	As 6 months. Dealing with final ending.

Source: Wells, 1997 and Beck, 1995

Therapy as a whole works to a structure, agreed at the beginning (a possible structure is shown in Table 6.1).

We start with identifying the client's goals, being as clear and specific as possible (Sanders and Wills, 2005; Westbrook et al., 2007). CBT then moves through a series of stages, depending on the individual client and formulation. A general 'formula' I keep in mind is to move therapy through assessment and formulation, looking at cognitive and behavioural factors maintaining the vicious cycles, looking at underlying assumptions and, if necessary, core beliefs, then moving towards ending therapy and relapse prevention.

The structured approach of CBT is one factor with which therapists from other disciplines have the most difficulties, with concerns about being dictatorial and not relationship-focused. In my experience, the vast majority of clients are happy to work in a structured way, and in good CBT the structure is implicit rather than laboured. When I first saw Beck at work, I thought his work was indistinguishable from that of Carl Rogers'. However, studying the video of his work in depth, the deep structure is clear: for example, Beck introduced the session time by saying 'We have 30 minutes to talk together, what would you like to focus on?', and maintained the focus by regularly summarizing his understanding so far.

Socratic method and guided discovery

One of the characteristic features of CBT is the use of Socratic questioning, or guided discovery, an investigative process whereby client and therapist work together in a collaborative way to explore different ways of viewing things. Socrates was a fifth-century Athenian philosopher and teacher, who used systematic questioning and inductive reasoning to arrive at 'truth' (Cartledge, 2001). Strong emotion, anxiety or depression narrow our way of thinking so our vision is limited and fixed; using Socratic questioning, we aim to help clients become aware of different perspectives, or information which they already know but have forgotten. An example is given below:

> Ken was feeling extremely low following bypass surgery and a long time off work. When he returned to his job as a street cleaner, he felt very anxious about seeing other people, thinking they would judge him as a 'cripple' and a 'waste of space'.
>
> *Therapist:* Is that what you think of yourself?
> *Ken:* Yeah, just a waste now. Good for nothing.
> *Therapist:* And it sounds like you think this is what other people are thinking of you?
> *Ken:* Yeah.

As a therapist, two avenues were possible: first, to enquire about the meaning of others thinking badly; and second, whether Ken also held a negative view about other people who had health problems. I started down the first line of enquiry:

Therapist: And if they were thinking this of you, what would that mean to you? What would be awful about it for you?

Ken: [long silence] Well, they'll all be talking behind my back. People do talk, don't they?

Therapist: Yes, people do discuss and gossip, but it sounds like you're assuming it would all be judgemental and negative – what is your evidence for that?

Ken:	Well, some guy said he'd had a neighbour who'd had a bypass and was up and running a few months later, why had it taken me so long to recover. That really upset me. I just walked off.
Therapist:	Have you met anyone else who has heart problems?
Ken:	Yes, loads I guess – in hospital and at rehab. [the hospital ran weekly gym sessions for cardiac patients]
Therapist:	And what do you think of them? Do you think they are all a waste of space?
Ken:	No, no, I don't think anything of them – they are just people like me. We have a laugh sometimes.
Therapist:	So what does this tell you?
Ken:	I never thought about them. I see what you're getting at. We're just all people who've been ill.

Socratic questioning is used in many different stages of therapy:

- During assessment to help the client formulate problems:

  When you felt terrified, what went through your mind?
  What did that mean to you?
  What is the worst that might happen?

- When looking for alternative ways of thinking:

  Is there a different way of seeing things?
  How helpful is it to think that way?
  Are there situations where this is not the case?
  What would you say to a friend in this situation?
  If you were not feeling so low, how might you interpret this?

- When solving problems:

  What else could you do?
  What have you tried in the past?
  How have you coped with this before?

- When working out behavioural experiments to test out beliefs:

  How could you test that out?
  What do you predict might happen?
  If the worst happened, what could you do?

- When ending therapy:

  What have you learned in therapy?
  What's been helpful, and unhelpful?
  What setbacks might you meet?
  What will you do then?

From the examples above, we are encouraging clients to broaden their vision, think through alternatives and throw light on strengths they may not realize they have. Guided discovery encourages a sense of curiosity in both client and therapist, as though we are detectives looking for the bigger picture. Throughout the process, we use empathic reflection and summarizing to check that we have fully understood. Once we have discovered information, synthesizing questions such as 'What do you make of that?', 'How does this information fit with you saying you're useless?' or 'How might these ideas make a difference to you?' enable the client to learn from the process (Padesky, 1993, 2003).

Parsimony and empiricism in CBT

CBT aims to be parsimonious, that is, the most work for the least effort. It therefore aims to be as short as necessary to help the target problems and meet goals, an aim which has been snapped up by NHS management who strive to find ever shorter ways of meeting targets. The brevity of the approach – 20 sessions maximum for depression, 10 for anxiety, or only 6 in primary care, regardless of the problem – leads to criticisms of superficiality and 'a job only half done'.

The answer is both yes and no. In much of routine practice, a huge amount can be done when the therapy is focused, the client plays an active part in recovery, and problems are relatively contained. Longer-standing problems may well require longer therapy, or more creative ways of negotiating time limits. For example, 10 sessions may be fine for people with depression arising from life events, without need for further therapy. For those with recurrent depression, stating 'I've been depressed most of my life', 10 sessions can give valuable tools and approaches to improve mood but leave the client at risk of relapse. In practice, I may offer 'blocks' of therapy: 10 sessions to address one set of problems, followed by a gap of a few months (or even a year or two in some cases), then another block to address another issue, and so on. Individual CBT can be supplemented by group work, such as mindfulness-based cognitive therapy groups for people with recurrent depression. In routine work, I deal with session limits by a Robin Hood approach – some clients need more sessions, some less, but by juggling them around I can mostly keep to my contracted session limits.

Empiricism implies that we measure what is going on. Once we have defined where we are going, it is very helpful to have a clear idea about how we will know when we have got there. Obviously what our clients tell us and what they are doing is one of the most important measures, but in addition, formal measurement helps both parties to evaluate progress. Measures can take many forms (Sanders and Wills, 2005), such as the Beck depression inventory. Simpler methods include asking a client to do a simple weekly rating out of 10 on problem areas:

Tracy found it very difficult to say just how she was feeling, and found filling in questionnaires difficult. She devised a 'global yeuch' measure, a 0–10 'yeuchometer', which gave us both useful feedback as to how she was getting on.

Other measures can be number of panic attacks and number of times avoided going out, measures of time someone is able to stay in a room without checking for the presence of spiders, number of obsessional thoughts, number of episodes of bingeing and vomiting, and so on.

Methods in CBT

The variety of methods used in CBT aim to help clients feel better by becoming more aware of their patterns of thinking and meanings given to experience, to think and assign meaning in a different, more helpful or realistic way and to make changes in behaviour. In some ways, this sounds relatively simple, and reading some CBT texts, one could be forgiven for thinking CBT can somehow offer a magic switch to enable people to literally change their minds. In practice, it is much more complex, and for some clients, an extremely difficult thing to do. Simply working cognitively does not work, and we need a range of cognitive, behavioural and emotional means in order to change minds, behaviours and feelings. Therefore, the methods used in CBT are many and varied, some unique to CBT, such as thought records and behavioural experiments, others borrowed or stolen from other disciplines, such as two-chair Gestalt methods or mindfulness, informed by Buddhism (Sanders and Wills, 2005; Westbrook et al., 2007; Wills, 2008).

The more technical aspects of therapy have led to criticisms of CBT: it is mechanistic, stressing tricks and techniques at the expense of emotions, concentrating on what methods to use rather than the process of therapy. Such criticisms contain a wealth of truth. Methods should not substitute for a good, collaborative therapeutic relationship, and should always be informed by a formulation specific to each individual client. However, such criticisms are anachronistic: recent developments in CBT looking at the therapeutic relationship and the role of emotion allow for a far more sophisticated approach, using a range of powerful tools of proven value to enable people to understand and tackle their particular difficulties. We also have more understanding of which methods work, and why, integrating emotional, cognitive and behavioural aspects in order to produce change. Old-style CBT, in a nutshell, may have said 'Tackle your crooked thinking and you'll feel better'; CBT today is focused on emotional change, on cognitive processes and using behaviour in order to change emotions, with greater integration of 'head' and 'heart' (Bennett-Levy, 2003; Bennett-Levy et al., 2004).

Thought	Evidence for	Evidence against
Other people think I'm a waste of space.	Roger's comments about his friend who'd had a bypass. It's what I think about myself.	I didn't stay around long enough to find out Roger's real opinion. I don't think the people in the gym are a waste of space – they're just people. Most people have been pleased to see me back and sound sympathetic. It's not my fault – lots of people get sick. I've got back to work – I have some use.

FIGURE 6.2   THOUGHT DIARY

Returning to Ken, above, two particular methods were helpful: the thought record and behavioural experiments. Ken kept a diary of his thoughts, and examined the evidence for and against his view of himself as 'a waste of space' (Figure 6.2).

In a short space of time, Ken was able to see his thought as biased. To carry on with this work, Ken used a behavioural experiment (Bennett-Levy et al., 2004), recording how many times people said negative or positive things to him. He discovered that most people were pleased to see him and sympathetic, and the only negative stuff came from work colleagues but was done in a spirit of joking and teasing rather than cruel judgements. He realized he was only paying attention to a certain range of evidence, whereas the questioning in the therapy session and keeping a diary of thoughts and reality helped him to feel better about himself, go out more and make a full recovery from depression.

Homework

Although the term 'homework' does not go down well with all clients or practitioners, working on therapeutic tasks between sessions is an essential part of cognitive therapy and is related to good outcome (Garland and Scott, 2002; Kazantzis and Lampropoulos, 2002). In my experience, most clients are happy with the term 'homework', but a few hate it, bringing back painful reminders of school. A negative client reaction can prove valuable:

> Donald, who worked for a large landscape firm, was dyslexic, although he had not told anyone all of his life. In his 50s, he developed severe anxiety, related to the introduction of computers and requirement to use email. In our first session, when we started talking about CBT and the value of trying things out between sessions, Donald visibly panicked. He felt 'paralyzed' and unable to 'think straight'. The idea of homework brought back painful memories of being humiliated by a teacher at school, who made him stand on a stool holding up his 'terrible' writing in front of the class. He was a brilliant gardener, but never learned to read or write properly, and had always managed to keep this hidden. Despite planning to keep it hidden from me as well, Donald and I focused on these issues during most of the therapy. As a result, he discovered a range of resources for adults with dyslexia, and began to learn to read and write for the first time in his life.

Homework tasks are very varied, and include:

- listening to a tape of the session
- reading information specific to the client's difficulties
- keeping a diary of symptoms
- thought diaries
- behavioural experiment tasks.

Making a record of sessions, using tapes or digital recordings, for the client to listen to between sessions, is invaluable to the process of therapy. The tapes allows for reflection, essential to making sense of and learning from therapy, as well as giving the client useful feedback. For example, a client who believed she presented a very muddled account of her difficulties was surprised at how clearly she was able to describe them; another person learned that whilst she said that she really wanted me to help her and kept on asking for my 'advice', she never really listened to anything I said.

NEW APPROACHES IN CBT: WORKING WITH COGNITIVE PROCESSES

The process of thinking, as opposed to content, is of great interest to 'third-wave' cognitive psychotherapy, particularly for people with generalized anxiety and worry, obsessive compulsive disorder, post-traumatic stress disorder and chronic relapsing depression (Harvey et al., 2004). Newer CBT approaches suggest we need to help both ourselves and our clients become more aware and mindful of these processes, and learn to accept and watch them in a non-judgemental way. Thoughts can be leapt on and challenged, talked to and modified, but a constant stream of thinking can be watched as though they are juggernauts passing by on a busy road or clouds scudding across the sky.

Such ideas are formalized in mindfulness-based cognitive therapy (Segal et al., 2002, Williams et al., 2007) for people with recurrent depression, who learn to identify and accept ruminative patterns of thinking as 'just thinking' rather than objective reality. By learning to watch the mind, rather than interact with or control it, we can see the huge variety of thoughts, memories and images which come and go, and regard these in a neutral way. These ideas are not new but have been embodied for centuries in Buddhist traditions and form the basis for many forms of meditation. The ideas and practice of mindfulness can be helpful for many problems and for life in general, and can be integrated into everyday practice.

CBT TRAINING AND COMPETENCIES

There are many ways in which CBT can be used, either integrating some of the methods and approaches into practice or training as a fully fledged CBT therapist, accredited through the BABCP (www.babcp.com). The competencies to deliver CBT have been described in the Department of Health report (Roth and Pilling, 2007). Competencies include, reassuringly, generic competencies in psychological therapies; the ability to form a trusting therapeutic relationship; and relating to people in a way which is warm, encouraging and accepting. Specific CBT competencies include maintaining structure and focus in sessions; using appropriate homework; Socratic questioning; working with exposure; behavioural experiments; and problem-specific skills such as activity scheduling in depression. The cognitive therapy rating scale (Young and Beck, 1980) is used to assess the competency of cognitive therapists in their work.

Rather than viewing CBT as the application of techniques and methods, reduced to a series of rote operations, meta-competency is knowing why and when to do something and being flexible, tailoring work to individual need: which, as a seasoned cognitive therapist, may come instinctively and intuitively rather than being conscious, moment-to-moment decisions. The Department of Health report (Roth and Pilling, 2007) has a helpful map of these competencies, is available from the British Psychological Society website (www.bps.org.uk).

APPLICATIONS OF CBT

Christine Padesky (1998) has said, possibly with tongue in cheek, that learning CBT was easy for her because there was at the time of her training, in the late 1970s, only one 'application': Beck's seminal work on the cognitive therapy of depression. In the

2008 British Association for Cognitive and Behavioural Psychotherapies conference in Edinburgh, there were a bewildering array of symposia of 40 or so different areas of application. It appears there is no problem known to humankind that CBT will not try to fix. CBT has been developed across a whole range of problems and is available in a wide range of settings. For each problem area, we can find general formulations and ideas about which methods might be effective.

As a counselling psychologist, knowledge of applications can both help and hinder the process of therapy. I find it very helpful to know the general formulations for problems such as depression and panic, where relatively 'standardized' interventions are, in my experience, helpful for many people: for example, activity scheduling is extremely useful in helping people through the heaviness and exhaustion of depression; using standard methods work well to enable people to find alternative explanations of their weird symptoms in panic. However, formulaic therapy is based on diagnostic categories which may or may not be helpful, and in general for the more complex the client I use highly individual formulation and highly individual therapy (Grant et al., 2004; Grant et al., 2008; Merrett and Easton, 2008; Sanders and Wills, 2005).

CBT AND COUNSELLING PSYCHOLOGY

There is little doubt that CBT is looked on very favourably, in initiatives such as Improved Access to Psychological Therapies (IAPT) and implementing Lord Layard's recommendation to train around 10,000 extra therapists offering CBT as therapy of choice. On the one hand, this is an excellent prospect. Depression, anxiety, psychological difficulties and mental health problems affect a huge number of people in the UK, and the need for help far outstrips supply. Most services struggle with waiting lists, which are demoralizing to clients and staff alike. There seems to be a move in two directions to improve supply of CBT: first, offering potentially 'diluted' forms of therapy, including computerized packages (www.livinglifetothefull.com and www.calipso.co.uk) and large-group format (White, 2000) to people with mild to moderate psychological difficulties; and second, to train graduates, with limited qualifications and experience, to offer relatively standardized forms of CBT. Time will tell whether such approaches to improve supply are appropriate. The research evidence so far suggests that brief interventions can be extremely effective when used appropriately, and computerized packages, such as those in health centres, can be useful. The Lupina project in Oxford is training psychology graduates to offer intensive CBT to people with agoraphobia and panic, and initial results appear promising (Turpin, 2007). On the other hand, however, such initiatives could be highly detrimental both to psychology as a profession and CBT. The risk is that most or all direct client work will go to relatively inexperienced practitioners, and those with most experience move to managerial and supervisory roles.

I think in reality CBT and its provision will move in various directions. Grant et al. (2004) suggest the varieties of practice under the umbrella of mainstream CBT might be plotted on a continuum. At one end is an explicitly technique-focused style, with standardized interventions based on experimentation and randomized controlled trials such as those described above. Unfortunately, I think CBT has branded itself at the technique end, as a uniform and unilateral approach, fitting with the rhetoric of evidence-based healthcare. In my career as a counselling psychologist and cognitive psychotherapist, I hear many arguments for and against CBT, and when I chartered as a counselling psychologist in the early 1990s, my allegiance to CBT was somewhat frowned upon, for the above reasons.

However, at the other end of our continuum sits formulation-based therapy, where we work with the richness and variety of individual experience. Here, we find experienced and highly-trained therapists working with people with complex needs, where we pay significant attention to moment-by-moment interactions and the relationship. In my CBT practice, and informed by being a counselling psychologist, I move between both areas. Some clients do well with an hour and a half assessment including a fairly comprehensive formulation of their difficulties, and guided self-help and biblio-therapy. For others, I work in a much longer-term way, with many sessions spent formulating and re-formulating their difficulties, using a variety of methods within a strong therapeutic alliance. For me, the richness of CBT lies in adapting my way of working to the individual. With its many new developments, CBT is in the process of rebranding itself; and counselling psychology's interest is expanding. I hope, in this chapter, to have shown how CBT is a complex and evolving form of psychotherapy, suitable to therapists from a variety of backgrounds, and fitting with the ethos of contemporary counselling psychology.

REFERENCES

American Psychiatric Association (2000) *Diagnostic and Statistical Manual of Mental Disorders*, 4th edn, Text Revision. Washington, DC: American Psychiatric Association.

Beck, A.T. (1976) *Cognitive Therapy and the Emotional Disorders*. New York: International Universities Press.

Beck, A.T. (1996) 'Beyond belief: A theory of modes, personality and psychopathology', in P.M. Salkovskis (ed.), *Frontiers of Cognitive Therapy*. New York: Guilford. pp. 1–25.

Beck, A.T., Rush, A.J., Shaw, B.F. and Emery, G. (1979) *Cognitive Therapy of Depression*. New York: Guilford.

Beck, J. (1995) *Cognitive Therapy: Basics and Beyond*. New York: Guilford Press.

Bennett-Levy, J. (2003) 'Mechanisms of change in cognitive therapy: The case of automatic thought records and behavioural experiments', *Behavioural and Cognitive Psychotherapy*, 31: 261–277.

Bennett-Levy, J., Butler, G., Fennell, M., Hackmann, A., Mueller, M. and Westbrook, D. (2004) *The Oxford Guide to Behavioural Experiments in Cognitive Therapy*. Oxford: Oxford University Press.

Cartledge, P. (2001) *The Greeks*. London: BBC Worldwide.

DoH (2007) *Commissioning a Brighter Future: Improving Access to Psychological Therapies*. London: Department of Health.

Ellis, A. (1962) *Reason and Emotion in Psychotherapy*. New York: Lyle Stuart.

Feltham, C. and Horton, I. (eds) (2006) *The Sage Handbook of Counselling and Psychotherapy*. London: Sage.

Garland, A. and Scott, J. (2002) 'Using homework in therapy for depression', *Journal of Clinical Psychology*, 58: 489–498.

Gilbert, P. (ed.) (2005) *Compassion: Conceptualisations, Research and Use in Psychotherapy*. London: Routledge.

Gilbert, P. and Leahy, R.L. (2007) *The Therapeutic Relationship in Cognitive Behavioural Psychotherapies*. London: Routledge.

Grant, A., Mills, J., Mulhern, R. and Short, N. (2004) *Cognitive Behavioural Therapy in Mental Health Care*. London: Sage.

Grant, A., Townend, M., Mills, J. and Cockx, A. (2008) *Assessment and Case Formulation in Cognitive Behavioural Therapy*. London: Sage.

Harvey, A., Watkins, E., Mansell, W. and Shafran, R. (2004) *Cognitive-Behavioural Processes Across Psychological Disorders*. Oxford: Oxford University Press.

Hayes, S.C. (2004) 'Acceptance and commitment therapy, relational frame theory, and the third wave of behavioural and cognitive therapies', *Behaviour Therapy*, 35: 639–665.

Katzow, A. and Safran, J.D. (2007) 'Recognising and resolving ruptures in the therapeutic alliance', in P. Gilbert and R.L. Leahy (eds), *The Therapeutic Relationship in the Cognitive and Behavioural Psychotherapies*. Hove: Routledge. pp. 90–105.

Kazantzis, N. and Lampropoulos, G.K. (2002) 'Reflecting on homework in psychotherapy: What can we conclude from research and experience?', *Journal of Clinical Psychology*, 58: 577–585.

Kelly, G. (1955) *The Psychology of Personal Constructs*. New York: W.W. Norton.

Kuyken, W. (2006) 'Evidence-based case formulation: Is the emperor clothed?', in N. Tarrier (ed.), *Case Formulation in Cognitive Behavioural Therapy*. London: Brunner-Routledge. pp. 12–35.

Kuyken, W., Padesky, C. and Dudley, R. (2009) *Collaborative Case Conceptualization*. London: Guilford.

Layard, R. (2006) *The Depression Report. A New Deal for Depression and Anxiety Disorders*. London: Centre for Economic Performance.

Layden, M.A., Newman, C.F., Freeman, A. and Morse, S.B. (1993) *Cognitive Therapy of Borderline Personality Disorder*. Boston, MA: Allyn and Bacon.

Linehan, M., Dimeff, L. and Koerner, K. (eds) (2007) *Dialectical Behavior Therapy in Clinical Practice: Applications Across Disorders and Settings*. New York: Guilford Press.

Merrett, C. and Easton, S. (2008) 'The cognitive-behavioural approach: CBT's big brother', *Counselling Psychology Review*, 23: 21–33.

Nelson-Jones, R. (2005) *The Theory and Practice of Counselling Psychology*, 4th edn. London: Sage.

Padesky, C.A. (1993) 'Socratic questioning: Changing minds or guided discovery?', Keynote address at the European Congress of Behavioural and Cognitive Therapies, London, September 24th.

Padesky, C.A. (1998) Keynote speech, European Association for Behavioural and Cognitive Psychotherapies, Cork, September, 1998.

Padesky, C.A. (2003) 'Guided discovery: Leading and following', audio CD, Centre for Cognitive Therapy, Newport Beach, CA. www.padesky.com.

Rogers, C.R. (1957) 'The necessary and sufficient conditions of therapeutic personality change', *Journal of Consulting and Clinical Psychology*, 21: 95–103.

Roth, A. and Fonagy, P. (2005) *What Works for Whom? A Critical Review of Psychotherapy Research*, 2nd edn. New York: Guilford Press.

Roth, A.D. and Pilling, S. (2007) *The Competences Required to Deliver Effective Cognitive and Behavioural Therapy for People with Depression and with Anxiety Disorders*. London: Department of Health.

Ryle, A. and Kerr, I. (2003) *Introducing Cognitive Analytic Therapy*. Chichester: Wiley.

Safran, J.D. and Segal, Z.V. (1990) *Interpersonal Processes in Cognitive Therapy*. New York: Basic Books.

Salkovskis, P. (2002) 'Empirically grounded clinical interventions: Cognitive-behavioural therapy progresses through a multi-dimensional approach to clinical science', *Behavioural and Cognitive Psychotherapy*, 30: 3–10.

Sanders, D. and Wills, F. (2003) *Counselling for Anxiety Problems*. London: Sage.

Sanders, D. and Wills, F. (2005) *Cognitive Therapy: An Introduction*. London: Sage.

Schon, D. (1983) *The Reflexive Practitioner*. New York: Basic Books.

Segal, Z.V., Williams, J.M.G. and Teasdale, J.D. (2002) *Mindfulness-based Cognitive Therapy for Depression: A New Approach to Preventing Relapse*. New York: Guilford Press.

Sequeira, H. and Van Scoyoc, S. (2001) 'Should counselling psychologists oppose the use of DSM-IV and testing?', *Counselling Psychology Review*, 16: 44–48.

Tarrier, N. (2006) *Case Formulation in Cognitive Behaviour Therapy*. London: Routledge.

Tarrier, N. and Calam, R. (2002) 'New developments in cognitive case formulation. Epidemiological, systemic and social context: an integrative approach', *Behavioural and Cognitive Psychotherapy*, 30(2): 311–328.

Turpin, G. (2007) *Good Practice Guide on the Contribution of Applied Psychologists to Improving Access for Psychological Therapies*. Leicester: BPS.

Wells, A. (1997) *Cognitive Therapy of Anxiety Disorders*. New York: Wiley.

Westbrook, D., Kennerley, H. and Kirk, J. (2007) *An Introduction to Cognitive Behaviour Therapy: Skills and Applications*. London: Sage.

Westbrook, D. and Kirk, J. (2005) 'The clinical effectiveness of cognitive behaviour therapy: Outcome for a large sample of adults treated in routine clinical practice', *Behaviour Research and Therapy*, 43: 1243–1261.

White, J.R. (2000) *Treating Anxiety and Stress: A Group Psychoeducational Approach Using Brief CBT*. Chichester: Wiley.

Williams, M., Teasdale, J., Segal, Z. and Kabat-Zinn, J. (2007) *The Mindful Way Through Depression*. New York: Guildford Press.

Wills, F. (2008) *Skills in Cognitive Behaviour Counselling and Psychotherapy*. London: Sage.

Young, J. and Beck, A.T. (1980) *The Cognitive Therapy Rating Scale Manual*. Philadelphia, PA: Center for Cognitive Therapy, University of Pennsylvania.

7

HUMANISTIC APPROACHES

Simon du Plock

The project of writing a coherent account of 'humanistic approaches' is a challenging one, in terms of determining which therapeutic orientations to include, of identifying common themes within the spectrum of therapeutic approaches which have been grouped under this rubric, and in terms of doing justice to the differences which exist between them. I am, moreover, acutely aware that my trajectory into this field is necessarily idiosyncratic: if I hope to embody the humanistic value of transparency in relationship which will be discussed further below, I need to identify myself at the outset as a counselling psychologist steeped in the existential-phenomenological tradition. While I believe Schoolism (characterized at its most extreme by a denial of the connections between different therapeutic orientations) to be an intellectual cul-de-sac, I own that the description of humanistic approaches that follows is, necessarily, filtered through an existential-phenomenological lens. In the postmodern world, the authoritative authorial voice is always suspect and to be regarded with caution. I am doubtless guilty of numerous omissions and lacunae; I hope that acknowledging my own values and biases enables readers to identify what I have illuminated, and also what I may inadvertently have thrown into shadow in what follows. My approach to writing this chapter parallels the stance of the humanistic practitioner who seeks to meet the client in an open, inquiring and creative way, as a skilful co-researcher of the client's world rather than as an all-knowing expert. The humanistic practitioner accepts a duty to provide the client with 'good enough' boundaries and support to undertake their therapeutic journey, at the same time striving not to enmesh the client in pre-conceived theories or diagnostic categories.

I will begin by suggesting that person-centred, existential-phenomenological and Gestalt psychotherapy constitute core orientations within the humanistic field. While other orientations, such as transactional analysis, might be included, the former three are those which most frequently feature in counselling psychology training programmes. Proponents of these have produced important critiques of each other's theoretical knowledge-bases and clinical practice; in doing so they have evidenced the way in which each operationalizes a fundamental philosophical perspective on what it means to be a human being. We might define this fundamental position as one which foregrounds subjective experience, personal meaning and self-worth. It also subscribes to organizing themes which include the primacy of optimal functioning and authenticity over a concern with objective measurement and notions of psychopathology.

These humanistic approaches offer counselling psychologists the opportunity to contribute to a deep understanding of therapy as fundamentally relational. Counselling psychologists who attempt to embody the values of humanistic approaches to therapy find themselves rethinking the therapeutic alliance and their work with clients in ways which can be characterized as democratic 'being with'. This may be contrasted to ways of working – particularly those influenced by medical models – which are implicitly about 'doing to', and the exercise of 'expert' knowledge to treat clients and promote change, or even 'cure'. Such ways of being a counselling psychologist, of embodying counselling psychology, can provide practitioners with a degree of confidence about their role vis-à-vis the client. Conversely, the adoption by counselling psychologists of a fellow-travelling relationship with clients involves the practitioner in a process of ongoing, sometimes uncomfortable, questioning both of their role and of the nature of therapy per se. It might be argued that this uncertainty – perhaps we might usefully think of it as a process of 'unknowing' – serves to open up a space in which counselling psychologists can rethink the therapeutic endeavour, and in doing so, create their own distinctive identity. This opening up of a space for philosophical exploration of what it means to be a therapist is invaluable for counselling psychologists as they increasingly attempt to formulate a distinctive value set and professional identity.

While the various approaches which have come to be identified as 'humanistic' largely hold a conception of what it means to be human in common, a fault line runs through them. This might, somewhat reductionistically, be thought of as a division between those which emerged from American humanistic psychology of the 1960s and 1970s, and which emphasize human potential, the core 'goodness' of human beings and their innate ability to grow and even self-actualize, and those approaches which owe more to European philosophical investigation of human *being*. Both largely developed in opposition to psychoanalysis, while American practitioners also particularly reacted to what they saw as the limitations of behaviourism. It will be interesting to consider in what follows the extent to which such a fault line can function to maintain critical awareness among humanistic practitioners, and encourage them in fruitful dialogue.

BASIC ASSUMPTIONS

It is probably not helpful to think of humanistic practitioners as proponents of a single or coherent 'humanistic model' since the various strands of thought which can be grouped within the humanistic camp attempt to encounter the client in their own way. That it constitutes a broad spectrum may be viewed as one of the characteristics of humanistic approaches which imbue it with a richness and diversity which can be attractive to potential clients. People seeking assistance with problems of living may feel their experience is mirrored more obviously by the being-qualities of a humanistic practitioner as against, say, a therapist who applies a cognitive-behavioural model or attempts to fit them to a psychoanalytic developmental model.

While there is diversity among humanistic therapists, it is possible to identify a number of basic assumptions, informed by principles of humanism, which unite them:

- *Focus primarily on the 'here and now':* Humanistic practitioners hold that the focus of therapy should be the client's currently lived experience, rather than past influences that may have led up to, or which might be thought to explain, their present position. In this way, practitioners seek to maintain an experiential focus on the 'here and now' of experience. In order to remain at the level of exploration that emphasizes current experience, humanistic therapists strive to focus on descriptive questioning and clarification and seek to avoid analytic questioning which ask 'why' the client feels something or acts in certain ways.
- *A holistic perspective:* Humanistic counselling psychologists tend to concentrate on the 'totality' of the client rather than emphasizing the client's presenting problem. By doing so they avoid a problem-solving orientation, in favour of the exploration of issues and concerns within the client's experience which give rise to, or are expressed as, problems. In this way the therapeutic relationship is able to provide 'the necessary freedom to explore areas of … life that are now denied to awareness or distorted' (Corey, 1991: 210).
- *Acknowledgement of the client's autonomy:* Humanistic therapists see the work of understanding or interpreting the client's experience as the responsibility of the client (assuming they wish to engage in such an endeavour), rather than the therapist. In this way, the therapist attempts to set aside theoretically based assumptions, biases and generalizations about human experience so that the client can be viewed in their uniqueness as generators of distinctive, singularly applicable meanings and world-views. The client is conceptualized as the 'expert' on the client: while they may need assistance in recovering (or even discovering) this basic truth, any attempt on the part of the therapist to take an expert role is likely to diminish the client's ability to become the author of their own life. Humanistic therapy emphasizes the client's freedom and ability to choose how to 'be' and what meanings to live by. In this way humanistic approaches act as a salutary reminder to the counselling psychologist that they should not present themselves as being more capable than clients of discerning or interpreting their experiences.

CONNECTIONS AND DISJUNCTIONS BETWEEN THE HUMANISTIC APPROACHES

I have argued that humanistic approaches hold a broadly phenomenological perspective on the therapeutic alliance in common. Rogers recognized the crucial importance in the therapeutic relationship of the client's perception of the therapist's attitude, and his work has contributed much to counselling psychologists' attempts to break through to those who experience themselves as radically separated from human contact. When the counselling psychologist tries to communicate to the client some of their (the psychologist's) experience of the situation and of the client, the client becomes aware of the phenomenal world of the therapist – which includes them. In Rogers' theory the client, aware of the possibility of being understood, is *ipso facto* less isolated.

There are a number of such links between the phenomenological ground of existential therapy and person-centred therapy. Perhaps most fundamental, as Spinelli has shown, is the use that person-centred therapy makes of the phenomenological notions of *noema* and *noesis* as 'the primary means with which to maintain unconditional positive regard' (1990: 19). This unconditional positive regard is the keystone of Rogers' approach:

> I can state the overall hypothesis in one sentence, as follows. If I can provide a certain type of relationship, the other person will discover within himself the capacity to use that relationship for growth, and change and personal development will occur. (1961: 33)

Unconditional positive regard remains central to person-centred therapy: it is the foundation, for example, of Frankland's (2001) model of person-centred supervision. This type of relationship can only be maintained if the therapist suspends judgement of the client's actions in favour of empathizing with the client's affects, or feelings – a distinction made by the phenomenologist Husserl. He posited that every act of intentionality (every mental act) is composed of two elements, the *noema* (the 'what') towards which we address our attention, and the *noesis* ('how' what happened is interpreted and 'felt'). By utilizing this contribution to phenomenological theory, Rogers was able to maximize the extent to which person-centred therapists are able to give unconditional positive regard.

Alongside these similarities there also exist significant differences – the fault line referred to in my introduction – between person-centred and existential ways of working. While person-centred therapists generally believe they suspend to a great extent their personal judgements about their clients, they do so against the background of a theory of human being which holds that humans are innately disposed to express their potential, and that change in the direction of expressing this potential – of self-actualizing – is central to the therapeutic process. Existential theory provides a critique of this stance on several levels. First, the underlying assumption of person-centred and other humanistic therapies that humans 'naturally' grow and develop, and struggle to do so even in the face of adverse environmental conditions, does not stand up to close scrutiny since while all living things struggle to live there is no reason to believe that they evince a predisposition to self-actualization. While we might agree with Rogers (1961) that potatoes will invariably shoot in the direction of light, we should not confuse the growth of vegetables with the spiritual or psychological life of humans. Further, while both person-centred and existential therapists see human experience as one of constant change and variation, the importance they attach to self-actualization leads them to value clients for their ability to change in this direction – a very different thing from the existential therapist's attempt to engage with clients in order to explore their way of being in the world. As Van Deurzen-Smith notes, 'people may evolve in any direction, good or bad … only reflection on what constitutes good and bad makes it possible to exercise one's choice in the matter' (1988: 56–7).

While the person-centred approach prides itself on its existential roots, it rarely pays due attention to the realities, limitations and consequences of human being in its overly-optimistic emphasis on freedom and potential. Person-centred and other humanistic theorists who attempt to dismiss British and European existentialism as pessimistic are really missing the point – that these approaches provide a healthy corrective to a simplistic view of human nature. The more rounded perspective on what it is to be human that the European tradition, in particular, affords should not be discarded too readily.

Though Rogers has wholeheartedly adopted a number of existential insights on the importance in therapy of relationship, his inspirational, positive-reinforcement mode of working is at variance with basic existential philosophy and so his identification with this approach is necessarily problematic. His own understanding of this is clear when he remarks:

> I was surprised to find, about 1951 … that the direction of my thinking and the central aspects of my therapeutic work could justifiably be labelled existential and phenomenological. It seems odd for an American psychologist to be in such strange company. Today these are significant influences in our profession. (1961: 378)

Rogers was not alone in consorting with 'such strange company': all the humanistic approaches have found themselves to a greater or lesser extent drawn to this philosophy, and each has adopted and adapted those aspects of it with which they felt the greatest sympathy. Fritz and Laura Perls intended the Gestalt therapy which they developed in the 1940s to be a synthesis of various aspects of psychoanalysis, Gestalt psychology and the existential/humanistic tradition. It has been innovative in the importance it accords to the 'here and now', to feeling as well as thinking, and to active awareness rather than the passive reflection of analytic approaches.

It shares, though, many of the difficulties, from an existential perspective, of its fellow humanistic therapies – in particular with regard to its emphasis on self-actualization and in its conception of the self. Kovel, an American commentator, makes the position plain:

> Gestalt therapy is an avowedly existential approach, though with none of the gloom of 'being-in-the-world' that characterizes European existential analysis. Rather it is thoroughly, positively American – positive in its assumption (with Rogers) that the obvious, most consciously held fact is the guide to truth, positive in its assertion that excitement and growth are the key processes of the human organism, and positive in giving active permission for the patient to express, openly and in public, all needs and resentments. (1978: 168)

Fritz Perls expresses his contempt for Freudian concepts of regression and the unconscious even more crisply:

> A good therapist doesn't listen to the content of the bullshit the patient produces, but to the sound, to the music, to the hesitations. (1972: 57)

Most existential therapists agree that a crucial part of therapy involves tuning into the client's world by attending closely not only to what is said, but also to the way in which it is said and, beyond this, to the client's demeanour as a whole. Perls's attitude to clients tended to be somewhat authoritarian, and he largely discounted the dynamics of the therapist–client relationship.

Gestalt therapy has been open to the criticism that its concern with the 'here-and-now' (a term first used, in fact, by the psychoanalyst Otto Rank) precludes any consideration of past or of future. Such de-emphasis on the client's temporal context is fraught with difficulties, as the phenomenologist Merleau-Ponty pointed out:

> Each present reasserts the presence of the whole past which it supplants, and anticipates that of all that is to come, and that by definition the present is not shut up within itself, but transcends itself towards a future and a past. (1962: 240)

The Gestalt Prayer, with its exhortation that each individual should take responsibility for getting their own needs met, is certainly far removed from the 'gloom of being-in-the-world':

> I do my thing, and you do your thing.
> I am not in this world to live up to your expectations.
> And you are not in this world to live up to mine.
> You are you, and I am I.
> And if by chance we find each other, it's beautiful.
> If not, it can't be helped.
> (Perls, 1976: 4)

There remains much work to be done to map precisely the areas of convergence and divergence between phenomenology and Gestalt therapy, but Clarkson (2000) has made an important contribution to this debate.

THE NATURE OF THE CLIENT–COUNSELLING PSYCHOLOGIST RELATIONSHIP

The nature of the client–counselling psychologist relationship lies at the heart of the therapeutic endeavour. Indeed, it may be more accurate to refer to the way in which two people (in the case of individual therapy) *encounter* each other and create a space in which both are able to come to a greater awareness of the way they create meaning in the world. Though the role of the counselling psychologist is to facilitate the client in clarifying their values and ways of being, they will themselves be changed by entering into relationship with the other.

A humanistic stance towards therapy seeks to promote a client–therapist relationship characterized by transparency rather than authoritative imposition and covert agendas. While there has been much debate among practitioners regarding the extent to which it is helpful or appropriate for the therapist to disclose personal attitudes, feelings or conflicts that arise from the encounter, such disclosure is not seen as invariably problematic as it is in those approaches which prioritize the application of a model over the therapist–client relationship. Psychoanalytic psychotherapy provides an important departure from this norm since here therapists resist disclosure but do prioritize relationship – albeit transferential relationship.

This transparency is indicative of a therapeutic approach which views the curative or positive benefits of therapy as arising from within the therapeutic process itself. Such a position requires that counselling psychologists adopt an accepting and caring stance towards the client, express congruent or genuine attitudes, and are able to accurately reflect the subjective experience of the client so that it is opened up to non-defensive exploration. This view is most fully expressed in person-centred therapy, with its emphasis on 'being', or attitudinal, attributes as both necessary and sufficient for a beneficial therapeutic encounter. These values run through all the humanistic approaches: Gestalt therapists, for example, often use skills-based techniques designed to promote self-challenge or emotional discharge, while emphasizing the therapist's 'being qualities' as essential constituents of the process which provide the necessary qualitative variables for the techniques to be both appropriate and successful.

Humanistic approaches hold that the problems or presenting symptoms that clients bring to therapy reveal an underlying experience of incongruence at the level of self-concept. As such, clients' own awareness of themselves is understood as being fundamentally divided in a variety of ways, all of which are focused on the self. So, for instance, clients may experience incongruence between the current view they hold of themselves and their ideal self, or between the self they believe they 'must' be as opposed to the self that 'is' (person-centred therapy); or they may have 'disowned', dissociated or depersonalized unacceptable, painful or contradictory aspects of their self (Gestalt therapy); or they may experience a disjunction between the way they experience themselves in the world and their self-construct, or story, they tell themselves about who they are (existential therapy). Seen in this way, the task of the humanistic counselling psychologist becomes that of integration, either by providing the means for increased self-congruence, or self-acceptance and validation, or a greater willingness and ability to 'own' one's experience.

CHANGE

Person-centred therapists view change as the outcome of a specific type of relationship – one in which certain attitudes and values, generally termed the 'core-conditions' – are actively communicated. The person-centred therapist must be able to empathically understand the client's subjective frame of reference, be an active transmitter of non-judgemental positive regard to the client, and stay real and genuine within the relationship. This relationship provides the conditions in which the client can become intensely aware of the incongruencies between their self-concept, with its internalized conditions of worth, and actual experience. As Kovel, in his classic 1978 text, states:

> The therapist tries neither to actively change this nor to interpretatively explain it … he merely reflects it back to the client filtered through his own subjectively benign state of unconditional regard – regard not for what a person does or says, but for what he *is*, for the wholeness within. (1978: 160, 161)

Rogers (1961) viewed change not as a discrete event but as a process whereby clients become progressively less defensive and more open to experiencing. Gillon describes this notion of change as being:

> not from one fixed state to another, but from a fixity in experiencing (i.e. rigid way of thinking/feeling) to a changingness (i.e. an openness to feelings and thoughts). Hence, effective therapy does not necessarily result in a client feeling 'good' about everything, but instead envisages that she is increasingly open to all her experiencing, able to accept it as a legitimate aspect of her personhood. (2007: 69)

As people are viewed within the existential approach as constantly in process, and without a fixed and permanent essence, the one thing of which we can be certain is that we are always changing. Clients generally enter therapy saying that they want to change, but it quickly becomes apparent in the context of the therapeutic relationship that they expend considerable energy attempting to maintain a stable sense of self and are, in fact, highly resistant to the possibility of being different. Why should this be so? For existential therapists the answer is that the possibility of change, of choosing to be other, provokes considerable anxiety. The role of the counselling psychologist is not, then, to encourage the client to change, but is to support them to reflect on the way they are living their life and creating themselves by choosing one way of being over another. This choice is seen as a constant process which occurs for all of us as we go about our daily business. Therapy can create a space for clients to pause in their habitual routines and consider how these either open up possibilities for engaging with life or close possibilities down.

Clients often experience themselves as having quite limited opportunities to exercise their freedom to choose how to be. Addiction provides an example of a presenting problem which is intimately linked with such a restricted sense of freedom. Humanistic counselling psychologists will focus on the particular ways in which the unique self-construct of their client functions to both open up and limit their 'way-of-being-in-the-world'. They engage in this process of clarification with the client not with the intention of helping them 'move on' in some way, but to enable them to engage as fully as possible in the therapy so that both of them can 'see what is there'. When the client can truly see the way they have constructed their 'way-of-being-in-the-world', they may elect to modulate it. (This is not, though, to underestimate how difficult this is likely to be, nor the degree of support they may require from the therapeutic alliance).

It might be objected that the counselling psychologist is duty-bound to direct the client towards accepting that their present behaviour is in some way injurious or dysfunctional and that, particularly when a client presents seeking to free themselves from an addiction, they must 'do' something to bring this about. Existential therapists counter that when the client is in a position to appreciate their role in creating their self-construct, they are also in a position to reflect on any changes they wish to make. The therapist will then be faced with the challenge of journeying with the client as they recover (or even discover for the first time) their freedom, and its attendant existential anxiety. There is a temptation on the part of therapists to, as Heidegger (1927) describes it, 'leap in' (*Einspringen*) to rescue clients in distress, rather than 'leap ahead' (*Vorspringen*) to return them to their responsibility for their self. The former, which can be thought of as the 'lifeboat' approach to therapy, *may* pull the client out of deep water, but does not enable them to reflect on how they navigate their way through life in order to avoid future perils. It may, worse, suggest to the client that there is an 'ultimate rescuer' at hand, and that they do not therefore need to strive to recover their own agency.

Such an attempt on the part of the therapist to 'be with' rather than 'do to' the client entails a qualitatively different encounter with the client's being, compared with that which is generally the case in working with addiction. It is more common for the therapist to relate to the client as an expert rather than enter directly and whole-heartedly into a relationship. The existential therapist must accept the obvious but discomforting fact that they are a part of the client's relational world.

This form of challenging engagement, if it is really to be an authentic relationship, demands much, perhaps as much, from the therapist as from the client. This reciprocal encounter with difference will lead them to question their own way of being and their own sedimented (fixed) beliefs about the world. It is crucial that the therapist monitors their response to this challenge and is open to exploration of the way they attempt to limit or dissociate this challenge.

We can make a more radical statement yet: we can say that the therapists need, if they are truly to enter the lived-world of the client to the greatest extent they are able, to accept values and beliefs that they may find alien or even repugnant. Because this is so, and may particularly be so when we meet with behaviour which seems purely negative and destructive, as is often the case when working with addiction, the therapeutic enterprise presents the opportunity for clarification for both parties. The therapist who seeks to enter the client's world via the acceptance of such beliefs and values *in the context of the client's world-view* opens themselves to the clarification of their own self-construct in a process which is remarkably similar to that which the client attempts.

An existential-phenomenological perspective on counselling psychology directs attention to the therapists' ways of 'being with' the client, rather than 'doing things to' them. While it is the quality of the relationship counselling psychologist and client co-create, which is held to be the *sine qua non* of therapy, it is helpful to think about certain key themes and skills which can inform and promote the work.

SKILLS AND STRATEGIES

Humanistic practitioners strive to enter into relationship with clients in a spirit of collaborative enquiry into the client's world-view. They are concerned to maintain an unbiased attitude which will enable the client to become increasingly aware of the way they are open, or closed, to the opportunities life presents. The cultivation of such a naïve attitude is supported by the phenomenological reduction, first formulated by Husserl and since adapted (Ihde, 1986; Spinelli, 1989) as: the rule of epoché, or bracketing, which requires us to set aside assumptions and biases; the rule of description, which requires us to describe rather than explain; and the rule of equalization, or horizontalization, which requires that we are open to all phenomena equally and do not order them according to our own sense of their importance. The consistent application of these three rules should be understood as a goal which the humanistic counselling psychologist will never attain. The attempt to do so, though, is fundamental to their endeavour to assist the client in uncovering what makes the client's world meaningful to them.

Human beings are always emotionally attuned to the world and attention to the client's emotions assists in clarifying their relationship with the world. Gaining a picture of this attunement will invariably lead on to clarification of the client's beliefs, values and their way of dealing with limitations. In bracketing their own assumptions and meanings about the client, the counselling psychologist models an attitude of curiosity for the client, who may, in turn, become curious about their self. The counselling psychologist is concerned to illuminate not only areas of difficulty, but also strengths and talents of which they may be unaware. At the same time he or she will take care to challenge the client where they fall into self-deception by denying their freedom. The client's memories of the past, their sense of the present and their vision of the future are all understood in terms of the life narrative, or story, clients tell themselves about themselves. The past is not seen as determining the present and future; rather, the client is considered to be an author of their own life, who might recollect themselves in new ways. Any emphasis on techniques at the expense of authentic relationship is anathema to both 'Rogerian' and existential approaches. Van Deurzen-Smith, while counselling against ways of working which rely on technique over description and exploration, has identified a number of major therapeutic strategies and techniques, including ways of cultivating a naïve attitude, identifying implicit themes, clarifying the subjective meaning of the client's choice of words, and exploring the client's values and deeply-held beliefs (1990: 12–14). Lobb and Amendt-Lyon note that Gestalt therapists draw on a wide spectrum of possible therapeutic interventions, which may include artistic materials and methods from both fine and performing arts. They remind us of Laura Perls' assertion that:

> Gestalt therapists may include a tremendous variety of therapeutic interventions in their work as long as these are *existential*, *experiential*, and *experimental*, and provided that adequate support for the experiment can be mobilized. Thus it is necessary to work phenomenologically, organizing recognized patterns into meaningful wholes, to be present-centred, and to spontaneously create custom-tailored experiments that will support figure formation within therapeutic interactions. (2003: viii–ix)

ASSESSMENT

Humanistic counselling psychologists mount a strong critique of assessment on philosophical and practical grounds. They argue that such formal assessment is based on a false dichotomy between health and illness, lack conceptual and predictive validity, and largely fail to capture the rich texture of the lived-world of clients. Humanistic practitioners are also concerned that attempts to diagnose the client will undermine those democratic and subjective elements of the therapeutic alliance which are held to be the most significant for positive outcome, however defined. For McLeod (1997a), the single area of humanistic work where assessment has a place is that where counselling psychologist and client together consider whether to make a commitment to work together. This is done on the basis of awareness and interpersonal skills, and does not rely on the use of diagnostic tools.

Rowan (2001) has highlighted an important contribution by Gestalt therapists to our way of thinking about assessment. He gives the example of Melnick and Nevis' work, which accepts the notion of assessment, but rethinks it in a way more congruent with Gestalt values:

> Consistent with the here-and-now focus on change is the Gestalt tendency to diagnose with verbs and not nouns. Seeing the world in an active and therefore potentially changing way, the clinician chooses words that emphasize behaviour. Thus, the description is of 'obsessing' rather than 'obsessive'. (Melnick and Nevis, 1998: 430)

Similarly, they argue for assessment as an ongoing process rather than a single event:

> Traditionally, Gestalt therapists have diagnosed by paying attention to the phenomenon in the moment. At some point an aspect of behaviour becomes interesting, something stands out, and a pattern emerges. The pattern might lead to a diagnostic statement such as, 'The patient appears to be retroflecting' (constricting his or her emotions). The remaining therapeutic work in that session might be focused on that retroflection. (Melnick and Nevis, 1998: 431)

Person-centred therapists argue that psychological distress has a single cause: lack of congruence between a person's self-image and their lived experience. This incongruence will have unique consequences for each client, thus making predictions on the basis of traditional diagnostic models irrelevant. They may, though, undertake assessment to determine the likelihood that they and the potential client will be able to form a person-centred relationship (Wilkins, 2005).

FAMILY, GROUP AND ORGANIZATIONAL APPLICATIONS

The focus of humanistic psychology on personal growth and empowerment has led to its wide employment by counselling psychologists engaged in private practice, where they may be working with individuals, but are also likely to work with couples and, to a lesser extent, families. The emphasis on the personal qualities of the counselling psychologist, such as their warmth, honesty and empathy, and on their ability to form and maintain the therapeutic alliance, has made this approach particularly attractive in the context of voluntary agencies.

While independence was posited by Carl Rogers as a key concept in defining psychological well-being, person-centred therapists have moved towards a more comprehensive theory of the human condition in the shape of 'family-centred therapy' for use with couples and families (Gaylin, 2001). Their shift from describing their approach as 'client-centred' to using instead the descriptor 'person-centred' is indicative of the extent to which Rogerian ideas about therapy and human development have been recognized as significant beyond psychotherapy. Such a holistic approach, which focuses on persons rather than the things they produce, offers a critique of contemporary life in the West. Natiello (2001) argues that person-centred practitioners are well-placed to offer alternatives to increasingly dysfunctional authoritarian structures in the workplace. She quotes Fletcher:

> The organization of the future … will need to move from hierachical systems of production and control to more team-based structures and reward systems … where information is shared freely and openly across divisions and functional barriers. These organizations will need a new kind of worker, one that is a continuous learner as well as a continuous teacher, who is willing to take responsibility for problems and work collaboratively with others to solve them. (1999: 2)

O'Leary (1999) provides a coherent integration of person-centred concepts and couple and family therapy.

A 'humanistic-experiential model' has been utilized for work with families and with highly disturbed clients (Lietaer et al., 1990; Greenberg et al., 1998; Lago and MacMillan, 1999). Humanistic therapy is increasingly seen as effective in work with clients presenting with complex conditions, including personality disorder. Many models of group work and organizational development have drawn heavily on humanistic theory, and humanistic ideas have been applied to a range of social and political problems (for example, Rogers, 1978). Person-centred groupwork is interesting for the way it functions as therapy for groups themselves, in response to the society-wide breakdown of social relationships. Natiello (2001) has propounded a way of thinking about groups as complex, living systems, which can be partially understood with the use of systems theory.

Existential theory's concern with the 'universals' of human existence as much as with individual experience has enabled its proponents to move beyond restrictive labels which categorize individuals in order to make significant contributions to the literature on the diversity of living as expressed in terms of culture, ethnicity, gender and sexuality. A number of existential writers have gone beyond illustrating ways of applying the existential approach to various ways of being human, and have begun to clarify psychological factors significant to any therapeutic work with such diversity. Van Deurzen has highlighted the value of the approach when working with young people who are attempting to create an identity, and people who are moving between cultures (1998). Eleftheriadou (1993), Asmall (1997) and Vontress and Epp (2001) have expanded on the potential for existential therapy with multicultural counselling. The founding fathers of existential therapy generally viewed sexuality as an aspect of choice, embodiment or freedom. More recently, British School existential theorists (Spinelli, 1997; Cohn, 1997; du Plock, 1998; Smith-Pickard, 2006) have been innovative in presenting an understanding of human sexuality and sexual orientation which transcend limited medically derived approaches which emphasize 'normality' and deviation from the norm.

Given the appreciation of the social world, or *mitwelt*, which underpins existential philosophy and therapy, it is perhaps surprising that, until recently, clinical practice has been almost entirely limited to individual therapy. Ludwig Binswanger, often referred to as the 'father' of 'existential psychiatry', was intimately concerned with family dynamics in producing his phenomenological analyses of the worlds inhabited by his individual patients. R.D. Laing's classic analysis (1969; Laing and Esterson, 1964) of family dynamics continues to be influential among existential therapists, though his work now receives little attention in the wider therapeutic community. Laing provides a critique of psychiatry rather than an account of clinical work with families. Yalom (1995) is influential in existential group therapy, though his approach owes much to person-centred therapy. The existential literature has been enriched by Hans W. Cohn's (1997) remarkably clear elucidation of an existential approach to group work which builds on Foulkes' (1964, 1975) group-analytic approach. Adams (2006) has provided perhaps the first succinct outline of an existential developmental theory.

Existential theorists have been astute at identifying the relevance of this approach to emerging areas of new and inter-disciplinary practice such as philosophical counselling and philosophical consulting (du Plock, 1999). Perhaps the most significant such development will be the impact of existential approaches (Strasser and Randolph, 2004) to the rapidly forming fields of coaching and mentoring; this promises to extend the influence of existential practice into areas which have not previously drawn to any great extent on therapeutic insights. The focus on 'meaning creation' and values makes the humanistic approaches particularly relevant for the development of business and executive coaching. As an example, Nevis (2001) has propounded ways of using Gestalt therapy to increase the creativity of corporate organizations.

RESEARCH

It is interesting to note that Rogers, together with colleagues at Ohio and Chicago, conducted among the earliest controlled outcome studies of psychotherapy and counselling in the 1940s and 1950s (Cartwright, 1957; Rogers and Dymond, 1954). Utilizing the Q-sort technique, these studies provided evidence of changes in self-concept as a result of person-centred therapy. The perceived self is more closely aligned with the ideal self, while the self as perceived becomes more comfortable and adjusted. Subsequent research has emphasized therapy outcomes less, as person-centred researchers have moved towards a phenomenological perspective which views 'outcome' as problematic:

We have come to the conclusion that 'success', no matter how it is phrased or described, is not a usable or useful criterion for research in psychotherapy … in every meaningful way we have given up the concept of 'success' as the criterion against which our research measurements will be compared. (Rogers and Dymond, 1954: 29)

During the next two decades, the majority of research focused on evaluations of Rogers' (1957) 'necessary and sufficient conditions' process model, rather than on the outcome research to be found in the universities. This may be in part a reflection of the core values of person-centred therapy and its critique of empiricist psychology (Georgi, 1987). A small but significant number of outcome studies have been completed. Horvath and Greenberg in their 1994 review of this literature, found strong evidence for the efficacy of humanistic approaches. There remains a need for further research to evaluate effectiveness with different client groups. As recently as 1997, McLeod was able to state that an:

absence of research activity places humanistic counselling psychologists at a growing disadvantage in a market place that increasingly demands accountability and evidence in relation to tightly defined groups or presenting problems. (McLeod, 1997a: 154)

Person-centred therapists have been energetic in response to this lack of empirical evidence to the extent that Cooper et al. (2007) are able to cite research findings which reposition their approach at the leading edge of evidence-based practice. They argue that person-centred therapy 'today has a depth and enjoys a variety of theoretical explanatory models that would make it the envy of many other therapeutic disciplines' (2007: xxi). Much of the significant research which has been completed has focused on the efficacy of the core conditions of person-centred therapy (Toukmanian and Hakim, 2007); their findings, in so far as they address the relational aspects of therapy, are relevant for practitioners of all theoretical orientations. Zimring (2000) has produced evidence of strong correlation between empathic understanding and the outcome of therapy; in their research study, Farber and Lane (2002) generate evidence for a statistically significant correlation between positive regard and therapy outcome. Elliott (2001) has developed a particularly innovative approach to case-study method, incorporating outcome measures and qualitative interviews, which allow him to generate evidence for the effectiveness of person-centred interventions. For an overview of research into the person-centred approach, readers are referred to Gillon (2007).

   Research has not until recently played a significant role in the development of gestalt therapy. It may be that an 'early, anti-intellectual bias meant that little academic research has been completed' (Ellis and Leary-Joyce, 2000). This situation has begun to change as a result of the movement of gestalt training institutes to university validation, and the concomitant requirement that trainees evidence the ability to undertake research on their approach.

It is remarkable that little over a decade ago Irvin Yalom was able, whilst considering revising his major text *Existential Psychotherapy*, to reject the plan, believing there to be no tradition of an evolving literature, no research to update and to review. It is often assumed that existential-phenomenological therapists have not conducted research on their approach because they are antagonistic to research per se. The existential-phenomeno-logical tradition, like the humanistic therapies, has until recently been found for historical reasons mainly outside the universities. There is still, consequently, more concentration on dissemination through pedagogy than on accumulation of knowledge via research, as has been the case in psychology since Wundt. Much depends, though, on what we mean when we use the word 'research', and this is a question which a therapy grounded in phi-losophy is well-placed to raise. A considerable amount of research may be said to exist in the form of case studies, and existential therapists increasingly conceptualize case work as research in practice in which the client is co-researcher. There is also a substantial, and grow-ing, body of qualitative research by trainees, many of whom utilize variations on standard empirical phenomenology (Colaizzi, 1978; Moustakas, 1994; Smith, 2003).

While it is the case that there exists remarkably little direct outcome research in exis-tential psychotherapy and counselling, a surprising amount of indirect evidence may be garnered from studies where existential factors are shown to be related to 'positive' out-comes (Bergin and Garfield, 1994), or from qualitative studies undertaken by researchers from other modalities (Rennie, 1992). Yalom's well-known conversion to existential therapy in his work with groups was a consequence of his early research on client change. Existential therapists have begun to take notice of research by therapists who are not explicitly existential-phenomenological in their orientation. As an example, the work of Johnstone (1992) provides considerable support for Laing's thesis that family dynamics rather than inherited genes play a significant, if not decisive, role in the devel-opment of schizophrenia. Research undertaken by person-centred therapists on those aspects of the person-centred approach (such as the therapist's ability to be genuine and authentic in the therapeutic relationship) which are shared with existential therapy, provide further indirect evidence of effectiveness. A number of innovative and relatively recent perspectives within qualitative research can have a useful dialogue with the existential-phenomenological approach. Among these may be counted the cluster of transpersonal research methods (Braud and Anderson, 1998), social-constructionist theory and discourse analysis (Potter et al., 1990) and narrative research (Josselson and Lieblich, 1999).

It may be that, in the past, existential-phenomenological therapists were mainly to be found in private practice where there was (relatively) less pressure to produce research. Therapists are increasingly finding that they need to build a portfolio of part-time appointments. Quality assurance, funding competition and ethical concerns in provider organizations tend to promote research, though not necessarily of an innovative nature. More recently pressure on counselling psychologists to produce evidence-based research themselves has led to an important debate in the existential community. This debate has not been about whether to engage in research or reject such activity as alien to existential therapy; rather, it has taken a creative turn as practitioners have come to ask what sort of research is congruent with, and supportive of, existential therapy. In the process of addressing this question, existential theorists have made a significant contribution to wider debate about the nature of qualitative research (Churchill and Wertz, 2001; Georgi, 1985; Karlsson, 1993).

Counselling psychology as a new professional grouping is itself engaged in discussion about what constitutes appropriate research and is open to questioning the notion of the scientist-practitioner as the single way forward. Existential therapists, perhaps because of their inherently sceptical stance to the world, are drawn to those arenas where debate about the nature and purpose of the therapeutic endeavour are located, and this arena is currently that of counselling psychology.

Existential counselling psychologists are well placed to critique published research. McLeod has drawn attention to the inevitability that writers 'impose a simplifying structure' when they report the lived experience of therapy:

> Freud constructs an account of therapy as if he was a detective: many cognitive-behavioural writers produce accounts written as if they were primarily scientists, and so on. The potential danger here is that the genre gets mistaken for the actuality. (1997b: 163)

A phenomenological perspective enables the researcher to uncover the assumptions implicit in the text, and to notice the ways in which 'unbiased' commentators re-write their clients according to their own script (du Plock, 1993).

Existential practitioners need to undertake research to clarify their position in relation to other orientations. Such research might both indicate what distinguishes existential-phenomenological therapy in terms of content and applicability, and say something useful about the nature of therapy itself. Outcome research is problematic for existential practitioners since they view success very differently compared with many other orientations, but this does not exclude them from research; rather, it spurs them to create forms of research congruent with their approach.

Qualitative researchers are increasingly recognizing the value of broadly phenomenological research methodology to investigate subjective experience of all forms of therapy, not just existential therapy. Some existential therapists have used phenomenological research methodology to investigate aspects of existential practice; examples of this are Kasket's (2003) work on the use of technology in existential practice and du Plock's (2008) research on the implications for existential therapists of a diagnosis of chronic illness. Research undertaken with the explicit purpose of investigating the efficacy of existential-phenomenological therapy is also on the increase. Though the number of such explorations is small, they may have a significant impact. Among current projects, de Sousa's investigation of therapist and client experience of significant events occurring during the therapeutic process may be noted. Readers who seek more detailed discussion of existential–phenomenological research methodology are referred to Colaizzi (1978), Georgi (1985), Mahrer and Boulet (2004), Moustakas (2001), Polkinghorne (1999) and Spinelli (2001).

CONCLUSION

The current political climate presents humanistic therapists with a number of challenges, principally with regard to engaging with demands for evidence-based practice. As we have seen, humanistic practitioners have a tradition of undertaking research congruent with their core values. They are able to raise important questions about the nature of research and lead the way in re-visioning research in ways which pay appropriate attention to the subjective world of the client, and to the nature of the co-constructed therapeutic alliance. The role of critic is a tradition for humanistic practitioners: therapists began to draw on existential philosophy in response to what they perceived as deficits in psychoanalytic theory; person-centred therapy emerged as a 'third force' to counter-balance objectification of what it means to be human; Gestalt therapy developed out of the need to engage with the emotional life of a whole person, rather than reduce them to a collection of psychological structures. It looks probable that such a holistic perspective will not find favour in an environment which defines evidence of therapeutic efficacy in terms of throughput and statistics. At the same time, it is important to remember that we practice in a world characterized above all else by constant change – it will be important for humanistic therapists to think about the shape of therapy over the next decades. It will also be important to be alert to opportunities to build bridges between humanistic approaches and those such as cognitive behaviour therapy which are, themselves, in a process of change and development. Perhaps the most crucial challenge for counselling psychologists who identify with orientations within the humanistic movement over the next decades will be to find ways to come together as a creative community, visible and attractive to potential clients, whether individuals, couples, groups or organizations. In doing so, such counselling psychologists will safeguard the concern to attend to *human being* which should constitute the core of any authentically therapeutic practice.

REFERENCES

Adams, M. (2006) 'Towards an existential phenomenological model of life span human development', *Existential Analysis*, 17 (2): 261–280.
Asmall, I. (1997) 'Existentialism, existential psychotherapy and African philosophy', *Existential Analysis*, 8 (2): 138–52.

Bergin, A., and Garfield, S. (1994) *Handbook of Psychotherapy and Behavior Change*. New York: Wiley.

Braud, W. and Anderson, R. (1998) *Transpersonal Research Methods for the Social Sciences: Honoring Human Experience*. Thousand Oaks, CA: Sage.

Cartwright, D.S. (1957) 'Annotated bibliography of research and theory construction in client-centered therapy', *Journal of Counseling Psychology*, 4 (1): 82–100.

Churchill, S.D. and Wertz, F.J. (2001) 'An introduction to phenomenological research in psychology: Historical, conceptual, and methodological foundations', in K.J. Schneider, J.F.T. Bugental and J.F. Pierson (eds), *The Handbook of Humanistic Psychology*. London: Sage.

Clarkson, P. (2000) *Gestalt Counselling in Action*, 2nd edn. London: Sage.

Cohn, H.W. (1997) *Existential Thought and Therapeutic Practice*. London: Sage.

Colaizzi, P.F. (1978) 'Psychological research as the phenomenologist views it', in R.S. Valle and M. King (eds), *Existential-Phenomenological Alternatives for Psychology*. New York: Oxford University Press.

Cooper, M., O'Hara, M., Schmid, P.F. and Wyatt, G. (2007) *The Handbook of Person-Centred Psychotherapy and Counselling*. Basingstoke: Palgrave Macmillan.

Corey, G. (1991) *Theory and Practice of Counseling and Psychotherapy*. Pacific Grove, CA: Brooks/Cole.

du Plock, S. (1993) 'Dialogue or diatribe? A brief comparison of the implications for client – therapist interaction of existential and cognitive analytic approaches', *Existential Analysis*, 4: 91–107.

du Plock, S. (1998) 'Sexual misconceptions: A critique of gay affirmative therapy and some thoughts on an existential-phenomenological theory of sexual orientation', *Existential Analysis*, 8 (2): 56–71.

du Plock, S. (1999) 'Today we have naming of parts: On the possibility of dialogue between philosophical counselling and existential psychotherapy', *Existential Analysis*, 10 (1): 72–81.

du Plock, S. (2008) 'Living ME: Some reflections on the experience of being diagnosed with a chronic "psycho-somatic" illness', *Existential Analysis*, 19 (1): 46–57.

Eleftheriadou, Z. (1993) 'Applications of a philosophical framework to transcultural therapy', *Existential Analysis*, 4: 116–23.

Elliott, R. (2001) 'Hermeneutic single-case efficacy design: An overview', in K.J. Schneider, J.F.T. Bugenthal and J.F. Pierson (eds), *The Handbook of Humanistic Therapies*. Thousand Oaks, CA: Sage.

Ellis, M. and Leary-Joyce, J. (2000) 'Gestalt therapy', in C. Feltham and I. Horton (eds), *Handbook of Counselling and Psychotherapy*. London: Sage. pp. 337–340.

Farber, B.A. and Lane, J.S. (2002) 'Positive regard', in J.C. Norcross (ed.), *Psychotherapy Relationships That Work*. Oxford: Oxford University Press. pp. 175–194.

Fletcher, J.K. (1999) *Disappearing Acts: Gender, Power, and Relational Practice at Work*. Cambridge: MIT Press.

Foulkes, S.H. (1964) *Therapeutic Group Analysis*. London: Karnac.

Foulkes, S.H. (1975) *Group-Analytic Psychotherapy: Method and Principles*. London: Karnac.

Frankland, A. (2001) 'A person-centred model of supervision', *Counselling Psychology Review*, 16 (4): 26–31.

Gaylin, N. (2001) *Family, Self and Psychotherapy: A Person-Centred Perspective*. Ross-on-Wye: PCCS.

Georgi, A. (ed.) (1985) *Phenomenological and Psychological Research*. Pittsburgh, PA: Duquesne University Press.

Georgi, A. (1987) 'The crisis of humanistic psychology', *Humanistic Psychologist*, 15 (1): 5–20.

Gillon, E. (2007) *Person-Centred Counselling Psychology: An Introduction*. London: Sage.

Greenberg, L.S., Watson, J.C. and Lietaer, G. (eds) (1998) *Handbook of Experiential Psychotherapy*. New York: Guilford Press.

Heidegger, M. (1927/1978) *Being and Time*. Oxford: Blackwell.

Horvath, A.O. and Greenberg, L.S. (eds) (1994) *The Working Alliance. Theory, Research, and Practice.* Chichester: Wiley and Sons.

Ihde, D. (1986) *Experimental Phenomenology: An Introduction.* Albany, NY: State University of New York Press.

Johnstone, L. (1992) 'Family management in schizophrenia: Its assumptions and contradictions', *Journal of Mental Health*, 2: 255–269.

Josselson, R. and Lieblich, A. (1999) *Making Meaning of Narratives.* Thousand Oaks, CA: Sage.

Karlsson, G. (1993) *Psychological Qualitative Research from a Phenomenological Perspective.* Stockholm: Almqvist & Wiksell.

Kasket, E. (2003) 'Online counselling: Some considerations for existential-phenomenological practitioners', *Existential Analysis*, 14 (1): 60–74.

Kovel, J. (1978) *A Complete Guide to Therapy: From Psychoanalysis to Behaviour Modification.* London: Pelican.

Lago, C. and MacMillan, M. (eds) (1999) *Experiences in Relatedness: Groupwork and the Person-Centered Approach.* Ross-on-Wye: PCCS.

Laing, R.D. (1969) *Self and Others,* 2nd edn. London: Penguin.

Laing, R.D. and Esterson, A. (1964) *Sanity, Madness and the Family.* Harmondsworth: Penguin.

Lietaer, G., Rombauts, J. and Van Balen, R. (eds) (1990) *Client-Centered and Experiential Therapy in the Nineties.* Leuven: University of Leuven Press.

Lobb, M.S. and Amendt-Lyon, N. (eds) (2003) *Creative License: The Art of Gestalt Therapy.* Vienna: Springer.

Mahrer, A. and Boulet, D.B. (2004) 'How can existentialists do research on psychotherapy?', *Existential Analysis*, 15 (1): 15–28.

McLeod, J. (1997a) 'The humanistic paradigm', in R. Woolfe (ed.), *Handbook of Counselling Psychology,* 3rd edn. London: Sage. pp. 140–160.

McLeod, J. (1997b). 'Reading, writing and research', in I. Horton and V. Varma (eds), *The Needs of Counsellors and Psychotherapists.* London: Sage. pp. 152–165.

Melnick, J. and Nevis, S.M. (1998) 'Diagnosing in the here and now: A Gestalt therapy approach', in L.S. Greenberg, J.C. Watson and G. Lietaer (eds), *Handbook of Experiential Psychotherapy.* New York: Guilford Press.

Merleau-Ponty, M. (1962) *The Phenomenology of Perception.* London: Routledge.

Moustakas, C. (1994) *Phenomenological Research Methods.* London: Sage.

Moustakas, C. (2001) 'Heuristic research: Design and methodology', in K.J. Schneider, J.F.T. Bugental and J.F. Pierson (eds), *The Handbook of Humanistic Psychology: Leading Edges in Theory, Research and Practice.* London: Sage. pp. 263–274.

Natiello, P. (2001) *The Person-Centred Approach: A Passionate Presence.* Ross-on-Wye: PCCS.

Nevis, E.C. (2001) *Organizational Consulting: A Gestalt Approach.* Cambridge, MA: Gestalt Press.

O'Leary, C.J. (1999) *Counselling Couples and Families: A Person-Centred Approach.* London: Sage.

Perls, F. (1972) *Gestalt Therapy Verbatim.* New York: Bantam.

Perls, F. (1976) *The Gestalt Approach and Eye Witness to Therapy.* New York: Bantam.

Polkinghorne, D.E. (1999) 'Traditional research and psychotherapy practice', *Journal of Clinical Psychology*, 55 (12): 1429–1440.

Potter, J., Wetherell, M., Gill, R. and Edwards, D. (1990) 'Discourse: Noun, verb or social practice?', *Philosophical Psychology*, 3 (2): 205–217.

Rennie, D.L. (1992) 'Qualitative analysis of the client's experience of psychotherapy: The unfolding of reflexivity', in S.G. Toukmanian and D.L. Rennie (eds), *Psychotherapy Process Research: Paradigmatic and Narrative Approches.* London: Sage.

Rogers, C.R. (1957) 'The necessary and sufficient conditions of therapeutic personality change', *Journal of Consulting Psychology*, 21: 95–103.

Rogers, C.R. (1961) *On Becoming a Person: A Therapist's View of Psychotherapy*. London: Constable.

Rogers, C.R. (1978) *Carl Rogers on Personal Power: Inner Strength and its Revolutionary Impact*. London: Constable.

Rogers, C.R. and Dymond, R.F. (eds) (1954) *Psychotherapy and Personality Change: Co-ordinated Research Studies in the Client-Centered Approach*. Chicago, IL: University of Chicago Press.

Rowan, J. (2001) *Ordinary Ecstasy: The Dialectics of Humanistic Psychology*. Hove: Brunner-Routledge.

Smith, J.A. (ed.) (2003) *Qualitative Psychology: A Practical Guide to Research* Methods. London: Sage.

Smith-Pickard, P. (2006) '*Transference as existential sexuality*', *Existential Analysis*, 17 (2): 224–237.

Spinelli, E. (1989) *The Interpreted World: An Introduction to Phenomenological Psychology*. London: Sage.

Spinelli, E. (1990) 'The phenomenological method and client-centred therapy', *Existential Analysis*, 1: 15–21.

Spinelli, E. (1997) 'Some hurried notes expressing outline ideas that someone might one day utilize as signposts towards a sketch of an existential-phenomenological theory of sexuality', *Existential Analysis*, 8 (1): 2–20.

Spinelli, E. (2001) *The Mirror and the Hammer: Challenges to Therapeutic Orthodoxy*. London: Continuum.

Strasser, F. and Randolph, P. (2004) *Mediation: A Psychological Insight into Conflict Resolution*. London: Continuum.

Toukmanian, S.G. and Hakim, L.Z. (2007) 'Client perception', in M. Cooper, M. O'Hard, P.F. Schmid and G. Wyatt (eds), *The Handbook of Person-Centred Psychotherapy and Counselling*. Basingstoke: Palgrave Macmillan.

Van Deurzen, E. (1998) *Paradox and Passion in Psychotherapy*. Chichester: Wiley and Sons.

Van Deurzen-Smith, E. (1988) *Existential Counselling in Practice*. London: Sage.

Van Deurzen-Smith, E. (1990) *Existential Therapy*. London: SEA.

Vontress, C.E. and Epp, L.R. (2001) 'Existential cross-cultural counselling: When hearts and cultures share', in K.J. Schneider, J.F.T. Bugental and J.F. Pierson (eds), *The Handbook of Humanistic Psychology*. London: Sage.

Wilkins, P. (2005) 'Assessment and 'diagnosis' in person-centred therapy', in S. Joseph and R. Worsley (eds), *Person-Centred Psychopathology: A Positive Psychology of Mental Health*. Ross-on-Wye: PCCS.

Yalom, I.D. (1995) *The Theory and Practice of Group Psychotherapy*, 4th edn. New York: Basic Books.

Zimring, F. (2000) 'Empathic understanding grows the person', *The Person-Centred Journal*, 7: 101–113.

8

A NARRATIVE APPROACH TO COUNSELLING PSYCHOLOGY

John Davy

In a sense, all talking therapies are narrative. A person experiencing some kind of dilemma or distress tells a therapist stories about their past, present and possible futures. The therapist listens, observes and responds, making sense of the stories told in relation to other narratives they have encountered in their professional training (for example, the meta-narratives of attachment theory, transference or evidence-based practice), previous clinical encounters, and through their wider life experience. A counselling psychologist's professional and personal knowledges provide lenses for construing (Hoffman, 1990). Their theories lend visibility and significance to some forms of life, and conversely minimize or exclude other aspects of the client's account. Through their responses, the therapist promotes elaboration and reflection on some kinds of story more than others.

This chapter examines a social-constructionist understanding of psychology and therapy in the condition of postmodernity. This involves more explicit attention to the narrative metaphor than is common in other forms of therapy, and a different concept of identity than that reproduced by modernist versions of psychology. I begin by offering some working definitions of story, narrative and discourse, then briefly trace a history of the narrative metaphor in psychology before contrasting the social-constructionist concept of identities with the essentialist notion of an inner-self. The second part of the chapter presents some therapeutic narrative practices developed by White and associates. The final section reflects on narrative and evidence, a distinction between narrative and narrativizing, and the limits of language.

SOME TENTATIVE DEFINITIONS

Narratives are about stories, which provide accounts of particular happenings. Cultures differ to some degree in what counts as a well-formed story (for example, Baerger and McAdams, 1999), but all stories involve events and encounters sequenced in time (Bruner, 1990, 1991), with a beginning, a middle and an end, and characters who are part of, and affected by, the events narrated. 'Narrative' is a broader term than 'story', since it also concerns the manner in which the story is told (for example, the viewpoint from which a story is narrated; cf. Mullan, 2006); considerations of audience; the integration of non-verbal communication alongside the words of a story; and how different stories involving similar material relate to one another.

Satisfying stories tend to require plot (Bruner, 1990: 44), a causal chain that explains the connections between events and protagonists and brings coherence. In Western cultures, the word 'story' is often associated with the idea of fiction or entertainment, but many important stories are neither. (Consider, for instance, the testimony of a Holocaust survivor's life story.)

The term 'discourse' is sometimes used in social-constructionist writing in preference to language, narrative or story to indicate a meaningful network of identities, relationships, roles, expectations, rights, and ways to express these (for example, actions, taxation, buildings, law, custom and ritual), a more inclusive framework than verbal language alone. Words have their meaning in use (Wittgenstein, 1958: PI 43 (20e)) within broader cultural and material contexts. These include, for example, images and stories circulated through a range of media about healthy and beautiful bodies in a world where money is made in the diet and health industries. Each of us is embodied and socially incited to monitor and discipline our bodies in comparison with those of others. (An instance of Foucault's 'normalizing judgement' as a technology of self in the operation of modern power; for example 1973, 1980, 1988; cf. White 2002.)

NARRATIVE METAPHOR AND PSYCHOLOGY

Psychology is not a unitary discipline, and the forms it takes are intimately connected with other contemporary cultural resources and practices. These provide metaphors which organize and focus theoretical thought within psychology, whilst also obscuring themes outside the reality constructed through the metaphor (Lakoff and Johnson, 1980; Gergen and Gergen, 1986). Early psychoanalytic theories drew on metaphors from hydraulic/Newtonian mechanics and Darwinian evolution in conceptualizing libido and drives, and the construction of the ego from the more primitive forces of the id (Schafer, 1980: 30–31). Humanistic psychologies borrowed from religious practices (McLeod, 1997: 7) and Western notions of liberal democracy and self-advancement.

Cognitive theories and early systemic thinking rested on metaphors of computation and cybernetics. Stiles and Shapiro (1989) argued that most psychotherapeutic research is constructed around a 'drug metaphor'.

From the 1970s onwards there has been a growing interest in the use of a narrative metaphor within psychological and social studies. Theorists including Shotter (1975), Schafer (1980), Sarbin (1986), Polkinghorne (1988) and Mair (1989) argue that positivist propositional knowledge provides an inadequate basis for understanding and intervening in human relationships situated within richly structured socio-historical contexts. They claim instead that personal and cultural experiences are constructed through the creation and performance of narratives. Drawing partly on the developmental psychology of Vygotsky (1962, 1978), Jerome Bruner (1986, 1990, 1991) has been a particularly articulate advocate of a cultural psychology with narrative as the building block of mind.

Concurrently, sociologists of science (for example Gilbert and Mulkay, 1984; Woolgar, 1988) have shown how psychology can itself be understood as a kind of meta-narrative. From a postmodern perspective, psychology does not find universal truths about the human mind. Rather, psychology is a kind of persuasive endeavour which both reflects prevalent societal ideas about mind, identity, relationships, distress and psychopathology, but also functions to produce and circulate particular versions of what it is to be human in the wider culture.

Postmodernism may be described as a pervasive position of 'incredulity to meta-narratives' (Lyotard, 1988), which places in question how 'taken-for-granted' or pre-eminent/ dominant theories and practices are constructed from others, teasing apart how claims to legitimacy are produced and noting the gaps and inconsistencies that are revealed in the process. Postmodernism incites a sceptical attitude towards claims of universal or general 'truth', emphasizing instead how knowledges (for example about psychology, therapy and identity) are produced and validated in local and contingent circumstances.

The relations between psychology and other cultural forms are complex and reciprocal. Rose's explorations of the 'psy-complex' (for example, 1989) demonstrate how psychological frameworks have infiltrated other domains such as the legal system, popular media and educational practices. This interpenetration can also be traced more specifically in relation to psychotherapy (for example, Parker, 1997). Stories about the 'right' way to be a psychologist influence the kinds of stories that psychologists tell about their work (for example, MacMillan, 1992; Davy, 2004). In turn, the stories that clients know about psychology and therapy influence what and how they narrate.

SOCIAL CONSTRUCTIONISM AND THE SELF

Psychotherapeutic psychologies in the West have helped to reproduce the notion of an autonomous, bounded self, striving to discipline and/or satisfy inner motivations and desire. Outward behaviours including language are taken as expressions of an inner essence, the self, whose structure could potentially be decoded through these outward signs to reveal the hidden psychological homunculus pulling our strings. In this structuralist paradigm, we 'act out', from inside. Decoding is viewed as a technical, expert matter in which psy-professionals can know someone else's inner being better than the person themself.

However, social-constructionists argue that this inner-self is an object constructed by the means of inquiry – something which psychologists and others have made seem real by the way they have looked and thought – rather than something which exists a priori at the core of our being. This post-structural position implies that 'surface' phenomena (behaviour, language, relationships and interaction) are not secondary but actually constitute life. Potentially, this stance democratizes psychology, since surface phenomena are shared and public rather than revealed through esoteric professional techniques. Instead of an inner-self acting out into the world, social-constructionists propose that our experience of identity is formed from our dealings and joint actions with others, a profoundly social view drawing on the symbolic interactionism of Mead (1934) and Goffman's (1959, 1961) sociological image of self as performance.

Language, and in particular narrative, is seen as a key substrate for organizing and interpreting experience, enabling 'access to the symbols necessary for thinking and acting as a self in a structured world of symbolic meaning' (Mead, 1934: 31). Constructionist psychology suggests that stories are the primary means by which we attempt to understand experience, and equally importantly that stories are the materials which build mind and identity. The stories I can tell about myself, the audiences available for these, and the validation, elaboration and cross-linkage to others' stories which these tellings meet, actually are my identity, continually (re)constructed through contextualized performances. The emphasis is on self in relationship to others, on self as something that entails action, agency, commitments and responses, and on self as fluid, multiple and contingent, rather than self as a private, singular essence.

Contexts, including relationships, are situations we act *into,* providing opportunities and constraints to express our lives in particular ways which fit with cultural, shared meanings, calling forth different versions of ourselves. An appointment in a hospital ward between a male psychologist in a suit and a female patient in bed offer different opportunities for meaning to be constructed, and different versions of identity to be shown and enacted, than a chance meeting at a children's crèche between two females, one a psychologist and one 'their' client, similarly dressed and present to collect their offspring. The 'same' action, such as a wink or a smile, is imbued with different meaning by the particular context, not just the actors' intentions or individual construing. Naming the behaviour in isolation is 'thin description' in Geertz's anthropological terms (1973), while a richly contextualized report is 'thick description', language used often in narrative therapy.

CONSTRUCTIVISM AND SOCIAL CONSTRUCTIONISM IN THERAPY

A modernist, constructivist (cf. Kelly, 1955; Piaget, 1955) interpretation of the narrative metaphor in psychology is the idea that persons hold internal representations of their experience in the form of stories or schemas. These encode memories and model the actual and anticipated world, with the related idea that people then use stories or draw upon particular discourses for rhetorical, persuasive effects when dealing with others (Potter and Wetherall, 1987). This framework posits stories as mental tools deployed strategically by an inner ghost in the human machine. The constructivist view does not problematize the idea of a bounded, individual agentic self, but focuses instead on the devices the self uses to interpret and influence the world.

Constructivist positions have been criticized by feminists, post-colonial theorists and others (for example, Bograd, 1984; Hare-Mustin, 1986; Callinicos, 1989; Dallos and Urry, 1999) for the implication that problems are produced by faults in the way that people think about things. This suggests that distress can be remediated by adjusting dysfunctional cognitions. For social-constructionists, this is an unacceptable privatization of politics which does not address issues of power and inequality. This kind of critique can be extended to psychotherapy in general (for example, Smail, 2005).

Social-constructionists argue a more radical position, positing a complex and reciprocal relationship between culture and the self, with identity being fashioned, and continually recreated and revised, from relationships with others and actions in the public, outer, world. Constructionists such as Henriques et al. (1984) propose that the process of story-making (and hence self-making/sense-making) depends critically on the cultural resources available for quotation and connotation, including particular forms of subjectivity and patterns of relationship.

Like constructivists, constructionists are interested in narrative, but tend to focus more on:

- the interrelationship between 'individual' narratives and the discourses and symbolic resources within a culture
- the social performance and functions of narrative (for example, audiences and the circulation of stories)
- how new narratives are produced through joint action, rather than the sense-making of the individual alone.

Social-constructionism recognizes a complex dialectic between individuals and culture. 'Top-down' contextual forces interact with 'bottom-up' implicative forces, since cultural forms and the material world shape and constrain available identities and potentialities for construing experience (cf. Bhaskar, 1989) but do not wholly determine individual expressions of life.

The cultures I inhabit provide a certain set of powerful stories and expectations about how lives are gendered. These often include the idea that gender matters as a key element of identity and 'should' be stable and unitary (Butler, 1990). These discourses are reproduced powerfully in language, and also in a myriad of other ways including family life (Chodorow, 1978), children's play, social divisions of space, work roles, public institutions, images of the body and beauty. Some discourses are more influential or 'dominant' than others, which can be termed 'marginalized' or 'subjugated' (White and Epston, 1990: 18–27; Foucault, 1980).

Gendered discourses affect the way I can 'perform' a masculine identity and co-ordinate with others. However, my performance of maleness has the potential to influence cultural stories about gendered expression, reproducing dominant discourse or giving life to more subjugated discourse. (For example: What kind of man am I when working with families affected by domestic violence? How might this influence them?) In Foucault's terms, I am subject to the disciplinary power of discourse, but I am also a site of potential resistance. Hence, 'the personal is political' (cf. Elliott, 2007: 21–24). Living as a 'text of identity' (Shotter and Gergen, 1989), I am both writer and written.

WHITE'S NARRATIVE APPROACH TO THERAPY

In the following sections, I describe some of the practices of a narrative approach based on social-constructionist theory and ideas developed by White and associates such as Epston (White and Epston, 1990).

These ideas partly grew out of White's early work as a family therapist. Family therapy and narrative practice share an emphasis on interpersonal and social experience; a relational emphasis; focus on meaning; and an understanding that problems, attempted solutions and meaning are contingent on multiple over-lapping contexts with complex patterns of reciprocal influence (cf. Dallos and Draper, 2000). However, narrative practice does not place special emphasis on families above other communities and groups which also constitute identity (cf. Minuchin, 1998), and narrative practice draws on many other traditions besides that of family therapy, including sociology, anthropology and literary studies. (The term 'practice' is often used rather than 'therapy' to problematize traditional power relations in psychotherapy and suggest the applicability of narrative ideas to other activities such as community work.)

Although all of the practices I describe can form part of a narrative conversation, the relative emphasis on each is not fixed. Some narrative work will only involve a few of these activities. All are intended as joint actions undertaken collaboratively between the therapist and the person consulting them. Borrowing from Bruner, White used the metaphor of maps to describe this work, conceptualizing the therapeutic encounter as a collaborative journey through the person's experience ('the territories of their own lives', White, 2007: 5) mapping lived experience more richly to offer a wider choice of destinations and routes.

White and Epston argue that

> in striving to make sense of life, persons face the task of arranging their experience of events across time in such a way as to arrive at a coherent account of themselves and the world around them. [...] The success of this storying of experience provides persons with a sense of continuity and meaning in their lives, and this is relied upon for the ordering of daily lives and for the interpretation of further experiences. (1990: 10)

Narrative therapists assume that clients often present for therapy when the dominant stories they tell about themselves lack coherence, omit too much of their actual experience, or cannot be shared with meaningful audiences.

EXTERNALIZNG CONVERSATIONS

Narrative therapists take a stance that the person is not the problem. Rather, the problem is the problem (White, 1989). Clients often describe the situation as though their own self were the problem ('I'm such an addictive person'), or as though the problem is an integral or internalized part of them ('I've been diagnosed as a depressive'). It is as if their conclusions about identity are largely defined by problems they are experiencing, and the stories they tell about their lives seem problem-saturated (White and Epston, 1990: 39). This may also be how others relate to them ('My next patient's a self-harmer', 'It's about my son, he's such an aggressive child'). This kind of internalized understanding of problems links with the modernist conception of an inner-self that narrative psychology rejects. From a Foucauldian perspective, internalizing problems is an effect of 'normalizing judgement':

> In a system of modern power, social control is established through the construction of norms about life and identity and by inciting people to engage in operations on their own and each other's lives to bring their actions and thoughts into harmony with these norms. For this reason, modern power is considered a system of 'normalizing judgement'. The very concept of 'autonomous and independent action' – and for that matter, of what it means to be a 'real' or 'authentic' person – is founded upon these constructed norms, and failing to reproduce these norms categorizes people as 'personal failures' in their own and each other's eyes. (White, 2007: 268).

If the person is conflated with the problem, this constructs the therapeutic task as changing a flawed individual, accepting that their spoiled self needs correction. White comments, 'If the person is the problem there is very little that can be done outside of taking action that is self-destructive' (White, 2007: 26).

Externalization has been taken up by some other therapists (for example, March and Mulle, 1996) as a cognitive reframing technique, a constructivist practice in which clients are encouraged to think about their problems in a different way which may be more 'functional' or 'accurate'. Using externalization as a technique to change the way an individual thinks is a different emphasis from the social-constructionist view on externalization. Narrative practitioners regard externalizing as one strand in a broader set of inquiries, which aim to develop richer understandings about a person's experiences, locating them in relation to other stories and structures in the culture around them and opening up options for new action.

White presented four types of inquiry in an externalizing conversation. The first category of inquiry attempts to negotiate a particular 'experience-near' definition of the problem, rather than an 'experience-far' problem definition derived from labels or categories in a professionally expert body of knowledge ('The doctor said I have a personality disorder') or particular social stereotypes ('I'm promiscuous'). For example, in working with a boy who was said to have ADHD (attention deficit hyperactivity disorder), White (2007: 11–22) was interested that the boy described himself as having 'AHD' rather than ADHD. He focused on investigating the characteristics of AHD as experienced by this particular child, rather than persuading the boy to accept the 'experience-far' child psychiatric label. The aim is for a personal definition, acting as an entry into rich, contextualized conversation about the person's lived experience, thick description (Geertz, 1973). This boy was not an expert on ADHD, but he knew more about his own AHD than anyone else in the whole world.

A classic example in White's early work concerns his externalization work with a child who soiled (1984). Identities brought into therapy were that the child was 'a soiler', or had 'encopresis' (medical discourse). Discussing how the problem was experienced and adapting to the child's language, White and the family began talking instead about a problem with Sneaky Poo. This unpleasant character crept out to cause trouble when least expected, sometimes tricking the child into colluding with concealing the mess, so causing other trouble.

One main aim in externalization is to negotiate a new problem definition that defamiliarizes the person from a habitual self-description reliant on categories borrowed or imposed from others (experience-far), in order to refamiliarize them with their own unique, situated experience of the problem (experience-near). Another intention is to introduce a playful 'as if' tone to a problem-saturated account, opening up room for experimenting with new possibilities. Sensitivity is required in negotiating an acceptable problem definition. Narrative therapists working with children often develop personified problem definitions, for example, 'Mr Fidget' instead of ADHD. On the other hand, a therapist who is too eager to suggest flamboyant, different terminology to define the problem, or who invents their own terms without sufficient reference to the client's language and self-description, may alienate the person consulting them. A shift from 'I'm depressed' to 'Sometimes depression tries to take over' may be therapeutically sufficient, with the depressive aspect transformed from a personal adjective to an independent noun.

This latter point connects with the second category of inquiry, mapping the effects of the problem. The narrative therapist is persistently curious about the effects a problem has in the life of the person(s) consulting them. For example, someone may present initially 'with a clinical depression'. Asking 'What kind of depression is it that visits you? How do you experience it?' might elicit an answer like, 'It's like I'm carrying a huge weight around, draining my energy'. This could become an experience-near definition, 'a heavy kind of depression, like a giant leech'. Questions to map the effects might then take the form, 'So when the leech is hungry, really draining you, how does that affect you? Who else would notice this? What would they see or hear?' 'Tell me about the times when you're feeling flattened by the weight of that greedy depression – how does it change the way you do things that matter to you?'

The intention is to be actively curious about the effects of the problem on the person's life, consistently talking 'as though' the problem and the person were two separate entities. This starts to deconstruct the truth status of the identity claims associated with the problem; for example, moving from a self-description of 'I'm a failure' to 'When the depression's got the upper-hand, it makes me feel like a failure' desediments the certainty involved in the ascription of failure. Other evidence and accounts of the self can then be considered.

Initially, the therapist is not focusing on efforts to resolve the problem, simply aiming to construct rich description of the problem's effects in varied domains (home, workplace, peergroup, family, one's relationship with oneself, the future possibilities someone imagines for themself and so on). However, as the conversation progresses, there may be some evidence that the person is 'experiencing a degree of separation from the problem definitions of their identity, and when they are beginning to give voice to intentions and values that contradict those associated with the problems' (White, 2007: 30). Then, emphasis shifts towards inquiry about the person's evaluation of the problem's activities. ('How do you feel about these effects that the self-hate has on your life?', 'Are these developments positive, or negative, or maybe a bit of both or neither, something else?', 'What's your position on the way the suicide attempt has affected you as a family?') The therapist should not impose their own evaluation through leading questions.

Gradually, the inquiry would then shift towards how the person justifies their evaluation, a set of 'why?' questions:

> 'You've explained that you don't like the way that cutting interferes with your relationship with your mother. Can you tell me, why does that matter to you?'
> 'I wonder, would you tell me a story about the history of your relationship with your mother to help me understand why you don't want cutting to get in the way?'

The therapist aims to help the person voice and develop intentional understandings about life, purposes, commitments, and to elaborate their values, skills and prized learnings. Inquiry about a person's evaluation of the problem's activities then leads into conversation about actions people have taken, or are considering, to diminish the influence of the problem so that they can more effectively pursue valued purposes. This is 'relative influence questioning', exploring the person's effects on the problem counter-posed to the problem's effects on them:

> 'What steps have you tried to give Mr Temper the slip?'
> 'How have you and your mother gone about keeping your connection, even though the cutting has tried to sever it?'

Discussion of the influence of the person over the problem need not be restricted to military metaphors founded on dominance or battle ('beating' or 'defeating' a problem). These run the risk of reproducing problematic dominant discourse whilst also setting the client up on a 'win or fail' trajectory (cf. White, 2002). Many other metaphors are possible, such as educating the problem, taming it, harnessing it, making friends or resigning from its influence.

RE-AUTHORING CONVERSATIONS

Therapeutic narrative conversations involve the inter-weaving of strands about the actions and events in a person's life (landscape of action) with other strands concerning their values, commitments, intentions, identity conclusions and attributions of meaning to the material of the landscape of action (landscape of consciousness), 'what those involved in the action know, think or feel, or do not know, think or feel' (J.S. Bruner, 1986: 14).

In literary theory, a readerly text (Barthes, 1974) is a story where the writer has already done the creative work. The reader simply needs to digest the preformed meanings contained within the author's text. Such stories make few demands on the reader, but also offer little scope for the reader's creativity and unique responses. By contrast, writerly texts are complex stories in which readers are invited to participate in the construction of textual meaning, filling in 'gaps' and indeterminacies of the texts' storylines through their own acts of interpretation and imagination. The meaning produced from such a writerly text is a joint creation of writer and reader, a performance of meaning in Bruner's terms. Narrative therapy uses this idea of joint work on a writerly text as a metaphor informing 're-authoring conversations'. The story of the client's lived experience is the text to be worked on. The therapist aims to highlight apparent gaps and inconsistencies in the storyline, fuelling curiosity about hitherto subordinate storylines and inviting the client into reinterpretations and performances of meaning around the events of their lives. The intention is to support the positioning of the client as the author of a rich and coherent story about their experience.

The therapist's role is decentred and editorial rather than authorial. The aim is to support the client in a writerly re-reading of their landscape of action and landscape of consciousness, not to supply the client with a 'better' story created by the therapist. The therapist tries to build:

> a context in which it becomes possible for people to give meaning to, and draw together into a storyline, many of the overlooked but significant events of their lives. These concepts also guide the therapist in supporting people to derive new conclusions about their lives, many of which will contradict existing deficit-focused conclusions that are associated with the dominant storylines that have been limiting of their lives. (White, 2007: 83)

Re-authoring conversations use the idea that 'life experience is richer than discourse. Narrative structures organise and give meaning to experience, but there are always feelings and lived experience not fully encompassed by the dominant story' (E. Bruner, 1986: 143). There are always new storylines that can be created around the events of our lives. Hence, identities are multi-storied. In the re-authoring process, some events that have previously been storied within a dominant but restrictive narrative may become re-storied within alternative plot lines that also account for them, but entail a different construction of self. Other life events which have previously been regarded as insignificant and left largely unstoried may be linked into storylines previously subordinate, but which can be elaborated and thickened to rival the initial dominant story.

The re-authoring stance is one of vigilance and curiosity about events (actions, decisions, relationships made and left and so on) that might contradict the problematic storyline, or which could not have been predicted from it. These exceptions from the dominant plot are known in narrative therapy as 'unique outcomes' (Goffman, 1961: 127). Sometimes these events come to light as the therapist works to deconstruct some of the current spoiled identity conclusions:

> 'I'd like to understand a bit more about this idea you've mentioned that you are a selfish coward. Can you tell me something about the part that cowardice has played in your life so far?' (NB: externalizing cowardice as a noun separate from the person),

while other such events may be mentioned during externalizing conversations. The therapist invites performances of meaning around unique outcomes through inquiries aiming to:

- negotiate a particular, experience-near definition of the unique outcome
- map the effects of the unique outcome (past, present, future)
- evaluate the unique outcome and its effects
- justifying the evaluation (the why): 'We've been discussing that one time when you did hit him back, and what that led to. Could you help me understand, looking back on that now, what's your opinion about your actions? If you could pick up a phone to call back in time to the person you were then, what might you want to say?'

A woman may initially tell a story about being an anxious and fearful person, who worries that she has harmed her child by staying with a violent partner for many years, concealing the abuse from others. The dominant story might be one of weakness and cowardice with considerable self-blame. However, there could be events not sufficiently accounted for by this dominant story. For instance: (a) times when the woman did think about leaving, and sought advice from friends; (b) times when the woman did take action to protect their child, such as finding excuses for the child to spend more time at a friend's house to avoid heightened domestic tension, or taking the blame for something the child had broken; (c) the action the woman is taking now to reveal the abuse and its effects. An alternative storyline could speak of well-founded caution, balancing risks and preparation.

Exploring the range of contexts and influences involved in such decisions would also be part of deconstructing the dominant story. Decisions about leaving violent relationships can depend on the possible reactions of family and friends, and the availability of alternative housing and other support services at short notice, rather than reflect personal courage alone.

In common with systemic family psychotherapists, narrative therapists are interested in negative explanations and restraints (Bateson, 1972; White, 1986), stories about other ways things could have happened but didn't. In his narrative work with men who are violent and abusive, Jenkins uses externalization questions to highlight and challenge attitudes and habits which may be holding a man back from taking more responsibility in relationships:

> Given his intentions: – What has stopped the man from taking responsibility to con-
> tribute to the relationship in ways that foster equity, mutual respect, sensitivity and car-
> ing? – What has stopped the man from taking responsibility for his violent behaviour?
> (Jenkins, 1990: 80)

Inquiries about externalized restraints on actions and identities are a deconstructive alternative to the internalized focus, 'Why is this man violent and abusive?'.

Storylines involve sequences of events in time, organized according to a plot. The therapist would be curious about the links between events in the landscape of action:

> 'What steps did you take to get ready to do that?'
> 'Were there other occasions before when you managed to distract him like that?'

and the landscape of consciousness:

> 'You mentioned a time when you plucked up enough courage to ask for a meeting with
> the Headteacher. What does that say about you, do you think?'
> 'When you insisted that you kept your own door key, what were you hoping for?
> Why was that important to you?'

and would also want to trace patterns of connections across time. For example, tracing a history of cautious preparation in the person's life:

> 'Can you tell me about a time when you were young that that was helpful to you?'

or exploring a history of the decision to speak about the abuse now:

> 'Thank you for talking to our trainees about your experiences. I'm curious, do you think that any of your school teachers might have predicted you would be the sort of person prepared to speak out in this way against the injustices you've experienced?'

Like the back-and-forth of a shuttle in a loom, tracing connections between landscape of action and landscape of consciousness in past, present and anticipated/imagined futures serves to weave densely patterned tapestries of storied experience. It is this sustained conversational process that co-creates alternative storylines, rather than attention to single exceptional events alone as a mutative process. Unique outcomes are points of entry into the development of rich stories about the person's life that link:

> [actions and events] with
> [multiple contexts including relationships and cultural discourses] with
> [intentions, values, choices and understandings] patterned through
> [time].

Re-authoring is not intended to smooth away traumas and loss that cannot be undone (cf. Fredman, 1997), putting things in a good light so that people feel happier. Work with the woman described above might not cancel regrets about possible mistakes made or decisions postponed, but could generate a richer and less self-blaming understanding about the range of factors involved in what had happened, highlight skills and knowledge about self-care and child-care that were being overlooked, and contribute to changing determinations about future relationships.

RE-MEMBERING CONVERSATIONS

The way that we come to experience ourselves is shaped by the way that others have viewed us, listened to us, responded to us, evaluated us, acknowledged or invalidated us. White refers to these others as a 'club of life'. Within this club of life, the views of some members will have been very influential, with others seeming less significant, of a lower membership status. Drawing on Myerhoff's work in cultural anthropology (for example, 1982), White developed a specific kind of recollection within narrative practice, 're-membering' (1997). This uses the metaphor of membership to open space for revisions to the status of those within the club of life.

For example, in tracing the histories of a belief that a person is worthless and stupid (deconstructing this idea's truth status through externalization, contextualization and a search for unique outcomes), the person may begin to think that this dominant narrative has been strongly informed by a step-parent's judgements (Russell and Carey, 2002). The therapist would discuss whether they were interested in downgrading the status of the step-parent in their club of life (or even revoking membership), and if there were others in the club whose voices they might want to promote to greater significance, which have previously been marginalized in the dominant deficit-focused account. Hence, re-membering is a deliberate process of re-evaluation and re-organizing rather than passive remembering.

One category of inquiry in re-membering concerns persons already identified as significant in the client's club of life. The client is invited to describe how this person has contributed to their life, what actions or words of theirs have been influential (landscape of action questions), combining this with curiosity about connections with the client's landscape of consciousness, for example:

> 'Why do you think your brother was so supportive of you when you separated, when you felt he'd been so distant before?'
> 'What difference do you think you may have made to the way that he thinks about his life, his relationships?'

Evaluation questions may then lead into decisions about re-membering, for example:

> 'Overall, what do you think about the influence he has had on your life?'
> 'Thinking about this now, would you want to change the weight you give to his opinions, to his voice in your life?'
> 'How might you want to make that change, or mark it?'

For some people, the conversation alone may be sufficient for them to feel they have re-membered the relationship as they wish. For others, further thinking about actions is useful. Therapeutic rituals can be planned, such as visiting a grave to honour someone whose views are to be promoted. The club of life can include members who have died but whose influence matters nonetheless. It can also encompass people who have not yet met the client but whose evaluation would signify, such as grandchildren as yet unborn or a future partner.

Sometimes, re-membering conversations mean that someone who was seen as a negative influence in the old dominant story comes to be understood in a different way. For example, a person might reflect on the constraints on a parent during their childhood, such as community expectations about gender roles and married life, and begin to think about that parent managing difficult dilemmas rather than simply being neglectful. The client might then wish to upgrade their relationship.

A second category of inquiry involves the search for members with little influence (or people entirely overlooked) in the dominant deficit-oriented narrative, who could contribute to preferred identity claims:

> 'You said that none of your family believed that you would be able to take this step, that they believe once a smack-head, always a smack-head. But here you are, two weeks into the programme. Who in your past would be least surprised to know that you'd been able to make this start?'
> 'What is that they knew about you that would have told them you could?'
> 'If they knew about what you're doing now, what might it mean to them?'

COUNTER-DOCUMENTATION AND DEFINITIONAL CEREMONIES

From a narrative perspective, identity is not simply about the stories we can tell about ourselves. It also concerns the way that others respond to our story, and the ways that our lived experience then makes a difference for others, how we become storied in the nets of other people's narratives. This highlights issues of audience, witnessing and circulation of preferred stories, and questions about the available contexts for performances of self. A therapist may be one important audience for an emerging self-story, but narrative therapists have developed rituals intended to thicken the alternative story through tellings and responses in more varied arenas involving a wider cross-section of the client's club of life.

> Although in the dominant culture therapy tends to be a secret enterprise [...] When therapy becomes a context in which people constitute preferred selves, they have nothing to hide, and much to show. (Freedman and Combs, 1996: 237)

From a social-constructionist perspective, many aspects of modern culture can be understood as dividing practices which reproduce dominant social norms by inviting persons to exercise normalizing judgement, measuring themselves against these norms. Some of these rituals result in documentation about a person's life (exam certificates, referral letters, therapists' file notes, CVs, probation reports) contributing to the reproduction of a particular identity.

Narrative practitioners use a wide range of counter-documentation to help amplify and circulate an emerging preferred story of identity. White and Epston (1990) describe the use of therapeutic letters, while Morgan (2000) discusses certificates (for example, 'Escape from self-doubt'), handbooks, notes from sessions, videotapes, lists and pictures as therapeutic counter-documentation. Counter-documents like letters and certificates of change can be circulated to significant others like school teachers or absent family members to publish the news (Freeman et al., 1997).

Definitional ceremonies are another kind of narrative therapeutic ritual derived from Myerhoff's research (1982) into the structured community support meetings of elderly Jews in Los Angeles. These aimed to build communal connection and coherent identity in the context of multiple losses and trauma. A definitional ceremony in narrative therapy involves convening a group of people to attend to the story of one or more of the group. One person talks with the therapist about a significant life story. The rest of the group are termed 'outside witnesses'. They may be friends, family, colleagues of the therapist (White, 1995) or others not yet known to the client who may be able to offer some relevant experience (for example, others who, like a client, have also had complex relationships with hearing voices; cf. James, 2001). The outsider witnesses then participates in a retelling of the story they have heard. Finally, there is a retelling of the outsider witnesses' retellings by the client.

The therapist is active in facilitating these tellings, inviting what White (2007) terms 'acknowledgement' (rather than applause, evaluation or hypothesizing). This involves the outside witnesses:

- commenting on particular expressions that caught their attention
- describing images and metaphors that came to mind as they listened, and how they thought these might relate to the client's values and purposes
- explaining their personal resonance, the witnesses' understandings of how their own history contributed to their interest in particular aspects of the teller's account
- speaking of ways in which they have been moved to a new perspective on their own identity or experience.

NARRATIVES OR NARRATIVIZING?

There is some tendency in the literature on narrative approaches to emphasize the co-construction of a preferred identity story as the engine of psychotherapeutic change. But is it more important to have a better story, or better story-telling skills? An unanswered research question relevant for resilience and long-term well-being concerns the extent to which narrative therapy changes the ongoing processes by which new experiences become storied into previous experience and identity, rather than simply changing current story content.

Arguing for the integration of attachment perspectives with narrative ideas, Dallos (2006) draws on Crittenden's dynamic maturational model of attachment (for example, 1997) to highlight that some individuals with difficult attachment experiences show persistent distortions in the way that events and relationships are interpreted, selectively limiting the material available for emplotment. Dallos suggests that an important therapeutic goal is the development of better narrativizing skills to connect different types of representational/memory systems (procedural, imaged/sensory, semantic, episodic, connotative language, working memory).

However, narrative practice does not rest on the idea that change is just a matter of cognitive change in the individual's head, whether of story or storying. Public and social changes in the network, in audience responses and acknowledgement, and in the way that a client's life is storied by others and reciprocally affects their stories, all matter. Memory and identity are seen as interpersonal and social accomplishments.

NARRATIVE AND THE LIMITS OF LANGUAGE

It is sometimes said that narrative therapy is too language-dependent, rendering it unsuitable for people with limited verbal skills. This criticism could be offered of any 'talking therapy', but the emphasis on story development can be seen as requiring sophistication. One response is to highlight again that narrative practice is oriented towards social and public conversations and expressions of identity. For instance, in narrative therapy with a child with significant learning difficulties and limited language, work with other people in the child's networks would also be important. However, this argument is double-edged, since narrative therapists still need to consider carefully how to privilege the voice of the child (or other less articulate/powerful consultees) rather than allow dominant others to speak for/over them (cf. Blow and Daniel, 2005).

The capacity of the therapist to adapt to the person(s) consulting them is crucial. White borrows Vygotsky's metaphor of scaffolding (1962) to highlight the flexible responsiveness needed to help clients explore the gap between what has been experienced, and what is known. Vygotsky termed the extent to which this is possible a 'zone of proximal development' (ZPD). The ZPD reflects an interaction between the style, skills and sensitivity of the scaffolder, the client's capacities, and the 'difficulty' of the material in the gap. If this work seems too hard, the scaffolder needs to adjust the style and complexity of their talk, and/or place more emphasis on other aspects of communication including drama, movement, humour, drawings and other props to create a 'theatre of possibilities' (Wilson, 2005). Sometimes acceptance is needed that exploration will be gently paced, particularly if traumatic experience is involved. This may inhibit both therapist and client (Smith, 2005).

A related argument concerns the importance of experience that is not represented in language or goes beyond words (for example, Dowling and Vetere, 2005: 9). I have tried to indicate how narrative work involves the use of rituals, attention to image and metaphor, social processes, and an orientation towards action in the lived world, not simply a constructivist verbal restorying of something inside someone's head. Rituals, images and metaphors have important social functions in connecting spoken and unspoken domains (for example, Van der Hart, 1983), and in expressing and honouring values and experience that cannot be easily contained in sentences. Narrative is a broader concept than verbal story.

NARRATIVE THERAPY AND EVIDENCE

Narrative practices derive from a range of fields including anthropology (for example, Myerhoff), literary studies (Barthes), social and political philosophy (Foucault), sociology (Goffman, Mead), cultural psychology (Bruner) and developmental psychology (Vygotsky). Feminist and post-colonial critiques of therapy and psychology have also been influential. The kinds of evidence given warrant in these traditions (such as fieldwork descriptions, action-research projects, discourse analysis, personal testimony and life-history) to construct validity tend to differ from the evidences valued within modernist empirical versions of psychology. Narrative therapy lacks outcome studies reflecting the kinds of rigour valued in positivist natural sciences. Narrative psychologists are critically curious about the interests and power relationships associated with a discourse of evidence-based practice, and the privileging and production of some forms of evidence over others (cf. Healy, 1999; Jackson, 2001).

Narrative practice principles are consistent with evidence from meta-analytic studies of psychotherapy which highlight common factors associated with beneficial outcomes. Narrative practitioners agree with an emphasis on the construction and maintenance of a good therapeutic relationship; orienting therapy to goals which matter to the client; using client language and expertise, working collaboratively; paying attention to supportive factors 'outside' therapy.

There is evidence already within positivist psychologies about the importance of narrative in human psychology. Examples include the use of stories in our memory systems (for example, Tulving, 1983; Crittenden, 1997); ways in which the language of others shapes the stories we tend to tell about our lives (for example, McCabe and Peterson, 1991); evidence that coherent stories about experience are associated with resilience in mental health (for example, Baerger and McAdams, 1999, Daniel and Wren, 2005: 128–129); as also is a capacity to mentalize (for example, Bateman and Fonagy, 2006), making sense of experience including one's own and other's actions in terms of affective and intentional state understandings of others and self (in narrative terms, the capacity to make connections between landscape of action and landscape of identity). The field of attachment in particular continues to produce considerable positivist evidence about the way that interactions with others shape our emotions, sense of self and capacities to relate to others, supporting many aspects of a constructionist, narrative approach to identity.

From a social-constructionist perspective, an emphasis on outcomes as the justification for a particular form of therapy reflects one particular kind of culturally situated value frame, a consequentialist ethic in which the end is said to justify the means (often associated with a drive towards productivity and economic efficiency; cf. Strawbridge, 2002; Layard, 2004). It is beyond the scope of this chapter to explore this, but there are other kinds of ethical meta-narratives that may interest psychologists, such as deontological ethics, virtue ethics, an ethics of relational responsibility

(McNamee and Gergen, 1999), an ethic of care (Gilligan, 1982) or an ethic of the Other (Levinas, 1989).

In considering whether to develop knowledge and skills in narrative approaches, a counselling psychologist could reflect on:

- their stance in relation to different forms of evidence and epistemology in psychology
- how a narrative psychologist can/should use modernist psychological expertise (for example, about attachment processes, lifespan developmental psychology, evolutionary psychology) without re-inscribing consultees into thinly described lives categorized in experience-far terms
- their intentions regarding employment contexts, and the forms of psychology and evidence which seem valued in those systems
- the preferences and values of people that the counselling psychologist wishes to serve
- which forms of professional practice will facilitate the expression of the psychologist's own preferred values.

REFERENCES

Baerger, D.R. and McAdams, D. (1999) 'Life story coherence and its relationship to psychological well-being', *Narrative Inquiry*, 9: 69–96.

Barthes, R. (1974) *S/Z: An Essay*. (Originally published 1970, trans. R. Miller) New York: Hill and Wang.

Bateman, A. and Fonagy, P. (2006) *Mentalization-Based Treatment for Borderline Personality Disorder*. Oxford: Oxford University Press.

Bateson, G. (1972) *Steps to an Ecology of Mind*. New York: Ballantine.

Bhaskar, R. (1989) *Reclaiming Reality: A Critical Introduction to Contemporary Philosophy*. London: Verso.

Blow, K. and Daniel, G. (2005) 'Whose story is it anyway?', in A. Vetere and E. Dowling (eds), *Narrative Therapy with Children and Their Families*. London: Routledge.

Bograd, M. (1984) 'Family systems approaches to wife battering: A feminist critique', *American Journal of Orthopsychiatry*, 54: 558–568.

Bruner, E. (1986) 'Ethnography as narrative', in V. Turner and E. Bruner (eds), *The Anthropology of Experience*. Chicago, IL: University of Illinois Press.

Bruner, J.S. (1986) *Actual Minds, Possible Worlds*. Cambridge, MA: Harvard University Press.

Bruner, J.S. (1990) *Acts of Meaning*. Cambridge, MA: Harvard University Press.

Bruner, J.S. (1991) 'The narrative construction of reality', *Critical Inquiry*, 18: 1–21.

Butler, J. (1990) *Gender Trouble*. London: Routledge.

Callinicos, A. (1989) *Against Postmodernism: A Marxist Critique*. Cambridge: Polity.

Chodorow, N. (1978) *The Reproduction of Mothering*. Berkeley, CA: University of California Press.

Crittenden, P. (1997) 'Truth, error, omissions, distortion and deception: An application of attachment theory to the assessment and treatment of psychological disorder', in S.M. Clany Dollinger and L.F. DiLalla (eds), *Assessment and Intervention Issues Across the Life Span*. London: Lawrence Erlbaum.

Dallos, R. (2006) *Attachment Narrative Therapy*. Maidenhead: Open University Press.

Dallos, R. and Draper, R. (2000) *An Introduction to Family Therapy*. Buckingham: Open University Press.

Dallos, R. and Urry, A. (1999) 'Abandoning our parents and grandparents: Does social construction mean the end of systemic family therapy?', *Journal of Family Therapy*, 21 (2): 161–186.

Daniel, G. and Wren, B. (2005) 'Families where a parent has a mental health problem', in A. Vetere and E. Dowling (eds), *Narrative Therapies with Children and Their Families*. Hove: Routledge.

Davy, J. (2004) 'The functions of case studies: Representation or persuasive construction?', *Counselling Psychology Review*, 19 (1): 22–38.

Dowling, E. and Vetere, A. (2005) 'Narrative concepts and therapeutic challenges', in A. Vetere and E. Dowling (eds), *Narrative Therapies with Children and their Families*. Hove: Routledge.

Elliott, A. (2007) *Concepts of the Self*, 2nd edn. Cambridge: Polity.

Foucault, M. (1973) *The Birth of the Clinic: An Archaeology of Medical Perception*. London: Tavistock.

Foucault, M. (1980) *Power/Knowledge: Selected Interviews and Other Writings 1972–1977*. Brighton: Harvester.

Foucault, M. (1988) 'Technologies of the self', in L. Martin, H. Gutman and P. Hutton (eds), *Technologies of the Self*. Amherst, MA: University of Massachusetts Press.

Fredman, G. (1997) *Death Talk: Conversations with Children and Families*. London: Karnac.

Freedman, J. and Combs, G. (1996) *Narrative Therapy*. New York: Norton.

Freeman, J., Epston, D. and Lobovits, D. (1997) *Playful Approaches to Serious Problems*. New York: Norton.

Geertz, C. (1973) 'Thick description: Toward an interpretive theory of culture', in C. Geertz (ed.), *The Interpretations of Cultures*. New York: Basic Books.

Gergen, K.J. and Gergen, M.M. (1986) 'Narrative forms and the construction of psychological science', in T.R. Sarbed (ed.), *Narrative Psychology: The Storied Nature of Human Conduct*. New York: Praeger.

Gilbert, G.N. and Mulkay, M.J. (1984) *Opening Pandora's Box: A Sociological Analysis of Scientists' Discourse*. Cambridge: Cambridge University Press.

Gilligan, C. (1982) *In a Different Voice*. Cambridge, MA: Harvard University Press.

Goffman, E. (1959) *The Presentation of Self in Everyday Life*. New York: Doubleday.

Goffman, E. (1961) *Asylums: Essays on the Social Situation of Mental Patients and Other Inmates*. New York: Doubleday.

Hare-Mustin, R.T. (1986) 'The problem of gender in family therapy theory', *Family Process*, 26: 15–27.

Healy, D. (1999) *The Antidepressant Era*. Cambridge, MA: Harvard University Press.

Henriques, J., Hollway, W., Urwin, C., Venn, C. and Walkerdine, V. (1984) *Changing the Subject: Psychology, Social Regulation and Subjectivity*. London: Methuen.

Hoffman, L. (1990) 'Constructing realities: An art of lenses', *Family Process*, 29 (1): 1–12.

Jackson, J. (2001) 'A lawyer's view of evidence', in C. Mace, S. Moorey and B. Roberts (eds), *Evidence in the Psychological Therapies*. Hove: Brunner-Routledge.

James, A. (2001) *Raising Our Voices: An Account of the Hearing Voices Movement*. Gloucester: Handsell.

Jenkins, A. (1990) *Invitations to Responsibility: The Therapeutic Engagement of Men Who Are Violent and Abusive*. Adelaide: Dulwich Centre Publications.

Kelly, G.A. (1955) *The Psychology of Personal Constructs*. New York: Norton.

Lakoff, G. and Johnson, M. (1980) *Metaphors We Live By*. Chicago, IL: University of Chicago Press.

Layard, R. (2004) *Mental Health: Britain's Biggest Social Problem? Report to the Cabinet Office*. London: HMSO.

Levinas, E. (1989) *The Levinas Reader*. Oxford: Blackwell.

Lyotard, J.-F. (1988) *The Postmodern Condition: A Report on Knowledge,* trans. G. Bennington and B. Massumi. Minneapolis, MN: University of Minnesota Press.

MacMillan, A. (1992) 'Communicating about clients: Speaking for myself and others', *Clinical Psychology Forum,* 49: 8–12.

Mair, M. (1989) *Between Psychology and Psychotherapy: A Poetics of Experience.* London: Routledge.

March, J. and Mulle, K. (1996) 'Banishing OCD: Cognitive-behavioural psychotherapy for obsessive-compulsive disorders', in E. Hibbs and P. Jensen (eds), *Psychosocial Treatments for Child and Adolescent Disorders.* Washington, DC: American Psychiatric Association.

McCabe, A. and Peterson, C. (1991) 'Getting the story: A longitudinal study of parenting styles in eliciting narratives and developing narrative skill', in A. McCabe and C. Peterson (eds), *Developing Narrative Structure.* London: Lawrence Erlbaum.

McLeod, J. (1997) *Narrative and Psychotherapy.* London: Sage.

McNamee, S. and Gergen, K.J. (eds) (1999) *Relational Responsibility.* London: Sage.

Mead, G.H. (1934/1974) *Mind, Self and Society.* Chicago, IL: University of Chicago.

Minuchin, S. (1998) 'Where is the family in narrative family therapy?', *Journal of Marital and Family Therapy*, 24: 397–403.

Morgan, A. (2000) *What is Narrative Therapy?* Adelaide: Dulwich Centre Publications.

Mullan, J. (2006) *How Novels Work.* Oxford: Oxford University Press.

Myerhoff, B. (1982) 'Life history among the elderly: Performance, visibility and re-membering', in J. Ruby (ed.), *A Crack in the Mirror: Reflective Perspectives in Anthropology.* Philadelphia, PA: University of Pennsylvania Press.

Parker, I. (1997) *Psychoanalytic Culture: Psychoanalytic Discourse in Western Society.* London: Sage.

Piaget, J. (1955) *The Child's Construction of Reality.* London: Routledge and Kegan Paul.

Polkinghorne, D.E. (1988) *Narrative Knowing and the Human Sciences.* Albany, NY: State University of New York Press.

Potter, J. and Wetherell, M. (1987) *Discourse and Social Psychology: Beyond Attitudes and Behaviour.* London: Sage.

Rose, N. (1989) *Governing the Soul.* London: Routledge.

Russell, S. and Carey, M. (2002) 'Re-membering: Responding to commonly asked questions', *International Journal of Narrative Therapy and Community Work*, 3: 23–31.

Sarbin, T.R. (1986) 'The narrative as a root metaphor for psychology', in T.R. Sarbed (ed.), *Narrative Psychology: The Storied Nature of Human Conduct.* New York: Praeger.

Schafer, R. (1980) 'Narration in the psychoanalytic dialogue', *Critical Inquiry,* 7: 29–53.

Shotter, J. (1975) *Images of Man in Psychological Research.* London: Methuen.

Shotter, J. and Gergen, K.J. (1989) *Texts of Identity.* London: Sage.

Smail, D. (2005) *Power, Interest and Psychology: Elements of a Social Materialist Understanding of Distress.* Ross-on-Wye: PCCS.

Smith, G. (2005) 'Children's narratives of traumatic experiences', in A. Vetere and E. Dowling (eds), *Narrative Therapies with Children and Their Families.* Hove: Routledge.

Stiles, W.B. and Shapiro, D.A. (1989) 'Abuse of the drug metaphor in psychotherapy process-outcome research', *Clinical Psychology Review*, 9: 521–543.

Strawbridge, S. (2002) 'McDonaldization or fast-food therapy', *Counselling Psychology Review*, 17 (4): 20–24.

Tulving, E. (1983) *Elements of Episodic Memory.* Oxford: Oxford University Press.

Van der Hart, O. (1983) *Rituals in Psychotherapy: Transition and Continuity.* New York: Irvington.

Vygotsky, L.S. (1962) *Thought and Language*, 2nd edn. Cambridge, MA: MIT Press.

Vygotsky, L.S. (1978) *Mind in Society*. New York: Cambridge University Press.

White, M. (1984) 'Pseudo-encopresis: From avalanche to victory, from vicious to virtuous cycles', *Family Systems Medicine*, 2 (2): 150–160.

White, M. (1986) 'Negative explanation, restraint and double description: A template for family therapy', *Family Process*, 25 (2): 169–184.

White, M. (1989) 'The externalizing of the problem and the re-authoring of lives and relationships', in M. White (ed.), *Selected Papers*. Adelaide: Dulwich Centre Publications.

White, M. (1995) 'Reflecting teamwork as definitional ceremony', in M. White (ed.), *Re-authoring Lives: Interviews and Essays*. Adelaide: Dulwich Centre Publications.

White, M. (1997) *Narratives of Therapists' Lives*. Adelaide: Dulwich Centre Publications.

White, M. (2002) 'Addressing personal failure', *International Journal of Narrative Therapy and Community Work*, 3: 33–76.

White, M. (2007) *Maps of Narrative Practice*. London: Norton.

White, M. and Epston, D. (1990) *Narrative Means to Therapeutic Ends*. London: Norton.

Wilson, J. (2005) 'Engaging children and young people', in A. Vetere and E. Dowling (eds), *Narrative Therapies with Children and their Families*. Hove: Routledge.

Wittgenstein, L. (1958) *Philosophical Investigations,* 2nd edn. Trans. G.E.M. Anscombe. Oxford: Blackwell.

Woolgar, S. (1988) *Science: The Very Idea*. Chichester: Ellis Horwood.

9

TOWARDS INTEGRATION

Maja O'Brien

This chapter is based on the book written jointly with Gaie Houston entitled *Integrative Therapy: A Practitioner's Guide* (2007) which was the product of our experience of over 40 years as practitioners of quite different theoretical backgrounds and informed by research in two broad areas of knowledge, namely: human development, and research on therapeutic process and outcome.

Integration is defined as a process which each therapist engages with during the course of her clinical practice (in this chapter the pronoun 'she' refers to the therapist and 'he' to the client). To facilitate reflection on practice and the theory that influences it or emerges from it, a framework for doing therapy is suggested. A belief inherent in an integrative stance is that no theory can fully explain the complexity of human beings, nor can any single therapeutic intervention account for therapeutic outcome. Each theoretical model or school of therapy has a valuable contribution to make. The three major orientations of cognitive-behavioural, psychodynamic and humanistic-existential therapy will be compared with reference to the components of the framework. Finally, it will be shown that the last two decades have seen a considerable convergence between different schools characterized by an emphasis on the relational dimension in therapy, a dimension which is the theoretical underpinning of the approach here advocated.

SOME PERSPECTIVES ON INTEGRATION

The field of psychological therapies

The last twenty years have been characterized by a trend towards the integration of ideas and ways of working across different models of psychological therapies. Thus integration can be seen as a corrective tendency in an over-fragmented field. On many sides there is disquiet with the compartmentalization into somewhat rivalrous and mutually exclusive schools, each with its own jargon and credo.

The British Association for Counselling and Psychotherapy (BACP) used to favour adherence to a core theory and sometimes frowned on multiplicity. It is interesting to note, therefore, the increasing number of integrative courses being accredited by this organization. The United Kingdom Council for Psychotherapy (UKCP) has eight sections, most of which define themselves in relation to a core theoretical model. Nevertheless, the Humanistic and Integrative Psychotherapy section welcomes 'interdisciplinary dialogue and an exploration of different psychological processes with particular emphasis on integration within the Section' (UKCP, 2002: IX).

Within the British Psychological Society, the Division of Counselling Psychology (BPS, 2007/8: 19) demands that the trainees will have an understanding and a working knowledge of two theoretical models of psychological therapy. The final examinations require them to demonstrate how they have integrated their learning into their personal and professional identity, thus suggesting a need for integration. It would appear, then, that a welcome move is being made in some parts of the establishment towards integration. It is still a controversial move as the departure of the psychoanalysts from the UKCP to form the British Confederation of Psychotherapists testifies. Nevertheless, the last two decades have seen a constant flow of publications on integration (Dryden, 1992; Evans and Gilbert, 2005; Hollanders, 2003; Lapworth et al., 2001; Mahrer, 1989; Norcross and Goldfried, 1992; Palmer and Woolfe, 1999; Scott, 2004; Stricker and Gold, 1993, 2003), including the *Journal of Psychotherapy Integration*, the official journal of the Society for the Exploration of Psychotherapy Integration.

Eclecticism vs. integration

A key point that distinguishes eclectic from integrative approaches lies in the role of theory. Stricker and Gold (2003: 320) describe these two ways of integrating as 'technical eclecticism' and 'theoretical integration'. They view technical eclecticism as the most clinical and technically oriented form of psychotherapy integration with the least amount of conceptual or theoretical integration. Multimodal therapy, developed by Lazarus (1992), is given as an important example. In contrast, and as the name implies, theoretical integration relies on a process of synthesis from two or more traditions of various theories about personality and human development, psychopathology or mechanisms of change. An early example is the work of Dollard and Miller (1950), who integrated psychoanalytic ideas with those from the learning theories. According to Stricker and Gold (2003), the most influential work on the theoretical integration of various psychotherapies has been the book *Psychoanalysis and Behavior Therapy* by Paul Wachtel (1977). Two other widely used integrative therapies in this country are cognitive-behavioral therapy, developed by Beck (Beck et al., 1979) and cognitive-analytic therapy, developed by Ryle (1990).

A variation of theoretical integration advocated by Stricker and Gold (2003) is 'assimilative integration', in which new techniques are assimilated/integrated into an existing conceptual model of therapy. In other words, new methods or interventions are being introduced whilst therapy proceeds according to the major theoretical orientation of the therapist. An example might be when a psychodynamic therapist, in her ongoing work, introduces a technique such as eye movement desensitization and reprocessing (EMDR). Stricker (2005: 233) suggests that the approach described by O'Brien and Houston (2000) falls within the 'rubric of assimilative integration'.

Common factors

Another perspective on integration has arisen from research on the effectiveness of therapy. Results based on the meta-analysis of hundreds of studies consistently showed negligible differences in outcome between different schools (Smith and Glass, 1977; Stiles et al., 1986). This equivalence of outcome has since been confirmed by a greatly increased number of studies (Lambert, 2004) and advances in research methodology (Lambert and Bergin, 1994). Overall, it looks as if there is little evidence to recommend one type of therapy over another.

If there are no noticeable differences in outcome from different models, then a possible explanation is that there must be some common or non-specific factors which occur in all therapies. Specific factors are techniques or interventions which are model-related. Research findings suggest that factors common across treatments are accounting for a substantial amount of improvement in psychotherapy clients, and may account for most of the gains that result from psychological interventions (Lambert and Bergin, 1994; Lambert, 2004).

Lambert et al. (2004) suggest three main traditional views that have been used to explain this phenomenon. The first derives from learning theory, which maintains that all behaviour (including mental disorders) is learned and therefore can be un-learned, and this view underpins the behavioural and cognitive therapies. The second derives from the humanistic, phenomenological perspective, which argues that the common factor in any therapy involves a caring relationship which is a 'condition' that makes change and growth possible. The third major perspective embraces the social psychology of persuasion and culturally defined social role behaviour first noted by Jerome Frank (1961). Here it is argued that 'all therapies provide a cathartic release of turbulent affect; a rationale or belief system of understanding and explaining one's troubles; a set of rituals or procedures for enacting an alternative, healthier life style; faith in the wisdom of the sanctioned healer' (Lambert et al., 2004: 810).

The above authors conclude that whilst all three of these views are seen to have merit and may apply to some degree, none offers a full explanation. A contemporary view amalgamates these viewpoints and suggests that common ingredients involved in producing change may be a combination of affective experiencing, cognitive mastery and behavioural regulation. However, 'there are, as yet, no precise descriptions of all these factors and no empirical tests of the effectiveness of combinations or integrations of the ingredients' (Lambert et al., 2004: 810).

The common-factors approach finds further support from research in neuroscience. Thus Cozolino writes:

> Although interventions can be based on any theory of change, I propose here that all forms of therapy, regardless of theoretical orientation, will be successful to the degree to which they foster neural growth and integration. Neural growth and integration in therapy are enhanced by:
>
> 1. The establishment of a safe and trusting relationship.
> 2. Gaining new information and experiences across the domains of cognition, emotion, sensation and behaviours.
> 3. The simultaneous or alternating activation of neural networks that are inadequately integrated or dissociated.
> 4. Moderate levels of stress or emotional arousal alternating with periods of calm and safety.
> 5. The integration of conceptual knowledge with emotional and bodily experience through narratives that are co-constructed with the therapist.
> 6. Developing a method of processing and organising new experiences so as to continue ongoing growth and integration outside of therapy. (2002: 27)

Integration as a process

The perspective advocated here is that integration is a process which takes place at an individual level. It evolves and changes over time through experience and the need to learn. This view is captured in the *Concise Oxford Dictionary*, which gives this definition for the verb 'to integrate': Complete (imperfect thing) by addition of parts; combine (parts) into a whole, derived from Latin 'integrare': make whole. Inherent in this definition is the desire or motivation to complete or make whole something yet unfinished or imperfect. However, the wish for wholeness needs to run alongside the awareness of it being unattainable, an illusion, as there is no single or ultimate truth nor final conclusion.

Integrative therapy must never be hijacked into becoming just one more brand of therapy. There is no place for hard and fast rules about precisely what to integrate and how to behave. Stricker and Gold make a distinction between 'integrative psychotherapy' and 'psychotherapy integration'. They favour 'a process of integration that guides psychotherapy rather than a single product or integrative psychotherapy that might become yet another sectarian approach' (2003: 317), a view very close to the one advocated in this chapter. However, what is emphasized here is integration that guides and is created by an individual psychotherapist rather than psychotherapy in general. This echoes the view of Lapworth et al. (2001) that integration requires developing a personal approach from available theoretical frameworks and strategies.

From this perspective there will be as many integrative therapies as there are therapists inclined towards integration. Each will have their own unique way of being, working and interacting with clients. However, they will share certain attitudes, beliefs and values. An integrative therapist will be acutely aware that her way of perceiving, believing and being in the world is but one of many possibilities. A wish to widen one's perspective is an essential precondition of becoming an integrative therapist. What is emphasized is that the basis for integration needs to be clinical practice guided by theory and supported by an attitude of critical inquiry. This process is usefully explored by Polkinghorne (1999).

INTEGRATING PRACTICE AND RESEARCH

There is much need for greater integration between practice and research. Psychological research and therapeutic practice have evolved apart from each other and often with little reference to each other. Yet they are both concerned with the same basic question: How do individuals develop and change over time? Here, two research based areas of knowledge addressing this question are chosen for their relevance to a practising therapist: the first is on human development and in particular the development of social relationships and the sense of self; the second derives from research on therapy process and outcome. Whilst it is impossible here to do justice to the extensive body of research into these two broad areas, a brief summary of factors, identified as important in facilitating change, is attempted below.

Human development: attachment and self

A particular contribution in this area comes from Bowlby and Stern, who are rare amongst practitioners in their commitment to empirical evaluation of their theories. Attachment theory (Bowlby, 1988), a variant of object relations, departs from both classical psychoanalytic and learning theory in that it asserts that the primary human motivational drive is to seek relationships with others. The central premise is that attachment to others is a universal biological need. In infancy it has a function of survival. Throughout life it reduces anxiety in danger and stress. From birth the infant is a social being, programmed to engage in interaction with the primary care-giver. Early bonding to the mother or carer is seen as the precursor of all later social relationships.

Bowlby's theory stimulated much empirical research on how development and the quality of attachment in infancy and early childhood predicts future functioning and to what extent secure or insecure attachments remain constant over time. The results of research studies on attachment seem to confirm the belief of most therapists that early years are particularly significant for people's capacity to form fulfilling relationships in later life (Ainsworth et al., 1978; Fonagy et al., 1991a; Main et al., 1985; Slade and Aber, 1992).

In their longitudinal study, Rutter and Rutter (1992) found that children raised in institutions or exposed to frequent changes of caretakers lacked the ability to form selective attachments during the first few years of life, which was found to be related to difficulties in later years in forming close relationships. But close relationships later in life may compensate for an earlier lack (Quinton and Rutter, 1988 cited in Rutter and Rutter, 1992). This finding supports the view that change is possible throughout the life-course.

The nature of parental influences plays a major role in attachment formation. Findings consistently show that security of attachment is fostered by factors such as the responsiveness of the caretakers to the baby's cues and by active interaction of care-givers with the baby. Development and the quality of attachment were also influenced by the individual characteristics of the child, such as capacities and temperament and how these are perceived and experienced by the parent. The 'mesh' or fit between parent–child, siblings and other relationships has been found to be influenced by these child properties (Rutter and Rutter, 1992).

In summary, research on attachment shows that what seems to matter to children, if they are to become able to feel secure and develop close relationships with those around them, is that the caretakers are reliable, consistent and engaged with them in a way which is tuned into their needs.

Similar findings have emerged from research conducted in the last two decades into the earliest time of life and from neuroscience. By using new methodology in infant research, an impressive body of evidence has emerged to show just how early infants become responsive to their social world. Stern (1985) brings together insights from psychoanalysis and experimental research, focusing in particular on the subjective experiences or what he calls the 'senses of self'. He demonstrates that the development of the infant (0 to 18 months) is anchored in the social interaction between him or her and the caretaker, and each sense of self defines the formation of a new domain of relatedness. This social interaction is characterized by mutual regulation, which is reciprocal. His findings strongly support the view of a child as an active player in his or her destiny from earliest times. The internal organizational change within the infant and the parental responses to this change are mutually facilitative. However, the role of the primary carer in this process is vital, particularly her or his ability for 'affective attunement' with the infant. Stern considers that sharing of affective states is the most pervasive and clinically core feature of intersubjective relatedness. More recent research from neuroscience further testifies to the importance of infancy and the transactions with the social environment in the development of psychic structures (Schore, 1994; Damasio, 2000).

Many of the findings from human development research find an echo in research conducted within the field of therapy process and outcome.

Therapy process and outcome

Process and outcome research addresses questions such as: What is it in therapy that produces change? Which aspects of therapy are responsible for change? Studies exploring these questions have been extensively reviewed by Orlinsky, Graw and Parks (1994: 270–365) and supported by Orlinsky et al. (2004).

Many specific and isolated variables were explored and their association with outcome measured. Looking through the findings overall, there are certain features which appear consistently in different contexts. The outcome of therapy is improved if:

- there is collaboration between therapist and client, such as agreement about goals and investment in the roles by both that is evidence of therapist–client teamwork.
- the therapeutic bond is characterized by good communicative contact or attunement (measured by the therapist's empathic understanding) and by mutual affect and affirmation. Orlinsky et al. conclude that:

  > After a period of continued intensive study since the last edition of this Handbook, the therapeutic bond still looms large as an aspect of process consistently associated with outcome. As a whole and in its several parts, the bond of relatedness between patient and therapist seems to be a central factor both in individual and in group psychotherapies. (1994: 339)

- client factors: the client is suitable for a particular treatment; ready and willing to engage in therapy; co-operative rather than resistant; his style of responding is open rather than defensive; he experiences 'affective arousal' (whether positive or negative) during treatment. These findings testify that the client's contribution to treatment is critical to the outcome.

Reflections on research findings

There are some striking similarities between the processes involved in the course of therapy and those involved in human development. The quality of relationships both developmentally and in the therapeutic encounter emerges as the single most consistent and important predictor of positive change. It is what the client (child) brings as well as how the therapist (carer) responds that matters. Infants/clients, research has shown, are active players in their destiny, constantly seeking to make sense of the world. What also matters to infants and clients alike is the carer's (therapist's) capacity for empathy, affective attunement and affirmation. Human relationships take place through mutual reciprocal engagement which is goal-directed, relevant to the task in hand and appropriate to the context in which it is taking place. Just what activities the protagonists engage in seems less significant. It is *how* they engage with each other that matters most.

Some of the above research findings are further elaborated below in relation to the components of the proposed therapy framework.

A FRAMEWORK FOR DOING THERAPY

Integration evolves from practice and requires reflection on what one is doing and why. In order to focus on this process, a structure or a framework for doing therapy is proposed and described below. It consists of components of therapy which each and every therapist, regardless of her orientation, is likely to consider in their work with clients. It is a structure readers may find useful in defining their own position, and the ways in which they need to adapt that position from time to time and person to person. To illustrate how different models may apply, the components and the issues that may arise for the process of integration, a fictitious client, Tessa, will be used and commented on at a number of points in the text.

> Tessa is a single parent of three- and five-year-old boys. She was brought up as an only child by a divorced mother, with infrequent contact with a father who she feels only took an interest in her once she was a teenager. She is 32, thin and wispy and dressed usually in ill-matching dull colours. She is referred to a therapist by her GP who describes her as depressed and non-coping. She asks for advice about parenting, and help with what she describes as her dreadful temper with the children.

Components of therapy practice

Social and organizational context

The context, background and setting of therapy is generally in place before the therapy begins. Orlinsky et al. (1994) remind us of many of these factors, including the characteristics and experience of both parties, their personal and professional networks and support systems. Increasing importance is now given to the influence of society and the cultural values and assumptions of therapist and client. At the beginning, and throughout their work together, the therapist needs to give vigilant respect to the possibility that her own beliefs and assumptions do not mesh with those of the person opposite. Peace of mind for the client might mean something quite other than for her. A smile, a stare, the asking of questions, can have different values for the client from those the therapist innocently intends. It is unwise to make the assumption that everyone speaks one language, with the same meanings for the same symbols. Moreover, it is also unwise to ignore the fact that, when confronted with difference, human beings tend to be suspicious and can become hostile. Prejudice is part and parcel of our human condition. As therapists, we owe it to ourselves and our clients to better understand those prejudices that we hold ourselves. It is part of the personal and professional development of a therapist to gain proper sensitivity and awareness in this area. Like individuals, organizations also operate within a set of beliefs and norms of behaviour and some understanding of organizational systems and how they operate is invaluable in assessing the impact of context in therapeutic work.

Personal awareness

Personal awareness is an important skill which needs to be addressed in the training of any therapy school. Anyone engaged in helping others will be called upon to do more than apply theoretical knowledge through skilled interventions. As ordinary human beings, they will encounter pain and distress which needs to be faced and contained, and therefore some provision for personal support and development of interpersonal sensitivity and self-awareness is vital.

Studies in human development testify to the importance of 'self-reflectiveness', for instance, in breaking habitual dysfunctional modes of relating (Fonagy et al., 1991b). It is interesting to note, also from the process-outcome research, that therapist's self-relatedness is positively associated to the therapeutic success under certain conditions and suggests that the therapist's ability to maintain an open or self-congruent state is beneficial.

Theoretical understanding

Theory has a powerful influence on what we perceive and how we intervene. This pertains to practitioner and researcher alike. In their writing on contemporary research, Alvesson and Skoldberg (2000) maintain that interpretation precedes data. It is vital, therefore, that the therapist is aware of her own theoretical assumptions. This will, to a large extent, influence which of the components in the framework she will emphasize and how she will apply them in practice. In other words, a practitioner needs to be familiar with the lenses through which she views and perceives the world. She needs also to be prepared, however, for the fact that at times the lenses she uses may not be adequate for what she is looking at. Integrating means recognizing and valuing many different aspects of what it is to be a person, including body, affect, cognition, behaviour and spirituality. Which of these is focused on varies between models. A therapist who rigidly adheres to one model may be limiting the richness that any one experience can provide. Her particular model of mind, if unquestioned, may result in clients being fitted into the theory. Broader knowledge and skill allow for greater choice when responding to a client's specific needs, temperament and circumstances.

Assessment

Assessment involves identifying and finding some explanations for the issues and underlying problems the client brings, with a view to formulating some goals and determining the therapeutic direction. What kinds of questions therapists ask and how they conduct the assessment is something that differentiates one school of therapy from another. It is strongly influenced by each respective therapist's theories about what it is to be human and about development. Consequently, there are certain expectations inherent in each model about goals, that is, changes in the client that need to take place if he is to get better. The therapist's goals will influence the way she listens and interprets the client's story and the presenting problems. The therapist's notion about health and ill-health will also be important. For instance, psychiatrists or clinical psychologists who tend to see clients within a medical setting will be listening to what the client says with an interest in making a diagnosis about signs and symptoms of possible mental illness as a first step in deciding what treatment to prescribe.

> So a psychiatrist who sees Tessa, described by her GP as depressed and not coping, may well assume and decide, on seeing her, that it is her depression which is making her unable to cope and will most likely prescribe an anti-depressant. In contrast, a therapist whose theoretical orientation is not primarily biological, but who believes that what matters is the nature of a person's current and past experience, is likely to make the opposite assumption – that she is depressed because she is not coping. She will be working towards helping Tessa cope better.

Different schools of therapy display a range of assessment criteria, from minimal attention to pathology in some of the humanistic models, to a requirement that therapists describe their clients in terms of psychiatric diagnostic categories. There is a radical difference in the attitude and approach of a therapist who assesses and works with a person who may also be obsessional or phobic and the therapist who focuses in her assessment and treatment on the disorder that the client brings.

Good assessment needs to include attention to suitability of approach to client. Outcome and process research show that, irrespective of orientation, what matters are therapist competence, client characteristics, and the interaction between these two with the techniques offered. So one of the important assessment questions for the therapist to investigate is about how she and the client are likely to get along together.

At the end of the assessment, the therapist will be able to form an overall picture or 'assessment formulation'. It contains more than a mere description of the information gathered in initial interviews, but rather conveys the way this information has been processed and understood by the therapist. This is the therapist's interpretation of the data. Being able to state briefly and concisely what it is that, in the therapist's view, ails the client and why is a difficult but important skill of any therapist. Assessment formulation will provide a rationale for the choice of the approach that the therapist will adopt to work with the client.

Therapeutic contract

Like any human activity, therapy happens within certain boundaries of space, time and role definition. All of these, and in particular the goals of therapy, will to a large extent be determined by the outcome of the assessment.

The research suggests strongly that the contractual process needs to be collaborative. The results show repeatedly that client co-operative participation with the therapist leads to favourable outcomes. This is reminiscent of findings on infant development that 'most of the infant's and parent's time together is spent in active mutual regulation of their own and the other's states, in the service of some aim or goal (Stern et al., 1998: 906).

Although some schools of therapy are uneasy with the notion of goal-setting, here goals are intended to suggest general treatment directions as well as the more programmatic goals favoured by some orientations.

Tessa is a frazzled and discouraged single parent with pre-school children. It may be that the length of time and the emotionality likely in some in-depth work on her own upbringing turn out not to be appropriate at the moment. Appropriate goal-setting may take into account the reality of her present predicament. She sounds as if she is eager to work in so far as her depression allows eagerness. Whatever the goals set, Tessa needs to understand and be in agreement with them if much useful work is to happen within the short time-span dictated by the needs of her children.

This process, although vital at the start of therapy, needs to continue throughout, and it is important for therapists to monitor and evaluate the interventions they make in relation to the overall purpose of therapy and the therapeutic movement during the work.

Working alliance

Working alliance is about establishing a productive working relationship. As research shows, the client's active participation and engagement bodes well for the therapeutic outcome, and the therapist's task when forging the working alliance is to facilitate such contributions and promote collaboration.

The idea of collaboration sits more easily with some models than others. Thus models which see the person as rational and which address the conscious aspects of psychological functioning would find no difficulty with this definition. If, on the other hand, humans are seen as irrational and largely driven by unconscious motivation, as psychoanalytic theory posits, then the working alliance, so defined, becomes problematic. It is a dilemma that any reflective practitioner is bound to ponder from time to time. Is it an adult sitting opposite her who knows what he wants, can say so and will stick to the agreements made, or is the client in front of her more like a confused, frightened and inarticulate child who will become more confused, frightened and inarticulate if asked what exactly it is he wants? As therapists, whether we address the coping adult or the hurt child are decisions we make from moment to moment and which we hope emerge out of the therapeutic encounter rather than from a prescribed theoretical model. How we do this has much impact on the kind of working alliance that evolves.

In the case of Tessa, for instance, although she herself seems to define her problems in terms of specific tasks and behaviours that may appear to be amenable to change, she may turn out to be so low-spirited about her parenting that she will stay feeling more like a helpless child. In this case, she may agree to all sorts of goals and tasks with the therapist, but then forget, fail to understand or not do her 'homework'. It seems possible that she would arrive late or miss sessions, and this may have a strong emotional impact on both parties. Tessa may feel yet more ashamed and hopeless, whilst the therapist may discover growing sulkiness or irritation in herself. If this is what happens, then the focus from goals and tasks may need to shift to the therapeutic relationship more directly. The therapist may enquire, for instance, how Tessa feels about coming for therapy and what she thinks is going on and how she experiences being with the therapist.

In the course of their work, therapists constantly move their focus from the task, the instrumental aspect of the therapeutic relationship, the 'doing', to the experience of 'being with' the client. They are indeed concurrent phenomena. The working alliance may be seen as a bridge between doing and being in pursuit of therapy goals.

Therapeutic activities: tools of the trade

Without good-heartedness, it would be difficult for the therapist to persist with the major generic skills which are part of almost every interactional therapy. These skills resemble closely two of Carl Rogers' (1951) core conditions: empathic understanding and unconditional positive regard. If the therapist manages to listen well and shows that she has accurately picked up the client's story and his inner, even out-of-awareness feelings and thoughts, this empathic and respectful responding is again likely to help the client stay with even painful experience, as well as to feel confident in the therapist.

Outcome research shows that some interventions traditionally associated with a single model, such as interpretation, experiential confrontation and paradoxical injunction, are particularly powerful. Yet each comes from a very different tradition. Interpretation is the sine qua non of analytic schools; experiential confrontation is widely used in Gestalt therapy, and paradoxical injunction in family therapy. This raises interesting questions for an integrative approach: should a therapist learn and apply techniques from orientations which have, as in this case, very different theoretical bases (as would be done in an eclectic approach), or should she be looking for a theoretical model or rationale which might explain the effectiveness of these different methodologies? According to Stricker and Gold:

> Perhaps the most critical strategic and technical questions in any integrative psychotherapy are when to move from one technique to the next and, correspondingly, to shift orientations and strategies from the behavioral to the experiential to the psychodynamic, and so on. (2003: 330)

Therapeutic relationship

The relationship between the therapist and client is in very many instances *the* therapy. All clients are extremely likely to need from the therapist some of the attitudes and behaviours of what we can loosely call 'good parents'. None of us, infants, children and adults alike, can discover and value what we truly are unless we feel sure that the person we depend upon cares enough, understands enough and is never going to diminish us by her judgements, but will give us secure space and time in which to be together. Orlinksy et al. (1994: 364) suggest that the therapeutic bond provides a leverage from within the therapeutic system itself to influence the conditions under which therapy can be effective. In the light of this, the statement 'the relationship is the therapy' proposes that the client's experience of the therapeutic relationship will have a profound impact, for better or for worse. This is not to diminish the importance of theoretical knowledge from which we derive our bearing, nor of technical expertise or skills. Just as with a great musician, technique is vital if the beauty of the music is to be conveyed, but technique alone is not enough.

The therapeutic relationship, like the parental one, involves two people in reciprocal interaction. As Sullivan (1953) pointed out long ago, the self is forged in interaction. Infant research supports these clinical observations and demonstrates the bi-directional influence between mother and child. This aspect of the therapeutic bond has not been extensively investigated in outcome research, but the few studies mentioned show that reciprocal affirmation between the client and therapist is constantly and positively related to outcome.

Working with the therapeutic relationship involves listening not only to what is being said, but also monitoring what is going on in the relationship, in the here and now, with regard to unspoken, under-the-surface thoughts and feelings and the roles which the therapist and client assume in relation to each other. The therapist may verbalize such observations if and when appropriate. To be able to do so requires sensitivity and evolves from practice and experience, yet we believe it is a skill all therapists should try to acquire.

How therapists use their observations and knowledge about what goes on in the therapeutic relationship is again something which differentiates between therapy models. The psychodynamic and the humanistic-existential models have always placed the therapeutic relationship at the centre of their work. The former emphasizes the transferential, and the latter the existential or real aspects of the relationship. Some examples with Tessa illustrate the different ways of working with the therapeutic relationship, starting with a psychodynamically orientated therapist.

> Let us imagine that, even after much endeavour on the therapist's part to convey that what she has to offer is not the giving of advice, Tessa nevertheless repeatedly makes such demands. Sooner or later the therapist will begin to feel useless or bullied, or helpless or irritated. Once she notes this, she wonders if she could be responding to Tessa's unconscious need once again to prove the carer as failing her, as someone she couldn't possibly rely on to protect her.

The therapist may say:

> 'Lately I noticed you have been making demands on me which I haven't been able to satisfy, and you are clearly disappointed and angry with me. Perhaps you feel that I, like your mother, cannot be trusted to take proper care of you. It's as if you are trying to convince both of us that no one could possibly bear your need.'

This is a typical transference interpretation based on the therapist's observation of her own inner state (her countertransference) in the interaction with Tessa and which she links to her knowledge of Tessa's history.

At the instant when the psychodynamic therapist wondered about whether Tessa was turning her into a depriving mother, a response from existential dialogue might be:

> 'When you folded your arms and looked down and stopped talking just now, I think I was scared of you. And I had a first impulse to act crossly, the way you've described your mother shouting at you to get a bit of backbone. And almost at the same moment I could feel a coldness inside me expanding to a sort of loneliness. It reminded me of when I was a child and I used to hide in the shed when I was upset, and how nobody came and looked for me.'

The invitation in this method is for the client to use it too so that there is an exploration of the actuality of the two people's responses to each other and of the implications of that in their own lives.

Contemporary therapists in both of these broad schools pay a great deal of attention to the relationship between client and therapist as it is experienced in the therapeutic session. It is assumed that, just as in infant development, what produces change is the mutually shared lived experience (Bollas, 1989; Erskine, 1989; Hycner, 1993; Kahn, 1991; Mitchell, 1988, 1994; Wright, 1991). Recent research on therapists' responsiveness to clients' interpersonal styles would seem to support this assumption (Hardy et al., 1998).

Although most of our knowledge about the therapeutic relationship is based on psychodynamic and humanistic-existential therapies, there is a growing recognition among cognitive therapists of the importance of the therapeutic relationship. Sanders and Wills (1999: 120) point out that there is substantial work being done by cognitive therapists who are developing cognitive interpersonal models of the therapeutic process and are focusing on 'how to use the relationship as an active ingredient in therapy.'

CONVERGING TRENDS

Although there are many differences in technique between psychodynamic and humanistic-existential models, recent developments in psychoanalysis brings them much closer together. Analytic theories and techniques have moved from emphasizing understanding or insight (that is, the cognitive/ego functions) to a more direct focus on emotion and the sense of self as they unfold and are re-experienced in the therapeutic encounter. The work is increasingly focused on the 'here and now' as a way of understanding the past, rather than the other way round, as used to be the case. Kohon writes:

> The psychoanalytic situation is always created and developed from the specific and unique interaction between the patient and the analyst

and

> The analyst is never an 'outsider'; he is part and parcel of the transference situation. In fact, one could argue that the transference is as much a function of countertransference as the countertransference is a result of the transference. (1988: 53)

This brings this model very close to the humanistic-existential viewpoint. There is a growing recognition in both models of the role that intersubjectivity plays in the therapeutic encounter. What is emphasized is both 'you and me'. Intersubjectivity is a concept which transcends intrapersonal and interpersonal psychologies and postulates that individual development cannot be separated from the context of living and interacting with others:

> Intersubjectivity is a field which is always there and makes possible experiences of closeness, distance, withdrawal and isolation, for all these experiences are only possible in relation to something or someone. In other words, these are modes of being that take place within an intersubjective space. (Diamond, 1996).

Stern (1985) points out that whilst psychoanalysis, in contrast to academic psychology, has always been interested in the subjective experience of the individual, it has not conceptualized intersubjective experience as a 'dyadic phenomenon'.

Buber (1970), with his existential ideas, had a particularly great influence on Gestalt therapists and other humanists. Rather than venture an interpretation, a humanistic-existential therapist might use what he calls a 'dialogic approach', which involves close attention to the present process between both parties. Whether or not the client joins in, Buber suggests that a dialogic attitude, and if necessary one-sided maintenance of this style by the therapist, demonstrates honesty and empathy and profound listening in a way likely to be of use to the client. He speaks of the moment of intimacy, the I–Thou which can suddenly illuminate such dialogue. By this he means a simultaneous moment of recognition and empathy between therapist and client which he sees as healing. This is very similar to what Stern et al. (1998) describe as 'non-interpretive mechanisms in psychoanalytic therapy', including 'moments of meeting' and 'now moments' which are seen as both more personal or intersubjective than interpretation alone, 'the something more'. They define the moment of meeting as:

> highly specific with each partner contributing something unique and authentic. When a moment of meeting is created the therapist's response cannot be routine or technical but rather he/she must use a specific aspect of his or her individuality that carries a personal signature. (1998: 913)

The change of focus during the last two decades from the intrapsychic to the interpersonal and intersubjective is usefully explored by Stolorow et al. (1987). Mitchell (1988) introduced the idea of the 'relational model', which offers a way of conceptually integrating a cluster of analytic theories, including British object-relations, interpersonal psychoanalysis and self-psychology, a development which he considers to be a major paradigm shift in psychoanalysis.

More often than is perhaps always made clear, analytic and humanistic-existential practice can be likened to two roads starting from and leading to the same places but running in parallel. At times an enlightened road-builder would do well to remove the partitions between the two roads and let them operate as one, more effective wide highway.

CONCLUSIONS AND IMPLICATIONS FOR TRAINING

The convergence of different schools is not surprising. It is consistent with the research findings that carers of young children and therapists have much in common when facilitating change. Therapists, like carers of young infants, respond unconsciously to the client's needs in a given moment and, if their responses are attuned to the client, a resulting shared experience will enable them together to produce the movement necessary for growth and development.

Theory will continue to be an essential foundation for the training of future therapists, but knowledge needs to be integrated with the practical skills and the personal qualities and attitudes of the practitioner. The findings presented here would indicate that a major emphasis needs to be placed on enabling the student to learn how 'to be' with their clients, regardless of the theoretical model adhered to. Whether or not the therapist pays attention to, reflects upon or deliberately uses her subjective experiences in the therapeutic encounter, such experiences are always present. Learning to attend to and reflect on these are essential in any therapy training. Learning to work 'relationally' has become a stated goal on many courses. Yet including both you and me in an intervention is one of the most difficult things for trainee therapists to master.

Good theoretical grounding is essential for any practitioner. To understand what is evolving in the therapy, and why, one can refer to more than one theory. If one way of theorizing the work with our clients makes most sense, then the integrative position is to allow that theory to inform what we do. It is also worth bearing in mind that human beings cheerfully function with several, often contradictory, psychologies at once. An integrative psychotherapy training offers a student from the beginning a variety of approaches and encourages a critical and evaluative stance. In this way the therapist is able to develop her own favoured approach derived from a broad theoretical base and tested and modified through practice. This is likely to lead to a sense of ownership and confidence in one's expertise and an ability to make an informed choice about the area of work, including the type of client problems.

To reiterate, learning of integration through practice involves constant vigilance about what one is doing and why. Action, a particular intervention, should be followed by observation of what has happened and reflection on the process and outcome. This in turn may stimulate the therapist to find some answers to theoretical questions about what is involved in the process of change. An integrative therapist will aspire to be, above all, a reflective practitioner and researcher.

REFERENCES

Ainsworth, M.D., Waters, M.C. and Wall, S. (1978) *Patterns of Attachment: Assessed in a Strange Situation and at Home,* Hillsdale, NJ: Lawrence Erlbaum.

Alvesson, M. and Skoldberg, K. (2000) *Reflexive Methodology: New Vistas for Qualitative Research.* London: Sage.

Beck, A.T., Rush, A.J., Shaw, B.F. and Emery, G. (1979) *Cognitive Therapy of Depression.* New York: Guilford Press.

Bollas, C. (1989) *Forces of Destiny.* London: Free Association Books.

Bowlby, J. (1988) *A Secure Base: Clinical Application of Attachment Theory.* London: Tavistock/Routledge.

British Psychological Society, Division of Counselling Psychology (2007/8) *Qualification in Counselling Psychology: Candidate Handbook.* Leicester: BPS.

Buber, M. (1970) *I and Thou.* New York: Scribners.

Cozolino, L.J. (2002) *The Neuroscience of Psychotherapy.* New York: Norton.

Damasio, A. (2000) *The Feeling of What Happens.* London: Vintage.

Diamond, N. (1996) 'Can we speak of internal and external reality?', *Group Analysis,* 29: 303–317.

Dollard, J. and Miller, N.E. (1950) *Personality and Psychotherapy.* New York: McGraw-Hill.

Dryden, W. (ed.) (1992) *Integrative and Eclectic Therapy: A Handbook.* Buckingham: Open University Press.

Erskine, R.G. (1989) 'A relationship therapy: Developmental perspectives', in B. Loria (ed.), *Developmental Theories and the Clinical Process: Conference Proceedings of the Eastern Regional Transactional Analysis Conference.* Stamford, CT: Eastern Regional Transactional Analysis Association.

Evans, K.R. and Gilbert, M.C. (2005) *An Introduction to Integrative Psychotherapy.* New York: Palgrave Macmillan.

Fonagy, P., Steele, H. and Steele, M. (1991a) 'Measuring the ghost in the nursery: A summary of the main findings of the Anna Freud Center – University College', *Bulletin of the Anna Freud Center,* 14: 115–31.

Fonagy, P., Steele, H., Steele, M., Moran, G.S. and Higgitt, A.C. (1991b) 'The capacity for understanding mental states: The reflective self in parent and child and its significance for security of attachment', *Infant Mental Health Journal,* 12: 200–18.

Frank, J.D. (1961) Persuasion and Healing: A Comparative Study of Psychotherapy. New York: Schocken.

Hardy, G.E., Stiles, W.B., Barkham, M. and Startup, M. (1998) 'Therapist responsiveness to client interpersonal styles during time-limited treatment for depression', *Journal of Consulting and Clinical Psychology,* 66: 304–312.

Hollanders, H. (2003) 'The eclectic and integrative approach', in R. Woolfe, W. Dryden and S. Strawbridge (eds), *Handbook of Counselling Psychology*, 2nd edn. London: Sage.

Hycner, R.M. (1993) *Between Person and Person*. New York: Gestalt Institute of Cleveland Press.

Kahn, M. (1991) *Between Therapist and Client: The New Relationship*. New York: Freeman.

Kohon, G. (ed.) (1988) *The British School of Psychoanalysis: The Independent Tradition*. London: Free Association Books.

Lambert, M.J. (2004) *Bergin and Garfield's Handbook of Psychotherapy and Behavior Change,* 5th edn. New York: Wiley.

Lambert, M.J. and Bergin, A.E. (1994) 'The effectiveness of psychotherapy', in A.E. Bergin and S.L. Garfield (eds), *Handbook of Psychotherapy and Behavior Change*. New York: Wiley.

Lambert, M.J., Garfield, S.L. and Bergin, A.E. (2004) 'Overview, trends, and future issues', in M.J. Lambert (ed.), *Bergin and Garfield's Handbook of Psychotherapy and Behavior Change,* 5th edn. New York: Wiley.

Lapworth, P., Sills, C. and Fish, S. (2001) *Integration in Counselling and Psychotherapy: Developing a Personal Approach*. London: Sage

Lazarus, A.A. (1992) 'Multimodal therapy: Technical eclecticism with minimal integration', in J.C. Norcross and M.R. Goldfried (eds), *Handbook of Psychotherapy Integration*. New York: Basic Books.

Mahrer, A.R. (1989) *The Integration of Psychotherapies: A Guide for Practising Therapists*. New York: Human Sciences Press.

Main, M., Kaplan, N. and Cassidy, J. (1985) 'Security in infancy, childhood and adulthood: A move to the level of representation', *Monograph of the Society for Research in Child Development*, 50 (1–2, Serial No. 209).

Mitchell, S.A. (1988) *Relational Concepts in Psychoanalysis: An Integration*. Cambridge, MA: Harvard University Press.

Mitchell, S.A. (1994) 'Recent developments in psychoanalytic theorizing', *Journal of Psychotherapy Integration*, 4(2): 93–103.

Norcross, J.C. and Goldfried, M.R. (eds) (1992) *Handbook of Psychotherapy Integration*. New York: Basic Books.

O'Brien, M. and Houston, G. (2000) *Integrative Therapy: A Practitioner's Guide*. London: Sage.

O'Brien, M. and Houston, G. (2007) *Integrative Therapy: A Practitioner's Guide*, 2nd edn. London: Sage.

Orlinsky, D.E, Graw, K. and Parks, B. (1994) 'Process and outcome in psychotherapy – noch einmal', in A.E. Bergin and S.L. Garfield (eds), *Handbook of Psychotherapy and Behavior Change*, 4th edn. New York: Wiley.

Orlinsky, D.E., Ronnestad, M.H. and Willutzki, U. (2004) 'Fifty years of psychotherapy process-outcome research: Continuity and change', in M.J. Lambert (ed.), *Bergin and Garfield's Handbook of Psychotherapy and Behavior Change*, 5th edn. New York: Wiley.

Palmer, S. and Woolfe, R. (eds) (1999) *Integrative and Eclectic Counselling and Psychotherapy*. London: Sage.

Polkinghorne, D.E. (1999) 'Traditional research and psychotherapy practice', *Journal of Clinical Psychology*, 55: 1429–40.

Rogers, C.R. (1951) *Client-Centered Therapy*. Boston: Houghton-Mifflin.

Rutter, M. and Rutter, M. (1992) *Developing Minds: Challenge and Continuity Across the Life Span*. Harmondsworth: Penguin.

Ryle, A. (1990) *Cognitive-analytic Therapy: Active Participation in Change*. Chichester: Wiley.

Sanders, D. and Wills, F. (1999) 'The therapeutic relationship in cognitive therapy', in C. Feltham (ed.), *Understanding the Counselling Relationship.* London: Sage.

Schore, A. (1994) *Affect Regulation and the Origin of Self.* Hillsdale, NJ: Lawrence Erlbaum.

Scott, T. (2004) *Integrative Psychotherapy in Healthcare: A Humanistic Approach.* Basingstoke: Palgrave Macmillan.

Slade, A. and Aber, J.L. (1992) 'Attachments, drives and development: Conflicts and convergencies in theory', in J.W. Barron, M.N. Eagle and D.L. Wolitzky (eds), *Interface of Psychoanalysis and Psychology.* Washington, DC: American Psychological Association.

Smith, M.L. and Glass G.V. (1977) 'Meta-analysis of psychotherapy outcome studies', *American Psychologist,* 32: 752–60.

Stern, D.N. (1985) *The Interpersonal World of the Infant.* New York: Basic Books.

Stern, D., Sander, L.W., Nahum, J.P., Harrison, A.M., Lyons-Ruth, K., Morgan, A.C., Bruschwiler-Stern, N. and Tronick, E. (The Process of Change Study Group) (1998) 'Non-interpretive mechanisms in psychoanalytic therapy: The "something more" than interpretation', *International Journal of Psychoanalysis,* 79: 903–21.

Stiles, W.B., Shapiro, D.A. and Elliott, R.K. (1986) 'Are all psychotherapies equivalent?', *American Psychologist,* 41: 165–80.

Stolorow, R.D., Brandchaft, B. and Atwood, G.E. (1987) *Psychoanalytic Treatment: An Intersubjective Approach.* Hillsdale, NJ: Analytic Press.

Stricker, G. (2005) 'Can something hard be made easy? A book essay', *Journal of Psychotherapy Integration,* 15: 224–237.

Stricker, G. and Gold, J.R. (eds) (1993) *Comprehensive Handbook of Psychotherapy Integration.* New York: Plenum Press.

Stricker, G. and Gold, J.R. (2003) 'Integrative approaches to psychotherapy', in A.S. Gurman and S.B. Messer (eds), *Essential Psychotherapies: Theory and Practice*, 2nd edn. New York: Guilford Press.

Sullivan, H.S. (1953) *The Interpersonal Theory of Psychiatry.* New York: Norton.

United Kingdom Council for Psychotherapy (2002) *National Register of Psychotherapists.* London: UKCP.

Wachtel, P.L. (1977) *Psychoanalysis and Behaviour Therapy. Toward an Integration.* New York: Basic Books.

Wright, K. (1991) *Vision and Separation: Between Mother and Baby.* London: Free Association Books.

PART III

DIFFERENCE AND DISCRIMINATION

Although historically the various theoretical traditions of counselling psychology have focused attention on individual psychology, counselling psychology, as a recognized branch of professional psychology, came to fruition in Britain in the 1980s in a climate of concern about difference and discrimination. The major traditions of therapeutic theory and practice were increasingly confronted by more sociologically and politically informed perspectives on inequality, discrimination and identity politics. Although we would not wish to underestimate the links between social and economic deprivation and psychological distress, by the 1980s the more traditional conceptions of class had become less of a focus for thinking about social inequality, and this remains so. However, coming to the fore, with the rise of identity politics, were challenges mounted in relation to race and culture, gender and sexual orientation and, later, physical and mental disability.

Whilst the differing traditions have addressed these challenges in various ways, it is perhaps the constructionist analyses focusing on discourses, narratives and systems that have been most influential in theorizing the relationships between social processes and individual psychology.

Social and economic inequalities, discrimination and oppression are linked to perceived difference and the dynamics of power. The chapters in this part of the book explore some of the issues posed by difference and discrimination in relation to counselling psychology theory and practice. Chapters 10, 11 and 13 address particular areas of difference in relation to the social construction of identities and power differentials. Chapter 12 focuses on relational aspects of power and the trauma that results from the abuse of power across a range of relationships characterized by inequality.

10

CROSS-CULTURAL COUNSELLING PSYCHOLOGY

Zack Eleftheriadou

The main focus of this chapter will be to outline the changes within psychology and the implications for counselling psychology practice. It will begin with an exploration of some commonly held notions surrounding cross-cultural therapy, including an exploration of the concepts of race, culture and identity. Experiences from cross-cultural therapeutic relationships will be used to illustrate the realities of cross-cultural counselling and to challenge existing stereotypes. Issues such as racial/cultural matching of client and counselling psychologist and how racial and cultural issues filter into the counselling psychology relationship will be explored. Case material will be used throughout the chapter to illustrate the dynamics at play, when the client and counselling psychologist share a culture or racial background and when they inhabit different worlds.

COUNSELLING PSYCHOLOGY AND THERAPEUTIC WORK

Counselling psychology is a newer branch of psychology, which bridges the applied, therapeutic aspects of psychology as well as the academic debates and research findings. Historically, counselling and psychology have moved their own separate ways, and in a way the discipline of counselling psychology has been a return to psychology. This has been particularly useful in the cross-cultural field as it means we can take on board theoretical issues and research findings to back up and even challenge therapeutic practice, especially from the disciplines of social psychology (Smith and Bond, 1998) and developmental psychology (Gardiner et al., 1988; Kagitcibasi, 2007) amongst others. The aim is to move away from rigid clinical practice to one that can be re-evaluated constantly. The importance for the psychologist to have a good level of personal awareness throughout the treatment process will become increasingly evident in this chapter, as difficult cross-cultural barriers have to be overcome.

The counselling psychologist has a choice in which school of thought to follow, shown by the plethora of approaches utilized throughout this book. This chapter aims to present cross-cultural ideas that a practitioner of any school of thought can follow, as these issues are increasingly present in all our work. However, the therapeutic practice followed in this chapter stems from predominantly psychoanalytic ideas, where the central notion in clinical work is based on the belief that there is an 'unconscious' (Bateman and Holmes, 1995; Lemma-Wright, 1995). This implies that there are behaviours and thoughts which are not in our conscious mind and they are unaccessible to us as they cause too much anxiety to consider within the conscious mind. They may have been pushed into the unconscious, as they are basically incompatible with other emotions or thoughts. In therapeutic work it takes a long time to uncover these and become conscious. They emerge through the person's narrative, as well as through the concepts of 'transference' and 'countertransference' (Bateman and Holmes, 1995). These concepts imply that there will be aspects of a client's early relationships that are unconscious and will be repeated in adult life without conscious awareness. An example of this repetition pattern is a woman who repeatedly becomes involved with the same type of person as her alcoholic father. During the therapy, it is common that the person places incorrect perceptions onto the relationship with the counselling psychologist, or at times evokes something in them, making them behave in ways like their early significant figures did. There are degrees of this unconscious communication process between the psychologist and the client which occur throughout the therapeutic process, and we all have to be aware of it by attending regular supervision and personal development. These types of dynamics occur however experienced we are, and they need to be understood slowly and carefully if significant and lasting changes are to be made in the client's thinking patterns. To summarize, both counselling psychology and contemporary psychoanalysis view the therapeutic relationship as 'relational', that is, the client is not speaking to someone who is a 'blank screen' or 'neutral', but both the psychologist and the client influence each other, consciously and unconsciously (Altman, 2005).

In cross-cultural work these concepts can be extended to what has been called 'pre-transference' (Curry, 1964), which can take place either towards the client or the psychologist. An example of this would be a client who has experienced racism in everyday life; when walking into our consulting room they will expect to be treated in the same way as other clients. Psychoanalysis helps us to comprehend how this process may emerge in a covert, hidden way, through statements or slips in conversation that people argue 'were not really meant' and yet they relay extremely significant information in understanding something about that person's emotional history. Furthermore, in cross-cultural work we find that many of our black and ethnic minority clients have had multiple racist experiences, that they might even begin to believe they are in some way 'inferior' or extremely 'different'. David, a West Indian client, from the beginning introduced racial stereotypes of others, letting me know indirectly how he had been labelled himself. He didn't expect me to think or treat him as an equal as he had never had any experience of this type of relationship. It is always a challenge to work with this therapeutically and not to become defensive, as this will inevitably stop the client from bringing any more material to the therapy. With David, I had to strike a balance between understanding his individual experiences and ensuring that I was not personalizing the racist issues. At the same time, I had to leave him adequate space and time to come to his own conclusions and to make any life (thinking or behavioural) changes he wished to rather than imposing any on him. The need to help clients, particularly those who may be socially excluded to some extent, like David, has to be resisted as it does not help anyone in the long term. It only serves to create dependency on the psychologist, and it reinforces the feeling that it is the majority culture psychologist who holds the power.

BACKGROUND TO THE CROSS-CULTURAL FIELD

In today's international community, cross-cultural issues filter into all aspects of our lives and inevitably have a significant role to play in therapeutic work. It is a time of paradoxes, where cross-cultural communication, contact and relationships have increased significantly, and yet we are faced with multiple wars and terrorism as hatred is directed towards particular religious groups and cultures. The whole area of cross-cultural counselling psychology has been investigated significantly less than other areas of psychology. Recently there has also been an increase in the number of therapists from different cultural/racial groups training in counselling psychology, although many more are required. To some extent, this has had an impact in the number of ethnic minorities seeking support. Centres like NAFSIYAT, the Inter-Cultural Therapy Centre, The Refugee Therapy Centre, and the Medical Foundation for the Care of the Support of Victims of Torture (based in North London, UK) have demonstrated that people of all cultures not only require but will also use appropriate therapeutic support. More mental health organizations are acknowledging (a) the need to consider implications for clinical practice and (b) the need for further professional training, in order to work effectively within cross-cultural relationships.

The intellectual debates have recently began to filter into the mechanics of clinical practice (see Eleftheriadou, 1997). Numerous academic journals, such as the American publications *Journal of Cross-cultural Psychology and Multicultural Counseling and Development* and *Journal of Cross-Cultural Psychology*, and an increasing number of books are being published every year in cross-cultural work. The reason for the huge expansion of literature in the cross-cultural field in the UK (and indeed around the world) has been as a result of the growing evidence that clients are being misdiagnosed, largely due to the misunderstanding of cultural factors and existing racism. Through vast clinical and research evidence, Littlewood and Lipsedge have concluded that the psychiatrist.

> has less clear expectations of how the patient is likely to behave and what, in different soci-
> eties, the limits of normality and abnormality are. In addition to his background and
> training, the psychiatrist's attitude to the minority patient will be formed by his own
> personal problems, conscious and unconscious racist assumptions and the particular
> setting in which the two meet. (1989: 13–4)

Although the above observations (see Bhugra and Cochrane, 2001 and Bhui and Bhugra, 2007, for more recent discussions) apply more to psychiatric assessments, as counselling psychologists we also need to be aware of how we understand another culture's norms and practices, hence the danger of labelling something as pathological because it is 'different'. Of course, the area of psychiatric assessment is complex and rather vast, therefore for the purposes of this chapter the focus will remain on psychological work. Nonetheless, as a result of these factors, amongst others, there has been considerably less use of the mental health services by ethnic minority clients. Even when people use the existing services there is still a higher drop-out rate from ethnic minorities (Fernando, 1991, 1995), which are issues still requiring much consideration.

Psychological research is still new and much more is required in order to really begin to understand the impact of race and culture in clinical practice. Thus far, the notion that if you have trained in one theoretical framework means you can work with people from all cultures, however, has been challenged. Undoubtedly, cultural issues cut across every approach of therapeutic work. The cross-cultural counselling psychologist has to keep these debates in mind and keep up to date with the research findings. Most importantly, though, we need to understand the impact of culture in our clients' lives as well as the meaning culture has in our own lives (Bhui and Bhugra, 2007). For a long time cultural and racial issues have been viewed as the client's 'issues', implying something that we are disconnected from and even problematic.

PSYCHOLOGY, CROSS-CULTURAL PSYCHOLOGY AND CULTURAL PSYCHOLOGY

The relationship between culture and psychology has been of interest for over a century, and yet it is only recently that psychology has been able to take a formal part in the academic debates and research. Currently, there are broadly two schools of thought within psychology which deal with cultural issues: cross-cultural psychology (Berry et al., 2002), and the relatively newer field that has been called 'cultural psychology' (Schweder, 1991; Stigler et al., 1990; Ratner, 2008).

The field of cross-cultural psychology compares concepts and events between different cultures, based on the premise that there is one inherent universal aspect across cultures. The latter takes a more anthropological view; that is, to examine a culture within itself. It takes the view that everything can be understood within its context and if the framework is removed, it becomes senseless. An example of cross-cultural psychology research might be to take a concept such as 'adolescence' and to explore it across cultures (see Berry et al., 2002). In the latter approach there would not be a preconceived notion of 'adolescence'. In fact, many would argue that it does not even exist as a concept as it is not seen as a distinct 'stage' of development. The other difference is that cross-cultural psychology has generally used Western measuring research tools, and researchers may have not belonged to that culture. This is changing, however, through the involvement of more countries in formulating research and assessment tools (see Suzuki et al., 2001). The latter approach uses 'insiders' or researchers who are part of the culture, or at least understand and speak the language, and will observe the process as such. Cultural psychology also comes from a different philosophical base where the observer is in interaction with the subject, hence the influence on each other, observer and subject, needs to be considered. Applied to clinical work, the philosophy of cultural psychology implies that there would be no usage of concepts which are considered to be universal, for example, asking a client to talk about their 'adolescent years'. Both approaches, cross-cultural and cultural psychology, are necessary if we are to have any type of comparison across cultures. Furthermore, if we are to work across cultures we also need to understand the object within its context. This has been demonstrated numerous times in the research of visual illusions where there is more than one image within a picture. At first glance, we can only see one image, but the longer that one observes the picture, so it alternates between one image and the other. Therefore, eventually we can see that both images are present, rather than one or the other. In the same way, if we translate this process to cross-cultural work, we can begin to see that culture is always present and part of the framework, and how we can become more sensitive to see an object within its context (rather than viewing it within a Western context, for example).

Cultural psychology has challenged the notion that all thinking mechanisms are fixed or that there is a central inherent mechanism across cultures which is universal. In fact, this *is* the main debate in this field; that is, whether deep down we are all the same and any variations are masked by culture. And if this is the case and we are all the same, then how can we really translate these across cultures? This will be examined throughout the chapter, but perhaps the most crucial element in cross-cultural work is accepting that there are differences and not all are bridgeable. This can be explored further by finding ways of opening up a dialogue about the meaning of culture.

ISSUES OF RACE, CULTURE AND IDENTITY

The concept 'race' is generally used to refer to unchangeable characteristics such as skin colour, hair, eye colour, facial characteristics, which are shared by a group of people who have the same ancestral origins. It does not refer to genetic differences between races, although, sadly, many still hold these views, and race often becomes a reason for political oppression. We live in a society that is racist and prejudiced, and this has a profound impact on the psyche. Ethnic minority groups continue to face discrimination, social, political, educational and economic disadvantage. We hear from our clients accounts of racism and culture blindness. As Thomas states:

> Racism, however, is not just a hatred of, or a conscious belief in the inferiority of, black people. Nor is it just physical violence. Disavowal of a person's 'different' existence is in itself a way of not recognising the degree to which this pervasive system operates in groups and in the individual. Inevitably, racism has a detrimental effect on social and personal relationships. Not only is this evident in relationships between black and white people but between black people themselves. (1992: 135)

So we need to be able to take into account the reality of racism and the impact it has on people. If we are open to it, then stories of race and racism will undoubtedly be recounted by our clients. The counselling psychologist needs to take responsibility to address this with the clients, who are often unsure whether it is safe enough to do so. Hence it often emerges in unconscious ways or disguised ways (Vannoy-Adams, 1996), unless triggered by a shocking media event and then people somehow feel there is 'permission' to discuss it and to be passionate about the issues.

Race is often extended to include cultural elements, implying that somehow people's behaviours or values are unchangeable. Sadly, it is not only at times of war that we find that people of the same race exhibit a strong prejudice (and even practice torture) towards others due to cultural factors such as religion or political beliefs; these differences become perceived, like race, as 'unbridgeable'. Although race and culture are often used interchangeably, in this context, culture is defined as something psycho-social and therefore changeable.

Culture can be defined as:

> a way of creating shared ways of functioning in order to communicate effectively ... we create shared events, practices, roles, values, myths, rules, beliefs, habits, symbols, illusions and realities. (Eleftheriadou, 1994: 1–2)

Culture includes the visible aspects such as dress-code, as well as all the invisible aspects such as the way we relate and think, and even 'culturally appropriate' ways of expressing emotions. Culture is such a part of us that it becomes incredibly difficult to

convey. For example, a client called Shenaz, on discussing her marriage and re
with her in-laws, got caught up in not knowing how much background infor
provide me with before launching into her life story, which was meaningful v
particular familial and cultural system. Later in the therapy, when more trust h
oped, she told me she feared she would be judged about not taking a mor
assertive stance with them, so she in fact took a great deal of time explaining 'cultural
structures'. Like Shenaz, it is not unusual that clients feel a sense of being overwhelmed
when they have to try to do this in counselling psychology. This is because much of
what constitutes culture is around us, we are part of it and require it, but it is not directly
observable. The individual and culture have a dynamic relationship. This can change
through time and with the arrival of newcomers or people returning to their culture
after exposure to new cultures and ways of living. Therefore, it is always the *relationship*
that we are interested in, not just the culture or only the individual. If we concentrate
on the culture we would be in danger of viewing the person within a stereotypical box
and, likewise, if we concentrate on the self only we would be trying to understand a
person without a context. In other words, we would not be viewing the whole, only
parts of it. At all times, the relationship between the triad – that is, the person, the familial
system and the cultural context – needs to be considered. If this framework can be kept
in mind, it will enable the counselling psychologist to keep a balance between the different aspects which contribute to people's way of being.

The distinction between various cultures is usually made in relation to dramatic and
obvious differences, but of course there are endless, often less marked distinctions. These
can be observed in everyday behaviours, for example: the way of relating to others such
as patterns of greeting, comfortable distance when in conversation with others, child
rearing values, dependence and independence, and all the ways one interacts with one's
social community (see Eleftheriadou, 2007). The challenge of cross-cultural work is to
have the sensitivity and the ability to enter a different world, or at least its significant
components, and not only understand it, but feel comfortable to challenge it.

Racial and cultural factors, together, form what we call our identity or the way we
define ourselves, psychologically and socially, in terms of our sense of belongingness
formed through adherence to one single culture. As Pedersen states:

> Culture's complexity is illustrated by the hundreds or perhaps even thousands of cul-
> turally learned identities, affiliations, and roles we each assume at one time or
> another. Culture is dynamic as each one of these alternative cultural identities replaces
> another in salience. (1997: 177)

Since it is a constellation of more than one culture, the counselling psychologist has to
be aware of which is the client's salient cultural identity, depending on the cultural
framework at the time. This idea of multiple identities (Thomas and Schwarzbaum,
2005) is increasingly supported by client accounts and research. For example, many
clients talk about how they feel about constantly being asked where they were born

when in fact they have been born in the majority culture. One American client, Laura, talked about how it 'throws her into feeling different again just when [she] was beginning to fit in'. Laura had had an international childhood, her father having been posted to a different country every few years. She desperately wished for some stability in her life. She came to therapy in order to explore her sense of self, as she felt it would change far too easily depending on her context of friends and surroundings. She felt as if she had become out of touch with anything constant, just like all the cultures she had experienced in her early years.

Ethnic minorities define their identity not only through the images and expectations of their own culture, but also by how they are perceived by the majority culture. If the cultural context and its influences are ignored, and indeed if the cross-cultural relationship is not mentioned, it dilutes the richness of the client and therapist relationship.

CLINICAL ISSUES

Challenging stereotypes

Working cross-culturally means raising and challenging awareness of some of the commonly held stereotypes around race and culture, such as those described below:

The distinction between 'them' and 'us'

The label 'they' is given to the racial/cultural grouping which is different from 'ours' as if one is the norm. Also neither 'they' or 'ours' are a homogeneous group. There is great diversity amongst any ethnic group, in terms of numerous factors such as socio-economic status, amongst many others. Cultural groups themselves can also use this as a defence, especially at times where defences are high, such as when abroad. This can result in groups holding on to cultural practices rigidly.

Hierarchies

There is often a 'poor them' attitude of pity for people of other races/cultures, which ignores the richness of their lives and becomes limiting. Interestingly, a hierarchy is created where the 'other' is seen as being 'less than' in terms of different factors such as education and social background. This is a common occurrence with minority groups, particularly with refugees. Somehow being a refugee is often perceived as people who *now have nothing, but also had nothing in their past.* This makes it difficult to remember that people had their own support networks and resources, perhaps a certain educational and professional status. For example, one particular client, Omar, who had been a judge in his own country, during sessions would constantly relay everyday situations where he would end up having disagreements with others. We explored this at length as it was difficult for him to see what he communicated to people and in turn how he was perceived as a refugee almost as if he had nothing to offer. It was hardly surprising how the loss of so much in his life, including his high status, was unbearable in the new country. Additionally, due to his poor English he was unable to take part in professional activities until he gained proficiency in English. His anger was getting in the way of relationships as well as preventing him from mastering the new language. Although not normally part of therapeutic practice, there are some circumstances where it is also significant to put people in touch with centres who can support them with practical issues. The cross-cultural centres mentioned earlier aim to support newcomers to the UK through these services, particularly refugees who may have urgent practical needs; they may need support with these before engaging with emotional support.

Negative images

The fear of the 'other' is portrayed in all kinds of media forms. The disturbing results are images of ethnic minorities who are often described as impulsive, irresponsible, dangerous and not to be trusted. Growing up amongst these images, they may be taken on board as if they belong to that particular cultural group.

Client seen as the racial/cultural group

This refers to the danger of seeing the individual client as representing the 'race' and 'culture'. This is common when anxieties are high, and in order to strengthen one's beliefs the client is seen to represent the whole group's behaviours and thinking. It is much more difficult for their individuality to be taken into account.

Suitability for therapy

Clients from different cultural backgrounds have often been seen as so different that they are 'untreatable' or as if they require specialist services. Of course, therapists communicate, both consciously and unconsciously, with their clients about their 'suitability' for therapeutic treatment.

All of the stereotypes result from our anxieties about working with difference and the often rather ethnocentric view of the world. 'Ethnos' is derived from the Greek word meaning 'nation', and the last part from 'centre', therefore meaning that one's own group is the centre of what is the norm and correct. Furthermore, there is the hierarchical judgement that one group is superior since what it carries represents the norm. Shifting ethnocentricism means reflecting on our behaviours, but challenging them can only take place with the right type of facilitation within a safe context. Although in today's international community cross-cultural interaction is inevitable, it can result in extremely powerful dynamics: it can significantly raise people's anxiety and increase defensiveness; raised anxiety can influence people's clarity of thinking and ability to understand others' behaviour, as well as to have insight into their own. As a result, people often do not reflect on their behaviour and simply do not understand how behaviours vary cross-culturally. In fact, sometimes issues of difference, namely racism, are so difficult to understand or to relate to without having personal experience, that people may choose to become emotionally detached from them. Another way of coping may be to feel that they are so unreal and overwhelming that one cannot take on board societal issues. Often, if expectations are more reality based (perhaps by being more informed about another culture), then there will be less disappointment or upset (Pedersen, 1997). Cross-cultural interactions can create these extremely complicated dynamics when people lose their familiar framework and do not feel safe.

Ethnocentrism also means shifting from the individualistic position of Western psychology and its clinical implications. 'Individualistic' refers to cultures which value, as stated, individualism or the person developing independently from the group. The individualism–collectivism distinction can be witnessed in every aspect of our lifestyle; for example, the degree of movement around the world for jobs is going to be largely guided by lifestyles and family expectations. For example, an individualist is more likely to travel in order to take a job many miles away, whilst a collectivist will remain closer to the family or community group (Berry et al., 2002). There will be a greater feeling of obligation to remain linked and near the collective.

Another example of the different value systems across cultures can be seen in the structure of cultural naming systems. For example, amongst the collectivist Balinese culture, personal names are rarely used. Personal and birth order names are used mainly to refer to children and adolescents. Balinese use tekonyms, or words which describe the relationship between two people, especially that between older and younger family members: when a child is born, the parents are known as the 'mother of' and 'father of' that particular child. In a more individualistic culture, the person will be known and there may be little mention of the connections to the rest of the cultural/familial group. These examples show that other cultures have different ways of relating (Perez Foster, 1998), which have implications for cross-cultural psychology and counselling. Similarly, a Southeast-Asian Muslim man will have a different name from his wife; for example, he may be called Mohammed Isha; the first name refers to his religious name and the latter to the personal name. Female Muslims also have two names, but there is a different structure; for example, in the name Fatima Bibi the first name is the personal one and the second one means 'Miss' or 'Madam' in English, therefore it would be meaningless to call someone 'Bibi' only (example taken from Eleftheriadou, 1996). However, this does not mean to state that every individualist or collectivist will behave in the same way, and indeed, there are many variations within one culture. It is perhaps more helpful to view it as a spectrum where some cultures show a greater degree of collectivism than others, and in different areas of life.

The counselling psychologist does not need to have information about all cultures; indeed, this would be an impossible task. The cross-cultural therapeutic process is about finding a way to work with the similarities and differences *at the same time*. There needs to be enough openness to challenge one's views and to consider diverse value systems.

CLINICAL ISSUES

Therapeutic goals

The therapeutic goals of cross-cultural counselling psychology work are:

- to take into account the role of race and culture(s) in the client's life
- to explore the client's relationship to their familial culture and how linked or differentiated they are from this
- to understand their choice of therapist and the meaning it holds, both consciously and unconsciously; despite similarities, the therapist may be experienced as the 'other' because of stereotypes (based on culture or religion) placed on them by the client
- to have clear awareness and challenge one's own ethnocentricism and any stereotypes evoked when coming into contact with other cultural groups
- to explore the client's conscious and unconscious relationship to the majority culture
- to be open to how the client presents their culture rather than the societal or media images of the culture
- to have some understanding of the client's journey, voluntary or involuntary to the new culture, such as conscious and unconscious motives for their wish to move away from their country of birth.

Non-verbal communication and language

A large part of cross-cultural work involves an awareness of cultural variation in non-verbal and verbal communication. In terms of the non-verbal aspects, for example, there are differences in the 'desirable' spatial distance across cultures, including the ideal conversational distance. In terms of kinesics, it has been found that people can decode body behaviour and facial expression more accurately when it is exhibited by those who share a common language, culture and race. Paralanguage, which involves tone, loudness of voice, pauses, hesitations, pitch and rate of speech, also differs across cultures. Similarly, it has been found that paralanguage is easier to comprehend by those who belong to the same culture. Paralanguage, kinesics and proxemics are so much part of everyday communication that they can provide stronger messages than the verbal. An attentive therapist can pick up a great deal of information from the body language of the client. Non-verbal behaviour is also more unconscious, hence more primitive than words, therefore can be more revealing than the verbal (Perez Foster, 1998).

In all therapeutic work, we need some awareness of the clients' historical background. Recalling something which was experienced at a younger age may be extremely difficult, especially if it is the first time it is being talked about and this has to take place in another language.

Generally, it is unrealistic to expect the counselling psychologist to find out exactly what the client would have said in their mother tongue. However, there may be times when meanings become too unclear due to language difficulties. It may be important to pause and ask the client to think/say the words in their own language. Even when there is confusion over finding the exact words or frustration of not being able to 'say it in English' at that point, this might still access the emotional experience. One Israeli client, Rayna, described the emotion attached to her story in a way that did not seem congruent with the content. When asked how she would say it in her own language, she said 'she would then sound sad'. This enabled her to discuss the frustration of having to convey these feelings in another language, and how she got in touch with the emotions she had avoided when speaking in English. As Perez Foster states:

> Anxiety or pervasive discomfort can accompany the bilingual's clinical presentation in a second language, especially when the bilingual is markedly more proficient in his or her native idioms. (1998: 93)

Cross-cultural communication may require a great deal of explanation, needing to be made more explicit, than if people shared a cultural background with the other. Where there are language barriers it may mean that therapeutic work can only remain at a particular level and not progress. However, when clients have mastered the 'new' language they may be able to relate their emotional life well, and sometimes even more explicitly than in their own language. This is because they may not have as rich a vocabulary and cannot intellectualize; they just have to use the first word which comes to mind. Using another language to one's 'mother tongue' in psychotherapy is complicated and can be a help or become a hindrance to the client, depending on the meaning attached to it.

Building the therapeutic relationship

Any relationship needs time to develop, and seeking help from a stranger is not to be underestimated. However, the added component of speaking to a stranger who belongs to a different culture/race needs careful consideration. During the initial meeting the therapist can gain insight into the reasons why the client needs support at that particular time in their life. The counselling psychologist can gain significant information through exploration of their journey to that particular therapist/therapy centre.

Counselling psychology is a delicate process because clients have to be understood within their cultural context. However, enquiry about cultural issues should not be the focus, unless it is the problem itself. A client can sense how the cultural information is asked and why. Counselling psychologists need to be clear that they are able to work with particular issues and certain cultural groups. This is because conscious and unconscious meanings and assumptions, such as strongly held religious or political beliefs, will be communicated to the client. As stated earlier, this is where cross-cultural training, supervision and personal development are crucial. If a therapist has not explored their prejudices and feelings about certain cultural groups and practices, then this can result in distancing the client and intensifying feelings of difference. During difficult times, the therapist who is attentive and knowledgeable about other cultures can provide a significant connection. I remember a Lebanese client of mine, Nawal, who was explaining to me about a relative's struggle with wearing the veil. Although I had said very little, she paused, saying 'I feel that you understand what I am saying by the way you have looked at me'. I had indeed understood and had lived in a country which required the veil, but had not disclosed this to my client at the time. Clients have a sense of whether we have an understanding (or wish to have an understanding) of what they mean or not. The way we word the comments/questions we use, pauses or even the non-verbal communication can signal a great deal of information. As the therapeutic work progressed with Nawal, it was interesting to understand how relieved she felt to be working with someone who was outside her culture, but who understood enough of the significant elements. Anyone engaged in cross-cultural work would need to have some familiarity with the socio-cultural context of our clients. Each group will bring their own issues and these need to be understood in order to separate what is internal in the client and what is external (and perhaps) group experience and probably out of the client's control (see Eleftheriadou, 1996). For example, when working with refugees the psychologist needs to have some sense of what it is like to be persecuted, to flee and to experience severe loss. Allowing clients room to convey their context means that they can bring in the aspects which they consider of importance. For example, a particular cultural element may not be brought into the session until there is an event back 'home', and then this will be on their mind. This process will include their assumptions of what the psychologist is familiar with or not.

These aspects are not unique to cross-cultural counselling work, but we know from research that the anxieties are usually intensified in cross-cultural contact (Ward et al., 2001). This is due to far too many uncertainties about the 'other'. Taking time and creating the space to understand, and allow for difference, is crucial to understanding the client's construction of meaning of the world. This may seem paradoxical as we need to understand enough of someone's background and yet to remain open to what they might bring or how it might be presented. Spinelli describes the process in the following way:

Although it may be impossible for us to bracket all biases and assumptions, we are certainly capable of bracketing a substantial number of them. In addition, even when the bracketing is not likely or feasible, the very recognition of bias lessens its impact upon our immediate experience. (1989:17)

Choice of therapist: racial or cultural matching

There is a long history of debate in counselling and psychology over whether there should be racial matching of client and therapist. All clients have ideas on whom they feel they can trust to work with. This can be discussed from the beginning of the relationship when anxieties are heightened. The client's qualitative account and hence preference reflects more accurately who they think (and trust) would support them best. This information would be useful for finding out where their identifications lie. For example, they may identify with the culture, the religion, the language, or the gender might be the most crucial factor. For one client, the most important factor was to work with a black female, whilst for another client, working with a Lingala-speaking counselling psychologist was of greatest importance.

There is controversy as to when and how the differences should be addressed. After all, when a man and woman are working together, or adult and child, this needs to be addressed, so why should two people from different races/cultures avoid it? As Kareem states:

a psychotherapeutic process that does not take into account the person's whole life experience, or that denies consideration of their race, culture, gender or social values can only fragment the person. (1992: 16)

For those whose race has been reflected as negative, it might be useful to work with someone from the same racial background. However, matching on racial background does not necessarily mean that the client and therapist are going to have exactly the same racial, cultural or psychological experiences. In fact, they are likely to have a rather different subjective meaning to their experience.

The research in this area is vast. For example, Sue and Sue (1999) believe that preference for a culturally-similar therapist does not apply to all cultural groups. There is also research to show that some people choose to go to a different ethnicity counsellor, but in the UK this research is still in its infancy. Some people wish to have someone who is not part of the in-group to ensure confidentiality and/or because they can identify with the host culture more than their own cultural background. For example, a Moroccan client, Nadia, wished to see a female therapist who spoke either Arabic or French, but didn't want someone from the same country. The fear was both about being known and, consequently, that it would somehow inhibit what she wanted to discuss in confidence. In later sessions, it emerged that her father was Moroccan and her mother was French and, interestingly, she had had a hierarchy in her mind about the superior culture being French, which was rather a surprise for her to admit.

Generally, a decision has to be made as to whether the client and therapist match should be made by taking into account a shared racial, cultural, language or gender background. Whether the client and the therapist are from the same culture or not, we need to explore what it means to be perceived by the client as being 'different' or 'the same'.

This raises the crucial question of whether clients can be helped in culturally different systems. For some clients, a cross-cultural relationship may be a more facilitating relationship. However, if the cultural distance is too great, then the outcome will not only be unfavourable, but it is also unlikely that clients will remain in the therapeutic relationship. Ethnic minority communities are very close, and if there is no trust in a particular service this quickly becomes known.

Understanding life stages across cultures

An interesting area to explore cross-culturally has been the whole notion of life-stage expectations. In this context, the concept of life stages is not used to mean strict guidelines on what is supposed to happen at each stage, but some idea of the community or cultural expectations. We know that expectations about development vary enormously across cultures (Baruth and Manning, 2002).

In counselling psychology practice we will get to know how our clients' expectations during a particular life age/phase are informed by the cultural context. Similarly, couple/marital relationships which are common and the norm in one country may be seen as inappropriate in another context (Georgas, 2006). Another area which has been researched widely in cross-cultural work is the whole area of child rearing and how parental expectations vary so significantly across contexts. In family work, for example, meanings have to be constructed taking into account the client's expectations, familial as well as their cultural norms. This is a delicate area and, as stated earlier, the information has to stem from the client in order to avoid gross generalizations taking place at the cost of the individual meaning for that particular client.

Working with interpreters

To some extent, language barriers can be overcome when working with interpreters. This is also particularly useful if one is working with young children who are not fully aware of all the socio-political facts. However, the interpreter in the room can also complicate dynamics when they see themselves (consciously or unconsciously) as inferior/superior to the client. It is interesting to observe who identifies with whom in the session (Perez Foster, 1998). Identifications are also interesting because these can provide useful information in the setting; that is, the therapist might feel as if they have a co-therapist in the room or that they are dealing with two clients who need support. Interpreters often have emotional difficulties around certain issues, especially when working with someone who shares a socio-political background, so it is something to be aware of. This was the case when working with one client who seemed to be experiencing a psychotic episode, and it took a long time to assess as she had very little English and the interpreter was being extremely protective. The interpreter blamed housing and other external issues for the 'distress', ending up in the position of justifying rather than directly translating the content of the client's material. Of course, what the interpreter was pointing out was that there were many contributing factors to the client's distress, but it was difficult to formulate a clear impression on how distressed the client was and whether they needed further (psychiatric) input. Overall, however, when working with a good interpreter it does provide additional information which can help the process, such as asking about how something was pronounced and picking up the emotional nuances of language. Often when working with refugees or asylum seekers, who may be quite (understandably) suspicious of disclosing difficulties to the therapist, interpreters may help them feel at ease.

CONCLUSION

This chapter has highlighted the key reasons why cross-cultural issues need to be taken on board by counselling psychologists. Although the cross-cultural work process still remains new territory for counselling psychologists, there has been more thinking about the issues (Sue et al., 1987). This is reflected in the numerous publications and events on the subject.

Since psychology has considered the issues relatively recently and the cross-cultural issues are about our private, psychological, as well as inter-personal group lives, we may need to step out of psychology and draw from the work of anthropologists, sociologists and many others who have observed the plethora of interpersonal interactions, particularly on a group/community level. The field of social psychology may also need to be incorporated much more as it has dedicated its work to understand and to take into account the power of the group on the individual (see Smith and Bond, 1998). It has provided useful information about the dynamics of groups and has brought a balance to the often rather individualistic Western view of general psychology. Issues of race and culture need to be taken into account, but it is, at all times, a delicate balance. That is, if we focus too much on race we make it into something concrete and unchangeable. We need to redefine our observations of cultural communications and meanings and to translate these to clinical practice guidelines.

Many of the cross-culturalist practitioners mentioned have provided us with good practice guidelines and ethics for clinical practice, and have also outlined research guidelines for cross-cultural work. The process is complex, but by no means impossible. Transcultural work has generally been portrayed as filled with barriers, and yet many clients who have engaged in a cross-cultural therapeutic relationship seem to find it a useful and creative process, but, and perhaps predictably, only when their culture is truly taken into consideration and respected.

For some clients cross-cultural work can be creative precisely because it takes the person out of the familiar context, where it is taken for granted that all is understood. In fact, the person can find the space to explore their cultural milieu, understand its influences, review them and as a result accept or reject them. This does not mean that every client will be willing to or that they 'should' do this.

This chapter has suggested that cross-cultural work is not about a specific theory, but about being open to people's different ways of thinking and behaving as a result of different socio-cultural experiences. The counselling psychologist and the client match does not have to be identical, but we need to be able to take on board the differences and similarities at the same time and 'consider ethnic/cultural/racial influences as central and necessary to the theory and practice' (Mishne, 2002: 240). Taking culture on board does not imply that it is problematic, but that it needs to be taken into account at every stage of the interaction if we are to have a good-enough understanding of our clients' way of being.

The purpose of this chapter was to emphasize that cross-cultural therapy is not a list of skills to be learnt. It is a way of thinking and relating in cross-cultural encounters that can only take place once we have undergone our own personal exploration of the issues, cross-cultural supervision and learning about other familiar and cultural practices and beliefs.

REFERENCES

Altman, N. (2005) 'Relational perspectives on the therapeutic action of psychoanalysis', in J. Ryan (ed.), *How Does Psychotherapy Work?* London: Karnac.

Baruth, L.G. and Manning, M.L. (2002) *Multicultural Counselling and Psychotherapy: A Lifespan Perspective.* Englewood Cliffe, NJ: Prentice Hall.

Bateman, A. and Holmes, J. (1995) *Introduction to Psychoanalysis: Contemporary Theory and Practice.* London: Routledge.

Berry, J.W., Poortinga, Y.H., Segall, M.H. and Dasen, P.R. (2002) *Cross-Cultural Psychology.* Cambridge: Cambridge University Press.

Bhugra, D. and Cochrane, R. (eds) (2001) *Psychiatry in Multicultural Britain.* London: Gaskell.

Bhui, K. and Bhugra, D. (2007) *Culture and Mental Health: A Comprehensive Textbook.* London: Hodder Arnold.

Curry, A. (1964) 'Myth, transference and the Black psychotherapist', *International Review of Psychoanalysis*, 45: 89–120.

Eleftheriadou, Z. (1994) *Transcultural Counselling.* London: Central Publishing House.

Eleftheriadou, Z. (1996) 'Notions of culture: The impact of culture on international students', in S. Sharples (ed.), *Changing Cultures: Developments in Cross-Cultural Theory and Practice.* London: UKCOSA.

Eleftheriadou, Z. (1997) 'Cultural differences in the therapeutic relationship', in I. Horton and V. Varma (eds), *The Needs of Counsellors and Psychotherapists.* London: Sage.

Eleftheriadou, Z. (2007) 'Skills for communicating with patients from different cultural backgrounds', in R. Bor and M. Lloyd (eds), *Communication Skills for Medicine*. Oxford: Churchill Livingstone.

Fernando, S. (1991) *Mental Health, Race and Culture*. London: Macmillan/MIND.

Fernando, S. (ed.) (1995) *Mental Health in a Multi-Ethnic Society*. London: Routledge.

Gardiner, H.W., Mutter, J.D. and Kosmitzki, C. (1988) *Lives Across Cultures: Cross-cultural Human Development*. Needhome Heights, MA: Allyn and Bacon.

Georgas, J., Berry, J.W., van de Vijuer, F.J.R., Kagitçibasi, C. and Poortinga, Y.H. (2006) *Families Across Cultures: A 30-Nation Psychology Study*. Cambridge: Cambridge University Press.

Kagitcibasi, C. (2007) *Family, Self and Human Development Across Cultures: Theory and Applications*. Hillsdale, NJ: Lawrence Erlbaum.

Kareem, J. (1992) The Nafsiyat Intercultural Therapy Centre: Ideas and experience in intercultural therapy', in J. Kareem and R. Littlewood (eds), *Intercultural Therapy*. Oxford: Blackwell. pp. 14–37.

Lemma-Wright, A. (1995) *Invitation to Psychodynamic Psychology*. London: Whurr.

Littlewood, R. and Lipsedge, M. (1989) *Aliens and Alienists*. London: Unwin Hyman.

Mishne, J.M. (2002) *Multiculturalism and the Therapeutic Process*. New York: Guilford.

Pedersen, P. (1997) *Culture-Centered Counselling Interventions*. London: Sage.

Perez Foster, R.M. (1998) *The Power of Language in the Clinical Process*. London: Aronson.

Ratner, C. (2008) *Cultural Psychology, Cross-cultural Psychology and Indigenous Psychology*. New York: Nova Science.

Schweder, R.A. (1991) *Thinking Through Cultures: Expeditions in Cultural Psychology*. London: Harvard.

Smith, P.B. and Bond, M.H. (1998) *Social Psychology Across Cultures*. Englewood Cliffs, NJ: Prentice-Hall.

Spinelli, E. (1989) *The Interpreted World: An Introduction to Phenomenological Psychology*. London: Sage.

Stigler, J.W., Shweder, R.A. and Herdt, G. (1990) *Cultural Psychology*. Cambridge: Cambridge University Press.

Sue, D.W. and Sue, D. (1999) *Counselling the Culturally Different: Theory and Practice*. New York: Wiley.

Sue, S.A., Kutsu, P.D. and Higashi, C. (1987) 'Training issues in conducting therapy with ethnic-minoritiy-group clients', in P. Pedersen (ed.), *Handbook of Cross-Cultural Counseling and Therapy*. New York: Praeger.

Suzuki, L.A., Ponterotto, J.G. and Meller, P.J. (eds) (2001) *Handbook of Multicultural Assessment*. San Francisco, CA: Jossey-Bass.

Thomas, A.J. and Schwarzbaum, S. (2005) *Culture and Identity: Life Stories for Counsellors and Therapists*. London: Sage.

Thomas, L. (1992) 'Racism and psychotherapy', in J. Kareem and R. Littlewood (eds), *Intercultural Therapy*. Oxford: Blackwell. pp. 33–145.

Vannoy Adams, M. (1996) *The Multicultural Imagination: 'Race', Colour, and the Unconscious*. London: Routledge.

Ward, C., Bochner, S. and Furnham, A. (2001) *The Psychology of Culture Shock*. London: Routledge.

11

FEMINIST PERSPECTIVES

Carol Tindall, Julia Robinson and Carolyn Kagan

This handbook constitutes an important space for the proliferation of counselling psychology values, the establishment of its identity and the updating of professional developments within the British context. It is in this way constitutive and the inclusion once again of a chapter on feminist practice could be seen as representing a continued call for counselling psychology professionals in a rapidly changing social world to divert attention away from individualizing ontological perspectives to consider more politically sensitive understandings of psychological distress. As educators and practitioners, we notice a waning of inequality awareness in contemporary society, particularly amongst some of our younger generations. Not only is feminism becoming increasingly unfashionable, but more concerning is the notion that political neutrality is a possibility.

   As a development from the chapter in the previous edition of this book, we aim to raise some contemporary issues for feminist work in counselling psychology and to follow this with an outline of the principles of practice which have remained the same. A detailed case study which threads these principles through to a discussion will hopefully illustrate ways of working, emphasizing the dilemmas and tensions which emerge. The chapter ends with some future directions for a feminist counselling psychology approach.

THE CONTEMPORARY CONTEXT

Historically, psychology as a discipline has been riddled with patriarchal values (Nicolson, 1992; Ussher, 1992). These values are implicit within the UK psychology's systems and emerge not only from within our own profession but also from other institutions with which we interact, particularly those which operate within medical settings. In its earlier days, counselling psychology forwarded itself as oppositional to the mainstream (Pugh and Coyle, 2000) and whilst pockets of enthusiasm remain (Martin, 2006), mechanisms of state control and the influence of wider ideological forces drive out opportunity for dissension and debate. Faced with these new challenges, a feminist approach can offer counselling psychologists a set of principles and values to buttress its own and guide us towards a creative interpretation of the political context. Feminism is relevant to all aspects of our work, inside and outside therapy, whatever the setting or client group. Raising awareness of feminism's application across contexts is increasingly relevant as counselling psychology is established as a profession and work broadens out into advisory, educational and managerial roles, roles we return to at the end of the chapter.

In the current climate, characterized by individualism and the collapse of community values, forwarding a more socio-political account of distress is quite a challenging task either from inside or outside psychology. Whilst counselling psychology makes claims to attend to the wider context, in practice this constitutes a somewhat idealized declaration as individualized accounts of being continue to subjugate more social accounts. A socio-political analysis does *not* focus on symptom reduction or quantification of happiness, and as such conflicts with the profit-making ethos which drives public sector services. Additionally, the individualized and rationalized accounts that clients bring to therapy present us with further challenges. Thatcher and Manktelow alert us to the difficulties with traditional methods and theories:

> Our theories of formulation and treatment, inevitably moulded by the society and culture of their origins are individualistic, interior and dislocated from their context. (2007: 31)

Despite facing obstacles at every turn, we remain committed to forwarding ways of working which place women at the centre and hold a positive vision for the future, a principle of feminist work. Thatcher and Manktelow (2007) are just two writers from a growing body (Proctor, 2002; Furedi, 2004; Smail, 2005; Johnstone and Dallos, 2006; White, 2006) who are similarly turning the focus to understanding the role of power in peoples' experience of distress.

Whilst the British context is our immediate concern, this cannot be seen in isolation from a wider global dynamic. Catalyzed by science and technology, capitalism continues to spread and mutate, creating rifts and new features in our social landscapes. Changing populations, technological advancements and tightening political structures contextualize our daily encounters. In the UK, the age of our population has been slowly increasing (Office for National Statistics, 2008), bringing new joys and challenges to our work. Women are typically the carers of the young and of older people, thus not only is the demographic constitution of our client base affected through an ageing population but there are also changes in roles, responsibilities and expectations for women across the life span. Globalization brings a necessity for counselling psychologists to understand the challenges faced by women both here and in other parts of the world. We see that to be informed is our responsibility, particularly as the potential to fund health research lies in the economically advantaged countries (Chung, 2005). As the movement of people across borders to escape from war and suffering continues, the social injustices which face us in the counselling room are not confined to those in our own localities. This returns us again to question appropriateness of our theoretical models and whether 'interior and dislocated' paradigms can meet the needs of women who have lived in communities based on collectivist principles (Chung, 2005). Although increasingly faced with pressures for manualized treatments and a one-size-fits-all philosophy, we must search for examples of good practice to learn from. Whilst there has been a response from some corners of psychology to understand, for example, the plight of female asylum seekers and refugees, there has been little output from the counselling or applied psychology literature that deals with relevant practice issues. This absence is mirrored in the American counselling psychology literature (Yakushko and Chronister, 2005). Yakushko and Chronister themselves offer some methodological ideas, forwarding the Bronfenbrenner model (1979) as the basis for socio-political analyses for work with female refugees. In Chapter 25 on community approaches we expand on this type of analysis and suggest further resources as starting points for therapeutic work.

The last five years has seen exciting and unprecedented technological changes which have increased the scope for global communication and widened spaces for the construction of identity. The ever-expanding gamut of social networking sites, whilst extending potential on an individual and community level, also brings new concerns and disruptions (Livingstone, 2008). Not only are computers assuming the role of therapists (a development which raises a number of issues around therapeutic models and relationships), but cyber communities now offer a choice for women to take their issues elsewhere; the 'pro-ana' cyber community is one illustration of this. This community is a particular response by young women which may challenge traditional notions of what is 'good' and 'therapeutic'. Typically consisting of around 400 websites, containing journals, blogs, discussion forums and non-professional advice, it is a community made by and for young people with 'eating disorders' (Giles, 2006). These sites have been the focus of much controversy as the type of advice available on these sites might include, for instance, how to sustain but conceal states of anorexia (Giles, 2006). Whilst this is not the space to consider the ethical debates surrounding the existence of such sites, and whilst these sites present cause for concern, their actuality may also tell us something important about the services that we offer young women and how these are arranged and received, and this in turn raises issues around regulation, authority and patriarchy. Within a growing culture of risk and accountability, social networking sites and other online forums may paradoxically (and in some cases worryingly) be providing the type of environment young women now seek for self-exploration, validation and experimentation around identity). Dilemmas are thus raised in terms of how to forward a feminist agenda. Our own feminist understandings may not coincide with those of different generations, yet we have a responsibility to listen, consider and try to understand young women. Working with young females may therefore present us with challenges. Gonick (2001) discusses the tensions that arise through exploration with young women, of the social constructions of femininity, gender relations and how women are positioned as a result of these. She offers the following questions for consideration:

> How far do I go in insisting on my own agenda if the girls are not only not interested in mine, but if mine suppresses theirs? How am I to be sure that what I think I have to offer them in terms of a feminist perspective is ethically and politically right for them? (2001: 168)

Gonick (2001) usefully highlights the difficulties arising from competing discourses of femininity and helps us to consider the notion that women's alienation may not only emerge from institutional practices but from within feminism itself.

The sense of alienation experienced by some women in public sector services is not a new issue, as the oversubscription to women's therapy centres set up in the 1980s was testament to. These voluntary sector services continue to be a popular choice for women, despite severe underfunding. Heenan (2001) suggests that the migration to such services may have something to do with the models of therapy which are offered within public sector services. She suggests that cognitive behavioural therapy, which focuses on symptom reduction, does not 'enhance a psychosocial understanding of women's mental health', but additionally it may be that the culture of the large organization makes the principles of feminist practice more difficult to achieve. In our look to the future at the end of this chapter we return to consider how feminist counselling psychology, at an organizational level, offers an alternative understanding of feminist intervention.

As counselling psychologists, we are required to be vigilant of change inside and outside the therapeutic encounter. It is not meant for continued population shifts, advancements in technology and the increase in state control to constitute an exhaustive list of changes since the last edition of this chapter. However, consideration of these issues can prompt us to reflect upon and monitor how changes in the social context impact on women and the services we offer them.

PRINCIPLES OF FEMINIST APPROACHES TO COUNSELLING PSYCHOLOGY

Feminist principles and values underpinning therapy work have remained constant, yet from within feminist psychology, shifts in the research gaze not only reveal something of contemporary politics and culture but also trends in feminist conceptualizations (Lee and Crawford, 2007). Whilst they hold relevance for counselling psychology, there is little space in this chapter to explore these theoretical and political debates (readers are instead directed to the journals *Feminism and Psychology* or *Feminist Review* for interdisciplinary feminist writing). However, some of these debates, such as the essentialist and relativist dilemma, resemble the theoretical tangles that our own discipline has historically found itself in.

Our feminist approach draws from a social-constructionist philosophy which is concerned with the way the self is moulded by the social world. Influenced by sociology, linguistics and philosophy, Burr also identifies a social-constructionist understanding as resting upon four key tenets: first, she describes a 'critical stance towards taken-for-granted knowledge'; second, she stresses the importance of 'historical and cultural specificity' to understanding; third, she emphasizes knowledge as 'sustained by social processes'; and fourth, that 'knowledge and social action go together' (1995: 3–5). We prefer to use the term 'social-constructionism' as opposed to 'postmodernism'; however, elements of both postmodernism and poststructuralism are incorporated into this perspective (Harper and Spellman, 2006). Social-constructionism does not constitute a single theory but a framework within which a diversity of feminist approaches sit. Ideas from social-constructionism also underpin other therapeutic approaches, such as narrative therapy, and therefore understandings from this chapter will chime with both the community counselling psychology and narrative therapy chapters in this book. Similarities are also visible with critical psychological approaches to working (Prilleltensky and Nelson, 2002).

Socio-political analysis

All schools of feminism start with the recognition of the inferior status of women and the fact of their oppression. Women's position in society and their experiences of relationships are shaped by external factors, by social structures and by cultural and ideological influences (Smail, 1991). These external structures are patriarchal, and feminisms in their different forms all offer critiques of patriarchy. In summary, women's social value and feelings of self-worth are anchored in patriarchal societal values and prescriptions about what it means to be female, and these must be understood and eventually changed.

Emphasis on gender and sex role stereotyping

As part of a critique of patriarchy, a useful distinction is to be made between sex (the biological embodiment of differences between men and women) and gender (the social expectations of the masculine and feminine). Some experiences women have may be linked to their sex – such as processes of reproduction and fertility. However, the meaning of these experiences is *socially* constructed, and thus linked to their gender. In most counselling psychology situations, it is the meaning of experience that is important, and thus it is with gender roles that we are concerned. Feminist counselling psychology aims to facilitate equality in personal power between men and women, and help clients to challenge culturally prescribed sex roles (Taylor, 1994).

Woman-centred focus

Women's lives and experiences are at the core of feminist work. Not only do feminist approaches seek to unmask and understand sex role stereotypes and their contribution to women's problems, they also undertake socio-political analyses of women's position, and importantly, highlight women's strengths and potential. Gender roles are acquired through the process of socialization; such socialization, coupled with women's relatively weak structural position, gives rise to some of the unique problems women face, and that feminist counselling psychology seeks to address. Elderly widowers, for example, will often receive more support and assistance from services than will elderly widows: not because their bereavement experiences are greater, but because of stereotyped expectations about their needs and capabilities.

Power and powerlessness

The exploration of power, powerlessness and gaining power[*] are common in one way or another to all feminist approaches. Power is a multi-layered concept, and is of interest not only in analyses of women's unequal access to social power in general, but also in considerations of the therapeutic relationship and processes. Power can be explored at the personal, interpersonal and societal levels, and it is important to understand that all analyses of power are tied in to particular historical and cultural contexts. Feminist approaches seek to identify different forms and sources of power and powerlessness and help clients to recognize their potential for gaining access to both personal and social power. Acknowledgement is made of the power (often wielded by counselling psychologists, feminist ones included) within the therapeutic process.

---

[*] We are deliberately avoiding suggesting that 'empowerment' is the feminist principle. Whilst it might be a feminist goal, we take the view that the process of empowerment, by which one person enables another to have power, is in and of itself disempowering a stance. People cannot be given power, they must acquire it.

Positive vision for the future

Feminist approaches share a commitment to work with women on their strengths, with a view to helping them develop their potential; this may be outside the restrictions of conventional sex role expectations. Central to this principle is the aim to help women gain a sense of worth, and be recognized as valuable persons in their own right. In addition to focusing on women's strengths and potential, feminist approaches offer a positive vision of the future for women. These visions are of a more equitable society, in which being female is valued and in which social resources are allocated equitably. In an unequal society, it is argued, women's self-image, ability to be self-directed and to be happy are constrained by their lack of access to external power. Thus feminist approaches help women dream of – and achieve – a future in which they can be who they want to be, not just who they are expected to be (Brown and Liss-Levinson, 1981).

Commitment to social action and social transformation

Key to feminism is a commitment to social transformation, in order to achieve the liberation of women. This usually goes hand in hand with a commitment to some form of collective action in order to actively contribute to and create social change. Yet without action, we have to recognize the limited contribution that counselling psychology might make to the position of women generally. Worrell and Remer put it thus: 'It is insufficient to fix women for functioning in a dysfunctional society' (1992: 24). What is needed is to create a more equitable society.

There are striking commonalities between the principles and values underpinning feminism and those underpinning counselling psychology, as both are infused with elements of humanism. As with feminist psychology, debate has been a rich and important part of counselling psychology's narrative and it is within both the process and substance of the debate that feminist principles and values are visible.

In the following case study we illustrate how the principles and values of feminist counselling psychology are threaded through to practice, and we follow this case study with a discussion of the relevant tensions and dilemmas that arise when working in this particular way in a contemporary context. The values and principles steering the process in this piece of feminist counselling psychology practice are highlighted in Figure 11.3.

ILLUSTRATIVE CASE STUDY

Mo is a fictitious client but the issues she presents were ones dealt with by one of us while working in a voluntary sector service supporting survivors of abuse. We have

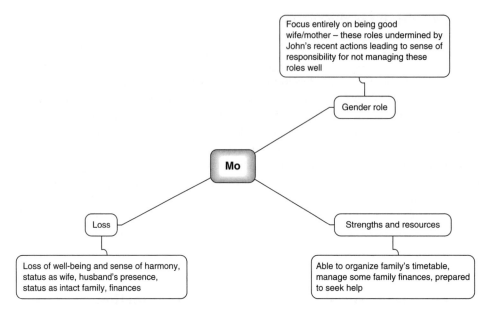

FIGURE 11.1   CASE STUDY: INITIAL FOCUS

retained the narrative characteristics of this account as we wanted the style to reflect the intrinsic values of feminist counselling psychology.

Case

Mo was a woman in her late 40s who turned up for counselling with a friend. This particular service offered drop-in sessions during which it was possible, if a counsellor was free, to have a 50-minute session. The service took the view that if a client needed another person with them initially, that was completely acceptable. Experience suggests that 'friends' attend for the first three meetings or so, which was the case here. Such friends often facilitate initial attendance and client engagement with the process. Both were well dressed, though Mo was dishevelled and obviously highly distressed. Her husband of more than 20 years had recently left to live with a younger professional woman with no children. Mo and John had a son of 16 and a daughter of 14. Mo felt responsible for what she called the break-up of the family.

Many issues were apparent from the first session (see Figure 11.1). Here we will deal with Mo's feeling of responsibility and her self-identified low self-esteem. First, her sense of responsibility for the break-up: the intention here was to challenge her notion of responsibility for this and offer her a different understanding of why she felt responsible and to find a more realistic view of what is needed to make relationships successful. This process is underpinned by the intertwined principles and values of socio-political analysis, power and powerlessness, egalitarian relationships and a woman-centred focus.

Initially exploring the reality of the current situation, we identified that Mo was taking care of the family and home alone. John had had no contact with her since leaving and as for as Mo was aware he had not contacted the children. Evidently she was being responsible, meeting the needs of the family despite her ongoing distress, whilst John was disconnected from the family and was taking no responsibility for aspects of family life, despite knowing that his leaving had confused and distressed his children. It was evident that Mo was doing her best in difficult circumstances to keep things as stable and routine as possible for the children. She was taking total responsibility for their well-being while at this stage John was not.

This exploration made Mo more aware of her position as central to maintaining family life and John's as more marginal in providing support, and in contributing to domestic tasks. Through this she was able to recognize that this pattern of contribution, highlighted by recent events, was entirely familiar. Indeed, far from being responsible for the disruption, she was enabling the family to continue functioning.

An aspect of working as a feminist is to focus on client strengths (see Figure 11.2). When asked about these, Mo had difficulty naming any of her positive qualities; this is not unusual. Here, breaking traditional therapeutic boundaries by allowing her friend to be with her was useful, as her friend was able to help Mo list many of the qualities that Mo was unable to clearly verbalize at the time. The friend's enabling of Mo could be likened to Vygotsky's (1962) concept of scaffolding. Confidentiality may be questioned but in this case, as in many others, Mo's friend knew Mo's innermost thoughts and worries at that time and had lived through the events alongside Mo. The friend knew a good deal more than the counsellor at this early stage. Taking this further by exploring both her and John's contribution to the family and couple over their 20-plus years led to a list demonstrating very clearly that she had made a wealth of contributions, much more so than John. Such 'evidence' provided by Mo with some help from her friend, enabled her to see that she had taken her responsibility to the family and couple seriously. When asked 'What more could you have done?', her honest answer was 'Little more'. Mo was also asked 'What more might John have done?' Again she was able to see that John had contributed little other than finances (which Mo valued highly) and company on family outings. According to Mo, John was a very successful businessman and a high earner.

Underpinning these explorations are the principles of socio-political analysis and a woman-centred focus. Here was an attempt via a reality check to value her contributions to their coupledom and family life. Women's contributions in these areas are often taken for granted or even devalued by society, thus positioning women as unimportant and powerless with little of worth to contribute. The focus here was to set in motion her ability to value herself and not dismiss her contributions as merely what is expected of wives and mothers yet often not expected of husbands and fathers. This was a potential

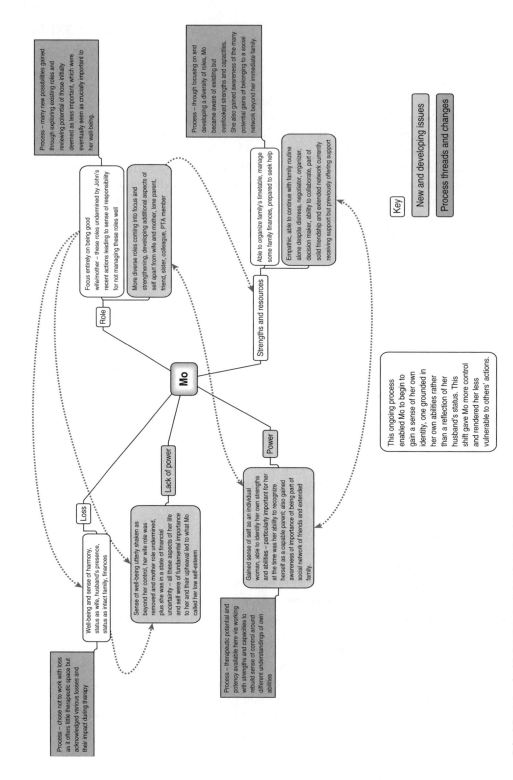

Process – many new possibilities gained through exploring existing roles and reviewing potential of those initially deemed as less important, which were eventually seen as crucially important to her well-being.

Process – through focusing on and developing a diversity of roles, Mo became aware of existing but overlooked strengths and capacities. She also gained awareness of the many potential gains of belonging to a social network beyond her immediate family.

Process – chose not to work with loss as it offers little therapeutic space but acknowledged various losses and their impact during therapy

Process – therapeutic potential and potency available here via working with strengths and capacities to rebuild sense of control around different understandings of own abilities

Mo

Role

Focus entirely on being good wife/mother – these roles undermined by John's recent actions leading to sense of responsibility for not managing these roles well

More diverse roles coming into focus and strengthening, developing additional aspects of self apart from wife and mother, lone parent, friend, sister, colleague, PTA member

Strengths and resources

Able to organize family's timetable, manage some family finances, prepared to seek help

Empathic, able to continue with family routine alone despite distress, negotiator, organizer, decision maker, ability to collaborate, part of solid friendship and extended network currently receiving support but previously offering support

Loss

Well-being and sense of harmony, status as wife, husband's presence, status as intact family, finances

Lack of power

Sense of well-being utterly shaken as beyond her control, her wife role was removed and mother role undermined, plus she was in a state of financial uncertainty – all these aspects of her life and self were of fundamental importance to her and their upheaval led to what Mo called her low self-esteem

Power

Gained sense of self as an individual woman, able to identify her own strengths and abilities – particularly important for her at the time was her ability to recognize herself as a capable parent; also gained awareness of importance of being part of social network of friends and extended family.

This ongoing process enabled Mo to begin to gain a sense of her own identity, one grounded in her own abilities rather than a reflection of her husband's status. This shift gave Mo more control and rendered her less vulnerable to others' actions.

Key

New and developing issues

Process threads and changes

FIGURE 11.2   CASE STUDY: BUILDING THE PICTURE

start to challenging the stereotype that women are solely responsible for making relationships and family life work by putting in place a more realistic view that both adults need to be actively engaged in a relationship if it is to be successful. This was quite a challenge to Mo's internalized gender stereotypes and societal norms. The main tension for the counsellor was around accepting and valuing Mo's reality while challenging her internalized gender stereotypes and acceptance of societal norms.

The specific aim was to enable Mo eventually to cut through these norms, to stand beyond the idea that women are responsible for making relationships work and to view this norm as a potential control mechanism, positioning women as powerless and ensuring that it is they who take responsibility both for the effort required to make the relationship work and the 'failure' of relationships. With such insights women can begin to free themselves of internalized norms and view relationships as joint ventures with joint responsibilities which then enables them to make their own choices and not follow the social scripts. Ussher (1991) highlights the need to be aware of the societal discourses which regulate and control women. Unless we offer this political analysis, women are left without ways of understanding that their experience is common for women and why their emotions are invalidated (Waterhouse, 1993). Without such analysis, non-political counselling approaches have the potential to socialize women into accepting social norms.

Issue two is Mo's talk of 'low self-esteem'; the intention here was to highlight sources other than personal deficit for her sense of low esteem and to facilitate her sense of power. The main principles and values underpinning this process are power and powerlessness, egalitarianism and care and commitment.

It seemed that no one, apart from her friend, took care of Mo. Like many women she was busy caring for everyone except herself. It seemed she had no free time. These beliefs and behaviours are likely to be driven by the internalization that women must nurture others. Mo was amazed and silent initially when asked who cared for her; eventually she responded with 'I'm not sure'. Often women do not expect to be nurtured. The intention was to enable her to value and take care of herself (encouraging self-care and commitment). Mo, with difficulty and with her friend's help, listed the things that made her feel good. It is important to encourage and give women permission to spend some time each day if possible doing something for themselves. Mo was asked to keep a diary of her choices, and in future sessions some time was spent reflecting on her experiences and their benefits or otherwise. Activities need to be realistic and preferably varied; it is crucial to be aware of client's resources, social contexts and other constraints so that choices are feasible and can become part of women's everyday lives. Mo was not short of financial resources (although she had difficulty in spending money on herself), and while this extends possibilities it is also possible to treat oneself in a host of ways with little or no money.

'Low self-esteem' is a popular term in twenty-first-century UK; this is yet another label for the disadvantaged which has absolutely no therapeutic potential. Many television programmes and self-help books encourage such labels, which are based on individualized notions of the self and a complete lack of awareness of the inherent socio-political structures and practices which advantage some and disadvantage others (Pilgrim, 1991; Proctor, 2002; Smail, 2005). Those who are structurally disadvantaged, usually without the means to access or exercise power, are then labelled as having low-self esteem, giving the individual total responsibility for their current lack of access to power, which is pathologizing. It is therefore not surprising that so many people view themselves, or are positioned by others, as having 'low self-esteem'. Mo and John followed the social norm of the time 'deciding' that Mo would care for the family and home while John worked outside the home as a businessman. His success was evident, he was a high earner and provided the family with all the material things that they needed. Mo's success was family based and less evident, invisible and taken for granted. John's decision to leave destroyed her sense of family success and identity and there was nothing she could do to make him return. He was all-powerful and she powerless in this situation. She was feeling wretched before she adopted the low self-esteem message, essentially that she should be more powerful and have more control, which ensured that she felt even worse. This could be seen as an example of Mo internalizing the norms that were her lived experience to the extent that she then provided her own surveillance to ensure that she conformed to the social and family norms of what it is to be a 'good' wife and mother.

Mo was disadvantageously positioned as a woman not engaged in paid work in UK's capitalist, patriarchal society which values earning power and personal control, neither of which she believed she had. Within the family, Mo believed that she had nothing important to contribute to decision making beyond issues concerning the children. John compounded this by making what Mo referred to as all the important decisions about money, the house and holidays alone. In a variety of subtle ways, it seemed that John was following his social script and therefore beyond his awareness, inadvertently undermining any belief Mo had in herself. The task here was to acknowledge Mo's reading of John's story as an important part of her situatedness and understanding of herself, not to explore John's story.

Mo's gender stereotypical qualities, values and contributions were overlooked and devalued by society and her husband as no more than expected, leaving her feeling unimportant. This was a realistic assessment of her current powerless, undervalued position as she was unable to exercise personal power and had no access to financial power other than John's earnings, which he carefully controlled. She was then labelled and pathologized as having low self-esteem, which undermined her tenuous position even further. Such constant systematic undermining drives some to depression. Mo was not depressed but was distressed and very confused; her world had been shattered by someone whom she trusted. Laing in the 1960s argued that such reactions, displayed by women, often referred to as 'symptoms' and identified as madness, are in fact the protests of the powerless, women's attempts to make sense of senseless situations and contradictory demands (Laing and Estersen, 1964), a perfect description of Mo's current situation.

Feminist counsellors and therapists will always work with people's strengths based on the value of care and commitment, something that is often overlooked in traditional approaches to counselling and therapy which tend to focus on problems. Working with strengths is a potent way to facilitate personal empowerment by offering therapeutic space and a positive focus. It is also a constructive way to avoid colluding with a client's sense of inadequacy, here Mo's low self-esteem label. Mo was a good organizer and communicator and eventually gained a place on the Parent Teacher Association at her son's school, using her organization and collaboration skills outside the home to affirm her abilities.

Working in her community also offered her important reference points beyond her immediate family, plus a new social network with possibilities of support and in novel social activities. Mo gloried in her efforts being appreciated and was eventually able to recognize her abilities beyond her role as mother and make use of her range of resources. Now in charge of all aspects of family life as a lone parent, Mo believed herself to be adequate, able to cope. Such valuing of herself and her abilities, especially as they had been tested and appreciated outside the family as well as within, began the process of experiencing feelings of personal power and belief in herself.

Counselling is never linear nor straightforward. It progresses as a tangle of personal meanings, practice issues, tensions and dilemmas which tend to increase in complexity throughout the process. Figure 11.3 demonstrates the growing complexity in Mo's story and how the process is first and foremost guided by a commitment to feminist values and principles. Instead of initial assessment, as feminists we have a commitment to work collaboratively with ongoing assessment as part of the therapeutic process. This involves both holding and making use of the increasing complexity and changes in emphasis; what initially seems important becomes less so as the picture builds.

DILEMMAS AND TENSIONS

There are a number of dilemmas and tensions which emerge in using a feminist counselling psychology approach such as in the case study above. These tensions are emphasized more in some contexts than others and revolve around, for example, the processes of professionalization of psychology, around the theoretical stance of the practitioner and around more fundamental questions as to whether therapy is social action.

Problems with professionalization

Searching for ways to incorporate feminist principles into modern-day institutional frameworks and processes of professionalization is an important and necessary quest.

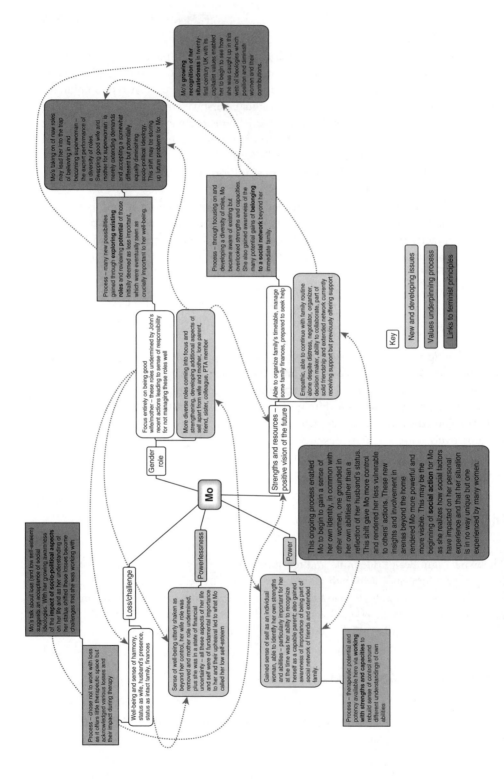

FIGURE 11.3 CASE STUDY: CONTINUED DEVELOPMENT

Modern public sector contexts and the institution of psychology demand particular ways of working which rest and feed upon characteristics of the capitalist economy, namely the pursuit of profit. The emphasis on rational scientific processes which support these political ideals are evident from within our own discipline, noticeable even between the editions of this book. The layout, language and emphases between the three editions reflect the 'technical' changes that structure our role. Whilst we are not suggesting that counselling psychology should not move with the times, it is important for us to evaluate and monitor the direction in which our discipline is moving, to maintain its original and distinguishing standpoint and raise awareness of the forces which move it.

On the British Psychological Society's website, the key tasks of a counselling psychologist include: assessment, formulation, planning treatment and evaluating outcomes of work. There are inevitable tensions here for a feminist approach, and we can illustrate this with the concept of formulation. The origins of formulation are particular to therapeutic approaches and stem back to the work of key psychologists: Eysenck and Meyer from the cognitive behavioural tradition and the work of Freud from the psychodynamic tradition (Johnstone and Dallos, 2006). However, formulation is rooted in a particular epistemological stance, sitting firmly within a positivist scientific way of working (Johnstone, 2006). It has been forwarded as a defining feature of psychologists' work (Kinderman, 2001), and whilst more benign than diagnosis (Johnstone, 2006), it has not emerged without criticism (see Johnstone, 2006; Smail, 2005; Harper and Moss, 2003). Within such critiques, formulation has been seen as a claim to expertise which predominantly serves the interest of psychology professionals as well as being symptomatic of patriarchal systems (Ussher, 1992). As a feminist counselling psychology approach is rooted in a social-constructionist understanding, the difficulties of 'shoehorning' the approach into a 'traditional formulation structure' immediately emerge (see Harper and Spellman's (2006) discussion of social-constructionist formulation). Between figures 11.1 and 11.3, it is evident that in the process of picture building, Mo's experience becomes more, not less, complex. The process is not causal or linear, it is not predictable and her experiences as a woman are not inevitable. What is vital is a broad awareness, knowledge and sensitivity in our understandings of clients:

> The task for us therapists and practitioners is … to grapple with the complexities of the lived experiences of our clients, without presuming any particular mapping between social category and lived experience. Here the current vogue for 'not knowing' is often put forward … we would caution against overstating the extent of 'not knowing', for we must know how to 'not know' and be vigilant about those (cultural and gender, for example) assumptions that we want not to know. (Burman et al., 1998: 293)

Although there are similarities between women, united as they might be by their position in an oppressive social system, there is no one system of feminist counselling practice, but reference to the socio-historical context as directly influencing client and counsellor experience is essential. The nature and role of power is central to feminist counselling psychology and it is therefore necessary for feminist practitioners to engage in a continual process of reflection, reconsideration and action. In contexts where formulation is required, a collaborative exploration of the values which underpin the formulation might accompany the process. As the example of Mo shows, formulations should be flexible and changes in the formulation should be negotiated throughout the therapy. Client and practitioner should always formulate together and within a socio-political account of distress.

Tensions arising from theoretical orientations

An integration of feminist values and principles is possible to achieve across a number of theoretical traditions; however, the precise mechanisms of integration are determined by the orientation of each individual counselling psychologist. Whilst the intention of this chapter has not been to explore the micro and dialogical processes of therapeutic work, readers from some orientations may be questioning compatibility with certain theoretical traditions. Theoretical and methodological challenges associated with the integration of feminist principles are not new to the counselling psychology profession (Strawbridge, 1992). Some feminists feel that humanistic models of therapy, with a focus on growth and empowerment, can integrate most easily with feminist practice in comparison with, for example, psychodynamic models where tensions have been more pronounced (Heenan and Seu, 1998). There remains some degree of choice for clients in some contexts, however, in terms of which theoretical model and which practitioner. Heenan and Seu remind us that:

> The idea of a single, unitary feminist therapy, as well as the belief that one model of therapy or one feminist stance can be privileged above others, is refuted. (1998: 1)

By way of contrast to the United States, in England it was the psychodynamic approaches which underpinned the first womens' therapy centre. This therapy centre was founded by Luise Eichenbaum and Susan Orbach, who worked with British object-relations theory developing the ideas of Nancy Chodorow, particularly focusing on the notion of the mother–daughter dyad (Heenan and Seu, 1998). There is a growing literature from feminist writers who explore some of the more theoretical and methodological issues of integration within their therapeutic traditions, and some write reflexively about the development of their own personal style (see White, 2006 for a humanistic account; Chaplin, 1998 for a 'cognitive' account; Heenan, 1995, 1998 and Seu, 1998, 2000 for psychodynamic accounts; and Swan, 1998, 1999 for narrative therapy accounts. With regard to specific dialogical interventions, Seu, 1998, 2000, in her explorations of the ideological function of language in psychotherapy, offers examples of a micro-analysis of feminist therapeutic processes using a psychodynamic framework, which some readers may find useful.) Between theoretical orientations and indeed between work with individual clients, there will be an inevitable variation in the feminist principles emphasized, and consequently in some pieces of therapeutic work other feminist values and principles may be less apparent.

Is therapy social action?

This feature of feminism is, perhaps, the most difficult to reconcile with counselling psychology, and certainly seems to be the principle least often put into practice (Chester and Bretherton, 2001; Mareck and Kravetz, 1998).

Some feminist counselling psychologists (for example in Chester and Bretherton's 2001 study) argue that therapy is a form of action in itself. A similar case for writing as a political strategy has been made by academic feminists (for example, Burman et al., 1996). Resolution of this issue may well depend on the extent to which action and social change is considered to be a legitimate goal of feminist counselling psychology. Enns (1992, 1993) outlines different patterns of feminist counselling over time, and suggests that the emphasis on collective action characterized earlier stages of feminist therapy, and features in radical and socialist feminist traditions.

The picture that emerges is somewhat cloudy and confused; the inevitable gaps between theory and practice are evident. Marecek and Kravetz highlight this point:

> Feminists who are therapists operate in a space of contradiction, ambiguity, and perhaps even incommensurability. (1998: 13)

The difficulties of reconciling action with therapy has led some to argue that therapeutic work, by definition, cannot be feminist (Kitzinger and Perkins, 1993). Scott (2004: 256) talks of the 'double movement' of feminism as the 'campaigning against patriarchal systems while also providing alternative support to women caught up in them,' and she advocates this particularly for women in prison settings. Some models of practice incorporate action within the counselling psychology method.

Holland (1988, 1992) presents a model of emancipatory psychotherapeutic practice (see also O'Hara, 1997) in which she challenges the split between inner strength and social action. She suggests that (in this case) depressed women may begin with individual therapy to explore and strengthen their self concepts, move on to group work with a view to helping them locate their difficulties within a social context, and experience commonalities with other women and then collectively engage in social action, highlighting mental health difficulties locally and developing facilities that may change some of the environmental conditions giving rise to depression in the first place. She describes this as helping women 'through psychic space into social space and so into political space' (Holland, 1988: 134). Her work makes explicit the legitimate role that therapeutic practitioners can play in supporting women in moves towards social action, reflecting the goals and principles of feminist practice. In our experience, it is not so much a matter of first finding personal strength and then proceeding to collective action; women may, for example, engage in collective action first and therein find personal strength.

FUTURE DIRECTIONS

Whilst moving between different levels of analysis, this chapter has been largely concerned with feminist counselling psychology interventions located at the therapeutic level. As the counselling psychologist's role expands, however, to include for instance the management of services, feminist intervention at organizational levels offer a new potential for women-focused work. As mental health service provision has typically been developed around white male needs, there is much work still to be done at this operational level, but examples of feminist approaches to service organizations are emerging from within the mental health arena. In 2002 the Department of Health recognized the need for a reorganization of services for women:

> Currently, much mental health care is not organized to be responsive to gender differences and women's needs consequently may be poorly met. (Department of Health, 2002: 7)

Women's needs have been particularly poorly met within forensic contexts, illustrated for instance by the route taken by women into high secure hospitals. The systems of administration and assessment which have been predominantly imported from North America and Europe as models of good practice are underpinned by gendered values from our psychiatric and criminal justice system and include, for example, use of the ICD-10 and the DSM-V classificatory systems (Aitken and Heenan, 2004). A way forward is for services to be woman-focused and for them to move away from 'gender-neutral derived models of mental health needs and risk' so as to avoid the perpetuation of oppressive practice and inadvertent re-experiencing of earlier and traumatic relational dynamics of power (Aitken and Heenan, 2004). The use of these types of assessment and administrative procedures, as mentioned in the previous section, are not confined to forensic contexts but are increasingly and rapidly spreading across mental health services.

Another site for the development of feminist counselling psychology practice lies within education. Traditionally academic feminists, particularly in the area of women's studies, have engaged with the politics of knowledge production and pedagogy, a task which Dever (1999) has identified as increasingly difficult in the current climate of economic rationalism. Prilleltensky and Nelson identify the way traditional education systems have marginalized women:

Feminist pedagogy has arisen in women's studies courses out of the need to provide an alternative to the dominant androcentric, sexist educational system. Historically, university professors have marginalized women in both the content of courses and the course processes. (2002: 39)

A feminist approach to counselling psychology education encourages students to develop critical skills to enable a deconstruction of foundational psychological knowledge, as well as offering a pedagogical approach which is enabling, collaborative and set within a non-hierarchical and student-centred practice. This may involve negotiated learning, a two-way dialogical process of collaboration (Dever, 1999). Along with anti-racist education, critical pedagogy and the work of Paulo Freire (2007), feminist pedagogy has contributed much to critical psychology teaching. With counselling psychology's attention to socio-political dimensions to practice this type of psychology teaching offers an appropriate model for counselling psychology training courses to follow.

CONCLUDING COMMENTS

It would seem appropriate to end this chapter on a point of reflexivity. The very project of writing this chapter has taken feminism as its aim and can usefully offer a means to illustrate feminism in action. There has been a care and a commitment to mutuality through processes of negotiation and the emphasizing of resourcefulness, whilst the making of space for both less and more experienced writers to work together offers an example of egalitarianism. The collaborative nature of our writing task has highlighted how individual engagements with feminism at different points in our lives and within the history of feminism leave us with diverse understandings and experiences of feminist practice. We have been open to learning from each other, and the chapter now appears quite different from the one we had planned at the start. We hope that our discussions have been reflected in the content of our writing. Diversity is not only valued per se, but rather for its capacity to dialectically progress understanding, and diversity of experience has, here, been very much valued.

REFERENCES

Aitken, G. and Heenan, C. (2004) 'Women in prison and secure psychiatric settings: Whose needs, whose dangerous', *Feminism and Psychology,* 14 (2): 215–19.

Bronfenbrenner, U. (1979) *The Ecology of Human Development.* Cambridge, MA: Harvard University Press.

Brown, L. and Liss-Levinson, N. (1981) 'Feminist therapy', in R. Corsini (ed.), *Handbook of Innovative Therapies.* New York: Wiley.

Burman, E., Alldred, P., Bewley, C., Goldberg, B., Heenan, C., Marks, D., Marshall, J., Taylor, K., Ullah, R. and Warner, S. (eds) (1996) *Challenging Women: Psychology's Exclusions, Feminist Possibilities*. Buckingham: Open University Press.

Burman, E., Gowrisunker, J. and Sangha, K. (1998) 'Conceptualising cultural and gendered identities in psychological therapies', *European Journal of Psychotherapy, Counselling and Health*, 1 (2): 231–56.

Burr, V. (1995) *An Introduction to Social Constructionism*. London: Routledge.

Chaplin, J. (1998) 'The rhythm model', in I.B. Seu and M.C. Heenan (eds), *Feminism and Psychotherapy: Reflections on Contemporary Theories and Practices*. London: Sage.

Chester, A. and Bretherton, D. (2001) 'What makes feminist counselling feminist?', *Feminism and Psychology*, 11 (4): 527–45.

Chung, R.C. (2005) 'Women, human rights, and counseling: Crossing international boundaries', *Journal of Counseling and Development*, 83: 262–68.

Department of Health (2002) *Women's Mental Health: Into the Mainstream: Strategic Development of Mental Health Care for Women*. London: Department of Health.

Dever, M. (1999) 'Notes on feminist pedagogy in the Brave New (Corporate) World', *European Journal of Women's Studies*, 6: 219–25.

Enns, C.Z. (1992) 'Towards integrating feminist psychotherapy and feminist philosophy', *Professional Psychology: Research and Practice*, 23 (6): 453–66.

Enns, C.Z. (1993) 'Twenty years of feminist counselling and therapy: From naming biases to implementing multifaceted practice', *Counselling Psychologist*, 21 (1): 3–87.

Freire, P. (2007) *Education for Critical Consciousness*. London: Continuum.

Furedi, F. (2004) *Therapy Culture: Cultivating Vulnerability in an Uncertain Age*. London: Routledge.

Giles, D. (2006) 'Constructing identities in cyberspace: The case of eating disorders', *British Journal of Social Psychology*, 45 (3): 463–79.

Gonick, M. (2001) 'What is the "problem" with these girls? Youth and feminist pedagogy', *Feminism and Psychology*, 11 (2): 167–71.

Harper, D. and Moss, D. (2003) 'A different kind of chemistry? Reformulating "formulation"', *Clinical Psychology*, 25: 6–10.

Harper, D. and Spellman, D. (2006) 'Social constructionist formulation: Telling a different story', in L. Johnstone and R. Dallos (eds), *Formulation in Psychology and Psychotherapy: Making Sense of People's Problems*. London: Routledge.

Heenan, M.C. (1995) 'Feminist psychotherapy: A contradiction in terms?', *Feminism and Psychology*, 5 (1): 112–17.

Heenan, M.C. (1998) 'Feminist object relations theory and therapy', in I.B. Seu and M.C. Heenan (eds), *Feminism and Psychotherapy: Reflections on Contemporary Theories and Practices*. London: Sage.

Heenan, M.C. (2001) 'Feminist therapy 'institutes' in England', *Feminist Review*, 68: 170–72.

Heenan, M.C. and Seu, I.B. (1998) 'Introduction', in I.B. Seu and M.C. Heenan (eds), *Feminism and Psychotherapy: Reflections on Contemporary Theories and Practices*. London: Sage.

Holland, S. (1988) 'Defining and experimenting with prevention', in S. Ramon and M. Giannichedda (eds), *Psychiatry in Transition: The British and Italian Experiences*. London: Routledge.

Holland, S. (1992) 'From social abuse to social action: A neighbourhood psychotherapy and social action project for women', in J.M. Ussher and P. Nicolson (eds), *Gender Issues in Clinical Psychology*. London: Routledge.

Johnstone, L. (2006) 'Controversies and debates about formulation', in L. Johnstone and R. Dallos (eds), *Formulation in Psychology and Psychotherapy: Making Sense of People's Problems*. London: Routledge.

Johnstone, L. and Dallos, R. (2006) 'Introduction to formulation', in L. Johnstone and R. Dallos (eds), *Formulation in Psychology and Psychotherapy: Making Sense of People's Problems*. London: Routledge.

Kinderman, P. (2001) 'The future of clinical psychology training', *Clinical Psychology*, 8: 6–10.

Kitzinger, S. and Perkins, R. (1993) *Changing our Minds: Lesbianism, Feminism and Psychology*. New York: New York University Press.

Laing, R.D. and Estersen, A. (1964) *Sanity, Madness and the Family: Families of Schizophrenics*. London: Penguin.

Lee, I. and Crawford, M. (2007) 'Lesbians and bisexual women in the eyes of scientific psychology', *Feminism and Psychology,* 17 (1): 109–27.

Livingstone, S. (2008) 'Taking risky opportunities in youthful content creation: Teenagers' use of social networking sites for intimacy, privacy and self-expression', *New Media and Society*, 10 (3): 393–411.

Maracek, J. and Kravetz, D. (1998) 'Power and agency in feminist therapy', in I.B. Seu and M.C. Heenan (eds), *Feminism and Psychotherapy: Reflections on Contemporary Theories and Practices*. London: Sage.

Martin, P. (2006) 'Different, dynamic and determined – the powerful force of counselling psychology in the helping professions', *Counselling Psychology Review*, 21 (3): 34–7.

Nicolson, P. (1992) 'Gender issues in the organisation of clinical psychology', in J.N. Ussher and P. Nicolson (eds), *Gender Issues in Clinical Psychology*. London: Routledge.

O'Hara, M. (1997) 'Emancipatory therapeutic practice in a turbulent transmodern era: A work of retrieval', *Journal of Humanistic Psychology*, 37 (3): 7–33.

Office for National Statistics (2008) 'Ageing: More pensioners than under-16s for first time ever'. Available at www.statistics.gov.uk/cci/nugget.asp?id=949, retrieved 27/05/09.

Pilgrim, D. (1991) 'Psychotherapy and social blinkers', *The Psychologist: Bulletin of the British Psychological Society*, (2): 52–5.

Prilleltensky, I. and Nelson, G. (2002) *Doing Psychology Critically: Making a Difference in Diverse Settings*. Basingstoke: Palgrave MacMillan.

Proctor, G. (2002) *The Dynamics of Power in Counselling and Psychotherapy: Ethics, Politics and Practice*. Ross-on-Wye: PCCS Books.

Pugh, D. and Coyle, A. (2000) 'The construction of counselling psychology in Britain: A discourse analysis of counselling psychology texts', *Counselling Psychology Quarterly*, 13 (1): 85–98.

Scott, S. (2004) 'Opening a can of worms? Counselling for survivors in UK women's prisons', in *Feminism and Psychology*, 14 (2): 256–61.

Seu, I.B. (1998) 'Change and theoretical frameworks', in I.B. Seu and M.C. Heenan (eds), *Feminism and Psychotherapy: Reflections on Contemporary Theories and Practices*. London: Sage.

Seu, I.B. (2000) 'Feminist psychoanalytic psychotherapy: Reflections on a complex undertaking', *Changes, an International Journal of Psychology and Psychotherapy*, 18 (4): 244–5.

Smail, D. (1991) 'Towards a radical environmentalist psychology of help', *The Psychologist*, 4 (2): 61–4.

Smail, D. (2005) *Power Interest and Psychology*. Ross-on-Wye: PCCS Books.

Strawbridge, S. (1992) 'How can I be a person-centred, psychodynamic, Marxist, feminist counsellor? Personal notes towards integration', *Counselling Psychology Review*, 7 (2): 7–9.

Swan, V. (1998) 'Narrative therapy, feminism and race', in I.B. Seu and C.M. Heenan (eds), *Feminism and Psychotherapy: Reflections on Contemporary Theories and Practices*. London: Sage.

Swan, V. (1999) 'Narrative, Foucault and feminism: Implications for therapeutic practice', in I. Parker (ed.), *Deconstructing Psychotherapy*. London: Sage.

Taylor, M. (1994) 'Gender and power in counselling and supervision', *British Journal of Guidance and Counselling*, 22 (3): 319–26.

Thatcher, M. and Manktelow, K. (2007) 'The cost of individualism', *Counselling Psychology Review*, 22 (4): 31–43.

Ussher, J.M. (1991) *Women's Madness: Misogyny or Mental Illness?* New York: Harvester Wheatsheaf.

Ussher, J.M. (1992) 'Science sexing psychology: Positivist science and gender bias in clinical psychology', in J.N. Ussher and P. Nicolson (eds), *Gender Issues in Clinical Psychology*. London: Routledge.

Vygotsky, L.S. (1962) *Thought and Language,* 2nd edn. Cambridge: Cambridge University Press.

Waterhouse, R.L. (1993) 'Wild women don't have the blues: A feminist critique of person centred counseling and therapy', *Feminism and Psychology,* 3 (1): 55–71.

White, B. (2006) 'The person-centred approach: A vehicle for acknowledging and respecting women's voices', in G. Procter, M. Cooper, P. Sanders and B. Malcom (eds), *Politicizing the Person-centred Approach: An Agenda for Social Change*. Ross-on-Wye: PCCS Books.

Worrell, J. and Remer, P. (1992) *Feminist Perspectives in Therapy*. Chichester: Wiley.

Yakushko, O. and Chronister, K.M. (2005) 'Immigrant women and counseling: The invisible others', *Journal of Counseling and Development*, 83: 292–8.

12

RELATIONAL TRAUMA

Lynne Jordan

In looking to write this chapter and doing a new literature search I was struck by the amount of papers that are being written around the concept of 'trauma'. In fact, mirroring the very heart of the issue it was all too easy to feel overwhelmed by the sheer volume of material available. 'Trauma' by its very nature interrupts life as we know it day to day. 'Relational trauma' (RT) also disrupts the formation and maintenance of relationships as we know them day to day. Allen (2001) proposes that a continuum of trauma from impersonal, through interpersonal to attachment trauma may help us in our understanding of the different kinds of trauma, and more importantly, the effects and consequences of those traumas long term. Broadly, a trauma is an event that is beyond the capacity to process within ordinary everyday mental functioning.

Examples of impersonal traumas are: road traffic accidents, floods, hurricanes, landslides, bombing; examples of interpersonal traumas are sexual or physical assault by a stranger. These are traumas that are usually outside a personal relationship. The psychological, cultural and relational effects of these traumas can be long-lasting. Attachment trauma is the aspect of trauma that is the subject of this chapter, in which a person is embedded in close personal relationships. In this chapter the reader will find reference to abuse in the context of RT and this refers the misuse of power and the betrayal of relationship which has a significant contribution to the RT overall experienced by an individual. Post traumatic stress disorder (PTSD) is a formal medical/psychological diagnosis sometimes given to a person. It can add another perspective to our understanding of trauma and the effects on an individual's psyche. The *Diagnostic and Statistical Manual* (DSM-IV) in diagnosing PTSD claims that a trauma is:

exposure to an extreme traumatic stressor involving direct personal experience of an event that involves actual or threatened death or serious injury, or other threat to one's physical integrity; or witnessing an event that involves death, injury, or a threat to the physical integrity of another person; or learning about unexpected or violent death, serious harm, or threat of death or injury experienced by a family member or other close associate. (APA, 1985: 435)

This chapter will endeavour to explore the concept of RT and abuse of relationship and see how it can be situated within the trauma field. We will look at some of the effects, specifically how RT affects a person's capacity for relationship, and look at some theories of why this might be. We will then look at the role of resilience and how this can be strengthened or undermined by the level of security of other attachments, including the role of the therapeutic, supervisory and trainer relationships. All the case vignettes presented here use pseudonyms and some details have been changed in order to protect anonymity.

RELATIONAL TRAUMA

The definition of RT is only partially covered by the DSM-IV criteria but with additional features of a threat to the self-identity and a profound undermining of safety in the world. There is an abuse and misuse of power in RT which includes a deep sense of betrayal of relationship (Freyd, 1996). People's sense of personal agency is undermined and there is often much confusion and mixed feelings about the relationship with the perpetrator. Trauma in general can be seen as a disruption to the attachment system (de Zuleta, 2004) and observed even more pervasively in RT. Grooming or the 'set up' process is part of the trauma of RT, and in fact it is important to understand as this is often experienced in retrospect as more traumatic than the abuse or violation itself. 'Trauma bonds' (Herman, 1997) or 'Stockholm syndrome' (Ochberg, 1982; Graham et al., 1995) are both concepts that seek to encapsulate the way a person entrapped in a traumatic relational dynamic will identify with the aggressor as a defence and in order to survive. There is a denial of the self and abdication to the self of the other. This is further complicated when a person is a vulnerable adult or a child, as the need for dependency for sustenance and survival is even greater.

RT includes all forms of child abuse: physical, sexual, emotional, verbal and neglect, bullying in schools and colleges, workplace and neighbourhood bullying, all forms of domestic violence: physical, sexual, emotional, verbal, financial and neglect as well as racial discrimination. It occurs basically when one person has power over another and uses that power to the detriment of the other person. In extensive prolonged RT there is a pervasive erosion of the cohesive self (Herman, 1997), where the person loses a sense of themselves. A key factor in extended and extensive RT is use of coercion to induce actual or perceived powerlessness. This, therefore, highlights the importance of a collaborative ethos in any therapeutic endeavour with survivors of RT or abuse. If we are not mindful of the need for collaboration, there is a great risk of falling into a dynamic where the abuse or trauma is played out between us as therapists and the client. It could be said that even with due care and attention given to this, it is inevitable that we will be pulled into some of the historic dynamic relations due to the pull by the client being so very strong. Coercive control in the use of power interpersonally works on the basis of the following:

- Violence and threat of violence so the victim is in a constant state of living in fear (DoH, 2002, 2006a, 2008).
- Control of bodily functions where the perpetrator decides, for example, when the victim is allowed to visit the toilet and if at all, or in the case of some survivors of sexual abuse causing the victim of unwanted sexual contact to be sexually aroused and to orgasm.
- Capricious enforcement of petty rules where the perpetrator places a lot of emphasis on small issues and yet ignores the big issues, leaving the victim with a sense of distorted perception of what is right and wrong and what is 'real'.
- Intermittent rewards which cause the victim to hold on to hope that things are improving, only to then slip back into the old patterns of control and ignoring of the victim's needs.
- Isolating the victim, thus allowing the perpetrator to be sure of the victim's silence and more secure in his 'reality' being the dominant one.
- Degradation through words and behaviour, for example, in calling the victim names such as 'slut' or 'bitch' or 'cunt' in a derogatory manner that implies hatred and total disrespect or, for example, urinating on the victim.
- Enforced participation in atrocities can be a really difficult issue when recovering from relational trauma or abuse as the victim can feel very shameful about this and responsible 'because I joined in'.

Relationship dynamics in RT are complex and give rise to complex trauma responses that are perhaps more accurately described as 'complex PTSD' syndrome rather than as PTSD (Herman, 1997). Complex PTSD is thought of as similar to a borderline personality profile with a profound sense of interpersonal alienation and instability of relationships. This chapter is not focusing on this aspect of trauma reaction, although many of the component criteria for a diagnosis of complex PTSD are embedded in this text as part of the attachment trauma effects. This is due to the additional relational aspects that can manifest as trauma bonds or 'Stockholm syndrome' where there is empathy between the victim and the perpetrator. This enables the victim to maintain the 'goodness' of the perpetrator and thus to deny any negative affect. Sometimes the victim's very safety and possibility of long-term survival may have depended on the child or vulnerable adult's ability to bond in this way to the perpetrator.

CASE VIGNETTE: JO

Jo came to see me after her long-term relationship with her partner broke up due to her lack of libido. She told a story of sadness and isolation and sexual confusion that stemmed from her childhood. When Jo's Mum died her father began to show an interest in her sexually. This manifested itself initially through appreciative comments about her blossoming womanhood. She was only nine years old but had begun to grow breasts and was aware that this was different to the other girls at school. The boys teased her at school and the girls called her 'booby queen'. Jo also found it difficult to concentrate at school and fell behind in her work. At home her father's attentions grew stronger over the first year after her mother had died and she found herself wishing her Mum was there so she could tell her what was happening. Her father touched and massaged her breasts, telling her it would help their development and that she would be used to a man's touch when she was older and so be better at knowing how to please a man. He was so nice to her and she found it impossible to say no to him even though she really did not like what was happening. He listened to her problems from school although she did not tell him about the 'booby queen' label as she feared he may laugh at her. In therapy we spoke a lot about her relationship with both her mother and her father and about the lack of any siblings. She felt a deep sense of both loyalty and shame towards her father and her memories of her mother were all but gone. We looked at photographs of her family when Mum was alive and at her and her Dad after her mother died. She found it very hard to sort through her feelings about the man who had cared for her as well as used her sexually, and it was important to look at the whole context of her growing up years in order for her to get an understanding of what her mixed feelings were about. We also looked at her coping strategies and how she had managed to survive and make a life for herself. The therapeutic relationship gave her a temporary secure base from which to work from to sort through the confusing and distressing experiences she had. Her father was a central figure in her growing up years, and it was very important as therapist to respect that relationship in spite of the abuse that occurred as she was very protective of him and would otherwise have quickly disengaged from therapy.

Dissociation, personality fragmentation and problems with identity including personality disorders, suicidality, eating disorders, substance abuse and self-harm along with a swathe of other mental and physical health problems are seen to be correlated with RT. The Department of Health's programme 'Tackling the health and mental health effects of domestic and sexual violence and abuse' (2006a) goes some way to outline this. Figure 12.1 demonstrates how the 'grooming process' can impact the effects

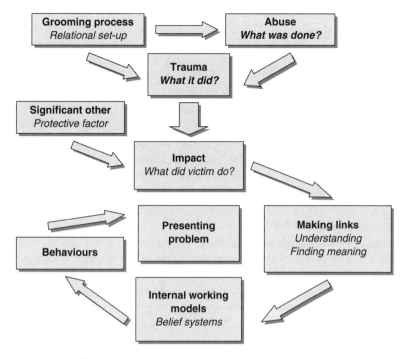

FIGURE 12.1 RELATIONAL TRAUMA DYNAMICS (INFORMED BY NURSE ET AL., 2005)

of abuse within RT and in fact becomes an important part of the trauma dynamics. The 'significant other' represents alternative attachment figures who operate as protective factors against the effects of the trauma. Conversely, a lack of alternative attachment figures increases risk for further abuse and make it more difficult to leave a current abusive relationship.

In considering the different forms of RT, it is important to be aware of cultural differences in attitudes to sex, the status of women and children in society and attitudes towards sexual activity between adults and children and between older and younger children. In addition, we should note the existence of various cultural, ritualistic practices which may clash with the laws of the land as in, for example, the Female Circumcision Acts (1995, 2003). The British Medical Association estimates that 3000 girls in UK annually undergo illegal female genital mutilation (FGM) or excision (FGE) with 10,000 girls at risk a year. FGM and FGE are seen by some as cultural rituals and not as sexual abuse; deMause (1991, 1993, 2002) argues that it is a form of incest and sadistic pleasure. Cultural differences are flagged for the purposes of this chapter, but warrant further discussion and should be borne in mind if working in cross-cultural contexts.

CASE VIGNETTE: SATHI

Sathi was 19 years old and of Indian origin, and she and her family had moved to Britain following some traumatic events where they were living in Pakistan. They were not asylum seekers but came to Britain because Sathi's doctor father got a job in a hospital in London. She had three brothers who were all older than her and had integrated into British way of life, but she had been more shy and although she had gone to a British school in Pakistan she felt out of her depth with her class peers and had only one friend. This friend was a girl of the same age as her who also found life at the school difficult as she had mild cerebral palsy and could not keep up with the rest of the class either academically or physically. From Sathi's point of view she was not worried about the lack of friends or the isolation from her peers. She came for therapy because she was always 'nervous' at home, especially when neither of her parents were there. On those occasions she never invited her friend to her house because she said her brothers teased her friend when the parents were not there. On further investigation it became evident that Sathi, as a very young child, had been victim to sexual assault by a friend of the family in Pakistan before emigrating to Britain, She had dismissed it as unimportant because she 'was safe' in Britain, but found that increasingly she could not cope with her brothers' horseplay in the family. This was making her feel anxious at home and very scared at going outside. She was having flashbacks of the assault and a lot of intrusive thoughts about the event and was catastrophising about what else might happen. She did not dare tell her family because she knew they would see it as a personal failure on their part. Part of her family culture was the importance of virginity before marriage, so she feared her family's rejection if she were to tell them. There was also a taboo on discussing anything sexual, so this made it even harder. Much of our work was about being a witness to what had happened and helping her to sort through her conflicting feelings about her family culture that had seemed to reinforce the effects of shame and self-disgust. She decided not to disclose to her family but did talk to her friend. We also worked at helping her to build more relationships with peers, giving her positive influences on her self-esteem.

EARLY EXPERIENCE AND ADULT MENTAL HEALTH

Relationships with 'significant others' seem to function as either protective factors for effects of abuse or risk inducing factors as seen by numerous researchers such as Briere and Runtz (1987), Finkelhor (1986), Furman (1997) and Jordan (2002, 2007b, 2008). They influence the extent to which traumatic aspects of life experience invade someone's psyche as a whole and therefore their mental health. Schore's (2001, 2003) work on the psychobiology of attachment importantly shows how the security and insecurity of early attachment affects the neurobiology of the developing brain and the subsequent ability to both manage stress and regulate emotion (see also Van der Kolk et al., 1996). Research testifies to our adult relationships being influenced by unconscious processes originating in early childhood through internal working models (Bowlby, 1988) and in the neurobiological development of the brain (Schore, 2001, 2003). As therapists, it is essential to understand our own early attachments and how they influence the therapeutic relationships we form. Security of attachment strengthens the self-reflective capacity, and this has a powerful protective mediating influence in how that person will cope with stress or trauma (Fonagy et al., 1991; Holmes, 2001; Schore, 2001, 2003). Relationality is clearly central to human well-being and functioning and, therefore, has a central role in effective therapeutic endeavours for therapist and as client, supervisee and trainee.

Abuse or trauma and neglect of all kinds especially in childhood is a core underlying issue of many mental health problems, and the most complex clients often present with a history of abuse. This has been highlighted though much research within therapeutic and medical fields, as seen in Briere and Runtz (1987), Harvey et al. (2000), Read (1997), Werner, (1989) and Winnicott (1965). Survivors often present with dissociative disorders, personality disorders, eating problems, self-harming, relationship difficulties and physical health problems.

Abuse in society goes back as long as history has ever been recorded. Yet it is only fairly recently that the connections between adult mental health problems and a history of childhood trauma and neglect and adult abuse and violence has been revisited and is now on government agendas. This is evidenced in the Department of Health's documents (2002, 2006a and b, 2008). What follows is a summary of some of the statistics drawn from these documents:

- Domestic abuse accounts for a quarter of all violent crime.
- 26 per cent of all women are victims of domestic violence.
- Two women a week are killed by partners/ex-partners, of which 30 per cent onsets or escalates during pregnancy.
- Thousands of children witness domestic violence every day, not just listening to verbal violence, but seeing their mothers being physically abused and sexually assaulted.
- Prevalence rates for childhood sexual abuse are high (20–30 per cent of girls, 5–10 per cent of boys).
- 20 per cent of children are subjected to physical violence regularly.
- In at least 40 per cent of domestic violence cases there is also childhood physical and sexual abuse involving the same perpetrator, usually the father or father figure.
- Rape is a significant element of domestic violence.
- The British Crime Survey (2001) found that 7 per cent of women suffer rape or serious sexual assault and that in 54 per cent of cases the rapist is the current (45 per cent) or ex (9 per cent) partner of the victim (Kershaw et al., 2001).
- Childhood sexual and physical abuse, domestic violence, and rape and sexual assault occur in all social classes and ethnic groups.

The long-term health and mental health effects of the RTs of child sexual abuse, rape and domestic abuse, plus sexual assault amongst adult men and women, are wide-ranging. There are significant correlations between these and a long list of conditions including PTSD/complex PTSD, personality disorders, depression and anxiety, panic, obsessive-compulsive disorder and phobias, suicide and para-suicide, and re-victimization. The list is endless: substance abuse, including smoking seen as 'health risk behaviours' (DoH, 2006a); eating disorders, self-harm, dissociation/fragmented identity, socio-economic problems, relationship difficulties of various kinds, sexual difficulties/risky sexual behaviour including prostitution, sexually transmitted infections/unwanted pregnancies including teenage pregnancies; irritable bowel syndrome, gynaecological problems, heart and circulatory disease, parenting problems (over/under protective or difficulty conceiving). The reader is urged to be mindful that this is not a checklist as there are other factors which interplay, including genetic predisposition. It should be remembered that the list does not imply direct causality but is rather a statement of significant correlation. Obviously, these effects are not normally all experienced by one person, and even if they are, they may occur at different times in life.

Various studies (Read, 1997) have reported that 50–60 per cent of inpatients and 40–60 per cent of outpatients in mental health services have been physically and/or sexually abused as children. A meta-analysis of 18 studies (Golding, 1999) found an average rate of PTSD among victimized women of 64 per cent, a rate of depression of 48 per cent and a suicide rate of 18 per cent. There are many studies showing that living in an environment of domestic violence inhibits children's emotional, behavioural and cognitive development. Its effects include anxiety, fear, withdrawal, highly sexualized and aggressive behaviour, reduced educational achievement, failure to acquire social competence, anti-social behaviour, and the use of drugs.

THE ROLE OF DISSOCIATION

'Dissociation' describes a state of altered consciousness, and there are various terms used by survivors: 'splitting', 'switching off', 'going blank', 'spacing out' and 'numbing'. Dissociation is a survival skill for people to cope with extreme experiences, which include various forms of RT/abuse and hostage situations. In fact, there have been found similarities between the manufactured trance states of prisoners in hostage situations and the dissociative skills of those coerced and entrapped in abusive relationships. Dissociation allows for removal of oneself in the mind from the immediate psychological and emotional impact of trauma even though the body is still present. As a client of mine said when in a child state of consciousness: 'It is OK because I was not there … nothing happened to me.' To the survivor it represents a way of keeping safe in the midst of danger – physical or psychological. As a child, to dissociate may have been an important way people survived the abuse, but as an adult there can be a high price to pay. This is due to the automatic way dissociation can be triggered when under stress or in certain situations. Extreme stress and danger, especially when experienced in early childhood, can severely interfere with the child's neurological development and has the power to resculpt the brain (Sanderson, 2006). This can reduce a person's resilience and therefore ability to cope with other stressors. Affect regulation is severely affected as the person has had her or his natural defences overwhelmed and overridden and he or she has not been able to learn the skills to manage emotions without cutting them off altogether.

Dissociation is on a continuum from a norm to extreme: the norm being when we drive a familiar route to the office and have not noticed the route and appear to have 'lost time' during the journey. The other end of that continuum is when the mind has dissociated so much that it fragments to separate selves, and different experiences are logged in different sections of the mind. The different sections may have opposing views of relationships and events and the person is motivated to keep these separate. Shengold (1989) describes the way the mind fragments to preserve 'the delusion of good parents'. This level of dissociation seen in dissociative identity disorder (APA, 1985) is almost always associated with a childhood history of extensive prolonged abuse (Putnam, 1985, 1989; Ross, C., 1980; Ross, B., 1991).

CASE VIGNETTE: LUCY

When I first met with Lucy, 22 years old, she really impressed me with her infectious laugh and lively manner. She had a zest for life and was very confused as to why she was referred to see me, which frankly I shared. Lucy lived with her parents and younger sister and worked in a nursery school. She was five months into an unplanned pregnancy with her now estranged boyfriend. She had never seen anyone in the 'helping services' previously and was referred by her GP due to problems with anxiety and finding it hard to get out of the house and go to work, and she was having 'emotional turns with angry outbursts' that were inexplicable. Her mother had persuaded her to go to her GP to have a physical check-up. There were no hormonal imbalances which had been suspected. In discussion with her, several facts emerged that were significant. She said she found items of clothing in her cupboard at times which she did not remember buying or even knowing as hers due to the different style; she was sometimes accosted by people she did not know who were very friendly and called her mate and by another name, she just assumed there was a case of mistaken identity. She also disclosed that she had a 'busy head'. When I asked her about this, it seemed she had internal dialogue about nearly everything and had ongoing conflict

(Continued)

(Continued)

of opinion and desires. She said 'It is driving me nuts … or am I nuts …?' During the course of the time spent with her, she continued in the lively mode until we spoke about her 'busy head' and then she looked panicked and completely different. I worked with Lucy over a period of several years but with numerous breaks. Our first task was to help her get some control of her anxiety symptoms and anger outbursts that seemed inextricably linked to the feeling of being overwhelmed with confusion at times. We also spent some time exploring her early attachment relationships, which were predominantly insecure, although there did seem to be a degree of over-protection by her mother in some ways whilst dismissing her needs and opinions at the same time. This had caused a split in Lucy and she had developed different ways of being that were inconsistent and she felt disconnected with herself and with others. She was unpredictable and could be anxious and fun-loving. She could be feisty and she could be relaxed. The therapeutic relationship had an important role in helping her to create an internal dialogue between the different parts of herself and to eventually find coherence and a co-working that gave her overall harmony and peace of mind.

TRAUMAGENIC DYNAMICS

Finkelhor's (1986) conceptual framework of 'traumagenic dynamics of child sexual abuse' is often used amongst mental health practitioners including therapists to help with understanding the broader context of effects of the RT of child sexual abuse. It is important to be sensitive in taking the principles of this theory in working cross-culturally as some differences will be found due to the diverse attitudes which may accentuate or undermine effects of abuse. Finkelhor describes four traumagenic dynamics: traumatic sexualization, stigmatization, betrayal, powerlessness.

- *Traumatic sexualization* is the process by which a child's sexuality is shaped in developmentally inappropriate ways. Sometimes there is an exchange of affection, gifts and privileges for sexual favours or contact. A child learns to use inappropriate sexual behaviour to get age-appropriate needs met. Parts of the anatomy are fetishized, and frightening memories can become associated with sexual activity. The perpetrator who evokes sexual response in the child or a child enticed to participate pro-actively has a more harmful effect. Children who have been sexually abused often have unusual amounts of sexual connections and awareness which can be surprising for their age.
- *Betrayal* is when children gradually or suddenly have the awareness that someone they love and depend on has hurt them. Children may realize they have been manipulated and lied to, or treated with contempt and disregard, and they experience a depth of betrayal and often rage at this point. Other family members/friends/teachers can also be

a part of the betrayal dynamic as they may not have protected the child or believed that child when they tried to disclose. The amount of betrayal is related to the amount the child feels tricked and also the family's response to disclosure.

- *Powerlessness* describes the way the child's will, desires and sense of efficacy are continually thwarted. The child has a learned helplessness response to the futility of trying to defend the self or to tell someone, or just a belief that it is simply too dangerous to do anything. Basic powerlessness occurs when a child's body and mind is invaded through coercive control. Powerlessness is increased through terror and fear and when she/he cannot make adults understand or believe what she/he is saying either through an inability to speak from a 'freeze' stress response or through lack of language or through an unavailability of anyone who is willing to listen. Threats or fear of consequences of disclosure entrap the child.

- *Stigmatization* comes from a deep sense of badness, shame and guilt, which are hallmarks of abuse experiences of children and adults. The perpetrator is held as good through splitting and dissociative abilities, whilst badness remains with the self. If the child's body responded to sexual abuse in arousal and or orgasm, the shame is even greater as the person feeling their own bodies have betrayed them. It is in the perpetrator's interest to see the victim feeling badness, shame and guilt, as this will minimize the likelihood of the victim blowing the whistle since the victim feels responsible for what has happened. Shame and guilt can be reinforced by familial or societal attitudes; for example, in the social construction of femininity it is more difficult for women to be seen as victimizers, as with the social construction of masculinity it is much harder for men to 'own' experiences of being victimized.

Recovery from any trauma needs to happen in the context of relationship since even in impersonal trauma the effects are interpersonal (Jordan, 2002, 2008; Pearlman and Courtois, 2005). These effects include:

- Avoidance of triggers which may be contained in people or in situations. However, avoidance causes people to isolate themselves, which inevitably will lead to isolation from others.

- People can avoid social situations or other people that remind them of a perpetrator or indeed situations that remind them of a place they were in when abused. This is a powerful factor in RT.

- Feelings of disconnection and estrangement from others, which can occur due to a sense that no one really understands and so people withdraw, becoming more frozen in the trauma.

- Restricted range of affect, with difficulty in having loving feelings due to the pre-occupation with the trauma and the shock and numbness that accompanies it. So much energy goes into this that people struggle with relating, to others, as the author has witnessed with many clients, as victims of domestic violence and child abuse.

- A sense of foreboding and a foreshortened future with no expectation of career, marriage or partnership or even normal lifespan due to the 'unthinkable' happening and the person's basic trust in the world blown out of the water. As a client survivor of date rape stated: '*it was like a nuclear blast! Everything was gone … at least it felt like that at the time and for a long time afterwards*'.

- Irritability and outbursts of anger, which the author has witnessed many times in clients who do not report having been angry people pre-trauma. It seems this can be anger at the self as much as anger at others, and sometimes is simply due to an overload of emotion that is difficult to name and which then spills out into anger and irritability.

The above factors also make it hard for others to relate to the survivors or victim of trauma, and in relational trauma particularly there is such a breach of trust that the person's ability to form and maintain relationships is severely compromised.

AN ATTACHMENT PERSPECTIVE

Attachment theory (Bowlby, 1988) tells us that a secure-enough base in childhood can make a huge difference to how people internalize the effects of trauma and abuse and is, therefore, intimately involved with development of resilience. Current research suggests that human beings' 'relationality' begins in the mother's womb way before birth and continues throughout life (see Righetti et al., 2005). Although attachment theory is not a model of therapy in itself, it could be argued that utilizing an attachment theory perspective will reinforce relational aspects of any model and will, therefore, strengthen therapeutic work. It is well understood that the quality of the therapeutic relationship is the most influential factor in therapy outcome. These theories can be transferable to the needs of staff who are working with survivors of trauma (see for example, Wosket, 1999). Holmes (2001) identified six attachment domains which can inform our working with survivors of RT through deconstructing the vital elements of attachment and its functions:

1. **Secure base:**
   - External secure base through 'an other'.
   - Internalized representation of that secure base within the self structure/internal working model.
   - 'Secure base' experience essential for recovery work in the therapeutic alliance.

2. **Exploration and enjoyment:**
   - The capacity for playful, sexual or intellectual pleasure is central to a secure base.
   - Many find a sense of humour a life-saver … staff as well as clients!
   - A sense of fun can, therefore, enhance resilience during the recovery process.

3. **Protest and anger:**
   - An attachment regulator to maintain attachment bonds and secure base.
   - Anger can be a central part of recovery as it enhances the self identity.

- It increases the sense of personal power and autonomy.
- Anger management strategies are important to build into the work in order to maximize self-control/agency.

4. **Separation and loss:**

- Central to much psychological distress and especially severe at times of crisis for those surviving any kind of RT.
- Attachment is only possible with negotiation of separation and the management of real or potential losses.
- Loss issues can be triggered through therapeutic relationship and life being settled.
- Related to a historic association between security and trauma.
- Breaks and pending ending of therapy are powerful triggers.

5. **Internal working models:**

- The shape of relationships, the 'who I am' and 'how I fit into the world' and 'how the world fits in with me'.
- Trauma destroys or undermines part of the attachment security regulating system (Schore, 2001).
- Therapy has a task of facilitating the building of new internal working models via relational working.
- Schore's work highlights the importance of having a bio-psychosocial perspective.

6. **Reflexive function and narrative competence:**

- Security of attachment facilitates reflexive functioning.
- Reflexive functioning enables the narrative process of therapy and the narrative process of therapy enhances reflexivity.
- Reflexivity capacity increases resilience and stress management capabilities.
- Increases continuity and cohesion and helps to heal dissociative self parts through internal dialog between self parts.

Herman (1997) explains how there is a fundamental need for safety before any trauma work is undertaken, mirroring the secure base principles of attachment theory. An attachment perspective assumes that basic emotional needs of security and support must be adequately met in order for people to learn and develop. Schore (1994, 1998a, 2000) proposes that early secure attachments are essential for right-side brain development, which has an enhanced sensitive period during the last trimester of pregnancy and the first three years of life. The right brain is crucial in 'not only processing social-emotional information, facilitating attachment functions, and regulating bodily and affective states' (Schore, 1994, 1998a), but also 'in the control of vital functions supporting survival and enabling the organism to cope actively and passively with stress' (Wittling and Schweiger, 1993). Schore also asserts that the maturing of the right brain development is centrally 'experience dependent', experience that is rooted in early attachments and that the quality of those attachments can positively and negatively influence development and, therefore, mental health both as an infant and in adulthood.

VULNERABILITY AND RESILIENCE

'Trauma', 'resilience', perpetrators and 'victims' are current 'buzz words' as we as a society seek to understand how we can possibly survive the atrocities that people commit against each other. In Freud's day it was considered sensational and preposterous to propose that a parent, particularly a father, could sexually abuse a child in his care, so much so that the seduction theory was refuted (Freud, 1896), and some may say that this has contributed to years of further denial continued en mass in society. A dominant narrative of this century amongst psychologists and lay people alike is that early childhood trauma affects adult functioning. The difference is, perhaps, that we are now aware that there is hope for recovery to a large extent from these traumatic events in childhood. Furman (1997) describes research that formed the basis for his book in which he had found overwhelming anecdotal evidence that the majority of people do indeed not only survive but also find ways to thrive beyond really difficult experiences. Although there are risk factors that affect vulnerability as to how much threatening events impact on a person's functioning, there are also protective factors which have similar effects.

People who have learning disabilities and physical disabilities are known to be more vulnerable to various forms of RT/abuse both as children, adolescents and adults, including physical, emotional, financial and sexual abuse (Hollins and Sinason, 2000; Kennedy, 1996). Therefore a disability could be seen as a risk factor or vulnerability factor, and so more protection is needed to compensate for this. There is some protection within statutory services via the 'vulnerable adults' policies, but it is important to be aware of the extra vulnerability. It could be that people with disability have less resilience and relational abilities that can be protective against trauma and thus to enhance resilience.

Resilience describes a person's ability to survive and recover from various threatening life events. Not only is this relevant for primary victims or survivors of trauma, but also for those in support roles. To mediate against vicarious trauma, support and reflection for carers and therapists are seen to act as protective factors, much like the therapeutic relationship can also act as a protective factor for clients (Jordan, 2008). In narrative research with women sexually abused in childhood, Jordan (2002) found that alternative relationships with others, apart from primary attachment figures, in childhood and adulthood acted as a secure base that facilitated positive growth, development and change. They were the strongest indicated protective factors against the effects of childhood abuse in adult functioning. A secure base and a reflexive capacity are known to be two of the six attachment domains considered vital for a healthy psyche (Holmes, 2001).

CASE STUDY: JIM AND JILL

Jim and Jill first met with me because Jill was not wanting to go to the day club she had previously attended and she said she was 'too depressed to be bothered'. Jill was born with a twisted spine and in spite of numerous operations still had to have a wheelchair to get around. Jim was her husband of 20 years and able-bodied. They were both in their mid-50s and very fraught when I first met them, with Jim exasperated and Jill resenting him. I was unsure at first why they had both come to the appointment as it was Jill who was referred by the GP in a primary care setting, so I had assumed Jim would help her into the room and then go and wait in the waiting area. Instead he sat down, looking expectantly at me. We all spoke together for the first part of the session and then agreed that Jim would wait outside for the remainder to give Jill a chance to talk through things alone. What emerged was a fascinating but very sad story about Jill's agreeing with all Jim wanted in order to please him, and she felt he wanted her at home because he was lonely and could not admit this. Jill also mentioned it felt the easiest thing in the world at first to go along with it since she had always done this at home with her parents. She felt bad about all the attention she had due to her 'problem' so she felt obliged to give in to everyone else's needs outside of the essential medical and practical care. The work that emerged was a piece with Jill to help her find her own feelings and wishes, her own self-identity. It also included Jim by way of helping her to be able to explain her feelings as she became aware of them. Jim was also referred for some individual work with a colleague, as it seemed to me that Jim was also depressed and needed some time to talk through things. Both partners demonstrated resilience in the way they had conducted their lives but had developed some unhelpful patterns. New patterns were developed through the therapeutic process.

The importance of secure attachments and secure base functionality is also seen in the needs of mental health workers and especially in the case of psychological therapists. They are potentially exposed to working with traumatized people every day, sometimes with very little support for their needs. Jordan (2008) found that the confidence of mental health staff and well-being improved greatly in their work with traumatized populations if they had adequate training and supervision and support for themselves in the workplace. Without this there is an increased risk of a vicarious trauma and burnout response.

McCann and Pearlman (1989) related what is needed as protection from vicarious trauma back to six 'fundamental needs'. These are much like Maslow's (1970) well-known hierarchy of needs that each of us have: safety, dependency, trust, power, esteem and intimacy. They also flagged up the coping strategies that can help to mediate against vicarious trauma developing:

1. Openly acknowledging feelings/supervision, support system.
2. Awareness of schemas or thoughts or beliefs challenged.
3. Balance of personal and work life.
4. Balance of case load.
5. Respect for own boundaries.
6. Awareness of limitations.
7. Need for self-nurturing met elsewhere.
8. Involvement in political social change agendas.
9. Need for non-victim activities that inspire hope and optimism.
10. Need for optimistic perseverance.

In training it is important for strategies to be included about how we encourage students to engage with their work. The principles link the concept of Maslow's (1970) hierarchy of needs and 'self-actualization' with Bowlby's (1988) concept of 'secure base' needing to be adequate in order for people to explore and develop and function properly. During training we are stretched to capacity and beyond and, therefore, there is an even keener need to find a good-enough secure base.

It could, therefore, be argued that personal therapy during training should be obligatory. Relationships with 'significant others' seem to function as either protective factors for the effects of abuse or risk inducing factors as seen by numerous researchers such as Briere and Runtz (1987), Finkelhor (1986), Furman (1997) and Jordan (2002, 2008). A therapist or counselling psychologist can operate as a temporary secure base with clients for sorting through issues in their lives or supervisees in their work. My own research demonstrated that by providing a 'secure base' of a good-enough training environment, trainees were more able to effectively reflect on their work with survivors. This enabled them to contain potential personal triggers and feel supported and safer in the work.

As counselling psychologists, it is important to take careful note of the interface between the personal and the professional. This interface is where we draw from our own experiences to empathize, but we are also are careful to keep those same experiences bracketed from being actively worked out in relationships with our clients, supervisees or trainees. We enter into any training as therapists first of all as human beings with life experience that can be more or less valuable as a reference point in our work with others. Therefore our internal working models of relationship can be seen as the baseline for any therapeutic or training work. Not only is the therapeutic relationship central to the process of change between therapist and client, but also between supervisor and supervisee or between trainer and trainee and between colleagues and within management hierarchies (Murphy and Gilbert, 2000; Paul and Pelham, 2000).

CASE VIGNETTE: SHEILA'S WORDS

'Into the light'

We have travelled a long way since the first footsteps we took together. We have seen the dark side of life that had been hidden away for so long. You took me through the jungle mass of thought, cutting away at the thickened creepers that barred my way.

As the brambles tugged at my sensitivities you soothed the hurt with quiet words urging me onwards into the clearing. I stumbled often, on the journey, over old memories and pain. The new shoot growth of the day's happenings barred my path but you made me see that they were young, not strong, and I could bend them away from my pilgrimage.

The destination seemed so far away at times, as the routes wound round and round. I often felt lost and as if I had backtracked to places without wanting to. The familiarity of the painful stops and starts of the journey did not make the voyage one to be enjoyed but still you urged me on.

You witnessed the struggles and the tears; you supported me in the dark frightening times when I teetered on the edge of submission, as the darkness surrounded me. You never let me be afraid and alone; you were always there with me.

It was a journey that you knew I had to make, for wholeness again. We knew there would be scars left at the end of the journey, but without them how would we be reminded of all that we had gone through to reach a liveable life.

When I hadn't enough strength to go on you showed me how to find the resilience to fight the despair I felt. You made the journey bearable when I thought it was too much.

Even as we are reaching the light and I falter, knowing soon the journey may end, you stay with me but encouraging me to make the sacrifice of losing a companion I have spent so much time with. The me you have given me back is not as damaged as I thought. The bruises and wounds are recovering now and do not appear so vivid as once they were. The injuries from the journey have been cared for gently and as they heal the scars are pale and insignificant, but we both know how they got there.

(Reprinted with permission from 'Brave Tears' by Llewellyn, 2008)

RELATIONAL THERAPY AND ATTACHMENT-BASED COUNSELLING

Research into therapy effectiveness and which model is 'best' also reveals that whichever model a therapist adheres to it is the quality of the therapeutic relationship which determines the effectiveness of that therapy. This is exemplified in the work of Beutler and Sandowicz (1994) and Orlinsky et al. (1994), in Dale (1999) and Hubble et al. (1999). They identified four key findings surrounding positive outcomes for clients which were more to do with personal characteristics of therapists and clients than with the therapeutic orientation or techniques. They concluded that some therapists, regardless of orientation, consistently produced either more positive or more negative results than others.

Although attachment theory is not a model of therapy in itself, it could be argued that utilizing attachment theory to enhance relational aspects of other models will strengthen therapeutic work. Attachment-based counselling (ABC) (Jordan, 2007b) offers a broad base for the integration of common factors across the models, which can be helpful when working in multi-disciplinary groups and with complex clients. ABC is mostly about an attitude to the work, a philosophical stance rather than prescribed ways of working. The philosophy can be flexibly adapted to suit most ways of working since the relationship in its different forms is at the core. ABC and other relational ways of working, for example, Holmes' 'brief attachment-based intervention' (BABI) (Holmes, 2001), can allow for flexibility of approach adapting to the attachment needs of clients as well as taking into account the resource demands and therapist level of competence.

It could be argued that survivors all need long-term help in the form of psychological therapy. In fact, although some will need long-term therapy many do very well with shorter-term interventions and actually prefer short-term work in several 'doses' as it is more manageable for them (Jordan, 2008). In this situation it is important to be very clear in contracting so that the expectations of either party are realistic, with a clear focus of what can and what cannot be achieved.

Clarkson (1995) illustrates clearly the way a therapeutic relationship can be many things at different times and with different people. She identifies five types of relationships that can be in operation: working alliance, transferential/counter-transferential, reparative/developmentally needed, person-to-person or the 'real relationship', and transpersonal. Her model offers an opportunity to see attachments at the heart of the working relationship in all the forms attachment can present. Using an adapted version of Malan's 'triangle of time' (1979), we can see how the therapeutic relationship moves around the triangle representing Clarkson's five different relationship modes for therapeutic practice (see Figure 12.2).

Focus on any one of the three corners of the triangle can open up information from the others if we are open to working flexibly. A survivor of RT needs the therapist to be flexible enough to utilize any one of these modes of relationship and aspects of the triangle at different periods in her or his therapy (Dale, 1999; Jordan, 2002, 2008). ABC is actually more a way of emphasizing common ground rather than differences between perspectives. It actually holds each approach as having something valuable to offer in a therapeutic encounter.

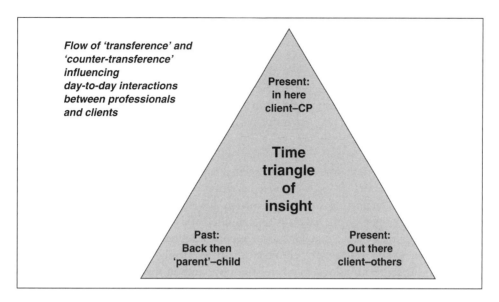

FIGURE 12.2   TIME TRIANGLE OF INSIGHT (ADAPTED FROM MALAN, 1979)

CONCLUSIONS

Herman (1997) explains how there is a fundamental need for safety before trauma work is undertaken. The principles of attachment theory can relate to the need for safety raised by Hermann in the form of the secure base. This also applies to those working with trauma to reduce vicarious trauma as well as with clients. In working with male and female survivors of abuse, having an attachment orientation can be an important springboard for the therapeutic work with survivors as we try to seek together to understand how the abuse had come to take place and in which ways its effects had impacted. As we have seen in this chapter, abuse most often happens in the context of relationships, and indeed it is there that the worst damage is done, so having a deep understanding of how early attachments or relationships are formed and disrupted can be invaluable to the work.

The need for a secure base continues to be important throughout life and is part of us, as therapists, actively healing ourselves. It seems vital that we learn the balance of 'inter-dependence', able to hold on to an internal sense of security as well as being able to be supported by someone else on the outside. Supervision and support are rated highly among the needs of workers in order to be able to feel safe enough to address the issues around violence and abuse.

It is from a secure base and a solid-enough sense of self that successful work can be done. The therapeutic relationship can be a tool of healing for people who have suffered primal hurts in their attachment system. RT can be treated and people can learn and heal from hurts that we can only wonder at how they even survived. Human beings are resilient and creative and have a drive towards health and life. In therapy, the client needs to have a good-enough attachment with a significant other even if temporary, until she or he can summon the courage to find others to reconnect with. RT is about disconnection and about feeling isolated and alone, terrified and ashamed. Therapy with this group of people is draining and inspiring, but aims to strengthen at the core of what it is to be human!

Creativity is at its best under circumstances of safety. If this is important for clients, then it is also important for us as counselling psychologists. There are then parallel worlds of the personal and professional narratives of discovering and developing a secure base and facilitating others' process in developing theirs. The journeys are distinctly separate but on the edge of one another, and intrinsically linked as the one continues to influence the other. Work with people, whether it be as therapist, supervisor, tutor, trainer, mentor, researcher, colleague or partner/family members has one thing in common, namely relationships. Life is relationships and on the edge!

REFERENCES

Allen, J.G. (2001) *Traumatic Relationships and Serious Mental Disorders*. Chichester: Wiley.

American Psychiatric Association (1985) *Diagnostic and Statistical Manual of Mental Disorders*, 4th edn. Washington, DC: American Psychiatric Association. pp. 435.

Beutler, L.E. and Sandowicz, M. (1994) 'The counselling relationship: What is it?', *The Counselling Psychologist*, 22 (1): 98–103.

Bowlby, J. (1988) *A Secure Base: Clinical Applications of Attachment Theory*. London: Routledge.

Briere, J. and Runtz, M. (1987) 'Post sexual abuse trauma: Data and implications for clinical practice', *Journal of Interpersonal Violence*, 2: 367–379.

Clarkson, P. (1995) *The Therapeutic Relationship in Psychoanalyis, Counselling Psychology and Psychotherapy*. London: Whurr.

Dale, P. (1999) *Adults Abused as Children: Experiences of Counselling and Psychotherapy*. London: Sage, commissioned by NSPCC.

Department of Health (2002) *Women's Mental Health; Into the Mainstream*. London: DoH.

Department of Health (2006a) *Tackling the Health and Mental Health Effects of Domestic and Sexual Violence and Abuse*. London: DoH.

Department of Health (2006b) *New NHS Guidance to Support Victims of Abuse*. London: DoH.

Department of Health (2008) *Healthier, Fairer and Safer Communities – Connecting People to Prevent Violence: Towards a Framework for Violence and Abuse Prevention*. London: DoH.

de Zueleta, F. (2004) 'Violence: Integrating psychology and biology.' Seminar at the Metanoia Institute, London.

deMause, L. (1991) 'The universality of incest', *Journal of Psychohistory*, 19, Fall: 2.

deMause, L. (1993) 'The history of child abuse'. Paper presented at the British Psychoanalytic Society, London.

deMause, L. (2002) *The Emotional Life of Nations*. London: Karnac.

Finkelhor, D. (1986) *A Sourcebook on Child Sexual Abuse*. London: Sage.

Fonagy, P., Steele, M., Steele, H., Moran, G. and Higgins, A. (1991) 'The capacity for understanding mental states: The reflective self in parent and child and its significance for security of attachment', *Infant Mental Health Journal*, 12: 201–18.

Freud, S. (1896) 'The aetiology of hysteria', *Wein Klin. Rdsch.*, Nos. 22–26. (ges. Werke, 1.)

Freyd, J.J. (1996) *Betrayal Trauma*. Cambridge, MA: Harvard University Press.

Furman, B. (1997) *It's Never Too Late To Have A Happy Childhood: From Adversity To Resilience*. London: BT Press.

Golding, J.M. (1999) 'Intimate partner violence as a risk factor for mental disorders: A meta analysis', *Journal of Family Violence*, 14 (2): 99–132.

Graham, D.L., Ihms, K., Rawlings, E., Foliano, J., Latimer, D. and Thompson, A. (1995) 'A scale for identifying "Stockholm Syndrome" reactions in young dating women: Factor structure, reliability and validity', *Violence and Victims*, 10 (1): 3–22.

Harvey, M.R., Mischler, E.G., Koenen, K. and Harney, A. (2000) 'In the aftermath of sexual abuse: Making and remaking meaning in narratives of trauma and recovery', *Narrative Inquiry*, 10 (2): 291–311.

Herman, J. (1997) *Trauma and Recovery: The Aftermath of Violence – from Domestic Abuse to Political Terror*. New York: Basic Books.

Hollins, S. and Sinason, V. (2000) 'Psychotherapy, learning disabilities and trauma: New perspectives', *British Journal of Psychiatry*, 176: 32–36.

Holmes, J. (2001) *The Search for the Secure Base: Attachment Theory and Psychotherapy*. Hove: Brunner-Routledge.

Hubble, M.A., Duncan, B.L. and Miller, S.D. (eds) (1999) *The Heart and Soul of Change: What Works in Therapy*. Washington, DC: American Psychological Association.

Jordan, L.F. (2002) 'A narrative analysis of the influence of child sexual abuse and subsequent therapy on the self-concept of five adult survivors'. In partial fulfilment of MSc in Counselling Psychology, Roehampton: University of Surrey.

Jordan, L.F. (2007a) 'Trauma, abuse and VVAPP', *Counselling Psychology Review*, 22 (2).

Jordan, L.F. (2007b) 'Attachment-based counseling … could this be an ABC of psychological therapies?', *Counselling Psychology Review*, 22 (1).

Jordan, L.F. (2008) 'Into the centre of the fire: working with adult survivors of abuse'. Unpublished doctoral project and final thesis for doctorate in Psychotherapy by Professional Studies at Metanoia Institute and Middlesex University.

Kennedy, M. (1996) 'Sexual abuse and disabled children', in J. Morriz (ed.), *Encounters with Strangers: Feminism and Disability*. London: The Women's Press.

Kershaw, C., Chivite-Matthews, N., Thomas, C. and Aust, R. (2001) *British Crime Survey 2001*. Home Office, England and Wales.

Llewellyn, S.J. (2008) *Brave Tears: A Personal Journey Through Therapy*. Bloomington, IN: Trafford Publishing.

Malan, D. (1979) *Individual Psychotherapy and the Science of Psychodynamics*. London: Butterworth.

Maslow, A. (1970) *Motivation and Personality*, 2nd edn. New York: Harper and Row.

McCann, L. and Pearlman, L. (1989) *Psychological Trauma and the Adult Survivor: Theory, Therapy and Transformation*. New York: Brunner/Mazel.

Murphy, K. and Gilbert, G. (2000) 'A systematic integrative relational model for counselling and psychotherapy', in S. Palmer and R. Woolfe (eds), *Integrative and Eclectic Counselling and Psychotherapy*. London: Sage.

Nurse, J., Garcia-Moreno, C., Phinney, A., Butchart, A. and Clarke, N. (2005) *A Global Perspective on Adolescent Sexual Relationship Violence: A New Understanding for Health Outcomes and*

Opportunities for Prevention Departments of Gender and Women's Health/ Violence and Injury Prevention. Geneva: World Health Organisation.

Ochberg, F. (1982) 'A case study: Gerad Vaders', in F. Ochberg and D.A. Soskis (eds), *Victims of Terrorism*. Boulder, CO: Westview. pp. 9–36.

Orlinsky, D., Grauwe, K. and Parks, B.K. (1994) Chapter 8 in A. Bergin and S. Garfield (eds), *Handbook of Psychotherapy and Behaviour Change*. New York: Wiley.

Paul, S. and Pelham, G. (2000) 'A relational approach to therapy', in S. Palmer and R. Woolfe (eds), *Integrative and Eclectic Counselling and Psychotherapy*. London: Sage.

Pearlman, L.A. and Courtois, C.A. (2005) 'Clinical applications of the attachment framework: Relational treatment of complex trauma', *Journal of Traumatic Stress*, 18 (5): 449–459.

Putnam, F.W. (1985) 'Dissociation as a response to extreme trauma', in R.P. Klupt (ed.), *Childhood Antecedents of Multiple Personality*. Washington, DC: American Psychiatric Press.

Putnam, F.W. (1989) Diagnosis and Treatment of Multiple Personality Disorder. New York: Guilford Press.

Read, J. (1997) 'Child abuse and psychosis: A literature review and implication for professional practice', *Professional Psychology: Research and Practice*, 28: 448–456.

Righetti, P.L., Avanzo, M.D., Grigio, M. and Nicolini, U. (2005) 'Maternal/paternal antenatal attachment and fourth-dimensional ultrasound technique: A preliminary report', *British Journal of Psychology*, 96: 1–10.

Ross, B.M. (1991) *Remembering the Personal Past: Descriptions of Autobiographical Memory*. New York: Oxford University Press.

Ross, C.A. (1980) *Multiple Personality Disorder: Diagnosis, Clinical Features and Treatment*. New York: Wiley.

Sanderson, C. (2006) *Counselling Adult Survivors of Child Sexual Abuse*, 3rd edn. London: Jessica Kingsley.

Schore, A.N. (1994) *Affect Regulation and the Origin of the Self: The Neurobiology of Emotional Development*. Mahwah, NJ: Erlbaum.

Schore, A.N. (1998a) 'Early shame experiences and infant brain development', in P. Gilbert and B. Andrews (eds), *Shame: Interpersonal Behaviour, Psychopathology, and Culture*. New York: Oxford University Press. pp. 57–77.

Schore, A.N. (1998b) 'The right brain as a neurobiological substrate of Freud's dynamic unconscious'. Unpublished keynote address at the conference, 'Freud at the Millennium', Georgetown University. Washington, DC.

Schore, A.N. (2000) 'Attachment and the regulation of the right brain', *Attachment & Human Development*, 2: 23–47.

Schore, A.N. (2001) 'The effects of a secure attachment relationship on right brain development, affect regulation, and infant mental health', *Infant Mental Health Journal*, 22: 7–66.

Schore, A.N. (2003) *Affect Regulation and the Repair of the Self*. New York: Norton.

Shengold, L. (1989) *Soul Murder: The Effects of Childhood Abuse and Deprivation*. New Haven, CT: Yale University Press.

Van der Kolk, B.A., McFarlane, A.C. and Weisaeth, L. (1996) *Traumatic Stress: The Effects of Overwhelming Experience on Mind, Body and Society*. New York: Guilford Press.

Werner, E.E. (1989) 'High-risk children in young adulthood: A longtitudinal study from birth to 32 years', *American Journal of Orthopsychiatry*, 59: 72–81.

Winnicott, D. (1965) *The Maturational Process and the Facilitating Environment*. London: Hogarth.

Wittling, W. and Schweiger, E. (1993) 'Neuroendocrine brain asymmetry and physical complaints', *Neuropsychologia*, 31: 591–608.

Wosket, V. (1999) *The Therapeutic Use Of Self: Counselling Practice, Research and Supervision*. London: Routledge.

13

SEXUAL IDENTITIES: MEANINGS FOR COUNSELLING PSYCHOLOGY PRACTICE

Colin Hicks and Martin Milton

Human sexuality has long caught the attention of philosophers, playwrights, poets and psychologists. It is one of the richest and most universal of human experiences while also being one of the most nebulous, complicated and personal. Our understanding of human sexuality is in a continual state of flux shaped by personal meaning, culture and history. One particular change has been in the construction of a person's sexual 'identity'. This concept is a fairly recent phenomenon, and it has evolved to denote a relatively stable aspect of the self with influence on inclusion within a social group.

As counselling psychologists, we cannot help but engage clients' sexuality. From assessment on, we ask clients about their current and historical relationship experiences. However, it is worth asking how much consideration we actually give to our understanding of a person's sexuality? While we read textbooks on various 'psychopathologies' and theoretical concepts, the same is seldom true when we engage a client who may or may not share a sexual identity with ourselves. Having said that, over recent years there has been a surge in 'affirmative psychotherapy' with lesbian, gay and bisexual clients. Despite this literature, the practitioner still needs to question what is meant by each of these terms and the idiosyncratic meaning that each label might have for a client.

This chapter invites you, the reader, to question your understanding of sexuality and consider how this penetrates and influences your practice with clients. This chapter is not designed to answer all possible questions. To do so would miss the point that sexuality is a rich, complex, relational phenomenon and requires elaboration, not premature knowing; understanding of process and meaning rather than simple assumption and classification. Therefore, this chapter encourages you to adopt a curious and passionate stance towards the domain of sexuality and hopes that the ideas posed here will inform other areas of clinical practice. First, the chapter examines the ways in which sexuality is understood.

CONTEMPORARY UNDERSTANDINGS OF SEXUALITY

Human sexuality holds an enigmatic quality for academics and clinicians. Whilst in Western society we consider everyone to have some 'form' of sexuality, academic discourse is rife with contrasting opinions as to the meaning of the very term 'sexuality' (Bohan, 1996). Lay people, however, are thought to hold a more consistent belief that a person's sexuality bears a direct relationship to the biological sex of their preferred choice of partner – male, female, or both – and view this 'as the most important single feature in the typology of desire' (Ross and Paul, 1992: 1283).

Western society widely accepts that people hold one of three sexual orientations: heterosexual (being attracted to people of the so-called 'opposite' sex); homosexual (also referred to as gay/lesbian where people are attracted to people of their own sex); or bisexual (being attracted to people of both sexes). Heterosexuality has become the default category to which people are assumed to fit unless they make a conscious effort to adopt a different classification, through a process commonly described as 'coming out' – or through a rejection of the classification system entirely.

It is important to reiterate that our current understanding of a person's sexual orientation, and more broadly their sexuality, is inextricably linked to our cultural and historical context (Bohan, 1996). Whilst same-sex sexuality has been documented since the ancient Greeks and Romans (Weeks, 1977, 2000) and is found worldwide in various forms and in different cultures (Rothblum, 2000; Weinrich and Williams, 1991), it is only within the last hundred years or so in Western society that an individual's sexual self has been defined in terms of the biological sex of his/her sexual partners. It is over that same period that the terms 'heterosexual' and 'homosexual' have come to be thought of as objective meaningful entities rather than just descriptors of behaviour. Prior to this, sexuality was defined in terms of class, age and gender roles (Rust, 1992). The implications of this is the shift from just describing the sexual behaviour to using the sexual behaviour to describe, or give some sort of insight into, an essential part of what it means to be a person (Epting et al., 1994). This opens itself up for multiple understandings of sexuality, some of which will be at odds with a society that values certainty and invests heavily in categorization. We seem to have moved to a point of being able to accept gay/lesbian and to a lesser extent bisexuality as viable alternatives to heterosexuality, provided one easily subscribes to a single identity and the stereotypical characteristics of each.

This understanding of an individual having a relatively stable sexual identity has lead, in both academic and mainstream discourse, to the assumption that there is some biologically predetermined aspect to a person's sexuality, with alternatives rarely discussed outside of the existential and social-constructionist literatures. This understanding sits comfortably in an age of empiricism, so-called scientific 'truth' and the concept of an objective reality. But of course, our understanding is inextricably linked to our culture and age and as such is only a meaningful construction. Whilst the idea of a biological marker for sexuality has proven a useful catalyst for political reform and the battle for equality for sexual minorities, it has given weight to the notion of sexually minority individuals as being different to heterosexual individuals based purely on their sexuality and with implications for their identity exceeding that of just their sexual preference. This raises a question that is as relevant for counselling psychologists as it is for anyone else. And that is, how well do we understand a person's sexuality when it encapsulates multiple dimensions including attraction, behaviour, fantasies, emotional, social and lifestyle preferences with people's experiences rarely fitting discretely under an identity label and the inferences it makes about behaviour? We will now go on to consider this question and some of the challenges that sexuality poses for our current understanding of people.

SEXUALITY AS MULTI-DIMENSIONAL

A frequently held assumption is that the different dimensions of attraction, behaviour and identity will be congruent with each other, or that such congruence is a desired end point, for example, heterosexual men will be attracted to and desire sex with women. Whilst for many this state of certainty exists, this is not a given. The sexual identity one might ascribe to oneself does not necessarily correspond to the lived experience of sexual orientation/preference or of one's sexual behaviour (Doll and Peterson, 1992; Dube, 2000; Higgins, 2006; Laumann et al., 1994), and nor should we expect it to. One survey of sexual behaviour found that only 45 per cent of men reporting same-sex sexual partners after the age of 18 self-identified as gay/homosexual/bisexual (Laumann et al., 1994). In addition, only 87 per cent of gay/homosexual/bisexually identified men reported same-sex sexual behaviour. This indicates a difference between behaviour and identity requiring us to think more critically, as this can have significant implications for individuals. For example, some may feel ill-equipped (or simply not feel the need) to integrate these different dimensions. Additionally, the society may not readily provide meaning-making systems for a person's own experiences. Unfortunately, a separate social process occurs for those who resist or cannot adopt this 'integrated' state and has led to constructions of categories of psychopathology.

The challenge for counselling psychologists is to recognize that assumptions cannot be made regarding the congruence of a person's sexuality, nor should clients be pushed towards identity foreclosure or the belief that identity, behaviour and attraction have to map onto the sex of a person and be consistent with each other. Instead, our role must be to work towards providing an environment in which an individual can explore different ways of constructing their own unique experiences and identity.

CASE VIGNETTE: MARIE*

Marie was a 24-year-old self-identified lesbian woman. Although Marie was in a long-term relationship, she still recognized her sexual attraction to both men and woman, having had relationships with partners of both sexes in the past. This was giving her partner some concern and precipitated Marie coming to therapy. For her partner, it was giving concern over Marie's identification as a lesbian as opposed to a bisexual woman, and supposedly denying her true identity (her partner self-identified as bisexual). This was causing friction in the relationship.

   Marie's therapy was spent exploring what it meant to her to adopt a lesbian identity. For Marie, her sexual identity was a transient label that purely described the sex of her current partner. She consciously rejected a bisexual label because, for her, it implied a desire to be in a relationship with a man and woman simultaneously. The latter part of therapy was spent exploring the language with which she could convey this to her partner to reaffirm her of Marie's commitment to the relationship.

SEXUALITY AS FLUIDITY

The assumption that a person's sexuality is a static fixed and desired phenomenon requires attention if therapists are going to work ethically with clients. People's experience and formal empirical research shows us that sexuality is fluid, changeable over time, and situation dependent (Diamond, 2000; Kitzinger and Wilkinson, 1995). It is not uncommon for people to move from what we understand as heterosexuality to being gay/lesbian. Equally for some people, they adopt a heterosexual identity and engage in a relationship with someone of the opposite-sex after years of being 'gay' and having a same-sex partner. Furthermore, others may construct their sexuality, not by the sex of the partner they are attracted to, but in terms of other more salient characteristics such

---

* All identifying information has been changed to protect client confidentiality.

as personality (Ross, 1984). These fluid realities are important for counselling psychologists to understand.

WHAT DOES KNOWING SOMEONE'S SEXUAL IDENTITY ACTUALLY TELL US?

The answer arguably is nothing. Knowing an individual's sexual identity does not automatically convey any information regarding a person's sexual behaviours or attractions, rather it might simply be a sign of a person's current identification with a particular social grouping. This can easily be seen with the use of the terms 'homosexual' and 'gay'. For many people these represent different sexual identities because an identity is both social and politicized, especially when it reflects membership in a minoritized group (Rust, 1992), and people who might subscribe to a gay identity may not subscribe to a homosexual one. The meaning of different identities also changes across time and culture (Rust, 1993). For example, the term 'homosexuality' has been most associated with medical discourse and the pathologising of same-sex sexual behaviour, whereas gay/lesbian sexual identity holds more political and activist origins. Furthermore, there is a greater societal recognition of a gay/lesbian sexual identity as being an alternative to a heterosexual identity than a bisexual one (Fox, 1996; Rust, 2001). However, even in this statement we are positing that 'gay' and 'lesbian' are terms that can be meaningfully interchanged on the basis of the sex of the individual we are discussing.

CASE VIGNETTE: WILL

Will was a 34-year-old self-identified heterosexual man. His long-term partner, James, also self-identified as heterosexual. Will acknowledged that whilst he was in a 'gay relationship', he felt this did not automatically mean he was a gay man. For Will, his sexual identity was constructed as representing where he felt he fitted in society. For him to accept a gay identity would mean identifying with a community that felt alien to him. Will was comfortable with this differentiation and recognized that other people may find it difficult to understand. Although therapy briefly explored his sexuality, its focus was on issues in other areas of his life. When issues of sexuality did arise, they were discussed with the therapist from a position of 'not knowing'.

As can be seen from the case vignettes, terms such as 'gay', 'lesbian', 'straight', 'bisexual', 'queer', 'questioning', 'homosexual', 'transsexual', 'transgender', 'nonconformist' … are all labels people can use to describe aspects of their sexuality in a personally meaningful way.

These labels are also a way of the individual conveying something about themselves to others around them. However, this process is not always that easy. How does a woman decide, when asked about her sexuality, whether she uses the term 'lesbian' or 'gay woman'. What will the other person make of the terminology used? What does she want to try to convey to the other person? And what happens if the available labels do not adequately describe her sexual sense of self? Increasingly, youths are using alternative labels to describe their identity or rejecting labels altogether in a move to embrace all sexual possibilities (Diamond, 2003). In some respects the terms 'gay' and 'lesbian' can be considered socio-political identities rooted in the mid- and late-twentieth century and, as such, only describe a particular identity then and do not accurately reflect the many same-sex behaving or desiring individuals today (Gonsiorek and Weinrich, 1991).

Different cultures have different concepts of sexuality and attribute very different meanings to sexual behaviour and identities than Western culture (Blackwood and Weiringer, 1999; Herdt, 1990; Weinrich and Williams, 1991). Whilst there is evidence that individuals engage in sexual behaviours with people of the same sex as well as people of the opposite sex, in many cultures this does not necessarily lead to an identity. In Latino culture, for example, homosexuality and heterosexuality are not determined by the sex of the person one engages in sexual relationships with, rather the role one plays in sex. In penetrative sex between two men, the inserter is seen as heterosexual maintaining the 'male active' sexual role, whereas the insertee is seen as homosexual taking an assumed 'female passive' sexual role (Carrier, 1985). These findings are not new. In fact McIntosh notes:

> The current conceptualisation of homosexuality as a condition is a false one, resulting from ethnocentric bias. Homosexuality should be seen rather as a social role. Anthropological evidence suggests that the role does not exist in all societies. Historical evidence shows that the role did not emerge in England until towards the end of the seventeenth century. (1968: 182)

In light of these studies, we need to recognize that there is a divide between the hallows of academic enquiry and people's experiences 'on the street'. For counselling psychologists, as both scientists and practitioners, we need to ensure that we make a link between the two.

PSYCHOLOGICAL THEORIES AND SEXUALITIES

Despite our critique of essentialist formulations of sexuality, as authors we have to engage with the turbulent relationship psychotherapy has with sexuality and the clinical implications of this. To do this we need to review literature and assumptions located firmly within this essentialist framework. To position this chapter at too far a distance from current social and clinical discourse would render the chapter impotent and as nothing more than a theoretical text with little clinical relevance. However, it is hoped that as we consider many of the upcoming issues we can attend to them from a slightly different place of understanding. Unsatisfactory as it is, the term 'non-heterosexual' has been used to denote a person who does not subscribe to a heterosexual identity. Its use is intended to be more inclusive than just using the terms lesbian, gay and bisexual (LGB), however, even with this terminology an artificial dichotomy has been created between the constructs of heterosexuality and non-heterosexuality.

Research indicates that LGB clients make substantial use of therapeutic services (Bieschke et al., 2000; Bradford et al., 1994; Cochran et al., 2003; Liddle, 1997), and that most psychotherapists report having seen at least one gay/lesbian client (Garnets et al., 1991). Despite this, the relationship between psychological theory and practice and non-heterosexual sexuality has been troubled – and remains so in some respects (Phillips et al., 2001; Taylor, 2002). Many theorists have constructed non-heterosexual sexuality in terms of pathology allowing practitioners (and some clients) to consider sexuality as something that needs addressing and that it is appropriate to try to change a client's sexuality to something more 'normal' and 'healthy'. And usually at this point heterosexuality is invoked. This distinction was largely a behavioural one (that is, who they had sex with) and made the assumption that knowing about a person's sexuality told one something meaningful about their psychology and apparent 'psychopathology'.

The pathologization of same-sex sexuality has been reinforced through religious, legal, cultural and medical beliefs, the latter reflected in its inclusion as a diagnosable disorder within the *Diagnostic and Statistic Manual of Mental Disorder* (DSM) (American Psychiatric Association, 1952). Homosexuality was formerly categorized as a psychiatric disorder but was downgraded to 'sexual orientation disturbance' in the DSM-II, 'ego-dystonic homosexuality' in the DSM-III and finally removed in the DSM-III-R. However, the diagnosis of 'sexual disorder not otherwise specified' for someone with 'persistent and marked distress about sexual orientation' (American Psychiatric Association, 1994: 538) remains, allowing practitioners and clients to prioritize sexuality as the cause of a client's struggle.

Whilst many practitioners have embraced a non-pathological understanding of non-heterosexual sexualities and a positive attitude to working with these clients, it has taken considerably longer for some schools of psychotherapy to reflect this change. The American Psychological Association has published guidelines on therapeutic work with LGB clients, emphasizing the acceptance of same-sex sexualities and denouncing suggestions of changing a client's sexual orientation as a therapeutic goal (American Psychological Association Division 44/Committee on Lesbian, Gay and Bisexual Concerns Joint Task Force on Guidelines for Psychotherapy with Lesbian, Gay and Bisexual Clients, 2000). The British Psychological Society is working on guidelines for ethical practice with sexual minority clients (Barker et al., forthcoming). Even prior to such explicit statements, counselling psychology training and ethical guidelines make explicit our commitment to work in ways which 'recognise social contexts and discrimination and to work always in ways that empower rather than control and also demonstrate the high standards of anti-discriminatory practice appropriate to the pluralistic nature of society today' (British Psychological Society, 2001: 2). Despite this, articles are still published in psychological journals that support the view of homosexuality as a psychopathology (Stone, 2000), or support the notion of conversion therapy (Nicolosi et al., 2000a, 2000b; Nicolosi and Nicolosi, 2002) despite evidence to suggest that it can actually be harmful to the individual (Shidlo and Schroeder, 2002).

This state of affairs causes confusion and conflict for some practitioners, where their school of thought is at odds with the anti-discriminatory stance. In fact:

> some therapists may not have amended their conceptualisations and practices in light of DSM and other changes – on the grounds that these changes were seen as resulting from political and social pressures which distort 'objective truth' – but instead adhere to the official view of same-sex sexualities that accorded with their personal outlook and/or the outlook espoused by their training or therapeutic professional body. (Milton et al., 2005: 185)

The tendency to pathologize non-heterosexual sexualities has been particularly evident in psychoanalytic formulations of homosexuality as 'inversions' (Freud, 1977) and indicators of developmental arrest and psychological immaturity; in Jungian interpretations of same-sex sexualities as a problematic over-identification with the contra-sexual (Hopcke, 1989) and the Kleinian perspective in particular supporting the notion that successful therapy is indicated by a heterosexual outcome (Ellis, 1997). Indeed, some branches of psychoanalysis still continue to view non-heterosexuality as pathological, both in the US (Socarides, 1995a, 1995b) and in the UK (Zachary, 1997).

Many therapeutic traditions have struggled – or failed – to recognize the social and cultural climate in which they developed and the social prejudice and assumptions this spawned (Ellis, 1997). While some argue that Freud's perspective facilitated an environment in which the pathologization of same-sex sexualities became acceptable (Spencer, 1995), others have suggested that Freud's attitude was both humanistic and liberal for its time and that it was Freud who made it legitimate to consider diverse forms of sexuality (Cohn, 1997).

As therapists we cannot escape the fact that we have trained in a heterocentric society in a historically conservative heterocentric profession (Pachankis and Goldfried, 2004). But recent literature within different schools of psychotherapy shows a reconsideration of same-sex sexualities and their relationship to psychotherapy. This has happened in a range of models including psychoanalytic/psychodynamic (Drescher, 1999; Izzard, 2000, O'Connor and Ryan, 1993), humanistic (Davies, 2000; Perlman, 2000), cognitive-behavioural (Martell et al., 2004), systemic (Laird and Green, 1996; Malley and McCann, 2002; Malley and Tasker, 1999) and existential-phenomenological (Milton, 2000, 2007; Spinelli, 1996, 1997). So logic, contemporary experience and empirical research indicate that we ought, and can, practise without the need to pathologize. What implications does this have for the work of the counselling psychologist?

NON-OPPRESSIVE THERAPY

In recent decades the topic of affirmative practice with non-heterosexual clients has become the focus of a relatively substantial body of literature (Campos and Goldfried, 2001; Davies, 1996; Eubanks-Carter et al., 2005; Pachankis and Goldfried, 2004; Perez et al., 2000). Affirmative therapy has been viewed in a variety of ways, although its core principle is that 'it affirms a lesbian, gay or bisexual identity as an equally positive human experience and expression to heterosexual identity' (Davies, 1996: 25) and as normal, natural and healthy (Halderman, 2000; Hitchings, 1994, 1997; Morrow, 2000). Another critical point of affirmative practice is that sexuality per se is not seen as the cause of psychological distress experienced by lesbian and gay clients (Garnets et al., 1991; Milton and Coyle, 1998), but rather it can be societal evaluation of same-sex sexualities which may cause or increase a client's distress and put non-heterosexual clients at increased risk of developing psychological disorders because of this social stigma (see Cochran et al., 2003).

Research has been conducted looking at the views and practices of clinical and counselling psychologists in working with lesbian and gay clients (Garnets et al., 1991; Milton, 1998; Milton and Coyle, 1998). In the UK study, reports of deficient practice centred around psychologists holding problematic and pathologizing views about lesbian and gay sexualities, which led them to over-emphasize the importance of sexuality in the presenting problems of lesbian and gay clients and to view changing clients' sexual orientations/preferences as an appropriate therapeutic aim. In contrast, in their accounts of exemplary, affirmative practice, participants pointed to instances where therapy was conducted within the context of accepting and affirming views of lesbian and gay sexualities, characterized by open-mindedness and delivered by therapists who were appropriately knowledgeable about lesbian and gay issues. Subsequent studies by Milton and Coyle (1999) and Milton et al. (2002) concluded that for any model of therapy, the therapist is central to the ethical potential of the therapy – they may engage creatively with the theory to produce affirmative practice or may use the theory to 'verify' anti-lesbian and anti-gay views.

Whilst considerable investment has been made into understanding the experiences of lesbian and gay clients, and some attention paid to bisexual clients, experiences of both transgender and heterosexual clients have largely been ignored in the psychotherapeutic literature. Transgender clients often have their experiences assimilated with those of LGB individuals, as suggested in the acronym 'LGBT'. This again serves only to reinforce the heterosexual/non-heterosexual divide and the notion of commonality of experiences between non-heterosexual individuals. However, the experiences of transgendered people require us to reconsider the concepts of sexuality and gender and what it means to be a man or woman (see Ettner, 1999; Milton, 2005).

Having commented on the contribution of psychological theory to working with clients' sexual identities, we will now move on to consider the qualities of a counselling psychologist that are important for practice in this area.

COUNSELLING PSYCHOLOGISTS' QUALITIES IMPORTANT FOR PRACTICE

Irrespective of theoretical orientation, there are a number of important qualities a counselling psychologist must have to work efficaciously with clients irrespective of their different sexualities. In working with non-heterosexual clients, authors and clients have suggested the qualities that are needed include an increased general awareness of LGB individuals and a position of openness to LGB issues without making presumptions concerning how a person constructs their sexuality and the possible relationship between an individual's sexual identity and their problems (Burckell and Goldfried, 2006). Pachankis and Goldfried (2004) also stress the importance for therapists to understand anti-homosexual/pro-heterosexual biases that operate in society in both obvious and subtle ways and that may not influence just the therapist's perception but also the client's perception of self. Whilst we recognize the value of these recommendations, our observation is that it is too easy to attend to this tokenistically and to fall back on societal stereotypes about how people 'should' act.

For counselling psychologists to work effectively with clients, we need to be able to step out of the dominant ideology of '*either* gay/lesbian *or* heterosexual' (and the associated sexual stereotypes) and consider the idea that this dichotomy is a remnant of a redundant taxonomy that is unnaturally constraining as it forces clients to subscribe or pin their colours to a mast which does not really represent their experience. Once we step out of the dichotomous thinking, counselling psychologists are more able to explore their own beliefs around sexuality, sexual identity, monogamous/non-monogamous relationships and the relationship between identity, behaviours and orientation (Dworkin, 2001; Falco, 1991; Hancock, 1995). This stance includes a non-defensive examination of their own sexuality and how the construction and understanding of their sexuality may influence their practice with clients who both have similar and different sexual identities (Morrow, 2000).

ISSUES IN THE CONSULTING ROOM

Whilst it is important to recognize that sexuality may present as an issue within the consulting room, one must remember that a client's sexuality is not automatically related to their presenting difficulties. What association there is has been suggested to be because of societal evaluation of non-heterosexual sexualities, more specifically that of stigmatization and prejudice as a cause of psychological distress rather than a client's sexuality per se, and placed LGB individuals at a higher risk of developing psychological disorders (Greene, 1994; Halderman, 2000; Pachankis and Goldfried, 2004). In workshops and other training contexts, when therapists are asked how often they question whether a client's distress is associated with their 'heterosexuality' the response is often 'rarely/never'. Yet therapists appear much more willing to consider that a client's non-heterosexuality *is* associated with their psychological distress.

The previous paragraph should not be read as encouragement to ignore sexuality in the exploration of a client's problems, even when to do so may reflect a laudable, if misguided, desire on the part of the therapist to avoid pathologizing the client's sexuality, particularly that which does not conform to heterocentric norms. It is indeed important to explore sexuality in the fullest way possible and is often very useful, especially when the counselling psychologist is able to develop an understanding of the context within which the client's presenting problems have developed and are experienced. It is simply that counselling psychologists need to be aware of the interaction between a person's sexuality and other characteristics of their personhood. For example, ageing individuals who identify as lesbian, gay or bisexual may have the effects of homophobia further compounded by that of ageism; religious clients may struggle to reconcile their sexuality with their religion (which may condemn homosexuality); and those from minority ethnic backgrounds will have to deal with both the dominant culture's racism and heterocentrism and their own ethnic group's heterocentrism (Greene, 1994; Pachankis and Goldfried, 2004).

This may sound reasonable enough, but it is important to note that a client may not automatically disclose anything about their sexuality to their therapist. Nor should it be assumed that the disclosure of a particular sexual identity will automatically reflect the totality of a client's sexual preferences, emotional attractions and sexual behaviours. Research suggests that some clients avoid disclosing their sexual orientation as a way to ensure unbiased care (MacEwan, 1994). If this is the case, it has been suggested that non-disclosure may result in less effective therapy (Cabaj, 1996). In addition, this may lead therapists to assume that every client who enters the consulting room is heterosexual unless the client presents evidence to the contrary, possibly leading them to apply heterocentric assumptions which may not be correct (Garnets et al., 1991). Of course, these assumptions may not 'fit' someone who identifies as heterosexual anyway!

THERAPIST'S SEXUALITY, DOES IT REALLY MATTER?

Along with the rise in affirmative practice came the question of whether a therapist who shared a similar sexual identity label as the client would be able to work more efficiently with clients who identified as non-heterosexuals. The literature presented a mixed picture, with some researchers suggesting that non-heterosexual clients have a preference for a non-heterosexual therapist (Isay, 1991; Kaufman et al., 1997; Liddle, 1997; McDermott et al., 1989), and that the sexual orientation and gender of the therapist was a significant predictor of participants rating therapy as beneficial (Jones et al., 2003). However, others have indicated that a matching in terms of a therapist and client's sexual orientation is not necessary for effective therapy (Jones and Gabriel, 1999) and may have possible disadvantages (Jones et al., 2003). Another perspective proposed is that particular benefits can be accrued from non-heterosexual clients working with a heterosexual therapist who can, to some extent, represent the heterosexual world within the therapeutic context (Milton and Coyle, 1999; Milton et al., 2002). Whatever the arrangement, it is important that all therapists have considered how their sexual identity will affect their practice with both heterosexual and non-heterosexual clients (Pachankis and Goldfried, 2004).

In summary, whilst some clients may gain a degree of comfort and confidence in the knowledge that their therapist shares the same sexual identity, and therefore may have a chance of a shared aspect of self, this may not necessarily be the case; two gay men are as likely to be different as two heterosexual men or a heterosexual man and a gay man. What is important is for a therapist to work to understand how their clients experience and construct their sexuality, what labels they feel comfortable using (without assumption as to the content of these), and not to project their own issues around sexuality onto their client.

AND AS FOR RELATIONSHIP STRUCTURES ...!

As sexuality is such a relational aspect of self, it is important to consider the implications that this has on relationship structures. Monogamous dyadic relationships have long been touted as being a prerequisite for the psychological health of the relationship and the individuals involved (especially in a society so firmly located in a capitalist framework which requires all adults to be economically productive). Yet, as counselling psychologists, we know that other cultures show a wide range of relationship structures including polygamy (Al-Krenewi et al., 2006; Slonim and Al-Krenewi, 2006), polyandry (Cassidy and Lee, 1989; Peters, 1982) and polyamory (Barker, 2005; Klesse, 2006; Ritchie and Barker, 2006). It is important to recognize that 'monogamy' is not a human universal at all. In fact, sociological and anthropological science suggests individuals can, and do, engage in different 'non-monogamous' and 'non-dyadic' relationships (Rust, 1996, 2001) without it being pathological for the individuals involved (Green et al., 1996). For therapists, this poses the challenge of understanding these relationships without invoking terms such as 'triangulation', 'difficulties with intimacy' and a heterocentric conservative framework to explain its occurrence. Instead, as counselling psychologists, we need to be more creative in our understanding of relationships and relish the development of new languages to discuss the full diversity of people's experiences;

languages that will come to reflect the joys as well as the anxieties, the advantages as well as the problems.

A NOTE ABOUT RESEARCH

Counselling psychologists are both generators and critical consumers of research. The problem with current research into sexuality is that we are conceptualizing sexuality through an essentialist scientific lens intrinsically linked to concepts of objectivity and truth, which are a product of our time and culture. Eliason (1996) criticizes the current understanding of sexual identity because of the ahistorical apolitical stance that researchers claim to take, leading to the assumption that sexuality can be studied as a discrete entity without regard to other sociological categories such as race and socio-economic status.

It is important to consider the research into sexuality and sexual identity critically, as much of it has operationalized different 'measures' of participants' sexuality; for example, some based on self-report sexual identity and others on sexual behaviour, yet tend to make the inference that they are measuring the same phenomenon. In addition, the definitions of sexuality are fundamentally guided by the singular characteristic of the sex of a person.

This has been a historical problem, often because of difficulties in recruiting sexually-minoritized clients, causing many studies to collapse lesbian, gay men and bisexual participants into a generic LGB group, which has meant each participant's experiences has been dissolved. Of course, this was more notable in quantitative rather than qualitative research. It is problematic as it offers the impression of validity to the categorizations of sexuality we critiqued earlier in this chapter. This is starting to change as researchers are more critical in the postmodern era, and cultural perspectives are allowing people to recognize that our clients' lives are proving to be so much richer and more complex than large-scale studies can encapsulate.

CONCLUSION

Markowe argues that:

> with continuing inequalities in support [...] for same-sex and opposite-sex relationships within European societies, lesbian and gay identities become necessary constructs, important socially, politically and on an individual level. ... While society continues to maintain gender divisions, it is creating a context in which the construction of lesbian and gay identities becomes a necessity – in part to maintain heterosexual identity (2002: 226).

As counselling psychologists, we have a duty not just to affirm, redress or work non-oppressively with all clients who experience stigmatization and prejudice, but also to consider the context and the framework of understanding in which these occur.

The ambivalent, often conflicting, attitudes towards non-heterosexuality experienced by therapists and in the therapeutic literature reflects current societal attitudes where debates are still going on about the legitimacy of non-heterosexual sexualities; see, for instance, debates about 'gay marriage' and 'gay parenting'. In addition, whilst the concepts of 'gay' and 'lesbian' have sat as the alternative to 'heterosexuality', this dichotomous classification has meant that people who would be referred to as 'bisexual' or who embrace a different understanding of their sexuality have been somewhat ignored.

The material presented in this chapter suggests that it may not always be straightforward for counselling psychologists to work with concepts of sexual identity in 'ways that empower and that accord with high standards of anti-discriminatory practice' (British Psychological Society, 2001). To do so can be a demanding undertaking, complicated by our immersion within social and professional belief systems that position non-heterosexual sexualities as negative and even pathological. If practitioners are to meet the standards of practice that our profession requires of us, it is necessary that a reflective stance is taken to the assumptions and beliefs that we hold and the way in which these impact on our understandings of sexuality and sexual identity. This is important for us all, not just as individuals but also as supervisors, researchers, trainers and providers of psychological services, particularly with many therapists reporting not feeling competent to work with LGB individuals (Anhalt et al., 2003; Doherty and Simmons, 1996).

No matter how complex or daunting the task, counselling psychologists should not flinch at the task. There is much research and practice-related work that has already been undertaken, both in Britain and internationally, which can inform and elaborate our reflections on sexuality and sexual identity – some of this has been cited in this chapter. There are also now clear and carefully formulated guidelines – prepared by the American Psychological Association – available to practitioners that describe the outlooks and competences required to work with lesbian and gay (and bisexual) clients (American Psychological Association Division 44/Committee on Lesbian, Gay, and Bisexual Concerns Joint Task Force on Guidelines for Psychotherapy with Lesbian, Gay, and Bisexual Clients, 2000). These will soon be complimented by those of the British Psychological Society (Barker et al., forthcoming). These guidelines examine the implicit biases that may be held by practising therapists and the need for practitioners to become more aware of them and to be prepared to address them if they are to work effectively with the sexuality of their clients. If counselling psychologists are to continue to lead the way in responding to the challenge of rethinking old assumptions and integrating new research and knowledge into their practice, counselling psychology may not only challenge outmoded, biased and damaging practices with clients of all sexualities but could also pioneer the development of more thoughtful, ethical and affirmative ways of working with a range of client groups.

REFERENCES

Al-Krenewi, A., Graham, J.R. and Ben-Shimol, J.S. (2006) 'Attitudes towards and reasons for polygamy differentiated by gender and age among bedouin-Arabs of the Negeu', *International Journal of Mental Health*, 35: 46–61.

American Psychiatric Association (1952) *Diagnostic and Statistical Manual of Mental Disorders.* Washington, DC: American Psychiatric Association.

American Psychiatric Association (1994) *Diagnostic and Statistical Manual of Mental Disorders*, 4th edn. Washington, DC: American Psychiatric Association.

American Psychological Association Division 44/Committee on Lesbian, Gay, and Bisexual Concerns Joint Task Force on Guidelines for Psychotherapy with Lesbian, Gay and Bisexual Clients (2000) 'Guidelines for psychotherapy with lesbian, gay, and bisexual clients', *American Psychologist*, 55: 1440–51.

Anhalt, K., Morris, T.L., Scotti, J.R. and Cohen, S.H. (2003) 'Student perspectives on training in gay, lesbian and bisexual issues: A survey of behavioural clinical psychology programs', *Cognitive and Behavioural Practice*, 10: 255–63.

Barker, M. (2005) 'This is my partner, and this is my … partner's partner: Constructing a polyamorous identity in a monogamous world', *Journal of Constructivist Psychology*, 18: 75–88.

Barker, M., Butler, C., Gibson, S., Hegarthy, P., Langridge, D., Leniham, P., Nair, R., Richards, C. and Shaw, E. (forthcoming) *Guidelines for Psychologists Working Therapeutically with Sexual Minority Clients.* Leicester: British Psychological Society.

Bieschke, K.J., McClanahan, M., Tozer, E., Grzegorek, J.L. and Park, J. (2000) 'Programmatic research on the treatment of lesbian, gay, and bisexual clients: The past, the present and the course of the future', in R.M. Perez, K.A. DeBord and K.J. Bieschke (eds), *Handbook of Counseling and Psychotherapy with Lesbian, Gay, and Bisexual Clients.* Washington, DC: American Psychological Association.

Blackwood, E. and Weiringer, S.E. (1999) *Female Desires: Same-Sex Relationships and Transgender Practices Across Cultures.* New York: Columbia University Press.

Bohan, J.S. (1996) *Psychology and Sexual Orientation: Coming to Terms.* New York: Routledge.

Bradford, J., Ryan, C. and Rothblum, E.D. (1994) 'National lesbian health care survey: Implications for mental health care', *Journal of Consulting and Clinical Psychology*, 62: 228–42.

British Psychological Society Division of Counselling Psychology (2001) *Professional Practice Guidelines.* Leicester: British Psychological Society.

Burckell, L.A. and Goldfried, M.R. (2006) 'Therapist qualities preferred by sexual-minority individuals', *Psychotherapy: Theory, Research, Practice, Training,* 43: 32–49.

Cabaj, R.P. (1996) 'Sexual orientation of the therapist', in R.P. Cabaj and T.S. Stein (eds), *Textbook of Homosexuality and Mental Health.* New York: American Psychiatric Press.

Campos, P.E and Goldfried, M.R. (2001) 'Working with gay, lesbian, and bisexual clients', *Journal of Clinical Psychology/In Session Psychotherapy in Practice*, 57: 609–13.

Carrier, J.M. (1985) 'Mexican male bisexuality', *Journal of Homosexuality*, 11: 75–85.

Cassidy, M.L. and Lee, G.R. (1989) 'The study of polyandry: A critique and synthesis', *Journal of Comparative Family Studies*, 20: 1–11.

Cochran, S.D., Sullivan, J.G. and Mays, V.M. (2003) 'Prevalence of mental disorders, psychological distress, and mental health services use among lesbian, gay, and bisexual adults in the United States', *Journal of Consulting and Clinical Psychology*, 71: 53–61.

Cohn, H. (1997) *Existential Thought and Therapeutic Practice: An Introduction to Existential Psychotherapy.* London: Sage.

Davies, D. (1996) 'Towards a model of gay affirmative therapy', in D. Davies and C. Neal (eds), *Pink Therapy: A Guide for Counsellors and Therapists Working with Lesbian, Gay and Bisexual Clients.* Buckingham: Open University Press.

Davies, D. (2000) 'Person-centred therapy', in D. Davies and C. Neal (eds), *Therapeutic Perspectives on Working with Lesbian, Gay and Bisexual Clients.* Buckingham: Open University Press.

Diamond, L. (2000) 'Sexual identity, attractions, and behaviour among young sexual minority women over a 2-year period', *Developmental Psychology*, 36: 241–50.

Diamond, L. (2003) 'Was it a phase? Young women's relinquishment of lesbian/gay identities over a 5-year period', *Journal of Personality and Social Psychology*, 84: 352–64.

Doherty, W.J. and Simmons, D.S. (1996) 'Clinical practice patterns of marriage and family therapists: A national survey of therapists and their clients', *Journal of Marital and Family Therapists*, 22: 9–25.

Doll, L.S. and Peterson, L.R. (1992) 'Homosexually and nonhomosexually identifying men who have sex with men: A behavioural comparison', *Journal of Sex Research*, 29: 1–24.

Drescher, J. (1999) *Psychoanalytic Therapy and the Gay Man.* Hillsdale, NJ: The Analytic Press.

Dube, E.M. (2000) 'The role of sexual behaviour in the identification process of gay and bisexual males', *Journal of Sex Research*, 37: 123–32.

Dworkin, S.H. (2001) 'Treating the bisexual client', *Psychotherapy in Practice: In Session*, 57: 671–80.

Eliason, M.J. (1996) 'Identity formation for lesbian, bisexual and gay persons: Beyond a minoritising view', *Journal of Homosexuality*, 30: 31–58.

Ellis, M.L. (1997) 'Who speaks? Who listens? Different voices and different sexualities', *British Journal of Psychotherapy,* 13: 369–83.

Epting, F.R., Raskin, J.D. and Burke, T.B. (1994) 'What is a homosexual? A critique of the heterosexual-homosexual dimension', *Humanistic Psychology*, 22: 353–70.

Ettner, R. (1999) *Gender Loving Care: A Guide to Counseling Gender-Variant Clients.* New York: Norton.

Eubank-Carter, C., Burckell, L.A. and Goldfried, M.R. (2005) 'Enhancing therapeutic effectiveness with gay, lesbian, and bisexual clients', *Clinical Psychology: Science and Practice*, 12: 1–18.

Falco, K.L. (1991) *Psychotherapy with Lesbian Clients: Theory into Practice.* New York: Brunner/Mazel.

Fox, R.C. (1996) 'Bisexuality in perspective: A review of theory and research', in B.A. Firestein (ed.), *Bisexuality: The Psychology and Politics of an Invisible Minority.* Newbury Park, CA: Sage.

Freud, S. (1977) *On Sexuality.* London: Penguin.

Garnets, L., Hancock, K.A., Cochran, S.D., Goodchilds, J. and Peplau, L.A. (1991) 'Issues in psychotherapy with lesbians and gay men: A survey of psychologists', *American Psychologist*, 46: 964–72.

Gonsiorek, J.C. and Weinrich, J.D. (1991) 'The definition and scope of sexual orientation', in J.C. Gonsiorek and J.D. Weinrich (eds), *Homosexuality: Research Implications for Public Policy.* Thousand Oaks, CA: Sage.

Green, R.J., Bettinger, M. and Zacks, E. (1996) 'Are lesbian couples fused and gay male couples disengaged?', in J. Laird and R.J. Green (eds), *Lesbian and Gays in Couples and Families.* San Fransisco, CA: Jossey-Bass.

Greene, B. (1994) 'Ethnic minority lesbians and gay men: Mental health and treatment issues', *Journal of Consulting and Clinical Psychology*, 62: 243–51.

Halderman, D.C. (2000) 'Therapeutic responses to sexual orientation: Psychology's evolution', in B. Greene and G.M. Herek (eds), *Lesbian and Gay Psychology: Theory, Research and Clinical Applications.* Thousand Oaks, CA: Sage.

Hancock, K.A. (1995) 'Psychotherapy with lesbians and gay men', in A.R. D' Augelli and C.J. Patterson (eds), *Lesbian, Gay and Bisexual Identities over the Lifespan: Psychological Perspectives.* New York: Oxford University Press.

Herdt, G. (1990) 'Developmental discontinuities and sexual orientation across cultures', in D.P. McWhirter, S.A. Sanders and J.M. Reinisch (eds), *Homosexuality/Heterosexuality: Concepts of Sexual Orientation.* New York: Oxford University Press.

Higgins, D.J. (2006) 'Same-sex attraction in heterosexually partnered men: Reasons, rationales and reflections', *Sexual and Relationship Therapy*, 21: 217–28.

Hitchings, P. (1994) 'Psychotherapy and sexual orientation', in P. Clarkson and M. Pokorny (eds), *Handbook of Psychotherapy.* London: Routledge.

Hitchings, P. (1997) 'Counselling and sexual orientation', in S. Palmer and G. McMahon (eds), *Handbook of Counselling.* London: Routledge.

Hopcke, R. (1989) *Jung, Jungians and Homosexuality.* Boston, MA: Shambhala.

Isay, R.A (1991) 'The homosexual analyst: Clinical considerations', *Psychoanalytic Study of the Child*, 46: 199–216.

Izzard, S. (2000) 'Psychoanalytic psychotherapy', in D. Davies and C. Neal (eds), *Therapeutic Perspectives on Working with Lesbian, Gay and Bisexual Clients.* Buckingham: Open University Press.

Jones, M.A., Botsko, M. and Gorman, B.S. (2003) 'Predictors of psychotherapeutic benefit of lesbian, gay and bisexual clients: The effects of sexual orientation matching and other factors', *Psychotherapy: Theory, Research, Practice, Training*, 40: 289–301.

Jones, M.A. and Gabriel, M.A. (1999) 'Utilization of psychotherapy by lesbians, gay men, and bisexuals: Findings from a nationwide survey', *American Journal of Orthopsychiatry*, 69: 209–219.

Kaufman, J.S., Carlozzi, A.F., Boswell, D.L., Barnes, L.L.B., Wheeler-Scruggs, K. and Levy, P.A. (1997) 'Factors influencing therapist selection among gay, lesbians, and bisexuals', *Counseling Psychology Quarterly*, 10: 287–97.

Kitzinger, C. and Wilkinson, S. (1995) 'Transitions from heterosexuality to lesbianism: The discursive construction of lesbian identities', *Developmental Psychology*, 31: 95–104.

Klesse, C. (2006) 'Polyamory and its "others": Contesting the terms of non-monogamy', *Sexuality*, 9: 565–83.

Laird, J. and Green, R. (eds) (1996) *Lesbians and Gays in Couples and Families: A Handbook for Therapists.* San Fransisco, CA: Jossey-Bass.

Laumann, E.O., Gagnon, J.H., Michael, R.T. and Michaels, S. (1994) *The Social Organization of Sexuality: Sexual Practice in the United States.* Chicago, IL: University of Chicago Press.

Liddle, B.J. (1997) 'Gay and lesbian clients' selection of therapists and utilization of therapy', *Psychotherapy*, 34: 11–18.

MacEwan, I. (1994) 'Differences in assessment and treatment approaches for homosexual clients', *Drug and Alcohol Review*, 13: 57–62.

Malley, M. and McCann, D. (2002) 'Family therapy with lesbian and gay clients', in A. Coyle and C. Kitzinger (eds), *Lesbian and Gay Psychology: New Perspectives.* Oxford: BPS Blackwell.

Malley, M. and Tasker, F. (1999) 'Lesbians, gay men and family therapy: A contradiction in terms?', *Journal of Family Therapy*, 21: 3–29.

Markowe, L.A. (2002) 'Lesbian and gay identity: European perspectives', *Journal of Community and Applied Social Psychology*, 12: 223–29.

Martell, C.R., Safran, S.A. and Price, S.E. (2004) *Cognitive-Behavioral Therapies with Lesbian, Gay and Bisexual Clients.* New York: Guilford.

McDermott, D., Tyndall, L. and Lichtenberg, J.W. (1989) 'Factors related to counsellor preference among gays and lesbians', *Journal of Counseling and Development*, 68: 31–35.

McIntosh, M. (1968) 'The homosexual role', *Social Problems*, 16: 182–92.

Milton, M. (1998) *Issues in Psychotherapy with Lesbians and Gay Men: A Survey of British Psychologists*. Leicester: British Psychological Society.

Milton, M. (2000) 'Is existential psychotherapy lesbian and gay affirmative psychotherapy?' *Journal of the Society for Existential Analysis*, 11: 86–102.

Milton, M. (2005) 'Political and ideological issues', in E. Van Deurzen and C. Penhallow (eds), *Existential Perspectives on Human Issues: A Handbook for Therapeutic Practice*. Basingstoke: Palgrave Macmillan.

Milton, M. (2007) 'Being sexual: Existential contributions to psychotherapy with gay male clients', *Journal of Gay and Lesbian Psychotherapy*, 11: 45–59.

Milton, M. and Coyle, A. (1998) 'Psychotherapy with lesbian and gay clients', *The Psychologist*, 11: 73–6.

Milton, M. and Coyle, A. (1999) 'Lesbian and gay affirmative psychotherapy: Issues in theory and practice', *Sexual and Marital Therapy*, 14: 41–57.

Milton, M., Coyle, A. and Legg, C. (2002) 'Lesbian and gay affirmative psychotherapy: Defining the domain', in A. Coyle and C. Kitzinger (eds), *Lesbian and Gay Psychology: New Perspectives*. Oxford: BPS Blackwell.

Milton, M., Coyle, A. and Legg, C. (2005) 'Countertransference issues in psychotherapy with lesbian and gay clients', *European Journal of Psychotherapy, Counselling and Health*, 7: 181–97.

Morrow, S.L. (2000) 'First do no harm: Therapist issues in psychotherapy with lesbian, gay, and bisexual clients', in R.M. Perez, K.A. DeBord and K.J. Bieschke (eds), *Handbook of Counseling and Psychotherapy with Lesbian, Gay, and Bisexual Clients*. Washington, DC: American Psychological Association.

Nicolosi, J., Byrd, A.D. and Potts, R.W. (2000a) 'Beliefs and practices of therapists who practice sexual reorientation psychotherapy', *Psychological Reports*, 86: 689–702.

Nicolosi, J., Byrd, A.D. and Potts R.W. (2000b) 'Retrospective self-reports of change in homosexual orientation: A consumer survey of conversion therapy clients', *Psychological Reports*, 86: 1071–88.

Nicolosi, J. and Nicolosi, L.A (2002) *A Parent's Guide to Preventing Homosexuality*. Downers Grove, IL: Intervarsity Press.

O'Connor, N. and Ryan, J. (1993) *Wild Desires and Mistaken Identities: Lesbianism and Psychoanalysis*. London: Virago.

Pachankis, J.E. and Goldfried, M.R. (2004) 'Clinical issues in working with lesbian, gay and bisexual clients', *Psychotherapy: Theory, Research, Practice, Training*, 3: 227–46.

Perez, R.M., DeBord, K.A. and Bieschke, K.J. (eds) (2000) *Handbook of Counseling and Psychotherapy with Lesbian, Gay, and Bisexual Clients*. Washington, DC: American Psychological Association.

Perlman, G. (2000) 'Transactional analysis', in D. Davies and C. Neal (eds), *Therapeutic Perspectives on Working with Lesbian, Gay and Bisexual Clients*. Buckingham: Open University Press.

Peters, J.F. (1982) 'Polyandry among the Yanomama Shirishana revisited', *Journal of Comparative Family Studies*, 13: 89–95.

Phillips, P., Bartlett, A. and King, M. (2001) 'Psychotherapists' approaches to gay and lesbian patients/clients: A qualitative study', *British Journal of Medical Psychology*, 74: 73–84.

Ritchie, A. and Barker, M. (2006) '"There aren't words for what we do or how we feel so we have to make them up": Constructing polyamorous language in a culture of compulsory monogamy', *Sexualities*, 9: 584–601.

Ross, M.W. (1984) 'Beyond the biological model: New directions in bisexual and homosexual research', *Journal of Homosexuality*, 10: 63–70.

Ross, M.W. and Paul, J.P. (1992) 'Beyond gender: The basis of sexual attraction in bisexual men and women', *Psychological Reports*, 71: 1283–90.

Rothblum, E.D. (2000) 'Sexual orientation and sex in women's lives: Conceptual and methodological issues', *Journal of Social Issues*, 56: 193–204.

Rust, P.C. (1992) 'The politics of sexual identity: Sexual attraction and behaviour amongst lesbian and sexual women', *Social Problems*, 39: 366–86.

Rust, P.C. (1993) 'Coming out in the age of social constructionism: Sexual identity formation among lesbian and bisexual women', *Gender and Society*, 7: 50–77.

Rust, P. (1996) 'Monogamy and polyamory relationship issues for bisexuals', in B.A. Firestein (ed.), *Bisexuality: The Psychology and Politics of an Invisible Minority.* Newbury Park, CA: Sage.

Rust, P. (2001) 'Two many and not enough: The meanings of bisexual identity', *Journal of Bisexuality*, 1: 31–68.

Shidlo, A. and Schroeder, M. (2002) 'Changing sexual orientation: A consumers' report', *Professional Psychology: Research and Practice*, 33: 249–59.

Slonim, N.V. and Al-Krenewi, A. (2006) 'Success and failure among polygamous families: The experiences of wives, husbands and children', *Family Process*, 45: 311–30.

Socarides, C.W. (1995a) *Homosexuality: A Freedom Too Far*. Phoenix, AZ: Adam Margrave.

Socarides, C.W. (1995b) 'On the Treatment of Homosexuality'. Invited talk in the School of Psychotherapy and Counselling, Regent's College, London, 28 April.

Spencer, C. (1995) *Homosexuality: A History.* London: Fourth Estate.

Spinelli, E. (1996) 'Some hurried notes expressing outline ideas that someone might someday utilise as signposts towards a sketch of an existential-phenomenological theory of sexuality', *Journal of the Society for Existential Analysis*, 8: 2–20.

Spinelli, E. (1997) 'Human sexuality and existential-phenomenological inquiry', *Counselling Psychology Review*, 12: 170–78.

Stone, M.H. (2000) 'Psychopathology: Biological and psychological correlates', *Journal of the American Academy of Psychoanalysis*, 28: 203–35.

Taylor, G. (2002) 'Psychopathology and the social and historical construction of gay male identities', in A. Coyle and C. Kitzinger (eds), *Lesbian and Gay Psychology: New Perspectives.* Oxford: BPS Blackwell.

Weeks, J. (1977) *Coming Out: Homosexual Politics in Britain from the Nineteenth Century to Present.* London: Quartet.

Weeks, J. (2000) *Making Sexual History.* Cambridge, UK: Polity Press.

Weinrich, J.D. and Williams, W.L. (1991) 'Strange customs, familiar lives: Homosexualities in other cultures', in J.C. Gonsiorek and J.D. Weinrich (eds), *Homosexuality: Research and Implications for Public Policy.* London: Sage.

Zachary, A. (1997) 'Psychotherapy of sexual deviation and perversion', *Current Opinion on Psychiatry*, 10: 251–55.

PART IV

DEVELOPMENTAL THEMES

Counselling psychology places an emphasis on the importance of developmental themes in thinking about practice and, in this way, directs attention away from pathologizing emotional difficulties towards perceiving them as located in normative human experiences. However, human development is a complex process that has been studied, often separately and without cross-reference, from differing disciplinary perspectives. These include developmental psychology, a significant field of mainstream psychology, as well as theory and research associated with psychotherapy, particularly the psychodynamic tradition, rather than psychology. These perspectives have particularly contributed to our understanding of infancy and childhood, although the notion of the 'life course' informs much current thinking. Similarly, sociology and cultural anthropology, focusing on socialization and cultural variation, have informed our understanding of development throughout the life course and have highlighted the significance of differing social worlds. It is, therefore, quite a task for counselling psychologists to draw upon, and integrate into practice, valuable insights from such contrasting bodies of theory and research.

The six chapters in this part of the book explore the creative tension between perspectives in relation to clients at different periods in their lives. The first chapter offers a model that provides an organizing principle for thinking about the life course overall and encourages the integration of learning from differing perspectives. Almost inevitably, there is a certain amount of overlap between chapters focusing on differing periods of life. Whilst at first sight two seem clearly distinct, namely those dealing with children and older persons, the remaining chapters examine adult life. This is a huge category in which the boundaries between various stages are arbitrary. When boys and girls of 13 are becoming parents, we might well ask where the boundary is between childhood and adulthood. Similarly, when 60-year-olds are climbing Mount Everest, we might ask what constitutes the boundary between adulthood and old age?

If these questions are difficult to answer, the task of differentiating between various stages of adulthood is even more complex, hence the degree of overlap between chapters. However, authors have addressed their tasks in different ways and with differing methodologies. The chapter on midlife focuses on the challenges commonly experienced at this time of life, whereas the chapter on young adults is more descriptive and based around the author's work as a therapist. The chapter on families encompasses all age ranges but has a particular focus on systemic approaches to working with families, also based upon the authors' practical experience.

14

THE LIFE COURSE: A FRAMEWORK FOR THE PRACTICE OF COUNSELLING PSYCHOLOGY

Léonie Sugarman

Counselling psychologists, irrespective of their specialism or theoretical orientation, need ways of encapsulating human experience that can be called on in the midst of practice. They need an applied understanding that provides action-oriented, flexible frameworks which are both sufficiently substantive to anchor the disparate elements that make up a client's experience, and also sufficiently malleable to accommodate the dynamic uniqueness of individually patterned lives. It is proposed here that adopting a life course perspective provides just such a pragmatic framework within which to locate practice.

Whoever your clients, all will be somewhere on the path from cradle to grave, and where they are in this journey will affect their needs. This is equally true of the counselling psychologist. In the therapeutic encounter, the lives of client and therapist touch each other at a particular point in the life course of each. Each will be working, both implicitly and explicitly, and with varying degrees of ease, on his or her developmental tasks (Sugarman and Woolfe, 1997). The framework of the life course can also, therefore, encase therapists' own life experiences and the implications for their therapeutic relationship and journey with particular clients.

THE LIFE COURSE PERSPECTIVE

The life course is defined here as *the rhythmic and fluctuating pattern of human life over time, marked out by expected and unexpected life events and by interactions between the self and the environment*. It includes all the stages, roles and key events a person experiences, along with his or her reactions to these experiences and the meanings attached to them. The metaphor of the river is instructive:

> The life course of each of us can be thought of as a river. On occasions turbulent, but at other times calm, it flows in a particular general direction, whilst deviating here and there from a straight and narrow path. It meets and departs from other rivers or streams along the way, having a momentum of its own whilst both influencing and being influenced by the environment through which it flows. (Sugarman and Woolfe, 1997: 22)

The notion of life-span developmental psychology came of age in 1980 when it first received the accolade of a paper devoted to it in the *Annual Review of Psychology*. Here life-span developmental psychology was defined as being 'concerned with the description, explanation, and modification (optimization) of developmental processes in the human life course from conception to death' (Baltes et al., 1980: 66). Whilst this definition still holds true today, its manifestation in research and practice has not remained static. Thus, 'descriptions' have tended to shift from the search for the universal to the understanding of the particular; 'explanations' have become increasingly contextualized and 'modifications' increasingly client-centred.

The life course perspective not only encases, but also transcends individual biographies (Dannefer, 2003), and to adopt a life course perspective is not to adhere to a particular, well-defined theory. Rather, it is to adhere, implicitly or explicitly, to a set of propositions grounded in the assumption of an active and agentic individual interacting with and moving through an influential and modifiable physical, cultural and interpersonal environment. The specific implications of this have been summarized in several overlapping sets of propositions that, together, can be thought of as a manifesto for the life course perspective (Baltes, 1987; Elder et al., 2003; Rutter, 1989; Shanahan et al., 2003):

1. *Development is a lifelong process*: Both ageing and development are defined as lifelong adaptive processes of 'acquisition, maintenance, transformation, and attrition' in psychological structures and functions (Baltes et al., 1999: 472). It is assumed that throughout life there is the potential for both continuous change, which is gradual, incremental, cumulative and quantitative, and discontinuous change, which is rapid, innovative, substantial and qualitative. This contrasts with earlier privileging within developmental psychology of childhood as the main period of growth and development – a period of 'becoming'; with adulthood assumed to be a stable plateau – a period of 'being' rather than becoming; and old age again a period of change, but this time characterized by decline and loss – almost a period of 'ceasing to be'.

2. *Development involves both loss and gain*:   Development is seen as a joint expression of growth (gain) and decline (loss). Thus, decision-making inevitably involves the closing-off of some options, moving forward inevitably involves leaving aspects of the past behind, and conditions of loss or limitation can provide a context for new forms of challenge or innovation. The life course perspective focuses attention on the gain:loss ratio in any particular situation, thereby providing a framework for understanding both post-traumatic growth (Calhoun and Tedeschi, 2006) and the experience of loss that frequently accompanies seemingly positive events.

3. *Development is multidimensional and multidirectional*:   Many different factors and dimensions contribute to a person's make-up, and these can change in different ways, at different rates, and with different outcomes; that is, the life course is multidimensional and multidirectional. It is recognized that different elements of the person – intellectual, social, career, family, for example – may follow different developmental trajectories. Indeed, some theorists have more or less abandoned stages for themes. Jacobs (2006), for example, shows how the issues of trust and dependency, authority and autonomy, and cooperation and competition emerge sequentially, but then stay centre-stage and find their place amongst the other themes, rather than fading from view whilst different issues take over.

4. *Development shows plasticity*:   Any life trajectory is one of a large, but not infinite, range of possibilities (Staudinger and Lindenberger, 2003), and 'plasticity' denotes the potential for a particular developmental path within a particular individual to be modified by life conditions and experiences. It refers to the potential for within-individual rather than between-individual variability.

   The developmental preoccupations of childhood are more likely to show greater correlation with age and less plasticity than those of adulthood. Perceptual, motor and cognitive development during the first years of life does follow a relatively fixed order and timetable, reinforced within any one society by regularities in child-rearing practices and education. Whilst still affected by social conventions and norms, adulthood is less bound by such ordered and timed processes. It is to be expected, therefore, that there will be a wider range of life course trajectories for adults. The limiting of options in late adulthood through both perceptual, motor and cognitive decline, and also through social exclusion, may reduce the plasticity and developmental possibilities of this life stage.

5. *Development as the outcome of individual-environment transactions*:   The life course perspective facilitates the promotion of an interactive, contextual or systems view of the person: an active organism within an active environment. Development is seen as an iterative process of person-context transactions, and psychological turning points as triggered by major life events, personally or socially significant role transitions, or symbolic indicators of ageing and mortality (Wethington et al., 1997). This draws attention to the need to look to the outer as well as the inner worlds inhabited by both client and therapist.

6. *Development is historically and culturally embedded*:   Development does not occur in a historical or social vacuum. Cultural contexts change over time, both in terms of specific events such as wars or economic recessions, which will be experienced by some generations but not by others, and also in terms of developments such as technological

advances and changing educational opportunities. The life course of someone born in 1950 will differ, for example, from that of someone born in the year 2000.

Similarly, the particular lifestyles that are condoned, sanctioned and expected vary across time and culture. Married women's participation in the work force was a case in point during the twentieth century, and Datan charts its progression through a qualitative as well as a quantitative shift: 'the exceptional becomes the scarce, the scarce becomes the infrequent, the infrequent becomes the acceptable, and finally, the acceptable becomes the norm' (1983: 41). An altered definition of 'normal' development is thus achieved. Whereas cultural differences serve to highlight the inappropriateness of transferring concepts of development from one social group to another, historical differences serve to make the past an uncertain and unreliable guide to the future.

7. *Development is a multilevel process*: The life course perspective encourages a consideration of the impact of a range of different systems of influence on development, including broad cultural influences, social institutions, immediate interpersonal relations, and intrapersonal psychological, cognitive and physiological factors. The life course perspective cuts across the disciplinary specialisms typically associated with these different levels of influence, instead seeing the life course as a dynamic system of interdependent and inseparable subsystems. Development is seen as involving the integration of changing relations among the multiple levels of organization (Ford and Lerner, 1992; Lewis, 2000; Smith and Thelan, 2003). From these interactions new qualities and capacities can emerge.

MODELS OF USEFULNESS

To adopt a life course framework is to embrace a range of alternative constructions of human experience across time. Rather than searching for some kind of single, grand, underlying truth, the concept of the life course is theoretical in the sense of offering what Mahrer (2004) terms 'convenient fictions' in the form of 'models of usefulness'. These models of usefulness are fictitious not in the sense of being wrong, but in the sense of being created. They are constructed with an eye to their effectiveness in achieving some purpose – in this case, reflection-in-action (Schon, 1995) and the development of a working knowledge that therapists can call on in the midst of their practice. Such models can help therapists construe clients' lives across time and be called upon irrespective of a client's life stage or situation.

Thus, the life course is seen here as a framework or metamodel for containing a number of pragmatic (Lynch, 1998) models of usefulness – although it is perhaps more accurately described as neopragmatic (Hansen, 2007; Polkinghorne, 1992) in that it embraces the postmodern notion of constructed rather than objective reality. Such models of usefulness have become increasingly important as the loss of life course certainties requires us constantly to re-fashion our sense of who we are. There are fewer hints and guidelines for us to follow than there were as we stumble our way through life.

In keeping with the definition of the life course posited earlier, models of usefulness will be considered that focus on: the rhythmic and fluctuating pattern of human life over time; expected and unexpected life events; and interactions between the self and the environment.

THE RHYTHMIC AND FLUCTUATING PATTERN OF HUMAN LIFE OVER TIME

The concepts of the life course and of life-span development are large and unwieldy, and metaphorical analogies represent alternative models of usefulness that can make it easier to grasp the Gestalt of what we mean. Since we frequently do not make explicit the metaphors we live and work by, the perspective we are taking on the nature of the life course may be hidden. Considering metaphorical images of the life course can help to clarify our perspective and assumptions.

Some metaphors are primarily visual. Thus, representing the life course as a ladder, an arc, a tapestry or a circle all create different images and bring particular assumptions and values to the fore. A ladder, for example, conveys the picture of a lone individual making stepwise progress toward some higher level – the solo heroic quest. An arc represents midlife as the pinnacle of development – preceded by growth, and followed by decline. A tapestry conveys the interlocking of many different threads – an image of connectedness rather than separation. A circle suggests that what goes around, comes around.

More complex metaphors include those drawn from the natural world, as when the metaphor of the river was used earlier to convey the human life course as dynamically embedded in its environment, powerful and directional. There are many images that could be invoked. Thus, Levinson (1996; Levinson et al., 1978) talks of the 'seasons' of life, Super (1990) of the life-career 'rainbow' and Jung (1972) of middle-age as the 'noon of life'. Another metaphor depicts life as a game of cards (Salmon, 1985), where we may be dealt a good or a poor hand, but to succeed we still need to 'play our cards right'. The metaphor of life as a journey reverberates through literature and daily speech as well as academic accounts.

Also evocative is the metaphor of life as a story (Salmon, 1985). Drawing, like many contemporary theorists of the life-span, on the work of Erikson (1980), McAdams (1993) suggests how, through infancy, childhood and adolescence the key features of our unique life story develop so that by the time we reach early adulthood we have available to us the tools we need to fashion our life experiences into a coherent, purposeful and meaningful story.

All these metaphors are instructive – and doubtless you will think of others. However, it is the image of the life course as a sequence of distinct stages that is perhaps the most pervasive. It has, in a variety of forms, dominated consideration of life-span development.

Life stages

Of course, accounts of the human life course did not begin with Baltes et al.'s landmark 1980 paper. From literature, Shakespeare's 'All the world's a stage' speech in *As You Like It* is often cited. Here we have, amongst other things, the infant 'mewling and puking in its nurse's arms'; the lover, 'sighing like a furnace'; and the soldier 'jealous in honour, sudden and quick in quarrel'. This depicts the life course, at least implicitly, as the 'natural' unfolding of stages assumed to be invariant, universal and cumulative.

An alternative view is expressed, less poetically, in the children's rhyme about Solomon Grundy: 'Born on Monday; Christened on Tuesday; Married on Wednesday', and so on and so forth. Again we have the inexorable passage of time, in this instance punctuated less by internally triggered drives and aspirations and more by external life events. The rhyme lists a series of 'normal' – in both the statistical sense and the sense of being age-appropriate – events which Solomon Grundy might be expected to experience. By implication we see Solomon Grundy as a metaphor for Everyman and, indeed, Everywoman.

However, for some time now, rigid timings in the organization of the life course have been softening. Indeed, it was back in the 1970s that Neugarten and her colleagues described how the sequence and rhythm of major life events has been changing, with puberty coming earlier than before, and death later. They describe how social timing is also changing, and how:

> Increasing numbers of men and women marry, divorce, then remarry, care for children in two-parent, then one-parent, then two-parent households, enter and re-enter the labor force, change jobs, undertake new careers or return to school. ... All this adds up to what has been called the fluid life cycle, one marked by an increasing number of transitions, the disappearance of traditional timetables, and the lack of synchrony among age-related roles. (Neugarten and Hagestad, 1976: 36)

Arguably, both the extent of this fluidity and its speed of flow have increased during the ensuing 30 years. Today we are less able to describe the 'normal' or 'natural' course of human life with the confident brevity of Shakespeare or of Solomon Grundy's anonymous biographer. We cannot assume the ordering or, indeed, the occurrence, of such events to be either invariant or universal.

In society as a whole, transitions between life stages are less frequently marked by shared rites of passage than previously. Gaining 'the key of the door' at age 21, or even 18, seems an outmoded and slightly quaint concept in this day and age. Marriage is no longer the key marker of the move out of the family home. The completion of full-time education, the onset of parenthood, the 'launching' of adult children, the age of retirement from work are all life events for which it is increasingly impossible to identify normative ages. But does that mean that we live, as has been suggested, in an increasingly age-irrelevant society? The answer is both 'yes' and 'no'.

Promulgating the idea of an 'ageless self' (Kaufman, 1986) can, at first blush, be seen as a laudable anti-ageist stance and as an appealing resistance to negative stereotypes of late adulthood, with age (especially 'old age') consigned to being nothing more than a mask concealing the essential identity of the person beneath (Bytheway, 1995; Featherstone and Hepworth, 1991). When old people talk about themselves, they will often express a sense of self that is ageless – an identity that maintains continuity despite the physical and social changes that come with age. However, it might be argued that the concept of the ageless self is itself ageist, denying the value of the experience with which our life time has been filled. Andrews rails against the tyranny of agelessness, arguing that we are not only as old as we feel, we are also as old as we are:

> While difference is celebrated in axes such as race, gender, religion and nationality, the same is not true for age. … [And yet] years are not empty containers: important things happen in that time. Why must these years be trivialised? They are the stuff of which people's lives are made. (1999: 309)

For Andrews, age is an important diversity. Stages can, therefore, be seen as useful 'convenient fictions' for considering its significance and implications.

Alongside the increase in unpredictability and diversity of life course patterns has been a burgeoning of claims for the existence of additional and more refined life stages. Two developments of significance to counselling psychologists in that they challenge taken-for-granted assumptions about particular life stages are Arnett's (2004) notion of emerging adulthood and Tornstam's (2005) concept of gerotranscendence.

Emerging adulthood

The transition from 'adolescence' to 'adulthood' is less clearly marked by normative life events than ever before, having become during the last three decades of the twentieth century a period of increasing demographic diversity and instability. The concept of 'emerging adulthood' (Arnett, 2004) recognizes that the onset of adulthood is beset with confusion and is a status acquired only by degrees. It acknowledges that, during this life stage, there are now no certainties, and few probabilities in relation to likely occupational, residential, marital or parental status.

Many young people move towards adulthood in the context of a diminishing support network (Apter, 2002), and this can leave them feeling isolated and vulnerable. Contact with parents and other relatives may diminish or be lost as family ties weaken or disintegrate through divorce, geographic dispersion and social diversity. Friendship networks may be unstable. They are less likely to have strong religious affiliation. Universities no longer operate *in loco parentis*. This state of flux, however, coexists with the assumption that those between the ages of 18 and 25 years should be and are 'grown up'. Labelled 'young adults', this implies that the status of adulthood has been reached, and can both be misleading and place a great weight of expectation on their shoulders. Our often unexpressed notions of what it is to be adult – possessing qualities such as psychological and financial independence, self-responsibility, maturity and a sense of perspective (Rogers, A., 1996) – represent aspirations that many at this point in their life feel unable to fulfil, leaving them with a sense of failure and inadequacy (Apter, 2002).

In sum, people of this age often exist in a context of alarmingly unsupported uncertainty where there is a contradiction between the assumptions presented about the nature of this life stage and the reality in which they find themselves. It behoves counselling psychologists working – perhaps in student counselling services – with 'emerging adult' clients to address these contradictions.

Gerotranscendence

Factors such as increasing longevity, improved health in later life and many people's gradual rather than sudden withdrawal from the world of paid employment, mean that the notion of 'emerging old age' is also a valid concept. Neugarten (1974) distinguished between the young-old and the old-old. Whilst the young-old are generally seen as those between, approximately, 65 and 80 years of age, and the old-old as those aged 80 and above, Neugarten argued for a functional rather than a chronological distinction between these two life stages – with the old-old experiencing increasing frailty, incapacity and dependence resulting from functional decline. This implies individual variation in the age of onset of very late adulthood – and argues against arbitrary age limits for exclusion from social roles, responsibilities and privileges.

Neugarten's notion of the old-old retains the 'hill-shaped' metaphor of the life course with its period of decline prior to death. However, the assumption of life changes as involving a loss:gain ratio leads to consideration of what positive aspects and potential for further psychological growth there may be in extreme old age. In his own late adulthood, this question engaged the attention of Erikson, whose eight-stage theory of lifespan psychosocial development (Erikson, 1980) is the touchstone from which much subsequent theorizing has developed. In a posthumously published edition of *The Life Cycle Completed* (1997), Joan Erikson, Erikson's widow and collaborator, proposed an extension to the theory in the form of a ninth stage during which individuals strive to transcend the everyday limitations of human experience and knowledge, instead confronting their own ageing self and seeking a more universal understanding of life. Her explication of this new stage drew extensively on Tornstam's (2005) theory of gerotranscendence, which suggests a potential stage of development in extreme old age where, rather than emphasizing decrements in physical capacity, there is a focus on continued growth in dimensions such as spirituality and inner strength. The gerotranscendent person is able to separate spiritual growth and development from physical deterioration.

The notion of gerotranscendence poses significant challenges for counselling psychologists working with older clients in that it reflects a qualitative break from a midlife rational and materialistic world-view in favour of a transcendent and cosmic one. We may be able to understand and empathize with the world-view of a child quite readily – we have, after all, all been children ourselves. But to empathize with the gerotranscendent world-view is, for the majority of us, to reach out beyond that which we know from our own personal experience. It demands that we question our assumptions about what we mean by 'successful ageing' (Baltes and Carstensen, 2003).

An understanding of life stage can help therapists orient themselves in relation to their clients' lives, recognizing how life problems take on a new hue in the psychosocial contexts of successive phases of life (Carlsen, 1988). It enables practitioners to help clients become aware of age-graded expectations within society and develop goals in relation to them. This does not imply conforming to all social expectations and agenorms, but rather that adherence to and deviation from them should be undertaken consciously, with consideration being given to the likely impact of so doing. Age norms operate as 'a kind of culturally specific guidance system' (Reinert, 1980: 17), and clients can be helped to choose whether to challenge or comply with its dictates.

However, whilst the concept of life stage is integral to the notion of life-span development, the life course perspective needs to be able to hold the tension between, on the one hand, the increasing diversity of life course patterns and, on the other, the identification of ever-more refined stages of life. A model of usefulness which recognizes this is that of the developmental task.

Developmental tasks

Developmental tasks (Chickering and Havighurst, 1981) represent tasks arising predictably and consistently at or about a certain period in the life of the individual, 'successful achievement of which leads to ... happiness and to success with later tasks, while failure leads to unhappiness in the individual, disapproval by the society, and difficulty with later tasks' (Havighurst, 1972: 2). Developmental tasks arise out of the interaction of maturational processes, cultural norms, and individual goals and aspirations. Because of the involvement of biological and psychological processes that are universal across people, time and place, there will be some commonality of developmental tasks for widely different individuals, families and communities. Because of the involvement of individual differences, varying aspirations, and cultural and social norms, the tasks associated with different life stages will, at the same time, also vary across individuals, cultures and epochs. Thus, each life course will include some developmental tasks that are shared with all other people, some shared with some other people, and some shared with none – 'If you could see your life's shape, you would find its features to be, like those on your face, universally human yet completely unique' (Rainer, 1998). This sets the scene for giving some credence to the notion of age-graded stages, but provides limits – making them guidelines rather than prescriptive strait-jackets.

Whilst Havighurst (1972) identified six to nine developmental tasks for each of six age periods ranging from 'Infancy and early childhood' to 'Later maturity', his recognition of the impact of social, cultural and historical change and difference led him to revise his list several times during his career. Normative developmental tasks are not written in stone. They change and evolve, and will never cease to need updating and revision.

Developmental sequences and patterns

Life stages may be cumulative and directional without being inevitable or age-related. Such sequences are developmental paths along which we will each progress at different rates and to differing degrees. The notion of being 'on time' or 'off time' is less relevant here, and there is less emphasis on the meeting of age-related developmental milestones. An example of particular relevance to counselling psychologists is Carl Rogers' (1961) account of how, in a series of 'moments of movement', a person experiencing the necessary conditions for psychological growth can move through successive stages from a position of fixity to changingness, from rigidity to flowingness, and from stasis to process. Rogers gradually came to discriminate seven stages in this trajectory of change, although they can more accurately be thought of as points on a continuum rather than distinct stages.

Developmental sequences propose a progressive path to the attainment of an improved way of being. In other words, later stages in the process are in some ways 'better' than earlier stages. They enshrine a concept of growth. Not all concepts of stage include this element – the 'seasons' of life are different from each other, but later ones are not necessarily 'better' than those which come before. Levinson (1990) proposes a developmental pattern in which the life course progresses through alternating phases of life-structure changing and life-structure building. The former, which typically last between three and five years, are periods of upheaval and decision making that involve terminating one life structure and initiating another. The latter, typically of five to seven years' duration, are periods of consolidation rather than upheaval and involve implementing and building on changes and decisions made during the transitional phase. This image not only suggests an underlying rhythm to the human life course, but also hints at rhythmic variations in the intervention needs of clients. Structure-changing phases suggest the need for support and exploration; structure-building phases for action planning and consolidation.

Having considered a range of convenient fictions that focus on the rhythmic and fluctuating pattern of human life over time, attention now turns to the second element in the definition of the life course posited at the beginning of this chapter: namely, the focus on expected and unexpected life events.

EXPECTED AND UNEXPECTED LIFE EVENTS

Life events are benchmarks that give shape and direction to a person's life. The occur-rence of some events is unpredictable, whilst others – even in our postmodern times – are age-graded, showing, in terms of onset and duration, a fairly strong correlation with chronological age. Still other events are related to the cultural and historical age in which we live.

Despite life events being one of the most basic elements of the life course (Willekens, 2001) we may still expect, at least implicitly, that our passage through life, especially once we reach adulthood, will be a smooth rather than a bumpy ride. We may always be searching for the calm after the storm. From this stance, disruptive life events, if they can-not be avoided, are treated largely as illnesses to be recovered from as quickly as possible, with the intervention goal being the restitution of 'health' (Frank, 1995). A life course perspective challenges this viewpoint, instead adopting a developmental stance, seeing both positive and negative life events as normative human experiences which pose a challenge and an opportunity for developmental adaptation and growth (Woolfe, 2001).

Life events are, therefore, more than benchmarks. They are also processes over time that can change us in significant ways and alter both the nature of our self-identity and the direction of our future life course. For counselling psychologists, the main focus of life events is their role as turning points and as triggers of psychosocial transitions.

Psychosocial transitions

The experience of many clients will have forced them into profound, often involuntary, and possibly sudden reassessments of their self-image – their sense of who they are. They will have experienced, or be in the midst of, a psychosocial transition – the process occur-ring whereby 'an event or non-event results in a change in assumptions about oneself and the world and thus requires a corresponding change in one's behaviour and relationships' (Schlossberg, 1981: 5). Amongst several possibilities (Ruble and Seidman, 1996), this definition of transition prioritizes changes in people's self-definition rather than their behaviour or social status. The inclusion of non-events (that is, hoped for or anticipated events that did not in fact occur) in the definition is also noteworthy, since it recognizes that failure to obtain an anticipated promotion or conceive a planned baby, for example, may provoke as significant a transition as the new job or baby would have done.

Kubler-Ross's (1997) work on death and dying has provided one of the most influ-ential and widely disseminated models of transition. It is a landmark example of a life event being viewed as a long-term process rather than a point-in-time occurrence. The model proposes five distinct, but overlapping stages in the process of facing and com-ing to terms with death: denial, anger, bargaining, depression and acceptance. Studies of other significant transitions have produced not dissimilar patterns, leading to the proposal (Hopson et al., 1988) that disruptions to our accustomed way of life trigger a relatively predictable cycle of reactions and feelings. First is a period of *immobilization* or shock, a sense of being overwhelmed, unable to plan or think logically. This leads into a sharp *reaction* to the event that, in turn, is followed by a period of *minimization* where the existence or impact of the event is denied or at least played down. This gives way, as the reality and implications of the event sink in, to a period of *self-doubt*, frequently manifested as depression, but possibly through other emotions such as anger or frustration. The next stage is reached as the person begins to *accept* the post-transition reality, thereby loosening the hold of the past on the present. This is followed by a period of *testing* as the person begins to try new ways of being in the changed situation. Next comes a phase of seeking to understand, learn from and *find meaning* in the experience; and, finally, the transition can be said to be complete when these new realities and understandings have become *integrated* into the life space.

Stage theories of transition have been both widely accepted and widely criticized. A main and general criticism centres around rejection of what is seen as their 'one-size-fits-all' mentality. The sequence of stages is seen as a denial of individual differences and an attempt to force people's experience into preordained categories rather than work with the unique experience of a unique individual. It is important, however, to see such frameworks as models of usefulness rather than universal truths, and to remember that they come laden with many qualifications and caveats. It must be recognized, for example, that passage through the cycle is rarely smooth and one-directional. People vacillate between stages and may be working on several stages simultaneously. No definitive guidelines can be given either as to the length of any one phase nor to the degree of vacillation of mood. Nor can it be assumed that all individuals will complete the cycle with regard to every transition. We may become 'stuck' – willingly or not – at any stage.

It is also important to recognize that in accepting the new reality and moving on, we do not 'put the past behind us' and leave it there. More usually, ties are loosened and renegotiated, rather than broken completely (Klass et al., 1996; Neimeyer, 2001). Consistent with this theorizing, Worden (1995) amended the fourth of his well-known list of the tasks of mourning. The first three remained: to accept the reality of the loss; to work through the pain of grief; and to adjust to an environment in which the deceased is missing. The fourth task was recast as the need to relocate the deceased emotionally and move on with life (amended from the earlier version (Worden, 1983) – withdrawing emotional energy from the deceased and reinvesting it in another relationship).

Although the transition cycle is a general pattern rather than a rigid sequence, and despite significant individual differences, it is sufficiently generalizable for most people to relate its stages to their own experience of at least some significant life events. The cycle serves to suggest how clients' needs may change as they move through its different stages. During the first part of the cycle, clients' preoccupations are primarily emotional, with an increasing involvement of cognitive processes as they move through the stages of testing and the search for meaning. Arguably, the focus of a counsellor's work should similarly change as a client moves through these stages.

Any particular transition must be considered in the context of the particular individual, the particular transition, and the particular social and personal circumstances – including life stage. However, whilst each person's experience is unique, this does not mean it shares nothing with any other experience – either the experiences of other people or other experiences of the same person. In the same way as age norms can provide guidance and a degree of comforting predictability as well as a set of constraining obligations and expectations, so, too, can knowledge of the transition cycle convey a sense of movement and direction. Recognizing that the sequence of emotions described in the transition cycle is 'normal' (that is, not inherently pathological) and 'normative' (that is, experienced by others as well as us) can be reassuring, helping to lessen loneliness of our suffering.

Zone of fertile emptiness

Taking a slightly different stance, Bridges (2004) suggested that transitions actually begin with an *ending*. This is followed by a period of *confusion and distress*, out of which *new beginnings* emerge. In describing the period of confusion and distress as a zone of fertile emptiness (although 'fertile chaos' might capture the experience more accurately), Bridges offers us an instructive model of usefulness. We can think of the time of fertile emptiness as a liminal zone, existing between an old past and a new future. Liminality is a threshold, a state of being betwixt-and-between, neither-this-nor-that, neither me nor not-me. It can be a scary and unnerving place to be, and the temptation is often to rush through the void or else try to return to the security of a former life structure.

But, liminality is also a place full of energy and potential. If we have the courage to stay in this space, we may be able to use it as a moratorium from our everyday routine that allows for personal reflection, reappraisal and redirection. An important role for counselling psychologists may be to help clients stay within this zone and rescue it from unmanageable anxiety in order to allow for the emergence of new beginnings.

INTERACTIONS BETWEEN THE SELF AND THE ENVIRONMENT

Much psychological discourse continues to discuss, understand and explain human existence in fundamentally individualistic terms. In the twenty-first century, when relationships are far less stable than in the past, there is a particular need to embrace more fully the inter-subjective turn, and start from the assumption that we are fundamentally and inextricably intertwined with others, and that our being is first and foremost a 'being-in-relation' (Mearns and Cooper, 2005).

Dynamic systems

Many of the metaphors invoked earlier encompass interaction between the self and the environment. Thus, the metaphor of a tapestry or a web emphasizes complexity and interconnectedness. Individual threads become meaningful and comprehensible by virtue of their position in the overall pattern. Rather than emphasizing separation and individuation, these metaphors focus on inter-subjectivity, and the relational nature of human experience.

Dynamic systems theory (Smith and Thelan, 2003) provides a meta-model of the life course that has the web metaphor at its heart. It proposes that we are inseparable from our environment and, therefore, that all experience and behaviour is a function of both the person and the situation, with development occurring through the dynamic, multidirectional interaction of personal and situational or contextual forces. Gottlieb et al. (1998) use the term 'coaction' rather than 'interaction' in order to emphasize the non-additive, non-linear and emergent nature of the interplay of developmental forces.

What distinguishes this perspective is its assumption that systems can generate novelty through their own activity, and its commitment to seeing individuals as self-organizing, self-constructing open systems fused with their environments. It embraces the key convenient fictions of *emergence*, *holism* and *agency*. It depicts the coming-into-existence of new forms or properties through ongoing processes intrinsic to the system itself (Lewis, 2000). Thus, the self is constantly under construction not just by the push of biology and the socio-cultural context, but also by the active process of self-construction. This echoes Havighurst's (1972) distinction between the three origins of developmental tasks – maturation, cultural norms and individual aspirations.

Personal life space

A life course perspective directs attention away from a boundaried self, towards a notion of self embedded in a multifaceted environment, with self and context being intermingled – separated, if at all, by a sea shore rather than a cliff face. The notion of self-in-context can be operationalized through the concept of the personal niche (Willi, 1999), life structure (Levinson, 1990) or life space – the self and the segment of the social, cultural and material environment that is meaningful to the person and with which he or she interacts. It is not merely the content of the personal life space that is important. Of even greater significance is the personal meaning of its elements and the relationships between them. A personal life space contains all those meanings (of people, experiences, belongings, relationships, events and so on) that a person has accumulated in life so far.

The personal life space can be represented visually as a map or a 'snapshot', with the relationships between the different parts of the map indicating how a person makes meaning of their world. Reflection on the map and dialogue between client and therapist can reveal personal values, assumptions and feelings that the person may have been unable to put into words directly. A person's life space is dynamic and changing, and comparing past and present life space maps can facilitate the exploration of change and loss. Similarly, life space mapping can also be used to help imagine and plan for the future. From maps of hoped-for selves, specific plans and action strategies can be developed to promote movement towards them (Shepherd, 1999). And likewise, concrete actions can possibly be taken to avoid or come to terms with feared future selves.

Stability zones

Many clients will have suffered a trauma that severely disrupts the stability and tranquillity of their personal life space. Thus, counselling is inextricably entwined with change – of behaviour, thoughts, feelings, awareness, understandings, interpretations. However, as tumults and upheavals cry out and grab our attention, it becomes all too easy to overlook that which might, by remaining constant, hold us steady. Elements within the life space that have not been lost or turned upside-down can assume enhanced significance during times of transition. They operate as anchors, or stability zones (Pedler et al., 2006), that we depend on when all else is confused, uncertain and frightening. Interventions in these circumstances may usefully include the development of new stability zones and the strengthening of those that remain.

More or less any element within the personal life space has the potential to operate as a stability zone. Frequently, however, they are associated with valued and enduring relationships with other *people*; *activities* that offer support or distraction; *ideas and values* that underpin personal standards and commitments to a philosophy, faith, profession, political ideology or cause; *places*, both large-scale (like a country) and small-scale (for example, a street or a particular room); *belongings*, in the guise of favourite, familiar, comforting possessions; and *organizations* such as professional bodies, work or other organizations with which we identify. The concept of stability zones provides a valuable lens through which to explore a person's life space map: How adequate is their repertoire of stability zones? How enduring? What should be retained and what needs changing? Have some elements outlived their usefulness? Are there any gaps?

Stability zones can never be sorted out once and for all. Needs, situations and roles change with time and life stage. Stability zones need, therefore, regular clarification and nurturing so that some are always available to provide reassurance, security and confidence when others are lost or discarded.

Support convoys

Life space maps and stability zone reviews are like snapshots, capturing a picture of the person at a particular moment. Introducing the idea of a support convoy (Kahn and Antonucci, 1980; Levitt, 2005) transporting the person across time is a model of usefulness that embeds these ideas in a life course context. A support convoy consists of a network of relationships that surrounds each of us and moves with us through life, both providing continuity in the exchange of support, and changing in structure over time. Support convoys can be visualized as a series of concentric circles, with the focal person at the centre, and with the most consistently important convoy members in the inner circle and the most transient on the periphery. Support convoys incorporate the concept of movement and change in that members can enter and leave the convoy and, within it, may move either towards or away from the focal person. They indicate the constantly evolving nature of supportive relationships.

CONCLUSION

The diversity of the life course in postmodern times makes the specification of normative life stages increasingly hazardous, but at the same time, we live in a more age-segregated society than previous generations. Many services – including those offered by counselling psychologists – use age and/or life stage, albeit inconsistently and at times implicitly rather than explicitly, as a gatekeeper guarding access to services and as a benchmark for allocating rights and responsibilities.

Adopting a life course perspective directs attention away from core theoretical orientations towards transtheoretical models of usefulness that therapists can call on across varying settings and client groups. As such, it facilitates the development of the varied and eclectic approach to practice that frequently characterizes experienced practitioners (Feltham, 1997; Skovholt and Ronnestad, 1995). Although emphasizing the pragmatic goal of utility, the life course perspective is saved from the postmodern 'vertigo of unlimited possibilities' (Gergen, 1991) by being grounded in a values base expressed in the explicit life course manifesto outlined earlier.

Taking a life course perspective is not, however, a simple option. It demands casting aside the blinkers of disciplinary specialism, tolerating ambiguity and living with the concept of 'both/and' rather than 'either/or'. However, by retaining an emphasis on the particular and the contextual, it can supplement rather than replace depth with breadth. It requires the ability to think dialectically – to resolve, albeit temporarily, contradictory factors in a particular situation. And this is something that denotes cognitive (for example, Commons et al., 1989) or personal (for example, Kolb et al., 2001) maturity, and is seen as the foundation for integration in therapeutic practice (Fear and Woolfe, 1996).

REFERENCES

Andrews, M. (1999) 'The seductiveness of agelessness', *Aging and Society*, 19: 301–318.

Apter, T. (2002) *The Myth of Maturity*. London: Norton.

Arnett, J.J. (2004) *Emerging Adulthood: The Winding Road from Late Teens through the Twenties*. Oxford: Oxford University Press.

Baltes, P.B. (1987) 'Theoretical propositions of life-span developmental psychology', *Developmental Psychology*, 23: 611–626.

Baltes, M. and Carstensen, L. (2003) 'The process of successful aging: Selection, optimization, and compensation', in U. Staudinger and U. Lindenberger (eds), *Understanding Development: Dialogues with Lifespan Psychology*. Boston, MA: Kluwer.

Baltes, P.B., Reese, H. and Lipsitt, L.P. (1980) 'Life-span developmental psychology', *Annual Review of Psychology*, 31: 65–110.

Baltes, P.B., Staudinger, U.M. and Lindenberger, U. (1999) 'Lifespan psychology: Theory and application to intellectual functioning', *Annual Review of Psychology*, 50: 471–507.

Bridges, W. (2004) *Transitions: Making Sense of Life's Changes*, 2nd edn. Cambridge, MA: Da Capo.

Bytheway, B. (1995) *Ageism*. Buckingham: Open University Press.

Calhoun, L. and Tedeschi, R. (2006) 'The foundations of posttraumatic growth: An expanded framework', in L. Calhoun and R. Tedeschi (eds), *Handbook of Posttraumatic Growth: Research and Practice*. London: Routledge.

Carlsen, M. (1988) *Meaning Making: Therapeutic Process in Adult Development*. New York: Norton.

Chickering, A.W. and Havighurst, R.J. (1981) 'The life cycle', in A. Chickering and Associates. *The Modern American College: Responding to the New Realities of Diverse Students and a Changing Society*. San Francisco, CA: Jossey-Bass.

Commons, M.L., Sinnott, J.D., Richards, F.A. and Armon, C. (eds) (1989) *Adult Development, Volume 1: Comparison and Applications of Developmental Models*. New York: Praeger.

Dannefer, D. (2003) 'Toward a global geography of the life course: Challenges of late modernity for life course theory', in J.T. Mortimer and M.J. Shanahan (eds), *Handbook of the Life Course*. New York: Kluwer.

Datan, N. (1983) 'Normative or not? Confessions of a fallen epistemologist', in E.J. Callahan and K.A. McKluskey (eds), *Life-Span Developmental Psychology: Non-Normative Life Crises*. New York: Academic Press.

Elder, G.H., Johnson, M.K. and Crosnoe, R. (2003) 'The emergence and development of life course theory', in J.T. Mortimer and M.J. Shanahan (eds), *Handbook of the Life Course*. New York: Kluwer.

Erikson, E.H. (1980) *Identity and the Life Cycle: A Reissue*. New York: Norton.

Erikson, E.H. (1997) *The Life Cycle Completed: Extended Version with New Chapters on the Ninth Stage by Joan M. Erikson*. New York: Norton.

Fear, R. and Woolfe, R. (1996) 'Searching for integration in counselling practice', *British Journal of Guidance and Counselling*, 24: 399–411.

Featherstone, M. and Hepworth, M. (1991) 'The mask of ageing and the postmodern life course', in M. Featherstone, M. Hepworth and B.S. Turner (eds), *The Body: Social Process and Cultural Theory*. London: Sage.

Feltham, C. (1997) 'Challenging the core theoretical model', *Counselling*, 8: 121–125.

Ford, D.H. and Lerner, R.M. (1992) *Developmental Systems Theory: An Integrative Approach*. Newby Park, CA: Sage.

Frank, A.W. (1995) *The Wounded Storyteller*. Chicago, IL: University of Chicago Press.

Gergen, K.J. (1991) *The Saturated Self: Dilemmas of Identity in Contemporary Life*. New York: Basic Books.

Gottlieb, G., Wahlsten, D. and Lickliter, R. (1998) 'The significance of biology for human development: A developmental psychobiological systems view', in W. Damon and R.M. Lerner (eds), *Handbook of Child Psychology, Volume 1: Theoretical Models of Human Development*. New York: Wiley.

Hansen, J.T. (2007) 'Counseling without truth: Toward a neopragmatic foundation for counseling practice', *Journal of Counseling and Development*, 85: 423–430.

Havighurst, R.J. (1972) *Developmental Tasks and Education*, 3rd edn. New York: David McKay.

Hopson, B., Scally, M. and Stafford, K. (1988) *Transitions: The Challenge of Change*. Leeds: Lifeskills.

Jacobs, M. (2006) *The Presenting Past: The Core of Psychodynamic Counselling and Therapy*, 3rd edn. Buckingham: Open University Press.

Jung, C.G. (1972) 'The transcendent function', in H. Read, M. Fordham, G. Adler and W. McGuire (eds), *The Structure and Dynamics of the Psyche, Volume 8: The Collected Works of C.G. Jung*, 2nd edn. London: Routledge and Kegan Paul.

Kahn, R.L. and Antonucci, T.C. (1980) 'Convoys over the life course: Attachment, roles and social support', in P.B. Baltes and O.G. Brim (eds), *Life-Span Development and Behavior, Volume 3*. New York: Academic Press.

Kaufman, S. (1986) *The Ageless Self: Sources of Meaning in Late Life*. New York: Meridian.

Klass, D., Silverman, P. and Nickman, S. (eds) (1996) *Continuing Bonds: New Understandings of Grief*. London: Taylor and Francis.

Kolb, D.A., Boyatzis, R. and Mainemelis, C. (2001) 'Experiential learning theory: Previous research and new directions', in R. Sternberg and L. Zhang (eds), *Perspectives on Cognitive Learning and Thinking Styles*. Mahwah, NJ: Erlbaum.

Kubler-Ross, E. (1997) *On Death and Dying: What the Dying Have to Teach Doctors, Clergy, Nurses and Their Own Families*, Reprint edn. New York: Simon & Schuster.

Levinson, D.J. (1990) 'A theory of life structure development in adulthood', in C.N. Alexander and E.J. Langer (eds), *Higher Stages of Human Development: Perspectives on Adult Growth*. New York: Oxford University Press.

Levinson, D.J. (1996) *The Seasons of a Woman's Life*. New York: Random House.

Levinson, D.J., Darrow, D.N., Klein, E.B., Levinson, M.H. and McKee, B. (1978) *The Seasons of a Man's Life*. New York: Knopf.

Levitt, M.J. (2005) 'Social relations in childhood and adolescence: The convoy model perspective', *Human Development*, 48: 28–47.

Lewis, M.D. (2000) 'The promise of dynamic systems approaches for an integrated account of human development', *Child Development*, 71: 36–43.

Lynch, G. (1998) 'A pragmatic approach to clinical counselling in context', in J. Lees (ed.), *Clinical Counselling in Context: An Introduction*. Oxford: Routledge.

Mahrer, A.R. (2004) *Theories of Truth, Models of Usefulness: Toward a Revolution in the Field of Psychotherapy*. London: Whurr.

McAdams, D.P. (1993) *Stories We Live by: Personal Myths and the Making of the Self*. New York: William Morrow.

Mearns, D. and Cooper, M. (2005) *Working at Relational Depth in Counselling and Psychotherapy*. London: Sage.

Neimeyer, R.A. (2001) 'Meaning reconstruction and loss', in R.A. Neimeyer (ed.), *Meaning Reconstruction and the Experience of Loss*. Washington, DC: American Psychological Association. pp. 1–9.

Neugarten, B.L. (1974) 'Age groups in American society and the rise of the young-old', *Annals of the American Society of Political Science*, 415: 187–198.

Neugarten, B.L. and Hagestad, G.O. (1976) 'Age and the life course', in R.H. Binstock and E. Shanas (eds), *Handbook of Aging and the Social Sciences*. NY: Van Nostrand Reinhold.

Pedler, M., Burgoyne, M.J. and Boydell, T. (2006) *A Manager's Guide to Self Development*, 5th edn. Maidenhead: McGraw-Hill.

Polkinghorne, D. (1992) 'Postmodern epistemology of practice', in S. Kvale (ed.), *Psychology and Postmodernism*. Thousand Oaks, CA: Sage.

Rainer, T. (1998) *Your Life as Story: Discovering the 'New Autobiography' and Writing Memoirs as Literature*. New York: Tarcher/Putnam.

Reinert, G. (1980) 'Educational psychology in the context of the human life span', in P.B. Baltes and O.G. Brim (eds), *Life-Span Development and Behavior, Volume 3*. New York: Academic Press.

Rogers, A. (1996) *Teaching Adults,* 2nd edn. Buckingham: Open University Press.

Rogers, C.R. (1961) *On Becoming a Person: A Therapist's View of Psychotherapy*. Boston, MA: Houghton Mifflin.

Ruble, D.N. and Seidman, E. (1996) 'Social transitions: Windows into social psychological processes', in E.T. Higgins and A.W. Kruglanski (eds), *Social Psychology: Handbook of Basic Principles*. New York: Guilford Press.

Rutter, M. (1989) 'Pathways from childhood to adult life', *Journal of Child Psychology and Psychiatry*, 30: 23–51.

Salmon, P. (1985) *Living in Time: A New Look at Personal Development*. London: Dent.

Schlossberg, N.K. (1981) 'A model for analysing human adaptation to transition', *Counseling Psychologist*, 9: 2–18.

Schon, D.A. (1995) *The Reflective Practitioner: How Professionals Think in Action*. Aldershot: Arena.

Shanahan, M.J., Hofer, S.M. and Miech, R.A. (2003) 'Planful competence, the life course, and aging: Retrospect and prospect', in S.H. Zarit, L.I. Pearlin and K.W. Schaie (eds), *Personal Control in Social and Life Course Contexts*. New York: Springer.

Shepherd, B. (1999) 'Possible selves mapping: Life-career exploration with young adolescents', *Canadian Journal of Counselling*, 33: 37–54.

Skovholt, T.M. and Ronnestad, M.H. (1995). *The Evolving Professional Self: Stages and Themes in Therapist and Counselor Development*. Chichester: Wiley.

Smith, L.B. and Thelan, E. (2003) 'Development as a dynamic system', *TRENDS in Cognitive Science*, 7: 343–348.

Staudinger, U.M. and Lindenberger, U. (2003) 'Why read another book on human development? Understanding human development takes a metatheory and multiple disciplines', in U. Staudinger and U. Lindenberger (eds), *Understanding Human Development: Dialogues with Lifespan Psychology*. Boston, MA: Kluwer.

Sugarman, L. and Woolfe, R. (1997) 'Piloting the stream: The life cycle and counselling', in S. Palmer and G. McMahon (eds), *Handbook of Counselling*, 2nd edn. London: Routledge.

Super, D.E. (1990) 'A life-span, life-space approach to career development', in D. Brown, L. Brooks and Associate, *Career Choice and Development*, 2nd edn. San Francisco, CA: Jossey-Bass.

Tornstam, L. (2005) *Gerotranscencence: A Developmental Theory of Positive Aging*. New York: Springer.

Wethington, E., Cooper, H. and Holmes, C.S. (1997) 'Turning points in midlife', in I.H. Gotlib and B. Wheaton (eds), *Stress and Adversity Over the Life Course: Trajectories and Turning Points*. Cambridge: Cambridge University Press.

Willekens, F. (2001) 'Theoretical and technical orientations toward longitudinal research in the social sciences', *Canadian Studies in Population*, 28: 189–217.

Willi, J. (1999) *Ecological Psychotherapy: Developing by Shaping the Personal Niche*. Seattle, WA: Hogrefe and Huber.

Woolfe, R. (2001) 'The helping process', *The Psychologist*, 14: 347.

Worden, J.W. (1983/1995) *Grief Counselling and Grief Therapy*. London: Routledge.

15

CHILDREN AND YOUNG PEOPLE

Sam Heywood

This chapter focuses on my work as a counselling psychologist working in an NHS community-based child psychology service. It is based in the Midlands and serves a working-class population in a deprived inner-city area. The service is atypical as there are few early intervention services nationally. I have therefore chosen to write about my role in a personal way to create a reflection of my experience (cf. Taylor, 1996).

This chapter is in three parts. In the first part of the chapter, the strategic context of psychological service provision for children and young people will be outlined by describing the current tier system. I will relate how my work differs from that in a specialist Child and Adolescent Mental Health Service (CAMHS), placing therapeutic work into a political context. In the second part, I will describe my particular approach to working with a typical family to illustrate some of the issues, dilemmas and tensions I encounter. This includes assessment, formulation and the complexity of families' competing needs during the intervention. By doing so, I illustrate the contrast between 'text book' and real life by using evidence-based research and examples of practice. The chapter ends with a short discussion of some clinical issues regarding training and practice.

PART 1: THE TIER MODEL

The first psychiatry-led Child Guidance Clinics were set up in the late 1920s, and by the end of the 1960s, social workers, educational psychologists and a few child psychotherapists were among the professionals employed in such teams. They were, however, isolated from other services and there was little emphasis on sharing information and skills with other professionals working with children. Over the last 30 years, the importance of addressing the mental health needs of children and young people has been increasingly recognized, and the growth of public and third sector services has reflected this. Currently, children's mental health services nationally are structured into four tiers (NHS HAS, 1995), starting at tier 1 for mild problems up to tier 4 for severe and persistent mental health difficulties. Each tier is outlined below, with further information about tiers 2 and 3, as these are the levels at which most counselling psychologists would be employed in the NHS.

Tier 1

Professionals in tier 1, including GPs, health visitors and school nurses, 'are in a unique position to influence parents from the start, raising awareness of health issues and encouraging them to seek help for themselves and their children' (DoH, 2004: 23). Problems can be identified early on, and children are signposted to other services in tiers 2 or 3 if they become too complicated for the professionals to manage at this level.

Tier 2

Professionals working in tier 2 include psychologists, speech and language therapists and social workers who work in the community. The focus is on more complex family problems, supporting the work done in tier 1 through training, supervision and consultation, as well as direct client work. The aim of this level of early intervention is to work with families before problems become too severe, and it is at this level that I work.

I moved to my current post after working in a tier 3 specialist CAMHS team. This shift for me fits with my inclination to lean toward a critical view of psychology with humanistic and feminist underpinnings. Some families need support with practical problems, like housing, which override the need to 'deliver' therapy for what may traditionally be seen as an intrinsic problem. Returning to my post after maternity leave, I remember discussing my role with the locum psychologist, who described 'feeling like a social worker rather than a psychologist' at times. I consider myself lucky to have the flexibility to work in what I consider to be a cutting-edge service.

On the whole, my work in specialist CAMHS gave me a solid grounding in working with children and families, partly due to the indispensable guidance and supervision I gained from colleagues. There were, however, downsides for me which included an 18-month waiting list, problems that were entrenched and difficult to change by the time the children were referred. In addition, children's difficulties were often seen as disorders (with DSM-IV diagnoses) rather than as being a product of environmental or social problems. Most CAMHS have traditionally been medically led by psychiatrists, following the old Child Guidance Clinic model. It is changing, but in some teams this remains the case. I am aware that for many practitioners in such teams there are tensions regarding a medical versus a social model of care.

My initial experience of working as a counselling psychologist in a new tier 2 service meant that I had some prejudice to deal with and was treated with suspicion and wariness by many families. As I could only offer a service if referrals came in, I began by focusing on developing relationships with parents and other practitioners. I spent some time simply meeting with mothers (as it was always mothers who attended) in groups such as baby clinics and playgroups, in order to 'get my face known' and become more accepted by the community. Once I was able to have conversations about their children, some of the mothers began to tell me their difficulties with tantrums, eating or sleep routines, after which I was able to work more therapeutically.

Within two years, I was part of a well-established team who knew what I did, referred regularly and asked for consultations and supervision. I was also a recognizable face in the community. The familiarity I had with some families' lives was enhanced by some of the work I did through supervision and consultation with other practitioners in tier 1, rather than direct clinical work. This allowed for easier access for families to the service I offered.

Tier 3

CAMHS is a service for children with specific mental health difficulties that are complex and persistent. A typical CAMHS team often consists of psychiatrists, psychologists, social workers, community mental health workers, nurses, play and/or art therapists and family therapists. Referrals are mostly from GPs, education welfare officers, school nurses, social workers and paediatricians.

CAMHS receive referrals for school-aged children and young people with problems such as anxiety, post-traumatic stress disorder (PTSD), depression, attention difficulties, psychosis, conduct disorder, eating disorders, autistic spectrum disorders and Tourette's syndrome. There are current NICE guidelines to treat problems such as depression, anxiety and PTSD, which would be utilized by CAMHS practitioners. There isn't sufficient space in this chapter to discuss interventions in any great depth, but *What Works for Whom?* (Fonagy et al., 2002) and *Drawing on the Evidence* (Wolpert et al., 2006) outline the most effective evidence-based ways of treating mental health difficulties in children and adolescents. Developmental difficulties and coping with pain or hospital admissions for physical illnesses (for example, cystic fibrosis or cancer) may be evident at a young age and require long-term support. These problems may be seen by psychologists in specialist teams within paediatric services or disability services for children. Although there isn't sufficient space to explore here, it is worth mentioning that there are child psychology services that may focus on working with other disadvantaged groups, such as ethnic minority groups (including asylum seekers), parents misusing drugs or alcohol,

TABLE 15.1   DIFFERENCES BETWEEN TIER 2 AND TIER 3 SERVICES

Tier 2	Tier 3
Mental health service from birth to school age.	Specialist mental health service for school-aged children up to 18 years in education.
Community-based, working in client's own home, children's centres, schools or clinics.	Clinic- or hospital-based, with some outreach work in schools or homes.
Work as a lone practitioner with few clinical staff.	More joint work with a variety of trained clinicians.
Social model.	Traditionally medical model.
High DNA and difficult to engage, often with low motivation to change.	Low DNA rates and more motivation.
Easily accessed by practitioners and parents alike.	Restricted criteria for referral into the service.
Preventive and clinical work with no crisis response.	Clinical work with complex and chronic problems, e.g. school refusal and crisis response for deliberate self-harm.

looked after children, and children with disabilities. These services are not necessarily a part of CAMHS, but are important to highlight.

Having worked in both tiers 2 and 3, there are clearly some differences between the services which I have summarized in Table 15.1. These are, however, pertinent to my experience and may vary nationally.

Tier 4

Tier 4 level of service is a highly specialized community or regional in-patient unit for severe and complex mental health problems, such as eating disorders. Professionals providing intensive support at tier 4 are often psychiatrists, psychologists, clinical nurse specialists, psychotherapists and family therapists.

PART 2: THERAPEUTIC WORK IN TIER 2 WITH CHILDREN AND PARENTS

Requests for help with child behaviour problems tend to be the dominant reason for referral. Sleep, toileting and feeding difficulties in preschool children tend to be dealt with by health visitors. A referral is made if the problem becomes chronic or when there are a number of other contributory factors, making the problem more complex, such as poor housing or abusive relationships. The work I do is mostly with parents (particularly given the young age of the children), and this may include enabling them to see their part in the child's problem. It could also involve addressing parental mental health difficulties, usually anxiety or depression, so that they are able to parent more effectively. Such referrals tend to be for mothers rather than fathers.

For the families I work with, using a psychological service can be challenging for a number of reasons. Parents and children rarely refer themselves, so may not wish to attend an appointment; parents may not understand my role (as I often have to rely on the referrer to explain), or the family live in a rather chaotic environment where appointments are often missed. These difficulties can manifest in high non-attendance rates, even though I arrange to visit families at a time and place that suits them.

Referral

Julie, a 23-year-old mum, was referred to me by her health visitor because of her low mood after the birth of her baby 10 months ago. Impacting on Julie's mood was the difficult behaviour of her 3-year-old, Bradley. The health visitor requested some support for Julie's parenting skills to help her manage the behaviour problems and also counselling for her low mood. Julie had recently broken up with the father of her two children, Carl.

It is worth noting that the family members are simply names I have chosen to represent the type of problem I might encounter. The story is based on no particular family that could be identifiable, so any familiarity is purely coincidental.

Initial contact

The first thing I did after the referral was to phone Julie to arrange a time and convenient place for us to meet and talk about her difficulties. I met Julie at her home, which is where most parents choose to meet me the first time, and I was greeted by her and her crying baby, Skye. Her small living room looked somewhat chaotic, with clothes everywhere, toys scattered on the floor, breakfast dishes piled up on the table and the television on. She described her 3-year-old son, Bradley, as a 'handful', never having grown out of the 'terrible twos'. He appeared to be a very active boy whilst I was there, often demanding his mother's attention.

Assessment

It was difficult to complete an in-depth assessment of Julie's needs, given the baby's distress and the interruptions to attend to Bradley. At an initial home visit, it is important to have an open mind and to work flexibly, as there may be more than one adult present (such as a friend or grandparent), a preschool child, the television on and a pet dog to greet you. This can often make an assessment rather difficult, but I have found it essential to allow the parent enough time to feel comfortable with a psychologist in their lounge, particularly if they are a family who wouldn't ordinarily access mainstream services. Thus, the assessment may take place over a period of time.

Confidentiality and consent

The issues of confidentiality and consent are an essential aspect of my initial visit. I make clear to parents the need to gain consent to share information when necessary, recognizing the limits to confidentiality. I explain that my role as a psychologist means I have an obligation to communicate information to other professionals if I have concerns of a child protection nature or if anyone is at risk of getting hurt. I do this at an initial visit to ensure that there is no confusion about it later on, and also because although information emerges as familiarity with a family grows, it is difficult to go back to the 'rules' once a good, trusting therapeutic relationship is established.

Ascertaining the problem

Perhaps the easiest place to start, and often what the parent wishes to talk about initially, is what the problem is and how the problem manifests itself. If the child is present, I look for evidence of this occurring during my visit. Julie identified that Bradley was her main source of stress and anxiety because she didn't feel able to control him at all, she didn't like him very much and she was worried that he would grow up to be 'like his dad': unable to hold down a job, taking drugs and becoming violent at times. She spoke of Bradley in negative terms whilst he was in the room, giving me the impression that it was usual for her to speak in that way. Julie also became tearful when she said that she'd 'tried everything' but nothing seemed to work and she didn't have the energy to keep going.

There are times when parents become distressed in the telling of their story and request support for themselves. The 'distress that is caused when difficulties make parents feel impotent is compounded by the realization that they themselves need caring for and that they need help' (Attride-Stirling et al., 2001: 185). At this stage therefore, it is important to acknowledge parents' struggles, to recognize the competing needs in the family and their attempts to solve the difficulties before they are referred to me. I can also gather clues as to how motivated they are to work with me, whether they have problem-solving skills and whether they are likely to want advice or information.

It is common for parents to struggle with a child's behaviour once they near school age. Therefore, as Julie described, 'terrible twos' were expected to be hard work but at 3 years old, a child is becoming their own person and starts to understand that their behaviour has an effect on others, namely parents and carers. If a parent has been inconsistent in saying 'no', for example, a 3-year-old may push harder to get what they want because they learn that eventually they'll get it by escalating their behaviour or noise levels. This was partly what was happening between Bradley and Julie.

Julie's immediate problem of Bradley's behaviour was not the only thing she mentioned, but I could see in their interaction how this behaviour was affecting them both. It is important to me to identify who the client is and whose problem it is, as often parents will perceive the child as being the problem, whereas the work I do may mean that the parents feel like my 'client' as they are doing the talking – not the child. The problem may be recognized by the parent as a result of poor attachment and bonding.

Developmental stages

During an assessment it is important to understand the developmental stages a child moves through from birth to adolescence (see Table 15.2). This is not an exhaustive list but merely a guide to my thinking in an assessment. Obviously children develop at different rates, but it is useful to understand what is 'typical' for their age range. Bradley's tantrums were not seen by Julie as being 'normal' for his age and she blamed herself for not being a good-enough parent to manage them. It was helpful to put her difficulties into context with her developmentally as well as within the family context to enable her to feel more empowered to change.

Another example to illustrate this is a child of 2 years bedwetting, which would be seen as a normal part of development. This would not be seen as typical in an 8-year-old. With the 2-year-old, some advice to the parent about how to progress out of nappies could be achieved by a health visitor and not require specialist help. With an 8-year-old, some exploration of the child's development, life events and other concurrent problems would be necessary to understand whether there may be a developmental delay. Alternatively, there might have been some trauma to explain why, after having been dry through the night, this child begins to wet the bed. Some difficulties can therefore be seen as part of normal development without diagnosing a problem unnecessarily, whereas those needing intervention are identified and worked with. This is clearly the role of assessment.

Formal assessment

Julie completed a number of questionnaires before the parenting programme, including the strengths and difficulties questionnaire (Goodman, 1997) and measures of how she perceived herself as a parent. Given that Julie also presented with depression, I used the Beck depression inventory to assess her level of mood and monitored this throughout my intervention. I rarely carry out formal psychometric tests as part of my assessment because

TABLE 15.2   DEVELOPMENTAL STAGES AND TYPICAL PROBLEMS

Age	Developmental stage	Typical problems presented
From birth to 7 years (early childhood)	Beginning to master physical independence, e.g. walking, talking but reliant on carer to ensure needs are met. Expresses emotion when needs not met, often through behaviour. Egocentric: the world revolves around them with little understanding of others' needs. Concrete thinking.	Feeding Toileting Sleeping Behaviour problems (e.g. tantrums and aggressive outbursts) Autistic spectrum disorders
8–12 years (middle childhood)	Less reliant on caregivers, more autonomous physically and able to reason, so some abstract thinking. Beginning to understand impact of self on others. Able to show more control over emotions and behaviour.	Conduct/behaviour Attention/ADHD Anxiety
13–17 years (adolescence)	Defining self as separate self/identity. Independent thinking and behaviour. Some return to egocentricity as preoccupied with self and appearance. Controlled emotional expression.	Depression Eating disorders Deliberate self-harm Substance misuse Psychosis

I generally see families in their homes, which is not conducive to the clinical conditions needed for testing. These are more likely to be used by my clinical psychology colleagues in hospital or clinic settings.

Assessment summary

During the first two visits, I was able to get much information from Julie about the current problems, early relationships and indicators of when the problems began. This helped me move towards a joint formulation of the difficulties and thus helped guide my intervention. My assessment with Julie highlighted the following areas:

- Bradley's aggressive and unpredictable behaviour, which had been apparent since he was 18 months old and restricted Julie to going out only for essential shopping because she felt embarrassed and unable to cope.
- Bradley was a child who 'screamed all the time' and was 'difficult from birth'. Julie thought this was because he was 'taken away' from her to be operated on as soon as he was born.
- Skye's sleep pattern was affecting Julie and she felt constantly exhausted. This was beginning to affect her relationship with the baby, as she felt angry. It also affected her relationship with Bradley as she was short-tempered with him.

- Julie was tearful and 'stressed' much of the time. She was not taking medication.
- Bradley's behaviour was not dealt with consistently, as reported by Julie.
- Julie's partner, Carl, left whilst she was pregnant with Skye following an incident of domestic violence. She thought Bradley may have witnessed some of this. Carl used to drink a lot, but they have no contact with him.
- Julie thought that Bradley had similar qualities to his father; she was unable to see any positives and was too tired to manage his outbursts.

Formulation

Pulling together a formulation is a key way in which counselling psychologists decide on the level and direction of their intervention. A formulation 'serves both as a map for therapy and a guide to which map to choose' (Aveline, 1999). Julie had identified her first goal as trying to manage Bradley's behaviour, so I drew out a formulation with her based on Carr's (2006: 42) framework (see Figure 15.1). This is analogous to the five Ps in a cognitive-behavioural therapy (CBT) formulation of presenting issues, precipitating, perpetuating, predisposing and protective factors. In my formulation with Julie, it also felt important to understand her feelings of sadness, hopelessness, guilt, loneliness and frustration, particularly as there is research to suggest that boys with depressed mothers showed a high level of behaviour problems at this age (Murray et al., 2003). Although I initially used a CBT model to formulate the behaviour problems, in my mind I recognized the importance of attachment theory as another way of understanding the difficulties with Bradley. Using the information about the distressing separation at birth, it felt important to incorporate this into my intervention.

Intervention

In thinking about my intervention, I continued to feel presented with a clinical dilemma about where to begin and had a number of questions in my mind: Do I focus on her parenting skills to help her feel more confident and in control? Do I think about her relationship with Bradley and work on this? Do I allow her some space to address her own feelings first? Before I go into detail about the intervention, I have summarized my work with this family in Table 15.3.

Julie's early relationship with Bradley was important to address, but I have learnt from experience that parents often want to know they are making a difference to their problems quickly by seeing some change in their child's behaviour. I make a clinical judgement when I meet parents about whether I attend to their relationship and early attachment through their responses to a child's behaviour (as in a parenting programme, for instance) or through emotional work using play, talking about and recognizing feelings. I therefore think about

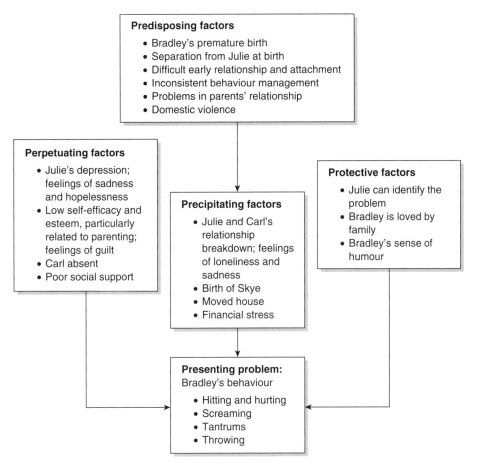

FIGURE 15.1   JULIE, CARL AND BRADLEY FORMULATION

the balance between symptom management of a child's behaviour and a perpetuating factor of a parent's style due to their attachment history.

Consultation

Although I could see that Bradley's behaviour was a huge source of stress for Julie, I also felt that her efficacy as a parent was being undermined by her level of exhaustion. Since changing behaviour requires a certain amount of energy, I suggested to Julie that we could work with the health visitor to help her develop a sleep routine for Skye. In addition, the health visitor referred Skye and Julie to a parenting practitioner (whose role is to support the health visitor) for baby massage. This level of intervention aimed to encourage

TABLE 15.3 SUMMARY OF INTERVENTION

Problem	Intervention	Outcome
Skye's sleep routine	Consultation and supervision with health visitor. Baby massage with parenting practitioner.	Sleep routine in place with increased number of hours sleep for Skye and Julie and quality time through massage to improve relationship.
Bradley's behaviour	Positive Parenting Programme.	More effective management of aggressive outbursts, fewer tantrums, improved self-efficacy re. parenting, enhanced relationship.
Julie's behaviour towards Bradley	Advanced level of parenting programme (Pathways) based on CBT model; referral to Domestic Violence Service.	Fewer angry outbursts towards Bradley and increased empathy.
Bradley's and Julie's relationship	Relationship play work with play specialist.	Warmer, more loving relationship.

bonding between Julie and Skye and also to help Julie gain more sleep. This enabled her to work effectively with me to increase her effectiveness in managing Bradley's outbursts.

Behavioural parent training

When working with parents I draw on parenting programmes, which are based on social learning theory, operant conditioning and CBT. This ensures modelling of a calm response from parents, rewards for good behaviour and non-attention to difficult behaviour, as well as rehearsal of new skills. Parent training has been suggested as one of the most effective ways of dealing with conduct-type disorders in children up to 10 years (NICE, 2006), and there are a number of evidenced-based programmes in use across the UK (Webster-Stratton, 1992; Sanders, 1999).

As I am trained in the Positive Parenting Programme (Triple P), I used this to provide support to Julie. The basic approach covers five key principles:

1. Providing a safe, engaging environment
2. Providing a positive learning environment
3. Using assertive discipline
4. Having realistic expectations (of parents and children)
5. Encouraging parents to take care of themselves

I invited Julie to my next group. The sessions take place over an eight-week period, incorporating the fundamental philosophy of working to improve relationships and increasing the behaviours parents wish to encourage, and then reducing behaviour they want to discourage. Parents set their own objectives and carry out homework in between sessions to rehearse newly acquired skills.

After an initially successful few weeks, during which Julie was practising her strategies, she began to have difficulty maintaining her good progress. This is not uncommon. It became apparent that Julie was struggling to manage her own feelings of anger and distress whilst also trying to think about Bradley's behaviour. She reported that she had not completed her homework on two occasions and eventually stopped attending the parenting group with me.

I arranged to meet Julie individually, and during this session she admitted to feeling 'stressed' whilst trying to implement the strategies from the parenting programme and she felt she wasn't making progress with Bradley. For instance, rather than keeping calm and using a logical consequence for Bradley's behaviour, she had ended up shouting and admitted to smacking Bradley on occasion. We explored what was happening at these times and it became apparent that it occurred mostly when Julie was feeling tired, lonely and angry. We agreed to focus further on her relationship with Bradley but at a level that would help her identify what happens to her behaviour when she's angry.

Child protection

A further tension in this work is around safeguarding children and making a decision about whether a child is safe in the care of his or her parents. After Lord Laming's inquiry into the death of Victoria Climbié, there were a number of reforms made in services to children which have been designed to ensure that similar tragedies do not happen again (DoH, 2003; HM Treasury, 2003). Unfortunately, given the well-publicized death of Baby P in Haringey, there is still much room for improvement for those working to safeguard children. The *Working Together* document (DoH, 2006) has made safeguarding children the concern of every professional working with a child.

At one point Julie told me about hurting her child. This sort of information is never easy to hear or witness and although I would not condone it, I made sense of it within the context of my assessment and formulation, as well as my relationship with her. I concluded that she and I needed to shift the focus of the work rather than make a referral to social care, and perhaps to think with her about who else could support her at this time.

If there is a concern about a child's safety in the care of a parent who might need more support, a meeting of professionals (such as health visitor, family support worker) with the parent and child, if he or she is old enough, should take place. The Common Assessment Framework (CAF) has been introduced as a model at a national level to do just this. The CAF is 'designed to enable practitioners across all agencies, after training, to follow the same process and achieve more consistent assessments that can be shared and understood by other agencies' in order to safeguard children as much as possible (see www.ecm.gov.uk/caf). It is important during a CAF to be able to gather information about a family's needs in a systematic way. This enables the professionals involved to be clear about where the gaps are and how to meet these needs. It is also important to be able to communicate this clearly and in a supportive way to a parent.

There is a question of what would happen if I *was* concerned about a child's welfare or a parent's inability to cope and provide basic care? If Julie had told me that she was regularly smacking Bradley, that she was constantly screaming at him, that she couldn't stand it any longer, that she wanted to leave or have him taken away or that she was suicidal, then I would have to act on that by contacting social care and refer Bradley as a child at risk. I would also assess the risk of Julie's suicide threat, take it to supervision, my line manager and would possibly need to refer on to adult mental health services. This, however, is when such a situation is fairly clear-cut.

Sometimes I may only have a hunch that things are not quite right. Gaining more accurate information and evidence to support this can be difficult, but I could be presented with a dilemma of having a feeling rather than a fact. The tension this creates can sometimes interfere with my clinical work as I become more vigilant about the information I'm hearing, perhaps trying to purposefully find out more by asking more questions around the relationship with the child. If parents are suspicious of social care due to their own experience or misunderstanding the role of a social worker, they are likely to pick up on the 'diversion' in the therapy. These families, in my experience, then begin to miss appointments and avoid me when in fact they are exactly the sort of family who need more support, not less. I have to try to maintain a relationship (and therefore the intervention) by being open and honest, yet also being mindful of the child's and the parent's needs. I cannot emphasize enough the need for supervision in this scenario, but ultimately, the child is my client and I may have to take this risk of losing a therapeutic relationship with a parent in favour of ensuring a child's welfare.

Enhanced parenting support using CBT

CBT seeks to work collaboratively with clients to help change their perceptions to healthier, more positive thought patterns. Julie's low mood and anger certainly played a part in how she believed she was behaving towards her children. As a result, I felt it important at this stage not only to help Julie with strategies to manage Bradley's behaviour, but also to offer support, given that 'personal control, empowerment, and self-determination are associated with positive mental health' (Prilleltensky et al., 2001: 143). I also see the importance in how a person's environment and previous experience can affect their level of distress, and Julie had experienced trauma and loss before giving birth. She was also struggling financially, had just ended a relationship that had been abusive and was raising two children on her own. Understandably, she described herself as feeling stressed and depressed and wanted to change her behaviour. She was able to recognize the effect her anger and low mood had on the children.

For this part of my intervention with Julie, I used an intervention called Triple P Pathways (Sanders and Pidgeon, 2005) which is used after, or in conjunction with, the group Triple P parenting programme. It is based on the understanding that a parent's mental health is impacting upon their parenting, and aims to address this rather than the mental health difficulty itself. It aims to enable parents to identify parent traps they fall into when with their children, to increase their empathy with their child's feelings, to help them understand the attributions they make about their child's misbehaviour and to encourage them to manage their own levels of stress using cognitive strategies.

I should make it clear why Julie was being seen by me rather than adult mental health services. There are a number of practical advantages in working within the context of a community-based child psychology service. For example, I am able to work flexibly and arrange a venue close to home, to organize childcare and transport if necessary. Furthermore, even though I am supporting Julie, at the heart of my work is the well-being of the children. Whilst encompassing and addressing Julie's mental health difficulties, my primary focus is on the way in which these affect her ability to parent effectively, and the impact these problems have on her children. This would not be the case in adult services.

Attachment work

Knowing more about Julie's relationship history over time, it was apparent that the early start to Julie's and Bradley's relationship was marred by a premature birth, subsequent separation, an abusive parental relationship and maternal depression. Whilst working with Julie at a behavioural level and helping her to see the positives about Bradley, I was struck by how little quality time she spent with him. It was possible that Julie's depression and exhaustion affected other aspects of her relationship with Bradley, such as quality of play.

Attachment theory is an influential aspect of my work as it emphasizes the importance of early relationships and their impact on behaviour in relationships later in life. It can help to make sense of behavioural difficulties emerging in early relationships. When children are young, they form a sense of themselves in relation to others through their primary carer. If early attachments are difficult in some way, this affects a child's sense of their own and others' behaviour, often leading to fear, distress and discomfort. Because attachment behaviour has evolved so that infants are protected, early exploration can be inhibited if their relationships and environment aren't safe, perhaps delaying development and increasing the child's need for protection: hence the need for a 'secure base' (Bowlby, 1988).

Often when I work with parents, their own attachment patterns are triggered by having a young child. This can lead to a repetition of disordered attachments, often manifesting in uncomfortable feelings and behaviour in themselves that they find difficult to deal with. As a result, I felt it important to shift the focus of the intervention to the early attachment and relationship by initially helping Julie feel more confident to play with Bradley. I am fortunate enough to work alongside play specialists who provide intervention using structured play activities to help build relationships between parents and young children. I suggested that the play specialist provide support to Bradley and Julie to model and thus facilitate a closer interaction, alongside the work I was doing with Julie on her emotional responses and behaviour towards Bradley.

The play specialist introduced the idea of playing together in close proximity over a number of weeks, gradually building up the intimacy between Julie and Bradley. Eventually Bradley was calmer and more settled when with his mum. He enjoyed sitting on her knee and singing with her, whilst Julie became more responsive toward him. She also found it easier to use the positive strategies we had worked on in the parenting programme, such as descriptive praise and attention.

This intervention has illustrated the multilayered approach I may use with a family by addressing various aspects of the difficulties in turn. This work may take a number of months to complete. The outcome for this family was positive: they were offered a number of interventions to address each of their needs, which were clearly not straightforward but relied on good engagement from the beginning. Julie, Bradley and Skye cannot, however, cover all the possible problems, dilemmas or levels of work that might be covered.

PART 3: CLINICAL ISSUES

One skill a counselling psychologist brings to work with children and young people is flexibility in thinking and practice, which I hope I have illustrated here. For those of you reading this who have never worked with children before, it felt necessary to highlight concepts like joint working, systemic thinking, and to demonstrate the complexities of working in a tier 2 service with a typical family. In this final section, I take a brief look at some of the tensions that I experience during my working life. These include local politics, research, supervision and training.

Political tension

A source of frustration for me occurs at the interface between services for children. The rather rigid criteria for referring into some services is an example of this, as it often means that I work with families who have complex problems and require a lot of liaison, and ultimately not very much direct work. The indirect client work I do, although is an essential component of my work, is not seen or recorded on the local Trust electronic system; this is only for face-to-face contact. There is, therefore, pressure for me to justify and report on the *direct* outcome with a family for the purpose of funding and targets.

Making psychological services accessible

Families who are most in need are least likely to access a service. In light of the recent *Improving Access to Psychological Therapies* (DoH, 2008) document highlighting a move towards accessible services, it's vital that we ensure children's services move towards meeting the mental health needs of families. 'In some organisations, the level of motivation required for people to access these services and resources is very high and effectively acts as a selection process, excluding those whose lives are too chaotic or whose motivation wavers' (Trevithick, 1998: 116). This seems particularly important to address. Providing a service in a family home, however, means that the power dynamic is altered. Psychologists reduce their power and increase risk to themselves, but ultimately families feel more comfortable.

Research in practice

I think it's important to acknowledge the role that research plays in our practice and when, for me, that can create tension and sometimes frustration. The Triple P parenting programme is well researched and is a government-recommended intervention. It is a resource that can produce some really good results for parents. This is particularly evident if parents understand that they play some part in their child's difficulties, if they are motivated to change and if they can attend a parenting group from beginning to end over the eight weeks. In practice, however, many of the parents I work with are like Julie in that they have more than one child, they are isolated, have no transport, may be struggling with their own depression or may have been 'sent' by other agencies. This makes the successful completion of a programme less likely, either because they find it hard to attend or because they don't want to, given that they see the child as 'the problem'.

What the research doesn't talk about is how, as a community practitioner, I work harder to engage these families, how I need to provide crèche and transport or how I may deliver the programme more creatively by offering catch-up sessions if parents do not attend. I often have to deliver a particular session over two weeks because some parents find the material overwhelming, thus making it a longer group. The complexities related to trying to meet the needs of many families whilst delivering a tried-and-tested model is not referred to in the training for the parenting programme, or in the research. Ultimately, it is reduced to either my clinical decision about a particular parent or a service-based decision about how many times a group should be offered before the family is discharged, how long the waiting list is and/or how well staffed the team is in relation to the number of referrals.

Some families do not engage, or opt out of the group after two or three sessions in spite of the flexible, accessible service, which is when frustration can build up for practitioners. This may be because parents have gained enough from the training to have dipped below their crisis point, or it may be that they found it hard to keep up with. In reality, we rarely gain feedback from parents who opt out, but I do try to contact them to offer another local group. Alternatively, I may offer work on an individual basis, as described with Julie.

This notion of measuring our outcomes to demonstrate what psychologists do, unfortunately, as I illustrated with my parenting groups, doesn't always fit with the intervention actually delivered. I don't remember being taught how to be flexible to a family's needs on my training to be a counselling psychologist, nor was it discussed very much on my parent training courses. I also work on a local Doctorate Clinical Psychology training course as a reflective group facilitator. During these groups, (particularly in the first year of training where trainees are being taught techniques for dealing with mental health difficulties), there is much discussion about how the text book doesn't fit with their experience of being in a room with a client. My response is often to say that people's lives are messy and theories are useful for providing us with structure, but there is an art and a skill to delivering therapy. Experience, rather than training, has taught me to worry less about the book but to understand how the book is important.

Supervision

After discussion with many colleagues, I think it is fair to say that there are very few simple, straightforward referrals made to children's psychological services any more, even though some may appear to be so at first meeting. Work with families can be complex and multifaceted, so it is essential to liaise with external agencies at times, to have regular supervision and to communicate with team members about your part in the life of the problem and the family you're working with. Although I have referred to liaising with other colleagues, I am aware that throughout this chapter, I have often used 'I' rather than 'we' to describe the work I do. On reflection, I think this has been a conscious decision to enable me to write in a way that is true to who I am at work. I think in part, it also reflects the autonomy I have that can sometimes feel isolating, which is when I value supervision most. One of the many challenges I face is to maintain a balance between working independently and holding clinical responsibility, whilst also feeling supported.

The importance of supervision, training, team support and awareness of risk to oneself on home visits as well as safeguarding children are paramount, particularly in making sense of the complexity of some families' difficulties. Being able to understand the wider context, and acknowledging that at times what we are faced with may resonate with our own experiences of parenting or of being parented, can help with separating our own feelings and experiences from theirs. In supervision it is important to look not only at management of workload but also at the impact that families have on us. Child protection work can be particularly harrowing. In addition, given that many situations tend not to be clear-cut, it is also important to develop your own internal supervisor and to practise as a reflexive, sensitive practitioner.

Training

Describing my work here gave me an opportunity to consider professional psychology training and whether or not it has equipped me for this particular type of work. Clearly, this is too big a question to answer here, but suffice to say, it is essential to have had additional training in child protection and useful to have done some sort of parenting training; a diploma in child and adolescent mental health will give more insight into this area of work. There have been times when I have been faced with situations, like being handed a baby to hold whilst a frantic mother tries to prevent a toddler from climbing out of the window, or having to talk to a mother about a sensitive issue whilst the rest of her extended family are present. On such occasions I have reflected upon my own training and realized that it hadn't taught me what to do in these situations! The idea of flexible boundaries came to mind and the question of how it is that we learn when it's acceptable to be less rule-bound about the way we work, which isn't described in a text book.

A sense of competency and what challenges this is another area I question and reflect upon. An example of this is whether or not it is possible to work sufficiently well with families if you have no children of your own, which is often a question parents ask, particularly when I'm delivering parent training. There are pros and cons for both sides of the argument, but certainly it is not essential to the job. It is essential, however, to be able to use basic counselling skills to engage with families, to be prepared to be playful (when talking with children) as well as calm and empathic (when talking with a parent), and showing flexibility in the way we approach problems. Being able to sit alongside a distressed parent yet also being able to give advice when it's requested are similarly important.

My job is interesting and multifaceted, as it includes delivery of teaching or training sessions, to provide supervision and receive it, to work with a 25-year-old parent as well as a 5-year-old child, to liaise with a social worker about concerns I have about a child as well as talking with a paediatrician about a child's toileting difficulties. These are all aspects of this work that make it exciting, challenging and sometimes complex. I hope this chapter has given some insight into this and will perhaps help to increase the numbers of counselling psychologists working in children's services in the future.

REFERENCES

Attride-Stirling, J., Davis, H., Markless, G., Sclare, I. and Day, C. (2001) 'Someone to talk to who'll listen: Addressing the psychosocial needs of children and families', *Journal of Community and Applied Social Psychology*, 11: 179–191.

Aveline, M. (1999) 'Introduction to formulation', in L. Johnstone and R. Dallos (ed.) (2006) *Formulation in Psychology and Psychotherapy*. London: Routledge.

Bowlby, J. (1988) *A Secure Base: Clinical Implications of Attachment Theory*. London: Routledge.

Carr, A. (2006) *The Handbook of Child and Adolescent Clinical Psychology: A Contextual Approach*, 2nd edn. London: Routledge.

Department of Health (2003) *Keeping Children Safe – The Government's Response to the Victoria Climbié Inquiry Report and Joint Chief Inspectors' Report Safeguarding Children*, Cm 5861. London: The Stationery Office.

Department of Health (2004) *Children's Health, Our Future*. National Service Framework for Children's Services (Ref. 277804). Available at www.dhgov.co.uk, accessed April 2008.

Department of Health (2006) *Working Together to Safeguard Children*. London: The Stationery Office.

Department of Health (2008) *Commissioning IAPT for the Whole Community – Improving Access to Psychological Therapies*. London: The Stationery Office.

Fonagy, P., Target, M., Cottrell, D., Phillips, J. and Kurtz, Z. (2002) *What Works for Whom? A Critical Review of Treatments for Children and Adolescents*. London: Guilford Press.

Goodman, R. (1997) 'The strengths and difficulties questionnaire: A research note', *Journal of Child Psychology and Psychiatry*, 38 (5): 581–586.

HM Treasury (2003) *Every Child Matters*, Cm 5860. London: The Stationery Office. Available at www.everychildmatters.gov.uk, accessed April 2008.

Murray, L., Cooper, P.J., Wilson, A. and Romaniuk, H. (2003) 'Controlled trial of the short- and long-term effect of psychological treatment of post-partum depression', *British Journal of Psychiatry*, 182: 420–427.

National Institute for Health and Clinical Excellence (2006) *Parent-Training/Education Programmes in the Management of Children with Conduct Disorders*. London: NICE. Available at www.nice.org.uk, accessed April 2008.

NHS Health Advisory Service (1995) *Together We Stand: The Commissioning Role and Management of Child and Adolescent Mental Health Services*. London: HMSO.

Prilleltensky, I., Nelson, G. and Peirson, L. (2001) 'The role of power and control in children's lives: An ecological analysis of pathways toward wellness, resilience and problems', *Journal of Community and Applied Social Psychology*, 11: 143–158.

Sanders, M.R. (1999) 'Triple P-positive parenting programme: Towards an empirically validated multilevel parenting and family support strategy for the prevention of behaviour and emotional problems in children', *Clinical Child and Family Psychology Review*, 2: 71–90.

Sanders, M.R. and Pidgeon, A.M. (2005) *Pathways to Positive Parenting, Module 2: Coping with Anger*. Brisbane: Triple P International.

Taylor, M. (1996) 'The reflexive practitioner: Feminist psychotherapy in action'. Unpublished PhD thesis, Manchester Metropolitan University.

Trevithick, P. (1998) 'Psychotherapy and working-class women', in I. Bruna Seu and C.M. Heenan (eds), *Feminism and Psychotherapy: Reflections on Contemporary Theories and Practices*. London: Sage.

Webster-Stratton, C. (1992) *The Incredible Years: A Trouble-shooting Guide for Parents of Children Aged 3–8*. Toronto: Umbrella Press.

Wolpert, M., Fuggle, P., Cottrell, D., Fonagy, P., Phillips, J., Pilling, S., Stein, S. and Target, M. (2006) *Drawing on the Evidence: Advice for Mental Health Professionals Working with Children and Adolescents*, 2nd edn. London: CAMHS.

16

PSYCHOLOGICAL COUNSELLING WITH YOUNG ADULTS

Cassie Cooper

This chapter focuses on clients aged between 16 and 24 years of age and, as such, traverses the boundary between adolescence and young adulthood. The years following adolescence are now recognized as an extended transitional period of emerging (Arnett, 2004), threshold (Apter, 2002) or fledgling (Sugarman, 2004) adulthood. The responsibilities, privileges and trappings of adult life are attained gradually and unevenly during this period, although by its end the majority of young people have made significant strides towards attaining a degree of occupational identity, residential security and/or the stability of an intimate relationship – all indicative markers of adult status.

Although the emphasis in this chapter is on the context with which I am familiar – the application of psychodynamic theory to counselling psychology – there are those who argue for the all-persuasive importance of social structures to counselling and psychotherapy, whilst others, particularly in the field of family therapy, maintain that the systems approach is of equal importance. There are also those counselling psychologists who place emphasis on consideration of single variables that may particularly affect this group; for example, race, body image, gender or drug use. A complex array of therapies, techniques, methodologies and arguments face the individual practitioner. If there is little agreement on any of these, the one thing of which we can be certain is that there are increasing numbers of young people in this age group who experience symptoms that cause distress to themselves, their families and their friends.

There is no consistent or universal definition of a young adult in the infrastructural institutions of the United Kingdom. The General Household Survey (Office of National Statistics, 2005) defines the pre-adult age group as being from 16 to 24 years. At 18 years a person is legally able to vote, buy cigarettes, marry, leave home, join the army, gamble, be arrested and tried in an adult court of law. At 16 you can leave school, although this is set to be raised to 18 in 2013, have hetero- or homosexual intercourse, take a full-time job, pay income tax and marry (with parental consent). With these inconsistencies, it is left for the individual to define the period of young adulthood as being only culturally and historically specific. Notwithstanding such inconsistencies, this young client group brings into sharp focus the fact that their parents are growing older, that the society their parents espoused is being supplanted and overtaken by new generations, and that these sexually developed young men and women are about to overtake their parents in forming external relationships that will eventually supplant and replace their families.

In a certain sense we can think of every young man and woman as a budding psychologist. The normal processes of maturation enable each and every one of us to develop a particular view of life and to operate strategies for predicting and responding to life events, however traumatic they may be. We learn as we go which major physical and intellectual developments are taking place. Psychological issues are generally concerned with personal difficulties occurring in relation to family and friends, the perception of the world, and around attitudes to their sexual development and identity. These problems, when they occur, can be characterized by feelings of anxiety or tension, dissatisfaction with their own behaviour, self-image or sense of failure to meet desired goals and ambitions in life. The pre-adult may present for help because they are urged on by a concern about their situation. Worried about relationships with family and/or teacher/employer, the young adult may bring problems of a personal nature relating to the way he or she feels and fears about internal struggles, sexual concerns, depression, self-destructive thoughts or behaviours such as self-harm or an eating disorder.

There may be times when clients themselves appear to be unaware that they have a 'problem', until significant others, who may be adversely affected by their behaviour, have cause to complain about the situation, after watching their loved ones become unhappy, lose hope or become self-destructive. Not infrequently, the teenager who comes for therapy is likely to have been encouraged to do so. For example, the worried parents of a young person who has become painfully thin and refuses to eat may be accompanied to the GP and consequently referred to an eating disorders unit despite their own protestations that all is well. In addition, young men and women in this age group seeking or being encouraged to come to therapy, may be experiencing difficult social contexts such as being unemployed, unable financially to leave home, in debt, facing discrimination by race, economic stringency, sexual, moral or religious demands or medical disability.

Yet for many years the field of psychology treated the topic of personality development in early adulthood and its ensuing problems with benign neglect. Psychologists concluded that, once the storms of adolescence had abated, the young adult would proceed to the calm of adulthood (Costa and McCrae, 2005). He or she having completed their schooling could go on to higher education, become a member of the workforce, leave home, get married and 'settle down'. Nothing more would be heard from them until they approached the periods highlighted by media spin – 'thirty-something' or 'mid-life crisis' and the generation gap which widens until the inevitability of old age and death. Psychoanalytic theories about independence have postulated that a successful transition from adolescence to young adulthood is achieved in individuation – a rejection of parental definitions of identity. Rejection means that at this time the young man or woman is torn between the longing to be regressive and loyal to past childhood association and facilitations and the alluring prospect of their own adult autonomy and networks of interdependence. Whatever occurs later in life has been considered largely as an elaboration or distillation of early childhood experiences.

Yet, more recently, both psychological and psychoanalytic theories acknowledge that the young adult of the twenty-first century does not enter or accept a period of tranquility, sameness and predictability, and it needs to be acknowledged that change also occurs in life outside adolescence and that flexibility and plasticity are characteristics of the human experience. In addition, personality formation theories, which echo the psychoanalytic theme of the need to 'break away' from childhood identities (the idea of leaving home, whether it be by one means or another), pose problems to this new state by their assumption of what is meant by dependence and the omnipotence of parents.

While this chapter reflects the author's experience in psychoanalytical practice, it will examine the theoretical perspectives which provide highly contrasting solutions to the problems listed below:

- The stormy and peaceful transitions in the individuation processes.
- Problems of separation – the development of independence/ego-strength.
- Failure to establish a work pattern either in education or employment.
- Ideas of success and failure.
- Suicide and self-harm.
- Developing the capacity to involve and develop intimate relationships.

THE INDIVIDUATION PROCESS

If you have been happily and securely attached to your family and to your parents, it is easier to establish your own identity and to leave home without things going wrong than if you are anxious about them or at war with them (Bowlby, 1979). Dependence is a prime characteristic of human nature, but as we reach adulthood the need to prove ourselves as independent becomes a priority. Independence is widely accepted as part of Western culture and philosophy, and is highly valued in current society. It is associated with powerful words and images such as strength, individualism and leadership. The notion of dependence is, in contrast, devalued and often associated with helplessness, indecision, weakness and childish behaviour. Dependence and independence are seen as opposite poles, delicately poised, which can tip in either direction, but the desirable weighting is seen to lie in the area of independence, the golden goal of achievement and growth. Although psychoanalytic theories stress the necessity for the child of an early period of dependence on his or her parents, it has never been seen as a positive goal. Dependence is viewed as a 'means to', a process which can lead to emotional security or ultimately to the achievement of independence.

However, rather than necessarily seeing the therapist's role as facilitating their young clients to become more independent, perhaps we need to ask whether any of us is ever truly independent. Fifty years ago, Kelly (1955) argued that adults, like children, are dependent too but that they extend their dependence discriminatingly to more people, more things and more institutions. More recently, Kagitcibasi (2005) questioned whether independence and relatedness are necessarily separate constructs. He went on to suggest that the attitude taken by 'helping professionals' should not be one of labelling clients as dependent and independent, but one where 'emphasis is placed upon variations in their dispersion', a salient aspect of personal growth.

According to Erikson's (1980) still influential theories of psychological development, the young adult is struggling to attain, and perhaps more important to retain, a sense of ego identity, a sense of self that is free and distinct from the experiences of childhood and adolescence. This task, says Erikson, is accomplished during a 'psychosocial moratorium' when the young person is free to experiment with new possibilities – for example, in careers or ideologies – without having to make a firm commitment to any as yet.

CASE STUDY: MINDU

The case of Mindu exemplifies a family's response to the experience of separation and loss related to the young adult's individuation process and the necessity for the counsellor to be ready and willing to meet this response in a flexible manner. In this case, the client was already away from home and her parents opposed the treatment because they found it threatening, in the same manner that they found her emerging autonomy threatening. There was no alliance with the family which could have helped the client had it existed.

Mindu, an intelligent university student, was referred for counselling because she had unsatisfactory relationships with men and performed poorly in one field of study after another. She had changed courses from Psychology to Business Studies, each time feeling inadequate and intellectually inferior. Her immigrant father, a wealthy and domineering businessman, had never allowed her to associate with young men of a different religion from his (Muslim) and could not understand why she was bothering to study at all. Her mother was also unsympathetic and called Mindu frequently to say that she was hurting her father who felt that, whilst Mindu was able to take his money, she did not really love him. If she loved him she would give up messing about in university and just come home. The father was part of a very large family business which had been built from scratch by the paternal grandfather. Having no sons, only daughters, he had focused on Mindu to follow him into the family business. He could not understand her needs and independent career aspirations, which seemed 'ridiculous' to him, and he devalued her fields of study as potentially leading to financial ruin.

I understood Mindu's failure in her studies as an expression of guilt over separation. Her parents fuelled her conflict, portraying her as a betrayer of family loyalties, attempting to thwart her moves towards independence and autonomy and wishing to ensure her safe return to the bosom of the family. Mindu verbalized this quite clearly: 'If I am not cut out for academic work and I do not have what it takes to get a reasonable degree, then perhaps I really belong back in the family business. Perhaps my father is right.' It was clear that Mindu was avoiding ambivalence and was daunted by the prospect of ever separating from the family

Shortly afterwards Mindu terminated her therapy. Mindu's confused mixture of loyalty and guilt forced her to seek a form of reparation for the difficulties between her father and his family. Splits in the family reinforced her own fear of becoming a success. Success meant that she became different from other members of the family, and this could be seen to be an abandonment of her relationship with them. Her fight for individuation and autonomy was regarded with suspicion and fear by her father and incompatible with his so-called ideas of 'femininity'. She was betraying her cultural and religious background by aiming to be like her non-Asian peer group.

As Summerfield and Babb point out, notions of the traditional family which conform to the roles, responsibilities and expectations of men and women as gender specific, are changing in terms of its dominant presence in most Western societies. Bearing witness to this change is the increasing proportion of households comprising couples without children, the massive increase in reconstituted families with complex familial relations and the increase in lone parent households. (2004)

However, despite changes in family structures, individuation remains a bottleneck through which each person has to squeeze individually and which, in most families, presents a potential crisis for all. Separation is a process that cannot be hurried – not simply an event, but a process which continues in a rather indefinite way.

Young people may be perplexed by their separation process and there are few guidelines. Is there a right time for this or that? A right age to leave, or are there only specific individual cases? Do our current cultural perspectives offer any means of assuring a smooth transition into adulthood – with no clear social norms? Who is to tell a parent that they are clinging too long to their sons and daughters or, erring in the opposite direction, pushing them out of the door too soon? It is not often appreciated just how important this transition is when young people break down at the very point when they should be taking off. Breakdown means not only mental breakdown, although that is included. For example, the highest incidence of first experience of schizophrenia is in the late teens and early twenties (Rethink, 2007). It may also, however, mean academic failure, drug abuse, self-harm, eating problems, criminal activities, unwanted pregnancies and other problems that are frequently associated with this age group.

SEPARATION

The defiant way to leave home is, of course, to run away, but while an abrupt exit is perplexing for all concerned, the inner dynamics of a gradual separation can be equally paradoxical. At the time of separation, when the young man or woman is striving for autonomy, there are conflicting thoughts about abandoning the home base. It is comforting to believe that there is a home base to return to in time of need. Here is the difficulty. In order to separate, it is necessary to acquire a psychological detachment from parents; the simultaneous wish for distinctness and approval. If you are 'different' from your parents, then you may feel separate from them. If, however, parents feel different from their sons and daughters, it could represent to the young adult the loss of the parents' love and support.

There is also the symptom of what could be termed 'paralysing apathy'. Haley (1997) traces many of these problems to the need to preserve the family by sacrificing one's own growth. The young student's failure, for example, often serves to keep parents from confronting issues in their marriage that might otherwise have led to a divorce. If children are unable to separate and thus able to keep their parents intensely involved with their own problems, then parents may neglect their own difficulties. Young men and women are prepared to pay a high price – their own emotional growth – for the sake of so-called stability in their family life.

Separation for the young adult may also be problematic in situations of parental need. The Government's report *Hidden Harm* (Home Office Report, 2003), for example, revealed that there were 350,000 children of problem drug users in the United Kingdom and more than one million children whose parent has a problem with alcohol. One of the consequences of such a situation in the family is 'parentification', that is, when children take on inappropriate parental roles:

> in trying to resolve unmet needs from their childhoods, children become parentified and take on overt and instrumental roles of domestic chores, and/or covert and expressive care-taking roles of confidante and mediator. This strategy is further established in adulthood where parentified individuals may enter helping professions, these roles representing

extensions of their childhood roles. The ultimate goal in the de-parentification process is to activate real self experiences unconsciously buried in the family system. In learning empathy for shamed identities, individuals can form relationships with others based on mutuality and respect. (Di Caccavo, 2006)

We understand these realignments of needs and wants as readjustments made necessary by increased anxieties and called forth by these acute life crises within the family. To label such reactions as 'pathological' or bad does not help to understand the problems. To help chart a purposeful course of action towards them, their inner psycho-logic, their rationale must be understood. This unfinished business of childhood provides a basis for adult development.

Maintaining childhood beliefs has the benefit of preserving our sense of security, but it also has a cost. We are confined by the rules that bound us as children. We cannot get free of these confining inhibitions without facing the illusory nature of some of our most fundamental beliefs and without giving up the security they provide. But when we do get free, we gain from this process real freedom to be our own person, in touch with our inner needs and passions, living a vital and meaningful life (Costa and McCrae, 2005). Thus, for the counselling psychologist, the work will likely be at this developmental level.

The critical developmental need of separation – individuation – is negotiated in the family setting. Successful maturation requires the helpful participation of the parents in providing a facilitating environment, a setting in which the young adult is emotionally supported whilst attempting to develop an integrated identity as a psychologically differentiated person. When parents themselves suffer unresolved narcissistic fixations rooted in frustrating relationships in their own early development, the threat of their own offspring's separation can induce regression in themselves. When this occurs, parents are less able to relate to their child as a separate and independent centre of their own, but tend to relate to him or her as an extension of themselves, a self-object whom they may attempt to possess and control. The resulting counter-separation attitudes and behaviour of parents present a profound interference to the nascent adult's developmental task.

A frequent scenario of this painful period is the abrupt and bitter exit from the family. Some of those who have to stay at home do so in a state of antagonism, and those who do leave home – for whatever reason – maintain a hostile dependent entanglement between offspring and parent. They may fail in key tasks of young adulthood. Even when living alone they neither form meaningful relationships outside the family nor embark on a career other than that of 'a problem'.

SUCCESS AND FAILURE

In an original piece of work, Super (1990) suggested some of the most respected theories of life-stage development, particularly in the areas of work and higher education.

In focusing on changes in the concept of self and how they affect inevitably the choice of education and career, Super delivered a theory of occupational development, and in relation to the age group 15 to 25 identified this as the first stage, one of 'exploration and trial'. But the world is changing fast and the age group 15 to 25 may no longer be a period of 'exploration and trial'. It is now less likely than in the past to lead to a period of stability and, even if it does, this stability may be shorter-lived and replaced by a further period of 'exploration and trial'.

FAILURE TO ESTABLISH A WORK PATTERN

How do we educate young men and women in preparation for the changing world of work that they will enter? School leavers and graduates worry about finding work and there are always too many young people between the ages of 18 and 25 who remain unemployed whatever government initiatives attempt to change. To be unemployed at the beginning of an adult work life is to head towards the term 'unemployable' – the vicious process of no experience/no work and so on. Society has been conditioned to believe that work is fundamental to our well-being. Most people want and need to work. Given the situation where we know that work is not obtainable, with signs that it may become scarcer still, by definition we have a large-scale mental health problem to face.

Sobering studies of unemployment in this and other age groups highlight particular psychological problems, and resulting family disturbances are frequently the problems with which the counselling psychologist is engaged. Schoon and Bartley examined the serious harm to physical and mental health and well-being caused by the experience of poverty and adverse life events: 'Socio-economic disadvantage, material hardship and family breakdown greatly increase the risk of developing adjustment problems later on, such as educational failure, behavioural problems, psychological stress or poor health' (2008).

The case history of a young chronically unemployed person can read like a description of clinical depression. The initial failure to find work and so-called 'success' may lead to a sense of personal failure, leading to frustration, apathy, immobilization and a sense of futility. Turned inwards, such experiences can result in depression and may be seen as integral to the rationale for the current Increased Access to Psychological Therapies (IAPT) agenda. Family distress too may be evident in a number of ways, with blame, cynicism, anxiety and helplessness being played out in a variety of destructive ways.

Successful stages of young adulthood, 'despite growing up in poverty, can be improved by facilitating and encouraging education achievement and participation across the life span' (Schoon and Bartley, 2008). However, the student whose parents expect a good result, or the student who has been financed, at great sacrifice, by parents or who has a feeling of inferiority that their exam result will confirm, is under pressures which may well be duplicated in later life. Anxiety and depression in students is increased by financial and other difficulties and can affect academic performance (Andrews and

Wilding, 2004). In addition, high levels of examination anxiety is associated with poor performance (Orbach et al., 2007).

CASE STUDY: ALAN

Alan, the eldest son of a northern working-class family, had a problem. He was a bright pupil at his primary school and was soon perceived as Oxbridge material at his secondary school. However, his parents were anxious about the possibility of him staying in school until 17 and then going on to University.

With donations from a charitable trust, Alan achieved 5 A-levels. Choosing Graphic Design, he decided to study in London, taking on part-time jobs in the holidays to buy himself some new clothes. Alan's parents were disappointed, hoping that he would change his mind, look for work and contribute to the family income.

Alan found student accommodation with a respected family near the University. Meeting Alan at a Freshers event you had to notice him: wearing an animal print jacket, hair glued into a dramatic quiff, leather collar around his neck, painfully thin, animated, contrasting with students dressed in T-shirts and jeans.

This course attracted students with middle-class, ambitious parents. Alan felt uncomfortable but, as a gifted designer, admired by staff and students, he was busy and successful.

At Christmas, the University contacted me. A student had returned in distress, needing to see a counsellor. It was Alan, white-faced, tearful, incoherent and shaking. Short of money he had not telephoned his parents, deciding to go home and surprise them, thumbing a lift on a nearby motorway.

His parents were surprised. He felt unwelcome. His bed had been sold and his young brother was sleeping in his former bedroom. His gear had been removed and stacked in the garden shed. Humiliated and distraught, Alan rushed away. After wandering the streets, he hitched a lift to London. His landlord invited him for Christmas dinner but Alan was too upset to accept. Fearing that he might become suicidal, his landlord drove him to the University for help.

I worked with Alan, initially to reconcile him to his parents' avoidant behaviour. Explaining their fear of a strange and different son so far removed from their own limited experience, split between feelings of inadequacy and abandonment, recognizing that Alan had grown further away from them. They were at a loss. Alan in turn experienced their coldness as punishment for the changes in him which were embarrassing the family. They had rejected him.

(Continued)

(Continued)

Alan admitted harbouring depressive feelings for many years. They had formulated during his time at secondary school, and he had considered the possibility of suicide. Attendant upon his depression was serious damage to his self-esteem, feelings of inequality, of uselessness, of never getting anywhere with his parents. Alan associated his 'differences' with fears of internal 'badness', of being unlovable and incapable of loving others.

Alan had anxiety about his homosexual identity, trying to cope with acute feelings of guilt, unable to communicate with anyone. Hiding his disturbance and shame about his parents' working-class background and his sexuality from his fellow students, with the inevitable effect of these pressures on relationships.

Adopting a 'couldn't care less' attitude to everyone only exacerbated his feelings of abandonment and isolation. The animal print jacket and leather collar disappeared, but the high hair style remained as a last line of defence.

In our mutual exploration of the conflicting processes within him, Alan could see that his subsequent behaviour made some kind of sense. There would always be the reality of his parents' poverty, a constant theme when assessing the outcome of our work together, and the responsibilities which lay ahead at his final graduation.

Alan grew attached to me, with an unconscious pressure for me to be there for him, to become more totally involved, not just in our weekly sessions. He needed someone to love him, hate him, reject him, punish him, take him home, fulfil all his needs for recognition, acknowledgement of his lonely existence and pain. Therapeutically, I persevered, leading Alan back to his mother and father, his mother who (whatever her later role in his life had been) had not abandoned him and had somehow been able to feed and physically care for him during his childhood and adolescence as best she could. Neither I, nor his parents, could fulfil his other needs. In leaving home, inevitably, separation had to occur. Perhaps his parents had felt a sense of relief to see him go but, in their confused and ambivalent way of understanding him, they had given up and were now in awe of his progress.

Alan found work in London. His parents were unable to attend his graduation. Alan stayed on with his former landlord, planning to travel to see his parents. He had saved money and intended to give it to his mother. He had survived and was starting to grow in real terms. We were beginning to move apart. His ability to earn his keep was sufficient to make him look forward to ending therapy in the right way. After going home Alan called, talking freely and at length about his parents. We both admitted that we were scared about what might have happened when he went back home, but I told him that I, at least, had considerable confidence that he was going to manage a lot better that he dared to think.

SUICIDE AND SELF-HARM

Suicide is a highly sensitive, controversial and stigmatizing issue, whether carried out, attempted or merely considered. The problem of suicide is enigmatic in many ways. Contrary to a still common belief, it is not dependent on a specific illness or mental state and it cuts across all diagnostic categories. The problem is complicated for the young adult because suicidal behaviour at this stage cannot be separated from the unique and challenging developmental processes of early adulthood and their tight connections with family dynamics and social context.

Although suicide is one of the foremost causes of death in young people (Gould et al., 2003), young people contemplating suicide do not usually seek help. Indeed, of young people aged between 10 and 19 who committed suicide between 1998 and 2003, only 14 per cent had been in touch with mental health services compared to 26 per cent of adults (Windfuhr et al., 2008). Furthermore, research data on suicide attempts may vary widely depending on how the information was obtained – from hospital out-patient departments, psychiatric hospitals and clinics or the Samaritans. In attempting to gain clarity, however, deliberate self-harm has been defined as 'intentional self-injury or self-poisoning, irrespective of type of motivation or degree of suicidal intent' (Hawton et al., 2003), and figures from the National Institute for Clinical Excellence (2002) suggest that rates of self-harm are considerably higher among young people, with approximately 25,000 young people admitted to hospital in the UK each year after deliberately harming themselves (Hawton et al., 2000).

We may feel so uneasy with the subject that we tend to deny, ignore and avoid confrontation. The violence and apparent irrationality of suicidal behaviours contribute to many of these observed individual or institutional defensive attitudes. In addition, the lack of specificity and poor predictive value of risk factors may be discouraging in clinical practice in spite of over 150,000 hospital attendances in Great Britain which relate to suicidal thoughts and behaviour (Winter, 2001). The same is true of the so-called warning clues, for example, failure in academic performance or obtaining a job and very often falling in or out of love. But suicide attempts are highly meaningful and are often dedicated symptoms of intense suffering. The acts appear to be a critical response to a usually long-standing series of unresolved overt or covert difficulties. One can only identify the presuicidal syndrome as a narrowing of personal capabilities and dynamic activities, the inhibition of aggression towards others and a turning of those feelings inwards, resulting in fantasies of death. The young adult recklessly driving a stolen car or experimenting with drugs is aware of death and destruction, often owing to 'bad/evil' feelings, including the power to hurt and destroy others and themselves: becoming more aware of the many ways in which other persons, even loved ones, have acted destructively towards them. What is worse, the realization comes that they may have done irrevocably hurtful things to parents, lovers, friends and rivals . . . but there is a positive aspect to this recognition of the capacity to be destructive.

By recognizing one's power to tear down things, you can begin to realize how truly powerful one can be in creating new and useful forms of life . . . powerful forces of destructiveness and of creativity coexist in the human soul and can be integrated in many ways, though never entirely (Levinson, 1980).

THE CAPACITY TO INVOLVE AND DEVELOP SOCIAL AND INTIMATE RELATIONSHIPS

Erikson (1980) put forward three adult identity phases: finding intimate relationships in early adulthood; establishing social links with different generations in middle adulthood; and engaging in a retrospective life review process in late adulthood. These were reflected by Kamptner (1989, 1995), who examined the material possessions most valued and treasured in these age groups. The young adults referred to the social significance that their cars, jewellery, music equipment, photographs and general memorabilia symbolized and the pleasures they provided. Changes occurred with age in the relevance of treasured possessions. Kamptner noted that the younger person's concern with functional items – status-orientated and reinforced by peer group fads and fashions – was gradually substituted for more personal items until in the 25 to 30 age group when it was replaced by items which indicated increasing concern with social networks and social history.

Obsession with style, with brand awareness, in young people is socially meaningful, and brands 'are often used as symbolic resources for the construction and maintenance of identity' (Dittmar, 2004), or may be seen as the defence mechanism of young people who feel powerless. Young people have wide choice in how to dress, what objects to have – choices which advertisers and manufacturers offer in abundance. Consumer choice has become a priority, offering a way of escape and a means of self-expression. We have a social fabric that is orientated towards social success, perhaps at the expense of our human need for love, respect and compassion. This may be a consequence of early life-histories of affectionless parenting, economic stress, past and present abuse and the rendering of young people into objects of glorification. However, dysfunctional communication can also occur in intact families where there is no history of abuse, neglect, violence or separation and it is not unusual to see young men and women who come into therapy in a state of being unable to conceptualize their affective state. Only later, in the course of therapy, do they recognize that in their family it was not possible to talk about feelings and interpersonal events and to understand them in a meaningful way.

The most important stage encountered in the developmental tasks of the young adult is that of establishing a workable and acceptable system of values and relationships, and this is by no means the prerogative of the most articulate and highly educated young people in our society. Young men and women who seek help from counselling show a genuine concern with moral issues, with questions of social justice, violence and discrimination. During the past 40 years, young people have indicated considerable concern, often at unconscious levels, with the threat of eventual annihilation. However, there is a real distinction between today's generation and that which preceded it. The focus of this concern in the twenty-first century has shifted to environmental relationship, possible pollution and degradation of 'space-ship Earth'. The awful predicament is the same, but the means to eliminate life are in the hands of man- and womankind. All periods involve change, but it is unquestionable that we have witnessed a culture of exceptionally rapid and complicated social change where society has manifested deep conflicts in its values and uncertainties in its attitudes to even the most fundamental aspects of human relationships. The basis of family life is itself subjected to reappraisal and criticism, and increased knowledge of the physical bases of bisexuality and androgyny is blurring what seemed to be clear-cut sexual distinctions.

The entry into young adulthood is marked by compromise. Compromise between what we think we might want and what our conscience allows us to live with. Earlier ways of feeling male or female are put under a new kind of stress. Previous experiences in childhood and adolescence of finding pleasure and feeling cared-for are put under pressure because of the presence of a sexually mature and developed body. It appears that society has tried to avoid a basic clarification. We are all seemingly aware of the differences between a male and female, and generally we can agree about the concepts of masculinity and femininity, but we have made the mistake of assuming that maleness signifies masculinity, whilst womanliness is construed as femininity. However, if people appear to conform to these expectations, they may well have been trained to do so. Gender schema theory attempts to explain how these misconceptions can occur. Gender schema processing suggests that there is a readiness on the part of children to encode and organize information according to how culture defines sex roles. For example, a child may observe that boys are usually described as 'strong' or 'brave', whereas girls are more usually described as 'nice' or 'sweet'.

Cultural notions of gender, therefore, become adopted via relationship with family, peer group and media (Leaper and Friedman, 2007). The child learns not only that the sexes differ, but more importantly that certain attributes are associated more with one sex than the other. 'The extreme degree in which our society classified behaviour and objects into masculine versus feminine only intensified the development of a gender scheme' (Basow, 1992).

The emphasis placed on only one side of our sexual make-up costs us dear. The young adult has to face up to this deficiency. In regarding himself as 'masculine', the young man has to conceptualize himself as being tough, an achiever, powerful and potent, as opposed to the feminine 'touchy-feely' orientation. The notion of androgyny still remains controversial since it was introduced into psychological literature in the 1960s. Basically, the word 'androgynous' is just a convenient way of defining those who are able to show a combination of high scores on both masculinity and femininity scales. Men who score high on the masculinity scale may well be classified as having higher self-esteem, higher achievement needs, to be dominant and aggressive. Femininity scales are related to differing behaviour – the ability to show empathy, social skills, sensitivity to other people's feelings. The androgynous person (by definition) has both sets of skills. This combination has shown itself to be most advantageous in the forming of long-standing relationships. In one set of studies, male and female subjects with various combinations of masculinity and femininity scores met each other in a waiting room. The results may contradict some common assumptions. The lowest level of interaction and enjoyment was found among the pairs sex-typed as high in masculinity and femininity. In contrast, when both persons were androgynous, levels of interaction and mutual enjoyment were high (Ickes and Barnes, 1987–88).

Men and women have been socialized to behave in sexist ways and they have difficulty in developing and integrating new roles that are compatible with non-sexist behaviour. Sex role strain (a major presenting problem) is the result of the rigid gender roles which restrict people's ability to actualize their human potential. Women are more likely to experience role conflict. They have limitations placed on them because of the pervasive ideas linked with the feminine sex role in our society – polarized between the page three 'bimbo', the mother of children or the high-powered executive complete with briefcase. Young men face differing sexual conflicts. Being a 'man' creates oppressive effects. Masculine mystique still implies that femininity is inferior to masculinity as a gender orientation.

Recent work has explored the role of social networking sites such as Facebook in the co-construction of social and gender identity. Facebook, MySpace and other social networking sites are extensively used by young adults, comScore (2008) suggesting that more than ten million emerging adults between 18 and 24 visit MySpace every month. More than half of MySpace visitors are now age 35 and older as the site's demographic composition continues to shift. Findings by Manago et al. suggest that here, too, 'offline gender scripts and roles guide expectations for appropriate behavior online' (2008).

CONCLUSION

The intention in this chapter has been to state my belief that the outcome of early childhood development and of its distortions becomes pronounced by the end of the period designated as young adulthood. In the past there will have been many occasions when psychological distress was allowed to accumulate without too much notice or concern, leaving the young man or woman to inherit severe distortions of their lives at best, with mental illness at worst. In working with the young adult we are made aware of a fundamental tension. On the one hand, many need not have reached the point of despair or illness that brings them to the therapist. Difference in their lives could well have been made earlier if they had been taken seriously and if their feelings had not been dismissed as a 'passing phase'. On the other hand, there is a strong desire not to categorize young adults with stigmatizing labels. The term 'pathologization of everyday life' is used by personal construct psychologists Burr and Butt, and they offer the following ways of resisting such categorizations:

- Avoiding traps for the oppression of clients as victims by a reconsideration of the therapist's stance as 'expert'.
- Recognition that human experience is diverse.
- Offering liberating ways of helping people construe their experience which do not carry a label.
- Seeing the role of language as more constructive than just a communication tool.
- Considering that the counselling ways of depicting causation when it comes to matters such as illness are limited because we participate in wider constructions of who we are.
- We should attempt to be experimental in how we depict histories. (Burr and Butt, 2000)

They add that psychologists need to know how to be enabling in helping clients 'to produce self-narratives which allow them to live at peace with themselves' (Burr and Butt, 2000). Depression and mental suffering are problems not only for individuals but also for groups and societies. It is not disputed that suffering sometimes involves biology or that there are individual variations and thresholds for becoming depressed, or that some depressions can be genetically loaded. What this chapter has tried to articulate is that the problems of the young adult are associated with roles and relationships, with self-organization and self-value. Our problem with young adults is often demoralization and a sense of hopelessness. Primary ingredients of these common, non-specific, factors is to respond with understanding, respect, interest, encouragement, acceptance, forgiveness – in short, the kinds of human qualities that since times immemorial have been considered to facilitate the human spirit.

REFERENCES

Andrews, B. and Wilding, J.M. (2004) 'The relation of depression and anxiety to life-stress and achievement in students', *British Journal of Psychology*, 95 (4): 509–521.

Apter, T. (2002) *The Myth of Maturity*. London: Norton.

Arnett, J.J. (2004) *Emerging Adulthood: The Winding Road from Late Teens through the Twenties*. Oxford: Oxford University Press.

Basow, S.A. (1992) *Gender Stereotypes and Roles*. Pacific Grove, CA: Brooks Cole.

Bowlby, J. (1979) 'Self-reliance and conditions that promote it', in J. Bowlby, *The Making and Breaking of Affectional Bonds*. London: Tavistock.

Burr, V. and Butt, T. (2000) 'Psychological distress and modern thought', in Dwight Fee (ed.), *Pathology and the Postmodern: Mental Illness as Discourse and Experience*. London: Sage.

comScore (2006) comScore analysis press release available at www.comscore.com/press/release.asp?press=1019, accessed 25/6/08.

Costa, P. and McCrae, R. (2005) *Personality in Adulthood,* 2nd edn. New York: Guilford Press.

Di Caccavo, A. (2006) 'Working with parentification: Implications for clients and couselling psychologists', *Psychology and Psychotherapy, Theory, Research and Practice*, 79: 469–478.

Dittmar, H. (2004) 'Are you what you have?', *The Psychologist*, 17 (4): 206–210.

Erikson, E.H. (1980) *Identity and the Life Cycle: A Reissue*. New York: Norton.

Gould, M., Greenberg, T., Velting, D. and Shaffer, D. (2003) 'Youth suicide risk and preventative interventions: A review of the past ten years', *Journal of the American Academy of Child and Adolescent Psychiatry*, 42: 386–405.

Haley, J. (1997) *Leaving Home: Therapy of Disturbed People*, 2nd edn. London: Routledge.

Hawton, K., Fagg J., Simkin, S., Bale, E. and Bond, A. (2000) 'Deliberate self-harm in adolescents in Oxford, 1985–1995, *Journal of Adolescence*, 23 (1): 47–55.

Hawton, K., Harriss, L., Hall, S., Simkin, S., Bale, E. and Bond, A. (2003) 'Deliberate self-harm in Oxford, 1990–2000: A time of change in patient characteristics', *Psychological Medicine*, 33: 987–96.

Home Office Report (2003) *Hidden Harm*. Available at http://drugs.homeoffice.gov.uk/publication-search/acmd/hidden-harm, accessed 12/6/09.

Ickes, W. and Barnes, R.D. (1987–88) 'The role of sex and self-monitoring in unstructured dyadic interactions', *Journal of Personality and Social Psychology*, 35: 315–30.

Kagitcibasi, C. (2005) 'Autonomy and relatedness in cultural context: Implications for self and family', *Journal of Cross-Cultural Psychology*, 36: 403.

Kamptner, N.L. (1989) 'Personal possessions and their meanings in childhood, adolescence and old age', in S. Spacapan and S. Oskamp (eds), *The Social Psychology of Aging*. London: Sage.

Kamptner, N.L (1995) 'Treasured possessions and their meanings in adolescent males and females', *Adolescence*, 30 (118): 301.

Kelly, G.A. (1955). *The Psychology of Personal Constructs*. New York: Norton.

Leaper, C. and Friedman, C. (2007) 'The socialization of gender', in J.E. Grusec and P.D. Hastings (eds), *Handbook of Socialization: Theory and Research*. New York: Guilford. pp. 561–587.

Levinson, D.J. (1980) 'Towards a conception of the adult life course', in N.J. Smelser and E.H. Erikson (eds), *Themes of Work and Love in Adulthood*. Cambridge, MA: Harvard University Press.

Manago, A., Graham, B., Greenfield, P. and Salimkhan, G. (2008) 'Self-presentation and gender on MySpace', *Journal of Applied Developmental Psychology*, 29 (6): 446–458.

National Institute for Clinical Excellence (2002) *Self-harm Scope Document*. London: NICE.

Office of National Statistics (2005) *General Household Survey*. London: Office of National Statistics.

Orbach, G., Lindsay, S. and Grey, S. (2007) 'A randomised placebo-controlled trial of a self-help Internet-based intervention for test anxiety', *Behaviour Research and Therapy*, 45: 483–496.

Rethink (2007) 'Schizophrenia'. Available at www.rethink.org/about_mental_illness/mental_illnesses_and_disorders/schizophrenia/index.html, accessed 12/6/09.

Schoon, I. and Bartley, M. (2008) 'The role of human capability and resilience', *The Psychologist*, 21 (1): 74.

Sugarman, L. (2004) *Counselling and the Life Course*. London: Sage.

Summerfield, C. and Babb, P. (2004) *Social Trends in Teenage Pregnancy and Parenthood*. London: Office of National Statistics. Table 34.

Super, D.E. (1990) 'A life-span, life-space approach to career development', in D. Brown, I. Brookes and Associates (eds), *Career Choice and Development*. San Francisco, CA: Jossey-Bass.

Windfuhr, K., While, D., Hunt, I., Turnbull, P., Lowe, R., Burns, J., Swinson, N., Shaw, J., Appleby, L., Kapur, N. and the National Confidential Inquiry into Suicide and Homicide by People with Mental Illness (2008) 'Suicide in juveniles and adolescents in the United Kingdom', *Journal of Child Psychology and Psychiatry*, 49 (11): 1157–1167.

Winter, David (2001) 'Self-harm and Reconstruction'. Paper presented at the BPS Centennial Conference, Glasgow, 29–31 March 2001.

17

WORKING WITH FAMILIES

Katrina Alilovic and Sarah Yassine

Working therapeutically with more than one member of a family presents both challenges and opportunities for counselling psychologists (Friedlander et al., 2006). This work is subsumed under the categories of couples (or marital) and family therapy, and this can have the unfortunate side-effect of restricting work of this kind to those who have undertaken specialist training such as family or systemic practitioners (Berman et al., 2006). Counselling psychology training places importance on the context of the individual and as such forms a strong base for practitioners to incorporate work with families.

Families exert significant influence on the health of individuals and thus warrant attention as a unit by our profession more broadly (Heru and Drury, 2006). Our aim in this chapter is to explore some of the dynamics, challenges and opportunities a counselling psychologist might encounter when they are involved in work with families. This chapter will outline principles central to working with families from a 'common factors' perspective and, in particular, provide information regarding the assessment phase and how to use genograms to support the work. A case study which focuses on a bereaved family is utilized to illustrate the theoretical aspects of working with a family without adhering to a specific model of family therapy.

INDIVIDUAL AND SYSTEMIC MODALITIES

The training of all BPS accredited counselling psychology programmes in the UK focuses on supporting practitioners to develop specialist skills in working with individuals with some input in other modalities (for example, groups, couples and families, and so on) (BPS, 2008). Individual courses will decide exactly what emphasis to give the other modalities, but this does not appear to have had the effect of encouraging significant numbers of counselling psychologists to work in modalities other than individual work. This is not to say that the systemic approach is not utilized. The value of systemic concepts to individual work has been elucidated in the literature (Bor and Legg, 2003; Street, 2003). In fact, it appears that it is not uncommon for practitioners to apply systemic theory to their practice. Athanasiades (2008) has written on how particular family therapy constructs can be used to positive effect in psychotherapeutic work with individuals. The ideas outlined in this work offer counselling psychologists practical ways of introducing the principles of systemic therapy into therapeutic work with individuals and builds on the work of others who have highlighted the value of systemic theory to the practice of individual therapy (Hedges, 2005; McGoldrick and Carter, 2001). However, these suggestions reside with a framework which maintains individual work as the primary focus of practitioners.

It is the authors' experience that relational issues provide the impetus for the majority of people who seek the services of counselling psychologists. It is also our experience that, in the main, counselling psychologists tend to work with these issues primarily at an individual level. The subjective experience of the authors is validated in the literature, which reiterates that the individual focus has characterized the fields of psychology and psychotherapy and continues to dominate the contemporary field (Anderson, 2005; Hedges, 2005). This is despite evidence supporting the use of alternate approaches such as family and group work with certain presenting issues and client groups (for example, Hubble et al., 1999; Roth and Fonagy, 2005).

This is not highlighted as a weakness as such but to draw attention to the fact that counselling psychologists are well situated to engage with the complexity associated with working alongside families. Kaslow et al. write that 'systemic epistemology entails a paradigm shift towards conceptualizing human behaviour in a fashion that integrates intraindividual, interpersonal, environmental and macrosystemic elements' (2005: 339). When Bor and Legg comment upon the potency of the systemic approaches in stating 'the strength of the systemic … approaches is that they stand in direct opposition to deficit models, focusing on creativity and resourcefulness of clients in the face of problems, rather than their limitations' (2003: 274), they could have been making reference to the values and philosophical underpinnings of counselling psychology which critique the biomedical approach and instead advocate a non-pathologizing approach (Strawbridge and Woolfe, 2003). The case is strong for the link between counselling psychology and systemic practice.

The reasons why counselling psychologists tend to work predominantly with individuals are many and varied. In part, this may be due to the long tradition of intervention at an intrapersonal level in the fields of psychiatry and psychotherapy (McLeod, 1998). It is helpful to know something about our own experience of our early work with families.

CASE STUDY: KATRINA'S EXPERIENCE

When I first learnt that I had been successful in securing a position with a service for children and families, my first response was to experience anxiety related to worries about intervening in the realm of the family and the complex dynamics that occur in groups. I had not undertaken specialized training in this field yet; the decision to employ me was made on the basis of existing skills and experience and that learning could and would occur 'on the job'. A quote by Dallos and Draper articulates my experience, '… the experience of working with a family embraces a variety of expectations and feelings ranging from apprehension to excitement, competence and impotence at the prospect of being able to assist with what at times appear to be insurmountable mountains of distress' (2005: 4). Upon commencing the work, I found myself experiencing a heightened sense of incompetence as the on-the-job learning exposed me to numerous challenges outside the range of my existing experience and my felt range of competence. Eventually the on-the-job training supported me to feel confident about applying what I already knew to this new work with children and their families. However, on reflection I know I did not consider my work as 'family therapy' or 'systemic therapy'. Interestingly, my experience appears to be mirrored by others who work therapeutically with families (Crago, 2006).

CASE STUDY: SARAH'S EXPERIENCE

After qualifying to work as a psychologist, I was employed by an open-access service that provided free and confidential counselling. My role within this position was to provide counselling to children, young people and adults. My interests were primarily with work with children, and consequently the majority of my case-load were children and young people. Parents referred their children for a range of reasons including anxiety, separation and divorce, depression, bullying, suspected or known sexual abuse, domestic violence or anger.

Since working in my current position in the bereavement field, I often think about the children that I worked with and how differently I would have done things based on my experience of working with families over the past years. More specifically, I wonder how my interventions with children and young people might have been more efficient and effective had I felt more confident to invite family members to be involved in one way or another.

(Continued)

(Continued)

Choosing not to involve the family in the past was, I genuinely believe, a decision based upon misinterpreting the term 'child-focused' (Wilson, 1998). I felt that to involve the child's family would be disrespectful to him or her and deny them the right to privacy and confidentiality. In fact, what I have learnt is that involving the family in a way that is respectful to the child can often mean empowering the family to support and nurture that child in his or her everyday life and therefore enhance therapeutic gains.

An additional and important reason to consider when reflecting upon the predominance of individual work is how families themselves formulate the reason(s) for the difficulties they experience (Byng-Hall, 2000). When a family member contacts a service or individual practitioner, one individual within the family is often identified as the one with the problem and the cause of the distress experience within the family. The family will have developed their own hypothesis, and this can be difficult for practitioners to reframe. As Bor and Legg state, 'it would be naive to believe that the individuals who have been referred are always the one with the problem' (2003: 265). Sometimes families are not open to considering family work, leaving practitioners in a position to work with an individual, without the option of exploring *with* the family *how* the family might be involved in maintaining the problem. Downey highlights this issue when stating that individual therapy 'might be the only therapeutic option available as the family are unable or unwilling to define the difficulty as a family … problem' (2003: 329). The following brief case example illustrates this occurrence and highlights a way of working individually that also makes room for involvement of a key family member. The authors invite readers to reflect on how they might begin to involve family members in their practice with individuals.

CASE STUDY: CERYS

Cerys (12) was referred by her mother as she was being bullied at school by a group of girls in the same class. After speaking with both Cerys and her mum individually and together, it became apparent that Cerys' mum was contributing unwittingly to the maintenance of Cerys' difficulties. In fact, it was suggested that mum might benefit from individual counselling. Mum had been bullied as a child and was re-experiencing difficult thoughts and feelings in response to Cerys' situation. Cerys had already been moved to a new school once and it seemed that Mum was leaning towards that option again. Unfortunately, Mum was unwilling to engage in counselling for herself, insisting that the issues lie with Cerys. The work continued with Cerys and she was supported to deal more effectively with the girls in her class and with her emotional and behavioural responses. Mum's choice not to have individual counselling was respected and instead she was included by inviting her in at the end of each session. Cerys was supported to inform her mum of what she was thinking and feeling, how she would like things to be different and specifically how she felt her mum could best support her. Cerys was able to tell her mum that she would like to stay at this school and to talk about her feelings. Mum was supported to hear from her daughter and respond empathically while managing her own anxiety.

GETTING TO GRIPS WITH 'FAMILY THERAPY'

Family therapy has a fascinating history spanning over 50 years and which consists of a melting pot of ideas, individuals and different locations in time (Gurman and Knisker, 1981, 1999). Unfortunately, the rich field of what is referred to as 'family therapy' is somewhat difficult to navigate, and its complexity may deter many practitioners. The label of 'family therapy' and the variety of approaches encompassed within the broad umbrella term of 'family therapy' may be off-putting or at worst intimidating to both new and experienced counselling psychologists. Asen (2002) suggests that the term 'family therapy' is misleading and prefers instead to use the term 'systemic therapy'. This assertion is based on the author's experience that it avoids the blame connotations that can be experienced by families when the term 'family therapy' is used and more accurately involves the wider context in which the family are situated.

MODELS/APPROACHES TO FAMILY WORK

Subsumed within the generic term 'family therapy' are a number of approaches which adhere to systemic principles. The approaches under the banner of family therapy include (but are not limited to) strategic, structural, Milan, post-Milan, feminist, Bowenian (also known as transgenerational family therapy), narrative, solution-focused and social-constructionist. It is easy to see why confusion can arise, given the plethora of approaches and resulting differences in emphasis. It has not been uncommon in researching this chapter to come across experts in the field acknowledging the complexity involved in gaining a sense of the overall field of family therapy. Over 25 years ago in the ground-breaking book *Handbook of Family Therapy* (Gurman and Knisker, 1981), the 'mystique' and 'muddle' are referred to in relation to the plethora of different viewpoints. This experience seems to have changed little over the past 25 years as British family therapists continue to document similar experiences (for example, Dallos and Draper, 2005) and are sympathetic to the difficulties entailed in trying to make sense of the various schools of family therapy.

Some of the confusion inherent in attempting to understand 'what is family therapy' is perpetuated by a focus on the history of the development of family therapy approaches in training programmes (Dallos and Draper, 2005). The current chapter aims to offer counselling psychologists a way of engaging with work with couples and families without necessarily having to serve an apprenticeship which involves learning the history of family therapy. The current authors toyed with the idea of bucking the paradigm by not including reference to history as a way of supporting the position asserted by, among others, Crago (2006) which focuses on the utility of common factors when working with families. However, it was decided that history has an important place, and therefore a summary is offered. Readers are invited to peruse the history while holding the focus on common factors.

The information presented in Table 17.1 provides a rudimentary outline of the systemic approaches to working with families and individuals. It is intended to contextualize a common factors approach to work with families and support practitioners to have an understanding of the ground and different levels of context in which we operate.

COMMON FACTORS APPROACH

A culture of convergence has been developing within the field of family therapy and is supported by research which purports that despite the assertions of difference between theories and models the actual practice of family therapists (from different schools) was more similar than not (Friedlander et al., 1987; Lebow, 1997; Sprenkle et al., 1999).

Reference to common factors by those who offer a more moderate view avoids the contention that all approaches are not of equal value and instead asserts that the differences in treatment outcomes (change) between effective psychotherapy approaches are relatively minor (Sprenkle and Blow, 1994). The common factors are those variables that are not specific to any one therapeutic approach and include factors such as client, therapist, relationship and expectancy variables.

FAMILY-SENSITIVE PRACTICE

'Family-sensitive practice' is an approach to working with families developed and used by the Bouverie Centre (Victoria, Australia) and fits alongside a common factors approach as opposed to being model-specific. Further information is available from the website

TABLE 17.1   SUMMARY OF APPROACHES TO FAMILY THERAPY

	Strategic	Transgenerational	Structural	Milan	Social-constructionism	Solution-focused
Major proponents	Hayley Madanes	Bowen Boszormenyi-Nagy	Minuchin	Palazzoli Cecchin	Cecchin Boscolo Anderson Goolishian	De Shazer
Central focus	Blend of structural and strategic (both confused in structure and in their patterns of interaction).	Patterns that develop in families in order to defuse anxiety.	The work is in the here-and-now, with change being brought about by the therapist changing sequences of interaction ('re-structuring') in the therapy room.	The therapist is interested in the rule-maintaining characteristics of communication and behaviours, and assume that the way to eliminate a symptom is to change the rules.	The therapist is interested in the language (not interactional patterns) used by the family as the difficulties experienced are seen to be constructed in and by the language system.	Solution-focused therapy emphasizes solutions over problems.
Key concepts	The goal of the strategic schools is to disrupt the self-reinforcing cycles that act to maintain the symptom and to introduce the conditions for more appropriate transactional patterns to develop.	The main goal is to reduce chronic anxiety by (1) facilitating awareness of how the emotional systems function; and (2) increasing levels of differentiation so that the focus is on making changes for oneself rather than on trying to change others.	Subsystems, hierarchy, boundaries, alliances and coalitions. Therapist is directive. Focus is not on feelings, beliefs or the past.	Hypothesizing, neutrality, positive connotation, paradox and counter-paradox, interventive questioning and the use of reflecting teams.	Therapist is not 'the expert' and adopts a 'not knowing' stance. Reflecting team conversations. Asking questions to develop expanded or alternative understanding. Facilitation of new language system.	1. If it ain't broke, don't fix it. 2. Once you know what works, do more of it. 3. If it doesn't work, don't do it again, do something different.

Source: Adapted from Carr, 2006

www.latrobe.edu.au/bouverie/mentalhealth/seven_principles.html. The introduction of yet another encompassing term such as 'family-sensitive practice' might elicit a groan of 'not another approach' or 'not another hybrid'. However, we would ask that you suspend your healthy cynicism for a brief while in order to consider how this might increase accessibility of services to individuals and families as a direct result of increasing confidence among practitioners to work alongside families without being aligned with a particular school of family therapy. It is not the intention of the authors to imply that specialist training in family therapy is not appropriate or necessary by focusing on the common factors approach and 'family-sensitive practice'. Rather, it is our intention to broaden the scope of counselling psychologists and perhaps encourage the profession to adopt a view that working with families is not synonymous with 'family-therapy' and an absolute requirement to complete an additional specialist training.

PRINCIPLES OF FAMILY-SENSITIVE PRACTICE

While an account of principles underpinning a particular approach does not give practitioners a prescribed way of working, it does, nevertheless, provide important information that informs the foundations of practice. The following seven principles, developed by the Bouverie Centre, reference the relationship between practitioners and families:

1. *Family and 'system' inclusive*: The aim is to involve as many relevant family members as possible. This may not always be possible, but should not exclude willing members of the family from receiving support. Flexibility in service delivery is key in attempting to engage family members in some way or another. For example, making contact via a letter or telephone conversation to explain what support is being offered, the possible benefits of their attendance and inviting them to join.
2. *Respect*: All members of a family deserve to receive a respectful service that acknowledges differences in culture, ethnicity, gender or socio-economic status. When working with a family, practitioners need to be respectful of individual differences within that family (for example, availability or expertise) as well as the core values, beliefs and routines a family might adhere to as a whole. An appreciation of the uniqueness that each family brings should underpin the practitioner's framework.
3. *Openness and honesty*: Transparent and consistent guidelines regarding privacy and confidentiality (and when this might need to be broken) should be outlined clearly at the beginning of any work with families. Such guidelines are important in developing trust and a sense of safety not only in the counselling room but also between family members.
4. *Information*: All family members should be given clear and coherent information about the service that is being offered, including options, consent, boundaries and where possible evidence for and against the potential benefits of the service provided. Developing a contract with the family prior to engaging in therapeutic work is one way of giving family members the opportunity to voice what it is that they need to feel safe and respected.

5. *Collaboration*: Working together and in co-operation with families towards a common goal underpins a collaborative approach which entails sharing knowledge, learning and building consensus. The practitioner facilitates the involvement of all members of the family on the premise that it is in pooling resources and stimulating reflexivity that effective outcomes will be developed. It is the practitioner's responsibility to attend to the power differentials so that there is consistency within the espoused approach and the actual behaviour.

6. *Empowerment*: One aim of any therapeutic relationship should be to empower the individual to make his or her own decisions and choices or be involved in the decision-making process about issues they are affected by. Differences in developmental, physical and intellectual capabilities between family members should be considered.

7. *Understanding subjective experiences*: Some families may view counselling as a negative experience and their referral to a service may have been unpleasant. Some may feel embarrassed or stigmatized at being referred to a therapeutic service and therefore may be reluctant to engage. The clinician should have an appreciation of the experience of families in coming to receive a clinical service. This may also serve as an important topic to discuss therapeutically.

The principles outlined above are consistent with approaches to family therapy, which place at their centre the client's constructions of their own meaning. This is a clear departure from the earlier schools of family therapy which advocated a structural and more directive approach to the interventions. However, is it possible that there remains a place within the newer approaches to family therapy for transmission to families of the accumulated knowledge of family practitioners? The postmodern approaches have been subject to some criticism which centres upon the possible 'withholding' of crucial information for families who are looking for signposting. It is important that practitioners working therapeutically with families find ways to communicate this knowledge without sacrificing the commitment to client-led work (Byng-Hall, 2000). However, proponents of this approach have countered with the assertion that the 'not-knowing' stance has been misinterpreted by some and that it was never intended as a tool of withholding but rather to characterize a stance which supports families to harness their own experience and consider a range of possibilities (Cottrell and Boston, 2002).

The philosophy supporting family-sensitive practice is consistent with the philosophical approach of counselling psychology that situates relational aspects as central (Strawbridge and Woolfe, 2003). Relational aspects could include the relationship between client and therapist and the client and their social and environmental contexts. As Hage states, 'It is the social developmental, contextual perspective … that we must embrace if we are to remain true to our roots and unique identity as counselling psychologists' (2003: 561). It is also suggested that practitioners need to find ways to side-step the ever-present pressure to practice in prescribed ways; that there is a preferred, optimal way of doing things and that this way should be adhered to without straying. While the value of evidence to support our practice is undisputed, the trend towards manualized therapy and quantifiable outcomes rather than a focus on the quality of the experience brings with it a danger of developing an approach that is impersonal and technically focused (Wampold, 2001). A move towards family-sensitive practice recognizes the importance of the contribution of the quality of the therapeutic relationship along with the skills and knowledge we have acquired, in creating a therapeutic experience for families that responds to their individual needs. Gianakis and Carey (2008) also highlight their observation that the role of the client tends to be overlooked in research which focuses on common factors in favour of therapist variables. It is the authors' view that the family-sensitive approach firmly prizes the role of the client(s) in achieving change and is consistent with Tallman and Bohart who conclude on the basis of their review of research evidence that 'the primary agent of change … is the client' (1999: 98).

An approach that is based on common features across the variety of systemic approaches means that, as practitioners, we can focus on the family and the work to be done. As a result, we can leave behind the differences in terminology and therapeutic emphasis. The shift is away from adhering to a particular school or approach and instead towards finding a way through the variety of 'schools' to devise an approach that is integrative. This means that the focus is not on getting the terminology to marry up with the right 'school' but freedom to adapt approaches to suit the families who present requesting our assistance. Families, we suspect, are not concerned that we adopt a purist approach, but they do want reassurance that the interventions will ease their distress. However, Smith and Southern (2005) draw attention to the confusion that has developed as a result of the variety of 'new' integrative approaches to family therapy which have sprung from a growing dissatisfaction with the 'schools' approach to family therapy.

ASSESSMENT ISSUES

The assessment stage of contact with an individual or family is characterized by the collection of a great deal of information. The delineation of assessment followed by appropriate interventions can be somewhat misleading, as a sound assessment provides a means of conceptualizing and guiding the work and is an intervention in and of itself (Bor and Legg, 2003; Deacon and Piercy, 2001). McPhatter (1991) suggests the following information is collected as part of a thorough family assessment:

- the problem (history, definitions, intensity across time, past solutions, and clients' motivation to solve the problem)
- family organization (membership, family history, power and hierarchy, socioeconomic status, cultural influences)
- family functioning (life-cycle issues, roles, rules, communication, problem-resolution skills, goals)

- family strengths and resources
- goals for therapy and change.

USING GENOGRAMS

An integral part of the assessment process can be realized through the construction of a genogram. The genogram is a tool for practitioners to use with families that fits within a relational and constructionist assessment framework instead of utilizing individual diagnostics (Iversen et al., 2005). A genogram is also referred to as a 'family tree'. In fact, the term 'family tree' is preferable as a way of talking about this important clinical tool to individuals and families. Using a term which is more accessible reduces the possibility of alienating the family from the process of constructing the diagram. Through the use of a genogram, 'therapists simultaneously learn about and intervene in families, empower the family, stimulate their involvement, level the therapist–client hierarchy through a more collaborative relationship, and make the process interactively enjoyable' (Deacon and Piercy, 2001: 355).

A genogram is a clinical tool used to support the assessment process to ensure that the support offered most closely matches what the family needs. It is a pictorial representation, using symbols and simple notations, of people, relationships, life-cycle events and patterns occurring in a family. It could be referred to as a system of shorthand for clinical purposes. A genogram can be as simple or as complex as is required by the setting and the purpose of the therapeutic situation. However, the genogram is not purely a tool for finding out and collecting information. It is a tool that permits practitioner and family to work collaboratively and explore together how family members understand their unit and to envision new and different possibilities. Iversen et al. suggest that the use of the genogram can fit neatly within a constructionist perspective as it 'invites the practitioner to question, displace and/or eschew the traditional position of authoritative voice in favour of a dialogic and collaborative orientation' (2005: 699).

How information is retrieved utilizing a genogram requires as much sensitivity as is required in any therapeutic assessment. The genogram can be a powerful tool which informs the focus of questions that may not have been pursued without the explicit task of constructing a genogram. As a result, information may be elicited which the client may not have been prepared for. The pacing of the assessment is an important consideration. When the genogram is constructed within the context of couple or family work, questions may be asked which prompt reluctance in answering or vague responses. This may be an indication that there is information that is not openly known within the couple or family unit. The practitioner will need to decide which lines of enquiry are pursued in the process of constructing a genogram and which areas are left for further investigation at a later point in the therapeutic process.

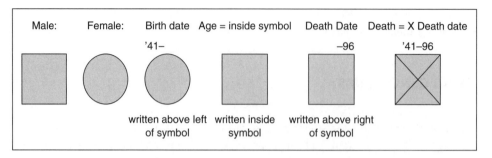

FIGURE 17.1 SYMBOLS TO DENOTE SEX AND SYSTEM TO RECORD BIOGRAPHICAL INFORMATION

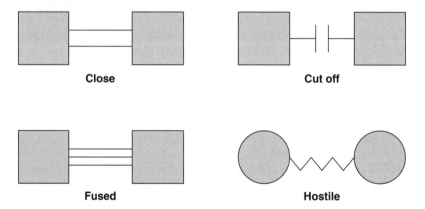

FIGURE 17.2 SYMBOLS DENOTING RELATIONAL PATTERNS BETWEEN PEOPLE

CONSTRUCTING A GENOGRAM

The process of constructing a genogram is supported by utilizing an established system rather than developing one's own system. However, practitioners are known to develop their own adaptations rather than conforming to a standard set of symbols. As long as the practitioner is able to remember the meaning of symbols and retain the integrity of the information, this does not tend to lead to difficulties. However, the adoption of a system that is uniformly utilized across practitioners is the ideal, as it assists in the process of communicating with other practitioners. Standardized symbols also support the process of research. If you decide that the construction of a genogram is of value, then your attention will need to turn to the practical issues of how to introduce it and how to manage the process of collecting information and recording it. Detailed practical guidance in using genograms in therapeutic work can be found in McGoldrick et al. (1999). A selection of symbols are presented in Figures 17.1 and 17.2.

REFLECTION POINT

Genograms are a most useful assessment and therapeutic tool for practitioners to utilize. However, their utility is hampered without sufficient experience or training. One way of familiarizing yourself with genograms is for practitioners to do their own genogram. It is most helpful if you enlist the support of a friend or colleague so you can experience some of what it feels like to be guided through the process of creating a pictorial representation of several generations of your family. Not only will you gain insight into the actual experience, but the activity will possibly generate enhanced self-knowledge that will also be beneficial in terms of strengthening your capacity to work alongside families. (Kaslow et al., 2005)

CASE STUDY

The following case study will be utilized to illustrate how using a genogram can assist practitioners in their work and one way for managing the tension between focusing on the individual and the family. In this example, a mother makes contact requesting individual support for her daughter following the father's death through suicide. The mother's approach to resolving the issues was to identify her daughter's behaviour as the cause of the family's current distress. It followed for her that if Kirsty had individual counselling she would learn how to deal more effectively with her emotions and the problems experienced in the family would be resolved. The practitioner who took the call from Pamela had a different way of conceptualizing the distress and approached the conversation with Pamela as an opportunity to suggest the possibility to working together as a family and to begin introducing the idea that the family might benefit from being supported together. The practitioner's thinking was influenced by her knowledge about the impact of a death on a family and the specific responses that can follow a death through suicide.

CASE STUDY: KIRSTY

Reason for referral

In May 2006, Pamela's husband Graham took his own life as a result of a drug over-dose. Their relationship had become increasingly difficult over the years and several

(Continued)

(Continued)

days before his death Pamela had told Graham that she wanted to separate. Graham's death came as a complete shock to Pamela and her two children, Kirsty (14) and Matthew (16).

Background information

Pamela was prompted to seek counselling for Kirsty after 'coming across' an email in which Kirsty had told a friend that she was 'sick of her life'. Pamela had confronted Kirsty who apparently 'flew off the handle', and told Pamela that she 'hated' her and wanted her to keep out of her life.

Pamela was very hurt by Kirsty's comments because she had always believed them to have a very close relationship, even describing Kirsty as her 'confidante' when times were difficult between her and Graham. She has always treated Kirsty as an 'adult' and since Graham's death lets her 'get away with much more than any of her other friends', including being allowed to drink and smoke – something Graham would have never allowed.

Pamela feels that she has done 'everything she can' and believes Kirsty needs to 'speak to a professional' about controlling her anger. When asked about Matthew, Pamela said that she had no concerns for him, describing him as a 'sweetheart' and 'man of the house'.

Through a process of assessment, which involved helping the family construct a family genogram, and both family and individual interventions, the family were supported to talk more openly about Graham's death. Matthew decided not to participate fully in the first meeting but was within hearing distance of the meeting. He was offered an individual meeting with one of the male practitioners and took this up. Later he did become involved in the group meetings. Although the children were both teenagers they had not been given detailed information about their Dad's death and had significant gaps in their knowledge. For Kirsty it proved important that she was able to ask her Mum about what happened and to talk about the misunderstandings that had developed. Kirsty had had an argument with her Dad just days prior to his death and was struggling with feeling she had caused her father to feel unloved. It also transpired that Matthew was worried about his Mum but also struggling with the weight of responsibility he now felt was on him. It was difficult for him to have Mum rely on him less, but in other ways it provided him with the freedom he needed to engage in other pursuits. The practitioner supported the family to communicate more openly about their thoughts and feelings and encouraged them to engage in a process of reorganizing themselves as a unit without Graham in their lives.

The genogram in Figure 17.3 illustrates the information that was gathered in the first meeting with the family. Kirsty and Pamela provided the most detail, with Matthew inputting from the sidelines occasionally. You are invited to use the information in Figures 17.1 and 17.2 to understand the information collected from the family in the assessment session.

GENOGRAM

The information presented in the case study outlines some of Pamela's concerns and gives us some idea of how Kirsty has been behaving. Naturally, we already begin to make assumptions about the reasons for Kirsty's behaviour. Taking an intrapersonal approach, we may assume that:

- Kirsty has difficulty controlling her anger
- Kirsty is grieving the death of her father
- Kirsty is abusing alcohol and possibly other drugs as well
- Kirsty is a 'typical' teenager
- Kirsty could even be suicidal.

Of course, this list is neither exhaustive nor exclusive.

A family-sensitive approach could enable us to understand the 'bigger picture' by inviting both Pamela and Matthew to join in the therapeutic process with Kirsty. One benefit of this approach is that Kirsty's role as the 'problem' is redefined as a role as part of a system with a problem, that is, a system which has been disrupted by a sudden and traumatic death. In adopting this approach, we can also begin to consider the historical and current interpersonal characteristics of the family. Futhermore, we can begin to think about Graham's death and how this has impacted on the family as a whole.

By constructing a genogram we can begin to engage the family (perhaps even as simply as asking Matthew what colour he would like it to be drawn in) and develop much deeper questions and hypotheses about Kirsty's current behaviour and how it is maintained. Focusing on the interpersonal, we might ask ourselves questions such as:

- Graham and Pamela's relationship was hostile, but to what extent? Was violence involved? Did the children witness arguments between them?
- Pamela describes her relationship with Kirsty as being 'very close'. Is their 'closeness' confused with 'enmeshment' where rules and boundaries are unclear? Has Pamela shared too much about her difficulties in her relationship with Graham? Does she fail to set limits around drinking and smoking?
- Does Kirsty feel guilty about her father's death due to a perceived alliance with her mother?

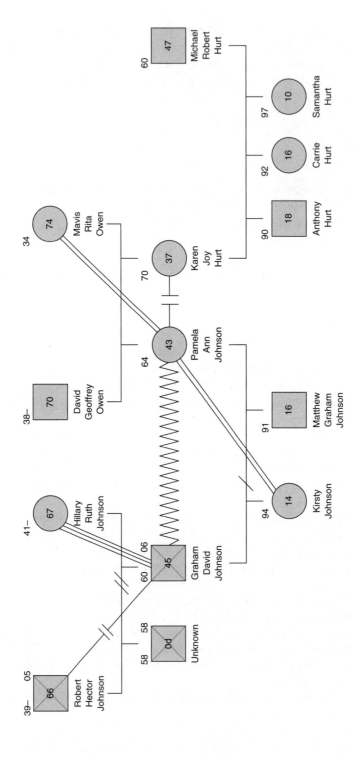

FIGURE 17.3   KIRSTY'S GENOGRAM

- Does Pamela's lack of respect for Kirsty's privacy (for example, reading her emails) result in her feeling suffocated? Is this indicative of the need for clearer boundaries?
- Can we consider Graham's estranged relationship with his father and enmeshed relationship with his mother as influential in his role as husband and father? Does this have implications for exploring the possible reasons for Graham taking his own life?
- What about Matthew? How is he feeling? How has he been affected by his father's death and the current difficulties within his family? How has he come to be 'man of the house' and is this appropriate?
- Pamela is cut off from her sister and her family. How much support does Pamela and her family have? Who does Pamela talk to?
- Is it difficult for Kirsty and Matthew to express their grief in front of Pamela for fear of upsetting her?

An advantage of exploring such questions in the context of the family as a whole is the opportunity to develop fuller therapeutic interventions. For example, in this family, work could be done around rules and boundaries, roles within the family and communication rather than only focusing on Kirsty and her anger.

Any case study necessarily simplifies the process and the authors are aware that this might convey a neat process from beginning to end. This was not the case, as any work with families is complex and requires a capacity on the part of practitioners to work flexibly to respond to the needs of the individuals in the family while holding the family as a whole as the focus.

RESEARCH EVIDENCE

Robust evidence is available to provide support for the contention that interventions at the level of family are worthwhile (Carr, 2000; Pinsof et al., 2008; Sprenkle, 2003). Shadish and Baldwin report the following conclusions from their meta-analysis:

> First, marriage and family interventions are clearly efficacious compared to no treatment. Second, those interventions are at least as efficacious as other modalities such as individual therapy, and perhaps more effective in at least some cases. Third, there is little evidence for differential efficacy among the various approaches to marriage and family interventions, particularly if mediating and moderating variables are controlled. Fourth, evidence that marriage and family interventions are effective in clinically representative conditions remains sparse, although there are some clear exceptions to that. (2003: 566)

Carr (2000) critiqued several important literature reviews and available effectiveness research (randomized control trials) for specific adult-focused problems and in doing so collated a base of solid evidence for the practice of family therapy. The current chapter highlights that there is scope for practitioners working on an individual level to incorporate family therapy ideas, strategies and techniques into their practice. This is supported by the evidence collated by Carr (2000). Carr goes further and suggests that 'there is [also] a strong argument for qualified clinicians to make learning such practices a priority when planning their own continuing professional development' (2000: 289).

Outcome research has identified four factors which together account for change in therapy: client/extratherapeutic factors (40 per cent); relationship factors (30 per cent); model/technique factors (15 per cent); and placebo, hope and expectancy factors (15 per cent) (Blow and Sprenkle, 2001; Lambert, 2003). Pinsof et al. (2008) conducted research focusing on the therapeutic alliance and concluded that the outcomes supported a systemic focus to individual psychotherapy. In addressing clinical implications they state that their research supports involving 'relevant others' in the therapy process as an important way of supporting clients to remain in therapy and to maximize the potential benefits of the therapy. This involvement could take the form of asking clients to talk about their sense of how important others support their therapy (or not) or of actual involvement in sessions. To some practitioners this may be a radical idea, and to others it may reflect current practice. The application of systemic theory to the practice of individual therapy is not a new idea. Perhaps it is the idea of involving important others in the therapy (as opposed to remaining individually focused) that represents the more radical challenge for practitioners. This is indeed the experience of the present authors, and underlines their invitation for counselling psychologists to explore further how they might actively engage in systemic practice.

Cottrell (2003) highlights that more evidence regarding outcomes of family therapy is needed. It is asserted that 'the real challenge for the future may not be evaluation of whole 'schools' of therapy that might be applied to a wide range of problems but the identification of those elements of current practice that may be used in combination with other techniques to target particular types of problems in particular contexts' (Cottrell, 2003: 414). This common factors approach to research is supported by a growing body of evidence (Hubble et al., 1999; Sexton, 2004; Wampold, 2001) and tends to produce research which practitioners can best apply to their own practice (Friedlander et al., 1994).

SUMMARY

Working therapeutically with more than one person at a time can feel like a daunting task for even an experienced counselling psychologist. However, it is hoped that this chapter has gone some way to highlighting that the training and theoretical and philosophical foundations of counselling psychologists (BPS, 2005) places practitioners in a prime position to make a significant contribution to families in psychological and emotional distress. Stratton asserts that as long as best practice related to family work is prioritized, 'much effective work with people in their families can be provided by those not formally accredited as Family Therapists or Systemic Psychotherapists' (2005: 5). Perhaps a dedicated special interest group or division of family psychologists might be an endeavour worth pursuing to promote the application of psychological theory and practice to couples and families. Interestingly, there is a dedicated division within the American Psychological Association but not within the British Psychological Society. Readers have been invited to reflect upon how they might combine ideas from the field of family therapy and their training in counselling psychology.

REFERENCES

Anderson, H. (2005) 'The myth of not-knowing', *Family Process*, 44 (4): 497–504.

Asen, I. (2002) 'Outcome research in family therapy', *Advances in Psychiatric Treatment*, 8: 230–238.

Athanasiades, C. (2008) 'Systemic thinking and circular questioning in therapy with individuals', *Counselling Psychology Review*, 23 (3): 5–13.

Berman, E.M., Heru, A.M., Grunebaum, H., Rolland, J., Wood, B. and Bruty, H. (2006) 'Family skills for general psychiatry residents: Meeting ACGME core competency requirements', *Academic Psychiatry*, 30 (1): 69–78.

Blow, A.J. and Sprenkle, D.H. (2001) 'Common factors across theories of marriage and family therapy: A modified Delphi study', *Journal of Marital and Family Therapy*, 27 (3): 385–401.

Bor, R. and Legg, C. (2003) 'The systems paradigm', in R. Woolfe, Dryden and S. Strawbridge (eds), *Handbook of Counselling Psychology*, 2nd edn. London: Sage.

British Psychological Society (2005) *Division of Counselling Psychology: Professional Practice Guidelines*. Leicester: British Psychological Society.

British Psychological Society (2008) *Membership and Professional Training Board: Criteria for the Accreditation of Postgraduate Programmes in Counselling Psychology*. Leicester: British Psychological Society.

Byng-Hall, J. (2000) 'Therapist reflections: Diverse developmental pathways for the family', *Journal of Family Therapy*, 22: 264–272.

Carr, A. (2000) 'Evidence-based practice in family therapy and systemic consultation. II Adult-focused problems', *Journal of Family Therapy*, 22: 273–295.

Carr, A. (2006) *Family Therapy*. Chichester: Wiley.

Cottrell, D. (2003) 'Outcome studies of family therapy in child and adolescent depression', *Journal of Family Therapy*, 25: 406–416.

Cottrell, D. and Boston, P. (2002) 'Practitioner review: The effectiveness of systemic therapy for children and adolescents', *Journal of Child Psychology and Psychiatry*, 43 (5): 573–586.

Crago, H. (2006) 'Family therapy's intimidating profile', *Australian and New Zealand Journal of Family Therapy*, 27 (1): iii–iv.

Dallos, R. and Draper, J. (2005) *An Introduction to Family Therapy: Systemic Theory and Practice*, 2nd edn. Maidenhead: Open University.

Deacon, S.A. and Piercy, F.P. (2001) 'Qualitative methods in family evaluation: Creative assessment techniques', *American Journal of Family Therapy*, 29: 355–373.

Downey, J. (2003) 'Psychological counselling of children and young people', in R. Woolfe, W. Dryden and S. Strawbridge (eds), *Handbook of Counselling Psychology,* 2nd edn. London: Sage.

Friedlander, M.L., Ellis, M.V., Raymond, L., Siegel, S.M. and Milford, D. (1987) 'Convergence and divergence in the process of interviewing families', *Psychotherapy*, 24: 570–583.

Friedlander, M.L., Escudero, V., Horvath, A.O., Heatherington, L., Cabero, A. and Martens, M.P. (2006) 'System for observing family therapy alliances: A tool for research and practice', *Journal of Counseling Psychology*, 53 (2): 214–224.

Friedlander, M.L., Wildman, J., Heatherington, L. and Skowron, E.A. (1994) 'What we do and don't know about the process of family therapy', *Journal of Family Psychology*, 8 (4): 390–416.

Gianakis, M. and Carey, T.A. (2008) 'A review of the experience and explanation of psychological change', *Counselling Psychology Review*, 23 (3): 27–38.

Gurman, A.S. and Knisker, D.P. (eds) (1981) *Handbook of Family Therapy, Vol I*. New York: Brunner/Mazel.

Gurman, A.S. and Knisker, D.P. (eds) (1999) *Handbook of Family Therapy, Vol. II*. New York: Brunner/Mazel, Publishers.

Hage, S.M. (2003) 'Reaffirming the unique identity of counseling psychology: Opting for the "road less traveled by"', *The Counseling Psychologist*, 31: 555–563.

Hedges, F. (2005) *An Introduction to Systemic Therapy with Individuals: A Social-Constructionist Approach*. Basingstoke: Palgrave McMillan.

Heru, A.M. and Drury, L. (2006) 'Overcoming barriers in working with families', *Academic Psychiatry*, 30: 379–384.

Hubble, M.A., Duncan, B.L. and Miller, S.D. (eds) (1999) *The Heart and Soul of Change: What Works in Therapy?* Washington, DC: American Psychological Association.

Iversen, R.R., Gergen, K. and Fairbanks II, R.P. (2005) 'Assessment and social construction: Conflict or co-creation?', *British Journal of Social Work*, 35: 689–708.

Kaslow, N.J., Celano, M.P. and Stanton, M. (2005) 'Training in family psychology: A competencies-based approach', *Family Process*, 44 (3): 337–353.

Lambert, M.J. (2003) 'Psychotherapy outcome research: Implications for integrative and eclectic therapists', in J. Norcross and M.R. Goldfried (eds), *Handbook of Psychotherapy Integration*. New York: Oxford University Press.

Lebow, J. (1997) 'The integrative revolution in couple and family therapy', *Family Process*, 36: 1–18.

McGoldrick, M. and Carter, B. (2001) 'Advances in coaching: Family therapy with one person', *Journal of Marital and Family Therapy*, 27 (3): 281–300.

McGoldrick, M., Gerson, R. and Shellenberger, S. (1999) *Genograms in Family Assessment*, 2nd edn. New York: Norton.

McGoldrick, M., Gerson, R. and Shellenberger, S. (2008) *Genograms: Assessment and Intervention*, 3rd edn. New York: Norton.

McLeod, J. (1998) *An Introduction to Counselling*, 3rd edn. Maidenhead: Open University Press.

McPhatter, A.R. (1991) 'Assessment revisited: A comprehensive approach to understanding family dynamics', *Families in Society*, 72: 11–21.

Pinsof, W., Zinbarg, R. and Knobloch-Fedders, L.M. (2008) 'Factorial and construct validity of the revised short form Integrative Psychotherapy Alliance Scales for family, couple, and individual therapy', *Family Process*, 47 (3): 281–301.

Roth, A. and Fonagy, P. (2005) What Works for Whom: A Critical Review of Psychotherapy Research. London: Guilford Press.

Sexton, T.L. (2004) 'Beyond common factors: Multi-level process models of therapeutic change in marriage and family therapy', *Journal of Marital and Family Therapy*, 30 (2): 151–157.

Shadish, W.R. and Baldwin, S.A. (2003) 'Meta-analysis of marriage and family interventions', *Journal of Marital and Family Therapy,* 29 (4): 547–570.

Smith, R.L. and Southern, S. (2005) 'Integrative confusion: An examination of integrative models in couple and family therapy', *The Family Journal*, 13: 392–399.

Sprenkle, D.H. (2003) 'Effectiveness research in marriage and family therapy: Introduction', *Journal of Marital and Family Therapy*, 29 (1): 85–96.

Sprenkle, D.H. and Blow, A.J. (2004) 'Common factors are not islands – they work through models: A response to Sexton, Ridley and Kleiner', *Journal of Marital and Family Therapy*, 30 (2): 151–158.

Sprenkle, D.H., Blow, A.J. and Dickey, M.H. (1999) 'Common factors and other nontechnique variables in marriage and family therapy', in M.A. Hubble, B.L. Duncan and S.D. Miller (eds), *The Heart and Soul of Change: What Works in Therapy*. Washington, DC: American Psychological Association.

Stratton, P. (2005) *Report on the Evidence Base of Systemic Family Therapy*. London: Association for Family Therapy.

Strawbridge, S. and Woolfe, R. (2003) 'Counselling psychology in context', in R. Woolfe, W. Dryden and S. Strawbridge (eds), *Handbook of Counselling Psychology*, 2nd edn. London: Sage.

Street, E. (2003) 'Counselling psychology and naturally occurring systems (families and couples)', in R. Woolfe, W. Dryden and S. Strawbridge (eds), *Handbook of Counselling Psychology*, 2nd edn. London: Sage.

Tallman, K. and Bohart, A.C. (1999) 'The client as a common factor: Clients as self healers', in M.A. Hubble, B.L. Duncan and S.D. Miller (eds), *The Heart and Soul of Change: What Works in Therapy*. Washington, DC: American Psychological Association. pp. 91–131.

Wampold, B.E. (2001) *The Great Psychotherapy Debate: Models, Methods and Findings*. New Jersey: Lawrence Erlbaum.

Wilson, J. (1998) *Child-focused Practice: A Collaborative Systemic Approach*. London: Karnac.

18

MIDLIFE ISSUES

Simon Biggs

While some may consider that the counselling psychology of midlife is simply the application of core adult psychological techniques, midlife, for both women and men, raises a number of specific issues. Evidence on the use of counselling psychology with midlife clients is limited. It is, nevertheless possible to identify issues that may be specific to midlife as a distinctive phase of the life course. These issues include the management of multiple demands on identity in the spheres of work, family and in personal relationships. They also include a series of existential priorities that emerge from an intensified subjective awareness of life as a finite progression, provoking an accompanying change in personal priorities. The coming together of these different trends has created a core tension for the psychology of contemporary midlife, between continuity and change. Continuity has been marked by the need for a continued youthful outlook, and change as the adoption of a mature identity adapting to personal and social aspects of ageing. These issues reflect the fact that midlife is socially, personally and biologically defined, and part of the therapeutic task is to examine the interaction of these multiple influences on psychological well-being.

Therapy with midlife clients may be subject to social and historical interpretation that lives both in the minds of clients and in the techniques of therapy itself. Two phenomena that affect the contemporary perception of midlife will be critically reviewed in order to assess their influence on the therapeutic situation. The first of these includes the medicalization of midlife, with a particular emphasis of the development of the 'male menopause' as a medical category. The second will review the notion of a 'blurring' of age-categories in midlife, which includes the view that different generations are becoming increasingly the same. While this may be the case in terms of lifestyle, it raises questions about avoidance of life course issues and the possibility of conflict between generational groups. Both of these phenomena have been influential in determining approaches to midlife in terms of technique, and also within wider organizational and policy systems that surround the therapeutic enterprise.

DEFINING MIDLIFE

It is very rare for a specific age to be placed on midlife. Some authors, such as Colarusso and Nemiroff (1985), have attempted to specify stages of midlife and fix them to chronological age. They have identified a period of midlife transition between 40 and 45 years, of entering middle adulthood (45–50), an age 50 transition (50–55), a culmination of middle adulthood between 55 and 60 years, and finally a late adult transition between 60–65 years. The therapeutic implication would be that clients' experience is judged according to its degree of fit with these stages. Neugarten (1968) examined the responses of 2000 Americans between the ages of 40–60 describing midlife as an 'awareness' issue. Neugarten was particularly interested in how adults 'clocked' themselves in relation to what their society, their friends, media images, conveyed as being 'age-appropriate' behaviour. If you were 'on-time' in terms of the cultural expectations of your part of the life course, you were likely to be less stressed than someone who was 'off-time'. Midlife emerges as a period of heightened sensitivity to one's position within a complex social environment, and where the reassessment of the self is a prevailing theme. She concluded, 'Middle-aged people look to their positions within different life contexts – body, career, family – rather than to chronological age for their primary cues in clocking themselves' (1968: 94).

However, such attempts may be over-determined and historically contingent on a particular view of established work and family-based expectations. A majority of later studies indicate that midlife is an uncharted period and, whilst there is a tacit everyday understanding that it exists, reactions depend largely on the subjectivity of the individual (Staudinger and Bluck, 2001). Ryff and Seltzer (1996) refer to midlife as those years when children grow up and into adulthood but parents are not yet themselves elderly, which, they maintain, is the longest period of the parental experience. However, an undue link between family and midlife processes fails to explain midlife issues that occur through relations beyond the conventional nuclear family. With changing demography, midlife is increasingly being defined in relation to an ageing senior generation. This 'sandwiched' position has been interpreted as a defining source of tension, and also as a means of continuing relationships between generations (Davis, 1981; Bengtson and Lowenstein, 2003). In terms of social policy, midlife is most commonly defined as a relationship to work (Biggs et al., 2007).

Midlife, then, can be identified through social processes as much as through chronological age, and can depend upon a combination of cultural factors and personal circumstances. A key issue here would be how far midlife issues are perceived to be open to change. Multiple interpretation may be the case, even when processes such as the menopause appear to be rooted in a defined biological process (Lock, 1998; Granville, 2000). Social processes can both define and represent mutable features of midlife. Shweder (1998), a social anthropologist who has studied midlife, points out, for example, that our 'cultural fictions are real things' which depend upon a shared point of view to make them a 'fact of experience'. These facts of experience are both socially contingent and cast a powerful influence over the options people perceive to be available to them at different phases of the life course. However, Gilleard and Higgs (2005) have argued that the expansion of consumerism has allowed a multiplicity of options, or 'cultures of ageing', to develop. Midlife, according to this perspective, should be considered to be more of a habitus or lifestyle than an age stage. In this sense, midlife has come to exemplify what Frosh (1991) considered to be a key problem of the contemporary self: a transition from too much structure to too little. The 'facts' of midlife experience can therefore easily become ones of indecision and of uncertainty. Bollas' (1997) work on 'generational consciousness' is particularly interesting here as he associates midlife with a transition from 'simple' to 'complex' states of mind. The former denote unreflective forms of life course awareness that occur when one is immersed in the dominant cultural ideals associated with youth. As adults grow older they 'become historical to themselves' and a tension between self-experience and cultural expectation provokes a more reflective mental attitude. This potential for a 'complex, reflecting self' becomes one of the markers of midlife development.

Midlife emerges from these attempts at definition as being multiply determined and contingent on cultural and experiential circumstances. It can be a period of considerable power and fulfilment, a period of intergenerational readjustment, or a period of reassessment of personal goals. Issues can become manifest in the public and the private spheres, in work or family relations, and both can be expected to arise in therapeutic situations. Indeed, one of the key issues for midlife would appear to be the psychological resources at hand for dealing with that complexity.

PROCESS AND CONTENT OF MIDLIFE COUNSELLING

The dominant psychological process in midlife has been variously described as the start of 'individuation' (Jung, 1967: Vols. 4 and 8), 'geotranscendence' (Tornstam, 2005) and as a process of integrative self-narration (Hooker and McAdams, 2003). Each places increasing awareness of the processes of adult ageing at its core. Biggs et al. (2006) have indicated that tension between a 'mature' self and a 'young' self can be a key feature of identity in midlife. The 'youthful self' position would be inferred from a looking back to youth and childhood, references to and continuities with one's own youth, identification with the younger generation and feeling young inside. The 'mature self' is reflected in a looking forward to the time one had left in life course terms, a focus on current issues, identification with a peer generation and feelings of satisfaction with actual chronological age. Both may exist simultaneously within the dynamic of midlife identity, and may be played out in the workplace as well as in relationships and in families.

A review of research evidence by Hill and Brettle (2006) indicates that counselling can have significant value for adults aged 50 and above, particularly in the treatment of anxiety, depression and in improving subjective well-being. The evidence indicates that 'individual, as opposed to group counselling, is the psychological treatment of choice' (2006: 281) amongst community dwelling clients.

Sherman (1994) suggests that adults make judgements about the ageing self on four dimensions:

- *Comparative self* draws conclusions about personal ageing by comparing oneself to others. These would include age-peers and the ageing of younger generations, of siblings and the observation of older kin. Peers, for example might be used to compare how well one is ageing relative to people in the same cohort. Family comparisons may be used to assess where one is on an intergenerational scale, which generation one belongs to.
- *Reflected self* would be sensitized to the views others are believed to hold about oneself. Here others are perceived to be judging the self according to age-appropriate criteria, which may include particular others or the general community.
- *Retrospective self* depends upon comparisons with former identities. Here, the past self acts as a sort of retrospective yardstick whereby bodily reminders such as changes in appearance, health and strength are logged. Often this increases awareness of any contradictions between how one feels inside and outward appearances.
- *Mature self* is identified as becoming freer, so that a client can construct his or her own identity. This final self allows movement beyond comparisons based on the other three.

Kleinberg has observed that clients 'Do not necessarily enter treatment to cope with a midlife issue. Instead they are interested in the relief of symptoms, in resolving family conflict, or in feeling more creative' (1995: 207).

In other words, issues that may be interpreted as midlife problems may not be presented in life course terms, and it is only through the therapeutic process itself that an awareness of the adult life course dimension becomes more sharply defined. Kleinberg has observed that in midlife, presenting problems often belie a personal feeling of senselessness and aimlessness, and that much of the therapeutic task consists of 'working through stagnation', and in this respect his work follows the Jungian transition between the first and re-vitalized second half of adult life (Jung, 1967).

Neugarten's (1968) early work identified a number of issues that link work, family and peer relations in midlife. These included: dealing with the different rhythms of life arising from different contexts such as the demands of work, family and relationships, plus being a bridge between generations and containing conflicts of interest. This is often accompanied by an increased awareness of mentoring and modelling roles. Also, a growing awareness of distance, emotionally, socially and culturally, between the midlife self and younger adults, marks one out as part of an ageing generation. An increased awareness of body health and the death of contemporaries, according to Neugarten, can lead to an increased sense of physical vulnerability, with life being re-thought in terms of 'time left to live' rather than 'time since birth'. Such changes in orientation intimate an increasing awareness of personal finitude and a spur to personal integration in what time one has left.

King (1980) has identified the following sources of anxiety and concern that she found to be indications of midlife disturbance:

- Fear of the diminution or loss of sexual potency and the impact this would have on relationships.
- Anxieties arising in marital relationships once the children have left home, and couples can no longer use their children to mask problems arising in their relationship with each other.
- At work, the threat of redundancy or displacement by younger people and awareness of the possible failure of professional skills.
- A feared loss of identity looming in retirement.
- An increased awareness of possible illness, and consequent dependence on others.
- A realization that they may not now be able to achieve life-goals with consequent feelings of depression or deprivation.

Kleinberg (1995) identified seven areas for initial assessment, which may indicate whether the client has begun to consider the process of midlife review. These include an increased awareness of:

- physical changes of ageing and their impact on work and other efforts
- increased awareness of mortality and finitude
- the extent to which a career is fulfilling and can continue to fulfil personal values
- current and future satisfactions and conflicts in intimate relationships
- needs for peer and mentoring relationships and means of fulfilling them in the future
- impact of family changes on role satisfactions
- a need to plan retirement years.

Writers such as Bengtson and Putney (2006) suggest that while family life can protect generations from external sources of conflict, midlifers are often pulled in three directions at once: between work commitments and the care needs of both younger and older generations. The tension between caring and working has been identified as a source of stress by the European Commission (European Foundation, 2008), and can be expected to be a presenting problem in therapeutic encounters.

MIDLIFE THEMES

Work and midlife

Part of the tension between continuity and discontinuity in midlife arises because it is perceived as a time of maximum capacity, but also a time of increased intergenerational competition. The contradictions that this and other factors can bring are encapsulated in the difference between wanting to be mature and wanting to feel young. The mid-lifer has a substantial repertoire of strategies to draw on and is 'no longer learning from a book', but at the same time faces challenges, such as changing technologies, that may be generationally identified (Edmunds and Turner, 2002).

Midlife issues, and the extension of mid-lifestyles ever more deeply into later life, have been identified as a drive toward 'productive ageing', which examines the question of ageing through the lens of economic usefulness (Hinterlong, 1999). Adherents of productive ageing maintain that productivity does not decrease with age, an approach that appears radical because it takes as its object the negative stereotyping of adult ageing. It is pointed out that rather than a steady slide into increasing incapacity, current generations are richer and fitter than those who preceded them (Metz and Underwood, 2005). To this is added the observation that there are many advantages for employers hiring older workers, including reliability, prior investment in skills and know-how, and company loyalty (Schultz, 2001). There is, it is argued, a basic connection between continued health and productivity, because 'engagement in productive behaviour requires a certain level of physical, cognitive and emotional functioning' (Butler et al., 1990). Rowe and Kahn (1998), the influential authors of *Successful Ageing*, claim that 'the frailty of old age is largely reversible ... what does it take to turn back the ageing clock? Its surprisingly simple ... Success is determined by good old-fashioned hard work' (1998: 15).

However, Gullette (2004) has argued that work is a restrictive source of midlife identity which can set later midlifers up to fail against younger workmates and contribute toward intergenerational conflict. Turner (1998; Edmunds and Turner, 2002) has drawn attention to intergenerational tension in the public arena of work. In addition to the traditional perception of later midlife being a time when individuals feel the pressure of a new generation attempting to replace them, midlife adults may actively build their own social defences which work to exclude younger adults. Workplace rivalries might therefore generate an oedipal-like situation imbued with fantasies of rivalry and usurpation. A key issue for counselling psychology would be the balance to be achieved between continuity and discontinuity of identity in terms of productive ageing, competition in the workplace and the need for a more individuated self.

Intergenerational families

Midlife relationships encompass a diversity of family structures, occasioned by divorce and new partnerships (Daatland, 2007), a move toward living alone or 'living apart together', and complex kin and step relations (De Jong Gierveld, 2004). The dramatic increase in life expectancy and lowered fertility, especially in more developed countries, has resulted in people living longer and more complex family structures, sometimes including four or more generations (Antonucci et al., 2007). However, this increased complexity has not been accompanied with strong normative frameworks to guide midlife behaviour. Two main areas of intergenerational relations have been identified in the literature that may lack established social norms: relationships with children and relations with ageing parents.

Looking at the parental experience of midlife, surprisingly little attention has been paid to how having and raising children affects parents themselves, as opposed to the effects of parenting on child development. Ryff and Selzer (1996) consider that midlife covers 'the most interesting time in the parental experience'. It includes the period in which children grow from adolescence to adulthood and how their strengths and weaknesses are played out in life choices, and thus when parents and children begin to develop adult–adult relationships.

It is also the stage when parenting (as compared to parenthood) ends, marked by a series of gradual transitions rather than an 'empty nest'. Leaving is a process and not an event, and this view gives a criterion for successful transition in terms of relationship rather than as an experience of loss. Gradually, attention changes to how children have 'turned out'. From this perspective, the achievements and adjustment of adult children constitute an important lens through which midlife parents evaluate themselves and their own accomplishments. The therapeutic task would inevitably privilege intergenerational factors in the achievement of adjustment and future well-being. Adolescent and midlife transitions often co-incide, giving rise to system tensions between emerging and declining sexuality, fertility and more global expressions of potency which require negotiation. The co-occurance between adolescent children and menopause has been suggested by Graber and Brooks-Gunn (1996) as an explanation of parental midlife conflict. Others (Dillaway, 2006), however, argue that menopause does not disrupt 'motherwork' and mothering experiences. Silverberg (1996) notes that parents' self-appraised mental health is strongly influenced by the development of adolescent children. The pubertal processes, peer influences and relationships, independence and autonomy, that emerge as issues during adolescence influence parental well-being. Factors would include the co-occurrence of daughters' and mothers' reproductive transitions, and also fathers' discovery of nurturant qualities which have hitherto been suppressed.

These changes take place at a time when a midlifer's own parents may be dealing with developmental processes involving life re-appraisal and personal re-evaluation, leading to interpersonal conflict. Nydegger and Miteness (1996) suggest that parental transitions from midlife into later life and personal ones into middle age act as pressures on the 'sandwiched' midlifers, raising questions of role reversal and changes in dependency, in addition to juggling multiple roles. This may not, however, be exclusively a source of stress, and can provoke a re-asssessment of parental relationships, now appearing on a more egalitarian footing. A midlifer's relationship with their own parents may develop from authority to friendship. It may not be until the mid to late 30s that individuals can establish true mutual autonomy with other adult generations, with successful renegotiation of generational relationships depending upon an established personal lifestyle. McIlvane et al. (2007) found that midlifers who were low in personal and social resources reported higher levels of well-being when they were in regular contact with their parents, when compared to those only with children or with both. They argue that with an increase in less traditional paths in life, such findings should be taken into account as sources of positive rather than negative value. Chang et al. (2007) indicate that social problem-solving techniques can be particularly valuable in reducing stress and increasing psychological well-being in middle-adulthood.

A key question for counselling psychology becomes whether the relational network can tolerate the anxiety of renegotiating powers and limits during this period that raise powerful feelings around autonomy and dependency.

Gender and relationship issues

A series of observations have also been made about changing gender identities and relationships in midlife. Guttman (1987) has observed that gendered attributes begin to 'cross over' in midlife, as individuals reclaim powers that fixed gender roles denied them in their younger adult years. According to this view, women become more outwardly assertive, taking up roles in the public sphere, whilst men discover their nurturant inner selves. This occurs in midlife (Huyuk and Guttman 1999) because the forced role specialization and stereotyping during the 'female window of fertility' and 'parental emergency' of the child-rearing years begins to recede. Sheehey (1995) refers to life course changes in gender identity as the 'sexual diamond'. Here it is claimed that from puberty until the mid-thirties, gender roles increasingly diverge, and then come together again in the late 50s. Around this period, women and men become more like each other, with a tendency for men to take on traditionally female attributes and women take on male ones.

Rosowsky (1999) has reviewed problems as experienced by couples in midlife. He observes that problems often arise around members' capacity to care. Joint goals and common focus or purposes may no longer appear to be viable as priorities change, which may produce a vacuum in couple relations. In such circumstances, a couple's relationship may easily become a repository of blame for unfulfilled goals and achievements. There is a strong link here with both a need to respond to changing personal gender identities and compensatory development for parts of the self that may have been suppressed in earlier phases of the relationship. According to Rosowsky, tasks for couples in midlife include:

- redefining important roles, for example, those of spouse, sibling, parent and adult–child, each of which may impinge upon relationship issues
- events precipitating a re-evaluation of relationships, such as retirement, the children being launched as independent adults, loss of one's parents, or the development of serious illnesses.

Each may lead to redefined goals for the individual and for their primary relationship, mutual disclosure and sense of trust. Henry and Miller (2004) indicate that the most common problems found in midlife relationships were financial matters, issues relating to children and sexual issues. Values, commitment, spiritual matters and family violence were the least common problem areas. Hollist and Miller (2005) argue that couples therapists can use emotionally focused therapy to address relationship problems in midlife. Their review of existing literature indicates that relative to young couples, studies of midlife relationships are minimal; however, a key task of midlife couples counselling is to move from insecure to secure attachment styles.

Failure to address these and related transitional issues may result in a form of narcissism noted by Kernberg (1989). This may present as:

- an inability to enjoy sexuality
- an inability to relate in-depth to other human beings
- a lack of awareness of ambivalence
- a lack of capacity for mourning and regret over previous acts of aggression toward those who are loved
- aggression may be denied and replaced by a display of naivity at the consequences of one's behaviour.

The literature on sexual orientation specific to midlife is minimal. This may, in part, result from a cultural focus on heterosexual marriage as the 'gold standard' of relationships, which can force lesbian and gay couples into the same mould. Research on the division of domestic labour in lesbian, gay and heterosexual relationships (Kurdek, 1992) suggest that heterosexual couples could adopt a wider spectrum of domestic strategies. Kurdek found three different styles: equality, balance and segregation. Equality, where tasks are shared and worked on as a couple, was found to be favoured by lesbian couples; balance, where the amount of tasks were divided up equally but with partners having their own areas of expertise tended to be used by gay couples; whereas segregation, where one partner shoulders the lion's share of household tasks, was most likely to belong to heterosexual married couples.

This overview suggests that midlife provokes reappraisal in the areas of personal identity, relationships and social roles. This is often concerned with life course transitions and requires the renegotiation of established roles and relationships. The co-occurrence of multiple transitions within and between different spheres of life would require considerable personal resources.

THERAPEUTIC APPROACHES TO MIDLIFE

King's psychoanalytic approach

King (1980) was one of the first psychoanalysts to specifically address midlife and adult ageing. She follows mainstream psychoanalytic thinking in seeing midlife issues as essentially a recapitualtion of oedipal problems, passed through the lens of adolescence. She argued that the therapist will often be younger than her client, a reverse of the traditionally assumed situation, and thus the resulting transference will not follow the more familiar route of parental therapist and client–child. She notes that:

- Midlife and older patients are unwilling to trust someone younger and less experienced than themselves, and that this itself may require relationship 'work' within the session.
- Therapists need to take into account what she calls the 'psychological timescale' within which a client may be functioning, with multiple possibilities for tranference which may reflect child–parent, parent–child, peer/lover relationships or grandparental experiences.
- Therapy may be particularly threatening to midlife adults because changes often appear as reversals, reflected in sexual, biological and role changes, when compared to earlier life-phases.

Reactions to these assaults and reversals include acting out and 'behaviour more reminiscent of adolescence than middle age', including sexual promiscuity and rapid changes in employment. In the session itself, an inability to commit to an enduring course of therapeutic action may reflect a fantasy that by avoiding change or therapeutic improvement, clients will be 'out of time and therefore avoid ageing and death'. The phantasy belief that therapy is 'keeping them alive' may also mean that midlifers can be both inconsistent and difficult to finish working with as clients.

Jung, individuation and masquerade

Jung (1967: Vols. 4 and 8) was the first psychotherapist to attempt a psychology of midlife. Key to Jung's view was the idea that the adult life course could be divided in two broadly different orientations, which he called the first and second halves of life. Midlife occurs as a transitional period, spanning the move from young adulthood to later adulthood. In the first half of life, a person's identity is said to consolidate around the personal will, and as part of this process the constraints of childhood are cast aside. It is in this sense that one can say that the first phase of adult identity looks backwards for its points of reference, even though it is experienced as a time of looking to the future. However, with the approach of midlife, the social conformity implied by the first half of life begins to become problematic and is increasingly experienced as having provoked a 'diminution of the personality' as personal potential has become supressed in the service of social achievements. At first, however, the midlife adult may become psychologically entrenched, clinging on to the familiar, if increasingly untenable, positions of the first half. Jung comments that, rather than a sign of psychological well-being, attempts to maintain the priorities of the first half of life into the second are an indication of poor life course adjustment, which he describes as a delusion: 'As formerly the neurotic could not escape from childhood, so now he cannot part with his youth' (1967: Vol. 8, 777).

For Jungian psychology, individuation is the core task of the second half of life. It constitutes a turning away form the external exigencies of early adult identity, and toward reflection on the inner world of the self. The person becomes, or has the potential to become, conscious in what respects she or he is both unique and at the same time holds in common with other human beings. As a part of the midlife transition to an individuated personality, the ageing adult begins to develop different existential priorities. First, as Stevens (2000) points out, midlifers have climbed to the top of life's hill, and can see both forwards and backwards. They can take in the complexity of diverse life course positions. Second, before them is a gentle decline, which invites an assesment of self in terms of 'time left to me' rather than 'time from childhood'. Thus life's projects are no longer open-ended, and the youthful phantasy of eternal life, and thus the possibility of eternal procrastination, has to be shed. Third, those shadow elements of the self that were previously projected onto older others begin to return and require acceptance. Fourth, there are those aspects of personal potential that had to be suppressed during the first half of life, which now have the possibility of expression.

Jaques (1965) placed the midlife transition, or crisis, as occurring between 35 and 65 years. He was at first interested in the changes in creative and most notably artistic production with age, observing the way in which the immediacy of paintings, plays and novels produced by writers early in their career – 'hot from the fire' – became more reflective and melancholy with age. 'The paradox is,' he claimed, one 'of entering the prime of life, the stage of fulfilment, but at the same time the prime and fulfilment are dated – death lies beyond' (1965: 512). The midlifer, then, looks both ways, back to early adulthood but also forward, becoming aware of finitude and that there is limited time left to achieve what they desire.

Whilst Jung saw midlife as a period in which the persona or social mask is dissolved, attempts to reconcile individuation with the effects of social ageism have given rise to the observation that midlife and older adults often deploy a masquerade in order to protect the emerging self from an ageist environment (Woodward, 1991; Biggs, 1999). The protective function of the persona is something which has been traditonally underplayed within this approach. Individuation then takes place, but has to be disguised if its public expression is anti-normative.

In terms of therapeutic process, the deployment of a masquerade in the mature years means that:

- The therapist may need to pay special attention to their own anti-ageist practice, in creating a facilitative environment for self-expression. This would require pychological work on attitudes to social and personal ageing.
- Masquerade may be positively protective of emerging individuation, rather than being exclusively an impediment to that process. The uses to which it is put may need to be explored as part of the therapeutic process.
- In addition to the enhancement of individuation itself, therapists would need to take into account the context within which individuated parts of the self will seek expression.

An awareness of the protective value of social masking has lead to a reconsideration of the value of this phenomenon in situations in which ageism impinges on personal identity.

McAdams and narrative approaches to midlife

In the late 1980s and 1990s an increasing awareness of diversity and the influence of consumerism on identity has produced a more fluid notion of midlife. Featherstone and Hepworth (1983, 1989) note that contemporary mid-lifestyles allow 'Individuals who look after their bodies and adopt a positive attitude toward life … to avoid the decline and negative effects of the ageing process and thereby prolong their capacity to enjoy the full benefits of consumer culture' (1989: 87). In Featherstone and Hepworth's view, midlife is no longer a period of transition from productivity to disengagement. Rather, it has become 'age less', a lifecourse plateau, buoyed up by consumer lifestyles and of continual reinvention. As Blaikie has observed, 'When older citizens are encouraged not just to dress "young" and look youthful, but to exercise, have sex, take holidays, socialise in ways indistinguishable from those of their children's generation … there are no rules now, only choices' (1999: 104).

Such observations fit well with McAdams' (1993) view that the therapeutic task is now to 'story' the life course from one's own resources. In life course terms, 'Defining the self through myth may be seen as an ongoing act of psychological and social respon-sibility. Because our world can no longer tell us who we are and how we should live, we must figure it out on our own' (1993: 35). Narrative therapies arguably provide tech-niques whereby a multiplicity of possibilities for identity can be negotiated in the absence of binding cultural guidelines.

McAdams (1993, 2001) has taken a particular interest in the construction of midlife identity, which he sees as a time of 'putting it together'. The hallmark of a successful midlife transition is perceived as 'integrating and making peace among conflicting images in ones personal myth'. The effects of this process can be seen in processes of psychological adaptation (McAdams, 2001) and attributional styles (Adler et al., 2006).

The images that McAdams refers to are alternative identities that are believed to have been collected by people in their 30s and early 40s Midlife, which is seen as stretching from the 40s to the late 60s, consists of a sorting out of these accumulated aspects of self, motivated by a fascination with one's own life story's denouement. By the time clients reach approximately 40 years of age, they are likely to have developed a much more articulated and realistic understanding of who they are and in what ways they have acquired a mature identity. Midlifers realize, in terms of love and work, that life is not simple and not fully under their control. The 'putting it together' in midlife must accomodate a 'curious blend of resurgence and decline', requiring a personal myth which changes in narrative tone from earlier versions of the self. The new narrative includes recognition and acceptance of contradictory or ambivalent positions, 'fundamental conflicts in the myth' that had previously been kept separate. According to this approach, individuals in midlife experience a 'growing realisation that good lives, like good stories, require good endings' (McAdams, 1993: 202).

Midlife narrative therapy simultaneously recognizes and attempts to re-write the life course script. As part of this process, McAdams draws on Erikson's (1982) life-stage model of midlife generativity. The 'Generativity script' states McAdams, 'is an adults' plan for what he or she hopes to do in the future to leave a heroic gift for the next generation. We recast and revise our own life stories so that the past is seen as giving birth to the present and the future, so that beginning, middle and end make sense in terms of each other' (1993: 227). McAdams' interest in generativity may reside in it as a concept binding the multiplicity of midlife narratives into a unitary self: 'human experience tends toward a fundamental sense of unity in that human beings apprehend experience through an integrative selfing process' (McAdams, 1997: 57).

The use of narrative approaches to understand midlife suggests a process that is triggered by a need to make sense of the multiple stories created during earlier phases of adulthood, and an increasing awareness of the contradictions between them. A new narrative emerges which better fits the social indeterminacy of contemporary ageing, yet grounds it in a sustainable narrative from. The integrative element of such narratives, as they impinge upon adult ageing, have been expanded by Hooker and McAdams (2003).

CONTEMPORARY NARRATIVES FOR MIDLIFE

While the therapeutic approaches outlined above emphasize the integrative and creative potential of midlife, these have to be placed in the context of powerful cultural narratives that will influence the demands and the concerns that midlife clients may bring to counselling psychology. The final part of this chapter will be used to examine two narratives that describe midlife to us in contemporary policy and popular literature. Both will form an influential backdrop to the presenting problems and perceived solutions that can be expected to appear in therapeutic situations. The first of these concerns the medicalization of characteristics associated with midlife and the second, a cultural blurring of age-identities.

Menopause, andropause and the medicalization of midlife

The debate on a medicalization of midlife has focused on the menopause (Day, 2002), and more recently a possible 'male menopause' or 'andropause' (Vainonpaa and Topo, 2005). Here, emphasis is placed on the ageing body and is closely linked to the development of pharmaceutical responses to life course problems previously associated with forms of midlife stress. In so far as biomedical solutions prioritize physical aspects of adult ageing and disease-based explanations of individual experience, they present a challenge to counselling psychology. Menopausal symptoms – male or otherwise – are, within the medicalizing agenda, not seen as a natural part of the life course, nor primarily subject to psychological interpretation and modification, with solutions based on personal agency. Rather, they are seen as physical problems that can be addressed by pharmacological solutions.

Feminist writers such as Day (2002) and Seaman (2003) had criticized the use of hormone replacement therapy (HRT) because it had failed to deliver the promised benefits and medicalizes an otherwise natural phase of the life course. A reduction in cardio-vascular stress, osteoporosis and Alzheimer's disease has not been supported by a critical examination of mortality and morbidity statistics (Meyer, 2001). It is perhaps a signal of the power of bio-medicalized discourse that there is little consideration of counselling approaches to menopause in this literature. Schultz-Zehden (2004), however, argues that for women counselling should form an important part of the response to menopause when it affects self-confidence, quality of partnership, job satisfaction and family relations.

The rediscovery of the male menopause, or andropause, first identified in the 1920s and subsequently discarded as a serious medical phenomenon (Siegel-Watkins, 2007), closely follows the popularization of the drug Viagara, used as a means of addressing reduced male sexual arousal and for recreational sexual activity (Marshall and Katz, 2002). These authors argue that sexual fitness had become a criterion for 'success' in responding to the ageing male body. Symptoms are associated with testosterone decline, which can be diagnosed through blood testosterone levels and treated by testosterone intake in a similar way that HRT had been prescribed for women.

The symptoms of andropause follow those traditionally associated with the menopause in midlife women. An Internet search of the phenomenon produced 1,830,983 hits, typical of which are an outline of characteristics on a BBC website: 'Common complaints as men reach middle age are poor sex drive, tiredness and fatigue, acknowledgement of ageing, hair loss and changes in body shape as they become less muscular and more rounded. Other symptoms include irritability, sweating, flushing, generalised aches and pains, and low mood, sometimes depression. Looking at these symptoms, it's easy to see why a comparison is made with the female menopause. Women may experience any or all of these symptoms' (BBC, 2008: 1).

The sexualization of midlife is, however, itself a historically contingent phenomenon (Marshall, 2007). At the turn of the twentieth century, Stall's *What a Man of Forty-five Ought to Know* identified a lowering of sexual drive as a boon such that 'the heart (becomes) more refined, the lines of intellectual and spiritual vision lengthened, the spheres of usefulness enlarged' (1901: 59). When in the 1920s testosterone-based therapies were popularized, Marshall (2007) notes that writers were concerned to emphasize social rejuvenation and potency and discouraged any association with sexual performance. Until the coming together of Viagara and mid-lifestyles, the common consensus, she tells us, was that symptoms were a result of midlife stress, a fear of loss of potency and changes in emotional attitude. She associates contemporary sexual anxiety in midlife to be the result of the spread of consumer culture to increasingly older parts of the adult life course. As such the identification of an andropause has contributed to a blurring of psychological and biological processes as they may emerge in counselling situations. While the research evidence is limited, it may be assumed that 'discovery' of andropause may lead to: increased pressure for 'youthful' sexual performance; avoidance of nurturing and relational aspects of intimacy; an eclipsing of accommodative processes toward natural life course change; and retreat into pharmacological 'solutions' rather than facing the challenges of psychological integration – each of which may emerge in counselling psychology sessions.

ADULT AGEING AND THE BLURRING OF GENERATIONAL CHARACTERISTICS

Midlife, and particularly late midlife, are presented as a time of potential fulfilment, in part because the current generation of midlifers and older adults are seen as being richer and fitter than previous generations (Metz and Underwood, 2005). A 'continuity' narrative is complemented by a popular view that differences between generations are becoming 'blurrred' in important respects (Hepworth, 2004).

Midlife, as represented by contemporary culture, has become a focus of interest for at least three reasons. First, it has become associated with the post-war 'baby-boomer' generation, credited as being the twentieth-century's 'first teenagers' and the harbingers of a characteristically 'youthful' approach to culture which has stayed with them as they have passed into midlife (Huber and Skidmore, 2003). Second, such a large cohort has not survived into later life in contemporary memory, and may be historically unprecedented. Individual members of large cohorts are driven, according to Stewart and

Torges (2006), to social and psychological expressions of individuality as a result of increased competition amongst age-peers. It may not be accidental that this generation is more psychologically literate than preceding ones and that their path to adulthood paralleled the growth of humanistic psychology. Third, spending the adult years in a period marked by rapid change in social attitudes toward gender roles, race and sexual orientation has raised the question of whether contemporary midlifers will also provoke changes in their attitudes and expectations of later adulthood. One result of this tension is that ageing and avoiding ageing becomes a core contradiction for psycho-social functioning in midlife. Woodward (1991) and Grenier (2007) have argued that rather than passively responding to age expectations, adults engage in active strategies that serve to position themselves in relation to intergenerational encounters.

Biggs et al. (2007) found that midlifers identified similarities between themselves and younger generational groups, both in terms of their own children and more widely as an age group, indicating, perhaps, a cultural shift as well as a perceived change in attitudes within families. This was particularly evident in areas of style, taste and social attitudes. Baby-boomers characteristically saw the 'blurring' of generations as something that had taken place between them and these younger groups; however, blurring was not extended to older generations, who were almost entirely seen as different in terms of attitude and culture. Personal ageing is seen as something that requires managing if its perceived consequences are to be successfully avoided. Maturity is evidenced in terms of comfort with current age and looking forward in terms of time left while feeling more youthful than actual age implies, supported by a blurring of differences with younger generations. The ageing midlifer, then, draws on a series of mature strategies to balance cultural and life-stage issues. A clear theme emerges in a desire to erase differences with younger generations, thereby reducing negative associations arising from the experience of their own parents. This extends to a rejection of associations with old age in general and ambivalence toward adult ageing and late-life experience.

Lessons for counselling in midlife might include an underscoring of anxiety about ageing as a driver for midlife identity, both in terms of attempts to disguise age difference with younger therapists and avoidance of 'deeper' concerns about the future. The presentation of self may be especially sensitive to age in the counselling relationship, with a tendency to focus on the priorities of the first half of life. In this context, counselling psychology could include encouraging a 'balanced' view of mature and youthful identities in the here and now, rapprochement with the legacy of older generations, and opening discussion of existential concerns and future planning.

CONCLUDING SUMMARY

It is possible to identify a number of issues that can arise in counselling psychology which may be specific to midlife as a distinctive phase of the life course. These issues include the management of multiple demands on identity in the spheres of work, family and personal relationships. They also indicate a series of existential priorities that emerge from an intensified subjective awareness of life as a finite progression, provoking an accompanying change in personal priorities. Midlife is therefore socially, personally and biologically defined. Therapy with midlife clients may be subject to social and historical interpretation that lives both in the minds of clients and in the techniques of therapy itself.

REFERENCES

Adler, J., Kissel, E. and McAdams, D. (2006) 'Emerging from the cave: Attributional style and the narrative study of identity in midlife adults', *Cognitive Therapy & Research*, 18 (2): 41–53.

Antonucci, T.C., Jackson, J.S. and Biggs, S. (2007) 'Intergenerational relations: Theory, research and policy', *Journal of Social Issues*, 63 (4): 679–694.

BBC (2008) 'Are men suffering in silence?'. Available at http://news.bbc.co.uk/1/hi/health/7358527.stm (accessed 12/6/09).

Bengtson, V. and Lowenstein, A. (2003) *Global Aging and the Challenges to Families*. New York: Aldine de Gruyte.

Bengtson, V. and Putney, N. (2006) 'Future "conflicts" across generations and cohorts?', in J. Vincent, C. Phillipson and M. Downes (eds), *The Futures of Old Age*. London: Sage.

Biggs, S. (1999) *The Mature Imagination: The Dynamics of Identity in Midlife and Beyond*. Buckingham: Open University Press.

Biggs, S., Phillipson, C., Money, A.-M. and Leach, R. (2006) 'The age-shift: Observations on social policy, ageism and the dynamics of the adult lifecourse', *Journal of Social Work Practice*, 20 (3) 239–250.

Biggs, S., Phillipson, C., Money, A.-M. and Leach, R. (2007) 'The mature imagination and consumption strategies', *International Journal of Ageing and Later life*, 2 (2): 61–90.

Blaikie, A. (1999) *Ageing and Popular Culture*. Cambridge: Cambridge University Press.

Bollas, C. (1997) *Being a Character*. London: Routledge.

Butler, R., Overlink, M. and Schecter, M. (1990) *The Promise of Productive Aging*. New York: Springer.

Chang, E., D'Zurilla, T. and Sanna, L. (2007) 'Social problem solving as a mediator of the link between social wellbeing and stress in middle adulthood', *Cognitive Therapy Research*, 10 (7): 106–19.

Colarusso, C.A. and Nemiroff, R.A. (1985) *The Race Against Time: Psychotherapy and Psychoanalysis in the Second Half of Life*. New York: Plenum.

Daatland, S.-O. (2007) 'Marital history and intergenerational solidarity: The impact of divorce and unmarried cohabitation', *Journal of Social Issues*, 63(4): 809–826.

Davis, R. (1981) *Aging: Prospects and Issues*. Los Angeles, CA: Andrus.

Day, A. (2002) 'Lessons from the women's health initiative', *Canadian Medical Association Journal*, 167: 361–62.

De Jong Gierveld, J. (2004) 'Societal trends and lifecourse events affecting diversity in later life', in S.-O. Daatland and S. Biggs (eds), *Ageing and Diversity*. Bristol: Policy.

Dillaway, H. (2006) 'Good mothers never wane: Mothering at menopause', *Journal of Women and Aging*, 18 (2): 41–53.

Edmunds, J. and Turner, B. (2002) *Generations, Culture and Society*. Buckingham: Open University Press.

Erikson, E. (1982) *The Life-Cycle Completed*. New York: Norton.

European Foundation (2008) *Working Longer, Living Better*. Dublin: Eurofund.

Featherstone, M. and Hepworth, M. (1983) 'The midlifestyle of George and Lynne', *Theory, Culture and Society*, 1: 85–92.

Featherstone, M. and Hepworth, M. (1989) 'Ageing and old age, reflections on the postmodern life-course', in B. Byetheway (ed.), *Becoming and Being Old*. London: Sage.

Frosh, S. (1991) *Identity Crisis*. London: Macmillan.

Gilleard, C. and Higgs, P. (2005) *Contexts of Ageing: Class Cohort and Community*. Cambridge: Polity Press.

Graber, J. and Brooks-Gunn, J. (1996) 'Reproductive transitions', in C. Ryff and M. Selzer (eds), *The Parental Experience in Midlife*. Chicago, IL: Chicago University Press.

Granville, G. (2000) 'Developing a mature identity: A feminist exploration of the meaning of menopause', PhD thesis, University of Keele. Available at http://en.scientificcommons.org/gillian_granville (accessed 12/6/09).

Grenier, A. (2007) 'Crossing age and generational boundaries', *Journal of Social Issues*, 63(4): 713–729.

Gullette, M. (2004) *Aged by Culture*. Chicago, IL: Chicago University Press.

Guttman, D. (1987) *Reclaimed Powers*. London: Hutchinson.

Hepworth, M. (2004) *Stories of Ageing*. Buckingham: Open University Press.

Hill, A. and Brettle, A. (2006) 'Counselling older people: What can we learn from research evidence?', *Journal of Social Work Practice*, 20 (3): 281–298.

Hinterlong, M. (1999) *Productive Aging*. New York: Springer.

Hollist, C. and Miller, R. (2005) 'Perceptions of attachment style and marital quality in midlife marriage', *Family Relations*, 54 (1): 46–57.

Hooker, K. and McAdams, D. (2003) 'Personality reconsidered: A new agenda for aging research', *Journal of Gerontology*, 58B (6): 296–304.

Henry, R. and Miller, R. (2004) 'Marital problems occurring in midlife', *American Journal of Family Therapy*, 32: 405–417.

Huber, J. and Skidmore, P. (2003) *The New Old: Why Baby Boomers won't be Pensioned Off*. London: Demos.

Huyuk, M. and Guttman, D. (1999) 'Developmental issues in psychotherapy with older men', in M. Duffy (ed.), *Handbook of Counselling and Psychotherapy with Older Adults*. New York: Wiley. pp. 77–90.

Jaques, E.. (1965) 'Death and the midlife crisis', *International Journal of Psychoanalysis*, 46: 507–14.

Jung, C.G. (1967*) Collected Works*. London. Routledge.

Kernberg, O. (1989) *Borderline Conditions and Pathological Narcissism*. New York: Aronson.

King, P. (1980) 'The lifecycle as indicated by the nature of the transference of the middle-aged and elderly', *International Journal of Psychoanalysis*, 61: 153–60.

Kleinberg, J. (1995) 'Group treatment of adults in midlife', *International Journal of Group Psychotherapy*, 45: 207–222.

Kurdek, L.A. (1992) 'Correlates of relationship satisfaction in cohabiting gay and lesbian couples: Integration of contextual, investment, and problem-solving models', *Journal of Personality and Social Psychology*, 61(6): 910–922.

Lock, M. (1998) 'Deconstructing the change', in R. Schweder (ed.), *Welcome to Middle Age!* Chicago, IL: Chicago University Press. pp. 45–74.

Marshall, B. (2007) 'Cimatcteric redux? Re-medicalising the male menopause', *Men and Masculinities*, 9: 509–529.

Marshall, B. and Katz, S. (2002) 'Forever functional: Sexual fitness and the ageing male body', *Body and Society*, 8 (4): 43–70.

McAdams, D. (1993) *The Stories We Live By*. New York: Morrow.

McAdams, D. (1997) 'The case for unity in the postmodern self', in R. Ashmore and L. Jussim (eds), *Self and Identity*. New York: Oxford University Press.

McAdams, D. (2001) 'Generativity in midlife', in M. Lachman (ed.), *Handbook of Midlife Development*. New York: Wiley. pp. 395–447.

McIlvane, J., Ajrouch, K. and Antonucci, T. (2007) 'Capturing the complexity of ontergenerational relations', *Journal of Social Issues*, 63 (4): 775–792.

Metz, D. and Underwood, M. (2005) *Older Richer Fitter*. London: Age Concern.

Meyer, V. (2001) 'The medicalisation of menopause', *International Journal of Health Services*, 31 (4): 769–792.

Neugarten, B. (1968) *Middle Age and Aging*. Chicago, IL: Chicago University Press.

Nydegger, C. and Mitteness, L. (1996) 'Midlife: The prime of fathers', in C. Ryff and M. Seltzer (eds), *The Parental Experience in Midlife*. Chicago, IL: Chicago University Press. pp. 533–560.

Rosowsky, E. (1999) 'Couple therapy with long married older adults', in M. Duffy (ed.), *Handbook of Counselling and Psychotherapy with Older Adults*. New York: Wiley. pp. 242–266.

Rowe, J.W. and Kahn, R.L. (1998) *Successful Ageing*. New York: Pantheon.

Ryff, C. and Seltzer, M. (1996) *The Parental Experience in Midlife*. Chicago, IL: Chicago University Press.

Schultz, J.H. (2001) 'Productive aging: An economist's view', in N. Morrow-Howell, J. Hinterlong and M. Sherraden (eds), *Productive Aging: Concepts and Challenges*. Baltimore, MD: Johns Hopkins. pp. 145–172.

Schultz-Zehden, B. (2004) 'Menopause as a challenge', *Psychotherapy*, 49 (5): 350–356.

Seaman, B. (2003) *The Greatest Experiment Ever Performed on Women*. New York: Hyperion.

Sheehey, G. (1995) *New Passages*. New York: Harper/Collins.

Sherman, S. (1994) 'Changes in age identity', *Journal of Aging Studies*, 8: 397–412.

Shweder, R. (1998) *Welcome to Midlife!* Chicago, IL: Chicago University Press.

Siegel-Watkins, E. (2007) 'The medicalisation of the male menopause in America', *Social History of Medicine*, 20 (2): 369–388.

Silverberg, S. (1996) 'Parents' well being and their children's transition to adolescence', in C. Ryff and M. Seltzer (eds), *The Parental Experience in Midlife*. Chicago, IL: Chicago University Press. pp. 215–254.

Stall, S. (1901) *What a Man of Forty-five Ought to Know*. Philadelphia, PA: VIR.

Staudinger, U. and Bluck, S. (2001) 'A view of midlife development from lifespan theory', in M. Lachman (ed.), *Handbook of Midlife Development*. New York: Wiley. pp. 3–39.

Stevens, A. (2000) *On Jung*. London: Penguin.

Stewart, A.J. and Torges, C.M. (2006) 'Social, historical, and developmental influences on the psychology of the baby boom at midlife', in S.K. Whitbourne and S.L. Willis (eds), *The Baby Boomers Grow Up: Contemporary Perspectives on Midlife*. New York: Lawrence Erlbaum.

Tornstam, L. (2005) *Gerotranscendence*. New York: Springer.

Turner, B. (1998) 'Ageing and generational conflicts', *British Journal of Sociology*, 49: 299–304.

Vainonpaa, K. and Topo, P. (2005) 'The making of an ageing disease: The male menopause in Finnish medical literature', *Ageing & Society*, 25 (6): 815–840.

Woodward, K. (1991) *Aging and Its Discontents*. Bloomington, IN: Indiana University Press.

19

PSYCHOLOGICAL THERAPY WITH OLDER ADULTS

Fiona Goudie

The last 15 years has seen the emergence of a substantial body of literature on the application of psychological therapy and counselling models with older people (see O'Leary, 1996; Terry, 1997; Knight, 1992, 1996; Hill and Brettle, 2004; Evans and Garner, 2004). The increasing emphasis on evidence-based approaches and treatment outcomes (NICE guidelines; Cochrane collaborations) more frequently includes older populations within the sampled populations or targets research and reviews specifically at them (Hill and Brettle 2004). There is good evidence that counselling and psychological therapy is effective with older people, particularly in the treatment of anxiety and depression. Outcomes are consistent across the life-span, with individual therapy being more favoured by older people than group approaches. In print at least, there has been much to challenge the assumption made by Freud (1905) that after the age of 50 personality structures were too rigid to change.

Along with the increasing research evidence for the effectiveness of psychological therapies with older people, there is also a projected increase in the ageing population. Those over retirement age currently make up 18 per cent of the ageing population. The numbers of people over 80 will increase by half and those over 90 will double by 2025 (Department of Health, 2001). Despite the evidence and the increasing numbers, older people continue to be under-represented on the case loads in psychology and psychotherapy departments (Murphy, 2000), and common mental health problems like depression and anxiety continue to be under-recognized and under-treated in primary care settings. Possible reasons for this range from ageism on the part of the referrer (Ford and Sbordone, 1980), to fear of dependency in the therapist (Martindale, 1989) or lack of knowledge about availability of psychological therapy among older people themselves. Woolfe (1998), in a study of counsellor's attitudes to working with older people, suggests that fear of dependency may affect both therapists and older people. Fears about their own mortality raised as a result of working on grief and loss issues, as well as being confronted with issues relating to their own parents and grandparents, may pose a threat to younger therapists. Whatever the reason, without sufficient experience of working with older clients in routine practice, individual therapists will be understandably nervous about addressing any complex issues that may arise in therapy. Counselling and psychological therapy services in general may be unsure about how to develop ways of working to meet the needs of more vulnerable older people. This will include those identified as priority groups such as those in hospital, people with stroke, mental health problems including dementia and frequent fallers (Department of Health, 2001, 2005; UK Inquiry into Mental Health and Well-being in Later Life, 2007).

The new UK initiative on Improving Access to Psychological Therapies (Department of Health, 2007) will see an increased investment in psychological therapists and training over three years to deliver increased treatment of depression and anxiety in primary care. It is expected that older people along with other groups will have better access to therapy. There is therefore a unique opportunity in the immediate future to increase therapists' opportunity and confidence in working with older people.

This chapter aims to provide a theoretical and practical framework using illustrative case examples to emphasize general models of psychological therapy which are valuable when working with older people while also referring to specific therapies or modifications which might need to be adopted with particular clients.

A MODEL OF AGEING FOR PSYCHOLOGICAL THERAPY

In all stages of life there are challenges to be overcome. Later life is not unique from that perspective. However, it is often assumed that loss and deficit are the most common challenges for the older client in psychological therapy. Knight (1992, 1996, 2004; Knight and Lee, 2008) has used the more positive developments from life-span developmental psychology to develop a trans-theoretical model of psychotherapy in later life in which older people are recognized as having losses and specific late life challenges, but also potentially greater maturity than younger ones, with a unique social and cultural set of experiences not always understood by younger people. They may be facing some of the hardest challenges of their lives – chronic illness, disability and bereavement. Therapeutic work needs to take account of birth cohort, socio-historical circumstances and immediate social environment as well as physical, cognitive and psychological declines and compensations. Knight's original model, the contextual, cohort-based, maturity, specific challenge model (CCMSC) model (1996, 2004) has been further modified to take account of more recent psychological developments in race and ethnicity (Gallagher-Thompson et al., 2000;

Hinrishen, 2006; Knight et al., 2002; Lau and Kinoshita, 2006). Knight and Lee (2008) have explicitly included culture as a new element to be considered as an inter-relationship with the other elements of the original model. The new model – the contextual adult lifespan theory for adapting psychotherapy (CALTAP) encourages therapists, regardless of their model, to include the key elements of context, cohort, culture, psychological maturation as well as decline and to conceptualize losses as specific challenges specific to each client's individual circumstances.

COGNITIVE BEHAVIOUR THERAPY

Cognitive behaviour therapy has the strongest evidence base with older populations. It has been demonstrated to be effective in treating older people with depression (Thompson et al., 1987; Teri et al., 1994; Scogin and McElreath, 1994), anxiety (Scogin et al., 1992) and chronic ill-health (Rybarczyk et al., 1992). Applications have been developed for groups as well as individuals (Yost et al., 1986; Beutler et al., 1987) and for special populations such as people with dementia (Teri et al., 1997).

A useful summary for using cognitive behavioural therapy (CBT) with older people is provided by Gallagher-Thompson and Thompson (1996). They have adapted the model developed by Beck and colleagues (Beck, 1976; Beck et al., 1979) for depression, which used techniques to help clients evaluate and challenge negative thinking patterns and develop more adaptive points of view. Written records of negative thoughts and modifications and use of homework tasks such as behavioural assignments to check out negative beliefs are key elements of the Beck model.

Gallagher-Thompson and Thompson have developed a 16- to 20-session process at the Older Adult and Family Centre, Department of Veterans Affairs Health Care System in Palo Alto, California. They emphasize that CBT is not a 'bag of tricks' but, like other forms of therapy, relies on a strong therapeutic rapport between the therapist and client. The first three or four sessions are spent on this as well as on 'socializing' the client into treatment. This includes explaining what therapy is and is not (that is, not a social visit, opportunity for medical review, or consultation about practical or financial support) as well as introducing certain techniques (recording forms, assessment questionnaires, behavioural tasks like activity scheduling). There will also be some discussion about how to stay on task with agreed goals of therapy, and 'rules of engagement' such as the therapist not being rude if they interrupt a long dialogue in order to stay on task and keep to time.

The treatment interventions in the early phase of therapy (possibly up to sessions 6–8) may be fairly behavioural and focus on concrete goals in the here and now. Monitoring links between activities and mood in order to plan ways of increasing pleasant activities or relaxation techniques to help cope with anxiety about socializing might be used. The middle phase will focus on links between events, thoughts and feelings. Various written and behavioural strategies are used to monitor, challenge and modify these. The client will be helped to practise and develop more adaptive ways in which to think and act when they are faced with a stressful situation.

The final phase involves helping the client to continue to use their new skills independently, with a written 'maintenance guide' for use when stressful situations occur. They also spend considerable time, as in other therapeutic approaches, exploring feelings and thoughts associated with termination of therapy. This is seen as one of the most important aspects of the work, as many older people will have found that therapy fills a significant gap in their lives.

Laidlaw et al. (2003) have further developed applications of the CBT model to cover depression and co-morbid medical problems such as stroke, Parkinson's disease, dementia and arthritis.

Yost et al. (1986) describe similar strategies for use in groupwork of older people. They adopt a psychoeducational approach with 'lecturettes' and the setting of homework as key elements of group sessions. Therapy is divided into four phases (preparation, collaboration and problem identification, cognitive change and consolidation/termination) over approximately 15–20 sessions. The advantages that can be derived from group therapy in general – socialization, altruism and universality of problems – are seen by Yost et al. as giving group approaches the edge over individual therapy with older clients.

PSYCHODYNAMIC APPROACHES

There has been a growing interest in the application of psychodynamic approaches to work with older people (Hildebrand, 1986; Knight, 1996; Semel, 1996; Evans and Garner, 2004). The Freudian position was that defences become more rigid and there is reduced motivation for change in later life (and therefore psychodynamic therapy may not be helpful). However, Hildebrand (1986), in his psychodynamic casework with older people, found that older people often took the long view in relation to their problems, had greater self-reliance and were more able to deal with therapeutic tasks on their own. This links to Knight's (1996) model described earlier. For example, while ageing presents challenges (memory changes, physical illness), continual growth towards maturity throughout the life-span may contribute to the greater self-reliance described by Hildebrand (1986). Maturity in Knight's sense means increasing cognitive complexity (the capacity to understand argument, social change and an appreciation that people hold differing points of view) and emotional complexity (better comprehension and control of emotional reactions). From this perspective, rather than the younger therapist making allowances for the slowness and rigidity of the older client, it could be argued that older clients at times have to make allowance for the lack of diversity and mature reasoning in younger therapists.

Critchley-Robbins, writing on brief psychodynamic therapy, suggests that brief therapy represents 'the central dilemma of late life: time, mortality and loss. It can give the opportunity to review life, rework their story, to embrace the life they have lived, to mourn and to accept' (2004: 147). She emphasizes the need to attend to potential obstacles or defences, including working on difficult issues with seemingly young or inexperienced therapists, use of denial or somatization and avoidance by focusing on the practical. Practical difficulties do need addressing (mobility, hearing loss), but Chritchley-Robbins would attend to them as possible defences in either the client or the therapist.

Those writing about psychodynamic work with older people have tended to adopt a case study format (Hildebrand, 1986). This may foster the impression that psychodynamic therapy is only suitable for verbal, articulate clients. While this view prevails in many areas, however, Terry (1997) has written movingly about their use with older people with dementia and their carers. He sees the aim of this work as helping the client resolve unconscious internal conflict underlying suffering and distress. He has undertaken psychodynamic work (through paying attention to his own responses and feelings) with a man who has severe dysphasia and 'behaviour problems'. He also describes support groups for staff to think about their own and their patients' feelings about being in an institutional setting, and to help them understand that some of their own feelings may be unconscious communications from their patients.

FAMILY THERAPY

The lives of older people are often deeply embedded within their families – the family they came from, those they have married into and the ones they have initiated through having children. Increased life expectancy makes three, four and five generation families more common, and we can expect to have relationships with our parents and siblings as adults which last longer than the years of parent–dependent child or child–child relationships. Divorce and remarriage also serve to make relationships more complex across the generations. How do grandparents fit in when a son and daughter-in-law divorce, she remarries and moves with the children to live near her new husband's parents 300 miles away?

While there has been limited research described within the family therapy literature on working with older people (see Qualls, 1996), practitioners from different 'schools' of family therapy *have* described and used clinical applications for ageing issues. The earliest dedicated text applied problem-focused brief therapy to older families (Herr and Weakland, 1979). Carter and McGoldrick (1980) acknowledged and described older age relationships as an important part of family culture and the life-cycle. The work of Boszormenyi-Nagy and Krasner (1986) explores the balance of family obligations that are transmitted across generations (for example, obligations about caring for elders).

Whatever model or school is adopted, it is likely that modifications to the approach are needed. It may be necessary to take account of complex relationships and their geographical spread (requiring telephone contact with important members of the network), physical limitations of key family members and the involvement of important people and organizations outside the family such as paid carers and nursing homes staff.

MODELS DEVELOPED SPECIFICALLY FOR USE WITH OLDER PEOPLE

Reality orientation

Reality orientation (RO) is not, strictly speaking, a model of psychotherapy. However, it is of historical importance as one of the earliest and most widely evaluated psychological interventions developed for use with older people. It originated in Veterans' Administration hospitals in the United States in the 1960s and was used with people with both long-standing psychiatric problems and those with dementia. However, research and practice has resulted in the approach being applied almost exclusively in dementia care settings.

The aim of the approach is to encourage people to remember and retain existing skills, abilities and sense of identity. Informal or 24-hour RO is the cornerstone of the approach. The emphasis is on staff interaction with clients to increase awareness and interest in what is going on around them. Attention is paid to reducing barriers to awareness (sensory deficits, poor lighting, background noise), enhancing staff communication skills (tone of voice, non-verbal communication, sentence structure) and modifying the environment (using memory boards, signposts, colour coding). Informal RO is supplemented by formal or group RO. These are structured sessions, which involve repetition and rehearsal of information relevant to group members (for example, names and addresses, life circumstances, current affairs). The mode of repetition and rehearsal means this approach has lent itself to evaluation. Woods (1992) summarizes the research on RO.

While there is evidence for the effectiveness of group RO, it has been criticized as rigid and encouraging clients to fail. However, this criticism is perhaps more appropriately aimed at those who have unthinkingly implemented the formal approach (focusing on endless repetition of day, date and weather, for instance) and paid insufficient attention to the informal approach (installing memory boards but not keeping them up to date, painting every door on a long corridor a uniform white instead of personalizing room doors or colour coding toilet doors).

Reminiscence and life review

Until the 1960s, reminiscence was seen as a negative activity, likely to over-emphasize past events and potentially cause distress to older people. Butler (1963) saw life review and related reminiscence activities as normative and undertaken by most people.

Reminiscence methods are used for a wide range of purposes including oral history, enhancing social contact, maintaining old skills, improving cross-generational and cultural understanding, life review, therapy and for fun (see Bender et al., 1999 for a summary of purposes). Reminiscence activities are usually carried out in groups but can happen on an individual basis. They are increasingly used with people who have dementia. The rationale for this has been that remote memories of childhood and early adulthood are relatively well preserved until later in the course of dementia. Drawing on these memories can help the person maintain a sense of themselves as a person and enable them to feel confidence in some areas of memory even if day-to-day events are difficult to recall. Open-ended discussion around particular themes (childhood, first job and family life) may be a useful approach with people who have little cognitive impairment. However, it is more common to use a range of triggers to stimulate recall. These commonly include music, videotapes, photographic material and everyday objects of historical interest. Drama, art and literary projects may also have reminiscence as the focus. Some approaches involve individuals writing, using tapes or diaries.

Bender et al. (1999) emphasize the importance of staff 'doing their homework' in advance by getting an individual life history of the clients they will involve in reminiscence. Goudie and Stokes (1990), in the same vein, discuss the importance of individual reminiscence profiles. This information is needed to ensure that the subject matter is something people will be familiar with. Those who conduct reminiscence need to be confident about using a variety of stimulus material and have good non-verbal as well as verbal communication skills. In addition, those running groups need good group-work skills and to be able to involve people with a range of cognitive abilities. At least two facilitators will be needed for a group of six. Certain people may not benefit from a group approach. Compulsive reminiscers (who may have unresolved feelings about an earlier life event) can dominate a group unhelpfully, and some people have no real interest in reminiscing. For others, certain topics if introduced without thought or awareness of the individual's life history can trigger distress (for example, playing the sound of an air raid siren for someone who experienced bombing during a war). Overall, however, such groups appear to be stimulating and enjoyable to those who participate and increase staff awareness of the lives of the people they care for. Research into group reminiscence for specific problems like depression is in its infancy, and a more structured approach which incorporates specific psychotherapeutic principles may be required (Fry, 1983).

Life-story work involves looking back over the past – usually on a one-to-one basis. It does not set out to resolve past or present problems, but can be used to help families and carers gain greater understanding of the person they care for, to have something for families to pass on to carers if someone moves into a residential setting, to orientate the person to the reality of their life. Some work can take the form of a life-story book, with sections decade by decade through the person's life, but could also be a visual record of photos and memorabilia. Murphy and Moyes (1997) describe good practice with people who have dementia.

Life review is a more focused and structured approach. The therapist and older person are usually working one-to-one on 'conflict resolution … self acceptance and coming to terms with life' (Garland, 1994). The technique of recalling specific events and re-evaluating them may involve painful experiences. It is a psychotherapeutic approach requiring a trained therapist with access to supervision. Both reminiscence and life review have demonstrable impact on well-being (Spector et al., 2003), but have not been found to specifically improve dementia symptoms.

Validation and resolution therapy

Validation therapy (Feil, 1990) was developed as a client-centred approach for listening to and understanding the apparently confused speech of people with dementia. Interpretation is linked to Feil's model of disorientation and the possibility of unresolved earlier life crises.

Resolution therapy (Goudie and Stokes, 1989; Stokes and Goudie, 1990) also emphasizes the use of Rogerian counselling skills (congruence, warmth and acceptance) to try to understand and respond to what the person with dementia might be feeling. The focus is on what is going on in the here and now to understand meaning and feeling. So, for example, if someone was insisting they must go home to cook their husband's tea (even though he has been dead for many years), the worker would *accept* that the person had been thinking about their husband and *reflect* this ('So you've been thinking about your husband and the meals you used to cook this afternoon?') while trying to *explore* what the current feelings behind this are ('It's very quiet here today, are you feeling bored?') and *resolve* them ('Would you like to give me a hand with the tea trolley?'). The idea is to use these skills to overcome the barrier to communication that dementia can pose.

These approaches emphasize the importance of the emotional life of people with dementia and are in line with the spirit of person-centred care for people with dementia. By using them routinely, those working in dementia care can help promote psychological well-being as well as establishing a basis for positive relationships on which to offer more focused help if it is needed. However, they do rely on the congruence – that is, two persons in psychological contact – for change to take place, and that becomes more difficult as dementia advances. Morton (2002) has worked on developing Prouty's (1976) model of 'pre therapy' – a way of working with people for whom psychological contact is difficult. The approach was developed for people with learning difficulties or psychosis to enable them and their therapists to meet the condition of psychological contact and then move on to using person-centred therapy. However, where this might not ever be achieved, the work focused more on psychological contact as the goal itself. Pre therapy works on using reflective techniques establish three 'contact functions':

- *Reality contact*: contact with the world, such as awareness of events, places and people.
- *Affective contact*: contact with ourselves, including awareness of thoughts, feelings and bodily sensations.
- *Communicative contact*: verbal and non-verbal communication with other people.

For example, reality contact would be enhanced by describing and naming situations, events and people. Describing non-verbal expressions – 'You look sad', 'Your hands look tense' – would aim to strengthen affective contact and word-for-word reflections, and body reflections would aim to build up communicative contact.

The overall purpose for using the reflective techniques is to 'intensify inner feeling to the point that an experiencing process is initiated' (Prouty, 1976).

KEY CLINICAL AREAS

The National Service Framework for Older People (Department of Health, 2001) identified a number of clinical areas as priorities for the National Health Service. These cover stroke, falls and mental health, including depression and dementia.

The aim of this section is to demonstrate (using a case study approach) how elements of the models described earlier can be used therapeutically with clients or carers who have experienced these health problems.

CASE STUDY 19.1: THE STROKE ADJUSTMENTS GROUP

The psychologist attached to a rehabilitation centre noticed that there was an increase in levels of depression among clients who had been attending for stroke rehabilitation and were to be discharged in the next four to six weeks. The physiotherapists and occupational therapist had noticed that some clients relapsed during this period while others became hopeless about the future ('I thought I'd walk out of here, now I won't – I'm such a failure, I'll never cope alone'), or angry with the team ('You've not done anything for me in a year, how can you discharge me?').

Because of the number of people who seemed to be experiencing similar feelings, the team felt that a group approach might be useful (Barton, 2007; Barton et al., 2002). They set up an eight-week stroke adjustments group run by two team members. The group aimed to enable members to draw support from each other at a time when many felt vulnerable about the future, share feelings about losses associated with stroke as well as considering previously established coping strategies outside their life as a 'stroke patient' and how these might help them move beyond the 'stroke patient' role.

Elements of the framework described by Yost et al. (1986) were used, such as socialization of the group to therapy, preparation, consolidation, termination as well as some of the techniques they suggest (the idea of turn-taking in 'rounds', mini lectures about cognitions and coping strategies).

After two or three sessions most group members were keen to speak during the rounds, both on their own behalf and in supporting and challenging each other, so the mini lectures were shortened. The facilitators still started each session with homework/

(Continued)

(Continued)

reflections on last week and introduced the agenda or theme for the session with handouts for some of them.

For many members, the group was the first time since their stroke they had been able to acknowledge that they would not regain their previous physical abilities or lifestyle. In relation to Knight's model, the stroke could be considered a 'specific challenge' not only to physical well-being but also continuity of lifestyle. For example, 'I was holding onto the idea that if I kept coming here I'd go back to normal eventually, even though I've been in a wheelchair for 14 months.'

The forthcoming discharge from the centre challenged such denial for group members and facilitators. For example, 'I think we've kind of ignored his wife's remarks about his poor concentration, because we were like him – desperately hoping he could start driving and being the treasurer of his social club again.'

Over half of the group's work was concerned with expressions of loss and regret. Members were often reluctant to consider the future, so a combined approach was used which allowed for reflection of feelings as well as more structured use of life review to consider previous ways of coping. This seemed to provide participants with a contained way of accepting the reality of their changed lives while maintaining continuity of strengths and resources (personal, social, material) to face their new life circumstances.

Certain themes emerged across a series of groups and were brought to peer supervision by the facilitators. These included dependency/autonomy and rank ordering (hierarchies) of group members by one another according to the severity of their stroke or its consequences. Many group members believed the philosophy of stroke rehabilitation was to encourage independence and saw themselves as failing to achieve this and not then being helped to accept that they needed to depend on others (people, aids, alterations to the environment).The group facilitators tried to encourage discussions about the balance between dependence and autonomy, but some members felt this was too little too late and had strong feelings of shame and betrayal. The wider rehabilitation team felt they needed to revise the messages they gave when people started attending. Information leaflets were re-written to include messages about appropriate support and sharing of care to modify the focus on maximizing independence.

There were some cross-cultural differences about dependency in a group with two male Asian members. Both men felt appropriately supported by their families and that at times the therapists had been urging them to become unnecessarily independent. One of them would continue to have a number of physical needs but could anticipate a future where he would continue to head his family and have an influence over the lives of his children and grandchildren. This contrasted with the often expressed and sometimes unrealistic desire among women members of the group to be 'totally independent' and 'not a burden on my family'.

The rank ordering or competitive hierarchy emerged with remarks like 'At least I'm not in a wheelchair' or 'Poor you having to go into a home'. The facilitators struggled at times with how to address the underlying feelings of fear. Early modelling by facilitators of supportively challenging remarks ('How did you feel when Elsie made the remarks about the wheelchair?') and generalizing comments ('Sometimes it is easier to put other people down than admit to what we're most scared of') seemed helpful, and many group members began to respond to such remarks spontaneously ('I used to feel like that too, Elsie, I fought the idea for a long time').

The difference between those facing residential or nursing home admission and those remaining in their own home seemed to be a gulf that was too difficult to bridge in a group of this sort, and the facilitators felt that in the future those going into care probably needed more space to reflect on the unique impact of this.

CASE STUDY 19.2: A COGNITIVE-BEHAVIOURAL INTERVENTION FOR FREQUENT FALLING

The consequences of falling, including the risks of hospitalization, increased risk of further falls and medical complications have been identified as key NHS targets within the National Service Framework. A national programme of falls clinics and falls rehabilitation programmes are being developed. These focus on medical risk reduction and physiotherapy-based rehabilitation. Psychological aspects of falling are infrequently considered, despite the fact that fear of falling attributions about the reasons for a fall may be important risk factors for future falls (McKee et al., 1999).

Mrs Jones was 84 and a widow living alone, with two daughters living nearby with their families. She had received a hip replacement 18 months previously and had never really gained the mobility she and the therapy team felt she would be able to. She spent most of the time sitting in her large armchair next to a commode with important items (newspaper, glasses, flask and TV remote control) on a table in front of her. Her muscles were weak and when she did rise from the chair she lurched dangerously from one large item of furniture to the next. She had had three further falls – usually when a family member was present. Her GP had suggested that she attend the new falls clinic at the nearby hospital, but she has said she is too afraid to attend and is generally too fearful to move very much. The practice counselling psychologist agreed to visit her at home in connection with the anxiety.

Mrs Jones had a range of negative thoughts about herself and her mobility. She felt that because she was old and scared the hip replacement operation had been a waste

(Continued)

(Continued)

of NHS time and money. The panic and fearfulness (which were at their worst when she tried to stand and move to the commode or the next-door bedroom) were not reducing. She put them down to old age and thought they would get worse in time. She believed her mobility problems were ruling every aspect of her life and that she was a nuisance to everyone.

The psychologist initially offered Mrs Jones a few one-to-one sessions to work on strategies for dealing with panic and alternative ways of thinking about herself and her mobility. Mrs Jones thought this might be a waste of the therapist's time (and the counselling psychologist felt some of these feelings herself), but was very interested in any alternatives to medication for the panic attacks.

During the second session one of the daughters called. It was clear that she shared many of the same cognitions as her mother about old age and falling. She remarked to the psychologist: 'It's nice of you to come and give mum a bit of company, but it would be better if you could sort a wheelchair for her – she'll need one soon enough.'

In supervision, the psychologist expressed her frustration about trying to carry out therapy in a home setting and also wondered if it would be better to pass Mrs Jones on to the district nurse or physiotherapist. Her supervisor reflected that perhaps the psychologist was experiencing and reacting to Mrs Jones' and her daughter's projections about ageing and hopelessness, and may also be feeling some irritation at having to see someone away from the contained office environment where interruptions can be controlled. At this point it is as if the challenges of ageing were becoming overwhelming for all involved. It was difficult to focus on the specific challenges of mobility and low mood or to draw on Mrs Jones' and her family's 'maturity' or life experiences.

At the subsequent session the psychologist suggested that a family meeting might be helpful. 'Why don't we invite everyone in the family who might be able to help us understand your fear of falling?' To her surprise, in addition to her two daughters, Mrs Jones suggested her 21-year-old grandson.

The meeting was arranged with Mrs Jones, her two daughters, her grandson and the psychologist. A problem-solving focus was agreed for the session in line with that proposed by Herr and Weakland (1979). For one daughter (Joyce) the ideal solution to Mrs Jones' difficulties was to get her a wheelchair and prevent her from putting herself at risk. She was frightened of the possibility of further falls, which could lead to hospitalization. The second daughter (Mary) was actually quite cross with her mother and sister and felt that her mother could do better and was 'putting on' the panic attacks for attention. The psychologist noted how they argued with each other and ignored their mother during the early part of the session. The grandson remained quiet through much of this. When asked to comment, he said 'This is just what it was like after Grandad died (five years previously) with mum and Aunt Mary arguing. But then Aunt Mary was blaming mum for not calling the ambulance quick enough and mum couldn't believe he might have had a stroke. Gran was wringing her hands and didn't know what to say.'

There was a lengthy silence at this point. Slowly both daughters acknowledged this had been the case. Joyce said 'I felt so guilty about dad that I want to wrap mum up in cotton wool.' Mary acknowledged that she couldn't bear to think of losing her mother and was therefore possibly playing down the implications of any genuine aspects of frailty. Jeremy, the grandson, had always been close to his grandmother and had been party to many disclosures from her about how concerned she was to keep the peace between them.

The therapist felt this family session was invaluable to help them all understand the family's attitude to ageing as well as the aspects of Mrs Jones' helplessness which were to do with feeling 'stuck' between her daughters. It was possible to set some practical goals and teach the family anxiety management strategies, which they could help Mrs Jones with. At three-month follow-up she was going out for regular trips in the car and visiting her daughters' homes. She had accepted a walking frame and had been able to clear the clutter of furniture from her lounge so that she could slowly but more confidently move between lounge, kitchen and bedroom. She continued to feel panicky in certain situations (for example, if someone unexpectedly knocked at the door), but felt this was a realistic fear she could cope with.

The psychologist felt that she had been able to offer something useful to the family and believed that supervision and awareness of her own feelings had been crucial in avoiding premature discharge and unhelpful collusion with the spirit of hopelessness.

CASE STUDY 19.3: DEALING WITH DIAGNOSIS IN EARLY DEMENTIA

The feelings associated with receiving a diagnosis of dementia or stroke are similar to those associated with a diagnosis of cancer or other terminal illness and with bereavement and loss. Giving a diagnosis and discussing implications can be stressful for health professionals and may generate feelings of panic, a desire to avoid the subject or pass on the task to someone they believe to be better qualified at dealing with bad news.

In services with a specific early diagnosis and treatment role, such as a memory clinic, the team may have developed their skills in pre- and post-diagnostic counselling. Grief counselling and therapy models such as Worden's (1991) can be valuable in relation to the post-diagnostic counselling work.

Many people with dementia never receive a diagnosis in the early stages of their disease. As their condition progresses, they attend hospitals or day centres with other

(Continued)

(Continued)

people who are obviously forgetful and have communication difficulties. Yet it is unusual for the treatment programmes in these settings to address directly the diagnosis and associated feelings for their service users themselves, even though support groups for carers may discuss the issues directly.

This case study describes the work between Mary (43), a nurse-therapist, and Ernest (80), an attender at a newly opened day hospital for people with dementia. The therapeutic programme was group-based and included reminiscence, general knowledge and word quizzes, social activities and skill-building (gardening, cooking).

Ernest was one of a small number of patients attending because they had been prescribed a new drug (cognitive enhancers for people with Alzheimer's disease). Some of the comments he made in groups during his first week included: 'I don't know why I'm here – I think my wife wants rid of me', 'I've been told I've got Alzheimer's and it would help coming here, but no one's told me what will help', 'Everyone is confused here, will I get like that?'.

Ernest expressed interest in weekly one-to-one sessions with Mary on the theme of 'Coping with forgetting' instead of one of the group activities. Mary was concerned that the service was ignoring and avoiding the fears clients had about dementia. She thought that new attenders in particular were confused by the purpose of some of the group activities. She had previously worked as a counsellor in a breast cancer unit and used a psychodynamic approach.

Early sessions were information-orientated at Ernest's request: 'I want to know why I'm taking these drugs.' He wanted this information written down to take home after the second session. The next morning his wife Violet phoned Mary to say that when Ernest had come home the previous evening with the information he had wanted to discuss it together. 'At first I was cross that he'd got hold of this himself, but then I realised we'd both been pretending to each other that everything was OK, ignoring the future but not really talking about now. We've always been so close. We cried together but it was such a relief.'

The sessions became more unstructured as Ernest gained the confidence to talk about his feelings of sadness about being denied information on his illness, anger at the early collusion between his wife and the health professionals and his fears and hopes for the future.

Ernest saw Mary weekly for eight weeks, then fortnightly for a further four sessions. The fortnightly sessions involved his wife. Mary was struck by the degree of support they were able to offer each other about marital tensions, the loss of their sexual relationship and certain friendships and the fact that Ernest had to stop driving. At times the couple joked about role reversal. Ernest had been the driver, the organized planner of trips and holidays and more confident socially. Now Violet was having to take on these roles. However, they were also able to express their frustration and resentment as well as their sadness. Violet had never liked driving and after a near miss got irritated with Ernest: 'If it wasn't for Ernest and his poor memory I wouldn't be driving.' Ernest was sad because he felt Violet was avoiding booking holidays: 'We'll never go abroad again. Violet feels embarrassed about me.'

Mary was able to reflect on these comments and suggest that at times they were projecting their own feelings onto the other. For example, Violet might feel irritated with herself about her neglected driving skills, and Ernest was perhaps embarrassed about his own memory lapses and lack of initiative in conversations.

They both felt positive about the sessions. Ernest felt they were no longer hiding things from each other, and Violet commented that they often carried on talking about issues that had come up in a particular session long into the evening. At six-month follow-up they were using more home support, but both felt that their relationship was still good and they could face the future together with the support of their family.

There were some issues arising from this work for Mary in supervision. She admitted that she feared once she began the one-to-one work with Ernest she would never be able to stop it and would have him on her case load until he was admitted to long-term care (see Martindale, 1989 for more on this theme). However, she was able to reflect on the possibility of these feelings for Ernest and use them in therapy directly. This enabled both Ernest and Violet to share their fears of dependency in the future as well as the reality now and not to catastrophize in advance. Instead of becoming dependent on Mary, Ernest was able to return to his confidante of a lifetime, Violet.

Mary had also been concerned about confidentiality and involving his wife in what had started out as individual work. However, it was important to acknowledge the reality of Ernest's memory problems and involve Violet in bearing witness to experiences he wanted to remember as well as helping with practical problem solving related to the consequences of Alzheimers' disease.

As someone with a psychodynamic background, Mary had thought Ernest would see her as a parent figure but instead had the sense that Ernest and Violet saw her more as a well-informed adult child who had to be let go. Biggs (1998) makes reference to the fact that therapy with older adults does not necessarily follow the psychodynamic tradition of transference, with the client projecting onto a 'parental' therapist. Indeed, Knight (1996) suggests that transference with older adults can take a number of forms (parent, child, grandchild, sexual partner) and the therapist needs to be alert to this.

CASE STUDY 19.4: DEPRESSION AND REACTIVATION OF WAR TRAUMA FOLLOWING ADMISSION TO RESIDENTIAL CARE

Post traumatic stress disorder (PTSD) has become increasingly recognized as a psychological consequence of war for service veterans and for many civilians living through war. Specific symptoms include flashbacks, intrusive thoughts, auditory and visual re-experiencing of traumatic events, nightmares and the tendency to be easily aroused or startled.

For many older people who have experienced trauma in earlier life, avoidance of memories has been made possible for many years by engaging in physically demanding activities, working long hours and using tobacco and alcohol. However, late life losses associated with bereavement, reduction in physical ability and early dementia can lead to the reactivation of traumatic memories which have been successfully repressed for many years (Goudie, 2002).

Mr Zimbrowski was an 84-year-old Polish man who had been resident in 'The Elms' for six months since the death of his wife. A combination of severe arthritis and Parkinson's Disease had made it difficult for him to look after himself in his own home. Staff at 'The Elms' were concerned about his behaviour. He was hostile to staff and would remove food from other residents' plates at meal times and hoard it in drawers and cupboards in his room. He was reluctant to eat his own meal in public. He appeared frightened of going to sleep and when he did go to bed, he wanted to use the furniture to barricade himself into his room.

The Head of Home and a visiting psychologist were able to develop enough of a relationship with Mr Zimbrowski and one of his daughters to find out that he had been a prisoner of war. He described how he survived starvation and death in the camp. He stayed awake at night to ensure his possessions were not stolen, and sought out and then hid any rations uneaten by the ill or dying. He had not talked about these experiences for decades, but the communal eating situation in the home and the noise of other residents and staff at night reactivated some of the old fears and behaviours. In the past he had been able to distract himself from certain memories by reading and watching TV late at night. His concentration now affected his enjoyment of these activities. He also found the group reminiscence sessions organized by the home's activity co-ordinator intrusive. Even though he avoided the groups themselves, he felt nervous when other residents and staff joked together about how the city had changed and mentioned the war years. He was not sleeping, his appetite was poor and he was feeling depressed by his new surroundings.

A number of strategies helped Mr Zimbrowski and those caring for him to cope better with his traumatic memories and reactions. He and the psychologist established together that it was important for him to try to stay in the 'here and now' rather than being drawn back into the past. However, it was also important for staff to understand enough of his background to be able to empathize with him, without Mr Zimbrowski having to explain his past to each new staff member. With his daughter's help, a life-story noticeboard was made with some of his mementoes and photographs. The board included recent photos of his children and grandchildren and information about work and hobbies as well as pre-war mementoes. It had two functions. It reminded staff of Mr Zimbrowski's Polish background and prisoner-of-war experiences and enabled them to empathize with him more readily. It also helped them to ground him in the here and now by drawing his attention to photos of his grandchildren, his long service award from the local steelworks and his membership card for the Polish Club he still attended occasionally with his son. His hoarding of food was reduced by giving him his meals on his own in his bedroom. He began to stay up late in the lounge with one or two other residents who enjoyed late-night TV. As far as possible, the same two key workers on nights would help him get into bed. They would regularly repeat a conversation about the here and now which included a reminder of the date, current news, any recent or planned visitors, who they were and that they would be looking after him and his belongings overnight.

Some difficulties remained, particularly when staff changed, but Mr Zimbrowski felt much more settled and the home felt more able to cope on a day-to-day basis. The psychologist continued to offer the Head of Home some supervision sessions over a period of a few months to enable her to reflect on and resolve any further difficulties.

CONCLUSION

This chapter has described the application of a range of approaches to psychological therapy and counselling with older people. The case studies illustrate some of the problems which older people and their carers may face and the different settings in which they can occur. While therapy with many older people will be little different to working with younger people, it has been the author's aim to demonstrate that psychological therapy and counselling can be of benefit to older people far beyond the confines of the one-to-one outpatient clinic room. This demands an openness to change and an alertness to ageist assumptions in potential therapists.

Generational and cultural factors – Knight (1996) refers to these as cohort factors – may mean that some older people have had little exposure to talking treatments and may not initially see its relevance. On the other hand, there will be those who have children or grandchildren with experience of counselling and therapy. It is important to explain treatment approaches and their relevance as well as the structure that will be followed in a session (that it will be time-limited, that particular topics will be agreed as the focus of the work and that the therapist will bring them back to the point if they get sidetracked). If sessions end up as sociable chats it may be because the enthusiastic practitioner, keen to get on with 'the work', has not taken sufficient time to explain the purpose of the work and how it will be done.

Supervision has been emphasized in the case studies described in this chapter. While this is important with all client groups, it seems to be given less emphasis in work with older adults among some professional groups. This is a great mistake – particularly *early on* in the career of the therapist and *early on* in the process of engaging in therapy with a particular client or group of clients. Early on in the career of the therapist it is important to become attuned to how the negative impact of ageism, relationships with parents and grandparents and fears about dependency and one's own ageing may affect the therapist's capacity to accept and work with older adults. Supervision is particularly important early on in the work with individuals or groups because it is at this point that most attention needs to be paid to clarifying what the relationship and therapeutic work are going to be about. Mutual avoidance of process issues (the feelings evoked in the client by the therapist and in the therapist by the client) at this stage can lead to premature discharge (as could have occurred with Mrs Jones in Case study 19.2) or, conversely, a feeling in the therapist that they need to carry on supporting a frail client forever as if they are a parent or grandparent.

Psychological therapy with older adults seems at times to engender apprehension in younger therapists. However, it can enrich our understanding of what life is like for older people now, and what it may be like for us in the future. The richness and diversity of relationships and experiences increase with age and can appear to pose a greater challenge when things go wrong. Nonetheless, there is an encyclopaedia of learning to draw on and use – if we will listen.

REFERENCES

Barton, J. (2007) 'Psychological aspects of stroke', in P. Kennedy (ed.), *Psychological Management of Physical Disability.* Hove: Routledge.

Barton, J., Miller, A. and Chanter, J. (2002) 'Emotional adjustment to stroke: A group therapeutic approach', *Nursing Times,* 98 (23): 33–35.

Beck, A.T. (1976) *Cognitive Therapy and the Emotional Disorders.* New York: International Universities Press.

Beck, A.T., Rush, J., Shaw, B. and Emery, G. (1979) *Cognitive Therapy of Depression.* New York: Guilford Press.

Bender, M., Bauckham, P. and Norris, N. (1999) *The Therapeutic Purposes of Reminiscence.* London: Sage.

Beutler, L.E., Scogin, F., Kirkish, P., Schretler, D. and Corbishley, A. (1987) 'Group cognitive therapy and alprazolam in the treatment of depression in older adults', *Journal of Consulting and Clinical Psychology,* 55: 550–556.

Biggs, S. (1998) 'The end of the beginning: A brief history of the psychoanalysis of adult ageing', *Journal of Social Work Practice,* 12 (2): 135–140.

Boszormenyi-Nagy, I. and Krasner, B. (1986) *Between Give and Take: A Clinical Guide to Contextual Therapy.* New York: Brunner/Mazel.

Butler, R.N. (1963) The Life Review: 'An interpretation of reminiscence in the aged', *Psychiatry*, 26: 65–76.

Carter, E. and McGoldrick, M. (1980) *The Family Life Cycle: A Framework for Family Therapy*, 2nd edn. New York: Gardner Press.

Critchley-Robbins, S. (2004) 'Brief psychodynamic therapy with older people', in S. Evans and J. Garner (eds), *Talking Over the Years: A Handbook of Dynamic Psychotherapy with Older Adults.* Hove: Brunner-Routledge.

Department of Health (2001) *The National Service Framework for Older People.* London: Department of Health.

Department of Health (2005) *Everybody's Business.* London: HMSO.

Department of Health (2007) *Improving Access to Psychological Therapies (IAPT) Specification for the Commissioner-led Pathfinder Programme.* London: Department of Health.

Evans, S. and Garner, J. (2004) *Talking Over the Years: A Handbook of Dynamic Psychotherapy with Older Adults.* Hove: Brunner-Routledge.

Feil, N. (1990) *Validation: The Feil Method*, 2nd edn. Cleveland, OH: Edward Feil Productions.

Ford, C.V. and Sbordone, R.J. (1980) 'Attitudes of psychiatrists toward elderly patients', *American Journal of Psychiatry*, 137: 571–575.

Freud S. (1905) *On Psychotherapy: Collected Works 7.* London: Hogarth.

Fry, P.A. (1983) 'Structured and unstructured reminiscence training and depression among the elderly', *Clinical Gerontologist*, 1 (3): 15–37.

Gallagher-Thompson, D. and Thompson, L.W. (1996) 'Applying Cognitive-behaviour therapy to the psychological problems of later life', in S.H. Zarit and B.G. Knight (eds), *A Guide to Psychotherapy and Aging: Effective Clinical Interventions in a Life Stage Context.* Washington, DC: American Psychological Association.

Gallagher-Thompson, D., Lovett, S., Rose, J., McKibbin, C., Coon, D. and Futterman, A. (2000) 'Impact of psychoeducational interventions on distressed family caregivers', *Journal of Clinical Geropsychology*, 6: 91–110.

Garland, J. (1994) 'What splendour it all coheres: Life review therapy with older people', in J. Bornat (ed.), *Reminiscence Reviewed: Perspectives, Evaluations, Achievements.* Buckingham: Open University Press.

Goudie, F. (2002) 'Trauma and dementia', in G. Stokes and F. Goudie (eds), *The Essential Dementia Care Handbook.* Bicester: Speechmark.

Goudie, F. and Stokes, G. (1989) 'Dealing with confusion', *Nursing Times*, 85 (39): 38–40.

Goudie, F. and Stokes, G. (1990) 'Reminiscence with dementia sufferers', in G. Stokes and F. Goudie (eds), *Working with Dementia.* Bicester: Winslow Press.

Herr, J.J. and Weakland, J.H. (1979) *Counselling Elders and their Families.* New York: Springer.

Hildebrand, P. (1986) 'Dynamic psychotherapy with the elderly', in I. Hanley and M. Gilhooly (eds), *Psychological Therapies for the Elderly.* London: Croom Helm.

Hill, A. and Brettle, A. (2004) *Counselling Older People: A Systematic Review.* Rugby: British Association for Counselling and Psychotherapy.

Hinrishen, A. (2006) 'Why multicultural issues matter for practitioners working with older adults', *Professional Psychology Research and Practice*, 37 (1): 29–35.

Knight, B.G. (1992) *Older Adults in Psychotherapy: Case Histories.* Newbury Park, CA: Sage.

Knight, B.G. (1996) *Psychotherapy with Older Adults.* Newbury Park, CA: Sage.

Knight, B.G. (2004) *Psychotherapy with Older Adults.* Thousand Oaks, CA: Sage.

Knight, B.G. and Lee, L.O. (2008) 'Contextual adult lifespan theory for adapting psychotherapy', in K. Laidlaw and B.G. Knight (eds), *Handbook of Emotional Disorders in Later Life: Assessment and Treatment.* Oxford: Oxford University Press.

Knight, B.G., Robinson, G.S., Flynn Longmire, C.V., Chun, M., Nakao, K. and Kim, J.H. (2002) 'Cross cultural issues in care giving for persons with dementia: Do familism values reduce burden and distress?', *Ageing International*, 27 (3): 70–94.

Laidlaw, K., Thompson, L.W., Dick-Siskin, L. and Gallagher-Thompson, D. (2003) *Cognitive Behaviour Therapy with Older People*. Chichester: Wiley.

Lua, A.W. and Kinoshita, L.M. (2006) 'Cognitive-behavioural therapy with culturally diverse older adults', in P.A. Hays and G.Y. Iwamasa (eds), *Culturally Responsive Cognitive Behaviour Therapy: Assessment, Practice and Supervision*. Washington, DC: American Psychological Association.

Martindale, B. (1989) 'Becoming dependent again', *Psychoanalytic Psychotherapy*, 4: 67–75.

McKee, K., Orbell, S. and Radley, K.A. (1999) 'Predicting perceived recovered activity in older people after a fall', *Disability and Rehabilitation*, 21 (12): 555–562.

Morton, I. (2002) 'Building therapeutic relationships with people who have dementia', in G. Stokes and F. Goudie (eds), *The Essential Dementia Care Handbook*. Bicester: Speechmark.

Murphy, C. and Moyes, M. (1997) 'Life story work', in M. Marshall (ed.), *State of the Art in Dementia Care*. London: Centre for Policy on Ageing.

Murphy, S. (2000) 'Provision of psychotherapy services for older people', *Psychiatric Bulletin*, 24: 181–184.

O'Leary, E. (1996) *Counselling Older Adults*. London: Chapman Hall.

Prouty, G. (1976) 'Pre-therapy: A method of treating pre-expressive psychotic and retarded patients', *Psychotherapy Research and Practice*, 13 (3): 290–95.

Qualls, S.H. (1996) 'Family therapy with aging families', in S.H. Zarit and B.G. Knight (eds), *A Guide to Psychotherapy and Aging*. Washington, DC: American Psychological Association.

Rybarczyk, B., Gallagher-Thompson, D. and Rodman, J. (1992) 'Applying CBT to the chronically ill elderly: Treatment issues and case illustration', *International Psychogeriatrics*, 4: 127–140.

Scogin, F. and McElreath, L. (1994) 'Efficacy of psychosocial treatments for geriatric depression: A quantitative review', *Journal of Counselling and Clinical Psychology*, 62: 69–74.

Scogin, F., Rickard, H.C., Keith, S., Wilson, J. and McElreath, L. (1992) 'Progressive and imaginal relaxation training for elderly persons with subjective anxiety', *Psychology and Aging*, 7: 419–424.

Semel, V.G. (1996) 'Modern psychoanalytic treatment of the older patient', in S.H. Zarit and B.G. Knight (eds), *A Guide to Psychotherapy and Aging*. Washington, DC: American Psychological Association.

Spector, A., Orell, M., Davies, S. and Woods, R.T. (2003) 'Reminiscence therapy for dementia' (Cochrane Review), in *The Cochrane Library*, Vol. 3. Oxford: Updated Software.

Stokes, G. and Goudie, F. (1990) 'Counselling confused elderly people', in G. Stokes and F. Goudie (eds), *Working with Dementia*. Bicester: Winslow.

Teri, L., Curtis, J., Gallagher-Thompson, D. and Thompson, L. (1994) 'Cognitive-behavioural therapy with depressed older adults', in L.S. Schneider, C.F. Reynolds, B.D. Lebowitz and A.J. Friedhoff (eds), *Diagnosis and Treatment of Depression in Late Life: Results of the NIH Consensus Development Conference*. Washington, DC: American Psychiatric Press. pp. 279–2910.

Teri, L., Logsdon, R.G., Uomoto, J. and McCurry, S.M. (1997) 'Behavioural treatment of depression in dementia patients: A controlled clinical trial', *Journal of Gerontology: Psychological Sciences*, 52: 159–166.

Terry, P. (1997) *Counselling the Elderly and their Carers*. Basingstoke: Macmillan.

Thompson, L.W., Gallagher, D. and Breckenridge, J.S. (1987) 'Comparative effectiveness of psychotherapies for depressed elders', *Journal of Consulting and Clinical Psychology*, 55: 385–390.

UK Inquiry into Mental Health and Well-being in Later Life (2007) *Improving Services and Support for Older People with Mental Health Problems.* London: UK Inquiry.

Woods, R.T. (1992) 'What can be learned from studies on reality orientation?', in G. Jones and B. Miesen (eds), *Care-giving in Dementia: Research and Applications.* London: Routledge.

Woolfe, R. (1998) 'Therapists' attitudes towards working with older people', *Journal of Social Work Practice*, 12 (2): 141–148.

Worden, W. (1991) *Grief Counselling and Grief Therapy*, 2nd edn. London: Routledge.

Yost, E.G., Beutler, L.E., Corbishley, A.M. and Allendar, J.R. (1986) *Group Cognitive Therapy: A Treatment Approach for Depressed Older Adults.* Elmsford, NY: Pergamon.

PART V

OPPORTUNITIES AND TENSIONS IN DIFFERENT CONTEXTS

The practice of counselling psychology takes place within political, economic and organizational contexts. These change over time as do the opportunities, issues and challenges they present. The contexts explored in this section represent some of the main employment settings currently available to counselling psychologists and illustrate some of the constraints and limitations the discipline faces as well as the potential for development that is afforded.

As counselling psychology has become more established in Britain, the NHS has grown in importance as a major employer. Chapter 20 explores the opportunities arising in this context as well as the constraints it imposes and the challenges it presents. The increasing domination of such a large and medically oriented setting raises issues not only for counselling psychology but also for psychology as a whole. These issues are likely to become more focused as the profession of psychology moves to regulation under the Health Professions Council.

It is, therefore, useful to recognize that perhaps in contrast to clinical psychologists, counselling psychologists work in a variety of settings such as those explored in the other chapters of this section. In some of these the construal of the discipline as a health profession and psychological distress as 'disorder' is inappropriate and may be damaging to both clients and the discipline. In some contexts counselling psychologists may work as coaches rather than psychotherapists, and in others they may work with communities. The future development of the discipline may be constrained if it becomes too closely allied to a single employment context. It is, therefore, important to consider the challenges presented by different settings in relation to the identity of counselling psychology defined in terms of its intellectual traditions, its values and approaches to practice.

20

COUNSELLING PSYCHOLOGY IN THE NHS

Pamela E. James and Alan Bellamy

This chapter traces the development of counselling psychology in the British National Health Service (NHS). It explores the relationship of this discipline with the organization itself, looking at how its philosophy inter-relates with the demands of working in the NHS. It considers how other professionals perceive counselling psychology and it identifies some of the critical points that occurred in the negotiations that have sought to establish the discipline within the NHS.

THE EARLY DAYS: 1993 TO 2005

In looking back to 1993 to see in what ways counselling psychology has contributed to the NHS, it is necessary at the same time to consider the development of the discipline of counselling psychology itself. A British Psychological Society (BPS) Section with a scientific interest in counselling had been set up in 1982; the Special Group in Counselling Psychology began in 1989. Palmer (1993) interviewed Richard Nelson-Jones, the first Section Chair, who expressed the view that the future for counselling psychology was in offering a 'life-skills helping approach' which could be available to the majority of the population. There was no mention in this interview of counselling psychology developing in the NHS.

In 1992, the BPS Membership and Qualification Board recognized the new Diploma in Counselling Psychology (now the Qualification), which is often referred to as 'the independent route'. Full divisional status followed in 1994; this allowed those holding the Diploma an eligibility for chartered status. During that year, Elton-Wilson's address to the BPS Annual Conference in Brighton spoke of the counselling psychologist as a practitioner scientist. The stance was one of working *with* the other person, which was understood as being in a 'non-expert role'. Elton-Wilson's (1994) address noted that counselling psychologists, as members of a new and emerging discipline, were not attached to any one public service or employment setting. She did, however, note that one of the future employment possibilities lay within GP practices in supervising counsellors and in working alongside clinical psychologists, 'especially in the management of counselling provision'.

Perceptions of counselling psychologists by other professionals in the NHS

Knight (1995) wrote about what counselling psychology could offer to general practitioners (GPs) in Primary Health Care settings. It could be argued that when counselling psychology entered the employment arena of the NHS, it became essential to distinguish between the similarities and differences of related professions, in particular counselling psychologists, counsellors and psychotherapists and clinical psychologists. One of the authors of this chapter describes his experience at this time:

> I began working as a counselling psychologist in the NHS in 1995. I took up a post that had been advertised as a clinical psychology position in an Adult Mental Health Clinical Psychology Department, but the requirements were to develop and deliver a staff counselling/stress management service at the local District General Hospital, and to provide a psychological consultation and counselling service at a large fund-holding general practice.
>
> This illustrates a number of facts about the early days of counselling psychology in the NHS. The first is that the post that I took was advertised as a clinical psychology post and existed in a clinical psychology department. In more recent years, counselling psychology applicants for posts advertised in such a manner have often found themselves disqualified at the first hurdle, that of having the correct title, but no objection was raised to my application back then.
>
> Second, the post involved activities that might today be considered the core activities of counselling psychology, but at the time it never occurred to anyone in the NHS to seek a counselling psychologist to do it. The vacancy was created within a clinical psychology department and it was automatically assumed that a clinical psychologist would fill it, and be the most appropriate person to do so. When I came on the scene,

it was apparent that I was well qualified to fulfil the requirements, and gradually I came to be accepted by my colleagues.

Over the following years I came to learn more about how my colleagues worked, and they learned about me. Gradually the rigid distinctions between our professions diminished and actual competencies became more important. Later I headed a service employing counselling and clinical psychologists and counsellors, all working alongside each other and complementing each other's skills across primary and secondary mental health care and physical health sectors.

The philosophy of counselling psychology, paradigm differences and employment issues

Woolfe et al. (2003) described the philosophy of counselling psychology and its historical development as a discipline. Perhaps one of the salient pillars of this philosophy is the appreciation of a person's life experience and the nature of the relationship in which the 'other' struggles to understand that person's perception. This is in contrast to the principles of a medical model that aims to diagnose, treat and hopefully cure. The entrance of counselling psychology's philosophy into the context of the NHS introduces another paradigm. The philosophy of counselling psychology finds similarity with that of counselling and psychotherapy. Clinical psychology, from a historical perspective, brings a confluence of both therapy and measurement and as a discipline has been in the NHS for much longer.

Looking back, it is clear that a number of dilemmas had the potential to develop. First, a clash of paradigms in terms of how to view people's experience with respect to their psychological well-being. Second, what was to be the employment status of this new discipline of counselling psychology in the NHS context? Considering the first of these, the 'clash of paradigms' refers to differences between those professionals that adopt a medical model and those that work from 'relational' philosophies. These differences become particularly significant when very different views are taken, for example, by some GPs and psychiatrists who see medication as the only response to people's distress, and some therapists who see the use of medication as irrelevant to people's sense of well-being. Furthermore, Woolfe (1996a) wrote about the nature of counselling psychology, emphasizing that it arose from a concern with developing a person's potential, not in relation to curing sickness and disease.

Second, given that counselling psychologists have entered the NHS, how can their employment status be negotiated in a way that allows fair placement amongst related colleagues? Some of the questions that were posed at that time, and are still in current focus, were about *competencies*, *clients groups* and *pay*. As counselling psychologists entered the

NHS during the 1990s, issues of pay posed some dilemmas. Were they to be paid at the same rate as counsellors, who themselves did not have an equivalent structure across the service? As counselling psychology was a new discipline, the debates about equivalent competencies with clinical psychologists had not yet been fully aired. Consequently, pay for the counselling psychologist was often similar to that of the counsellor, although there may have been some local variation.

The competency focus in 1995 and in subsequent years has highlighted the question of the differences and similarities between counsellors, psychotherapists, clinical and counselling psychologists. In the 12 years or so since that time, much has been written in further attempts to clarify; there has also been a cross-fertilization of ideas, theories, research and working practices. It could be argued that the result is an overlap of competencies, where many colleagues in these professions are dual and triple qualified. The Division of Counselling Psychology published their competencies in *Counselling Psychology Review* in November 2001, representing the first formal statements. Within the discipline of psychology, it was apparent that there was much overlap with clinical psychology competencies. However, in terms of underlying philosophy, it was difficult to identify a formal statement of the philosophy of clinical psychology as a discipline, although in our experience, some clinical psychologists would share the philosophy of counselling psychology. Later in the chapter, the formal structures that have been erected to explore these positions will be discussed.

In 1995, counselling psychologists were counselling clients in GP practices and supervising counsellors who had worked in primary care for some time. The advent of fund-holding meant that GP practices could, if they so wished, commission in-house counselling services, and there was a blossoming of innovative schemes. They were able to draw on the whole legacy of counselling and psychotherapy research in primary health care (Bor, 1995); many counselling psychologists were also qualified counsellors, as the former training may include the latter. Knight (1995) described the work of the counselling psychologist in the primary health care multidisciplinary team in GP practices. In many areas these services have continued, and a colleague writes about working as a counselling psychologist in primary care today:

> There is something of a myth that the work of psychology in Primary Care is with the, rather insultingly phrased, 'mild to moderate' client group but my experience is that people bring complex difficulties, often longstanding, that pose frequent challenges and that are always fascinating. The challenge of Primary Care is how to meet these needs, to offer a 'good-enough' service, within a time-limited frame. Our service offers appointments outwith the specialist departmental base, closer to peoples' homes, usually in GPs' practices. This means we are working away from our colleagues and our base for most of our clinical work.
>
> The Primary Care service is within a large inner-city department of Clinical and Health Psychology in which I am the only Counselling Psychologist.

I am lucky to work in a very thoughtful team in which there is a culture of discussion of our practice, of how best to meet the needs of the diverse population with whom we work and of questioning bureaucratic demands. My colleagues have been especially committed to considering the needs of those from black and ethnic minority groups, refugees and asylum seekers. While the local training course for Clinical Psychology is noted for its emphasis on cognitive therapy, within our team there is a range of therapeutic models and a particular interest in the psychodynamic interpersonal model, formerly the conversational model, and cognitive analytic therapy.

So what do I bring as a Counselling Psychologist? At first glance I could see little except occasionally that I serve as the grit in discussions about, for example, diagnostic categorization, or suggesting the place for practice-based evidence alongside evidence-based practice. On a practical level, I offer a placement for trainees that brings a sense of professional continuity and reminder of the diversity within psychology.

During this time, many colleagues were asking what this professional mix meant for clients. From the position of practice-based evidence, in the writers' view, this can be seen in many forms. In terms of advantages, clients had an increased opportunity to see a counsellor or counselling psychologist in primary care. A wider range of ways of working psychologically was made possible, although clients are not usually aware of professional differences. However, clients can be confused whether the medication that they take will 'cure' their distress; they ask how can 'just talking' help, which therapy is preferred, and should they continue taking medication? Prescribed medication for psychological issues has been an area in which counselling psychologists have taken an informed view. Hammersley's contribution is notable in this area, and in Hammersley (2000) she brought to attention certain named medications and their effect on a person's functioning. She noted Parry's (1996) research on the necessity for therapists' skills in working with people taking certain psychotropic medications, with respect to their ability to work in the therapeutic relationship. The dynamics of the relational issues that can arise between client, psychiatrist, GP and therapist (counselling psychologist) are well set out by Johnstone (1989).

Training

In the later part of the 1990s, training courses in counselling psychology were developing. There was a taught doctorate at Surrey University and an MSc and Post MSc at City University. Crawford-Wright and Hart (1997) discussed their experience in setting up the then MSc in Counselling Psychology at Wolverhampton. In this article they brought to light some of the dilemmas, challenges and potential benefits from working alongside NHS-based clinical psychology colleagues. Meanwhile, the BPS Diploma in Counselling

Psychology was attracting more trainees; many were looking for training placements and practice opportunities in the NHS. In total, Woolfe (1996a) wrote that there were 250 chartered counselling psychologists, but the number working in the NHS in 1996 was not known at this time. Smallwood (1996) wrote about her own training experience in Scotland as a candidate on the independent route. She began her placement experience in a department of Consulting and Clinical Psychology (secondary care) on a volunteer basis, which led to the post of psychology assistant; this was followed by her being sponsored by the psychology department for the duration of her training. Needless to say, funding training in this way was a rare opportunity. Most trainees funded their own training.

A paradigm shift, pay and working conditions: events leading up to the Advance Letter 2001

During 1996/7, as more counselling psychologists came into the NHS in primary and secondary care settings and became embedded in the multi-professional milieu, some were questioning whether a paradigm shift might be occuring. Woolfe (1996b) reflected on possibilities that traditional frameworks were being queried and challenged, and ideas and values of one system becoming inter-mingled with another in the formation of new systems.

By 1999, the issue of parity of pay and working conditions for counselling psychologists in the NHS was reaching a more formal footing. Jordan and Tholstrup (1999) wrote that the MSF Trade Union in November 1998 had agreed to establish grading criteria, related to clinical psychologists' and child psychotherapists' pay scales. This was to be the precursor for future developments, described in more detail in a further article by Thomas et al. (1999), and a position paper was written by Hammersley on Pay and Conditions of Employment. Meanwhile, the need to adopt an integrative stance remained the challenge for NHS counselling psychologists who were now beginning to work across a variety of client groups as well as in adult mental health, such as learning disabilities, oncology, brain injury rehabilitation, eating disorders and child and family work.

As more counselling psychologists looked to working in the NHS, it became necessary to clarify their professional and employment status. At the same time as individuals were attempting to do this in their own employment contexts, there were two organizational bodies also becoming increasingly involved. The first was the Division of Counselling Psychology (DCoP) of the BPS. The Division Committee was becoming concerned at reports from members of discriminatory employment practice, and a number of the committee's officers began working to tackle this matter and the related issue of the absence of funding for counselling psychology training.

The other body was the Psychology Occupational Advisory Committee (OAC) of the MSF Trade Union (later to become Amicus). This committee, which negotiated with the Department of Health on pay and conditions, was supportive of counselling psychology from the beginning, and adopted the term 'family of psychology' to describe the way in which its constituency had widened from being composed solely of clinical psychologists.

Counselling psychologists on the OAC and on the DCoP Committee also began to take up seats on the BPS Professional Practice Board (PPB) and Standing Committee for Psychologists in Health and Social Care (SCPHSC). Through these different channels they became heavily involved in arguing for equal treatment with colleagues from clinical psychology.

A substantial breakthrough in the pay negotiations for psychologists came in 2001, when the Department of Health Advance Letter (DoH, 2001) advised about the employment conditions for chartered psychologists other than clinical psychologists. Written guidance was given in the Advance Letter; this was to inform employers during the transition period until the government set up the Agenda for Change. The implications of the Advance Letter for applied psychologists working in the NHS were that when an employment situation was described, where applicants could show that they had equivalent competencies, then equivalent pay and employment conditions should follow. As a result, posts began to be advertised as for Clinical/Counselling Psychologists, usually at the level of Grade A, although eventually at Grade B (consultant level).

After the Advance Letter 2001: developments between 2000 and 2005

The turn of the millennium could be seen to be the beginning of changes within the NHS that would in turn affect the employment of NHS counselling psychologists. Needless to say, the expansion of work with different clients continued. The changes in pay, status and conditions of employment were more about the development of counselling psychologists as a profession. Subsequent discussion at the level of committee work in the BPS, and also at government level, now referred to applied psychologists in health and social care. By 2001, a list of assessors/advisers was being set up to act as external assessors for NHS appointments. In 2000, the NHS Plan for England was launched.

The government announced that 1000 new graduate primary care mental health workers would be funded and enter the English employment market. In this initial phase, it was not clear who these people would be or what they would do. Gradually it emerged that they could be graduates from any subject, but in practice were likely to be from psychology or nursing, they would have a funded in-service training and would work in GP practices in a psycho-educational role. In hindsight, there were parallel streams of activity during 2000–2005. Counselling Psychology was becoming more established in different departments within the NHS. Milton (2001) writes that trainees on placement were in 'older adults', community mental health teams, primary care, psychotherapy, eating disorders and learning difficulties. There were insufficient chartered counselling psychologists to offer supervision to trainees. This task was being undertaken by clinical psychologists and psychotherapists. Whilst a valuable learning experience, it was preferable that the main supervision came from a chartered counselling psychologist who could hold the trainee in the philosophy of the discipline. The profession itself was being discussed within the committee structure of the BPS, namely the Professional Affairs Board (which became known as the Professional Practice Board) and its standing committee: Psychologists in Health and Social Care. These discussions centred around competencies, conditions of work and equity across the applied psychologies working in health and social care. The authors of this chapter were members of these committees in the early years after the millennium; they were also Chairs of the Division between 2001 and 2004.

Statement of competence

By 2001, the Division of Counselling Psychology published its Review Statement of the Areas of Competence in Counselling Psychology. This became a helpful document that served as information and guidance both within and without the NHS, for employers and commissioners of services, trainers and trainees. Some aspects of working in the NHS arena with colleagues from a multi-disciplinary base threw up issues that were debated at length: for example, should counselling psychologists oppose the use of the DSM-IV and psychometric testing (Sequira and Van Scoyoc, 2001). Questions such as these were to continue to be debated for the next few years; such debates are of particular interest as they challenge the under-pinning philosophy of counselling psychology that is in essence non-diagnostic.

Benanti (2002) asked if there was a clinical apartheid within the NHS. This question arose as a result of the anecdotal feedback from colleagues about the difficulties regarding posts, consultancy and research opportunities in the NHS. Benanti pointed out that there must be a willingness to modify counselling psychology training in line with NHS needs; the onus, she said, is on the trainers and NHS training placements must be mandatory and not optional. This viewpoint has been discussed within the Counselling Psychology Divisional Committee. Whilst it is now accepted that placement experience in the NHS is encouraged, it is not mandatory. Also, as not all counselling psychologists work in the NHS, there is a view that training should be broad enough to encompass different work settings.

Funded training

The year 2001 was a time of increased activity regarding pay, conditions of employment and training. One of the issues of equity was the funding of counselling psychologists' training. The cross-divisional BPS Standing Committee for Psychologists in Health and

Social Care and the BPS/Amicus Joint-Liaison Committee were considered to be the appropriate forum for discussion. The passage of the events surrounding the quest for funded training were outlined by James (2004) in an invited keynote address to the BPS Annual Conference in London. She traced the events that took place between 2001 and 2004. Both the authors of this chapter represented counselling psychology through the succession of meetings that were to result from the extended involvement with the Department of Health.

In October 2002, the Amicus Union liaised with the Department of Health to set up a meeting with one representative from each of the Divisional Committees in Health and Counselling Psychology. This initial meeting served to inform the government about the nature of the disciplines of health and counselling psychology; it included the discussions about equity for funding training. The government was interested to know more about the relationship of the work of counselling psychology to the NHS Plan (2000) and National Service Frameworks. Two further meetings with ministers from the Department of Health took place in 2003.

The NHS Plan (DoH, 2000) had stated that there was a need for more NHS psychologists. This in itself had been a response to the demand for more 'talking therapies' and a realization that across England there were ever-increasing waiting lists for this kind of therapy. The cross-divisional Standing Committee for Psychologists in Health and Social Care approached the Department of Health (DoH) National Institute for Mental Health England to develop a working liaison. Meetings were arranged on a quarterly basis at the BPS London Office. The first of these was in January 2003; the agenda concerned policy and strategy issues related to applied psychologists working in the NHS. Numbers of psychologists in the workforce became an item of consideration. In July 2003, a BPS cross-divisional one-day conference was arranged at the London BPS office, where the competencies of clinical, health and counselling psychology were stated and discussed. Clinical psychology colleagues invited counselling and health representatives to join their well-established Workforce Planning Committee.

During 2003 there was a flurry of activity amongst representatives of counselling psychology aimed at gathering information, writing documents, presenting arguments for the funded training and employment of NHS counselling psychology. Viewpoints were represented in the recommendations of the Mental Health Care Group Workforce Team Report (2003) and Lavender and Paxton's (2004) Adult Mental Health Service Model, Clinical/Applied Psychology Demand. The English Survey of Applied Psychologists in Health and Social Care and the Prison and Probation Service was carried out by BPS/DoH and published in 2004. Based on what was estimated as a 65 per cent response rate, it reported that there were 149 chartered counselling psychologists working in this context.

Looking back at this time, the growth and development of counselling psychology as a discipline working in the NHS was continuing. However, there was no clear response from the government saying that training for counselling psychologists would be funded.

Instead, there were changes in the way in which the government structured the administration of resources. This was almost an anti-climax. There was also the beginning of a realization that not only were there insufficient courses (estimated from clinical psychology) to produce enough psychologists to meet the demand, but the training of the numbers required would be too expensive.

Parallel meetings were being held during this period with the devolved governments in Scotland and Wales, and with some local variations a similar story was emerging. In Wales one of the authors of this chapter had been invited to represent counselling psychology on what was then called the Clinical Psychology Advisory Committee to the Welsh Assembly's Medical Committee, and had met with the Health Minister and NHS Wales leaders to discuss applied psychology workforce funding generally as well as the particular difficulties facing counselling psychology trainees.

The demand–supply gap

One of the responses by clinical psychology colleagues to this situation was to look again at the development of the training of what were loosely described at the time as associate psychologists. During the latter part of 2004, a series of BPS cross-divisional meetings began between BPS and DoH to discuss the development of associate psychologists. Questions ranged around what would be their competencies, how would trainees be funded and where would they be trained. Counselling psychology reflected on the outcomes for these meetings. How could their training syllabus that had been recently restructured to reflect a three-year, full-time integration of theory, practice, research and personal development be seen to have 'step-off points' which might constitute the training for an associate psychologist? What would be the competencies of a counselling psychology 'associate'? The views from counselling psychologists discussed in BPS meetings at this time included the rejection of the use of manualized cognitive behavioural therapy delivered from protocols (this was being suggested as one of the main roles of associate psychologists). Other points stressed that the training of a psychologist to be fully appraised of being a therapist could not be achieved in one year's full-time training, so plans for becoming an associate would represent a possible devaluing of the therapist's contribution.

The focus of attention for the development of government-funded posts had shifted to the way in which psychology graduates could be trained to deliver therapy and work in a psycho-educative way at a level below chartership. In 2004, feedback from the DoH in BPS/DoH meetings was that if counselling psychologists were to achieve government funding, then this might be achieved by a 'bottom-up' approach. This meant that Local Development Plans in NHS Trusts would reflect the need for counselling psychologists, which might in turn lead to their commissioning. Higher Education Institutions would need then to bid for their training. Although this was discussed within counselling psychology at the time, the process itself was not taken up. One of the objections voiced within the Division was that the freedom of content of the training syllabus would then be lost, as there would be an expectation that the DoH could impose what was taught.

Applied psychologists working together?

In February 2005, there was a one-day conference that was hosted by the BPS/DoH NIMHE in Birmingham. This was a cross-divisional conference and was intended to bring NHS applied psychologists and their service managers together to look at shared and specific ways of working across health and social care. The conference aimed to look at ways of influencing strategic health authorities regarding commissioning, to look at choice for service users in terms of mental health professionals and to address the career structure of applied psychologists. As a part of this, one of the authors of this chapter gave a presentation on the knowledge, skills and potential roles of Counselling Psychologists in the NHS. There was some consternation in the audience, many of whom were clinical psychology heads of departments, as it dawned on them that what was being claimed was that counselling psychology had as important a role to play in the core services of the changing NHS as did clinical psychology, and that in any case there was considerable overlap in knowledge and skills. This is reported by Turpin (2005) and also by James (2005), who noted the inter-group tensions that arose between the applied psychologists present. She commented on the parallels with other situations in social psychology research where there was competition for scarce resources. By July 2005, the sequence of meetings of the Standing Committee for Psychologists in Health and Social Care that had taken place between the DoH and BPS applied psychologists gave birth to a new group. This group consisted of people from the DoH and BPS Applied Psychologists, meeting in Manchester in July 2005. It was co-chaired by Rosyln Hope (DoH) and Tony Lavender (BPS) and was to form the outline for the New Ways of Working for Applied Psychologists project, which published its report in July 2007.

Ongoing professional issues

Meanwhile, whilst professional issues were continuing to be debated during the years 2000–2005, NHS counselling psychologists were working and publishing on practice issues. Contentious issues included the use of psychometric testing, diagnostic criteria and the interpretation of evidenced-based practice. *Counselling Psychology Review* has set aside entire issues for the discussion of evidence-based practice (August 2003) and psychological testing (November 2004).

In the working environment of the NHS, these issues come to the fore, as the counselling psychologist will be working alongside other professionals who have different belief systems. Turner-Young (2003) debated the use of diagnostic criteria. She stresses the contrast of Natural Sciences and Human Sciences, saying that the latter is akin with the philosophy of counselling psychology that emphasizes the therapeutic relationship. Stern et al., (1998) wrote that in relationship, the client's perception of self can alter as a result of authentic person-to-person connection. The training of counselling psychologists aims to foster people who can work in this way. Hence the dilemma or challenge emerges regarding working alongside other professionals who are trained to work with diagnostic labelling. Their viewpoints may be more focused on how to describe a person, and as a result what intervention is appropriate from a previously ordained guideline, for example, that of the National Institute for Clinical Excellence (NICE). Yet the NHS counselling psychologist works in this arena and has the opportunity to influence and challenge the process in a meaningful way. A counselling psychologist who works in learning disabilities describes how she views her role:

> Working within the NHS as part of a Learning Disability Community Team involves being part of a large and varied multi-disciplinary team, contributing to team working via supervision, training and service planning and development.
>
> As a counselling psychologist, I bring a humanistic or person-centred values base, which complements the prevalent ideology in Learning Disability Services, of valuing and finding ways to promote empowerment of the individual. Despite this values base, within the NHS there is undoubtedly a continuing dependence on medical models of thinking which can pathologize and disempower. There is then an ongoing challenge to the counselling psychologist of promoting a more holistic way of thinking and working.
>
> One way that this can be achieved is by promoting the involvement of service users in self-advocacy organizations such as People First. Also, by developing partnerships with such organizations to undertake participative research, enabling the voices of those labelled as learning disabled to be heard within services and within the wider population.
>
> My role within the organization does not differ greatly from that of other applied psychologists in Learning Disability Services. I carry out assessments of eligibility for access to the service such as IQ and functional skills assessments, and Autistic Spectrum Disorder screening assessments.
>
> I also do assessments of cognitive function, both with respect to identifying neurological disorders and with respect to cognitive deterioration. I carry out psychological interventions and appropriate follow-up including individual, group and family interventions, and also work with staff groups, and in a consultative capacity to other team members.
>
> In addition to this more traditional type of psychology role, I am also concerned to develop a more proactive way of working with psychological distress for this client

group. This involves developing working partnerships with other statutory and voluntary agencies, which may help to support people to live independent lives with minimal appropriate service involvement, for example, working with child protection and family support teams.

THE PRESENT: 2005 TO TODAY

The New Ways of Working for Applied Psychologists project

The New Ways of Working for Applied Psychologists (NWW for AP) project was established in July 2005 as part of a wider NIMHE programme for New Ways of Working in Mental Health, and reported back in July 2007. There were seven psychology project groups, focusing on new roles, career pathways, improving access to psychological therapies, training models in applied psychology, organizing, managing and leading services, working in teams, and mental health legislation. Throughout the project an applied psychology stance was taken and there was full involvement by the counselling psychology representatives in all the project groups. Indeed, the use of the term 'applied psychology' throughout the final report represents the distance travelled in working for equal consideration for counselling (and health) psychology in the NHS, and no distinction is made between the various applied psychologies in most of the report. However, the Training Models group was different in that it reviewed the similarities and differences between the different training routes, and recommended that all applied psychology training courses should explore sharing modules and placements where appropriate, that they develop training programmes at assistant and senior assistant levels, and that the BPS Membership and Professional Training Board be asked to initiate a project to 'identify commonalities, complementary areas of practice and differences between the applied Divisions in their training curricula and learning outcomes' (BPS, 2007: 19). The group also looked at proposals for integrated training programmes across the applied psychologies but stopped short of recommending any of these at the time, considering that such a proposal would be premature. This reflects one of the difficulties faced by this group; its remit was to look at training from an NHS perspective, and of course counselling psychology extends well beyond the NHS environment.

The whole reason for the NWW project is to 'modernize' the NHS workforce, and this includes all aspects of the applied psychology profession; training programmes, career structures, roles and responsibilities. One of the authors of this chapter was a member of the Core Group for the NWW-AP project and she particularly recalls the contributions from service users during the meetings of the project. The emphasis here was to keep in focus the needs of service users, and to be mindful of the direction in discussions which had the tendency to become over-focused on development and organization of the applied psychology profession.

For applied psychologists outside the NHS, the requirements and demands of the NHS are not relevant to a significant number of members and there is a danger in allowing those requirements to dominate the development of those professions. For counselling psychology in particular, this is an acute difficulty because we estimate that around half of the profession work for at least part of their time in the NHS, which means that half do not, and the profession itself is founded on values and philosophies that sometimes sit uneasily alongside NHS practices. Therefore engagement in NWW-AP and similar NHS projects, working parties and committees is never going to be straightforward for counselling psychology. Nevertheless, such engagement, and fair consideration of combined training routes with clinical psychologists, is going to be vital if counselling psychology is to have a future in the NHS.

The National Assessors and the Letter re Nomenclature in Advertising Jobs

Another forum where these tensions have been felt is the NHS National Assessors group. The National Assessors advise employing Trusts on consultant psychologist grade appointments, from the writing of job descriptions to the interviewing and selection of applicants. Initially a purely clinical psychology group, comprised of senior clinicians divided according to specialty, there has for several years now been a counselling psychologist, one of the authors of this chapter, on the Lead Assessors committee. A frequent comment has been that the competencies of a post seem appropriate for a counselling psychologist but the advertisement or job description refer only to clinically qualified applicants, and so counselling psychology applicants have been disqualified. Employment law is complex in this area, and the National Assessors can only advise employers, but it has been clear that there has been cause for genuine grievance in some cases.

After much difficult debate, the National Assessors agreed in May 2007 to support the dissemination of a letter, signed by the chairs of SCPHSC and PPB, reminding employing Trusts that the competencies of all the applied psychologies should be considered when vacant posts are advertised, and that adjectival titles only used if justified by the requirements of a particular post. Part of the statement reads:

Recent years have seen great changes in the profile and status of psychology in health and social care. Clinical psychologists have been joined by other applied psychologists, such as health psychologists and counselling psychologists in providing psychological services and consultation in the NHS. Each has particular competencies to contribute to healthcare as well as a set of shared psychological knowledge and skills. The competencies and perspectives that are shared by applied psychologists are often greater and more important than the specific issues that distinguish our areas of specialism.

Traditionally, NHS psychology posts have been advertised with particular adjectival titles: 'clinical psychologist', 'counselling psychologist', 'health psychologist' etc. Clearly, in some cases, this is appropriate. If, for instance, the duties of the post-holder map squarely onto the accepted competencies of a specific specialist (such as health psychologist), or if the post requires, as an essential element, competencies that are not found across specialties, then clearly it is right to make that clear in advertisements.

Given, however, the greater overlap of perspectives and skills outlined above, the British Psychological Society's Standing Committee for Psychologists in Health and Social Care (representing the applied Divisions of the Society), Amicus and the National Institute for Mental Health in England (NIMHE) recommend that managers should ensure that the competencies of each individual role are described and each post advertised appropriately. This may be best achieved through phrases such as 'Clinical or Counselling Psychologist' […] The use of competencies will differentiate between those posts which may be more appropriate for one branch of the profession rather than another, without excluding potential candidates on the basis of adjectival title. (BPS, 2007: 1)

More generally, the DoH workforce modernization agenda is proceeding rapidly and having an increasing effect on the availability of psychology posts. Applied psychologists are expensive to employ – only psychiatrists cost more – and so must be able to offer 'added value' over and above the contribution made by less expensive colleagues such as community psychiatric nurses and CBT therapists. This added value is likely to be seen in terms of supervision, consultancy and clinical leadership. Chartered clinical and counselling psychologists will be expected to develop and support the psychological thinking of non-psychologist colleagues, and it is they who will be doing most of the direct client work.

THE FUTURE

NWW for AP could be seen to represent the coming together of *parallel streams* in that it aimed to address a response to people's need to 'speak to someone' (one expression of this is large waiting lists), whilst looking to modernize the workforce to meet the need. It is likely that there will be a continuation and strengthening of two apparently contradictory trends. The *first* of these is towards an increased recognition of the part played by psychological factors in both physical and mental health, and a consequent acknowledgement of the importance of psychological understanding and skills in treatment planning and delivery.

Two examples of this are the Improving Access to Psychological Therapies project (IAPT) and the changes to professional roles and responsibilities seen in the new Mental Health Act (DoH, 2007). Turpin (2007) has given a thorough discussion of the IAPT project as it applies in England. Beginning with the recommendations of Layard (2004, 2006) and initial outcome data from two pilot sites, IAPT envisages a network of psychological therapy centres in primary care where short-term CBT will be widely available to the public as part of a stepped-care mental health and well-being structure. The government has pledged £300 million funding over three years for this programme, and as Turpin states:

> The IAPT programme represents a major opportunity to create good quality psychological therapy services that are evidence-based, accessible and provide real choice of treatments for NHS users. Modelling the workforce to deliver such a major redesign of services presents a formidable challenge to those engaged in workforce planning. (2007: 8)

The new Mental Health Act of 2007 replaced the role of Responsible Medical Officer with that of Responsible Clinician (DoH, 2007), with the expectation that senior applied psychologists in the NHS will take on the role in addition to consultant psychiatrists. The Act thereby recognizes the place of psychological understanding alongside psychiatric expertise.

The *other trend* is towards an increasingly streamlined workforce, with more generically trained workers providing shorter and more standardized treatments as cost pressures mount across the NHS. The emphasis on short-term CBT in IAPT and the increasing number of posts for generically trained 'psychological therapists' are examples of this.

It may be that the future for applied psychologists in health lies outside of the NHS, in private consultancies with whom the NHS may contract to manage, supervise and/or deliver services. The challenge to counselling psychology will then be to hold on to its core philosophy in a more commercial environment. However, it should also be remembered that devolution is already leading to diverging NHS priorities in each of the devolved nations. The head of the NHS Confederation said in January 2008 that there were now four different health services operating in the UK, and that the differences between them were likely to increase. Dr Gill Morgan, the organization's chief executive, told the *Guardian*: 'We basically have four different systems, albeit with the same set of values.' Morgan said it was too early to say which system was more successful as each had its advantages, but she said the differences were expected to become even greater (Morgan, 2008).

There is, however, one *parallel theme* that is important to the process of change and development that can become almost silenced in the apparent excitement of the process of development. This is expressed in the voices of practitioners from both clinical and counselling psychology who are relating their clinical experience and noting the complex needs of some clients. For example, clients who are described as having a borderline personality, and those with both mental health and drugs and alcohol problems, often have complex needs. There is an ongoing role for applied psychologists in the NHS to constantly be shaping the use of the workforce where their thinking is driven by psychological information and practitioner experience. So counselling psychologists' voices are a reminder of these issues, a re-statement of the relational focus as a factor in the origin of distress and in the response to that.

Discussions about the Statutory Regulation of Psychologists with the Health Professionals Council, planned to occur during 2009, is bringing to a focus the need to have registration at chartered level. Chartered applied psychologists in the NHS are able to take leadership positions (both clinically and in administrative management), and design the workforce in response to overall client need in mental and physical health. The concept of accredited pre-chartered training is currently being explored in the BPS; their statutory registration has yet to be considered.

Pre-chartered applied psychologists, who include existing assistant psychologists, will continue to offer psycho-education; run anxiety and stress management groups; identify those with complex needs; deliver CBT programmes under supervision; assist in preventing the onset of psychosis; and offer active listening where appropriate using basic counselling skills. All these tasks would occur under the supervision of a chartered psychologist.

So, given the above, how can we summarize the contribution that counselling psychologists have made to the NHS, and will make in the future? Apart from numerically, one way of looking at this is that counselling psychologists provide a continuing reminder that patients are people, and that people exist in relationship. It is all too easy when faced with long waiting lists, severe distress and disturbance, and the demands of a large bureaucratic organization, to adopt a dehumanizing medical model of treatment. Clinical psychology colleagues have defended a humanistic position in the NHS for many years, and counselling psychology, less rooted in NHS culture, has been able to reinforce that and extend it further. This is a philosophy that supports the view that people's experience develops in relationship, that is, the way in which other people have related with them, influences the way in which they perceive themselves. It follows, then, that this can be made aware in relationship; it can be understood in relationship and possibly it can be changed in relationship, or at least its damaging effects contained. The counselling psychologist is more likely to be an integrative therapist than a purist, and has a firm rationale as to why this is so. In addition, those colleagues who wish to extend their therapeutic roles are able to transfer these concepts into management, leadership and supervision.

The constant threat to the development of NHS counselling psychology will probably be in the form of tensions produced by competition and professional jealousies in an atmosphere of difficult work-related content and diminished resources. Can this be contained? Work by Obholzer and Roberts (1994) is helpful in looking at dynamic factors in organizational development. The challenge is to hold on to all that is good in our profession whilst fully engaging with the requirements and opportunities of a cash-limited, open-to-all public health system.

REFERENCES

Benanti, J. (2002) 'Are counselling psychologists experiencing a "clinical apartheid" within the NHS?', *Counselling Psychology Review*, 17 (1): 28–32.

Bor, R. (1995) 'Bibliography: Psychological counselling in primary health care', *Counselling Psychology Review*, 10 (3): 38–40.

British Psychological Society (2007) *New Ways of Working for Applied Psychologists in Health and Social Care. Summary Report.* Leicester: British Psychological Society.

British Psychological Society Professional Practice Board (2007) Letter re nomenclature in the advertising of posts in Applied Psychology. Leicester: British Psychological Society.

British Psychological Society and Department of Health (2004) *English Survey of Applied Psychologists in Health and Social Care and in Prison and Probation Service.* Leicester and London: British Psychological Society and Department of Health.

Counselling Psychology Review (2003) Special Issue: Evidence-Based Practice, *Counselling Psychology Review*, 18 (3).

Counselling Psychology Review (2004) Special Edition on Counselling Psychology and Psychological Testing, *Counselling Psychology Review*, 19 (4).

Crawford-Wright, A. and Hart, N. (1997) 'Developing a training course', *Counselling Psychology Review*, 12 (3): 117–121.

Department of Health (2000) *NHS Plan.* London: Department of Health.

Department of Health (2001) *Advance Letter (SP) 4.* Available online at www.doh.gov.uk/coin.htm, accessed 20/10/08.

Department of Health (2007) *The Mental Health Act.* Available online at www.opsi.gov.uk/acts/acts2007/ukpga_20070012_en_1, accessed 20/10/08.

Division of Counselling Psychology (2001) '"Chartered Counselling Psychologists' training and areas of competence". Statement from the Division of Counselling Psychology', *Counselling Psychology Review*, 16 (4): 41–43.

Elton-Wilson, J. (1994) 'Letter from the chair', *Counselling Psychology Review*, 9 (1): 3.

Hammersley, D. (2000) 'Developing a policy on drugs and alcohol for psychotherapeutic service', *Counselling Psychology Review*, 15 (3): 18–25.

James, P.E. (2004) 'On the road to funded training for counselling psychologists', *Counselling Psychology Review*, 19 (3): 32–35.

James, P.E. (2005) 'Group dynamics in a professional setting: The challenge for applied psychologists. Reflections after the NIMHE/BPS Conference in Birmingham, February 2005', *Counselling Psychology Review*, 20 (2): 52–55.

Johnstone, L. (1989) *Users and Abusers of Psychiatry.* London: Routledge.

Jordan, R. and Tholstrup, M. (1999) 'Report from the working party on parity of pay and working conditions for counselling psychologists in the NHS', *Counselling Psychology Review*, 14 (1): 22–23.

Knight, L. (1995) 'Explaining what counselling psychology is and what it can offer to GPs in primary health care settings', *Counselling Psychology Review*, 10 (4): 2–4.

Lavender, T. and Paxton, R. (2004) *Estimating the Applied Psychology Demand in Adult Mental Health*. Leicester: British Psychological Society.

Layard, R. (2004) *Mental Health: Britain's Biggest Social Problem*? London: Cabinet Office.

Layard, R. (2006) 'The case for psychological treatment centres', *British Medical Journal*, 332: 1030–1032.

Mental Health Care Group (2003) *Workforce Team Recommendations: Access 2003 Report to the Workforce Numbers Advisory Board*. London: Department of Health.

Milton, M. (2001) 'Counselling psychology placements: Reflections from the Health Service', *Counselling Psychology Review*, 16 (2): 4–10.

Morgan, G. (2008) 'Devolution and the NHS', *Guardian Unlimited*, 2 January.

NIMHE (National Institute for Mental Health England) (2007) *New Ways of Working in Mental Health*. London: Department of Health.

Obholzer, A. and Roberts, V.Z. (eds) (1994) *The Unconscious at Work*. Routledge: London and New York.

Palmer, S. (1993) 'Editorial: Changes', *Counselling Psychology Review*, 8 (1): 2.

Parry, G. (1996) *NHS Psychotherapy Services in England: Review of Strategic Policy*. London: NHS Executive.

Sequeira, H. and Van Scoyoc, S. (2001) 'Divisional Round Table 2001: Should counselling psychologists oppose the use of DSM-IV and testing?', *Counselling Psychology Review*, 16 (4): 44–48.

Smallwood, J. (1996) 'A year in the life of a trainee counselling psychologist in the NHS', *Counselling Psychology Review*, 11 (4): 19–25.

Stern, D.N., Sander, L.W., Nahum, J.P., Harrison, A.M., Lyons-Ruth, K., Morgan, A.C., Bruschweilerstern, N. and Tronick, E.Z. (1998) 'Non-interpretive mechanisms in psychoanalytic therapy: The "something more" than interpretation', *International Journal of Psycho-Analysis*, 79: 903–921.

Thomas, A., Tholstrup, M. and Jordan, R. (1999) 'Parity of pay and conditions for chartered counselling psychologists: A report from the Working Party', *Counselling Psychology Review*, 14 (4): 22–26.

Turner-Young, L. (2003) 'Counselling psychology and diagnostic systems: Do they have a place in our philosophy?', *Counselling Psychology Review*, 18 (1): 53.

Turpin, G. (2005) 'New ways of shaping and delivering psychology services. Reflections after the NIMHE/BPS Conference in Birmingham, February 2005', *Counselling Psychology Review*, 20 (2): 56–57.

Turpin, G. (2007) *Good Practice Guide on the Contribution of Applied Psychologists to Improving Access for Psychological Therapies*. Leicester: British Psychological Society.

Woolfe, R. (1996a) 'Counselling psychology in Britain: Past, present and future', *Counselling Psychology Review*, 11 (4): 7–18.

Woolfe, R. (1996b) 'The nature of counselling psychology', in R. Woolfe and W. Dryden (eds), *Handbook of Counselling Psychology*. London: Sage.

Woolfe, R., Dryden, W. and Strawbridge, S. (eds) (2003) *Handbook of Counselling Psychology*. London: Sage.

21

COUNSELLING PSYCHOLOGY IN THE WORKPLACE

Stephen Palmer and Kristina Gyllensten

Work is a part of life and much time is spent in the workplace. This is true for counselling psychologists and for many of their therapeutic clients (Hesketh, 2000). Although the workplace may not be the most traditional area of work for counselling psychologist, there is an increasing number who practise in this sector (Carroll, 1996; Orlans, 2003). According to Orlans (2003), the bridging nature of counselling psychology, with its openness to different traditions and methods of practice, is a reason why it can be valuable in work settings.

The fact that counselling psychologists are involved in the workplace is also recognized by the British Psychological Society (BPS). Within the BPS' (2001) statement regarding counselling psychologists' areas of competence, it is stated that counselling psychologists work in both Employment Assistance Programmes (EAPs) and Occupational Health Departments. Furthermore, the BPS (2008) explains in the Regulations and Syllabus for the Qualification in Counselling Psychology 2008 that counselling psychologists in training should work in a wide range of modalities, one suggestion being that they work within organizations. Indeed, counselling psychologists may be involved in different areas in the workplace, including providing counselling, coaching, consultation, career development, supervision, setting up and running stress management programmes, and conducting research.

HEALTH AND WELL-BEING AT WORK

We are currently in an era characterized by globalization, corporate reorganization, the introduction of new technologies, increased workforce diversity and increased expectations in the workforce. Organizations have downsized and fewer people are doing more work. The culture has subsequently moved towards short-term contracts and freelance workers, with fewer employees regarding their employment as secure. Demands for job-skills are also changing, and the need for a more flexible workforce has placed importance on multi-skilling, with individuals increasingly expected to pursue multiple careers during their working life. Of these changes, many bring with them prosperity, but also carry risks of work-related stress (Cooper et al., 2001; Cooper et al., 1996).

There is empirical evidence showing that jobs in Britain are becoming more time-consuming and stressful and thereby less satisfying (Taylor, 2002). The survey 'Self-reported work-related illness in 2003/2004' (SWI03/04) (Jones et al., 2004), commissioned by the Health and Safety Executive (HSE), found that stress, depression and anxiety was the second most prevalent type of work-related health problem in the UK. All five SWI surveys (from 1990 to 2003/2004) (Jones et al., 2004) indicated that, after musculoskeletal disorders, work-related stress and related conditions were the most common type of work-related health problem. Estimates from SWI03/04 indicated that half a million people in the UK believed that they were suffering from stress, anxiety or depression related to their work. It was further estimated that 12.8 million days were lost due to work-related stress, anxiety or depression (Jones et al., 2004). The Sainsbury Centre for Mental Health (2007) published a policy paper on developing a business case. It estimated the costs of mental health problems at work to be much higher than the HSE estimates: reduced productivity costs £15.1 bn; sickness absence £8.4 bn; and staff turnover, £2.4 bn.

Key interventions organizations and counselling psychologists that can undertake to address these problems include the provision of counselling within Employee Assistance Programmes (EAPs), stress counselling, stress prevention/management programmes, stress auditing, coaching and coaching training programmes.

EMPLOYEE ASSISTANCE PROGRAMMES (EAPS)

Counselling within organizations has a long history in the UK (Orlans, 2008). Workplace counselling has been defined as 'the provision of brief psychological therapy for employees of an organisation which is paid for by an employer' (McLeod and Henderson, 2003: 103). It is commonly offered to employees who have suffered ill health as a result of conditions in the workplace and may often focus on dealing with stressors and life difficulties influencing the job (Cooper et al., 2001).

Often counselling within an organizational setting is provided by an EAP. EAPs have been developed to help employers and employees to manage issues affecting performance, productivity and well-being. Although counselling is the most utilized resource within EAPs, these programmes can also offer other forms of assistance and advice on a systematic basis, including financial support, legal advice and health information (Winwood and Beer, 2008).

The Employee Assistance Professionals Association states that 'In the US, over 97% of companies with more than 5,000 employees have EAPs. 80% of companies with 1,001–5,000 employees have EAPs. 75% of companies with 251–1,000 employees have EAPs' (EAPA, 2009a). This emphasizes the popularity of EAP services. The essential components of EAP services as declared by the EAPA are:

1. Consultation with, training of, and assistance to work organization leadership (managers, supervisors, and union stewards) seeking to manage the troubled employee, enhance the work environment, and improve employee job performance, and outreach to and education of employees and their family members about availability of EAP services;
2. Confidential and timely problem identification/assessment services for employee clients with personal concerns that may affect job performance;
3. Use of constructive confrontation, motivation, and short-term intervention with employee clients to address problems that affect job performance;
4. Referral of employee clients for diagnosis, treatment, and assistance, plus case monitoring and follow-up services;
5. Consultation to work organizations in establishing and maintaining effective relations with treatment and other service providers and in managing provider contracts;
6. Consultation to work organizations to encourage availability of, and employee access to, health benefits covering medical and behavioural problems, including but not limited to alcoholism, drug abuse, and mental and emotional disorders; and
7. Identification of the effects of Employee Assistance services on the work organization and individual job performance. (EAPA: 2009b)

This highlights the range of services that EAPs may offer. The EAPA has branches around the world, including in the UK.

Organizations may be more or less involved in the day-to-day running of the EAP, and an important issue such as confidentiality may be handled in different ways, depending on the organization (Orlans, 2008). Counselling psychologists may be involved in EAPs in different ways. They may provide counselling to employees or they may provide supervision, and they could also be involved in the development and management of the EAP.

It can be difficult to evaluate interventions in the workplace using what is sometimes suggested to be the highest band of methodological rigour, as it may not be possible to use control groups or randomization. Nevertheless, evaluations of counselling in the workplace have been conducted. McLeod (2001, 2007) conducted a review of all English-language research investigating counselling in the workplace. It was found that workplace counselling helped to reduce symptoms of stress and depression in two-thirds of the studies and that workplace counselling services at least cover their costs. A well-known study investigated the effectiveness of stress counselling that was introduced in the Post Office. Although weaknesses in the design were recognized, it was reported that absenteeism and psychological well-being was improved in the participants (Allison et al., 1989; Cooper and Sadri, 1991).

POTENTIAL AREAS OF CONFLICT

According to Firth-Cozens and Hardy (1992), counselling appears to be effective in rehabilitating employees suffering from stress, but changes are likely to be short-term if employees return to an unchanged work environment. This is clearly an important point and raises a number of ethical and boundary issues about the roles and responsibilities of counselling psychologists.

In the case of the EAP, the latter is just one stakeholder in a complex series of relationships. These include the client, the EAP and the sponsoring company which funds the EAP. It is tempting to assume that the interests of all the parties coincide, but this may not always be the case. There may be situations where these may not be identical. For example, from the point of view of the EAP, it is important that the client feels satisfied with the counselling experience in order that the funder can feel justified in their continued financial support of the EAP. However, counselling may often involve helping clients to confront unpalatable aspects of their lives. A client might benefit from the experience but feel angry with the counsellor for placing them in this position, and in response to a request for feedback from the EAP might blame the counsellor for this rather than accepting responsibility for themselves. This can result in the counsellor being subject to enquiry about the quality of his or her work from the EAP. In a similar vein, the result of the counselling might be that a client becomes less rather than more satisfied with the work environment. The counsellor might feel a job well done and the client might be pleased with the insights gained and the outcome is a decision to think about leaving the company. However, the sponsoring company might not feel too happy about the prospect of a valued employee returning to work less motivated than previously. This is then presented to the EAP as a failure of counselling and the counsellor once again may be questioned about the quality of his or her work.

These issues are not just confined to the EAP situation but are also relevant to the workplace situation more generally, and perhaps even more powerfully, when counselling is provided on an in-house basis. The question of confidentiality arises if there is any concern about information being fed back to the line manager. More generally, Kinder (2007: 32) suggests that the practitioner will need to answer the following questions:

> 'Whose side is the practitioner on?'
> 'Can the practitioner balance the demands of the client and the organization, particularly when these two conflict?'

'Should the practitioner purely be concerned about issues that are affecting work performance?'

'How should a practitioner respond when a manager sends a client to be sorted out?'

Kinder puts it neatly when he suggests that counselling psychologists in the workplace need to 'spend their time with two ears open – one on the client and the other on the organization' (2007: 33).

It may be that for some workers who seek counselling, their symptoms of depression or anxiety resulting from the presenting work issue obscure the simple fact that the work environment is itself oppressive/bullying. In this sense, they can be said to be victims of an unsupportive work environment, and to focus on the depression or anxiety simply individualizes and thus obscures bigger social issues about the quality of the workplace and its impact upon staff. The counselling psychologist thus treads a narrow line in having to pay attention both to easing the symptoms of depression/anxiety and on a wider agenda of thinking about the depression/anxiety in the context of work roles and environment. There are complex issues here about boundaries and ethical dilemmas that may not appear so sharply in other contexts in which counselling psychologists operate.

STRESS COUNSELLING AT WORK

A range of different therapeutic approaches are used in stress counselling. Most suited to stress counselling are cognitive-behavioural or solution-focused approaches. These approaches can provide strategies and facilitate the development of solutions to dealing with workplace issues and also personal problems. They are also adaptable to brief or session-limited counselling. In this section we will briefly describe one cognitive behavioural therapeutic approach: multimodal counselling. This approach is easily adapted to individual and workplace stress as it provides a basic framework for assessment and a flexible therapeutic programme (for a more in-depth explanation of the approach, see Palmer and Dryden, 1995; Palmer et al., 2003a). According to Lazarus (1981), the multimodal approach should be customized to the individual client and their situation. A basic assumption within this approach is that clients are often troubled by a variety of problems that should be dealt with by a variety of treatments. Considering the great number of therapeutic techniques that can be applied, Palmer and Dryden (1995) highlight that it is important that the counsellor carefully considers the most suitable set of interventions for the individual client.

Lazarus (1981) suggests that personality can be divided into seven modalities: behaviour, affect, sensation, imagery, cognition, interpersonal and drugs/biology. These modalities form the acronym 'BASIC ID' and the modalities are systematically examined in the therapeutic assessment. Following the assessment, a number

TABLE 21.1   MODALITY PROFILE: CLIENT WITH PERFORMANCE ANXIETY AND A
NUMBER OF ADDITIONAL AREAS TO BE ADDRESSED IN COUNSELLING (OR COACHING)

Modality	Problem or issues	Proposed counselling or coaching programme
Behaviour	Avoidance of giving presentations	Behavioural practice of giving a presentation, exposure programme and cognitive restructuring
Affect	Anxiety	Breathing exercises, relaxation training
Sensation	Tension	Relaxation training, swimming
Imagery	Images of failing the presentation	Coping imagery
Cognition	'I must do a perfect presentation', 'The others will laugh'	Cognitive restructuring
Interpersonal	Unassertive with colleagues	Assertiveness training
Drugs/biology	Lack of exercise	Swimming

of suitable interventions are applied in the therapeutic programme. The information that is obtained in the assessment helps the counselling psychologist/counsellor and client to complete a modality profile. Table 21.1 provides an example of a completed profile. The modality profile consists of the identified problems in each modality and the suggested treatment interventions. The profile can be reviewed and modified during the therapy. The interventions should take the client's wishes and expectations into account. For example, if the client believes that relaxation exercises will be effective in dealing with stress at work, then this should be offered to the client. The counselling psychologist could adapt a relaxation script for the client, and it could be used and recorded in the session so that the client can listen to it as an in-between session task or homework exercise. A commercially available CD or download could be another alternative. Otherwise, a suitable referral may be made to a practitioner who can assist.

INTERNAL VERSUS EXTERNAL COUNSELLING

Counselling at work could be both internal or external. The counselling psychologist may work for the occupational health department, although this may vary depending upon the organization. Advantages of using an internal counselling psychologist include that he or she is more likely to be aware of the organization's policies, politics, history and organizational culture. This may provide a more empathic position during the counselling from which to understand the client's perspective about how organizational issues impinge upon his or her well-being. The counselling psychologist may also be a familiar figure to the employees, and this may make him or her more approachable and thereby more likely to seek an appointment. It is also possible that in internal counselling psychologist could have more opportunity to feed back any organizational issues that may have a negative impact upon employees' health. However, employees may be worried about breach of confidentiality within the counselling (Gyllensten et al., 2005), and this worry may be increased if the counselling psychologist is internally employed. Thus, one advantage of external counselling could be that employees might feel more secure in disclosing sensitive issues. However, disadvantages of external counselling psychologists could be that they are unaware of how the organization is structured and that they may have little opportunity to influence any negative organizational issues.

UNDERTAKING A STRESS RISK ASSESSMENT

As stated previously, stress in the workplace is a serious problem in the UK and the HSE, which is working to reduce workplace stress within the UK, suggests that organizations should conduct risk assessments focusing on stress. Since the first landmark stress case in 1995 when a social worker, John Walker was awarded £200,000 by the High Court (accepted £175,000 out of court) after suffering from two work-induced nervous breakdowns, companies have taken stress prevention far more seriously. This landmark case highlighted that employers have a legal duty of care to their employees regarding their physical and mental health. There are a number of laws and regulations relating to health and safety which are also applicable to stress. Also disability discrimination issues can arise when work-related stress has led to long-term sickness. The following section will outline the steps involved in such an assessment but will first present a model of workplace stress and provide some background to the HSE's approach.

When discussing stress it is important to be aware that there are many different definitions of stress at work. According to the HSE, stress is defined as 'the adverse reaction people have to excessive pressures or other types of demand placed on them' (2001: 1). The American National Institute for Occupational Safety and Health defines work stress as 'the harmful physical and emotional responses that occur when the requirements of the job do not match the capabilities, resources or needs of the worker' (NIOSH, 1999: 6). In cognitive definitions of stress, there is a focus on a person's individual view of what is stressful. Palmer et al. propose the following definition: 'stress occurs when the perceived pressure exceeds your perceived ability to cope' (2003a: 2).

After undertaking extensive research of work conditions, the HSE has identified six distinct hazard or stressor areas (for example, Mackay et al., 2004). These stressor areas are:

- *Demands*: refers to workload, work patterns, and the working environment.
- *Control*: refers to employee involvement with how they do their work, for example, control balanced against demands.

- *Support*: refers to the encouragement, sponsorship and resources a person is receiving from the organization and colleagues.
- *Relationships*: refers to the promotion of positive practices at work and management of unacceptable behaviour such as harassment or bullying.
- *Role*: refers to how much a person understands their role within the workplace and whether the individual has conflicting roles.
- *Change*: refers to the way organizational change is managed and communicated.

The HSE has developed and published management standards for each area which are applicable for all workplaces. Each area can be assessed when investigating stress within organizations and the HSE has developed guidelines for standards to be achieved (Cousins et al., 2004). As well as a basis for a systematic stress assessment, the six stressor areas could also be the basis for a less formal initial discussion about workplace stress. The model of work stress presented in Figure 21.1 (adapted Palmer et al., 2001) is based on the six stressors and highlights the relationship between these stressors/hazards, symptoms and causes of stress.

As stated previously, the HSE (2001, 2007) suggests that the six stressor areas should be included in a risk assessment for workplace stress. Indeed, both the HSE (2001) and

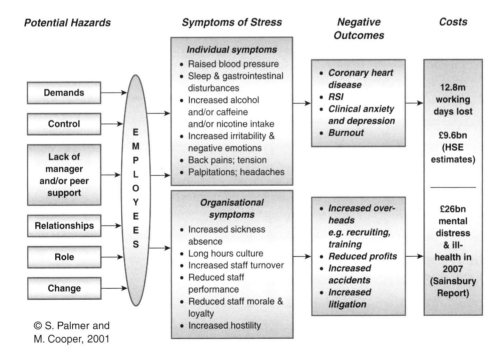

© S. Palmer and
M. Cooper, 2001

FIGURE 21.1   THE MODEL OF WORK STRESS (PUBLISHED WITH PERMISSION OF PALMER ET AL., 2001)

various researchers (Briner, 1997; Cooper and Cartwright, 1997; Cox, 1993) have suggested that organizations should conduct risk assessments or stress audits to manage stress. The risk assessment helps organizations to identify potential stressors, guide to appropriate action, and to review the process at relevant intervals. It is important that the assessment involves employee participation (HSE, 2001, 2007).

The HSE (2007) recommends that organizations should conduct a five-step stress risk assessment. However, initially management and employee commitment to a stress prevention programme needs to be gained through key stakeholder meetings, which may include employee representatives, trade union officers and key staff from human resources, occupational health, and health and safety. A stress policy can also be developed at this stage. The five steps are:

1. *Identify the hazards*: the six stressor areas should be assessed, and data could be collected from many sources including informal talks to employees, performance appraisals, focus groups, productivity data, sickness/absence data and turnover data.
2. *Decide who might be harmed and how*: stress may affect individuals differently, and it is important to find out what individuals/groups are vulnerable to stress and how they are affected.
3. *Evaluate the risk and decide if enough is being done*: assessment of what action is already taken and what further action is needed. Communicate results and provide feedback to the staff. (This can involve focus groups to provide feedback and also ask staff for their suggestions in how to tackle work-related stress.)
4. *Record the significant findings of the assessment and develop an action plan*: a record should be kept of the significant findings of the assessment and of which groups have been identified as being particularly at risk.
5. *Review the assessment at appropriate intervals, evaluate effectiveness and revise where necessary.*

This approach is now well documented on the HSE website, which provides case studies and support material including a manual on how to facilitate stress focus groups and a 35-question stress indicator tool which is also available as downloadable electronic programme that can be used to undertake the stress risk assessment (see www.hse.gov.uk). The HSE recommended approach is a continuous improvement model so that organizations can strive for improvement in areas that need to be addressed.

DEVELOPMENT OF STRESS MANAGEMENT AND PREVENTION PROGRAMMES

The content of stress-management programmes vary greatly. They may focus on stress awareness training, assertiveness training, dealing with stress-inducing thoughts, education, exercise, relaxation, biofeedback and meditation (Cartwright and Cooper, 2005; Palmer, 2003). The duration of these programmes may also vary from one-day workshops to longer programmes. When developing a programme it is important to assess the needs of the particular group or organization. It is useful to ask 'Why do they need a stress-management intervention?' and 'What activities have they used previously?' It is also important to consider the culture of the organization or the area of business. In some fields it is likely that there may be a stigma of stress and employees may be reluctant to attend any stress-management activities. In other fields there may be an awareness of the problem and the employees may be open to learning more about stress. It may be necessary to adapt the terms to make them less clinical and more business-like. For example, Neenan and Palmer (2001) use the terms 'PITs' (performance inhibiting thoughts) and 'PETs' (performance enhancing thoughts) instead of 'dysfunctional thinking'. This approach is applied in counselling, coaching and training in the workplace. Finally, if there are serious organizational stressors or hazards affecting the employees, it is likely that stress-management interventions may not be very effective in reducing stress. The organization has a responsibility to address these hazards if practicable.

THE EFFECTIVENESS OF STRESS MANAGEMENT PROGRAMMES

The research evidence of the effectiveness of stress management training is confusing and imprecise, according to Cooper and Cartwright (1997). In a review of the stress management literature they found no change in levels of job-satisfaction, blood pressure or work stress, but modest improvements in strain and symptoms. The British Occupational Health Research Foundation (BOHRF) (2005) conducted a review of studies evaluating a range of stress-management interventions, and it was concluded that there was moderate to limited evidence of the effect of these interventions. Cooper et al. (1996) have suggested that stress management programmes can help employees to cope with workplace stressors. However, it has also been suggested that stress management training may be insufficient if the stressors are structural (Cooper et al., 2001). Van der Klink et al. (2001) conducted a meta-analysis and reported that stress management interventions are effective, in particular cognitive-behavioural interventions. Indeed, a randomized controlled trial found that stress symptoms were significantly reduced in a group of managers using a cognitive-behavioural self-help manual, whereas there were no changes in a control group (Grbcic and Palmer, 2006). In summary, the evidence for the effectiveness of stress management training is mixed.

ORGANIZATIONAL INTERVENTIONS

Organizational interventions can be undertaken at primary, secondary and tertiary levels. Table 21.2 summarizes the interventions.

TABLE 21.2   A CONCEPTUAL FRAMEWORK FOR STRESS MANAGEMENT AND PREVENTION INTERVENTIONS

Level of intervention	Examples of activities
Primary	Job redesign
	Flexible work schedules
	Structural changes
	Improve resources
Secondary	Stress awareness or stress/pressure management
	Training or coaching programmes
	Relaxation and biofeedback training education
	Health promotion
Tertiary	Counselling and psychotherapy
	Outplacement or career counselling/coaching
	Medical interventions
	Rehabilitation

Following a risk assessment it may become apparent that individual interventions, including counselling and stress-management, are not sufficient to improve employee well-being. Rather more organizational changes are needed. Organizational interventions are also called 'primary interventions', and the aim of these interventions is to modify or eliminate sources of stress inherent in the workplace (Cartwright and Cooper, 2005). One intervention could be to redesign the actual job or to make the work schedules more flexible. Another example is reorganization of certain departments or of the whole organization (Cooper and Cartwright, 1997). In the case of reorganization, it is important that the employees are informed about the changes and are supported through the change period, as change is a potential workplace stressor (HSE, 2001). Problems concerning relationships at work, and in particular bullying by peers or managers, should always be addressed. Such incidents can trigger stress and in some situations can lead to post traumatic stress disorder (PTSD), which has been diagnosed in employees who have suffered from being bullied. The HSE stress risk assessment tool will specifically highlight any report of bullying. Although policies and relevant training for staff are important, in some cases the only successful resolution of the problem is to deal directly with the person exhibiting bullying behaviour. This has sometimes been difficult to manage when the person is in a senior position in the company.

It has been suggested that primary interventions are likely to be the most effective interventions in dealing with stress in the workplace in the long-term (Cartwright and Cooper, 2005).

COACHING AT WORK

Coaching is a popular intervention that is used by individuals and organizations (Neenan and Dryden, 2002; Palmer et al., 2003b). Although employees may be somewhat resistant to receiving counselling, they tend to view coaching in a more positive light (Gyllensten et al., 2005). Coaching can focus on individual issues such as career development, transition, improving performance, enhancing resilience, dealing with procrastination, improving communication skills and dealing with criticism. It can also help key personnel to focus on more organizational issues, such as identifying and changing stressors, processes and team development. A number of different coaching definitions have been proposed. Grant defines coaching in the workplace as 'a solution-focused, result-oriented systematic process in which the coach facilitates the enhancement of work performance and the self-directed learning and personal growth of the coachee' (2001: 8). Moreover, Grant defines life coaching as 'a collaborative solution-focused, results oriented and systematic process in which the coach facilitates the enhancement of life experience and goal attainment in the personal and/or professional life of normal, nonclinical clients' (2003: 254).

There is some ambiguity regarding the difference between counselling/therapy and coaching. A commonly suggested distinction between coaching and therapy is that therapy deals with individuals who have a high psychopathology and low functionality, whereas coaching deals with individuals who have a low psychopathology and high functionality (Grant, 2001). Thus, therapy is focusing on treating psychopathology and coaching is focusing on improving performance or life-experience (Grant, 2001). However, this distinction may not always be straightforward, considering the fact that individuals with mental health problems may seek coaching rather than therapy or counselling (Cavanagh, no date). Figure 21.2 illustrates some suggested differences between therapy, counselling, psychological coaching, coaching and mentoring in a continuum.

Bachkirova and Cox (2004) suggest that coaches emphasize differences to counselling in order to distinguish themselves from counsellors and thereby make coaching sound more attractive. From a different perspective, counsellors/therapists tend to argue that the difference is only superficial and coaches are viewed as competitors without extensive training. According to Bachkirova and Cox (2004), both groups tend to have their own agendas and over- and under-emphasize some factors. For example, some coaches suggest that a difference between counselling and coaching is that counselling focuses on the past and coaching on the future. However, there are several counselling approaches that focus on the present and future goals, such as cognitive-behavioural and solution-focused therapy. Counsellors may fail to highlight important differences, including the context of coaching and accountability. Bachkirova and Cox (2004) suggest that the coaching field could be enriched and gain important understanding by examining and learning from certain issues in the counselling field, including theoretical grounding, evaluation research and understanding of the dynamics of the relationship. Moreover, it is also important to recognize that coaching is attracting individuals who may not use counselling/therapy.

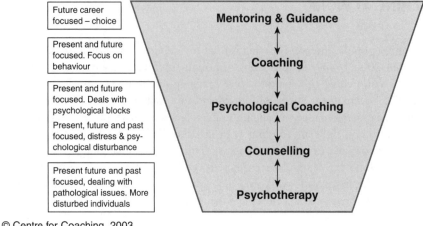

© Centre for Coaching, 2003

FIGURE 21.2   PSYCHOLOGICAL COACHING: A CONTINUUM (REPRINTED WITH PERMISSION FROM THE CENTRE FOR COACHING)

There are many different forms of coaching, and coaching practitioners are influenced by concepts and methods from a number of areas including traditional organizational development, adult education and management training (Kilburg, 1996). Grant (2001) suggests that the discipline of psychology has a lot of offer the field of coaching, both in terms of research practice and theoretical grounding. Certainly, coaching psychology is becoming established in the UK and in 2004 a Special Group in Coaching Psychology was formed within the British Psychological Society (Palmer and Whybrow, 2006). Its members are drawn from occupational and, to a lesser extent, counselling psychology, with some from the remaining areas of professional psychology practice. The following definition has been proposed: 'Coaching psychology is for enhancing well-being and performance in personal life and work domains underpinned by models of coaching grounded in established adult learning or psychological approaches' (adapted from Grant and Palmer, 2002). Considering that counselling psychologists are taught both clinical skills and techniques and research skills that could be useful in coaching, they could contribute to the area of coaching psychology. Counselling psychologists who are looking to broaden their area of work could become involved in coaching.

Although there is still a lack of good research studies on the effectiveness of coaching, some research has been conducted. Studies have found a mixed result regarding the effectiveness of coaching. Gyllensten and Palmer (2005) addressed this issue in their study. Coaching effectiveness was measured by one Likert scale item, where a score of 1 indicated not at all effective and a score of 7 indicated very effective. Figure 21.3 reports the frequencies of each score. Participants reported a high level of coaching effectiveness with a mode and median of 6, and a mean of 5.64. Surveys by leading professional bodies have also found similar results.

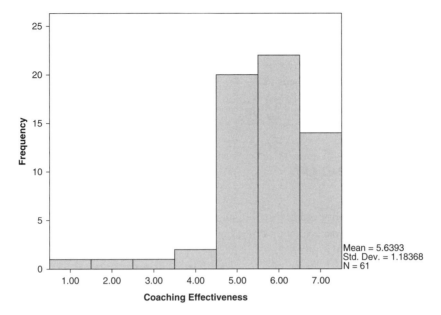

FIGURE 21.3   COACHING EFFECTIVENESS

One of the early studies in the field of workplace coaching by Gorby (1937) found that when experienced, older employees coached newer employees to reduce waste, profits could be increased which then maximized profit-sharing bonuses. This was probably one of the earliest studies that indirectly considered 'return on investment' in coaching in the workplace. Grant (2003) found that coaching was effective in facilitating goal attainment. When solution-focused, cognitive-behavioural coaching is being applied, a number of studies have found that measures of mental health, such as depression, anxiety and stress, show a significant improvement even though these were not being targeted for change in the intervention (for example, Green et al., 2006; Green et al., 2007).

An in-depth review of the coaching research is beyond the scope of this chapter; for more information see Palmer and Whybrow (2006) or Grant (2001).

THE COUNSELLING PSYCHOLOGIST AS TRAINER OR FACILITATOR IN THE WORKPLACE

In this chapter, we have illustrated a number of areas where there are opportunities for a suitably trained counselling psychologist to provide workplace training to employees. For example, in the field of stress management and prevention, they can run stress management training workshops and courses, and facilitate focus groups as part of a stress risk assessment. Additional areas can include conflict resolution at work and mediation. Whereas in the 1980s counselling psychologists may have trained managers to use counselling skills, during this decade they have also been instrumental in training supervisors, managers and executives in coaching and mentoring skills. These courses have often been externally university accredited and/or recognized as leading to National Vocational Qualifications (NVQs), which are vocational awards in England and Wales gained through assessment and training.

SUPERVISION AND CPD

Supervision is always important for counselling psychologists, and this is also true for practitioners in the workplace. In addition to the standard issues that counselling psychologists need to consider in their practice, counselling psychologists in the workplace need to consider the organizational system and possible stressors. In some instances it may be more effective to deal with the stressor and the cause of the problems rather than 'treating' the individual. Supervision may be a good opportunity to become aware of and discuss these issues. In some cases, depending upon the intervention being made, supervision may sometimes be enhanced by engaging additional supervision from an occupational psychologist.

Counselling psychologists practising in the workplace may benefit from continuing professional development (CPD) in areas relating to stress management and prevention, coaching, leadership, groups dynamics, organizational systems and conflict resolution. Work may not always be related to the problems and clinical disorders clients may bring to counselling, and counselling psychologists still need to have CPD and ongoing supervision on a range of topics.

CONCLUSION

Currently, counselling psychologists have posts working in EAPs and also as practitioners working with employees providing a counselling service for organizations. They undertake a variety of other services too, such as stress management training. In the UK psychologists will need to be registered on the Health Professions Council (HPC) register, which will eventually approve post-degree qualifications in psychology leading to HPC registration. It is important that the counselling psychology profession ensures that registration does not limit the field in which counselling psychologists can practise to just individual client work or group therapy. Counselling psychologists have a lot to offer both employees and organizations in terms of individual, group or consultancy work. This knowledge can be gained with relevant post-qualification training or ongoing continuing professional development and supervision.

REFERENCES

Allison, T., Cooper, C. and Reynolds, P. (1989) 'The post office experience', *The Psychologist*, 2: 384–388.

Bachkirova, T. and Cox, E. (2004) 'A bridge over troubled water: Bridging together coaching and counselling', *The International Journal of Mentoring and Coaching*, 2 (1).

Briner, R.B. (1997) 'Improving stress assessment: Toward an evidence-based approach to organizational stress interventions', *Journal of Psychosomatic Research*, 43: 61–71.

British Occupational Health Research Foundation (2005) 'Workplace interventions for people with common mental health problems: Evidence, review, and recommendations'. Available at www.hse. gov.uk/sress/research.htm, accessed 15 May 2008.

British Psychological Society (2001) 'Chartered counselling psychologists' training and areas of competence', *Counselling Psychology Review*, 16: 41–43.

British Psychological Society (2008) *Regulations and Syllabus for the Qualification in Counselling Psychology 2008*. Leicester: British Psychological Society.

Carroll, M. (1996) *Workplace Counselling*. London: Sage.

Cartwright, S. and Cooper, C. (2005) 'Individually targeted interventions', in J. Barling, E.K. Kelloway and M.R. Frone (eds), *Handbook of Work Stress*. London: Sage. pp. 607–622.

Cavanagh, M. (no date) 'Mental-health issues and challenging clients in executive coaching'. Available at www.groups.psychology.org.au/Assets/Files/article_cavanagh.pdf, accessed 9 May 2008.

Cooper, C.L. and Cartwright, S. (1997) 'An intervention strategy for workplace stress', *Journal of Psychosomatic Research*, 43: 7–16.

Cooper, C.L., Dewe, P.J. and O'Driscoll, M.P. (2001) *Organizational Stress: A Review and Critique of Theory, Research and Applications*. Thousand Oaks, CA: Sage.

Cooper, C.L., Liukkonen, P. and Cartwright, S. (1996) *Stress Prevention in the Workplace: Assessing the Costs and Benefits to Organisations*. Dublin: European Foundation for the Improvement of Living and Working Conditions.

Cooper, C.L. and Sadri, G. (1991) 'The impact of stress counselling at work', *Journal of Social Behaviour and Personality*, 6: 411–423.

Cousins, R., Makay, C.J., Clarke, S.D., Kelly, C., Kelly, P.J. and McCaig, R.H. (2004) 'Management standards and work-related stress in the UK: Practical development', *Work and Stress*, 18: 113–136.

Cox, T. (1993) *Stress Research and Stress Management: Putting Theory to Work*. Sudbury: HSE Books.

EAPA (2009a) 'Employee Assistance Professionals Association'. Available at www.eapassn.org/public/pages/index.cfm?pageid=825#EAP, accessed 6 August 2009.

EAPA (2009b) 'Employee Assistance Professionals Association'. Available at www.eapassn.org/public/pages/index.cfm?pageid=869, accessed 6 August 2009.

Firth-Cozens, J. and Hardy, G.E. (1992) 'Occupational stress, clinical treatment and changes in job perceptions', *Journal of Occupational and Organizational Psychology*, 65: 81–88.

Gorby, C.B. (1937) 'Everyone gets a share of the profits', *Factory Management and Maintenance*, 95: 82–83.

Grant, A.M. (2001) 'Towards a psychology of coaching'. Available at www.psych.usyd.edu.au, accessed 12 May 2003.

Grant, A.M. (2003) 'The impact of life coaching on goal attainment, metacognition and mental health', *Social Behaviour and Personality*, 31: 253–264.

Grant, T. and Palmer, S. (2002) 'Coaching psychology workshop'. Annual conference of the Division of Counselling Psychology, British Psychological Society, Torquay, 18 May.

Grbcic, S. and Palmer, S. (2006) 'A cognitive-behavioural manualised self-coaching approach to stress management and prevention at work: A randomised controlled study'. Research paper presented at the First International Coaching Psychology Conference, City University, London, 18 December.

Green, L.S., Oades, L.G. and Grant, A.M. (2006) 'Cognitive-behavioural, solution-focused life coaching: Enhancing goal striving, well-being and hope', *Journal of Positive Psychology*, 1 (3): 142–149.

Green, S., Grant, A. and Rynsaardt, J. (2007) 'Evidence-based life coaching for senior high school students: Building hardiness and hope', *International Coaching Psychology Review*, 2 (1): 24–32.

Gyllensten, K. and Palmer, S. (2005) 'The relationship between coaching and workplace stress: A correlational study', *International Journal of Health Promotion and Education*, 43 (3): 97–103.

Gyllensten, K., Palmer, S. and Farrants, J. (2005) 'Perception of stress and stress interventions in finance organisations: Overcoming resistance towards counselling', *Counselling Psychology Quarterly*, 18: 19–29.

Health and Safety Executive (2001) *Tackling Work-related Stress: A Manager's Guide to Improving and Maintaining Employee Health and Well-being*. Sudbury: HSE Books.

Health and Safety Executive (2007) *Managing the Causes of Work-related Stress: A Step-by-step Approach Using the Management Standards*. Sudbury: HSE Books.

Hesketh, B. (2000) 'Prevention and development in the workplace', in S.D. Brown and R.W. Lent (eds), *Handbook of Counselling Psychology*. New York: Wiley. pp. 471–498.

Jones, J.R., Huxtable, C.S. and Hodgson, J.T. (2004) *Self-reported Work-related Illness in 2003/2004: Results from the Labour Force Survey*. Sudbury: HSE Books.

Kilburg, R.R. (1996) 'Executive coaching as an emerging competency in the practice of consultation', *Consulting Psychology Journal: Practice and Research,* 48: 59–60.

Kinder, A. (2007) 'Counselling psychologists in the workplace', *Counselling Psychology Review*, 22 (1): 32–34.

Lazarus, A.A. (1981) *The Practice of Multimodal Therapy*. New York: McGraw Hill.

Mackay, C.J., Cousins, R., Kelly, P.J., Lee, S. and McCaig, R.H. (2004) 'Management standards and work-related stress in the UK: Policy background and science', *Work and Stress*, 18: 91–112.

McLeod, J. (2001) *Counselling in the Workplace: The Facts: A Systematic Study of the Research Evidence*. Lutterworth: British Association for Counselling and Psychotherapy.

McLeod, J. (2007) *Counselling in the Workplace: The Facts: A Comprehensive Review of the Research Evidence*, 2nd edn. Rugby: British Association for Counselling and Psychotherapy.

McLeod, J. and Henderson, M. (2003) 'Does workplace counselling work?', *British Journal of Psychiatry*, 182: 103–104.

National Institute for Occupational Safety and Health (1999) 'Stress'. Available from www.cdc.gov/niosh, accessed 11 April 2003.

Neenan, M. and Dryden, W. (2002) *Life Coaching: A Cognitive Behavioural Approach*. Hove: Brunner-Routledge.

Neenan, M. and Palmer, S. (2001) 'Cognitive behavioural coaching', *Stress News*, 13 (3): 15–18.

Orlans, V. (2003) 'Counselling psychology in the workplace', in R. Wolfe, W. Dryden and S. Strawbridge (eds), *Handbook of Counselling Psychology*. London: Sage. pp. 536–551.

Orlans, V. (2008) 'Counselling and coaching in organisations: An integrative multi-level approach', in A. Kinder, R. Hughes and C.L. Cooper (eds), *Employee Well-being Support: A Workplace Resource*. Chichester: Wiley. pp. 175–182.

Palmer, S. (2003) 'Whistle-stop tour of the theory and practice of stress management and prevention: Its possible role in postgraduate health promotion', *Health Education Journal*, 62: 133–142.

Palmer, S., Cooper, C. and Thomas, K. (2001) 'Model of organisational stress for use within an occupational health education/promotion or wellbeing programme: A short communication', *Health Education Journal*, 60: 378–380.

Palmer, S., Cooper, C. and Thomas, K. (2003a) *Creating a Balance: Managing Stress*. London: The British Library.

Palmer, S. and Dryden, W. (1995) *Counselling for Stress Problems*. London: Sage.

Palmer, S., Tubbs, I. and Whybrow, A. (2003b) 'Health coaching to facilitate the promotion of healthy behaviour and achievement of health-related goals', *International Journal of Health Promotion and Education*, 41: 91–93.

Palmer, S. and Whybrow, A. (2005) 'The proposal to establish a special group in coaching psychology', *The Coaching Psychologist*, 1: 5–11.

Palmer, S. and Whybrow, A. (2006) 'Coaching psychology: An introduction', in S. Palmer and A. Whybrow (eds), *Handbook of Coaching Psychology: A Guide for Practitioners*. London: Routledge.

Sainsbury Centre for Mental Health, The (2007) 'Mental health at work: Developing the business case', Policy Paper 8. Available from http://website.scmh.org.uk/80256FBD004F3555/vWeb/flKHAL79TMEC/$file/mental_health_at_work.pdf, accessed 1 September 2008.

Taylor, R. (2002) *The Future of Work–Life Balance*. London: Economic and Social Research Council.

Van der Klink, J.J.L., Blonk, R.W.B., Schene, A.H. and van Dijk, F.J.H. (2001) 'The benefits of interventions for work-related stress', *American Journal of Public Health*, 91: 270–276.

Winwood, M.A. and Beer, S. (2008) 'What makes a good employee assistance programme?,' in A. Kinder, R. Hughes and C.L. Cooper (eds), *Employee well-being Support: A Workplace Resource*. Chichester: Wiley. pp. 183–200.

22

WORKING IN PRIVATE PRACTICE

Jacqui Porter

When I was asked to write this chapter on 'working in private practice', my first thoughts were 'How long will it take?' and 'Will I get paid?'. If you are self-employed, these are important questions. When you are on holiday, at a conference, on a training course or having supervision, you are not earning an income. This does not, of course, mean that you shouldn't do these things. On the contrary, it is very important that you do. The point is that they all have to be costed and factored into your business plan. As Weitz (2006) notes, some therapists find it difficult to think in these terms because they feel it suggests that the work they do is the same as 'selling widgets'. However, there is one simple truth you have to remember if you are working in private practice: you are running a business (Howden Professionals, 2007). And as Prichard (2006) emphasizes, the ultimate objective has to be to make money. If you don't, your business will fail.

It follows that if you are considering setting up your own practice, one of the first questions to ask is 'Do I have enough business experience?' If the answer is 'no', then find out what training and specialist advice is available. You should be able to get information from local banks or colleges or from the Internet about initiatives in your area to help small business start-ups. Some of the business and financial issues you will need to consider include how you structure your business, where you work, what income you need to live on, what your costs will be and what you are going to charge for your services. Another key question is 'What products am I going to offer?' This will depend partly on the range and depth of your training and experience, but also on what products are 'in demand', who your competitors are, what differentiates you from others and how you let potential clients know about your practice. A third question to ask yourself is 'Do I have the stamina and health to run a business, cope with the downturns and sustain a reasonable work/life balance?'

After defining what we mean by 'private practice', we will look briefly at all these issues. Whether they feel like positives or negatives will depend on your personality, training, experience, setting and circumstances. Working on your own; being in control of your own time; being accountable for your clinical work; and being responsible for your own sales, marketing, finance and administration – this may sound attractive, challenging, daunting, frightening or all of the above. In her 'Reflections of a counselling psychologist in private practice' (2007), Staples draws a picture of the 'truly appealing ... dream' of being a private practitioner, before going on to describe the reality of her own experience. As she notes, all our experiences of private practice differ. But if you are imagining leisurely mornings reading the paper in the garden before seeing a small number of interesting, wealthy and psychologically-aware clients who provide you with a reliable and regular income – you might want to read a little more before taking the plunge!

It is impossible to cover all of the issues in detail in one chapter. You will not, for example, find detailed information here about how to develop a business plan, keep accounts, work out tax and so on. There are some very good, specialist 'how to' books available on these and other aspects of running your own business, and I have listed a selection of these at the end of the chapter. Included in this list are the guidelines produced by the British Psychological Society for psychologists in private practice (BPS, 2008b). These guidelines include some key points from the Society's *Code of Ethics and Conduct* (BPS, 2006) and *Generic Professional Practice Guidelines* (BPS, 2008a), which should underpin the practice of all professional psychologists. They also provide an invaluable source of advice and information for psychologists who are working independently, including contact details for an online private practitioners' discussion forum.

What you will find in this chapter is an overview of some of the key questions any therapist needs to consider before setting up in private practice, with, when appropriate, reference to the particular challenges and opportunities these issues represent for counselling psychologists. You will not find a long list of academic references at the end. It is an essentially practical chapter, drawing largely on my own experience of running a private practice for some 12 years and on the anecdotal experience of colleagues. You will find as many questions as answers, because much will depend on your individual circumstances and objectives. By asking questions, I hope to raise your awareness of the issues you need to consider and to encourage you to find answers that are right for you.

For those of you who are at the beginning of your careers as counselling psychologists, I am ending this introduction with some words of caution. If you are thinking of private practice as a possibility for the future, I hope this helps you evaluate whether it will be right for you at some point, and identify some of the experience and skills you will need to acquire along the way. However, if you are considering setting up private practice as soon as you have qualified, I hope this increases your understanding of what will be involved and causes you to stop and think. *If* you have already had business experience in a 'previous life', and *if* in the course of your training you have had an unusually wide range of clinical experience, and *if* you can afford to take financial risk, and *if* you know that you really are someone who is happy working in isolation, then setting up a private practice straight away could be a good option. But these are a lot of '*ifs*' and I would generally advise a newly qualified practitioner to extend her clinical, professional and business experience first, then build up a private practice over time. This chapter might, of course, help you decide that you will *never* work in private practice. Either way, I hope it will encourage you to question any stereotypes you might have about the private sector and give you a more realistic view of what it is actually about.

Finally, I am using the female gender in this chapter purely for convenience – everything I have written is equally relevant to both male and female counselling psychologists.

KEY POINTS

- If you are running a private practice, you are running a business.
- There are many business, financial and clinical questions to consider before setting up a private practice.
- You will need to consider whether you have sufficient business and clinical experience, and whether private practice is right for you.

WHAT DO WE MEAN BY 'PRIVATE PRACTICE'?

If a therapist is working in private practice, it is generally assumed she is self-employed and has clients for whom she provides some form of counselling or psychotherapy. In defining the term 'private practice', Thistle notes that practitioners 'earn all or part of their income directly from their clients, working professionally in the context of a therapeutic relationship' (1998: 3). As we will note later, the nature of their training means that counselling psychologists can potentially offer a wide range of therapeutic services. Much of the literature on working in private practice relates specifically to the provision of counselling or psychotherapy, but whether we are providing counselling, coaching or consultancy, many of the issues are the same.

The fact that a client pays you directly for your services is, as Field and Hemmings (2007) note, one of the defining characteristics of private practice. This 'exchange of money' not only has practical implications for the business in terms of accounting and administration, but it also impacts the work in a range of different ways. Money has a different meaning for each of us, and this will inevitably have an effect on the therapeutic relationship. It can affect clinical decisions about theoretical approach, aims and length of treatment, and may raise issues for both client and therapist in relation to the power differential, the value they put on themselves and each other, and the beliefs they hold about the concept of private practice. One of the tensions of private practice, for example, is the notion of 'fiscal dependence', with the risk that the therapist's financial dependence on the client impacts clinical decisions and length of treatment. These and other dilemmas are explored more fully by Field and Hemmings (2007) in their chapter entitled 'The role of money in the therapeutic relationship'.

Taking one dilemma as an example, in some parts of the UK patients currently have to wait a long time to obtain psychological treatment for mental health problems through the NHS. Usually the only alternatives to a waiting list are voluntary counselling agencies or the private sector. Within the private sector there can be a significant difference in the fees charged by individual private practitioners. Some practitioners charge fees affordable only by people on high incomes or with private medical insurance. Some have a sliding scale, offering lower fees to people on lower incomes. For people who are unwaged or on a small income, the private sector may always be unattainable, and their only option is to wait for the psychological help they need.

If your business is the provision of psychological counselling, then coming to terms with this situation and deciding where you want to position your practice is key. As Thistle (1998) notes, you must check your personal priorities at the outset. You need to decide where your primary objective lies on a continuum between the extremes of 'making as much money as possible' and 'offering psychological services to as many people as possible'. If you are uncomfortable making this sort of compromise and don't like dealing with money, then working in the private sector is not for you. The fees you charge will directly impact the number of hours you will need to work to achieve your desired level of income; it may affect your health, energy levels and how you feel about your work and your clients; it will determine who can afford to see you; and it will have clinical implications. For example, if a client can only afford to see you for six sessions, this will significantly influence the treatment you can offer.

You can, of course, have clients in your private practice who don't pay you themselves. Your services can be paid for by someone else, for example, by their employer, by an Employee Assistance Programme (EAP), by a private medical scheme insurance, or as part of compensation agreed following an accident. However, you will be engaging in a direct 'exchange of money' with some – if not all – of your clients, and you will need to consider carefully what that means for you and your therapeutic practice.

KEY POINTS

- Being in private practice means that clients pay you money for your services.
- Money has a different meaning for us all, and the fact there is an 'exchange of money' may have clinical, business, political and personal implications.
- If you are uncomfortable with those implications and with 'dealing with money', then private practice is not for you.

SELF-EMPLOYMENT

Working in private practice does not necessarily mean you are fully self-employed and spend 100 per cent of your time on private work. You can, of course, be both self-employed and employed at the same time, as long as your employment contract does not preclude you from doing both. For example, you could be in full-time employment and see a couple of private clients in the evening; or you could be self-employed for two days a week and be employed part-time by an organization for three days. Another possibility is that you are fully self-employed but only spending part of your time seeing private clients. The rest of the time you could be working on contracts under the terms of which you are providing services to organizations rather than directly to clients. As Tyler (2003) notes, the question of whether you are employed, self-employed or both is of much interest to the HM Revenue and Customs (HMRC) and there will be implications for your tax and national insurance contributions, how you treat expenses and how you keep your accounts. Tyler's book *Money Matters for Therapists* sets out these issues clearly.

Whether you are employed or self-employed, if you are seeing private clients then you have a 'private practice', and from an administrative and financial perspective it is essential that you keep separate records. However small your practice, the issues raised in this chapter still apply; for example, where you see clients, security, insurance, clinical supervision and so on.

Whether you start with a couple of private clients and build up your practice over time or start a full-time private practice straight away, you will need to decide on the structure of your business. As Weitz (2006) notes, there are essentially four types of business – sole trader, limited company, partnership and cooperative – and she gives an explanation of the differences. The most common structures for private practitioners are 'sole trader' and 'limited company', and a number of commentators – including Weitz (2006) and Tyler (2003) – set out some pros and cons of both. Most private practitioners begin as sole traders and for many this will continue to be the best option. There are fewer formalities required to set up as a sole trader, and the legal, accounting and taxation requirements are less stringent. If you decide to set up a limited company, it is a separate legal entity; you will need a 'registered office', your accounts have to be set out in a certain way and filed at Companies House, and you become an employee of that company. If you are considering this route, you should certainly take advice from an accountant.

Most of the books listed at the end of the chapter provide comprehensive guidance on all aspects of setting up your own private practice, including details of how to manage financial matters. We will identify a few of the key financial considerations in the next section.

KEY POINTS

- You can be both self-employed and employed at the same time, but each is treated differently in terms of tax, national insurance contributions, expenses and so on; and it is essential that you keep separate records.

- Even if you only have two private clients, you still have a 'private practice' and the issues raised in this chapter still apply.
- You will need to decide on the structure of your business. Many in private practice choose 'sole trader', but it will depend on your circumstances and you should take professional advice.

SOME KEY FINANCIAL CONSIDERATIONS

As McMahon notes 'many self-employed people get into a dreadful mess handling and controlling their money' (1994: 33) – they lose receipts, don't keep financial records up to date, and mix personal and business finance. Teaching yourself the basics, keeping on top of the paperwork and getting good professional advice will all be important factors in the successful running of your business. Whether you decide to use an accountant to prepare your accounts and tax returns or do it yourself will depend on the size of your business and of the accountant's fees, as well as your ability and desire to do the work yourself. At the very least, you will be well advised to find a good book-keeper, the best source of which is likely to be personal recommendation. As Weitz (2006) notes, this will leave you free to concentrate on what you are good at: the provision of psychological services. At the same time your accounts will always be up to date and you will know how your business is doing.

Deciding what products you are going to offer in your practice is key, and we will look at some marketing issues in the next section. From a financial perspective, a good starting point is to consider how much income you need. As Tyler (2003) notes, this is a fairly fundamental point. It will depend on a range of factors: your personal circumstances, whether you have other sources of income, what products you are able to offer and how many hours you want to devote to your practice. Once you have decided your desired income level, you should then calculate what is achievable. The three key variables to consider are the fees you charge for your services, the hours you work and the costs of running your practice.

Fees

The fees that you can charge will be determined by a range of factors. We have already noted there are some social and political considerations which may influence where you position your practice. Other factors include the nature and quality of your products, the demand that exists in the marketplace, what your client group can afford, how many similar products are already available, who your competitors are and what they charge.

Hours

In calculating the hours you work and how many are chargeable 'client hours', you need to be realistic about the time you will need for administration, making client notes, dealing with telephone calls, having supervision, keeping up to date with clinical developments, taking breaks, attending training courses and so on. McMahon (1994) calculates that if you are doing 20 one-hour sessions with clients per week, your average working week can be around 50 hours, once you have taken account of the time you need for all other aspects of running your business.

In separating dream from reality, Staples warns how simple it is to calculate: 'If I charge £60 per hour and work 40 hours a week, I can earn £120,000 a year' (2007: 35). This is the dream. In reality, if you are doing an average of 20 sessions of psychological counselling per week, not only will you be working long hours but you will also be doing well in your practice. If the average client attends for, say, 10–12 sessions and you work for, say, 46 weeks per year, you will need around 75 new clients per year to sustain this average. If you achieve this, based on Staples' figure your income from fees will be around £55,000 for the year, from which you have to deduct the costs of running your business and then account for things like tax, national insurance, pension contributions and so on. You will also need to take account of the fact that you will not be earning income when on holiday; and that self-employed people are not paid statutory sick pay. The actual fees charged by different psychologists will, of course, vary significantly. According to the BPS guidelines (2008b), anecdotal evidence suggested a very wide range of fees, from £80 per hour upwards. This includes all categories of psychologists and the actual fees charged by counselling psychologists in your areas of interests may be higher or lower depending on the nature of the work, the personal choices and circumstances of the psychologists, their geographical location, and the economic climate of the time. However, the basic calculations you need to carry out are the same. If they do not leave you with sufficient net income, you will need to rethink your business plan and either increase your fees, work longer hours or reduce your costs – or some combination of the three.

Running costs

In calculating the costs of running your practice, you need to take account of a whole range of factors which can include rent, cleaning, heating, lighting, telephones, insurance, stationery, postage, journals, books, professional subscriptions, supervision, training, conferences, advertising, travel, fees for accountant/book-keeper and so on. You will also need to consider whether costs are 'variable' (only occur if you are working) or 'fixed' (do not vary according to the number of hours you work), and whether for taxation purposes they are 'allowable expenses', that is, 'wholly and exclusively for the operation of the business'.

Once you have considered all these factors and decided on your products, you can then finalize your business plan, draw up a cash-flow forecast and set up some financial systems. On a practical level, you will need a separate bank account for your business. You must keep records of all money paid in, whether by cheque, cash or debit/credit cards. If you want to offer the facility of taking cards, you should discuss this with your bank or financial adviser as it can be a costly option. You must also keep records of all money paid out, with relevant receipts. You will need to ensure that you are putting money aside for income tax and – if you are registered – for VAT. The requirement to register for VAT depends on level of income and on profession. At the time of writing, psychology practices are not exempt and this may or may not change in the future for psychologists when they are on the Health Professions Council's Register. This illustrates the importance of keeping abreast with changing professional and HMRC regulations. The BPS guidelines (2008b) contain useful telephone and website contact details where you can obtain up-to-date information.

All these financial issues, and more, are covered in detail in a number of the publications listed at the end of the chapter and are essential reading before setting up your practice.

KEY POINTS

- It is very important to keep on top of paperwork and keep accounts up to date, and you should consider using the services of a book-keeper and/or accountant.
- You must decide what level of income you need. The income you can achieve will be broadly determined by three variables: fees, hours and expenses.
- It is easy to underestimate the number of hours needed to run a private practice, the number of new clients you will need and the costs involved in running the practice.

DECIDING WHAT PRODUCTS TO OFFER

Deciding on what products you will offer is a key decision when planning your private practice and it is likely to change, not only as your areas of expertise and interest develop, but also as the prevailing 'zeitgeist' changes. Hudson-Allez (2007) describes how developments in the 'wider field' can impact therapists in private practice in her chapter 'The changing status of counselling'.

As McMahon et al. (2005) note, every business has to determine its range of products or services, and psychological counselling is no exception. We have to make decisions about whether to specialize or generalize; there can be a strong temptation when we first set up a practice to 'see everyone and offer everything'. As already noted, counselling psychologists can potentially offer a wide range of products because of the nature of their training. According to the BPS website, counselling psychologists work almost anywhere there are people – in industry, commerce, the prison service, education, mental health services, research, teaching and consultancy. Frankland (2007) describes counselling psychology as 'the trade for the Portfolio Professional'.

Within the broad area of 'therapeutic services', the products a counselling psychologist can offer in private practice include psychological counselling, clinical supervision, clinical training, stress management and coaching. You can also include consultancy services, research and writing in your 'portfolio'. However, the risks of trying to become an 'all round provider tackling any psychological task in sight' are noted by Staples (2007: 36), and a number of commentators (for example, McMahon, 1994; Thistle, 1998; Weitz, 2006) suggest some questions which will help you to be more specific about the products you are going to offer in your private practice. These include:

> What experience, skills and specialisms can you offer; or could develop with further training?
> What are you good at and enjoy doing?
> What is 'unique' about what you can offer?
> What is your 'catchment area'?
> What do people in your catchment area want? At what price?
> What are they likely to want in the future? Are there any clear market trends?
> Who are your competitors? And what will differentiate your practice from that of your competitors?

These questions should encourage you to think about two broad areas: supply and demand. On the demand side, defining your 'catchment area' and determining what people want, what they are prepared to pay, who your competitors are, what they offer – these are all aspects of 'marketing research' which are explored in detail by a number of commentators, including McMahon (1994), Weitz (2006) and McMahon et al. (2005). Sources of market information can include national and local newspapers, professional journals, websites, local counselling networks, colleagues and friends. The importance of market research cannot be underestimated. As Weitz (2006) states, 'No clients, no business'.

On the supply side, the questions will help you decide what products you can offer. In terms of 'specialisms', there are many possibilities just within the field of psychological counselling. For example, you could specialize in working with individuals, couples or groups; provide short-term or long-term therapy; use a specific therapeutic approach; work with adolescents, adults or elderly people; or work with particular mental health issues. It doesn't, of course, have to be 'either/or'. You may decide to work with individuals *and* couples; to provide both short- *and* long-term therapy; and to specialize in *a number of* mental health issues. The important thing is that you have thought about the options and made a considered decision, and that in reaching that decision you have asked yourself whether you have sufficient levels of expertise and competence.

As well as specializing within psychological counselling, you may decide to extend your range of products to areas such as supervision, training, coaching and consultancy. If you do, there may be some additional questions to consider in terms of the 'synergy' that exists in your product range: how well do they 'fit' together therapeutically, commercially and practically? As an example, when I first became self-employed I spent two days a week providing consultancy and coaching in organizations. Much of this work was in London and involved long hours away from my Bristol base. Whilst lucrative and enjoyable, it was tiring and it limited the number of hours I could offer to clients in my counselling psychology practice at home. I eventually decided to stop offering coaching and consultancy, focusing instead on expanding my counselling psychology practice and developing new products – clinical supervision and training.

I also decided to develop a 'specialism' in cognitive behaviour psychotherapy, partly because it was an approach that interested me and partly because in my geographic area demand was high and supply limited. Whilst my counselling psychology enabled me to draw on and integrate theory and research from a number of models including CBT, I knew there had been developments in the field of cognitive therapy and I needed to gain more in-depth knowledge and expertise to specialize in the approach. I therefore embarked on further training which eventually enabled me to practise as a cognitive psychotherapist and to teach and supervise others in CBT. Whilst lengthy, costly and time-consuming, the training enabled me to differentiate my private practice from others in my area. As a counselling psychologist with specialisms in CBT, supervision and training, I had a 'synergistic' mix of products which was both interesting to me and 'in demand' by others.

The factors determining your decision about products will be different from mine, but the questions to ask yourself are the same. Once you have answered them, you will need to think about how you are going to develop and advertise your business, which we will look at next.

KEY POINTS

- Counselling psychologists can potentially offer a wide range of products and services, but may have to resist the temptation to 'see everyone and offer everything'.
- Options include specializing within counselling psychology and extending to other product areas such as supervision, training, coaching or consultancy.
- It is essential to decide what products you will offer. Asking yourself a range of questions will help you decide what is in demand and what you are qualified and competent to offer.

DEVELOPING YOUR BUSINESS

Having done your market research and decided what products you are going to offer, you will be faced with what Suss (2007) describes as the thorny questions of 'Where will I get my clients?' and 'How will people get to know what I offer?'.

Many people looking for therapists search the online registers of professional organizations such as the BPS, BACP (British Association of Counselling and Psychotherapy), UKCP (United Kingdom Council for Psychotherapy) and BABCP (British Association for Behavioural and Cognitive Psychotherapies). Therefore keeping your registrations and accreditations up to date is essential. People also ask their GPs, and I recommend that you send brief details of your qualifications and product offerings to local surgeries. Other potential sources of business include private medical insurance companies, injury compensation schemes, occupational health schemes and Employee Assistance Programmes (EAPs).

The best source of new referrals is undoubtedly word of mouth. It takes time to build up a practice and to 'get known', but if clients have a good experience of your services, they may pass your name on to friends and colleagues. In my experience, the more synergistic your products, the greater the impact of the 'word of mouth' effect across your business. For example, people attending your training courses may recommend you as a therapist or a supervisor; a supervisee may recommend you as a trainer or therapist, and so on. There are some potential downsides to this. First, you need to bear in mind the opposite effect – as Suss notes, 'all it takes is a few disgruntled clients to spread rumours of your incompetence or unethical practice and potential clients will stay away' (2007: 23). Another potential problem is that if clients, supervisees and trainees recommend you to their colleagues and friends, boundary issues are likely to arise at some point. It is therefore important in private practice to build up a list of colleagues to whom you can refer clients. This is not only if a boundary issue prevents you from seeing a client: sometimes you may not feel qualified to deal with a specific issue, you may feel a colleague would be more appropriate for a particular client, or you may be fully booked.

Whatever your product offering, you will need to consider whether, where and how you advertise your business. For many, the most successful way to advertise is through their own website, and there are plenty of people offering website design services. You may decide to sign up to one of the many counselling forums which offer lists on the Internet, or consider advertising in newspapers, professional journals and the yellow pages of local phone directories. This can be costly and you will need to monitor how much business you get from different forms of advertising. If you are going to advertise widely, it is important to consider your personal security. You may feel more cautious doing an assessment with someone who has seen your advert in a paper and 'walked in off the street', as opposed to someone who has been referred by their GP or via a personal recommendation. You also need to be clear about the BPS guidelines on advertising (BPS, 2008b) and consider the image you wish to present. These and other aspects of advertising are explored by Suss (2007) and McMahon (1994). McMahon emphasizes the importance of professional image, not only in how and where you advertise, but how you treat clients, how you run your practice, what your stationery looks like, how you dress and so on. As she notes, clients pay money for your services and some may struggle to afford your fees – 'they have a right to receive a professional service in return' (1994: 62).

KEY POINTS

- There are a range of possible business sources you can contact.
- People looking for therapists increasingly use the Internet to search for individual websites and look up the registers of professional bodies such as the BPS.
- There are many ways to advertise. Some can be costly and you should monitor their effectiveness. How you present your image is particularly important.

AN EXAMPLE OF BUILDING A PRIVATE PRACTICE OVER TIME

Bearing in mind that everyone's situation is different, I can use my personal experience to illustrate one example of building a private practice over time. At the time of writing, I have been self-employed for some 15 years, prior to which I was employed by an organization. When I decided to become self-employed, my work was my only source of income, so from the outset I had to think in terms of 'a business'. Ensuring that I had sufficient funds to cover my start-up costs and any temporary shortfall in my projected income whilst I was building up the practice was essential. Becoming self-employed is always a risk, made easier for me because I did not have any financial dependants. Having financial dependants does not, of course, preclude you from starting a private practice, but you may be more cautious.

From the outset I was fully self-employed and I set up my business as a sole trader, eventually becoming a limited company on my accountant's advice when the business was established and expanding. Initially, I split my time between part-time contracts and private work. My part-time contracts were with organizations providing coaching, consultancy and psychological services and they provided a reliable source of income whilst I expanded my clinical and commercial experience and slowly increased the number of clients I saw in my private practice. Over time, the emphasis in my business shifted from 'mainly contract' to 'mainly private' to 'fully private' as it is today.

There were a number of objectives I had identified in my original business plan. I needed a source of income while I was developing my private client base and 'getting myself known'. At the same time, I needed to expand my clinical and business experience, both of which were essential to the future success of my practice. I also wanted to invest in further training to increase the range of products and services I could ultimately offer. Deciding whether to invest now in something which you hope will bring benefit in the future is one of the dilemmas you face in any business. Investing in your own training is a prime example. Continuing professional development (CPD) is, of course, essential for all counselling psychologists if they are to keep their skills and knowledge up to date and meet the standards of organizations such as the Health Professions Council. If you are self-employed you have to fund your CPD yourself, whether it is time spent reading, going to conferences, reflecting on practice or attending training courses. Training can be costly in terms of course fees, books, travel and time, so it should be of interest both personally and professionally, providing you with skills which will improve the quality and range of your products. Attending a training course may also reduce the number of hours you have available to work, so your costs will increase and your income will go down, unless you decide to increase your fees, work longer hours or change the products you are offering. As we have seen, all of those decisions have implications for the kind of practice you run, the clients who can afford to see you, and your own levels of stress and work/life balance. Finding a way to resolve such dilemmas is key in setting up a successful private practice. As McMahon notes, you have to be able to resolve 'the potential clash of three conflicting elements' (1994: 6):

- running a business
  (while)
- working as a professional counselling psychologist
  (and considering)
- your own needs.

KEY POINTS

- It is essential to develop a business plan of how you will develop your practice over time, both financially and in terms of the products you will be offering.
- The costs of further training can be high, but if it enables you to expand your knowledge and skills in areas that are in demand, it is an investment for the future.
- In building up your private practice you will need to manage the sometimes conflicting needs of your business, your profession and your self.

SOME PRACTICAL REALITIES OF WORKING IN PRIVATE PRACTICE

When I was researching the literature on working in private practice, I found some informative books but not a lot of anecdotal information from practitioners out there working independently. I belong to an informal network called Counsellors and Psychotherapists in Private Practice (or CAPPP), set up by local practitioners to provide mutual support and assistance. The membership of some 150 includes counsellors and psychotherapists plus a small number of counselling and clinical psychologists. I sent members an email explaining that I was writing this chapter and asking them three questions: (a) the best things about working in private practice; (b) the worst things about working in private practice; and (c) three things they wished they had known before they started. Some 30 practitioners replied.

The most commonly cited **best things** were:

- *Autonomy* – being able to make my own decisions across a range of clinical and business issues.
- *Flexibility* – in terms of managing my own time.
- *Lack of organizational things* – like politics, hierarchy and bureaucracy.

The most commonly cited **worst things** were:

- Isolation and loneliness.
- Insecurity and unpredictability of work.
- Having to do everything myself.
- Working long and late hours.
- Having to 'sell' myself.
- Not having any paid holidays or sick pay.
- The amount of time and energy it takes up.

The things that people most **wish they had known** at the outset included:

- The time it will take to build up a practice.
- The long hours I will have to work.
- I will need lots of energy and stamina.
- It can be lonely.
- I will have to pay constant attention to matters such as marketing and advertising.
- I need to allow for business downturns, as well as the costs of training and development, in my budget.

Significantly, a number said that if someone had told them how 'fantastic' and what 'fun' it would be working in private practice, they would have done it sooner.

We will now look at a few of these themes in more detail.

Doing everything myself

An important reality of self-employment is that, unless *you* arrange it, there is nobody else to provide or do things for you. As already noted, you will not receive a salary or any benefits. No one pays you when you are sick or on holiday; nor funds your pension plan; nor organizes and pays for your clinical supervision, training, professional journals and books. There is no one automatically on hand to fix your computer, purchase stationery, issue invoices, keep accounts, calculate your tax and national insurance deductions and do the filing. It will be up to you to arrange the professional indemnity, public liability and other insurance cover you will need, and you will have to ensure that you comply with the Data Protection Act, Health & Safety legislation and so on. You will also need to sort out and pay for heating, telephones, photocopier, cleaning, coffee and so forth. Even if you are capable of doing all these things yourself, you will have to decide whether it is cost effective to do so, or whether you will be better paying others to do all or some of them for you whilst you spend your time seeing clients. These are decisions you will have to make for yourself, and there are no right or wrong answers. What is important is that you are aware that: (a) all these things need arranging or doing; (b) if you pay someone else to do them your costs will increase; and (c) every hour you work with clients you are earning income (and every hour you spend fixing the computer you are potentially losing income). How you balance this equation will depend on your circumstances.

Being responsible for all the decisions

A second practical reality of working in private practice is that you are responsible for all decisions. This includes business, financial, marketing and clinical decisions. You will have to decide what products you offer, what fees you charge, what hours you work, where you advertise, what computer you buy, what you will have on your website and what your stationery looks like. You will also be responsible for deciding whether or not to see a client when they make that initial contact; for carrying out assessments; and for deciding whether you have the clinical experience and skills to deal with a specific case. You will need to assess whether a client is a suicide risk and what steps you will take if there is a crisis with a patient during a session. You will need to make decisions about whether to refer on, and if so to whom; whether a client is a risk to you, and if so how to handle it. Also what theoretical models and treatment plan would be appropriate for a specific client; what to do if a client brings a complaint against you; and what actions to take if a client does not pay you. The list seems endless and the responsibility daunting. However, as evidenced in the survey responses, many practitioners feel that having autonomy and freedom to make their own decisions is the best thing about working in private practice. Of paramount importance is that you have both the business and the clinical experience on which to base your decisions, and that you know where to get advice and when to refer on to others. Having good clinical supervision and knowing the limits of your own competence are essential.

Working at home or away

A third practical reality is that, whether you are planning to do two or twenty hours of private work per week, you need somewhere to do it. Options can include renting space on your own or with others, which will increase your costs. Rentals obviously differ between locations, but Field (2007) suggests that for some private practitioners rent can amount to as much as one-third of their fee. On the plus side, renting space will help you to avoid some of the disadvantages of working at home, and if you rent with others you will overcome some of the problems of security, isolation and loneliness.

Like many in private practice, I set up my office and consulting room in my house. A major advantage, of course, is that you don't have to pay rent. It can also be very convenient. However, it is not a decision to make lightly. Seeing a client in the corner of the sitting-room is not acceptable professionally, ethically or practically. You will need space for a dedicated office and consulting room with easy access from the street. You will also need to consider other factors, such as a waiting area, access to a toilet, privacy, noise, security (of your home contents, your business, your documents and of yourself), insurance, decor, furniture, how to store confidential files, whether you are accessible by public transport, car parking and so on.

If you are working from home, you must also consider boundary issues, both for yourself and for the people you live with. If you live alone, it is easy for the boundaries between work and non-work to become blurred, both physically and psychologically: doing your invoices after supper on a kitchen table covered in computers and papers is not conducive to a stress-free life. If you live with others, the boundaries become even more complicated. You will have to consider whether it is either possible or desirable to ask children, animals and partners to keep quiet and out of sight in their own home whilst your clients are on the premises. This may be a particular problem if you work in the evening – and many clients only want evening appointments.

Some potential effects of working from home on the therapeutic relationship are highlighted by Field (2007), who describes the concept of 'client envy'. Whether clients feel 'envy' or 'curiosity', they will undoubtedly notice things about your house, the car parked outside and the glimpses of your life they see through a window. They will know much more about you than if you see them in a separate office, and it is important that you are aware of the impact this can have on the therapeutic relationship. The extent to which you use this in the therapy will, of course, be influenced by the theoretical model you are using.

There are considerable advantages of working from home. At a practical level, you can catch up on the accounts or the gardening when you have a client who cancels, and you can empty the dishwasher in between appointments. Most importantly, you can control your working environment. Being able to make your own decisions about how you decorate, furnish and utilize the space in your consulting room, and having the freedom to use tools that suit your therapeutic approach – whether this is using flipcharts, paints, stones, music or toys – were all identified as significant benefits in the survey responses, and are not always possible if you are renting your space from someone else.

Working alone or with others

Once you have decided where you are going to work, you will need to decide whether to work alone or with others. Isolation and loneliness were the most commonly cited problems of working in private practice but are not the only consideration. McMahon (1994) identifies some pros and cons of different working arrangements, such as a partnership with another practitioner or a 'loose arrangement' with a group of practitioners. Of course, just because you have chosen to work from your home does not necessarily mean you have to work alone. If you have the space, you could consider letting a room in your house to another practitioner, although you will need to check whether there are implications for insurance, health and safety and so on.

If you are working in a building on your own, it is essential to consider your own personal security, as stressed in the BPS guidelines (2008b). Deciding what you would do if you feel threatened by a client is of crucial importance. This might include thinking about where you sit in your consulting room in relation to the door, whom you would contact if you needed help and how you would let them know. For example, you might decide to have a panic button installed which links directly to a security company.

You should also consider whether you are sufficiently disciplined to work alone, without the support of colleagues. Personality type can be an important consideration. If you have a preference for 'extraversion', you may need to think about how you are going to recharge your batteries and get sufficient external stimulation. Alternatively, if you have a preference for 'introversion', you may withdraw too much and have insufficient contact with the outside world, both professionally and socially. We all need to think about with whom we are going to laugh – or cry – when we have just seen 'the client from hell', or carried out the worst session in our career.

Working in private practice is not an easy option, and if you are working alone it is essential to have a network of support and advice. This includes advice on business and financial matters, supervision on your clinical work and support from colleagues. The latter is not always easy, because when you are in private practice you need to be aware that your colleagues are also your competitors. You will need to find a good accountant who is familiar with small businesses, and choose an experienced clinical supervisor who is both sympathetic to your theoretical approach and understands private practice. Joining or creating a peer supervision group of experienced clinicians working in similar settings and finding a supportive local network of colleagues working in the same field will also be key. These factors are important to all who are setting up in private practice, but particularly so if you are working on your own.

Equally important is ensuring that you have time for yourself and have a healthy balance between home and work; maintaining this discipline can be more difficult if you are working alone. Engaging in physical, creative and social activities will be essential if you are to maintain the high levels of energy and stamina needed to run a private practice.

KEY POINTS

- A survey of private practitioners suggested that the best things about private practice are autonomy, flexibility and lack of bureaucracy. The worst things include loneliness, insecurity, long hours, having to do everything and being responsible for all decisions.
- Some key decisions include whether to work alone or with others, and whether to work at home or rent space. Both have financial and clinical implications.
- It is essential to have legal and financial support, good clinical supervision, support from colleagues and a healthy work/life balance.

SUMMARY

Working in private practice is not an easy option. You will be running a business and will need good commercial and organizational skills as well as extensive clinical experience. It will be important that you enjoy taking responsibility, are able to live with uncertainty, can work long hours and have high levels of stamina. There is a range of questions you will need to consider before setting up your practice: what products are in demand; what products you are able to offer; what will differentiate your practice from others; what you will charge; where you will work; and how you will let people know about your products. As well as financial and marketing considerations, you will be responsible for clinical decisions and having good supervision will be essential.

As already noted, this can all sound terrifying, exciting or both. If it doesn't put you off and if you are attracted by autonomy, flexibility and challenge, then you could find working in private practice stimulating, rewarding and enjoyable. Like me, you could look back one day and realize that when you decided to become self-employed and set up your own practice, you made one of the best decisions of your professional life.

USEFUL INFORMATION AND RECOMMENDED READING

Independent/Private practice as a psychologist – Guidance, published by the Professional Practice Board of the British Psychological Society, INFO3/07.2008 (see www.bps.org.uk/ppb).

Private practitioners discussion forum – email ppbchair@bps.org.uk if you wish to join.

Bond, T. and Mitchels, B. (2008) *Confidentiality and Record Keeping in Counselling and Psychotherapy.* London: Sage.

Bond, T. and Sandu, A. (2005) *Therapists in Court: Providing Evidence and Supporting Witnesses.* London: Sage.

Field, R. and Hemmings, A. (2007) *Counselling and Psychotherapy in Contemporary Private Practice.* Hove: Routledge.

McMahon, G. (1994) *Setting Up Your Own Private Practice in Counselling and Psychotherapy.* Cambridge: NEC Trust.

McMahon, G., Palmer, S. and Wilding, C. (2005) *The Essential Skills for Setting Up a Counselling and Psychotherapy Practice.* Hove: Routledge.

Thistle, R. (1998) *Counselling and Psychotherapy in Private Practice.* London Sage.

Tyler, R. (2003) *Money Matters for Therapists.* London: Worth.

Weitz, P. (2006) *Setting Up and Maintaining an Effective Private Practice: A Practical Workbook for Mental Health Practitioners.* London: Karnac.

REFERENCES

British Psychological Society (2006) *Code of Ethics and Conduct.* Leicester: British Psychological Society.

British Psychological Society (2008a) *Generic Professional Practice Guidelines*, 2nd edn. Leicester: British Psychological Society.

British Psychological Society (2008b) *Independent/Private Practice as a Psychologist: Guidance Published by the Professional Practice Board of the British Psychological Society*, Info3/07.2008 (revised edn). Leicester: British Psychological Society.

Field, R. (2007) 'Working from home in independent practice', in R. Field and A. Hemmings (eds), *Counselling and Psychotherapy in Contemporary Private Practice.* Hove: Routledge.

Field, R. and Hemmings, A. (2007) 'The role of money in the therapeutic relationship', in R. Field and A. Hemmings (eds), *Counselling and Psychotherapy in Contemporary Private Practice.* Hove: Routledge.

Frankland, A. (2007) 'Counselling psychology: The trade for the portfolio professional', *Counselling Psychology Review,* 22 (1): 41–45.

Howden Professionals (2007) 'Top tips for psychological therapists working in private practice', *Counselling Psychology Review,* 22 (4): 74–77.

Hudson-Allez, G. (2007) 'The changing status of counselling', in R. Field and A. Hemmings (eds), *Counselling and Psychotherapy in Contemporary Private Practice.* Hove: Routledge.

McMahon, G. (1994) *Setting up Your Own Private Practice in Counselling and Psychotherapy.* Cambridge: NEC Trust.

McMahon, G., Palmer, S. and Wilding, C. (2005) *The Essential Skills for Setting Up a Counselling and Psychotherapy Practice.* Hove: Routledge.

Prichard, D. (2006) 'Setting up in private practice', *Counselling at Work*, Winter: 26–29.

Staples, J.L. (2007) 'Reflections of a counselling psychologist in private practice', *Counselling Psychology Review,* 22 (1): 35–40.

Suss, L. (2007) 'Advertising', in R. Field and A. Hemmings (eds), *Counselling and Psychotherapy in Contemporary Private Practice.* Hove: Routledge.

Thistle, R. (1998) *Counselling and Psychotherapy in Private Practice.* London: Sage.

Tyler, R. (2003) *Money Matters for Therapists.* London: Worth.

Weitz, P. (2006) *Setting Up and Maintaining an Effective Private Practice: A Practical Workbook for Mental Health Practitioners.* London: Karnac.

23

COUNSELLING PSYCHOLOGY IN FORENSIC SETTINGS

Clive Sims

This chapter, for the third edition of the *Handbook*, reflects the continuing development of counselling psychology as a profession. Traditionally, and in the UK it is only a short tradition, counselling psychology has largely concerned itself with working with clients to explore the issues underlying a wide range of psychological, social and relationship problems. In the main, these problems would not easily fit within the boundaries of 'mental illness' as defined in DSM-IV (American Psychiatric Association, 1995) or in ICD-10 (WHO, 2007), or as defined in the Mental Health Act 1983 (Department of Health, 2008a). Indeed, many counselling psychologists would reject the concept of mental illness altogether, particularly when there is no demonstrable neurological substrate, and regard it as a social construct referring to problems in living. Some may echo Thomas Szasz and regard it as a myth used to justify social control (Szasz, 2007). The fundamental philosophy of counselling psychology is one of evidenced-based practice and can be broadly defined as being 'an active, collaborative relationship which can both facilitate the exploration of underlying issues and can empower people to confront change' (Division of Counselling Psychology, 2008). With this definition of counselling psychology the problem of the existence, or otherwise, of mental illness is neatly side-stepped as the focus is quite clearly on the individual rather than upon any actual or hypothesized biological dysfunction. It also emphasizes the empowerment of the individual to make changes themselves rather than the change being the result of an external agency or substance. However, the biological substrate cannot be totally ignored. The training of all applied psychologists, including counselling psychologists, on the integration of theories and models of functioning places them in the unique position, amongst mental health professionals, of being equipped to integrate psychological, social and biological models of mental and emotional distress and of well-being. They are able to link together the many facets of research and apply them to the problem presented by the client before them (Gallo and Leuken 2008).

With increasing recognition of the value of counselling psychology, within both the statutory services and the private sector, opportunities are opening up in many different areas, some of which are already 'inhabited' by other professional groups of psychologists. In this chapter we will look at forensic settings: what they are, who inhabits them, where counselling psychologists fit in and what new perspectives they add. But first we must define our terms and address that most misunderstood term, 'forensic'.

SO WHAT IS 'FORENSIC'?

To the layperson, who has been nurtured on a diet of popular criminal investigation shows on television, the term 'forensic' will conjure up images of dead bodies, morgues and strange people in white coats doing arcane things with microscopes and probes. On more than one occasion I have been asked why I, as a psychologist, see dead people. This is disconcerting. Those with slightly broader tastes and who are familiar with the 'Cracker' series or 'Wire in the Blood' imagine that the forensic activities of psychologists either involve bullying interrogation techniques, amazing leaps of intuition on the flimsiest of evidence, or surviving regular attempts on our lives. Just like the Canadian Mountie we, the 'forensic' psychologists, always get our man even though the odds may be hugely stacked against us. To add further confusion to the public's misconceptions, the psychologists involved almost invariably have significant mental health issues and, in the case of the lead character in 'Cracker', a significant addiction problem. The serious issue of fitness to practice would, in real life, be quickly brought into question. Whilst both series make good television viewing, they are poor advertisements for professional psychology in general and the practice of psychology in forensic settings in particular.

To place counselling psychology in a forensic context, we must first define what we mean by the term 'forensic' in the real world rather than the fictional world of books or television. This is actually quite straightforward. The term 'forensic' derives from the Latin word 'fora', meaning in this context 'the Courts', so anything that is described as being 'forensic' pertains to the Courts and, by implication, the legal system in general. This can be any Court, criminal, civil, family or any legal tribunal such as Mental Health Act or Employment Act. The connection may be close, as in giving evidence; it may be distant, as in carrying out the instructions of the Court or tribunal; or may simply be any involvement with the legal system, however remote, such as treating a patient who is detained under the Mental Health Act 1983. Indeed, psychologists are often involved in 'forensic' practice without being aware that it is the case, as they regard it as simply being part of their day-to-day activities. Unfortunately, many psychologists are not as aware of the legal implications of these activities as they should be, nor are they necessarily aware of their legal obligations either under common law or under relevant Acts, such as the Mental Health Act 1983. Thus an individual psychologist may, inadvertently, fall foul of the law through ignorance, and ignorance, unlike a genuine mistake, is no excuse under the Law.

Whilst all professional psychologists may, to a greater or lesser degree, interact with the legal system there have been, until recently, three professional groups that have had direct involvement with the legal process to a significant degree. These have been forensic psychologists, clinical psychologists and educational psychologists. All three have professional Divisions within the British Psychological Society. Newer arrivals have been counselling psychologists and investigative psychologists. Whilst counselling psychology also has Divisional status, investigative psychology is currently subsumed under, and overlaps with, forensic psychology, although it has a distinct area of functional expertise and many investigative psychologists would consider it to be a discipline in its own right. All can be considered to be engaged in 'forensic' work, as defined above; however, their areas of activity only overlap to a limited extent. The nature and degree of overlap largely depends on the organization or organizations within which the individual psychologist works; this can range from the police through to forensic psychiatric units and from prisons through to secure children's homes. Potentially, counselling psychologists may be involved with, either directly or indirectly, any of these environments. However, due to the relative youth of the profession when compared with forensic, clinical and educational psychology, it is only quite recently that counselling psychologists have been employed within the statutory services or by their non-statutory equivalents.

PROFESSIONAL PSYCHOLOGY

Professional applied psychology in the UK has a relatively short history. A glance at the *Annual Report of the British Psychological Society* will show that the first professional divisions were only set up following the Second World War, and initially had very small memberships (British Psychological Society, 2008). Both the number of divisions and their memberships have grown over the past 20 years. Counselling psychology only achieved divisional status in the last decade of the twentieth century, having previously been a Section and then a Special Group. It was only with the founding of the Special Group in Counselling Psychology that any distinction was made between members who were practitioners and general, non-practitioner members. Therefore it is not surprising that there has been very limited exposure to forensic settings. The two main professional groups with whom counselling psychologists are likely to come into contact within forensic settings are forensic psychologists and clinical psychologists. This contact is likely to be within the context of the prison service, the probation service, the police and forensic psychiatric services. They may come into limited and probably indirect contact with educational psychologists in the context of Child and Adolescent Mental Health Services (CAMHS). This, however, is a rarity at present and so will not be specifically addressed in this chapter. As there is likely to be a considerable overlap of activities with the first two groups, it will be useful to take a necessarily brief overview at what forensic and clinical psychologists do before proceeding to the unique perspective and contribution that counselling psychologists can make to the practice of psychology in forensic settings.

FORENSIC PSYCHOLOGY

There are approximately 800 chartered forensic psychologists in the UK. Some will also be chartered in other professional divisions, such as the clinical division and, in a few instances, the Division of Counselling Psychology. The majority are employed within the prison service, with a few engaged in research and development activities with the Home Office. Others may be employed within the Probation Service either as probation officers or, less frequently, specifically as forensic psychologists. Fewer still are employed by the police, where frequently they are serving police officers, and by universities in an academic capacity. Many of the latter carry out consultancy work in forensic settings. Additionally, forensic psychologists may be employed in the National Health Service (NHS) or private healthcare facilities although, in the main, these psychologists are also chartered as clinical psychologists and, increasingly, as counselling psychologists.

Forensic psychologists work with offenders and with victims applying psychological knowledge to offending behaviour. A primary activity is harm reduction through risk assessment using assessment tools to profile prisoners and thereby to assess the probability of re-offending on release from prison. As a result of such an assessment a prisoner may enter a behavioural modification programme, such as a drug and alcohol programme or a violence reduction programme, the purpose of which is to reduce the risk of re-offending on release from prison. Such programmes are frequently manualized and run by prison officers, or other specialist staff, under the direction and supervision of the forensic psychologist. Two further important areas of work are in the formulation and delivery of the Prison Service's strategies on the awareness of suicide and self-harm and its prevention, and in the management and prevention of bullying. As a consequence of these activities, the psychologist is frequently required to advise the Courts and Parole Boards in relation to the suitability of individual prisoners for early release into the community and the level of supervision that they will require. Additionally, forensic psychologists are involved with staff training, with a view to promoting psychological mindedness, and with research. A comprehensive account of the role of forensic psychologists was published by the Division of Forensic Psychology in 1999 and much remains relevant today (Towl and McDougall, 1999).

A more specialist area is offender profiling, which is usually carried out by forensic psychologists engaged in investigative work either directly employed by the police or, more frequently, brought in on a consultancy basis. An even smaller number of psychologists may be involved in advising and training the police on hostage negotiations, and may even be brought in as an adviser in actual hostage situations, although they are never the active negotiators who are invariably serving police officers.

FORENSIC CLINICAL PSYCHOLOGY

Forensic clinical psychology is the scientific application of the principles of psychology, particularly clinical psychology, to offenders with mental health problems. The mental health problems may be a direct contributory factor to the offending behaviour or may be co-existent and independent. As with general clinical psychology, the aim is to reduce personal mental and emotional distress and to promote positive psychological well-being within the individual and within the population being served. Individual psychological therapy usually takes place within the context of the multi-disciplinary team, either within an in-patient setting or in the community, and can be initiated at any stage of the patient's overall treatment programme. Initially the patient will be assessed using a variety of methods which may include psychometric tests, interviews, direct observation, interviews with carers and reviews of the medical records and any court and prison records that may be appropriate and relevant. Following the assessment process, a formulation of the problem will be made and a treatment plan drawn up in collaboration with the patient and carers, including professional staff. The fact that the patient is detained in prison or in a secure forensic mental health facility does not detract from the need to engage him or her in a collaborative endeavour. Any attempt to impose psychological therapy, for example, as a condition of release, is doomed to failure and makes a mockery of the therapeutic alliance. Psychological treatment is invariably carried out within a multi-disciplinary team approach; thus a patient may be receiving psychiatric treatment in the form of medication, may be receiving support within the community from a community psychiatric nurse, may have an occupational therapy programme and may be having social-work input in addition to psychological therapy. All these strands are pulled together and co-ordinated in multi-disciplinary team meetings and, specifically within health-care settings, in the Care Programme Approach (CPA) (CPA Association, 2004). Currently there are two tiers of CPA, one which is common to all service users and an additional Enhanced CPA process for those with complex mental health and social needs. The main features of CPA are:

- A system to assess the health and social needs of patients.
- A care plan that identifies the health and social care that is required and the agencies and individuals who will supply that care.

- The appointment of a care co-ordinator, acceptable to the patient, who will maintain continuity of contact and monitor and co-ordinate care. It is unusual, in forensic settings, for the psychologist to be nominated as care co-ordinator, the role usually falling to a community psychiatric nurse or to a social worker. The psychologist is, however, one of the key care providers.
- The care plan is reviewed regularly and updated and changed as necessary. The key to the success of this approach is the care co-ordinator, who brings together all the strands and who produces, with the team and with the patient, a care plan detailing all the therapeutic interventions and ensuring that these interventions take place (CPA Association, 2004).

The great majority of forensic patients, whether in hospital or in the community, are on Enhanced CPA as they have complex mental health needs requiring input from both the health and the social services. Frequently forensic patients will have a complicated mix of clinical conditions, including drug and alcohol problems in addition to mental health issues, and are usually difficult to link with services and with whom maintaining contact can be a serious problem with potentially serious consequences, in view of the risk that they may pose to the general public. The care plan for all service users will include how services will intervene and agreed goals within an agreed timescale, action to be taken should a crisis occur and the date and time of the next review (CPA Association, 2004). Additionally, for those on Enhanced CPA, the care plan will include arrangements for the management of any risk to the service user and to others, and a proposed plan of action to be taken if necessary. This will include a comprehensive crisis plan. Persons on both Standard and Enhanced CPA will often have many other needs that require attention, and these can be addressed through the care plan. They may include physical health issues, substance misuse, poverty, social exclusion, accommodation issues, work, education and spiritual and cultural issues (CPA Association, 2004). Whilst the psychologist's input may be direct intervention, it will also include contributions to all of the above in order to create psychological mindedness within the team.

I have focused on the Care Programme Approach because it emphasizes the need for a holistic, multi-disciplinary approach rather than individual and unrelated packages of care. For the majority of forensic patients within the hospital and community, as opposed to the prison settings, the changes in the Care Programme Approach proposed in *Refocusing the Care Programme Approach: Policy and Positive Practice Guidance* (Department of Health, 2008b) will have minimal impact. From October 2008 there is only one tier, which is simply called the Care Programme Approach. Effectively, this will serve the same client group as the former enhanced CPA, that is, all persons with mental health problems who have a wide range of needs from several services and who are most at risk. Those with lower, more straightforward levels of need who do not require complex levels of support and with whom only one agency is involved, continue to be entitled to have a needs assessment and the development of a care plan, with a review process built in as part of good professional practice, but the formal designated paperwork for care planning and the review process is no longer required. Mental health services in prisons usually focus on this level of care as, ideally, those prisoners with complex mental health needs and who requires the Care Programme Approach should be treated within the forensic psychiatric system at the appropriate level of security.

Clinical psychologists who work in forensic settings fall into two groups. The prison population is usually served by a general clinical psychologist attached to the Prison In-Reach Team. This psychologist, who is not necessarily qualified as a forensic clinical psychologist, will usually be line-managed by the team manager and professionally managed by the lead forensic clinical psychologist, if the NHS trust that provides the In-Reach team has a low or medium secure service. If not, then the lead psychologist for adult mental health will normally fulfil that role. Forensic clinical psychologists work within what are frequently described as the Criminal Justice Mental Health Services. They may work in in-patient high-security units, which include the special hospitals Broadmoor, Rampton and Ashworth in England and Carstairs in Scotland, in medium secure units that are usually regionally based or in low secure units that are trust-based. The proportion of in-patient and community-based work will vary with the individual service, but, in general, the higher the level of security, the greater the proportion of in-patient work. In addition to direct work with patients forensic clinical psychologists will offer consultancy to other mental health services, to learning disability services and to other agencies including the police, the probation service, the social services and the Crown Prosecution Service. They will frequently provide reports for the Mental Health Act Tribunals that regularly hold hearings to review whether a patient should continue to be detained in hospital, whether they should be discharged, when they should be discharged and under what conditions, if appropriate. They will also often provide reports for the Courts either as an independent expert witness or, if they have been directly involved in the treatment of the alleged offender, as a professional witness. In both these circumstances the psychologist will normally be required to attend the Court in person and to give evidence on oath.

The public is often confused about the different roles that psychologists can take as witnesses in criminal proceedings, and this confusion can often extend to members of the profession who may have had limited forensic training. Besides being witnesses of fact, where they, like anyone else, may be cross-examined on the facts of a case in which they were directly involved, they may be professional witnesses or independent expert witnesses. The difference between these two roles is important but can lead to confusion which, at worst, can have a detrimental effect upon the case in question and may lead to a judicial reprimand in extreme instances. The psychologist as professional witness will normally have been directly involved in the case before the Court, usually having been a member of the team treating the defendant or, in some instances, the victim. As such they cannot be regarded, in Law, as being independent. Cross-examination is limited to the facts of any assessment and treatment carried out in the course of normal practice. The psychologist is not permitted to venture any opinion outside those limits. In contrast, the psychologist as 'expert witness' is expected to provide the Court with independent assistance by giving an expert opinion drawn from the facts of the case, to enable it to reach a just conclusion. Such assistance will also include facts based on any assessments or interviews carried out by the psychologist and are underpinned by research. It will also include opinion based upon those facts. It is solely at the expert's discretion to decide which facts will be relied upon and which facts will be considered and subsequently rejected as being either unreliable or irrelevant. Provided that justification is provided as to which facts are included and which excluded, then there is wide discretion for basing the evidence on whatever the expert considers to be both essential and verifiable. Both are subject to testing by cross-examination.

Few forensic clinical psychologists are involved with Children's Mental Health Services (CAMHS), although some may work with adolescents either in secure residential accommodation or prisons for young offenders. Most forensic clinical psychologists will offer advice and consultation services to CAMHS, usually as part of a comprehensive package offered by the Criminal Justice Mental Health Services. They may also provide professional supervision where required. This is particularly appropriate where there is a complex relationship between mental health issues and offending behaviour.

COUNSELLING PSYCHOLOGY

I have, I hope, not wasted the reader's time by describing the roles and functions of other professional psychologists within the forensic context, as these will be the colleagues with whom counselling psychologists will work. Counselling psychology in the UK is new and, as such, brings a new philosophical perspective. An operational definition of counselling psychology would emphasize its competence in the psychological therapies, being firmly rooted in the discipline of psychology, whilst, at the same time, emphasizing the importance of the therapeutic relationship and process over simple technical expertise. The practice of counselling psychology, of whatever theoretical persuasion, requires a high level of self-awareness and competence in relating the skills and knowledge of personal and interpersonal dynamics in the therapeutic context.

Counselling psychology competencies are grounded in values that aim to empower those who use their services, and place high priority on anti-discriminatory practice, social and cultural context and ethical decision making. Whilst not unique to counselling psychology, their primacy serves to differentiate it from other areas of applied psychology.

This definition of the competencies required for professional practice particularly embodies the move away from the medical model of mental ill-health which emphasizes diagnostic categories, pathology, often of dubious validity, and illness as the opposite of well-being. As such it distinguishes counselling psychology from clinical psychology and this distinction remains, despite increasing numbers of counselling psychologists working in mental health-care settings, and derives from the very different historical and philosophical origins of the two disciplines (Woolfe, 1996).

Whilst clinical psychology tends to follow, albeit not slavishly, the medical model, counselling psychology applies the humanistic phenomenological model to therapy.

Both disciplines adhere to the 'scientist practitioner' model and both emphasize the concept of the 'reflective practitioner' (Schon, 1983), but bring different philosophical assumptions to those models. The philosophical origins of clinical psychology lie firmly within the same empirical-positivistic tradition as medicine and the social sciences (Bryant, 1985), whereas counselling psychology has it roots in phenomenology (Bozarth, 1990). As a result of these different roots, the orientation of practitioners tends to be different. Counselling psychologists, through their commitment to the reflective practitioner model, utilize personal reflection as the means of personal development, thereby eschewing the more technical approach that is the inheritance of clinical psychology from the empirical-positivistic tradition. Thus psychological therapy for counselling psychology is as much an art as a science, and the counselling psychologist brings 'artistic, intuitive processes ... to situations of uncertainty, instability, uniqueness and value conflict' (Schon, 1983: 49). This is not to say that the counselling psychologist practitioner disavows empiricism. On the contrary, the empirical values of the scientist practitioner model underpin, but do not overwhelm, the psychologist as reflective practitioner. As such, counselling psychology will, hopefully, be able to remain true to its philosophical origins and maintain its identity within the broadly defined world of psychology applied to forensic settings.

FORENSIC CHALLENGES

Any counselling psychologist entering into a job that interfaces with the Criminal Justice System is entering a strange world where many treasured assumptions and profound beliefs are going to be called into question. The first casualty is going to be the belief in the primacy of the client. Within the forensic setting, whether secure or in the community, the immediate focus is on public safety, hence the emphasis on risk assessment and risk management. Once the management plan is in place, the focus turns to the client's needs. Throughout the course of therapy change is measured not only in terms of the individual but also in terms of level of risk to the public.

Risk assessment invariably involves some form of psychological assessment. This can range from cognitive functioning through to repeat measures of symptom strength in order to demonstrate symptom reduction. For many counselling psychologists in the past, the use of psychometric assessments has been anathema. However, in forensic settings the psychologist has to be able to demonstrate to outside agencies, such as the Courts, the Ministry of Justice and Mental Health Review Tribunals, that change has taken place and that, consequently, the risk of harm is reduced. Unfortunately these agencies have little or no understanding of the psychological formulation model used by counselling psychologists and are not impressed by opinions that are not backed by measurements that are usually based on the medical diagnostic model. There are also specific risk assessment tools, such as the Historical, Clinical Risk Management-20 (HCR-20) (Webster et al., 2003), which require specialist training. The HCR-20 identifies risk markers which are organized into factors that concern the past (Historical), dynamic factors that concern the present (Clinical) and factors that may increase or decrease risk in the future (Risk management). These are usually multi-disciplinary assessments to which the counselling psychologist would be expected to make a contribution. Whatever the opinion of the individual counselling psychologist, these are likely to be the expectancies of the agency within which they work. Psychometric assessment is a useful tool, particularly in the forensic setting where wrong opinions, however well justified, may have disastrous consequences for the client, for society and, by no means least, for the individual practitioner.

Counselling psychologists expect to work collaboratively with their clients. They expect them to have engaged in therapy voluntarily and to be open and motivated to change their lives. Most clients in forensic settings are subject to some legal detention or direction, either as a sentenced prisoner, or detained under a section of the Mental Health Act 1983 or are subject to a Probation Order. Whilst the majority who engage in therapy do so willingly, a few try to 'play the system'. As a result they may lie, cheat, sabotage therapy, pursue hidden agendas, be threatening even to the point of violence and make a mockery of the whole concept of the therapeutic alliance. All of these can happen within forensic settings and present counselling psychologists with a big challenge. It is easy to become cynical in such situations, and this is where the philosophical underpinning of counselling psychology is important. To be able to see the client in front of you as a human being and to engage in a therapeutically positive manner and build a therapeutic alliance despite all the barriers that the client may put up is the sign of a good forensic counselling psychologist (Cordess, 2002). The psychologist is there for the client and is focusing on 'the power of the therapeutic relationship, (being), rather than the application of specific skills or techniques, (doing)' (Woolfe, 2002).

Most counselling psychologists who work in forensic settings will be functioning within a healthcare context, whether private or NHS. They will usually work in forensic secure units or in prison in-reach services where, alongside individual and group therapy, they will contribute to CPA, Mental Health Act Review Tribunals, Parole Boards and the Courts. Invariably they will be working alongside clinical psychologists and, to a lesser extent, forensic psychologists. It is important, therefore, that counselling psychologists maintain the essential features and characteristics that differentiate them from those professions (Woolfe, 2002). Without them there will be little to distinguish between the professions, and the unique approach which characterizes counselling psychology will be lost.

THE FUTURE

As a profession, counselling psychology is continuing to grow and with that growth there are increasing opportunities available both for the newly qualified and for the experienced practitioner (Woolfe, 1996). There will be increasing opportunities for employment within forensic settings alongside clinical and forensic psychologists, where they will contribute to the strong multi-disciplinary teams recommended for low secure units (Beer, 2006) and, increasingly, to prison in-reach services. Of particular relevance to future development is the recently recognized need to address the psychological issues facing an ageing prison and secure hospital population (Sims, 2008). Further opportunities for counselling psychologists will be provided by the government initiative for improving access to psychological therapies (IAPT). Although currently focused on the community general practice population of working age it is likely to be rolled out to include prisoners, following the publication of the report by the Sainsbury Centre for Mental Health *From the Inside* on the urgent need to address prisoners' mental health issues (Durcan, 2008). Predicting the future is always fraught with difficulty, but I would also expect to see increasing numbers of counselling psychologists working in the National Probation Service, either as probation officers or as psychologists.

Working in forensic settings will provide a host of new opportunities and challenges for counselling psychologists, and I am sure that the profession is ready for them. Working in collaboration with other healthcare professionals, they will bring a unique perspective to the care, treatment and rehabilitation of offender clients.

REFERENCES

American Psychiatric Association (1995) *Diagnostic and Statistical Manual of Mental Disorders*, 4th edn. Washington, DC: American Psychiatric Association.

Beer, M.D. (2006) 'Managing challenging behaviour', in G. Roberts, S. Davenport, F. Roberts and T. Tattan (eds), *Enabling Recovery: The Principles and Practice of Rehabilitation Psychiatry*. London: Gaskell. pp. 211–228.

Bozarth, J.D. (1990) 'The essence of client-centred therapy', in G. Liataer, J. Rombauts and R. Van Balen (eds), *Client-Centred and Experiential Psychotherapy Therapy in the Nineties*. Leuven: Leuven University Press. pp. 59–64.

British Psychological Society (2008) *Annual Report 2007*. Leicester: British Psychological Society.

Bryant, C.G.A. (1985) *Positivism in Social Theory and Research*. New York: St Martin's.

Care Programme Approach Association (2004) *The CPA Handbook*, April 2004. Chesterfield: The CPA Association.

Cordess, C. (2002) 'Building and nurturing a therapeutic alliance with offenders', in M. McMurran (ed.), *Motivating Offenders to Change: A Guide to Enhancing Engagement in Therapy*. Chichester: Wiley.

Department of Health (2008a) *Mental Health Act 1983*. London: The Stationery Office.

Department of Health (2008b) *Refocusing the Care Programme Approach: Policy and Positive Practice Guidance*. London: The Stationery Office.

Division of Counselling Psychology, BPS (2008) *Guidelines for the Professional Practice of Counselling Psychology*. Leicester: The British Psychological Society.

Durcan, G. (2008) *From the Inside: Experiences of Prison Mental Health Care*. London: Sainsbury Centre for Mental Health.

Gallo, L.C. and Lueken, L.J. (2008) 'Physiological research methods in health psychology: Applications of the biopsychosocial model', in L.J. Leuken and L.C. Gallo (eds), *Handbook of Physiological Methods in Health Psychology.* London: Sage.

Schon, D.A. (1983) *The Reflective Practitioner: How Professionals Think in Action.* New York: Basic Books.

Sims, C.A. (2008) 'Elderly mentally disordered offenders. What next?', *PSIGE Newsletter*, 102: 76–78.

Szasz, T. (2007) *The Medicalization of Everyday Life: Selected Essays.* Syracuse, NY: Syracuse University Press.

Towl, G. and McDougall, C. (eds) (1999) 'What do forensic psychologists do?', in D. Forbes and J. Bailey (eds), *Issues in Forensic Psychology*, *1.* Leicester: British Psychological Society.

Webster, C.D., Douglas, K.G., Eaves, D. and Hart, S.D. (2003) *HCR-20: Assessing Risk for Violence (Version 2).* Burnaby, BC: Simon Fraser University, Mental Health, Law, and Policy Institue.

Woolfe, R. (1996) 'Counselling psychology in Britain: Past, present and future', *Counselling Psychology Review*, 11 (4): 7–18.

Woolfe, R. (2002) Letter to *The Psychologist*, 15 (4): 168.

World Health Organization (2007) *The ICD-10 Classification of Mental and Behavioural Disorders.* Geneva: World Health Organization.

24

COUNSELLING PSYCHOLOGY IN EDUCATIONAL SETTINGS

Dee Danchev

Whilst in training, counselling psychologists often have a placement involving counselling schoolchildren either in a school or working for one of the organizations from the charitable sector that provides psychological care and support to schoolchildren. A few counselling psychologists go on to make a career within educational establishments. This area is slowly expanding and the skills and training of counselling psychologists are well-suited to this setting.

This chapter provides an overview of educational settings and highlights UK research relating to this area. Counselling is more established in colleges and universities than in schools; the focus of this chapter reflects that history, and the stronger body of literature and research it has generated. Counselling psychology interventions with particular age groups and developmental stages are dealt with in more detail in Part IV of this *Handbook*. This chapter concentrates on the development of counselling and counselling psychology in educational settings and on the particular issues encountered when working in this environment.

Working therapeutically within the educational sector encompasses particular challenges and rewards. The intake is unfiltered, and the counselling psychologist can be confronted with some severe presentations without the back-up of a medical team. In schools and further education colleges, practitioners may be working alone and may be faced with feelings of personal and professional isolation. On the positive side, counselling psychologists often have the freedom to practise in the way they feel is most effective without the constraints of a medical model. There are also opportunities for proactive and holistic work. Institutional practices that impact negatively on well-being can be highlighted and positive practices enhanced.

HISTORY

The provision of pastoral care has always been a part of academic institutions and until the latter decades of the twentieth century was seen as integral to the role of teachers and lecturers; no additional professional support was felt to be necessary. In the 1960s, Tony Bolger, one of the pioneers in the field of counselling within both education and psychology, led a course at Keele University that provided school teachers with counselling training (Bolger, 1985). The impetus for university training in counselling had arisen alongside the changes in education following the *Newsom Report* (Ministry of Education, 1963). Keele and Reading Universities provided the first training programmes, and some of the graduates from these courses initiated the provision of counselling in schools. There was an expansion of school counselling into the 1970s, but then this initiative dwindled during the late 1970s and 1980s and trained school counsellors became a scarce resource (Hooper and Lang, 1988). Baginsky (2004) has explored this decline and cites the resource restrictions of the late 1970s and 1980s, and the strengthening of the idea that pastoral care should be provided by the teaching staff, as reasons for the retrenchment. In recent years there has been a resurgence of trained counsellors in schools. This has been linked to the substantial increase in administrative and assessment duties for teachers (Baginsky, 2004), a decline in the mental health of young people and an increase in behavioural problems (Leach, 2008), and a growing realization that professional training is needed to provide effective support for troubled children and young people. A further reason may be linked to the expansion of therapeutic training and the incremental but significant impact of trainee counsellors and counselling psychologists who secured unpaid placements in schools, proved themselves to be indispensable and were retained in a paid capacity after qualification.

Nationally, the mental health of children and young people is a cause for concern (Cole, 2006). At least 10 per cent have mental health and conduct disorders of a level of severity that affects their ability to achieve (Leach, 2008). Mental health services for children in the UK have been under-funded and under-resourced; there has been a paucity of people trained in the expertise needed to work effectively with children. In recent years the establishment of the Child and Adolescent Mental Health Services (CAMHS) has sought to provide more comprehensive mental health care (Kramer and Garralder, 2000). The role of psychological therapy in achieving these aims is acknowledged by the National Institute for Health and Clinical Excellance (NICE) guidelines. Over the past ten years the government has rationalized its school careers and support services into *Connexions*;

each young person has a named adviser and some support for personal issues is provided. However, the advantages of an on-site professional therapeutic service with its ease of access, understanding of context, early intervention and preventative work are clear. Bor et al. (2002) emphasize the need for practitioners to move away from viewing dysfunction in individual terms and work systemically with the family, school and social context of the child.

In further and higher education there is a similar history of the emergence of professional counselling in the 1960s. However, there are many strands to this emergence; Bell (1996) provides a thorough historical review. Unlike the schools' experience, the establishment of college and university counselling provision has been characterized by steady, if slow, growth. In the mid-1990s, college and university counselling services experienced a substantial increase in demand. This increase in numbers of students requesting counselling was matched by an increase in the severity of mental health issues encountered (Association for University and College Counselling (AUCC), 1999; Waller et al., 2005). The following factors may have contributed to the increase in demand and continue to impact on student life:

- *Financial pressures:* These increased over the previous decade. It is not unusual for students to be working as well as trying to complete full-time academic courses, and this has been linked to poorer mental health (Roberts et al., 1999).
- *Prolongation of childhood:* The financial cost of education means that many students are dependent on their families for financial support. In some cases, parents have specified the courses that they are prepared to pay for. The transition to independent adult life has become more complex and can be a lengthier process.
- *Widening access to education:* The government and academic institutions have worked hard in recent years to provide equal opportunities by increasing access to further and higher education. The government target is to increase participation to a level of 50 per cent by 2010 (DfES, 2003), and The Disability Discrimination Act (2001) has strengthened the rights of people with disabilities to access education. These are positive changes; however, many widening access students have neither the financial nor the social support available to enable them to take full advantage of these opportunities, and the increase in student numbers has not been matched by an equivalent expansion in university and college support structures to keep pace with these developments (AUCC, 2004; Baker et al., 2006).
- *Modularization:* Whilst modularization is a positive step in terms of increased choices and flexibility, it has disadvantages in that students no longer go through their undergraduate life with the same peer group and staff in their teaching sessions. Each new semester may involve a change in peer groups and staff. Friendship bonds can be disrupted and the supportive aspects of a stable learning group substituted by more transient links.
- *Pressures on academic staff:* In order to fulfil requirements for research, teaching assessments and increasing administrative duties, academics find that they have less time to form mentoring and supportive relationships with students. It is, therefore, possible for individual students to be relatively unknown to academic staff, whereas in the past a decline in their emotional health may have been noticed by staff at an earlier stage.

- *Restricted external services:* The pressures on NHS primary care and community mental health teams may be reflected in people seeking other sources of psychological care. In particular there has been a lack of provision for child and adolescent mental health services (AUCC, 1999).

The unexpected increase in the levels of students seeking psychological care at the end of the 1990s raised the fundamental question: Does the current higher education system contribute to poor mental health? A Royal College of Psychiatrists' (RCP) working party was convened and the resulting report (RCP, 2003) found that, whilst there was no research evidence to suggest that students were more likely to develop a mental illness than their peers, students did report more emotional and behavioural symptoms. The RCP suggested that the transitions and stresses of student life may underlie this additional layer of emotional and behavioural disturbance. This view is borne out by Sinclair et al.'s (2005) study utilizing the Clinical Outcomes for Routine Evaluative system (CORE), which found 12 per cent of their participants to be in the clinical population prior to university entry, 20 per cent in the clinical population in the first and second years, and 25 per cent in the third year. A similar pattern of increased depression was found by Andrews and Wilding (2004) using the Hospital Anxiety and Depression Scale.

WORKING WITHIN AN EDUCATIONAL INSTITUTION

The primary focus of the work of counselling psychologists is to promote good mental health and work with people to restore it when problems have arisen. This is not the primary aim of academic institutions; academic success and achievement are the focus. It is important for the counselling psychologist to be wholehearted about the primary aim to work successfully within the institution (Carroll, 1996), but this does not mean that she should collude with practices that may be detrimental to clients. Whilst most educational establishments are liberal institutions and are concerned with the well-being of their young people, students and staff, there may be practices inherent in the educational system that work against good mental health (Andrews and Wilding, 2004; Sinclair et al., 2005). Counselling psychologists can play an important part in identifying and drawing the attention of the organization to such issues. Effecting change may not be an easy matter, particularly if current practices are viewed as contributing to academic success. A systemic approach is vital. Egan and Cowan (1979) emphasize that if, within an organization, people are falling into the stream up-river and the counselling service finds that they are pulling them out down-river, then there is a duty to go up-river, find out what is happening, and stop them falling in in the first place. It is not possible to be effective within an educational setting by operating as if you are in private practice. You are part of the process of the organization and a thorough understanding of the context is needed (Egan, 2004). This raises the question of boundary management.

In order to understand an educational institution you need to be sufficiently embedded to feel the stresses, strains and joys, but maintain enough distance to be able to reflect critically on the organizational processes. This is a fine line to tread, as practitioners are often expected to take part in the life of the institution, for example, to attend ceremonies, celebrations and social events. These events provide an opportunity to absorb important information about the atmosphere, implicit values, tensions and positive aspects of the school, college or university. On the other hand, your presence at such events can raise anxieties about confidentiality, and the counselling psychologist can never be 'off duty'. Boundaries must be clear and firm enough to maintain confidentiality and convey trust but flexible enough to cater for particular situations. A certain degree of visibility and informal contact helps to get the message across that you are available for everyone and inclusive of minority groups. As well as in informal settings, this will also be conveyed by your advertising material, and participation in inductions, information sessions and workshops on relevant issues.

CURRENT PROVISION

The Department for Children, Schools and Families has no current statistical data on the provision of counselling in schools (DCSF, 2008). There are a variety of ways that counselling is delivered in the educational sector, but in schools three patterns of delivery predominate:

- Teachers provide counselling/pastoral care. Teachers may take on therapeutic training and have an additional counselling role.
- Counselling is provided by an external agency. This is provided either in school or at an external location.
- The school employs a counsellor. These are often short-term contracts and the role can also embrace welfare issues as well as counselling. Counselling sessions are often less than 50 minutes; 30 minutes has been found to work well with the attention span of children and young people (Baginsky, 2004). Counsellors in schools rarely have their own room and ensuring suitable accommodation that is soundproof can be difficult to achieve.

Counsellors in further (FE) and higher education (HE) are almost always employed by their college or university, but part-time work is the norm and some practitioners may be on term-time only or short-term contracts. Provision in FE is more limited compared to that in HE due to resource constraints. A counsellor working in FE may be restricted to 30-minute sessions due to the heavy nature of the demand rather than the needs of the client. A typical day for an FE counsellor described by Leach (2008) involves seeing nine students, several consultations with academic staff, a discussion group, two journeys to different campuses, and administration. Leach estimates that she sees between 50 and 60 students a week. The hours are long and practitioners working in FE may be the only person providing professional therapeutic care in the institution; nevertheless, Leach underlines that her heavy workload is far outweighed by the positive feelings gained from being a part of facilitating change in the lives of young people.

University settings are the best funded, and most of the university sector provides free counselling for its students. Fifty-minute sessions and five sessions booked per day are the usual practice. Some services see only students; others see all members of the academic community, including catering staff, administrators and so on, as well as academics and students. Practitioners usually work as part of a team from a designated counselling service with specific counselling rooms that are appropriately furnished; administrative support and reception services are provided. Some counselling services have a separate building, whilst others work within 'one-stop shop' student services departments. At large universities there may be extensive student services departments with over 50 members of staff including accommodation services, careers, financial advice, disability services, an international student office and health advice. Whilst there may be some overlap, in practice these roles are usually fairly well-defined and cross-referral often occurs. On occasion, clarification about role boundaries and methods of liaison are needed. However the service is structured and located, it needs to be fit for purpose. It must be quiet and soundproof and have a comfortable, calm atmosphere. There are advantages and disadvantages of all forms of provision, and ease of access and confidentiality are often deployed as arguments for and against siting. Similar discussions take place in relation to the siting of the service within the institutional hierarchy. In the past, counselling provision was often viewed as a peripheral function and located on the margins of the institutional structure. Today the 'student experience' involves a progression through the system that is mapped from initial application to alumnus status and mirrors a customer/provider relationship. The emerging emphasis on 'service' and 'provision' has led to an increasing recognition that college and university support structures must be located more centrally within the organizational structure in order to attract and retain students and meet educational targets.

At present the counselling services may be managed by medical services, student services, human resources, health and safety or report directly to a headmaster, college head, senior tutor or vice-chancellor. The counselling psychologist has a part to play in ensuring that they are contained within the institution in a way that best serves the needs of their clients, and in arguing for structural repositioning if this proves not to be the case.

REFERRALS

In schools, potential clients may refer themselves; teachers and school staff may identify a possible need; parents may raise concerns; or external agencies such as social services or medical practitioners may refer. In further and higher education, most clients refer themselves. Less frequently encountered referral sources are academic staff, residential staff, campus medical services, chaplaincies, other student services, friends and families.

WAITING LISTS

Demand often exceeds supply and managing over-demand is an important task for practitioners. Pressure tends to build up as terms progress and specific times of year such as Christmas and exam periods are particular pressure points. Pressure can be especially great in areas where local mental health services have long waiting lists and there is little provision or spare capacity in voluntary organizations. Waiting lists are usually managed centrally, but in some places a waiting list is allocated to and managed by each counsellor. Some operate a strict first come first served basis, with information given about alternative local sources of counselling at times when the waiting list is long. Others triage by assessment; some utilize a mental health measure such as CORE to assess severity; some offer an initial assessment session with a counsellor and prioritize severe presentations whilst supplying less urgent clients with information about alternative sources of help. One institution with an ongoing heavy demand is experimenting with an assessment session followed by a single intensive extended counselling session (Cowley, 2007).

ASSESSMENT

Assessment follows the usual pattern for therapeutic work in accordance with the theoretical orientation of the practitioner. Some institutions use formal assessment instruments such as the Hospital Anxiety and Depression Scale and the Beck Depression Inventory, however, increasing numbers of services are using CORE as part of the assessment process. The 34-item CORE-OM includes a 6-item risk score as well as functioning, problem and well-being domains; Reeves and Coldridge (2007) underline its usefulness for suicide assessment when used in conjunction with the therapeutic discourse.

Research with student populations has shown that social support systems, trauma screening, alcohol intake and gender role conflict are important factors to include in the assessment process (Connell et al., 2006). Suicide risk is an especially important part of every assessment and the increased suicide risk for males aged 14–25 underlines the need for careful screening. There does not appear to be an increased suicide risk for students and studies have shown that the suicide rate amongst university students, and even those in high pressure academic environments, is not significantly different from the 15–24 age group in the general population (Collins and Paykel, 2000). In a study of attempted suicides, Hawton et al. (1995) found that during the years between 1976 and 1990, 216 university students (119 females and 97 males) were referred to hospital because of suicide attempts (254 in all). The rate of attempted suicide during university term-time was 106 per 100,000 and lower than the 164 per 100,000 rate for attempted suicide found in people of a similar age in the same city. The difference in the female rate was markedly lower at 178 per 100,000 for students and 269 per 100,000 for the general aged-matched female population. Hawton et al. (1995) suggest that the lower rates found in the students may be partly due to their generally higher socio-economic status. They also concluded that very few of the attempts were failed suicides. The most common precipitating factor for student suicide attempts was interpersonal issues and associated with partnership problems in particular. Academic concerns were the second highest group and related to difficulties with coursework rather than examinations. Approximately 30 per cent of the students who had attempted suicide had psychiatric problems, with depression and personality disorders being the most common. In another study, examinations were also not found to be associated with excess suicide rates (Collins and Paykel, 2000). Despite these findings suggesting that academic environments may not be linked with higher than normal suicide and attempted suicide rates, the death of any young person is a tragedy and as well as making careful risk assessments, prompt and easy access to help should be available. In 2007 a qualitative study was study commissioned by PAPYRUS, a group founded by parents of students who had committed suicide. The cases of twenty students who had committed suicide were explored by interviewing the family, friends, colleagues and staff involved with each student. The results included findings that most of the people who had committed suicide were young men, 75 per cent were in a transition phase at the beginning or end of an academic year, and two-thirds had diagnosed mental health problems. Relationship difficulties, heavy alcohol and drugs use, financial and academic problems, and perfectionist tendencies were factors that interacted with their mental health problems. 'Many of the students were experiencing a web of problems which appears to have left them feeling trapped at a time of change' (RaPSS, 2007b: 2). The inclusion of an exploration of the above factors and an awareness that they may be linked to suicide risk is an important part of the assessment process.

PRESENTING ISSUES

The composition of schools and FE colleges usually reflects the local population and the positive and negative aspects of those areas are often represented in the issues brought to therapy. In areas of deprivation, issues relating to unemployment, poverty, poor housing, poor health and teenage pregnancy may be prevalent and complicate the more general issues of transition, life, and developmental problems encountered by the various age groups. Universities tend to draw populations from wide geographical areas and often have diverse international populations; representatives from over 100 countries within one establishment are not unusual.

Presenting issues in schools can include family and peer relationships, behavioural problems, bullying, the concerns of puberty, and risk-taking behaviours. In colleges and universities, relationship difficulties, anxiety and depression are the most frequently encountered problem areas (AUCC, 2007). Many of the issues encountered in educational settings mirror those encountered in external services. However, there are some particular factors encountered in this setting that warrant further discussion.

ADDITIONAL FACTORS

An overriding feature of this setting is that therapeutic work is structured by the rhythms of the academic year. At the the start of the year anxiety may predominate as young people and students adjust to a new life pattern. Some may be living away from home for the first time and adapting to independent living, including learning how to live in close proximity with others who may be strangers. Homesickness is often encountered and for non-UK resident students there may be an additional layer of culture shock to come to terms with. Some students return from studies abroad and find that they have difficulty in settling back into the UK system – a form of reverse culture shock. Their previous friendship constellation may well have shifted and their expectation that they will slip back into previous routines with former friends and partners can be disappointed and result in disorientation, isolation and low mood.

At times, attending college or university may be seen as the start of a 'new phase in life' for refugees, people who have been in prison, undergoing gender reassignment, or have had long-term physical or mental health problems. They may have been made redundant from work, recently been divorced, or be seeking a complete change of direction. The anticipated 'new life' is often idealized and the stresses and strains of academic work and student life are not taken fully into consideration. The fantasy that previous problems can be completely left behind is rarely realized. Sensitive pre-arrival information can encourage people with pre-existing mental health problems to make contact with the disability services who can then ensure that their needs are properly assessed and plans put in place to support their academic endeavours. Counselling psychologists can play a significant role by providing short-term work to cover the adjustment periods on arrival and by ensuring that vulnerable students are familiar with service provision should problems arise.

Mindfulness of academic rhythms is an important factor, and therapeutic work needs to be paced to ensure that it is not working against the academic interests of clients. Exam anxieties have lessened with the trend towards modularization, but some examination hurdles still have to be negotiated and the appropriateness and depth of therapeutic work may need to be adjusted to ensure that energy for study is available.

CASE STUDY: JANE

During a lecture on child abuse Jane realized that the behaviour of a favourite uncle amounted to sexual abuse. She was referred to the counselling service and during a first tearful session with the counselling psychologist it was agreed that they would explore what this meant to her. A warning that this exploration may be painful and take up emotional energy was included. Jane had exams in three weeks' time and on reflection chose to postpone in-depth work until after the exams. The first three sessions focused on how she might deal with the immediate realization and contain her feelings so that she could concentrate on her work. The later in-depth exploration was helpful; Jane finished her course successfully and reached a position in relation to the abuse that meant that it was no longer taking up emotional space and energy.

Occasionally people develop severe mental health problems and refuse medical referral. In these situations a careful assessment needs to be undertaken and a decision has to be made as to whether it is feasible to offer support. This is not a simple decision as one person exhibiting disturbed behaviour, especially in a residential setting, can impact negatively on the mental health of a number of other people. It is important to ensure that the best interests of the client are balanced with the interests of other people who may be affected. In extreme cases it may be necessary to suspend the student until they can satisfy the school, college or university medical officer that they are fit to resume their studies. In some cases fairly severe levels of mental illness can be supported, but co-working with local psychiatric services is essential.

CASE STUDY: JIM

Jim developed paranoid symptoms at the age of 20 in his second year at university. He sought counselling and described his fears of others living in his hall of residence. His condition rapidly deteriorated and having no insight into his condition he rejected all medical help and was sectioned to a local community psychiatric unit. The unit provided excellent support and Jim formed positive relationships with his psychiatrist and the staff and was able to return to university after several months. A care plan was devised which involved regular sessions with the community psychiatric nurse, the campus GP, the psychiatrist and the university counsellor. His parents visited often

(Continued)

(Continued)

and maintained email and phone contact. The university counsellor saw Jim once a week on a long-term basis and provided occasional emergency sessions when he was feeling low or disturbed. She also liaised with and provided consultation for his academic department head who, when necessary, adjusted the timescales for Jim's coursework submissions. Jim went through the usual cycles of improving so much on medication that he would cease to take it and then be readmitted to hospital. However, despite two readmissions, he was able to complete his coursework and was thrilled to receive an upper second class honours degree.

Interpersonal work forms another important facet of the work. McLeod (1997) emphasizes the role of counselling in enabling people to belong and be core members of and participants in a social world. In academic settings the breakdown of relationships with peers, academic and administrative staff can occur through fear, anger or dispute. Therapy can facilitate the re-negotiation of relationships and the re-establishment of trust. Bullying causes particular distress and disturbance, and as well as providing individual therapy, counselling psychologists can assist in the development of anti-bullying policies and mentoring schemes. Relationships with family, friends and partners also go through ruptures and repair. Surviving the painful feelings that accompany the ending of love can be particularly difficult in situations where the person has to work with and be part of a social world that still contains the ex-partner: 'Just when I'm beginning to feel a bit better I walk round a corner and bump into her; she is everywhere.'

In an academic environment, perfectionism and its allied difficulty of procrastination are often encountered. The therapeutic task involves helping the person to retain the high level of adaptive perfectionism that is needed to do excellent work and develop a more balanced view of the areas that are maladaptive. Maladaptive behaviours often involve the generalization of perfectionism to other areas of life and can result in a raft of additional problems including the rejection of behaviours that might balance academic work stress, such as exercise: 'I can't play tennis because I never beat anyone.' Unhelpful polarizations are also encountered, such as viewing work as dreadful because the teacher or lecturer has written one mildly worded suggestion for improvement amongst many positive ones on the feedback sheet.

A final issue to highlight is the feelings of inadequacy that practitioners can encounter when working with very bright people. It can be daunting to have a PhD student look at your bookshelf and say 'Well, I don't know very much about psychotherapy but I've read Lacan'. Students do challenge you on philosophical subtleties and make wide reference to arts and literature. Viewing references to intellectual matters as diversionary tactics may be helpful at times in terms of process, but if you are going to form a solid working alliance with your clients you do have to communicate with them and engage with their concerns in a way that speaks to them, but it is not possible or necessary to be an expert in all fields.

TYPES OF INTERVENTION

In most educational establishments, short-term therapy is the usual mode of operation. A small percentage of people have chronic mental health problems and need long-term therapeutic support. Longer-term work is often important in terms of containment and helping clients to balance their self-care with their academic work.

Counsellors from all theoretical orientations work in education. With younger people expressive therapies aid communication; art and play therapy are often utilized. For good accounts of the range of interventions and brief forms of working with school children, see Bor et al. (2002) and Lines (2006). In relation to orientation, the question that has been asked is whether some interventions are more helpful than others with this age group. A scoping review of counselling in further and higher education (Connell et al., 2006) reports findings of limited effectiveness for CBT with anxiety and unresolved traumatic experiences, and preliminary evidence for the effectiveness of psychodynamic therapy and short-term therapy. However, this research evidence does not provide us with a solid basis to operate from, as Connell et al. underline the paucity of research in this area and recommend a co-ordinated UK national study of high methodological quality.

Counselling psychologists can offer a range of interventions in this setting depending on their training, experience and expertise. Apart from individual work, couple counselling, small group work and larger group work are all part of the challenges encountered. The predominance of relationship difficulties means that couple work is an important facet of the work. Work with small groups of friends or flatmates following a rupture in relationships can be very helpful. Events such as assaults, accidents or a death by accident, illness, murder or suicide have a considerable impact on communities and those close to the student in particular. Meetings and aftercare for people affected by deaths and traumatic incidents require skills in defusing and a knowledge of PTSD symptomology (Tehrani, 2004). Counselling psychologists can also contribute to the wider understanding of mental health issues within the institution by providing training and workshops for teachers, academics and staff.

In one school it was noticed that administrative staff were sometimes providing listening support for pupils. A listening and boundary skills session which underlined the importance of self-care and appropriate referral was much appreciated by the staff.

The counselling psychologist can also act as a change agent within the organization. You may identify issues that need attention and it may be possible to raise them yourself.

However, change is more easily effected if you can associate yourself with initiatives that come from other parts of the organization or co-ordinate with people who have similar concerns. Egan (1994) draws our attention to the shadow-side of organizations. We need to know the formal hierarchy, but it is also important to understand where power lies – which committees or people are influential. It is important to have a voice on committees such as welfare, equality, disability, and to be involved in policy and emergency planning groups. Any aspects of the institution's practices that may have implications for mental health should be the concern of the counselling psychologist. Through their work, practitioners can be in a good position to identify good practices that can be shared more widely, and deficits in provision that impact significantly on mental health. It is necessary to present information and arguments in ways that will be heard, and it may be that quantitative and financial arguments weigh more heavily than qualitative, psychological or medical arguments. Times of crisis are often key moments to achieve change, but this needs to be well-thought through rather than simply reactive.

> After a student attempted suicide in a hall of residence the counselling psychologist was able to argue successfully for a greater level of training and support for residential staff; a need that they had highlighted previously but had not been taken up at that time by the administration.

Young people are technologically skilled and these resources are part of a well-functioning service. Text messaging systems can be used to remind clients of appointments. An attractive website with links to mental health information, a database of local NHS, private and voluntary sector provision and links to specialist areas aimed at young people (for example, www.talktofrank.com) is essential. Whilst it is rarely an effective substitute for face-to-face contact, e-counselling can be useful for maintaining contact during holidays and whilst studying abroad (Evans, 2007). It is also of great value in helping potential clients who have reservations about counselling to make initial contact and begin building a relationship that enables them to make the move to face-to-face work.

A good range of age-appropriate, easily accessible self-help books provides an additional means of intervention. These can range from evidence-based self-help literature to clients and peers developing their own lists of helpful, sustaining and inspirational reading. These can be listed and described on the website and kept in the institution in an easily accessed location such as the library.

Peer support is a growing feature of educational institutions. It complements professional support, and there is persuasive evidence that these systems are valuable (Cowie and Wallace, 2000; Greenland et al., 2003; Smalley et al., 2005). Mentoring and peer support systems can be especially helpful in reducing bullying and its effects (Cowie and Hutson, 2005; McGowan, 2002). Counselling psychologists can be involved in initiating and supporting such schemes. These can range from phone helplines such as the student managed system 'Nightline' to individuals trained and identified as peer supporters. In a university setting, Ford (2004a) selects and trains peer supporters in active listening, assertiveness and referral for counselling or to other professionals. The duration of the training is 30 hours and is offered in 10 three-hour sessions. Peer support interventions can range from befriending/counselling support to mediation and conflict resolution, peer tutoring, advocacy and information giving. Peer supporters make themselves known to their colleagues and then wait to be contacted. Safeguards are careful selection, an emphasis on when and how to refer, confidentiality, and ready access to professional advice. Peer support is seen not only as filling in gaps in provision, but also as a genuine alternative that may enable students to consult at an early stage. Regular supervision and provision for emergency consultation is an important part of the scheme. One university peer support scheme has found that 9 per cent of students contact peer supporters (Cooper and Dasgupta, 2008). Ford (2004b) also provides valuable information and advice for setting up peer support systems with the 15–18 age group.

As well as organized appointments, drop-in times or space for emergency sessions, ensure that those with urgent issues can be seen promptly. A 'drop-in' time also caters for clients who prefer a more informal initial contact. Young people and students may think that their concern is not important enough to take up counselling time, and this form of access can help to dispel their concerns.

LIAISON

The counselling psychologist has a role to play in helping teachers and academic staff understand the types of issues that affect their pupils and students, and how these issues may impact on their ability to study and perform academically. This can be done via training courses and school or departmental meetings. Counselling psychologists can also offer consultation either by telephone, email or face-to-face. In consultancy work the bounds of confidentiality need to be carefully drawn and consultations may often involve requests for advice without names or contextual factors being included. The counselling service of a large multi-site university has a 9–5 weekday staff call line to support staff and advise if they have concerns about students.

A level of trust has to be built up with academic staff so that on occasion practitioners can intervene on a client's behalf (with their permission) without having to specify the problem. It is not unusual for clients to be ambivalent about letting teachers or academic staff know about their problems and mental health concerns. There are also a few issues that they almost never wish staff to be made aware of; these can include rape, termination of pregnancy, drug addictions and criminal proceedings.

> One student was appearing as the accused in court in the weeks immediately preceding his finals. The counselling psychologist was able to write a letter to the head of his department that underlined that the student had significant problems that were affecting his ability to study without disclosing the reason.

Alerting staff to difficulties before events such as exams is important as the retrospective identification of mitigating circumstances is less likely to be taken into consideration by exam boards.

Establishing effective working relationships with external support services is vital: an emergency is not the time to be making professional links. It can help smooth the process and obtain the best service for your clients if the local doctors, A&E department, community mental health team and social services department know who you are and what you do. There may be a community psychiatric nurse (CPN) designated to your geographical area who might prove to be a useful liaison person. Some community psychiatric services will take direct referrals from counselling psychologists working in educational settings and will dispatch a CPN to investigate the situation if there is serious concern. An important part of liaison is to ensure that the mental health teams understand the bounds of support that are available. They may assume that there are residential tutors available on-call 24-hours a day when in fact the institution has switched to a hotel-style residence management. Leaving information leaflets at the local A&E department, where attempted suicide or self-harm may be presenting, can help to ensure that young people and students in distress are aware of your services. The child protection link person in school and college settings is a source of expert advice. The safety of the child or young person takes precedence over confidentiality, and at these times consultation with a supervisor who understands the context is vital. Bor et al. (2002) provide excellent guidance on managing cases of suspected or actual child abuse.

EVALUATION

A key task is to make the work of the service visible. One of the problems with providing a successful service is that at an organizational level it appears that everything is running smoothly, and the contribution of the counselling psychologist to this happy state may not be apparent. The institution may then believe that there are no significant problems and that a counselling service is unnecessary, and the service then becomes vulnerable to cuts in times of financial pressure. Up-to-date statistics that demonstrate effectiveness and the production of an annual report reminds the hierarchy of the value of your work. It also provides an opportunity to highlight any institutional or educational practices that may be detrimental or beneficial to mental health. When presenting data it is important to be aware of the current goals of the institution and, if possible, to demonstrate the ways in which the service you provide is contributing to these efforts.

Retrospective evaluation is usually part of the counselling process. If practitioners are working effectively, they will be reflecting on the helpfulness of the therapeutic process with their clients and holding regular review sessions. An 'after end of therapy' question-naire with ample space for comments and anonymity guaranteed can be very helpful, not only to reflect on the effectiveness of counselling but also to ask about views on the referral process, reception area and location of the service.

Prospective evaluation is more powerful. Mark Phippen at Cambridge University devised the INFORM system to collect demographic data and record presenting issues, appointments, attendance, DNAs, cancellations, course, level of study and other relevant variables. CORE is becoming more widely used for assessment and evaluation purposes and can be used as an integral part of the therapeutic process. The resulting data can then be used in many ways. As well as demonstrating therapeutic effectiveness and making explicit the service's role in retention, it can be used to identify 'hot spots' in the institu-tion; particular classes, departments or courses may be associated with counselling service attendance and/or high CORE scores, indicating the need for exploration of the possible causes. Statistics can also be used to monitor that the service is accessible to all. The client profile should match that of the institution. Disparities can indicate that sections of the edu-cational community may be being excluded by omission or commission of the service.

LEGAL ISSUES

Mindfulness of the legal framework is as important in educational settings as elsewhere. In particular, a thorough understanding of child protection and mental health laws and procedures is necessary. The Disability Discrimination Act, equality legislation and the Data Protection Act underpin daily working practices, ensuring that the service is acces-sible to all and that client information is recorded and stored safely.

CONCLUSION

In this chapter I have attempted to map the development of counselling in educational settings and provide an overview of the challenges and stimulating aspects of this envi-ronment. Academic institutions strive to achieve high standards for academic success; there is every reason for mental health to be included within these high standards. Counselling psychologists have three years of post-graduate training at doctoral level; they are skilled at individual work, they think systemically and they are research-minded. These are excel-lent attributes for this setting. Although there are not yet many counselling psychologists working in education, this career pathway is a viable option for those who wish to work outside NHS settings. Counselling psychologists are encouraged to take their place along-side their counselling and psychotherapy colleagues and be at the forefront of ensuring that mental health is prioritized within the educational agenda.

REFERENCES

Andrews, B. and Wilding, J.M. (2004) 'The relation of depression and anxiety to life-stress and achievements in students', *British Journal of Psychology*, 95: 509–521.

AUCC (1999) *Degrees of Disturbance: The New Agenda*. Rugby: British Association for Counselling and Psychotherapy.

AUCC (2004) *Guidelines for University and College Counselling Services*. Rugby: British Association for Counselling and Psychotherapy.

AUCC (2007) *Annual Survey of Counselling in UK Colleges and Universities*. Rugby: British Association for Counselling and Psychotherapy.

Baginsky, W. (2004) *School Counselling in England, Wales and Northern Ireland: A Review*. London: NSPCC.

Baker, S., Brown, B.J. and Fazey, J.A. (2006) 'Mental health and higher education: Mapping field consciousness and legitimation', *Critical Social Policy*, 26 (1): 31–56.

Bell, E. (1996) *Counselling in Further and Higher Education*. Buckingham: Open University Press.

Bolger, A.W. (1985) 'Training and research in counselling', *British Journal of Guidance and Counselling*, 13 (1): 112–124.

Bor, R., Ebner-Landy, J., Gill, S. and Brace, C. (2002) *Counselling in Schools*. London: Sage.

Carroll, M. (1996) *Workplace Counselling*. London: Sage.

Cole, A. (2006) 'Inquiry opens into the state of childhood in the UK', *British Medical Journal*, 333: 619.

Collins, I.P. and Paykel, E.S. (2000) 'Suicide amongst Cambridge University students 1970–1996', *Social Psychiatry and Psychiatric Epidemiology*, 35 (3): 128–132.

Connell, J., Cahill, J., Barkham, M., Gilbody, S. and Madill, A. (2006) *A Systematic Scoping Review of the Research on Counselling in Higher and Further Education*. Rugby: British Association for Counselling and Psychotherapy.

Cooper, J. and Dasgupta, C. (2008) 'From bystanding to standing by', *AUCC Journal,* March.

Cowie, H. and Hutson, N. (2005) 'Peer support: A strategy to help bystanders challenge school bullying', *Pastoral Care in Education*, 23 (2): 40–44.

Cowie, H. and Wallace, P. (2000) *Peer Support in Action*. London: Sage.

Cowley, J. (2007) 'Stepped care: The Cardiff model', *Association for University and College Counselling Journal*, December: 2–5.

DCSF (2008) Personal communication: a response to an email enquiry requesting statistical data relating to counselling provision in schools.

Department for Education and Skills (2003) *The Future of Higher Education*. Norwich: The Stationery Office.

Egan, G. (1994) *Working the Shadow Side: A Guide to Positive Behind-the-Scenes Management*. San Francisco, CA: Jossey-Bass.

Egan, G. (2004) *The Skilled Helper: A Problem Management and Opportunity Development Approach to Helping*, 7th edn. Chicago, IL: Wadsworth.

Egan, G. and Cowan, M. (1979) *People in Systems*. Monterey, CA: Brooks Cole.

Evans, J. (2007) 'A pull-out guide to online counselling and psychotherapy in universities and colleges', *AUCC Journal*, December.

Ford, A. (2004a) *Peer Support in Colleges and Universities: A Training Manual*, 2nd edn. Rugby: Pettifer.

Ford, A. (2004b) *Peer Supervision in Teenagers Aged 15 to 18 Years Old*. Rugby: Pettifer.

Good Child Inquiry, The (2008) Available at www.childrenssociety.org.uk, accessed 27/5/09.

Greenland, K., Scourfield, J., Smalley, N., Prior, L. and Scourfield, J. (2003) *Young People, Gender and Suicide Prevention: Helpseeking in 17–18 Year Old Men and Women*. Cardiff: Draft Report for the Wales Office of Research and Development in Health and Social Care.

Hawton, K., Haig, R., Simkin, S. and Fagg, J. (1995) 'Attempted suicide in Oxford University students, 1976–1990', *Psychological Medicine*, 25 (1): 179–188.

Hooper, R. and Lang, P. (1988) 'Counselling revisited', *Pastoral Car*e, 6 (2): 27–32.

Kramer, T. and Garralda, M.E. (2000) 'Child and adolescent mental health problems in primary care', *Advances in Psychiatric Treatment*, 6: 287–294.

Leach, G. (2008) 'Helping students achieve', *AUCC Journal*, March: 15–19.

Lines, D. (2006) *Brief Counselling in Schools*: *Working with Young People 11–18*. London: Sage.

McGowan, M. (2002) *Young People and Peer Support: How to Set Up Peer Support Programmes*. Brighton: Trust for the Study of Adolescence.

McLeod, J. (1997) *Introduction to Counselling*. London. Sage.

Ministry of Education (1963) *Half Our Future*. A report of the Central Advisory Council of Education (England). Chairman: John Newsom. London: HMSO.

National Institute for Health and Clinical Excellence (NICE) Clinical Guideline for Depression in Children and Young People. Available at www.nice.org/nicemedia/pdf/cg028fullguideline.pdf, accessed 8/8/09

RaPSS (2007a) 'The responses and prevention in student suicide'. Available at www.rapss.org.uk, accessed 27/5/09.

RaPSS (2007b) 'The responses and prevention in student suicide: Summary of findings'. Available at www.rapss.org.uk, accessed 27/5/09.

Reeves, A. and Coldridge, E. (2007) 'A question of balance: Using CORE-OM when assessing suicide risk', *AUCC Journal*, March.

Roberts, R., Golding, J., Towell, T. and Weinreb, I. (1999) 'The effects of economic circumstances on British students' mental and physical health', *Journal of American College Health*, 48 (3): 103–9.

Royal College of Psychiatrists (2003) *The Mental Health of Students in Higher Education, CR112*. London: RCP.

Sinclair, A., Barkham, M., Evans, C., Connell, J. and Audin, K. (2005) 'Rationale and development of a general population well-being measure: Psychometric status of the GP-CORE in a student population', *British Journal of Guidance and Counselling*, 33 (2): 153–174.

Smalley, N., Scourfield, J. and Greenland, K. (2005) 'Young people, gender and suicide: A review of the social context', *Journal of Social Work*, 5 (2): 133–154.

Tehrani, N. (2004) *Workplace Trauma*. Hove: Brunner-Routledge.

Waller, R.M., Mahmood, T., Gandi, R., Delves, S., Humphrys, N. and Smith, D. (2005) 'Student mental health – how can psychiatrists better support the work of university medical centres and university counselling services?', *British Journal of Guidance and Counselling*, 33 (1): 117–128.

USEFUL WEBSITES

www.student.counselling.co.uk   This website was set up by the Heads of Student Counselling Services in UK Universities. It provides information and has links to counselling services and other sources of help.

www.studentdepression.org   This website was set up by the Charlie Waller Memorial Trust in consultation with the Association for University and College Counselling. It is a user-friendly site with clearly presented information and students' own accounts of recognizing and coping with depression.

www.thecalmzone.net   A site aimed at young people and black men in particular.

25

COMMUNITY PSYCHOLOGY: LINKING THE INDIVIDUAL WITH THE COMMUNITY

Carolyn Kagan, Carol Tindall and Julia Robinson

In 2002 a group of women activists from a housing estate in North Manchester who have worked with both Carolyn and Carol, met with Isaac Prilleltensky, one of the most prolific writers on critical and community psychology. They told him they had tried to read some of his work but found it difficult. They advised that if people like them were to understand community psychology, we (community psychologists) would be better writing in the style of questions and answers to an 'agony aunt'. So this is the format we have chosen. Whilst we recognize that we have still strayed into a professional writing register, we hope the format of the chapter makes some of the key issues come alive for students, counselling psychologists, and those experts by experience who may find themselves the clients of counselling psychologists. In particular, we have stressed the social justice agenda characteristic of community psychology, and linked this to counselling psychology. This approach makes explicit a political agenda underpinning our practice, challenging any notion of psychology's political neutrality. We have referred to this approach as 'community counselling psychology'.[1]

---

[1]All case scenarios are based on real situations, anonymized so that identification is not possible.

Dear Carolyn, Carol and Julia,

I am a trainee counselling psychologist and am getting frustrated at the way models of counselling psychology focus on individual change, whilst at the same time we are expected to take clients' contexts into account. I read something recently in the *Counselling Psychology Review* that suggested that community psychology might have something to offer. What is community psychology?

Yours,
Puzzled Trainee Eddie

Dear Eddie,

We think you must have read the article by Thatcher and Manktelow (2007), in which they highlight the limitations of the emphasis on individualism in counselling psychology. Community psychology is an approach that focuses more on system change than individual change. Whilst it has different roots in different places (Reich et al., 2007), it is frequently offered as an alternative to individual ways of working to promote psychological health and wellness. Indeed, community psychology develops critiques of the individual focus within psychology and highlights the psychological damage done through living in those societies that over-value competitive individualism and which are characterized by asymmetrical power relations and distribution of resources, underpinning processes of oppression (Nelson and Prilleltensky, 2005). Community psychologists have called for conceptualizations of distress and personal change that:

> … involve an analysis of how social power produces and sustains social inequity of the psychological, spiritual, or material implications of dehumanization, marginalization and disenfranchisement. (Watts et al., 2003: 185–6)

In our community psychological practice, we emphasize working with those who have been marginalized by the social system in order to create self-aware social change. This work is underpinned by clearly articulated values linked to a social justice agenda, participatory work and the development of alliances (Kagan and Burton, 2005a, 2005b; Burton et al., 2007).

> It is *community* psychology because it emphasises a level of analysis and intervention other than the individual and their immediate interpersonal context. It is community *psychology* because it is nevertheless concerned with how people feel, think, experience, and act as they work together, resisting oppression and struggling to create a better world. (Burton et al., 2007: 219)

This approach might well offer you a way of resolving the paradox you find yourself in. If you thought a full-blown community counselling psychology approach was too big a step to take in one go, you might want to pick up on some of the suggestions of how to integrate a critical perspective into counselling settings, made by Prilleltensky and Nelson. They make the important point that:

> critical alternative approaches are not for everyone. While mainstream mental health services have not been helpful for disadvantaged client groups, we recognize that some clients might be better served by more mainstream approaches. All clients should have a range of services from which to choose. (2002: 91)

Nevertheless, they highlight the advantages for some clients of assuming that causes or consequences of some problems reflect political and psychological oppression, to be relieved by structural as well as personal solutions. In practice this leads to encouraging clients to pursue personal and collective empowerment. They also suggest a broadening of values underpinning practice to include diversity, collaboration, support of community infrastructure and social justice.

> Dear Carolyn, Carol and Julia,
>
> My husband is a successful, highly paid futures dealer, and travels abroad every month. I don't work and could go with him, but have a phobia about flying so cannot go in a plane. Would seeing a community counselling psychologist help me?
>
> Fear of flying, Zarina

Dear Zarina,

We don't think it would, Zarina. Community psychology practice is underpinned by sets of explicit values. Whilst different community psychological practitioners assert slightly different underpinning values, there is agreement that the pursuit of social justice guides practice (Kagan and Burton, 2000, 2001; Prilletensky, 2001). Lee unpacks the concept of social justice:

> … social justice involves promoting access and equity to ensure full participation in the life of a society, particularly for those who have been systematically excluded on the basis of race/ethnicity, gender, age, physical or mental disability, education, sexual orientation, socioeconomic status, or other characteristics of background or group membership. (2007: 1)

Thus, a focus on social justice is a focus on social exclusion and marginalization. A concern for social justice is not limited to community psychology, and it is at the core of the organization of Counselors for Social Justice (see http://counselorsforsocialjustice.com/), reiterated by Crethar et al.:

> Social justice counseling represents a multifaceted approach to counseling in which practitioners strive to simultaneously promote human development and the common good through addressing challenges related to both individual and distributive justice.

Social justice counseling includes empowerment of the individual as well as active confrontation of injustice and inequality in society as they impact clientele as well as those in their systemic contexts. In doing so, social justice counselors direct attention to the promotion of four critical principles that guide their work; equity, access, participation, and harmony. This work is done with a focus on the cultural, contextual, and individual needs of those served. (2008: 271).

Social justice is undermined by a number of destructive social forces which effectively marginalize people from the social system (Kagan and Burton, 2005b). Examples of such destructive forces include: increasing social inequality leading to wider societal schisms; the grip of neoliberal economic policies, resulting in the commodification of people, communication and human relations; repression, reflected in increased harshness towards minorities; deregulation and privatization, leading to the privatization of public and community space and a withdrawal from politics; and environmental destruction with the consequent unequal use of natural resources and threats to sustainability (Kagan and Burton, 2001).

Our community psychological work needs to side with resistance to these destructive forces. As community counselling psychologists, we work to achieve equitable distribution of social justice: this means that we cannot make our services equally available to all, but need to focus on those with most inequitable access to social resources, and the most socially marginalized. From your letter, you are in a position of social privilege, with wealth and opportunity. The only benefit you might get from a community counselling approach is one wherein your position of privilege is explored, along with possibilities for meaningful social roles and activities beyond those of your husband's wife (see Chapter 11 in this book on Feminist Perspectives). A community counselling approach might encourage you to examine flying as a global phenomenon and its contribution to climate change. If we were to work with you on these issues (rather than the one you identified of flying phobia), we would be aiming to enable you to be part of a group in order to increase knowledge and understanding about your social position in relation to others, with a view to moving towards some action leading to social change: not so you lose all your privileges, but so that others gain some.

Dear Carolyn, Carol and Julia,

I am in year 10 in a secondary school. I am finding it hard to make friends as my timetable means that I don't get to mix with people I like. I am really unhappy at the moment. I am being bullied in some of my lessons and sometimes in the breaks, so nowadays I go home for lunch as it means I escape from school for a bit. My head of year has suggested I see the community counselling psychologist who is visiting from CAMHS. Will she be able to help me?

Yours,
Miserable, James

Dear James,

We are sorry you are feeling so unhappy. Seeing the community counselling psychologist might be useful; certainly it usually helps to talk things through. But how you are feeling is not your fault, and the community counselling psychologist will help you understand how the ways schools are organized cuts through friendships and often fails to build on the strengths and assets of the pupils. One of our own studies has shown that how pupils feel is closely linked to the organization of the school (Sixsmith et al., 2005). The organization of lessons promotes well-being if it affords opportunities to talk with and interact with your friends, but if not, pupils dislike school.

One of the things that contributed to positive well-being in schools from our study was pupil participation. If you went to the community counselling psychologist, it is likely that she or he would explore with you ways in which you might get involved in other activities in the school, beyond your lessons. This doesn't just mean sport. You might want to stand for election on the school council, for example, or join the choir or take part in some other club. This way you would get to meet other pupils out of lesson time, and school might become more enjoyable. It is surprising how enjoyable it is getting to know other pupils during extra-curricular activities, as our evaluation of an intergenerational project in schools has shown (Siddiquee et al., 2008). Feeling good about yourself is as much about what you do as what others do to you, so a community counselling approach would be able to help you find ways of getting involved in things that matter to you and the school. If you talk with your friends out of school, you might come up with lots of ideas of other kinds of things that you could do together in school. For example, you might want to develop an Internet link with a school in a different part of the world, or organize fundraising for a charity. These will give you other roles to play in school and may well make you feel better, and you may find that other pupils respect you more, particularly if they think the things you are doing are worthwhile. The counselling psychologist will help you find other people to help you with doing these things – through this you will become empowered. Key to a community psychological approach to counselling is empowerment.

Empowerment is not just about you, as an individual being able to do things. It is also about the extent to which you are able to control things and have valued roles (Chinman and Linney, 1998). Perkins and Zimmerman (1995) discuss empowerment at individual, organizational and community levels. In relation to bullying at the organizational level, the school should involve pupils in monitoring and implementing any anti-bullying policy. However, bullying is a symptom and it is often the case that the bullies need help, not punishment. Drewery (2004) presents compelling evidence of the success of a restorative approach to bullying wherein constructive conversations are introduced throughout the school. These conversations are characterized by mutual respect and can take place between teachers, teachers and pupils or pupils and pupils. Support for constructive conversations throughout the school is something the counselling psychologist could initiate, and this would lead to a positive change in school culture. If this is to be done effectively, the counselling psychologist would need to initiate a programme of staff development, taking her away from one-to-one work with pupils, but in the long run strengthening the school and preventing further pupil distress. Empowerment at community level might involve the development of close alliances between different schools or between schools and other local agencies concerned with behaviour and respect between young people.

Bullying is a problem in many schools, but should not be tolerated. If the bullying policies are not being implemented properly, the counselling psychologist can help you decide what to do about this. She may be able to mobilize the resources within the school to ensure that pupils are fully involved in anti-bullying and positive relationships within the school. She will need to see the issue as not being just a problem for you, but rather a problem of and for the school. Being bullied often makes you feel powerless and worthless, so another approach would be to find ways of involving you in activities that give you a sense of pride and achievement. Clearly, these things require the counselling psychologist to undertake different kinds of activities from those usually expected of a counsellor, and to play different roles herself. Her new roles might include advocate, alliance builder, resource procurer, trainer, networker, participation-enabler, roles more familiar to community psychologists than to counselling psychologists (Kagan et al., 2005).

> Dear Carolyn, Carol and Julia,
>
> I am a GP working in the inner city. I see quite a number of men – sometimes their wives rather than the men themselves – who are unemployed and getting weighed down by mounting debt. Those men I have seen I would say are definitely depressed. I think they would respond well to medication, but before prescribing thought I would find out what you thought might help. If they were women I would recommend the Well Woman self-help group, but the men are not interested in meeting other men in the same position. I would welcome your opinion as a community counselling psychologist.
>
> Yours,
> Dr Dilemma

Dear Dr Dilemma,

Thank you for contacting us – we are delighted to see the way that you are thinking about depression amongst your male patients, and recognize some of the social factors contributing to their depression. The social context in which depression emerges is one that community psychologists are keen to emphasize, particularly in the current context of government support for talking therapies.[2] Indeed, some of us feel so strongly about this that we recently issued a press release, challenging the individual approaches being proposed to deal with high levels of mental distress (Burton and Kagan, 2008). The statement issued was:

---

[2] http://nds.coi.gov.uk/environment/, press realese 27 November 2007.

> Cognitive behaviour therapy and associated approaches are comprehensively problematic. Primary prevention is the only way to substantially reduce socially, economically and materially caused distress. To be effective primary prevention must involve social rather than cognitive change. Reducing income inequality in our society would be one of the most effective ways to reduce psychological distress and ill health. (*UK Community Psychology Network, 2008*, cited in Burton and Kagan, 2008)

There is a growing concern about the links between debt and mental health, as highlighted by a recent MIND survey (MIND, 2008). Whilst the relationships are difficult to disentangle, they argue that being in debt undoubtedly affects mental health, whilst living with a mental health problem increased the likelihood of falling into debt. Debt has been associated with self-harm (Hatcher, 1994; Taylor, 1994) and even with suicide attempts (Hintikka et al., 1998). Sharpe and Bostock (2002) also highlighted the problems and suggested that in general, health professionals did not have the knowledge or awareness of how to deal with clients in debt. Although Fitch et al. (2007) give information to professionals about debt to enable them to work better with clients, you might be better making strong links with a debt counselling or citizens' advice service, which has been shown to be beneficial to patients (Galvin et al., 2001). The Citizen's Advice Bureau will also help with ensuring that people get the benefits to which they are entitled. This would be rather similar to the placing of employment advisers in GP surgeries that has been piloted recently (Sainsbury et al., 2008). If you did this you would be creating a new social setting, which is a longstanding community psychological strategy (Sarason, 1972). Another way of thinking about this would be to say that you were making alliances in order to benefit patients, which would be part of what Zimmerman (2000) considers to be a community level aspect of empowerment. It would be well worth your while encouraging your practice community counselling psychologist to try to set up one of these projects, utilizing her community skills of resource procurer, networker and facilitator of alliances. You need to be aware, though, that whilst debt and lack of money contribute to ill health, relying on benefits or getting an unfulfilling job may not improve matters. Fryer points out that:

> receipt of State benefit money was described [by unemployed people] as redolent with indecency, humiliation, stigma and depression. The passivity and lack of any reciprocity, of an exchange relationship, with unemployment benefit was especially thoroughly explicated. By contrast, money earned from work on the side was experienced quite differently: there was a reciprocal relationship between the hard work done, the payment received and the entitlement to spend it … (2003: 23)

Sixsmith (1999), too, highlights the positive mental health gains from working in the 'hidden economy'. What we are suggesting is that whilst addressing the income and money issues, it will also be necessary to find ways of ensuring that the men are occupied with meaningful work from which they can get satisfaction, identity and status – preferably paid, but unpaid would be better than nothing.

You are right to suggest that men may be more reluctant to seek self-help or social support from people with similar experiences (Boneham and Sixsmith, 2003). However, Melluish and Bulmer (1999) found that through forming an alliance between a psychological therapist and community development worker, men who were experiencing psychological distress were able to build a gardening project – with support – which then provided them with employment. Their work drew on that of Holland (1991, 1992), who has shown how psychotherapy can be the springboard to social action and wider social change for women experiencing psychological distress and living in areas of multiple deprivation. A rather different approach was taken by one of our psychology and counselling students in working with unemployed men, who were depressed, in an inner city area. Instead of even trying to help them recognize that they needed psychological help, some free sessions at a local gym were set up. The men went along and worked out, although they hardly spoke to each other for several months. Gradually, though, they began to talk to each other and see that they had life experiences in common. Our project ended at this point, but we heard later that they still meet up. Whilst you are right that men are unlikely to go straight away to any sort of self-help group, if they form ties with other men through other activities, they may indirectly get and give the social support that is needed.

Dear Carolyn, Carol and Julia,

I have a four month old baby. I am at my wit's end, getting to be so tired. I have been to my GP who has referred me to a counselling psychologist. What good will this do me?

At the end of my tether,
Rachel

Dear Rachel,

What a shame that your tiredness is stopping you enjoy the company of your new baby. If you are being referred to community counselling psychologists, it may help. Their approach would be to help you see that your feelings are not due to some failure of yours to cope. Rather, as we discussed in Chapter 11 on Feminist Perspectives, it is to do with your position as a woman and a mother in a society that constructs clear ideals of the perfect (super)woman. Your circumstances are not unique to you, and are shared by other new mums. It would probably be helpful if you met with other mums in the same position as you. As you get to talk, you will become aware of the wider social forces that add pressures on you to cope. It will also enable you, perhaps, to share looking after each other's children so you get a bit of a rest sometimes. Milne (1999) highlighted the ways in which social support can be seen as an intervention to preserve and enhance mental well-being. A community counselling psychologist should be able to help you get information about what groups there are locally, or if not, put you in touch with someone who can help you set up a group. Contemporary English society has been said to lack what is known as 'social capital', which in turn depletes people's health. Putnam is, perhaps, the most widely accepted proponent of social capital as a useful idea and defines it as follows:

> 'Social capital' refers to features of social organization such as networks, norms, and social trust that facilitate co-ordination and co-operation for mutual benefit. (1995: 67).

These benefits are both social and psychological and, according to Putnam, increase physical and mental health. Not everyone agrees with this (Pearce and Smith, 2003), and some commentators suggest that income inequality in a society is what produces ill health, although the mechanisms for this are not understood. Even so, community counselling psychologists can work in ways that serve to strengthen and preserve social capital. One way is to encourage awareness and social support. Another would be to develop other forms of support that utilize the strengths of other community members.

O'Connor (2001) describes the advantages of a 'community mothers' project. Older women who are experienced with children volunteer to get to know and befriend young mums in order to help them out, give advice and support and, of course, a much needed rest when required. This kind of project demands a number of skills of the community counselling psychologist, first in gaining funding and support, then publicizing the project and recruiting and supporting volunteers – not the usual substance of a counselling psychologist's role. However, such a project has the added advantage of making the wider community aware of the strain that some of its members are under. Lewis and Arnold (1998: 59) argue that counsellors are well placed to know the problems that exist in a community, and to know when negative environmental factors (such as isolation) impinge upon people's lives. They suggest that counsellors can facilitate action for change by taking three steps to support communities in their empowerment efforts: making communities as a whole aware of specific problems affecting its members; alerting existing community organizations that might be interested in joining an alliance to work on a particular issue; and participating with other individuals and groups to act as allies for people who are fighting for change on their own behalf.

The aim of this kind of work is to prevent other young mums getting into the position you find yourself, but doing this in ways that give both individuals and communities as much control over their own lives as possible. Counselling psychologists may well consider that this kind of work is beyond their remit, in which case they could concentrate on forming alliances with local community development workers and others who are working towards supportive communities and the well-being of children, in order to advocate and lobby for such projects to be established.

The advocacy and policy roles being suggested here will probably be necessary if any change for new mothers is to be long term and contribute towards transformative change (rather than what is known as ameliorative, or 'sticking plaster' change) and prevent other young mums getting to the position you find yourself in.

Dear Carolyn, Carol and Julia,

My little boy, Ahmed, is 8 years old. He has been suspended from school and may well get permanently excluded as his behaviour is so bad. He punches the other children, steals things from them and the teacher. I don't know what I can do with him. He won't listen to me. His other five brothers and sisters have been no trouble and get on with each other, even though we have gone through difficult times leaving Sudan and are all squashed into a two-bedroom house. I am coming to see the community counselling psychologist from the CAMHS team next week and am really hoping they will be able to do something for him. Do you think they can sort him out?

With out of control son,
Amani

Dear Amani,

Life must be very difficult for you at the moment. The approach of the community counselling psychologist will be to look at the problems you are faced with holistically. She will be sensitive to your cultural background when talking with you about your family and your life circumstances and will use an ecological perspective to make sense of your son's difficulties. The best way to explain this is to think of an onion. In the centre is Ahmed, but close to him are his family members and the other people he meets at school or in the community – his friends and teachers, neighbours, other family members and so on. The next layer out is the linking of his family with the school, the family with the housing officers and so forth. Right on the outside, holding it all together are the policies and practices of government that impinge upon you – this may include policies linked to children, families, migration, housing, income support, education and so on. All of these things will affect Ahmed directly and indirectly. This way of thinking is called a 'nested systems approach' (Bronfenbrenner, 1979). It is an ecological approach because what she will be trying to do is understand the difficulties you face, and Ahmed's behaviour *in context*, before looking at any individual factors that might be affecting Ahmed. In doing this, she may well ask about the family and yourself, as well as the school and what happens in the classroom, because it will be difficult for her to make sense of what is happening to Ahmed without doing this.

You have told us that you all live in a two-bedroom house. We know that overcrowding puts pressure on people, and it may be this that is the root cause of the problems. Some people are more resilient than others, and Schoon and Bartley note that:

> socio-economic disadvantage, material hardship and family breakdown greatly increase the risk of developing adjustment problems later on, such as educational failure, behavioural problems, psychological distress or poor health. (2008: 24)

Not everyone, however, is affected in the same way. Poor housing is one of the stressors on families they identify, and it is likely that through her analysis, the community counselling psychologist will see this as a starting point. With your permission, she could engage in assertive advocacy, and all that that entails, including persistence and the mobilization of additional advocates, such as local councillors, service managers or members of parliament where necessary.

Vera and Speight (2007: 376) outline three forms of advocacy: helping clients to advocate for themselves; advocating directly with institutions or policymakers; or advocating indirectly through training or educating professionals who work with people living in areas of multiple deprivation, underserved by services. In your case we would expect she will undertake direct advocacy, but follow this through with helping you to advocate for yourself.

If we are right, and she manages to get you re-housed, you might find Ahmed's problems disappear and he becomes able to engage fully with school again. If not, at least you will be in a better position to then work out what else might be contributing to his behaviour. It could be argued that you will be disempowered if the counselling psychologist undertakes the advocacy. However, it is more likely that if it is successful, you will have a lot more strength to deal with issues affecting the family.

Vera and Speight (2003, 2007) argue that advocacy, alongside prevention and outreach, are critical components of a social justice agenda for counsellors. Each must be grounded in a commitment to social justice, which in turn requires a foundation in the psychology of oppression and liberation (Speight and Vera, 2004; Moane, 1999). Vera and Speight propose that three interrelated activities characterize effective outreach: relationship building, collaborative efforts and needs assessments. They suggest that there is sometimes confusion about the purpose of therapists engaging in outreach and argue that it is more than breaking down barriers so that previously underserved clients will learn to seek out the services of professional community counselors:

> Rather it involves collaborating in partnerships with existing community organisations to bring services to where the people are. [These efforts] will be largely unsuccessful if done without the involvement of the community members from the inception of the idea. (Vera and Speight, 2007: 379)

When initially engaging in outreach activities, they advise affiliating with a trusted member of, or establishment within, the community. It is not professional training that will enable the growth of trusted relationships with a community, but rather the personal integrity of the counselling psychologist. A recent UK-based community counselling and clinical psychology project, Building Bridges, worked in this way (Thorp, 2007) offering the following guidelines for outreach work with minority communities:

- Recruit staff who are from the same ethnic backgrounds as your service users. It will help you to make stronger connections with your target community.
- Work in partnership with other services; mainstream service providers should not disengage from the service user after you have accepted a referral.

- Encourage self-referrals – families are less likely to engage with you if the idea has been imposed upon them.
- Community engagement is crucial – you need to understand what challenges different ethnic communities are facing.
- Act as a complement to other services, not a replacement. Ethnic minority families could be marginalized if they do not have access to mainstream services.

Rojano (2007) goes further in outlining valid roles for therapists. He argues for a model of community family therapy, wherein the therapist becomes a 'citizen therapist', partnering with the community in various forms of social actions in low-income neighbourhoods, where families have multiple problems. He outlines several stages in the process of becoming a 'citizen therapist':

a) awareness – the therapist needs to be aware of situations where some citizens are actively working on one or more civic projects; b) familiarity – to be civically minded requires detailed knowledge of and specific information about the issues, facts and other reasons that led to the development of a civic campaign, struggle or project; c) engagement – therapists must maintain a minimum level of connection with individuals and groups in the community; and d) activism – a citizen therapist is one who is an active volunteer in one or more civic projects. (Rojano, 2007: 259)

Dear Carolyn, Carol and Julia,

I am becoming increasingly desperate. My life is really not worth living. All my life I have been fat and ugly. I hate myself. I don't have any friends and I am not surprised as I'm not nice to know. I wouldn't like to be my friend. I don't think I'll ever have a boyfriend – this is all I've ever wanted. Sometimes I feel as if I am about to explode – at these times I get great relief by cutting myself with a razor blade – I feel better as soon as I see the blood. Can you help (no-one else can)?

Yours,
Never-look-in-the-mirror, Yasmin

Dear Yasmin,

It sounds as if you are having a horrible time, but you have realized that things are getting out of control and are seeking help. We are community counselling psychologists, and this means we would work with you to help you understand your situation and the social pressures that contribute to how you feel about yourself; encourage you to make links with other people who have or have had similar experiences; and find new ways to enjoy life a little more. Let's look at these things in a little more detail.

You say you are fat and ugly. You live in a society that promotes a particular view of what is good and beautiful – for both men and women – and yet is full of contradictions. There is a societal preoccupation with appearance, with a strong emphasis on individual responsibility. Thus those of us who do not conform to these social ideals (which is most of us) are considered entirely responsible, and this leads to a 'victim-blaming culture' which in turn makes us feel even worse about ourselves. Wherever we look there are advertisements for food (much of which is unhealthy), cosmetics, interventions to address imperfections, such as plastic surgery, hypnosis and so on. It is no wonder that we begin to get preoccupied with how we look and whether anyone will like us. Indeed, rather than see concerns about weight and appearance as individual problems, some argue for a social justice approach:

> A social justice approach pushes the boundaries of problem definition beyond the individual to consider larger systemic influences. ... we need to stop trying to foster change within a system that supports eating disorders and obesity, and look to transforming the larger systems that create the problem in the first place. (Russell-Mayhew, 2007: 9, 7)

Working with you to develop awareness of the food, cosmetic and fashion industries and how they affect our lives whilst making large profits would be a process of 'consciousness raising', or what Freire (1990) calls 'conscientization'. This is seen as the first step in taking action for change. Even better would be to encourage you to join a group of people who have similar concerns – the solidarity gained from others as well as the support and encouragement is one of the reasons why self-help groups work.

Some practitioners argue that awareness-raising should include understanding the historical context of different social phenomena and a reclaiming of culture and creativity, which in many advanced capitalist, as well as colonized, societies has been lost (Kagan, 2008). Moane (1999, 2003) draws on the experiences of women in Ireland to outline liberation psychology approaches. She suggests a cycle of liberation, wherein personal, interpersonal and political levels of change are all interconnected, and equally important. Personal-level change is about building strengths, and may include assertiveness, positive images and role models, developing a sense of history, exploring sexuality, cultivating creativity and developing spirituality. The interpersonal level is about making connections and includes support, solidarity, handling conflict, valuing diversity and cultivating community. The political level is about taking action and includes developing analysis (which starts with awareness), exploring options, gaining a broader understanding of change and developing strategies to work towards a vision of a different future.

You haven't told us much about what you enjoy in life. It's likely that there are some things. If you had a go at doing some of the things that you enjoy, you may meet like-minded people: but the most important thing is that you enjoy the activity. For example, if you like walking, you could join a ramblers' group; if you like art, join an art group. Your problems might not go away, but you might feel better about yourself. We have researched a number of arts projects involving people under stress and with mental health problems (for example, Lawthom et al., 2007; Kilroy et al., 2007), and several people have told us that although their problems had not gone away they were now an artist, photographer, sculptor and so on. What all of these kinds of activities do is give you a sense of control over your life, which is often something that helps young people who harm themselves as you are doing (Spandler and Warner, 2007).

If you cannot at the moment face other people, you might find, as countless other young people have, that an Internet forum where you can discuss your feelings and impulses with others who have similar experiences, helpful. Take a look at one of these – it is called Recover Your Life and offers a safe place to share as well as contribute ideas to help others (www.recoveryourlife.com/).

So, as community counselling psychologists, we would be thinking about personal, interpersonal and political levels of change, with an emphasis on looking at the social construction of body image and finding ways in which you can take other kinds of control over your life. Political change usually involves some kind of action, and you might end up challenging some of the more destructive policies and practices concerning food. We, as counselling psychologists, also have a responsibility if we are working within a social justice framework, to become active and resist some of the societal pressures that we know contribute to clients' distress. The Food Commission, for example, mobilizes campaigns linked to some of the hypocrisies of food and health policies, and this might be a place for us to contribute to wider social changes.

> Dear Carolyn, Carol and Julia,
>
> We are revising our programmes in training in applied (particularly counselling) psychology and would like to address some of the skills for working as counselling psychologists within a social justice framework. Do you have any ideas that might help us?
>
> Yours,
> Counselling Psychologists moving towards social justice frameworks, Fred and Doreen

Dear Fred and Doreen,

It is great to hear about the changes you are thinking of making. We have been able to do some thinking about what might be needed on training courses to enhance counselling psychologists' abilities to work within a social justice framework, borrowing from the growing literature (for example, Goodman et al., 2004; Toporek and McNally, 2006; Vera and Speight, 2007). Some of these might already be present on some counselling psychology programmes as there has always been a critical edge to counselling psychology in the UK. Goodman et al. define the social justice work of counselling psychology in the following way:

> We conceptualize the social justice work of counseling psychologists as scholarship and professional action designed to change societal values, structures, policies, and practices, such that disadvantaged or marginalized groups gain increased access to these tools of self-determination. (2004: 795)

Thus they advocate a critical approach to counselling psychology practice and thereby training. Prilleltensky and Nelson (2002) suggest that key skills for critical psychological work can be distinguished at different levels. Personal-level skills include personal reflection and consciousness raising, basic communication and assessment skills. Group-level skills include group facilitation, organizational development and evaluation. Societal-level skills include community development, community organizing and social policy analysis – not usually found in the repertoire of counselling psychologists, but essential for social justice work.

Goodman et al. (2004) outline six principles to be considered in preparing counselling psychologists for social justice work, and these are commensurate with the skills for critical psychology work outlined above:

- Ongoing self-examination
- Sharing power
- Giving voice
- Facilitating consciousness raising
- Building on strengths
- Leaving clients the tools to work towards social change.

Another way of thinking about training is in terms of knowledge, skills, self-awareness (of trainee) and attitudes and values.

Knowledge will include historical and sociological understanding of the phenomena that affect trainees and their clients. In terms of social justice, this must include understanding of processes of oppression and marginalization. It is sociology and the critical psychology literature that provides rich understanding of these processes, as well as exposure of the damage done by deficit models of human functioning and the way that power, oppression and resistance both operate and can be mobilized for change. Corcoran (2007) has examined the utility of adopting a discursive understanding to counselling in educational settings.

Attitudes and values are closely linked to self-awareness. McWhirter and McWhirter (2007) discuss these in relation to what they describe, after Prilleltensky, as an 'emancipatory communitarian' approach to psychological practice (EC). The five values that are embedded into EC, and seen as in balance with each other, include caring and compassion; self determination; human diversity; collaboration and participation; distributive justice. In training, students can be encouraged continually to re-visit these values and examine how they affect their practice, including problem definition, role of the client, role of the helper, type of intervention, time of intervention, and assessment of efficacy of intervention.

Self-awareness is primarily about positionality. Trainees are encouraged to examine themselves in terms of privilege, power and access to resources, and to articulate how the power they have impacts upon their clients. The idea is to develop critical consciousness throughout training and continuing into practice, and to adopt the same type of ecological thinking about themselves that they will go on to apply to clients. Self-awareness will also need trainees to examine where they stand on global political and social issues, and their own possibilities and limitations for social action (Sloan, 2005).

There is wide agreement that skills development for social justice work is best achieved through work with community intervention projects (Adams, 2007; Ali et al., 2008; O'Brien et al., 2006). It is through practical experience that students will gain the skills of outreach work, collaboration, advocacy and prevention, all key to social justice approaches. One of the most difficult skills to enable trainees to learn is how and when to take no action. Sometimes it suffices to accompany those living in conditions of oppression (Moane, 2003); Edge et al. put it thus:

> We are suggesting a process of walking alongside, listening to and witnessing the realities of the lives of people living poverty – a process of accompaniment. It is just this support and solidarity that may offer itself as a different form of psychological work. Instead of rushing in to use our expertise to help people or their circumstances change, it is often enough to walk alongside them and publicly witness their struggles. (2004: 30–31)

It is important to remember, though, that a social justice curriculum needs to be underpinned by an appropriate pedagogy. Due attention needs to be paid to power and power sharing, collaboration, decision making, learning by doing, group facilitation, the use of participative learning and development techniques, an attitude and climate of openness to learning and continual self-awareness and responsiveness to feedback from students.

There will be some experienced practitioners who want to extend their knowledge and skills in the direction of community counselling psychology. Several psychology departments now teach community psychology and it may be possible for practitioners to take individual units for continuing professional development (CPD) purposes (see the community psychology resource websites www.cphe.org.uk and www.compsy.org.uk). Professional doctorates offer opportunities for new and reflexive practice, and a number of universities offer these, too. However, perhaps more in the spirit of community practice would be a self-designed CPD activity where practitioners take on a new, more community oriented project, and seek either the supervision of a community counselling psychologist or a group of peers, via an action learning set – interprofessional, if possible.

It will not be easy to change the training curriculum as there is still not widespread agreement that a social justice agenda should be adopted by counselling psychologists, and there will be organizational and individual barriers to change. The reasons to work towards acceptance of a social justice curriculum are compelling, as Lewis et al. (1998: 23–24) suggests (in relation to counsellors, but equally applicable to counselling psychologists):

> Their work brings … counsellors face to face with the victims of poverty, racism, sexism and stigmatization: of political, economic, and social systems that leave individuals feeling powerless; of governing bodies that deny their responsibility to respond; of social norms that encourage isolation. In the face of these realities, counsellors have no choice but to promote positive change in those systems that directly impact the psychological well-being of their clients or to blame the victims. (1998: 23–24)

REFERENCES

Adams, E.M. (2007) 'Moving from contemplation to preparation: Is counseling psychology ready to embrace culturally responsive prevention?', *The Counseling Psychologist*, 35 (6): 840–849.

Ali, S.R., Liu, W.M., Mahmood, A. and Arguello, J. (2008) 'Social justice and applied psychology: Practical ideas for training the next generation of psychologists', *Journal for Social Action in Counseling and Psychology*, 1 (2): 1–13.

Boneham, M. and Sixsmith, J. (2003) 'Older men's participation in community life: Notions of social capital, health, and empowerment', *Ageing International*, 28 (4): 372–388.

Bronfenbrenner, U. (1979) *The Ecology of Human Development*. Cambridge, MA: Harvard University Press.

Burton, M. and Kagan, C. (2008) 'Making the psychological political – challenges for community psychology'. Paper presented to the World Congress on Community Psychology, Lisbon, 4 June.

Burton, M., Kagan, C., Boyle, S. and Harris, C. (2007) 'History of community psychology in the UK', in S.M. Reich, M. Riemer, I. Prilleltensky and M. Montero (eds), *International Community Psychology: History and Theories*. London: Palgrave. pp. 221–239.

Chinman, M.J. and Linney, J.A. (1998) 'Toward a model of adolescent empowerment: Theoretical and empirical evidence', *The Journal of Primary Prevention*, 18 (4): 393–413.

Corcoran, T. (2007) 'Counselling in a discursive world', *International Journal for the Advancement of Counselling*, 29 (2): 111–122.

Crethar, H.C., Rivera, E.T. and Nash, S. (2008) 'In search of common threads: Linking multicultural, feminist, and social justice counseling paradigms. (Expanding cultural considerations)', *Journal Counseling and Development*, 86 (3): 269–278.

Drewery, W. (2004) 'Conferencing in schools: Punishment, restorative justice, and the productive importance of the process of conversation', *Journal of Community & Applied Social Psychology*, 14 (5): 332–344.

Edge, I., Kagan, C. and Stewart, A. (2004) 'Living poverty: Surviving on the edge', *Clinical Psychology*, 38: 28–31.

Fitch, C., Chaplin, R., Trend, C. and Collard, S. (2007) 'Debt and mental health: The role of psychiatrists', *Advances in Psychiatric Treatment*, 13: 194–202.

Freire, P. (1990) *Education for a Critical Consciousness*. New York: Continuum.

Fryer, D. (2003) 'What makes critical health psychology critical? A critical community public health psychological perspective', *Health Psychology Update*, 12 (3): 20–24.

Galvin, K., Sharples, A. and Jackson, D. (2001) 'Citizens Advice Bureaux in general practice: An illuminative evaluation', *Health & Social Care in the Community*, 8 (4): 277–282.

Goodman, L.A., Liang, B., Helms, J.E., Latta, R.E., Sparks, E. and Weintraub, S.R. (2004) 'Training counseling psychologists as social justice agents', *The Counseling Psychologist*, 32 (6): 793–836.

Hatcher, S. (1994) 'Debt and deliberate self poisoning', *British Journal Psychiatry*, 164: 111–114.

Hintikka, J., Kontula, O., Saarinen, P., Tauskanan, A., Koskela, K. and Vünamäki, H. (1998) 'Debt and suicidal behaviour in the Finnish general population', *Acta Psychiatrica Scandinavica*, 98 (66): 493–496.

Holland, S. (1991) 'From private symptom to public action', *Feminism and Psychology*, 1 (1): 58–62.

Holland, S. (1992) 'From social abuse to social action', in J. Ussher and P. Nicholson (eds), *Gender Issues in Clinical Psychology*. London: Routledge. pp. 68–77.

Kagan, C. (2008) 'Arts, social identity and health: From individual to collective gain?' Paper presented to BPS seminar 'Arts and Health: Psycho-social perspectives on arts for well-being and social inclusion. Day 1: Psycho-social understandings of arts for health', Manchester, 19 May.

Kagan, C. and Burton, M. (2000) 'Pre-figurative action research: An alternative basis for critical psychology?', *Annual Review of Critical Psychology*, 2: 73–88.

Kagan, C. and Burton, M. (2001) *Critical Community Psychological Praxis for the 21st Century.* Manchester: IOD Research Group.

Kagan, C. and Burton, M. (2005a) 'Community psychological perspectives with people with learning difficulties', *Clinical Psychology*, 150 (June): 31–36.

Kagan, C. and Burton, M. (2005b) 'Marginalization', in G. Nelson and I. Prilleltensky (eds), *Community Psychology: In Pursuit of Wellness and Liberation.* London: Macmillan/Palgrave. pp. 293–308.

Kagan, C., Duckett, P., Lawthom, R. and Burton, M. (2005) 'Community psychology and disabled people', in D. Goodley and R. Lawthom (eds), *Disability and Psychology: Critical Introductions and Reflections.* London: Palgrave.

Kilroy, A., Garner, C., Parkinson, C., Kagan, C. and Senior, P. (2007) 'Towards Transformation: Exploring the impact of culture, creativity and the arts on health and wellbeing'. A consultation report for the Critical Friends event, Manchester, Arts for Health.

Lawthom, R., Sixsmith, J. and Kagan, C. (2007) 'Interrogating power: The case of arts and mental health in community projects', *Journal Community Applied Social Psychology*, 17 (4): 268–279.

Lee, C. (2007) 'Social justice: A moral imperative for counsellors', *Professional Counselling Digest. ACAPCD-07.* Available at http://counselingoutfitters.com/ACAPCD/ACAPCD-07.pdf, accessed 23 June 2008.

Lewis, J.A. and Arnold, M.S. (1998) 'From multiculturalism to social action', in C.C. Lee and G.R. Walz (eds), S*ocial Action: A Mandate for Counselors.* Alexandra, VA: American Counseling Association and ERIC Counseling and Student Services Clearinghouse. pp. 51–65.

Lewis, J.A., Lewis, N.D., Daniels, J.A. and D'Andrea, M.J. (1998) 'Community counseling: Empowerment strategies for a diverse society', Pacific Grove, CA: Brooks/Cole, cited in J.A. Lewis and M.S. Arnold, 'From multiculturalism to social action', in C.C.Lee and G.R. Walz (eds), *Social Action: A Mandate for Counselors.* Alexandra, VA: American Counseling Association and ERIC Counseling and Student Services Clearinghouse. pp. 51–65.

McWhirter, B.T. and McWhirter, E.H. (2007) 'Toward an emancipatory communitarian approach to the practice of psychology training', in E. Aldarondo (ed.), *Advancing Social Justice Through Clinical Practice.* Mahwah, NJ: Lawrence Erlbaum.

Melluish, S. and Bulmer, D. (1999) 'Rebuilding solidarity: An account of a men's health action project', *Journal of Community & Applied Social Psychology*, 9 (2): 93–100.

Milne, D.L. (1999) *Social Therapy: A Guide to Social Support Interventions for Mental Health Practitioners.* Chichester: Wiley.

MIND (2008) *In the Red: Debt and Mental Health.* London: MIND. Available at www.mind.org.uk/NR/rdonlyres/B8ACA0C3-C16C-45DE-886D-4F0745A1C9D/0/Mw08reportWeb.pdf, accessed 5 July 2008.

Moane, G. (1999) *Gender and Colonialism: A Psychological Analysis of Oppresison and Liberation.* Basingstoke: Palgrave Macmillan.

Moane, G. (2003) 'Bridging the personal and the political: Practices for a liberation psychology', *American Journal of Community Psychology*, 31 (1–2): 91–101.

Nelson, G. and Prilleltensky, I. (2005) *Community Psychology: In pursuit of Liberation and Wellbeing.* Basingstoke: Palgrave Macmillan.

O'Brien, K., Patel, S., Hensler-McGinnis, N. and Kaplan, N. (2006) 'Empowering undergraduate students to be agents of social change: An innovative service learning course in counseling psychology', in R.L. Toporek, L.H. Gerstein, N.A. Fouad, G. Roysircar and T. Israel (eds), *Handbook for Social Justice in Counseling Psychology: Leadership, Vision and Action.* New York: Sage. Ch. 5.

O'Connor P. (2001) 'Supporting mothers: Issues in a Community Mothers programme', *Community, Work & Family*, 4 (1): 63–85.

Pearce, N. and Smith, G.D. (2003) 'Is social capital the key to inequalities in health?', *American Journal Public Health*, 93 (1): 122–129.

Perkins, D. and Zimmerman, M.A. (1995) 'Empowerment theory, research and application', *American Journal Community Psychology*, 23 (5): 569–579.

Prilleltensky, I. (2001) 'Value based praxis in community psychology: Moving toward social justice and social action', *American Journal of Community Psychology*, 29: 747–78.

Prilleltensky, I. and Nelson, G. (2002) *Doing Psychology Critically: Making a Difference in Diverse Settings*. New York: Palgrave Macmillan.

Putnam, R.D. (1995) '"Bowling Alone": America's declining social capital', *Journal of Democracy*, 6 (1): 65–78.

Reich, S., Rimmer, M., Prilleltensky, I. and Montero, M. (eds) (2007) *International Community Psychology: History and Theories*. New York: Springer.

Rojano, R. (2007) 'The practice of community family therapy', in E. Aldarondo (ed.), *Advancing Social Justice Through Clinical Practice*. Mahwah, NJ: Lawrence Erlbaum. pp. 245–263.

Russell-Mayhew, S. (2007) 'Eating disorders as social justice issues: Implications for research and practice', *Journal for Social Action in Counseling and Psychology*, 1 (1): 1–13. Available at www.psysr.org/jsacp, accessed 4 July 2008.

Sainsbury, R., Nice, K., Nevill, C., Wood, M., Dixon, J. and Mitchell, M. (2008) *The Pathways Advisory Service: Placing Employment Advisers in GP Surgeries*. London: Department for Work and Pensions Research Report, No. 494/York, SPRU.

Sarason, S. (1972) *The Creation of Settings and the Future Societies*. San Francisco, CA: Jossey-Bass.

Schoon, I. and Bartley, M. (2008) 'The role of human capability and resilience', *The Psychologist*, 21 (1): 24–27.

Sharpe, J. and Bostock, J. (2002) *Supporting People with Debt and Mental Health Problems: Community Psychology*. Northumberland: Health Action Zone.

Siddiquee, A., Kagan, C., de Santis, C. and Ali, R. (2008) '"We can find ourselves in them and they can find themselves in us." Evaluation of *INTERGEN*: Intergenerational understanding, wellbeing and social capital.' Manchester: RIHSC.

Sixsmith, J. (1999) 'Working in the hidden economy: The experience of unemployed men in the UK', *Community, Work and Family*, 2 (3): 257–277.

Sixsmith, J., Duckett, P. and Kagan, C. (2005) '"I leave me outside when I come in school and pick myself back up on the way home." Young people's perspectives on healthy schools', *PlayRights*, XXVI (2): 26–32.

Sloan, T. (2005) 'Global work-related suffering as a priority for vocational psychology', *The Counseling Psychologist*, 33 (2): 207–214.

Spandler, H. and Warner, S. (eds) (2007) *Beyond Fear and Control: Working with young People Who Self Harm*. Ross-on-Wye: PCCS books.

Speight, S.L. and Vera, E.M. (2004) 'A social justice agenda: Ready or not?', *The Counseling Psychologist*, 32 (1): 109–118.

Taylor, S.J. (1994) 'Debt and deliberate self-harm', *British Journal Psychiatry*, 164: 848–849.

Thatcher, M. and Manktelow, K.I. (2007) 'The cost of individualism', *Counselling Psychology Review*, 22: 31–88.

Thorp, S. (2007) 'Spanning continents: Practice: Liverpool project Building Bridges supports people from ethnic minorities who face social exclusion', *Community Care*, 22 February. Available at www.communitycare.co.uk/Articles/2007/02/22/103528/practice-liverpool-project-building-bridges-supports-people-from-ethnic-minorities-who-face-social.html, accessed 8 August 2008.

Toporek, R.L. and McNally, C.J. (2006) 'Social justice training in counseling psychology: Needs and innovations', in R.L. Toporek, L.H. Gerstein, N.A. Fouad, G. Roysircar and T. Israel (eds), *Handbook for Social Justice in Counseling Psychology: Leadership, Vision and Action.* New York: Sage. Ch. 3.

Vera, E.M. and Speight, S.L. (2003) 'Multicultural competence, social justice and counseling psychology', *The Counseling Psychologist*, 31 (3): 253–272.

Vera, E.M. and Speight, S.L. (2007) 'Advocacy, outreach and prevention: Integrating social action roles in professional training', in E. Aldarondo (ed.), *Advancing Social Justice Through Clinical Practice.* Mahwah, NJ: Lawrence Erlbaum.

Watts, R.J., Williams, N.C. and Jagers, R.J. (2003) 'Sociopolitical development', *American Journal of Community Psychology*, 31 (1–2): 185–194.

Zimmerman, M.A. (2000) 'Empowerment theory: Psychological organizational and community levels of analysis', in J. Rappaport and E. Seidman (eds), *Handbook of Community Psychology.* New York: Springer.

PART VI

PROFESSIONAL AND ETHICAL ISSUES

Whatever the theoretical approach or client group, there are a number of areas of professional or ethical concern that apply to all areas of practice. The chapters in this part address some of these important aspects of practice. Both the British Psychological Society and the British Association for Counselling and Psychotherapy have recently revised their respective ethical guidelines and placed emphasis on thinking issues through in terms of ethical principles and values in contrast to more codified rules of conduct. This is also apparent in the approach adopted by the HPC. The shift in emphasis is significant and is sometimes characterized as a move away from a 'prescriptive' towards an 'aspirational' approach to ethical practice. The implications of this are explored in Chapter 26, whilst Chapter 27 highlights the importance of familiarity with the legal frameworks that constrain practice. Legal issues often relate to, and may even conflict with, ethical concerns and some, such as those arising in relation to confidentiality, are of general concern whilst others are more specific to particular areas of practice, such as acting as an expert witness or working with children.

The future direction of counselling psychology will be affected by decisions taken about training, and Chapter 28 explores some of the issues and controversies relating to the training of the next generation of practitioners. There are continuing debates about the role of personal development, including personal therapy, in the training and continuing professional development of counselling psychologists and these are considered in Chapter 29, whilst Chapter 30 reflects on the value of supervision and raises some challenging questions about this requirement.

26

ETHICAL ISSUES IN COUNSELLING PSYCHOLOGY

Carol Shillito-Clarke

Over the last four years, there has been an average of nine complaints a year made against counselling psychologists (BPS, 2008). This represents a small proportion of the membership of the Division, but even nine complaints each year are too many. So if counselling psychologists are not renowned for behaving unethically, what is the purpose of this chapter? Many of us feel strongly that ethics is about more than resolving dilemmas and avoiding being the subject of a complaint; it is at the heart of evolving best practice. So this chapter is about promoting and reinforcing ethical attitudes and behaviours, and understanding what underlies them.

A FRAMEWORK FOR THINKING ABOUT ETHICS

The background

Since the time of Aristotle, people have debated the nature of the person and what it means to live a 'good' life. Ethics, or moral philosophy, concerns the study and development of guidelines by which human character, relations and actions may be judged as good or bad, right or wrong. But the nature of ethics is neither simple nor static, and what is considered 'ethical' varies between professions and evolves over time, reflecting developments in thought and practice. Professional ethics are usually defined in the relevant professional body's public statement of appropriate ethical conduct. Such published statements change over time. Indeed, as of 1 July 2009, the Health Professions Council (HPC) has taken over the regulatory functions of the BPS. The HPC's *Standards of Conduct, Performance and Ethics* now supercedes the BPS *Code of Ethics and Conduct* (BPS, 2006) and all subsystems' published *Guidelines*. The HPC state that: 'The standards are written in broad terms and designed to apply to all registrants as far as possible. However, we recognise that some of the standards may not apply to all the professions we regulate or to the practice of some of the registrants' (HPC, 2008: 4). So how the *Standards* will be interpreted for, and applied to, the practice of psychology remains to be seen.

Although the status of the BPS *Code* is now aspirational rather than obligatory, it is still the best guide to ethics for all psychologists. In particular it emphasizes the importance of ethical awareness and reflective practice rather than mere unthinking adherence to a set of rules. As the *Code* makes explicit: 'thinking is not optional' (2006: 6) and ethical decisions should be based on rational principles. Accordingly, I begin this chapter with a model of ethical reasoning. I go on to consider the concept of the ethical practitioner: their values and how they conduct themselves and their relationships, whether with therapy clients or others in supervision, training, management or consultancy. I will also consider some of the key areas of ethical difficulty in practice and outline the model of decision making proposed by BPS 2006. In some sections I have included examples of ethical dilemmas and it must be emphasized that although these are based on experience, they do not refer to actual people or incidents.

A model of moral and ethical reasoning

The model of ethical reasoning devised by Beauchamp and Childress (1989) is the starting point for conceptualizing ethics in counselling psychology. This model describes the relationship between individual conscience, rules, principles and philosophical theories and offers a structure for reasoning and problem solving. The model consists of two levels of ethical reasoning: the intuitive level and the critical-evaluative level.

The intuitive level

The intuitive level represents the immediate response of the individual's conscience. This is based on their moral upbringing and experience. While this is often a sound guide for ethical behaviour in simple circumstances, it is unlikely to be sufficiently well articulated to cope with more complex and challenging circumstances. For example, under time pressure, in the face of cultural differences or when subjected to special pleading, emotions may confound rather than inform thought.

The critical-evaluative level

The critical-evaluative level is therefore required in order to illuminate, refine and guide moral reasoning. It comprises three hierarchically related sub-levels:

- Rules, specific laws and codes of conduct.
- Principles, or universally applicable values of equal merit.
- Theories, or philosophical ideas about the nature and meaning of human existence. This may be extended to include the values underpinning such theories.

Rules

Rules or professional codes of conduct provide an extrinsic, regulatory framework that is primarily for the protection of clients. They identify baseline standards of ethical practice that are acceptable to the majority of members and with which all members must comply or face sanctions.

However, codes of conduct have their limitations. A code can provide only a broad framework for ethical behaviour, overlooking the more subtle ethical conflicts of interests. Therefore it is possible to comply with the broader obligation of a code while behaving in a way many would consider unethical. Uncritical conformity itself may actually be unethical (Pattinson, 1999). A code may not even address some of the basic aims and methods of the profession (Thatcher, 2006). Codes of conduct rarely provide guidance on how ethical dilemmas may be prioritized and resolved and may themselves be the source of ethical problems. For instance, an exploitative, vengeful or disturbed client may seek to use the code unfairly against a practitioner (Holmes et al., 2000).

Principles

Principles are more abstract than rules. Different authorities prefer different moral principles. Beauchamp and Childress (1989) considered that respect for autonomy, beneficence, non-maleficence and justice had prima facie validity. In addition, Kitchener (1984) considered the principle of fidelity to be of particular importance for psychologists.

e BACP's *Ethical Framework for Good Practice in Counselling and Psychotherapy* has :luded self-respect: 'fostering the practitioner's self-knowledge and care of self')07: 03). Recently, Bond has also suggested that therapeutic ethics are missing an intrinsic 'ethic of trust' to complement other ethical principles. He defines it as 'one that supports the development of reciprocal relationships of sufficient strength to withstand the relational challenges of difference and inequality and the existential challenges of risk and uncertainty' (Bond, 2005: 82). The BPS (2006), following both the Canadian Psychological Association and the European Federation of Psychologists' Associations (EFPA), has chosen *respect, competence, responsibility* and *integrity* as its key principles:

- *Respect* recognizes the dynamics of power and promotes anti-oppressive practice by upholding individuals' autonomy. Standards of respect include the maximization of the client's informed choice and self-determination and their right to privacy and confidentiality. The concept of choice also raises theoretical and practical questions about the individual's ability to know, and distinguish between, their conscious and unconscious desires.

- *Competence* relates to the personal and professional knowledge and skills of the psychologist, including their ethical reasoning. It requires awareness of the limits of professional knowledge, skill and experience, both pre-and post-training, and the ability to recognize physical or psychological impairment adversely affecting performance. The practitioner's competence is an important contributor to avoiding harm, as is their awareness of the differences between themselves and their clients. Competence also underlies the requirement for continuing professional development (CPD), supervision and ethical behaviour.

- *Responsibility* covers the use of power and the avoidance of harm and exploitation in the name of psychology. Responsibility also includes an awareness of the need to manage and terminate work appropriately. The principle is considered particularly important in the conduct of research and the protection of participants in research work, from initial contracting to debriefing.

- *Integrity* is about being honest, clear, accurate and fair both in what is offered and to whom. It recognizes that personal and professional relationships may be hard to keep separate and require strong boundaries. Integrity also covers the avoidance of conflicts of interests and the appropriate exercise of power. It precludes sexual exploitation and harassment.

- *Fidelity*, the principle emphasized by Kitchener (1984) as especially important for counselling psychologists, is not included explicitly in the BPS *Code* but is implied in the previous four principles. It is considered fundamental to the therapeutic relationship, which depends on trustworthy and unpretentious communication, clear boundaries and respect for the individual's autonomy. Good contracting, informed consent and confidentiality are relevant not only to the therapeutic work of counselling psychologists, but also to all the domains in which they work. How these five principles relate to counselling psychology practice is explored throughout the chapter.

Theories

Theories provide the third and most abstract level of the Beauchamp and Childress model. The two types of ethical theory that have traditionally been used to address ethical questions are: teleological or consequentialist theories and deontological or principle-based theories. In recent years, virtue ethics has also become an important theoretical framework (Tjeltveit 1999).

- *Teleological or consequentialist theories* consider that the aim of ethical action is to maximize happiness and well-being and that it is the consequences of acts that determine the extent to which they may be considered 'good'. Arguments against these theories emphasize that happiness is not the only thing that matters, that it is very difficult to calculate and predict consequences, and that maximization of happiness does not necessarily imply fairness and justice.
- *Deontological or principle-based theories* propose that morality should be consistent, impartial and based on reason rather than authoritarian decree. They suggest that rules, which can be stated as principles, are not absolutes but prima facie obligations (that is, each principle is binding unless, in a given situation, there is a more significant principle that overrides it).
- *Virtue ethics* go beyond the teleological or deontological approaches by considering the nature of the person and the ideals to which practitioners should aspire. Being a good, moral person is considered more important than acting correctly according to some abstract rules. The virtuous agent is one who 'is motivated to do good; possesses vision and discernment; realises the role of affect or emotion in assessing and judging proper conduct; has a high degree of self-understanding and awareness; and, perhaps most importantly, is connected with and understands the mores of his or her community and the importance of community in moral decision making, policy setting and character development and is alert to the legitimacy of client diversity in these respects' (Meara et al., 1996: 28).

Meara et al. (1996) also propose four key virtues for psychologists. These are prudence, integrity, respectfulness and benevolence. These would seem very close to the values underpinning the BPS ethical principles and also the 'Personal Moral Qualities' suggested by BACP (2007: 4), which also include: empathy, sincerity, resilience, humility, competence, fairness, wisdom and courage. Given the importance that virtue ethics places on the person of the practitioner and their context, I would suggest that complementing principle ethics with virtue ethics is particularly relevant to counselling psychology. This proposal will be developed in the section on the person of the counselling psychologist.

The hierarchical structure of Beauchamp and Childress' model is important for moral reasoning and problem solving. Because the levels are interrelated, the solution to an ethical problem, which is difficult at one level, may become clearer at a more abstract level. For example, how the counselling psychologist addresses an individual's right to commit suicide (a legal rule) will be influenced by the principles of respect for the client's autonomy and the principle of responsibility to avoid harm. These principles, in turn, reflect different philosophical theories about the meaning and sanctity of life.

VALUES, ETHICS AND POWER IN COUNSELLING PSYCHOLOGY

Values and ethics

Values underpin all ethical theories and principles. Because a person's values direct their thinking and behaviour, consciously and unconsciously, it is important to explore their relationship to ethical practice. As with ethics, there is no single definition of 'value'. Values vary according to the philosophical and religious beliefs of the individual and the time and culture within which they operate (Holmes and Lindley, 1991; Tjeltveit, 1999). Each individual builds up a value system through cultural socialization processes and experience, mediated by history and environment. Many values are introjected or accepted without question in childhood. So it may be difficult to judge the extent to which our values and our positive or negative perceptions of others' values are shaped by our individual context. Where values are questioned and reflected upon, they may be affirmed or they may be rejected and different values substituted. In an increasingly pluralistic society, values vary widely, even within a single community. Neighbourliness may be perceived as nosiness; individuality may be construed as abdication of social responsibility.

> Before you read on, review your own values and what you know of the values of others with whom you work and the context in which you work.

Counselling psychology practitioners differ from one another, from their clients and from other professionals in how they conceive and value psychological health and dysfunction. The values inherent in preferred theoretical models determine the kinds of therapeutic interventions made, such as those promoting rationality or spontaneity, emotional expression or impulse control, subjectivity or objectivity. Such differences can lead to ethical problems. Additional ethical problems may arise from the divergence in the value systems of scientific psychology and practice-based psychotherapy; what Meara et al. (1996) call the 'language of evidence'. Science values objectivity, accuracy, quantification and predictability. Therapy values subjectivity, description and the meaning and consequences of actions.

The situation is further complicated by the value systems of politics and commerce, which determine the context in which most practitioners work. With recent government initiatives such as Increased Access to Psychological Therapies (IAPT) and the economically-driven insistence on the use of evidenced-based therapies, predominantly cognitive-behavioural therapy (CBT), old ethical questions have re-emerged. What constitutes 'well-being' and what is the role of therapy? For instance:

> Monica is referred by her GP for therapy for anxiety and depression. Her partner's insurance scheme agrees to fund six sessions of therapy. In the course of therapy it becomes clear that Monica's problems are located in her relationship but her partner refuses to accept any responsibility, blaming her work. Monica's parents are also concerned about the outcome. At the end of the six sessions, Monica has techniques for managing the anxiety and some insight into the aetiology of the depression. She believes she can return to work but feels she needs to continue taking medication. Her GP agrees. Although Monica says she would like to continue, she refuses further therapy because her partner will not support private fees.

Although the counselling psychologist has behaved ethically throughout, such a case raises a number of ethical issues. Monica is enabled to return to work after the contracted number of sessions, has a better awareness of her difficulty, is better able to manage her symptoms and is apparently making a choice about her relationship. But has Monica's therapy done more harm than good by questioning and potentially destabilizing the nature of the relationship; by giving her means to manage her symptoms without facilitating their removal; and by colluding with a model of therapy provision that emphasizes brief intervention and seeks to individualize the problem? To what extent should practitioners compromise their integrity if their preferred therapeutic model is different from that of their employers?

Counselling psychologists with managerial responsibility may have particular ethical concerns about balancing the needs of the clients, trainees or supervisees against those of the institution or organization. To what extent should they defer to organizational values with which they disagree? For example:

> A Primary Care Trust is keen to bid for funds for a new treatment initiative. As the lead psychologist, Liz is responsible for the submission. If successful, she believes her department could help a large number of people. However, she is also aware that her department does not meet the pre-conditions required for the bid. If she is to be successful, she will have to be less than honest in how she presents the proposal. Her manager thinks she is being overly principled and not considering the needs of the patients and the longer-term effects on waiting lists.

Counselling psychology cannot be value-free. The promotion of personal values and beliefs as being those of counselling psychology is contrary to the profession's core values. Any action or attitude that discriminates on the grounds of race, gender, disability, class or religion, is unethical and illegal. The key issue thus becomes: who determines which values will predominate? This is where awareness of the ethical exercise of power becomes critical.

Power and ethics

Whenever there are differences in values and beliefs, and differences in perceived power, there is the opportunity for one person to abuse or exploit another. Counselling psychology upholds anti-oppressive practice, that is, practice which addresses 'interconnections between issues of power within the therapeutic relationship and the cultural and socio-political contexts' (Strawbridge, 1994: 6). Hence the fundamental importance of the principles of responsibility and integrity in all counselling psychology practice.

In therapeutic practice, as in all branches of the 'caring' professions, the practitioner is in a position of power relative to the client. The client is psychologically vulnerable by virtue of having a problem or difficulty which he or she feels cannot be resolved unaided. The client who wishes to be helped must give the practitioner personal information about him or herself. Such knowledge, often about something of which the client is afraid or ashamed, gives away further power. It is therefore important that the client can trust the practitioner to use that knowledge to help or empower them rather than use it against them. There is a parallel position of vulnerability for the supervisee in relation to the supervisor, especially whilst in training.

A practitioner also holds power by claiming experience, expertise and the right to be paid. Counselling psychologists whose values are rooted in the humanistic tradition may wish to argue for a position of equality with their clients. However, it must be remembered that the client may have a different perception of the relationship, particularly at the beginning of the work. Indeed, endowing the therapist with the power to heal may be an essential part of some people's culturally determined perceptions of the counselling psychologist's role. The label 'psychologist' itself carries numerous fearful connotations, and may be confused with the label of 'psychiatrist' or 'psychoanalyst' by lay people. This confusion may be compounded if psychometric tests or medical language are used.

A further point to be considered here is that of exercising power in the guise of responsibility *for* rather than responsibility *to* the client. The desire to assume some responsibility for the client and 'make it better' is one way, common among helping professionals, of construing – or misconstruing – the 'duty of care'. As Guggenbuhl-Craig points out: 'In general, the power drive is given freest rein when it can appear under the cloak of objective and moral rectitude' (1971: 10). Again, some clients expect their therapist to take a degree of responsibility for them. However, taking such responsibility may conflict with respecting the client's autonomy. Many counselling psychologists will, at times, struggle with the finer distinctions between their professional responsibility, their personal desire to take control for the client and trusting the client to know what is best for him or her self. The ethical imperative for all counselling psychologists is therefore to be self-aware, particularly in relation to the use of power (Lakin, 1991).

As I have suggested in the section on virtue ethics, the person of the counselling psychologist is a significant factor both in what they do and how they relate to others. In the next section I discuss the foundations of the person of the counselling psychologist under the headings of competence, fitness to practice, self-care, and ethical mindfulness. In the following section, I explore aspects of ethical relationships practice under the following headings: defining the client; respect for the client's autonomy; clear contracts; obtaining informed consent; confidentiality; sensitivity to dual and multiple relationships; and sexual relationships.

THE PERSON OF THE COUNSELLING PSYCHOLOGIST

Competence

I discussed competence earlier as an ethical principle, but it is also a practical requirement. Throughout practice, unexpected issues arise that challenge the competence of the practitioner. For example:

> Tony is a trainee-counselling psychologist who has been working with a client who unexpectedly discloses her deep desire for gender reassignment. Tony feels he is not yet adequately trained to work with the client and would prefer to refer her to a specialist. However, the client feels that she has, for the first time, established a therapeutic relationship which can be trusted. Tony's manager is not aware of any local facilities to which the client could be referred and is happy for Tony to continue to work with her. Tony's supervisor has no experience of working with, and is personally unsympathetic to, gender reassignment, and has reservations about Tony working outside his current area of competence.

This example raises a number of questions. To what extent are knowledge and skills of working with a specific problem important if the client trusts the therapeutic relationship and there is little other help available? What kind and how much training are needed to claim 'competence'? How does one become truly competent without experience gained from mentored practice in what Vygotsky described as the 'zone of proximal development' (1986)?

Fitness to practise

Fitness to practise could be regarded as a subset of competence. Recognizing impairment, together with the courage and humility to own it, is intrinsic to being ethical. Given the intersubjective nature of the therapeutic relationship, a vulnerable client may be put at risk if the therapist's ability to perceive and respond appropriately is even temporarily reduced. For instance:

Although the break-up of his primary relationship has devastated and depressed Sam, he insists on coming to work. Despite an increasing number of mistakes and obvious tiredness, he claims that his experience is making him more sensitive to his clients and that it would be unethical to take time away from two or three whom he regards as being at risk.

The question here is: when is 'good enough' not good enough ethically? Any lack of awareness of, or disregard for, the 'shadow aspects' of personal limitations may increase the practitioner's vulnerability. He or she risks sliding or being coerced into unethical behaviour to protect personal self-image or esteem (Guggenbuhl-Craig, 1971; Page, 1999). Challenging others' perceived impairment and providing good remedial support are ethical requirements in developing competence (Forrest et al., 1999; Lamb, 1999).

Self-care

Counselling psychology encourages reflexive practice, recognizing that in any interaction between client and practitioner each will affect the other. The effect is not always positive. Schore (2003), Wilson and Thomas (2004) and Rothschild (2006) amongst others, cite research on the effects of prolonged exposure to clients in states of high affect and the subsequent negative consequences for the health of the practitioner.

Sadly, not all clients are well-intentioned towards their practitioner. Holmes et al., (2000) suggest that stalking of therapists is an under-reported problem. Bullying and harassment by colleagues are not unknown. Recognizing and dealing with such psychological attacks against the self and bringing allegations of misconduct against a colleague or employing organization (whistle-blowing) can be seen as upholding the principle of integrity. However, such actions may also be perceived as contravening the principle of responsibility by 'bringing the Society or the reputation of the profession into disrepute' (BPS, 2006: 17). Anyone involved in such dilemmas may benefit from the advice available from charities such as Witness (the former POPAN) or Freedom to Care. BPS further advises all psychologists to carry personal indemnity insurance over and above any provision made by employers. In all such difficulties, keeping clear records, regular monitoring and asserting the boundaries around personal as well as professional accessibility become essential. Using supervision and finding as much personal support outside the work relationship as possible, including personal therapy, is part of an ethical response (BPS DCoP, 2005, 2007).

Ethical mindfulness

Being consciously aware of our values and asking moral questions of ourselves, of our practice and of our professional relationships, as a matter of routine not just when decisions may be controversial, has been termed 'ethical mindfulness' (Bond, 2000: 242). Counselling psychologists have always taken a strong position within the BPS over the importance of self-awareness and working reflexively within the relationship. Which is why personal psychological therapy and regular, ongoing supervision are considered to be essential requirements for ethical mindfulness and best practice (BPS DCoP, 2005).

ETHICAL RELATIONSHIPS

Counselling psychology is now an established branch of applied psychology, requiring a combination of good psychological and therapeutic practice skills. At its heart lies the relationship between the practitioner and the client – the person or persons for whom the practitioner is working. The quality of the relationship between the counselling psychologist and their client is a key factor in determining the success of the work (Roth and Fonagy, 1996; Meara et al., 1996). This applies to relationships with therapy clients, supervisees, trainees, employees and employing organizations, colleagues and other professionals. So who is the client?

Defining the 'client'

BPS defines clients as: 'any person or persons with whom a psychologist interacts on a professional basis' (2006: 5). So despite the theoretical emphasis on the therapist/client dyad, many other people may be implicated in the work of the counselling psychologist as in the cases of Monica and Liz described above. Partners, family members, employers of the client and the practitioner, supervisors, health-care referrers, insurance companies, training institutions and accrediting bodies such as the BPS may be 'secondary clients' (Shillito-Clarke 2003) or 'stakeholders' in the outcome, exerting overt or covert pressure on the counselling psychologist (Carroll, 1996).

Respect for the client's autonomy

The principle of respect requires recognition of others' autonomy and human rights. However, respect for the client's autonomy may challenge personal values and beliefs about the professional's duty of care and responsibility, particularly when an employing organization is also involved. For example:

> You work as a counselling psychologist in a rehabilitation unit's group home. Zara, who is recuperating from a serious head injury, has formed a close friendship with another patient and they want to become lovers. Neither patient has been sectioned and the ethos of the home is about normalization. Many of the staff disapprove, but should they attempt to dissuade them? Should the staff tell Zara's husband? How do you react and what do you think your role should be?

An ethical dilemma may easily arise when clients' beliefs, values, morals, needs, goals and understanding of their situation differ from those of the counselling psychologist and/or other interested parties. Differences of opinion may be exacerbated if practitioners are not aware of, and respectful towards, the clients' historically determined construction of their world and their racial and cultural beliefs. This is particularly significant in the case of the Western theoretical emphasis on the self, which undervalues the importance of self in relation to family, community and culture. The questions 'Whose "best interests" do I favour?' and 'Would I work differently if the client was of a different race/culture/ gender (or other significant 'difference')?' are crucial here and should be a part of the assessment of every dilemma.

Ethical issues relating to autonomy may also arise as a result of the practitioner's theoretical approach to the client (Spinelli, 1994). For example, a counselling psychologist trained in psychodynamic psychotherapy may believe that she or he is in a better position to interpret the client's unconscious processes than the client. To what extent is the client free to challenge or reject the interpretation? To what extent is a client receiving cognitive-behaviour therapy in a position to reject the concept of rational thought and choose what the therapist considers 'irrational' behaviour? The humanistic models place particular emphasis on respecting the client's autonomy. However, do all clients necessarily want or know how to use the responsibility of defining their own needs? Such questions may be easy to answer theoretically but the answers may be difficult to incorporate into practice. Ethics become important when the client challenges the perceived wisdom of the theory, or the authority of the counselling psychologist, or when the client does not respond to treatment or precipitates an unexpected outcome.

Clear contracts

A contract is a written or spoken agreement intended to be enforceable by law (Concise Oxford English Dictionary, 2000). Good ethical practice requires that a clear contract should be negotiated with each client. Such a contract recognizes that the parties involved have needs to be met and it draws a firm boundary around those needs. However clear the initial contract may be, unexpected circumstances can challenge the boundaries agreed and a review and renegotiation may be necessary. For example:

James was referred for therapy following a car accident for which he was not responsible. In talking about the trauma, James worked through a significant earlier experience, the emotional impact of which he had hitherto denied. Now James' solicitors require the release of his case notes for a legal hearing. The notes contain information about the earlier experience, which could be used to weaken James' current claim for compensation, and which could identify and compromise others. How do you proceed?

The ethical dilemmas that arise from such a case relate, in part, to the information James was given in the original therapeutic contract about the limits of confidentiality and his understanding of, and consent to, working within that contract. There are also broader questions about the rights of individuals to decide what personal information to withhold or to make public, and to whom.

Obtaining informed consent

For a contract to be meaningful, the client must be able to give 'valid consent' to the intended procedures and, where appropriate, confirm that they have been 'given ample opportunity to understand the nature, purpose and anticipated consequences of any professional services or research participation' (BPS, 2006: 12). The concept of obtaining consent may be clear in theory but less so in practice. There is a need to balance the client's right to freedom of choice against their ability to understand the arguments, evaluate the risks of participation and the consequences of refusing. This will depend in part on their motivation and their emotional and psychological state at the time.

Children, older people and those with learning difficulties may require special consideration. In such cases it is important to include the concepts of limited and intermittent competence in the decision-making process (Kitchener, 1984). Limited competence usually refers to those who have a limited capacity for making rational decisions, such as children and impaired adults. Intermittent competence refers to a fluctuating state of rationality, as may occur with Alzheimer's disease or psychosis. Such cases still require that the individual's choice be respected when possible and supported by responsible others.

The counselling psychologist has primary responsibility for identifying and eliminating or minimizing physical and psychological risks to the client. Because such risks depend largely on the individual's construction of the situation they may change over time. Unfortunately, our ability to accurately predict our future responses is generally poor (Gilbert, 2006). What to the client, or indeed the practitioner, seemed a good idea at the start of therapy may subsequently be regarded very differently.

Carroll (2005) also draws attention to the 'psychological contract'; the beliefs, assumptions and expectations that each person brings to any contract. Much of the psychological contract will be unspoken and un-negotiated but the client will carry the expectation of it being fulfilled and will feel let-down and perhaps deceived if it is not. Within the context of a team or an organization, where many people will have different ideas about the work and different values, the opportunities for such misunderstandings are multiplied.

Making clear contracts and gaining informed consent are ethically important in all the relationships in which counselling psychologists engage. Having made the parameters of the work clear and negotiated a contract for that work with the client, the ethical responsibility of the practitioner is the maintenance of the agreed boundaries and the protection of the client's confidentiality.

Confidentiality

The success of all 'talking' therapies rests on the premise that what one person says to another will be treated with respect and kept private. However, promising total confidentiality to the client is impractical and unethical. While a policy of confidentiality appears to uphold the principle of respect, it does not ensure the principle of responsibility and may threaten the principle of fidelity. If total confidentiality is impossible, a number of questions arise. Who determines the boundaries to protect the client and facilitate practice? Where are they drawn? What happens if the original situation changes over time as in the cases of Zara and James?

Confidentiality and the law

The relationship between ethics and the law is complex and subject to change. Practitioners have an ethical responsibility to avoid illegal activities (Bond, 2000). In Britain today there is a legal obligation for practitioners to disclose information concerning terrorism (Terrorism Act 2000) and drug trafficking (Drug Trafficking Act 1994). Under the Children Act (1989) the obligation to disclose information concerning child abuse is regarded somewhat differently unless one is working for one of the public authorities (Bond, 2000; Jones, 2000). Practitioners are also legally obliged to disclose information when summoned as a witness or subpoenaed by a court of law. The Data Protection Act 1998 and the Human Rights Act 1998 have both affected the interpretation of the laws concerning confidential information, with significant implications for practitioners. For instance, authorities such as the police, the Crown Prosecution Service or the Health and Safety Executive have the right to subpoena all forms of notes held by therapists and supervisors that identify a specific client. Such 'unused material' may be interpreted in a different light from that in which it was recorded for therapeutic purposes.

Counselling psychologists are advised by the BPS to be aware of the specific legal and ethical context of their work, the general legal requirements concerning giving and withholding information, and to inform their clients appropriately. The Divisions of Clinical Psychology and Counselling Psychology, and the BACP, have all prepared guidelines on confidentiality and case notes. But because legal requirements change, organization members are strongly advised to seek professional support and guidance as necessary (see also Jenkins, 2005). This is another aspect of self-care.

Holding confidentiality in exceptional circumstances

One of the most difficult ethical questions is when to break a client's confidentiality against their wishes when there is no legal imperative to do so. The principle of responsibility to oneself has to be weighed against respect for the client's autonomy (or that of a potential victim's) and the fidelity of the relationship. When is the exercise of such power genuinely beneficent?

While one can contract for emergency disclosures at the start of a relationship, it is particularly difficult, in highly-charged emotional situations, to know whether one is under- or over-reacting. Codes seem to agree that breaching confidentiality is acceptable if the practitioner has tried, and failed, to get the client's consent and if there has been consultation with an experienced colleague. But what of the 'duty of care' once a contract has ended? For example:

> Mary was working with Tom and Viv over the breakdown of their marriage. Viv was very depressed but refused to seek medical support or allow Mary to contact her GP. After many weeks, things seemed to be resolving and the couple decided to end therapy. Now Viv turns up at Mary's door, angry and very distressed. She says that if Mary won't help her, she will kill herself by crashing her car. What is Mary's responsibility and what can she do?

Counselling psychologists accountable to others for their work need to be aware of all relevant policies and legal requirements, as well as any discrepancy between their own values and attitudes and those of their employers.

Confidentiality and other relationships

Different contexts, cultural values and expectations concerning privacy of information need to be taken into account in considering where the boundaries of confidentiality should be drawn. During training, use of client material is needed to demonstrate the student's developing competence. Similarly, client material is sometimes used in research or other publications. In each circumstance the counselling psychologist takes on a dual role in relation to the client. An ethical conflict of interest may develop between the needs of the client and those of the practitioner. If material is used without the client's informed consent, the fidelity of the relationship is jeopardized. This applies as much to a student's 'client study' as to a thesis or research project. It is also difficult to predict whether a client, or other person mentioned in material placed in the public domain, will be recognized.

Care to preserve anonymity needs to be taken, not only in the recording of information about clients but also in its transmission, transportation and storage. This is particularly important with audio and videotapes and the use of the Internet. As with case notes, the ethical tension is between protecting the clients' confidentiality, sharing essential information and holding evidence to validate one's work. The falsification or suppression of information about clients to protect the practitioner is, of course, always unethical.

Confidentiality after death

Dealing with an unexpected end to therapy or supervision is not a matter that is usually discussed in the initial contract, although it is a significant part of the fidelity of the relationship. The client's confidentiality continues after their death 'unless legal and ethical considerations demand otherwise' (BPS DCoP, 2005) and may be a matter of discussion. The death of the practitioner is rarely considered, although it can have enormous repercussions for the client. Counselling psychologists are expected to make provision for emergency disclosure of information in the event of their own death or prolonged, involuntary absence, perhaps owing to a serious accident. In keeping with the principle of responsibility, appointing a professional colleague as an executor to take over a practice may be the most efficient way to support the practitioner's clients and family.

Sensitivity to dual and multiple relationships

Confidentiality is just one aspect of practice that may be ethically compromised when the practitioner holds one or more relationships with another person. The Good Work Project found that the wearing of 'too many professional hats' simultaneously or trying to switch between possibly incompatible 'hats' was a cause of ethical conflict and 'compromised work' (Seider et al., 2007). But not all dual and multiple relationships are avoidable or unethical. Woskett (1999) cites other writers' good arguments for holding them. In some communities it may be difficult to avoid meeting clients or supervisees in another capacity. Indeed, in some cultures it would be considered strange or even antisocial to refuse to work with a colleague's friend or relative.

Some personal relationships may pre-date the professional relationship. For example, partners, one or both of whom are counselling psychologists, may be involved in the same course or may elect to work or do research together. The problem is that dual relationships may call into play subtle and not always conscious forces. They can then involve others, such as colleagues or course participants, who may feel professionally compromised or disadvantaged if they do not have the power and status to make their disquiet explicit.

While Pearson and Piazza (1997) suggest that most dual and multiple relationships can be managed, some arise unexpectedly and may give rise to an ethical dilemma. For example:

> Your partner has an accident and is admitted to hospital. The senior ward nurse that night turns out to be a client of yours. Among the issues you have focused on with her are her concerns about the competence of the consultant whom you now recognize as having responsibility for your partner's care. What can you do?

At times of unexpected emergency and heightened vulnerability, it is hard to remember professional boundaries and not be influenced by previous knowledge, however speculative. Fortunately such events are rare, but when relationships and roles get blurred or confused, when there is an emotional involvement, mistakes and ethical difficulties become more likely. Reviewing, clarifying and strengthening boundaries is a task for supervision, particularly if they involve sexual concerns.

Sexual relationships

The BPS, reflecting the Human Rights Act 1998, takes a very strong line on all forms of sexual harassment, abuse or misuse of clients by practitioners. Engagement 'in any form of sexual or romantic relationship with any persons to whom they are providing professional services, or to whom they owe a continuing duty of care, or with whom they have a relationship of trust' is precluded (BPS, 2006: 21). However, relationships characterized by a power imbalance can be hard to challenge, particularly if your primary source of consultancy is involved. For example:

> Ellie is completing her final training placement in your specialty. She is clearly a sound practitioner but you find her interpersonal interactions with you very awkward. When you address this with her, she gets very distressed and blurts out that her previous supervisor, head of the division and a senior colleague of yours, sexually harassed her during that placement. When she tried to address the problem with the supervisor, she was told that it was she who was behaving in a sexually provocative manner, that the supervisor had no sexual interest in her and that if she pursued the matter in any way it would seriously jeopardize her final assessments. What do you do?

Sex, sexuality, gender and erotic desire are all aspects of being human. But because sex is such a fundamental and emotionally powerful element in any relationship, it is one that is open to misinterpretation, exploitation and abuse – by both practitioner and client (Hunter and Struve, 1998). Counselling psychologists have to be able to deal with issues relating to sexuality, whether or not it is the main focus of the work. So how can they ethically manage themselves, their work and their relationships without either defensively avoiding all sexual issues or sliding down the 'slippery slope' to gross malpractice?

It is important to be able to distinguish between sexual attraction *towards* a client and sexual feelings *with* the client resulting from an exploration of their material (Wosket, 1999). Such a distinction also requires honesty to oneself and to one's supervisor in acknowledging any feelings of sexual attraction towards the client. Spinelli (1994: 113) further argues that if the sexual attraction is directly towards the client, the practitioner should not deny their feelings but 'choose an act of sacrifice' accepting, but not acting on, their desire in favour of the fidelity of the therapeutic relationship. The same applies to other relationships in counselling psychology, supported by supervision and personal therapy as necessary.

ETHICS AS PART OF TRAINING AND CPD

Awareness of sexuality, boundaries, power and the other aspects of ethical practice, together with the skills to work with them, will be developed first in training. If, as

I have argued, ethical mindfulness is more than an academic exercise, it needs to be reflected in every aspect of training and the promotion of best practice. Trainers, supervisors, managers and personal therapists therefore have a particular responsibility to model ethical behaviours and attitudes. For instance:

Jas, a second-year trainee on a counselling psychology course, is struggling despite concerted efforts to help him. While he has passed the academic component of his course, his tutors and supervisor feel he lacks the necessary level of awareness of interpersonal processes and sensitivity to others' perspectives. Jas does not agree. The senior tutor feels caught. Are the staff failing in their duty to him if he is allowed to continue with a poor chance of qualifying as a practitioner? Are they putting his clients at risk? Or should they trust Jas' assessment of his competence and allow him to continue in the hope he can develop the necessary awareness? The student group is split in their support for Jas. The institution is concerned about its reputation but also about its pass rates. What do you think needs to be done to resolve this situation?

Reviewing and reinforcing ethical mindfulness may be even more important postqualification. How often are ethical dilemmas made public? How often are ethical issues researched or discussed in CPD activities? What skills do we need to develop to become competent in facing up to ethical challenges?

DEALING WITH ETHICAL CHALLENGES

Lakin suggested that 'whereas ethical dilemmas in the practice of psychotherapy are inevitable, unethical actions and behaviours are not' (1991: 11). But is it possible to avoid unethical practice completely? Palmer Barnes (1998) suggests four levels of unethical behaviour: mistakes in otherwise good practice; poor practice in which the overall standard of work is inadequate; negligence or wanton lack of care; and malpractice which is intentionally exploitative and abusive.

Anyone, regardless of their training and experience, can, and probably will, make mistakes during their career. Hopefully most will not be serious. However, every mistake should be taken seriously. Bond (2005) suggests that awareness of a mistake and careful handling of the consequences by the practitioner may make the difference for a client at an early stage. Open curiosity about, and a willingness to explore, what has happened is preferable to defensive behaviour with the implication that it is someone-else's fault. BPS is clear that an apology 'for any negative outcome' may be the most appropriate acknowledgement of a client's distress and does not necessarily admit liability (BPS, 2006: 8). Repeated mistakes herald decline into poor practice. Recognizing and dealing with them requires a high level of self-awareness and personal integrity, sensitivity to declining standards and humility in consultation if charges of negligence and malpractice are to be avoided. Unfortunately, fear and shame are powerful deterrents to seeking help. We need to foster a climate in which acknowledgement of, and involvement in, the resolution of ethical dilemmas is regarded without prejudice. Systematic investigation of the outcomes of ethical decisions could help clarify and define future decision making under similar circumstances (Forrest et al., 1999; Bond, 2000).

Professional guidelines and codes may be helpful in defining an ethical challenge but are ultimately inadequate in resolving it. Different people perceive and react to the same situation in very different ways. The pressure to act quickly from the intuitive level may be strong but the BPS *Code of Ethics and Conduct* (2006: 8) emphasizes that 'thinking is not optional' and proposes the following steps for ethical decision making:

- Identify the relevant issues:

  – What are the parameters of the situation?
  – Is there research evidence that might be relevant?
  – What legal guidance exists?
  – What do peers advise?

- Identify the clients and other stakeholders and consider or obtain their views.
- Use the *Code of Ethics and Conduct* to identify the principles involved.
- Evaluate the rights, responsibilities and welfare of all clients and stakeholders.
- Generate the alternative decisions preferably with others to act as a sounding-board.
- Establish a cost/risk–benefit analysis to include both short- and long-term consequences.
- Make the decision after checking that the reasoning behind it is logical, lucid and consistent.
- Document the process of decision making.
- Assume responsibility and monitor any outcomes.
- Apologize for any negative outcomes that result. Many formal complaints are often a client's only way of obtaining acknowledgement of distress. Saying 'sorry' does not automatically admit liability.
- Make every effort to correct any negative outcomes and remain engaged in the process.
- Learn from the process yourself, for others and the Society.

Francis (1999) further suggests two quick tests for urgent decisions:

- Could you defend your decision in a court of law?
- Would your family still be proud of you after you had explained your reasoning?

CONCLUSION

I began this chapter by identifying the moral principles of respect, competence, responsibility and integrity that underlie the ethical decisions that must be taken by counselling psychologists in their daily life and work. I went on to suggest that different ethical interpretations are inevitable because of the different values held by clients and counselling psychologists alike – our different upbringings, cultures, experiences, understanding and working contexts. Different theoretical approaches to counselling psychology also embody different values, which need to be taken into account. All such differences must be recognized and respected. The codes of ethics and practice of relevant professional bodies such as the HPC and BPS offer sound guidelines but may not be able to account for the subtle nature of many ethical dilemmas.

Bell suggests that ethical living is 'a process you go through so that as each new situation arises, the inclination to choose ethically is stronger in you, even if the right path is less clear' (2002: 36). I have suggested that counselling psychologists should be trained and encouraged to develop a conscious ethical mindfulness, an awareness of ethical issues and boundaries, both within themselves and between themselves and those with whom they work, as a matter of everyday practice. Use of professional consultation, careful analysis and informed reflection are all-important. Debate about ethical dilemmas needs to be encouraged and more investigation and research should be conducted into the process and outcomes of their resolution. Above all, I would argue that the profession should foster a climate in which ethical practice is regarded as a mark of excellence and something to be proud of rather than a way of avoiding complaints about negligence or malpractice.

REFERENCES

Beauchamp, T.L. and Childress, J.F. (1989) *Principles of Biomedical Ethics*, 3rd edn. New York: Oxford University Press.

Bell, D. (2002) *Ethical Ambition: Living a Life of Meaning and Worth.* London: Bloomsbury.

Bond, T. (2000) *Standards and Ethics for Counselling in Action.* London: Sage.

Bond, T. (2005) 'Developing and monitoring professional ethics and good practice guidelines', in R. Tribe and J. Morrissey (eds), *Handbook of Professional and Ethical Practice for Psychologists, Counsellors and Psychotherapists.* Hove: Brunner-Routledge.

Bond, T. (2008) 'Toward a new ethic of trust', *Therapy Today*, 19 (3): 30–35

British Association for Counselling and Psychotherapy (2007) *Ethical Framework for Good Practice in Counselling and Psychotherapy.* Lutterworth: BACP.

British Psychological Society: Division of Counselling Psychology (2005) *Professional Practice Guidelines for Counselling Psychology.* Leicester: BPS.

British Psychological Society (2006) *Code of Ethics and Conduct.* Leicester: BPS.

British Psychological Society: Division of Counselling Psychology (2007) *Guidelines for Supervision.* Leicester: BPS.

British Psychological Society (2008) *The 2007 Annual Report.* Leicester: BPS.

Carroll, M. (1996) *Workplace Counselling.* London: Sage.

Carroll, M. (2005) 'Psychological contracts with and within organisations', in R. Tribe and J. Morrissey (eds), *Handbook of Professional and Ethical Practice for Psychologists, Counsellor and Psychotherapists.* Hove: Brunner-Routledge.

Forrest, L., Elman, N., Gizara, S. and Vacha-Haase, T. (1999) 'Trainee impairment: A review of identification, remediation, dismissal and legal issues', *Counselling Psychologist*, 27 (5): 627–686.

Francis, R.D. (1999) *Ethics for Psychologists: A Handbook*. Leicester: BPS.

Gilbert, D. (2006) *Stumbling on Happiness*. St Ives: Harper Perennial.

Guggenbuhl-Craig, A. (1971) Power *in the Helping Professions*. Woodstock: Spring.

Health Professions Council (2008) *Standards of Conduct, Performance and Ethics*. London: HPC.

Holmes, D.A., Taylor, M. and Saeed, A. (2000) 'Stalking and the therapeutic relationship: On-going research', *Forensic Update*, 60.

Holmes, J. and Lindley, R. (1991) *The Values of Psychotherapy*. Oxford: Oxford University Press.

Hunter, M. and Struve, J. (1998) *The Ethical Use of Touch in Psychotherapy*. London: Sage.

Jenkins, P. (2005) 'Client confidentiality and data protection', in R. Tribe and J. Morrissey (eds), *Handbook of Professional and Ethical Practice for Psychologists, Counsellors and Psychotherapists*. Hove: Brunner-Routledge.

Jones, C. (2000) 'What should counsellors consider when contacted by persons such as solicitors or the police and other authorities in connection with client work or when clients request such assistance on their behalf?', in C. Jones, C.M. Shillito-Clarke, G. Syme, D. Hill, R. Caseuare and L. Murdiu (eds), *Questions of Ethics in Counselling and Therapy*. Buckingham: Open University Press.

Kitchener, K.S. (1984) 'Intuition, critical evaluation and ethical principles', *Counseling Psychologist*, 21 (3): 43–55.

Lakin, M. (1991) *Coping with Ethical Dilemmas in Psychotherapy*. New York: Pergamon.

Lamb, D.H. (1999) 'Addressing impairment and its relationship to professional boundary issues', *Counseling Psychologist*, 27 (5): 702–711.

Meara, N.M., Schmidt, L.D. and Day, J.D. (1996) 'Principles and virtues: A foundation for ethical decisions, policies, and character', *Counseling Psychologist*, 24 (1): 4–77.

Page, S. (1999) *The Shadow and the Counsellor: Working with Darker Aspects of the Person, Role and Profession*. London: Routledge.

Palmer Barnes, F. (1998) *Complaints and Grievances in Psychotherapy: A Handbook of Ethical Practice*. London: Routledge.

Pattinson, S. (1999) 'Are professional codes ethical?', *Counselling*, 10 (5): 374–380.

Pearson, B. and Piazza, N. (1997) 'Classification of dual relationships in the helping professions', *Counsellor Education and Supervision*, 37 (2): 89–99.

Roth, A. and Fonagy, P. (1996) *What Works for Whom?* London: Guilford.

Rothschild, B. (2006) *Help for the Helper*. London: Norton.

Schore, A. (2003) *Affect Regulation and the Repair of the Self*. London: Norton.

Seider, S., Davis, K. and Gardner, H. (2007) 'Good work in psychology', in *The Psychologist*, 20 (11): 672–676.

Shillito-Clarke, C.M. (2003) 'Ethics in supervision', in D. Hill and C. Jones (eds), *Forms of Ethical Thinking in Therapeutic Practice*. Buckingham: Open University Press.

Spinelli, E. (1994) *Demystifying Therapy*. London: Constable.

Strawbridge, S. (1994) 'Towards anti-oppressive practice in counselling psychology', *Counselling Psychology Review*, 9 (1): 5.

Thatcher, M. (2006) 'Are ethical codes ethical?', *Counselling Psychology Review*, 21 (3): 4–11.

Tjeltveit, A.C. (1999) *Ethics and Values in Psychotherapy*. London: Routledge.

Vygotsky, L. (1986) *Thought and Language*. Cambridge, MA: MIT Press.

Wilson, J.P. and Thomas, R.B. (2004) *Empathy in the Treatment of Trauma and PTSD*. Hove: Brunner-Routledge.

Wosket, V. (1999) *The Therapeutic Use of Self: Counselling Practice, Research and Supervision*. London: Routledge.

27

LEGAL FRAMEWORKS

Diane Hammersley*

Legal settings are not the main context within which counselling psychologists usually operate, because their training is focused primarily on therapeutic work with clients. However, there is no reason why a therapeutic training should be a barrier to working in these contexts and many psychologists from a variety of applied backgrounds find that they have skills and knowledge which are useful within them. For example, a number of counselling psychologists work in the criminal justice system in prisons, conducting assessments, writing reports and carrying out individual and group therapeutic interventions. As chartered psychologists, we are all scientists with theoretical knowledge about human beings, research methods and academic skills, and experience of communicating this knowledge to others. Counselling psychologists can add specialist skills in relating to others, therapeutic insights, qualitative methodology and an understanding of the importance of subjectivity and the impact of different contexts.

In the broadest sense, many psychologists carry out assessments after accidents in the workplace, or in road traffic accidents on people who have suffered physical and psychological injury for compensation. They also assess people with learning disabilities and special needs to ensure their human rights or entitlement to assistance are respected. Working with people who have sought political asylum, or are refugees, or in other ways find themselves displaced, brings psychologists into contact with our legal system and involves working within that framework. Psychologists who might directly or indirectly be in contact with children are aware of a special legal duty to be concerned for their protection, and that includes us all.

---

* The author wishes to acknowledge the contribution of Dr Muriel Churchill to the discussion of this chapter.

This chapter will focus first on some of the complex professional and ethical issues which arise from counselling people within a legal framework, such as confidentiality and conflicts of interest. Second, it addresses the special area of expert witness work and uses as an illustration the assessment of parents and relatives involved in child protection and parental contact. This work comes under the jurisdiction of the Family Court system. The third area of focus explores some of the processes which underpin the complex system of relationships within which a counselling psychologist must operate and the interpersonal dynamics which result from a relational stance rather than an objective stance to working within legal frameworks.

DIFFERENT ROLES

Jenkins (2005), in a paper which explores some of the key aspects of psychotherapy and the law and especially confidentiality, makes the point that the relationship between a psychologist and a client is not a privileged one, like the solicitor–client relationship. Also criminal and civil proceedings may be different in that the burden of proof in criminal cases is 'beyond all reasonable doubt', whereas in civil cases it is on 'the balance of probabilities' (2005: 46). In addition, it is likely that psychologists have been trained to establish what facts are, but mostly that is the prerogative of the court to determine, and even expert witnesses are merely giving opinions at various levels of certainty or confidence. Jenkins also shows how issues such as informed consent and negligence may be subject to the Bolam test, which is used in medical negligence case law as a failure to act 'in accordance with a practice of competent respected professional opinion' (2005: 48).

Confidentiality

Whatever our role within a legal framework, there are important ethical issues to consider both for ourselves and others. Different roles imply different ground rules or assumptions, and these may need to be made explicit. An important one is the issue of confidentiality, but wherever there is more than one client there is a potential conflict of interest and both of these are significant in working with other professions whose ground rules may be different. The uneasy relationship between therapy and the law is discussed by Jenkins (2007), who explores the legal contexts within which therapists may work, the legal tradition in England and Wales, and the court system.

Working therapeutically with a client usually means that the psychologist has a duty of confidentiality to the client, except in certain circumstances such as when there is a danger to the client or others, especially children, when the psychologist may be obliged to limit that confidentiality and make a limited disclosure. Criminal acts may also limit confidentiality because the psychologist has a duty to disclose information, so that the duty to the public is greater than the duty to the individual client. Problems can arise when the boundaries are set at the beginning, and then the client or the client's solicitor asks for a report for reasons of providing evidence to a third party such as an employment tribunal, in divorce or family proceedings, or for an insurance compensation claim. It may seem straightforward enough to agree to the disclosure of notes or a report, but there may be problems because the disclosure was not agreed in advance.

Notes, however carefully and conscientiously written, may not have protected other people who have been named, and the psychologist may not have protected themselves sufficiently by including speculations, reflections on the process and counter-transference material. Therefore, unless disclosure has been agreed in advance, it is a change to the contract and the psychotherapeutic frame, and the psychologist should consider whether to refuse to release notes to legal practitioners unless ordered to do so by a county court judge. An alternative which may suit the legal professionals just as well is to consider writing a report after therapeutic work has started, but that might also change the therapeutic frame and diminish the quality, effectiveness and dynamics of therapy by introducing another agenda. Perhaps writing a report after therapeutic work has ended may reduce the impact of that second agenda.

One example of a contract which illustrates combining roles is when a client is seen as part of an educational and assessment programme, such as in a residential family assessment centre:

Sue was a woman who had had five previous children taken into care and adopted because of conflict and violence in her relationships with her partners, and the neglect of the children. She was in a new relationship and had a young baby and had been referred by a Social Service department and the family court for a 12-week residential assessment with her partner. The Legal Services Commission will not fund therapy but will sometimes fund an assessment which may have a therapeutic element. The court wanted a psychological assessment of how Sue had understood her own experiences of poor attachments, conflicted relationships and abuse, and what she had learned and integrated from the social work programme that might indicate she had changed. I had complete therapeutic freedom as usual to allow us to explore any issues which came up.

As the psychologist, I was separate from the staff of the centre but dependent on them to provide me with a room and a time to see Sue for an hour a week during her stay. A mutually respectful relationship between the staff and me was very important in making this kind of arrangement work. They would suggest to Sue that issues that came up in their sessions might be discussed with me, and they gave me an updating briefing before I saw her each week. What was very helpful was that I was under no pressure to disclose anything to the staff unless I wished to and had talked to Sue about that first. On the basis of our sessions I then wrote a report for the court, which was read alongside the centre's assessment and recommendations.

A second example of a contract is when the court explicitly requests therapeutic work to be undertaken at the client's expense and asks for a report on the outcomes. Separating the assessment element of the first and last sessions means that those can be funded as part of the report, while the client pays for therapeutic sessions at a rate which is usually charged to private clients:

Mike and Lucy had been married with two sons, but divorced shortly after the birth of their second son. Lucy had remarried to Colin and the boys lived with them. Only the younger son saw his birth-father for a day out once a fortnight, the older son having refused to see him. This was a private family law case in that the Local Authority through the Social Services department was not involved or concerned. Problems had arisen over Mike's contact with his sons and he blamed Lucy and Colin for turning his sons against him. Lucy claimed she did her best to persuade the younger son, aged 8, to go but he rebelled and pointed out that his brother who was 11 was not forced to do so. Mike had been trying to gain increased contact with his sons through the courts for several years.

The planned therapeutic work focused on each of us seeing all the parties first and then either working with the couple or the birth-father with a view to developing trust and a common framework so that we could come together to work systemically on the communication problems and move to mediation over the contact arrangements. In order to accommodate travelling and work commitments, we agreed to see the parties for two hours once a fortnight at the children's solicitor's office. This plan of work was changed when it became clear that joint sessions would not be appropriate as Mike had alcohol problems and features of a borderline personality. Although all the parties had previously been assessed by a forensic psychologist, the real issues became much clearer when a therapeutic intervention revealed the underlying problems in reaching agreement. It also informed my understanding of the children's positions when I subsequently met them to hear their views on contact, and they may have responded better to a less formal style of interview.

A third example of a contract to work therapeutically is one that allows therapeutic work to take place without the requirement to write a report for the court. In this case, confidentiality is much closer to the normal contract between a counselling psychologist and a client. The court has to be satisfied that the work is being done, and the following case illustrates one way that this can be negotiated. However, there is still a dual role because the client has 'been sent':

Simon was referred to me by his solicitor, originally with a request that I see him for psychodynamic therapy which had been recommended by a psychiatrist who had assessed him. I was asked to see the court papers before accepting him, and the judge

---

in the family court asked whether I would agree to see Simon on the understanding that I would not write a report, but that the psychiatrist would assess him again in 6 months to determine whether Simon had made any progress, before being allowed access to contact with his son aged 5. Simon was to pay me for therapy himself if we both agreed at the first session that we thought we could work together.

Simon was aware from the outset that I had in one sense been chosen by the judge as his therapist and this led to issues of trust between us, with Simon constantly challenging me that I was 'going to put it in my report'. Simon had experienced a lot of loss in his early life which he had interpreted as rejection by his parents, and his adult experience of the breakdown with his partner which he had interpreted as abandonment and betrayal added to his anger. Following an argument which led to violence, he had served a term in prison, had various psychiatric diagnoses and was taking antipsychotic medication and had been using cannabis and alcohol intermittently. It was not really a surprise when he 'walked out' on me during the second session, but he walked back in again the next week. How much his return was really due to the court's requirement that he attend therapy in order to see his son is difficult to tell.

Further ethical considerations

Respect is an ethical principle that counselling psychologists try to apply in all their work, but legal contexts may sometimes provide less familiar dilemmas. Many of the people we assess have considerably less social standing and power than we do because of age, social class or learning disability in particular. Working with young parents in child-care proceedings means that clients are in their teens or early-20s, may be receiving financial benefits or have a learning disability. Several clients have commented to us on their experience of professionals, including psychologists, as being condescending and making derogatory comments about them. So while it may be appropriate to address people by their first name in therapy or during an assessment, we believe that reports should use formal titles unless in reported speech. The language and tone of reports is also important, especially if it is relevant to comment upon people's appearance and other personal matters. References to psychiatric diagnoses are not always expressed in the most respectful of terms and we try to avoid any pejorative language.

When counselling psychologists are assessing their competence to carry out work in legal settings, they may believe that they need to have attended a training course first. This is not the only or even the best way to become competent, and however experienced we may be we are still likely to encounter new challenges in almost every case. Life and work experience such as teaching, social work or nursing may also be relevant. Certain knowledge may be important, for example, in assessing the effects of physical injury or domestic violence, abuse of all kinds, children and young people, drugs and alcohol, prisoners and learning disabilities. Much of this knowledge can be gained by working alongside someone more experienced in the field and through appropriate supervision.

Responsibility

Operating within a legal framework carries special responsibility for ensuring that the effects of the assessment or therapy do not harm the client or lead to misunderstandings. We have made a point of asking clients we assess for their feedback on the assessment process and how they have experienced it. The role of the counselling psychologist is a very powerful one and when the outcome of our interventions may have life-changing consequences for clients, such as the return of their children, we cannot take our responsibility lightly. The law requires psychologists who are involved in children's cases to put the best interests of the child first; deciding that when the children may not be able to speak for themselves adds an extra dilemma in weighing up the possibilities for their future care.

Integrity

It goes without saying that we should try to make honest and accurate assessments of people, taking into account all the evidence that is available to us. Where there are several clients in an adversarial system, it is inevitable that psychologists are faced with conflicts of interest and need to be aware of other people seeking to influence their judgements. Personal boundaries are an area where counselling psychologists might consider that they 'have the edge' over other psychologists, but being a relatively new profession without the same established reputation, there is a temptation to be seduced by the relatively high fees and high status accorded to some experts. Grandiosity can blind people to their weaknesses, and it is important to 'have the edge' in terms of personal awareness too.

THE EXPERT ROLE

In some circumstances, a psychologist is approached in order to provide an assessment and report for legal purposes and in this case 'there is no confidentiality at all' (BPS, 2007). Issues of confidentiality still need to be discussed in advance, making it clear that what is disclosed or discovered in the assessment will be disclosed in the report, although clearly the psychologist still has an ethical duty of respect to the client (BPS, 2006).

Perhaps this could be described as 'limited confidentiality', applying the principle of respect by saying that what is disclosed will not be confidential but be treated with discretion. This means writing respectfully of third parties, not including anything which is not relevant and not disclosing any of the information elsewhere where people can be identified.

A particular example of this is where a psychologist is approached as an independent expert, agreed by all the parties to conduct an assessment, provide a report and if necessary attend court in order to give evidence. The BPS guidance (2007) on the independence of the psychologist points out that this needs to be maintained if the report is to be useful. In child-care proceedings in the family courts, disclosure of the proceedings requires the court's permission and a different level of confidentiality is maintained. In the family courts, although the clients may be the Local Authority or parents, it is made explicit that the expert's first duty is to the court and the best interests of a child or children must be given priority.

Problems may arise where a person's ability to give their informed consent to an assessment is questioned because of their mental health or capacity (BPS, 2005). A further ethical dilemma may arise over whether the client in legal settings has a real choice in consenting to an assessment, or a limited one, or has virtually no choice at all. In the case of family divorce proceedings, claims for compensation, attempts to reverse decisions about redundancy and claims about discrimination, for example, clients will probably be following the advice given to them by their legal advisers. To some extent they could agree to settle early, or give up the case because a financial loss may be easier to bear than the dispute. However, where the issue is the return of a child or children who have been removed, or where there is a dispute between parents over contact with a child, parents may be under much greater pressure to consent because the alternative is too terrible for them to contemplate.

WORKING THROUGH A CASE

Before undertaking expert work of this kind, the BPS guidelines for expert witnesses (2007) provide a clear framework for the various stages of the process. They establish ways of understanding what an expert is, ways of deciding whether a psychologist has sufficient competence to act as an expert witness, and the processes involved in agreeing to act in this capacity. It is encouraging to read that 'the courts recognise that all experts have to start somewhere and gain experience cumulatively' (2007: 4). Other psychologists may offer advice on the process or support for the role, although the expert is not expected to need supervision for their opinion. Courts and lawyers may be helpful in explaining unfamiliar legal processes, but care is needed in not becoming vulnerable to robust cross-examination in what is essentially an adversarial process.

Preparing to accept instructions

It may be useful to consider what counselling or therapeutic experience might be relevant in advance of being approached. In the examples in this chapter, many of the instructions have been for providing expert opinions for the family court, but they will be relevant for other cases. The following experience is often useful: assessing child–parent attachment styles, the impact of personal and family histories, drug and alcohol use, prescribed medication, intellectual functioning, childhood abuse, mental health histories and treatments, understanding parenting, parenting skills, learning disabilities, personality styles, criminal behaviour, couple relationships, divorce and its impact on children, bereavement and loss.

Many of these issues come up in the course of therapeutic work and particular settings, such as drug and alcohol agencies or NHS settings, provide opportunities to gain experience. The solicitor who enquires about your suitability will usually ask whether you have experience in the particular areas which are needed; you do not have to have had specialist placements in learning disabilities for example during your training as clinical psychologists might be expected to have done. Similarly, one does not need to have attended a course, but some experience of practice is what is asked for.

The second task in order to be ready to respond is to have prepared a suitable CV for which you will be asked, in order for all the solicitors to agree that you are a suitable expert to instruct. This document needs to be very different from one written for a job application! It is not an opportunity to sell yourself to a potential employer but should be more of a professional and academic statement, listing posts held, research and publications, the breadth and depth of your therapeutic experience and your experience as an expert.

The other main questions to prepare for are availability to include a timescale for completing the work, fees and availability to be called to any hearing. You will have to allocate time to reading documents, interviewing clients, observing contact with children, conducting tests and so forth, and it might be reasonable to offer to complete these within a month of receiving instructions, with a period of perhaps a further month in which to write the report. The amount of work you can undertake may be affected by your employment or other work, and in particular whether psychometric tests are used which require less time to write up than interviews and observations. So a timescale of two months from receiving instructions to delivering a report is usually acceptable to the court. Fees are usually quoted in hourly or day rates as appropriate.

Receiving instructions

Having secured an expert, instructions may be agreed within hours or take several days for a jointly appointed expert. Sometimes the written instructions deviate from earlier discussions and since this may greatly increase the workload, it necessitates additional discussions if the objectives are to be met. It may be that solicitors anticipate a standard process, particularly if they have instructed other psychologists previously and may not anticipate that counselling psychologists may vary the process considerably for the particular clients involved. This expectation may have arisen through prior experience of working with other psychologists more reliant on a standard package of psychometric tests. Working with the family courts, a greater variety of methods may be accepted, especially when the assessment involves children.

Example of a case outline:

Bernice and Arthur are a couple who have two children currently in foster care. Bernice is thought to have learning difficulties because she was not able to organize feeding and looking after the children since having the second child. It has been suggested that she suffers from post-natal depression. Arthur has been a heavy drinker and he has a few convictions for possession of cannabis, and he has been getting advice on his drug and drinking habits from his general practitioner. Bernice has a history of childhood sexual abuse and Arthur's mother left his father when he was 10 and he lived with his grandmother who found him difficult to control.

The psychological assessment requires an exploration of how their personal histories may be impacting on their parental abilities, questions about their ability to form attachments with their children, an assessment of Bernice's cognitive functioning and what help she may need to learn parenting skills, an assessment of Arthur's addiction to drink and drugs and whether he will be able to abstain in future. It also requests an opinion about which of them would be able to parent alone if they cannot maintain their partnership, whether either or both of them is in need of any treatments or counselling and who might provide such treatment or counselling and the timescales involved.

A second case example:

Alicia had a baby when she was 16 years old and she lived with her mother and her mother's new partner for about 18 months. She does not get on with her mother's partner and their relationship has broken down, so Alicia left to live with her boyfriend, leaving her baby son with her mother. She wants to have her baby back to live with her and her boyfriend but the social worker is concerned about Alicia's immaturity, and inability to take care of her son because whenever she runs out of money she

(Continued)

(Continued)

goes home to borrow from her mother or leaves her son with his grandmother. There were concerns about the child's safety when Alicia and her boyfriend had a row and he hit her. Grandmother has asked the court for a residence order because she does not think that Alicia can take care of the baby as well as she can.

A psychological assessment is required to assess the level of understanding of the child's needs by Alicia, her boyfriend and her mother. The child's attachments to all four people involved in his care are to be assessed, and whether he is developing any psychological problems from being passed between his mother and grandmother's care. The health visitor and the social worker have both prepared reports and the expert is asked to give an opinion about the respective abilities of the mother and grandmother to care for the baby and to assess whether they can co-operate with each other, the health visitor and the social worker. The expert is asked to recommend any further assessments or work which should be undertaken with Alicia or to enable the family to work together.

Planning the assessment

A letter of instruction sets out the background to the assessment, the contract being agreed with the expert, the proposed timescale and costs and the questions which the expert is to respond to in the report. These questions will have been circulated to and agreed by all the solicitors involved in the case. This is a jointly appointed independent expert role, which means the expert is not acting as an advocate of the party commissioning the report. At the same time, the expert will usually be sent all the documents, consisting of court orders, reports from social workers or drug workers, statements by the parents requesting a residence order or contact arrangements, possibly medical or criminal records and any other expert reports which have been submitted in the past. This is known as 'the bundle'. The reading of the bundle can take at least two hours and sometimes longer, and it raises questions which can guide the investigation later in the assessment process itself. Of course, it may also create assumptions in the mind of the expert, who must beware of being too influenced by what others have written or said. The expert must bring an open and enquiring mind to the task.

There are practical matters to be arranged, such as days and times and places where the assessment can be conducted. Solicitors will often offer a meeting room at their offices, which may be convenient for the clients and is a suitably private setting and perhaps less daunting for some people than clinics and hospitals. However, clients may need to be visited in prison, at a family assessment centre or at home, and these settings provide problems which sometimes draw on the counselling psychologist's ability to think on their feet and improvise! Children may be seen at school or nursery, or observed with the parent at a family centre, playground or park depending on their age.

Methodology

There are two main approaches to assessment: quantitative methods rely upon standardized tests and measurements which can be statistically analysed, whereas qualitative methods rely upon a wider variety of sources for a rich and detailed description which can be analysed and is unique to each case. Whichever approach is chosen, assessments nearly always contain some qualitative element such as a semi-structured interview, but in part the instructions themselves may determine the methodology. For example, an instruction 'to conduct a full psychological assessment of cognitive functioning' leaves little doubt that formal testing using an instrument such as the WAIS (1998) is required. Often psychometric tests simply confirm what is already known and tell the court less than a detailed exploration of client history and other exploratory methods. At times earlier assessments may suggest poor intellectual functioning which cast doubt on the client's capabilities. In practice, such assessments can be simply an indication that without rapport some people do not co-operate with psychologists and other professionals (Axline, 1964).

An example of the importance of establishing the necessary relationship is Katie:

Katie had received a brain injury at birth and had a baby who was in foster care while her capacity to parent the child was being assessed. Katie's learning difficulty was acknowledged and she had received special assistance during her education. Nevertheless, an assessment of cognitive functioning was requested by the court. The first test in the WAIS (1998) asks what is missing from a picture. Katie was angry and offended, and when asked what she was feeling angry about, she said that she thought the question was too simple and she was being asked it because she was simple.

When Katie understood that everyone is asked the same questions in the test, regardless of how well they have done at school, she became more relaxed and agreed to continue. She told us that on previous occasions she had felt 'talked down to' and did not try. Rapport is necessary in administering even the most standardized psychometric tests, otherwise the person may not co-operate or try.

A semi-structured interview

The interview needs to be constructed around both The Questions and the evidence in the bundle, in order to collect information, opinions, explanations, reasons and insights from the person being assessed. To some extent the client may have prepared their answers perhaps by previous interviews, and some probing may be required such as asking for examples or asking about an incident from another person's point of view. Other more creative methods could include asking a person to draw themselves and then to add into the drawing the people closest to them. What is included in the drawing or left out, the scale of the figures and their proximity, whether the bodies have substance or are stick figures, the expressions on the faces as well as the commentary made while doing the drawing can all be richly revealing. In addition, clients can be asked for their favourite story or fairytale character from childhood, which can represent a heroic figure or a tale with strong symbolic connections with the person's past.

When the assessment is about parents' attitudes to children, one way of exploring their awareness and understanding is by using soft toys to represent the child and other people. Of course, children themselves will often construct stories using dolls and toys, but some clients find it helpful and enjoyable to use their imagination in this way. It has proved to be invaluable in working with clients with learning difficulties of various kinds. Before the assessment, a story can be written to include everyday scenarios which involve empathy, emotional awareness, being able to guess what might happen in any situation, situations of conflict and disagreement, and these stories can be read a short section at a time to the client and followed by a question. Even without the toys, imaginary scenarios which pick up themes from the case can be presented, and this is especially useful when parents or a couple are being assessed together as well as separately. This can be used to assess their relationship and how they support or complement each other.

An example of using toys in a creative way is the following Teddy exercise:

Introduction: Teddy belongs to me and sometimes he is looked after by my friend. He represents a child in these exercises. I shall ask each of you questions in turn and may invite you to add something to the other person's answer.

I am getting Teddy ready to go out in the morning because we are going to meet my friend in town. He's being a bit grisly and won't drink his milk and struggles when I try to get his coat on. What do you think is going on for Teddy? What is he thinking and feeling?

When I get to town and meet my friend, I pass him over to her while I go into a shop. Teddy starts to cry. Why is Teddy crying? What would you do to stop him? What do you think Teddy is thinking and feeling?

After we've been shopping, we decide to go to a café for some lunch. What do you think Teddy needs? When he starts throwing his food on the floor, what should I do? What should my friend do?

We take Teddy to the park and my friend takes him on the swings on her lap, which he seems to like because he screams with delight and doesn't want to stop. How do you think she should get Teddy off the swings?

We are tired so we put Teddy in his buggy to watch the ducks while we have a sit down and a chat. What do you think we need to do before we settle down to our chat?

My friend comes home with Teddy and me after our day in town. What should we do when we get home and in what order?

An example of using stories imaginatively is 'The Clinic' scenario:

> You arrive at the baby clinic for a regular check-up and the receptionist says that there is a note to say that the specialist wants a word with you. She won't say what it is about and tells you to sit in the waiting room. How might you be feeling and what would you say to each other while you wait?
>
> The nurse takes you into the treatment room and starts examining and checking the baby. She seems to be taking a long time and doing things you have never seen the nurse do before. She tells you things but because she is foreign, you don't really understand what she is saying. She goes off to have a word with the doctor. How might you be feeling?
>
> When the doctor comes in he tells you he is a bit worried about the baby and asks you if you have noticed anything unusual. You can't think what he means. He says he thinks the baby had better go to the hospital for further tests. What might you be feeling?
>
> When you get home you talk about what the nurse and doctor meant. Who would you turn to for help and advice?

The assessment

The assessment should start with introductions of those who are conducting the assessment, an explanation of the purpose of it and how long it is planned to take, and information about breaks and facilities at the venue. It may be helpful to give clients a timetable for the day. Then it should be explained that clients can ask for questions to be repeated, or explained or put another way, because they may be unused to being interviewed in a formal manner or setting. Differences of background, culture, ethnic origin, gender, age, disabilities and language may need to be explored and discussed in order to ensure that the clients understand the process. For example, when a client with learning disabilities was accompanied by an advocate, she was invited to discuss this with the advocate who also met her during the breaks and helped the client form and ask questions. It is important that confidentiality is explained, particularly since family court proceedings cannot be reported outside the court (The Lord Chancellor, 2008), but clients are usually aware that a report will be written for the court.

By being very clear with clients as to the role and responsibility of the expert, and by checking that whatever their intellectual ability the client comprehends the task and process, a clear contract based on trust can usually be established. Transparency of process, and a clear set of mutually agreed objectives, reduces the tension and allows for constructive exploration of the client's history and a fair assessment of skills and potential. This is important if the expert's report is to provide clear indications when required as to how clients can best be supported in the future. Even standardized psychological tests cannot be relied upon if the client is very frightened, unwilling or offended and therefore under-performs.

However, two groups pose difficulties: clients with addictions, and those whose behaviour and approach suggest features of personality difficulties. In the former case, the client may not have previously admitted the extent or severity of their addiction and may be reluctant to undermine their case. In the latter case, the challenge is to discriminate between the clients' hopes and fantasies, and a more objective assessment based on a structured analytic approach. Some clients 'forget' that the independent expert has access to all relevant materials, and can ask for additional information if necessary. For example, some clients who fail to reveal prior convictions and are otherwise 'economical with the truth' about their behaviour, which is a matter of record, cannot be considered to be co-operating. When the situation demands an exploration of omissions or specific relevant allegations such as pimping or prostitution, the expert might anticipate a degree of hostility which is best met with calmness and determination.

It is important at the end of the assessment to thank clients for what may have been an exacting experience and to invite their feedback. If they have had similar experiences, it may or may not have been what they expected. Sometimes they say it was enjoyable and they often refer to the Teddy exercises or the drawing exercises. Then they need to know what will happen next, when their solicitor will receive the report and when they will know what it contains. This is a useful reminder that whatever is written about people, they will have to hear it and it may have therapeutic potential or the opposite effect. Some solicitors and guardians see the assessment process as primarily having a therapeutic value in confronting people with the nature of their difficulty which they may have avoided or denied.

The report

The first stage in writing a report is to gather together all the material which is to form the data or evidence. Tests have to be scored and the results analysed, and a mini-report of that section of the assessment is written in the form recommended by the test publisher. If someone assisted by taking notes of the interviews and exercises, it will help when writing a summary of the interview if they follow the same structure as the interview with the same headings, and have indicated where speech is recorded verbatim. This allows for the interview to be illustrated with the client's actual words at important moments in the interview, and lends it credibility. As well as recording the content of interviews and exercises, it is also relevant to consider process issues such as the impact that the questions might have had or the client's demeanour and body language while being interviewed. The interview is a relational process and counselling psychologists bring awareness of process dynamics into the assessment, which can help with the interpretation of the evidence.

The key part of the report is the responses to the questions which were agreed by all the parties. This represents the expert's considered professional opinion and it requires each statement of opinion to be underpinned by the evidence from the assessment and reference to major theoretical and research evidence. In that way, the court can see how the opinion was arrived at and on what it was based. Sometimes, if there is evidence for different conclusions, that should be outlined, with the emphasis given to the stronger case. It is perfectly reasonable to decline to answer a question, particularly if it has not proved possible either for reasons beyond the expert's control or because of shortage of time to collect the evidence. However, it is important to show what attempts were made to try to fulfil the requirement to give an answer. Sometimes the expert is invited to recommend whether further assessments are appropriate or to recommend what actions might be taken next to facilitate progress in the case.

An example outline for a report is as follows:

- A summary of how, when and by whom you were instructed as an expert
- Details of any tests you were asked to administer
- A list of the questions you were asked to address
- A statement about the author, qualifications and brief summary of experience
- Those who assisted in the assessment and their qualifications
- The methods used in the assessment
- Results of tests and findings from interviews and other observations
- Responses to the questions and opinion
- Statement of Duty to the Court and Statement of Truth
- Signature and date
- References.

Professionals' meetings and court hearings

Professionals' meetings may take place after the report has been submitted and the clients and their solicitors have had time to consider their positions and perhaps submit statements. The purpose is for the parties such as clients, guardian and solicitors or barristers to meet the expert to clarify some part of the report. On occasions, clients may be invited too. The meeting is usually chaired by the lead solicitor, who often represents the children through the Guardian ad Litem. The tone of these meetings may vary from a respectful discussion to a more confrontational style because the legal representatives are involved in an adversarial process and they are looking for the best way to present their client's case. Notes are taken of the meeting and usually circulated for correction and approval. It is very important to check these notes carefully to ensure that they represent the expert's views accurately. This is where impartiality is important since some clients may be represented by inexperienced or less assertive solicitors, while others may have an experienced litigator who is sizing up the expert with a view to cross-examination in court.

The hearing may not take place until several months after the assessment was carried out and requires careful preparation of the bundle and other documents so that the expert has it at their fingertips. Expert witnesses are not always called to give evidence but the more contentious the case, the more likely they are to be called. It can involve waiting around while discussions are taking place between others, but people are around to explain what is happening. Sometimes the case 'collapses' during the first day and then the expert is not called at all, leading to a lot of frustration and wasted journeys. Surprisingly, there seems to be no formal mechanism for informing the expert witness what the outcome of the case was. Perhaps other experts are not interested, but not only does the case lack closure for counselling psychologists but a valuable learning opportunity is missed as well.

PROCESS ISSUES

Relationships with solicitors

It is fairly obvious that solicitors want a professional job done as per instructions, with a usable report delivered on time and under the budget limit. In the field of family law, however, many solicitors are much more personally involved with their clients and cases, and that may be an area where counselling psychologists can make a connection with them. They may go to extraordinary lengths to assist vulnerable people engage with this process, by visiting them at home, telephoning them to remind them of appointments, sending or paying for taxis to get their client to the assessment, delivering documents by hand, escorting them to collect medical notes, making cases for a second chance, for example. Behind this care for their clients with which we may empathize, we have discovered that solicitors sometimes think psychologists' reports are incomprehensible or state the obvious. On being asked to interpret a report by another psychologist, it sometimes reads as very familiar language but it is difficult to discern what it means, or what use it is. Both psychologists and solicitors use their own jargon and have to work at making meanings understood.

What psychologists want from solicitors is clarity about the process without sudden changes of direction. A clear outline of the case when instructions are being discussed helps us to identify whether this is the sort of case that suits our approach and style. There is no standard way of conducting a psychological assessment, and although other specialist psychologists may have established norms for their branch of applied psychology, that does not mean that those ways are better or worse than counselling psychology's approach. Some solicitors are unaware of these differences and may expect an approach with which they are more familiar. We sometimes need and value advice from people who are much more experienced in this field than we are, such as specialist family law solicitors and experienced Guardians ad Litem.

The client's experience

Few clients are likely to relish a legal case because of the demands of assessments and court hearings. Furthermore, for some, their prior experience of 'professionals' and their expectation of not being heard, experiencing prejudice or discrimination can make anticipation and the process of assessment very demanding. For example, for those who have been brought up in care and not been protected, any suggestion that social services might now enter their lives again because they have a child and are not considered to have 'good enough' parenting skills may produce considerable hostility towards the process and predictable concern about their child should the court decide that he or she should be taken into care. The cycle of deprivation can be extremely difficult to break, but empathy and respect from the expert and a fair hearing can be the first step towards real healing and change.

In addition to past experiences in the care system, some clients have suffered abuse, deprivation, trauma, addictions and personality difficulties or learning disabilities. They find themselves once more in a less powerful position than others, and under pressure may act accordingly. Counselling psychologists who work in this field are like other psychologists, more vulnerable to allegations of professional misconduct or complaints to solicitors or the police, especially when people are angry and want to hit out at others. Psychologists can use professional distance to protect themselves, but in this field may be willing to take some risks and engage with clients more closely.

The dynamics of the process

The very term 'expert' conjures up such powerful images of importance and being treated with respect or deference that it is easy to see how delusions of grandeur can seduce a psychologist into becoming over-important or believing their own rhetoric. In legal settings when other professionals behave with charm and courtesy, or seem to be hanging on every word of our opinion, it is tempting to believe that we know or understand far more than we do. While on the one hand we must seek to avoid colluding with one point of view rather than another, particularly when it is the 'safe' opinion, we also have to dare to be different on other occasions. It is inevitable that we shall be challenged, and we have to become comfortable with welcoming that challenge as a proper thing for others to do in order for the legal system to determine the facts of the case.

One particular challenge is that of holding a different view from another expert, especially another psychologist. Other psychologists may have procedures and processes that they adhere to and be sceptical of a more fluid approach which does not rely entirely on guidelines. Guidelines are not rules and cannot be used to negate, or as a substitute for, professional judgement. Counselling psychologists are used to managing and containing uncertainty and bring this as a different strength to the role of expert.

CONCLUSIONS

Perhaps the most important qualities for any counselling psychologist entering this arena are the ability to convey respect, to build relationships quickly, and to keep a sense of direction and boundaries when under pressure. A strong ethical underpinning of practice is vital in this work, and it is probably a sense of social justice which provides much of the motivation for doing it. While as a practitioner one might be motivated by a desire for justice for the clients, the nature of the role means this may not be the expert's responsibility alone. Working within legal frameworks makes demands on the psychologist to hold a position of independence while others are working differently to make their case. This requires resilience whether working alone or in a team, and support from colleagues who share this same vision.

REFERENCES

Axline, V. (1964) *Dibs In Search of Self*. London: Penguin.

British Psychological Society (2005) *Mental Capacity Act 2005: Short Reference Guide for Psychologists and Psychiatrists*. Leicester: BPS.

British Psychological Society (2006) *Code of Ethics and Conduct*. Leicester: BPS.

British Psychological Society (2007) *Psychologists as Expert Witnesses: Guidelines and Procedure for England and Wales*. Leicester: BPS.

Lord Chancellor, The (2008) *Practice Direction: Experts in Family Proceedings Relating to Children*. London: The Lord Chancellor's Office. Available at www.bps.org.uk.

Jenkins, P. (2005) 'Aspects of the external frame: Psychodynamic psychotherapy and the law', *Psychodynamic Practice*, 11 (1): 41–56.

Jenkins, P. (2007) *Counselling, Psychotherapy and the Law*, 2nd edn. London: Sage.

Wechsler, D. (1998) *Wechsler Adult Intelligence Scale (WAIS)*, 3rd edn. London: The Psychological Corporation.

28

TRAINING AND PROFESSIONAL DEVELOPMENT

Peter Martin

A SUMMARY OF THIS CHAPTER

I begin this chapter by positioning myself within the debate that this chapter is designed to stimulate. I then outline briefly the history and the current state of initial training and continuing professional development (CPD) in counselling psychology (factual information has kindly been readily supplied by officers of the British Psychological Society (BPS) and more is available on the frequently updated website). The chapter next questions what is distinctive about training as a counselling psychologist. In the third section, the question of what the training is for is addressed in terms of the issues of licensing and professionalism. It goes on to critique the current syllabus and the present basis of CPD, concluding by identifying some possible ways forward.

MY PERSONAL POSITION

I write as a member of the profession, a practitioner and an academic, who is excited about the future of counselling psychology. I have had a small hand in its present state and thus I own some responsibility for that which I also critique. If we are to move towards a viable and vigorous future, we need to be radically and continuously adventurous in our critique of the status quo. We are morally required to regard nothing as sacred and everything as up for questioning and debate. That is how learning renews itself and how institutions respond to the world that they attempt to serve. Accordingly, the chapter asks difficult questions about the tensions which inevitably arise in such an explosive area as training and development. The reader is invited to become part of that debate.

WHAT CONSTITUTES COUNSELLING PSYCHOLOGY TRAINING?

The origins of counselling psychology in this country relate closely to its pioneer history as a radical new force in therapeutic psychology. The evolution of the Division, first as the Counselling Psychology section, then as a Special Group and since 1994 as a Division continues (Walsh et al., 2004). Initially, experienced working counselling psychologists were 'grand-parented' in. Others took the old Diploma in Counselling Psychology, which is now superseded by the present system of training outlined below.

The regulations governing the BPS represent the only way to becoming a Chartered Psychologist in Great Britain and Northern Ireland. The training requirements of chartered applied psychologists consist of a specified initial qualification, followed by CPD for as long as a psychologist holds a practising certificate. All intending trainees must have the Graduate Basis for Chartered Membership (GBC). The initial training for counselling psychology is in acquiring and demonstrating the competences set out either in the BPS's *Criteria for the Accreditation of Doctoral Training Programmes in Counselling psychology* (BPS, 2005) (for approved courses) or *Regulations and Syllabus for the Qualification in Counselling psychology* (BPS 2006) for the independent route.

Training through approved courses

There are currently 12 institutions which offer training recognized for Chartered status, of which 8 are in the London area and 1 only in Scotland. Since 2005–6, all new training courses have been designated as Doctoral level. At present there are no BPS accredited courses in Wales or in Northern Ireland. One institution in Scotland is currently working towards accreditation.

Training by the independent route

Accreditation is also obtainable via the Independent Route (BPS, 2007a, 2007b). This recognizes that psychologists have diverse pathways towards chartership. Some trainees have partially completed other relevant qualifications, or have experience and qualifications which, although of the required standard, are not sufficient for accreditation. Prior accreditation for some components of the syllabus can be applied for on the basis of previous experience and training. There is an anomaly at the time of writing in that such candidates are not able to qualify with a doctorate since the BPS is not a degree-awarding body.

The requirements of continuing professional development

Since 2005 all chartered counselling psychologists are mandated to identify and fulfil their learning needs on a yearly basis if a current practising certificate is to be issued. The CPD activities pursued must contribute to at least two development needs each year that are linked to the appropriate Key Role(s) of the National Occupational Standards for Applied Psychologists (NOS, 2006), ethics, practice, research and evaluation, communication, training and management (BPS, 2008) Activities need to take a minimum of 40 hours' input over the year, recorded electronically by the practitioner. A proportion of such records are audited by the Society. The hours may consist of courses, reading, peer discussion and so on.

WHAT IS DISTINCTIVE ABOUT A COUNSELLING PSYCHOLOGY TRAINING AND CPD?

I have elsewhere (Martin, 2006) spoken of the need for each counselling psychologist to identify essentials of counselling psychology if it is to be a distinctive force within the field. It would follow that training and CPD for this profession would reflect these emphases. They are as follows:

Counselling psychology as an applied aspect of psychology with the consequent claim to an evidence base

Other therapy trainings may not require an initial academic background at all, or may simply specify that the applicant must be a graduate or equivalent. Counselling psychology as an applied aspect of the discipline of psychology, insists on a first degree substantially in mainstream psychology. A common set of understandings, tests and disciplines forms an important start point in understanding what is required of a counselling psychology training (Dienes, 2008).

Hallmarks of psychology are in its focus on psychological knowledge. Psychology is defined as 'the study of mind and behaviour' (APA, 2008). The discipline of psychology emphasizes mental processes such as memory and perception, complex social behaviour all within the influence of prevailing social forces. Such a version of traditional psychology may not be very useful to therapists who place a high priority on feelings and emotions. It can be argued that the counselling psychologist's interest in subjectivity and intersubjectivity and in phenomenology in general may shed light on the general problem all psychologists have in studying human behaviour and human internal processes. The psychologist is, after all, part of that phenomenon being investigated. In this respect, therapeutic concerns within psychology not only derive from this dilemma, but perhaps also inform mainstream psychology.

Characteristic also of psychology is the scientific method of formulating a theory, testing by experiment and by observation the revision of hypotheses on the basis of further data, as well as the more subjective methodologies associated with qualitative research. Implicit in all these practices and thought forms is the need to treat humans differently than objects, and so the ethical dimension of both experiment and practice is highly significant in psychological endeavour.

Consequent upon the discipline's scientific basis is the collection of evidence. The evidence base of counselling psychology, however, needs to be flexibly and imaginatively interpreted. The question 'What constitutes evidence?' must be asked in the context of the other core values of the discipline. The epistemology of so-called evidence needs a sharp focus in all psychological trainings if such concepts are not to be reified (Monk, 2003).

While counselling psychology shares much with other applied psychology trainings, it also needs to maintain its distinctive ethos as a *specific* applied psychology. There may be a case for the a generic training for all applied psychologists, as proposed by the *New Ways of Working* training report (BPS, 2007c). This arrangement, however, poses important difficulties. Generic training of applied psychologists seems to imply the need to further fragment the syllabi of the applied psychologies. The components would presumably then be developed as discrete units in a university setting or in a distance learning context. Such disparate 'modules' can be taken in many combinations, making it hard to maintain a unifying philosophy which represents a particular applied psychology. It would be harder to *suffuse* a training with the *values* of counselling psychology, and in particular its reflexive and intersubjective core, if the components of the syllabus are dealt with piecemeal. The generic training initiative may well prove to be a blow against an organic training with a *philosophy of persons* as its inspiration. The considerable downside of segmentation needs to be taken into account before decisions are made (Brecher, 2005).

Counselling psychology's interest in social context and lifespan issues

Social psychology is a dynamic and fertile source of inspiration to the counselling psychologist. Here society and the individual interact. Through this focus we can question both intrapsychic and interpsychic phenomena and arrive at fertile dilemmas and theoretical and clinical formulations for the benefit of ourselves and for the wider psychological community. So we need theoretical clarity.

At present many compendia of counselling psychology, counselling and psychotherapy have impressive sections on 'contexts' in terms of varieties of experience and expertise in 'Arenas' and 'Settings' (for example, Dryden, 1989). These chapters attempt to embrace and explore the multiplicity clinical modalities and situational environments in which therapy takes place. What we lack is a coherent map from which theory can be generated in this field. The point is to help the counselling psychologist to understand, interrogate and respond positively to these hidden interrelationships in *specific* situations in the service of the therapeutic relationship and outcome. This is a hard skill to come by, but a very important one.

Examining issues of philosophical assumptions is one way of generating theory about diverse and multiple therapeutic settings, modalities and cultural backgrounds. Questioning, for instance, underlying *values* of a specific voluntary organization set up, say, for gay men might well reveal notions of oppression, of belonging or not belonging. Thus the truth claim (or 'epistemology') might well centre on the validity of subjective experience. Behind all this there might perhaps be a seemingly contradictory stance that inequality is an essential condition of being (or 'ontology'). A specific service for this client group within the NHS might well espouse similar *values*, but in the present climate its epistemology is likely to be based on hard statistics (or a 'positivistic' truth claim), and its ontology is perhaps more likely to be about striving for health as essential to being rather than inequality as essential to being. We would end up in either case with a complex but rich conceptual framework from which we are able to respond to a client in the therapeutic encounter.

Philosophy matters. Counselling psychology does not happen in a vacuum: ideas count, and intrude mightily on the nature of the therapeutic encounter. Training is charged with helping people to learn to think analytically and creatively about the principles of valuing, knowing and believing. If counselling psychologists make a claim to take social psychology seriously for libertarian and other reasons, this discipline needs to be the bedrock of training and CPD, and not a sideshow.

Similarly lifespan issues, again a specific interest of counselling psychology, needs to breathe the oxygen of relevance to clinical situations (Savickas, 2007). Theory can meet practice here, as suggested by Sugarman (2004) in her postmodernist take on what has previously been a slow traipse through the alleged stages of man.

Were we to examine these perspectives across the syllabus, we would have a more integrated and organic learning model. The questions and dilemma raised by a living relationship between, say, lifespan issues and ethical dilemmas, or the psychodynamic model, or some supervised counselling work would facilitate *active* learning. An organic model of learning would therefore emphasize the *system* that the client and counsellor operate within by reflecting that system in the syllabus/pedagogical environment. In terms of contextual awareness, all client work could, for instance, start with the question 'To what degree does the context in which this client and you meet in relationship, affect the meaning that you together generate?'

Counselling psychology's emphasis on the primacy of the relationship between the therapist and the client

All counsellors place heavy emphasis on the importance of relationship in successful counselling (Grencavage and Norcross, 1990; Wampold, 2001). Counselling psychologists and their clients in their turn are co-creators of meaning (Horvath and Greenberg, 1994). Subjectivity is the basis of all therapeutic interaction.

There is an opportunity within training and CPD to hold clinical, theoretical and research perspectives on intersubjectivity in a fertile and holistic way. We need to grasp this opportunity.

Counselling psychology's two dominant models: the scientist-practitioner and the reflexive practitioner

The scientist-practitioner

Counselling psychology owes much to sister discipline clinical psychology for the scientist-practitioner approach. Dallos and Cullen differentiate between two streams that fed into early clinical work: (i) the 'emphasis on the application of techniques'; and (ii) 'operating within the framework of general scientific method ... The scientist-practitioner model embodies the idea of progressive hypothesising' (1990: 752; emphasis in the original). Shapiro identifies five features of this methodology: critical assimilation of research; a holistic awareness of the patient; scientific eclecticism in the selection of explanations; an attention to the practitioner's own needs; and 'a continuous attention to both idiographic and nomothetic evaluation of both assessment and treatment procedures' (1985: 10). Certainly many of these skills can be taught and learned using the traditional pedagogical methods of science in our universities and training institutions.

The characteristics of clinical methodology which are identified above *can* encompass also the aspirations of the reflective practitioner (Schön, 1983), but they are probably different in emphasis.

The reflexive practitioner

Learning to be a reflexive practitioner is not easy. It consists in the ability to consult with new data and to reform ideas and understandings on the basis of consulting with current input. The notion of reflexivity is another facet of the well-proven scientific method of observation applied to the limitations of human experience.

Usher et al. (1997) summarize Schön's (1983) definition of the philosophical skill base which undergirds much skills teaching in any domain. They call it 'technical-rationality' which is 'a positivist epistemology of practice'. It is 'the dominant paradigm which has "failed to resolve the dilemma of rigour versus relevance confronting professionals"' (1997: 147). Usher then explores Schön's view of consequent implications for learning and teaching reflexivity for practitioners and for those who teach them: 'Donald Schön ... looks to an alternative epistemology of practice "in which the knowledge inherent in practice is be understood as artful doing"' (1983, quoted in Usher, 1996: 147).

Schön advises all involved in learning counselling psychology to move away from the *theory* of reflexivity into the pedagogy of a *living experience*, one which is allied to art as well as to science. It is hard to work with the lived experience in a training ethos unless we are to use our own process as the subject matter of how we learn. There is a need to introduce new ideas by teaching, but there is also a need for the learner to progressively translate evolving learning into privately relevant data. This tension is ever-present for the counselling psychology trainer.

In the same talk to teachers, Schön goes on to attack the categorization of knowledge that is used only as a tool, and consequent 'molecular knowledge'. He says the alternative to this kind of fragmentation is found in 'knowing in action'. He means that *knowing* remote from *doing* is meaningless. This is a potent warning to all in the training world. For instance, it is relatively common for a counselling psychology trainee to learn how to do clinical assessments as a discrete skill. 'Knowing in action' would instead *embed* this skill in specific relationality within specific institutional contexts. This kind of knowing requires the learner to make the generalizations themselves, in an atmosphere where mistakes are the building blocks of learning. This model is admittedly in some ways at odds with the world of academic prowess.

Schön has many critics (Harris, 1989; Richardson, 1990; Russell and Munby, 1991). Usher et al. (1997: 149) accuse him of failing to interrogate his own method, for instance. This may be so, but arguments against proponents of active learning do not necessarily invalidate the concept per se. If Schön's basic thesis is valid, it would follow that all learning in a training for counselling psychology could do well to focus on the client–practitioner interaction. Theory, even theory about learning, needs an outcome. The outcome (or *praxis*) of Schön's theory is learning that involves the whole self of the learner in a context of the client as a whole person, facilitated by trainers prepared to engage in holistic involvement.

Such learning is hard to provide in a training situation. It is more a state of mind as well as a 'theory in use' (Argyris and Schön, 1978). Intersubjectivity, the product of reflexive relating, is fleeting and hard or impossible to bottle. There is an argument, therefore, that the whole nature of training and CPD should be based on intersubjective encounters, a far cry from the regulated hurdle-jumping that characterizes our most common university-dominated training environments. This kind of learning experience would entail a commitment to experiential work that was issue-based and which took as its main stance processing interpersonal relationships; a kind of democratized form of extended analysis. In the days of distance learning and earn-as-you-learn postgraduate education, all this would be hard to achieve. Yet it may be possible to achieve this in quality if not in quantity, with more privileging of block learning as opposed to sequential 'drip' teaching, where the philosophy of what it is to be a counselling psychologist could be experienced and absorbed more holistically.

Another component in the syllabus which possibly contributes to learning reflexivity in the trainee is the mandatory inclusion of personal development (Galbraith and Hart, 2007). Mearns, however, points out that 'Simply stating a requirement for personal therapy without exploring the functions it meets is inadequate' (2007: 27). The structure that *requires* a minimum of 40 hours' therapy in counselling psychology training must also keep focus on the *function* of such personal development in the service of reflexivity. This clearly has important repercussions on the *kind* of personal therapy the training institutions encourage and on the briefing of both trainees and potential therapists. The requirements of confidentiality and the need for therapy to be apt for purpose can often be at odds. What is clear is that the nature of such therapy needs to encompass the relationality that is characteristic of Schön's position if it is to increase the capacity of the trainee to interact in this way with his or her client.

We have, however, divided our syllabus into discrete and manageable bundles. The courses which are offered to deliver the syllabus reflect this fragmentation that Schön is opposing. This regrettable position is likely to be exacerbated by the understandable demand from the universities (the main providers of training) for high academic standards for the now mandatory practitioner doctorates (Lester, 2004) with their mainly modular structure.

The opportunity to work out this theoretical stance in real terms is, for the trainee, highly dependent on their practice opportunities. It is notoriously difficult to find agencies that are able to offer the right environment where intersubjectivity can be wrought. Often trainees need to be pragmatic about the clinical practice they engage in. Many such placements on offer are of high quality in most respects but are vague about what exactly a counselling psychologist is. *The Interim Report* (sadly there was no funding available for a final report) *to the Department of Health on Initial Mapping Project for Psychotherapy and Counselling* (Aldridge and Pollard, 2005) quotes The Health Professions Council standards, which require that placements be 'integral to the programme'. Regrettably this is rarely the case, so there is much work to be done in joined-up learning for the trainee. There is little systematic research here, but there is an apposite and thorough longitudinal American study. Neimeyer and Keilin (2007) examine the provision of internships in relation to the espoused learning model of interns over a 30-year period. It shows an appreciable relationship between intern outcome where the model learned by the intern is matched with the model employed by the intern's placement. There is a need for such thorough British studies. Appropriate placements are essential seedbeds for such subtle learning.

If reflexive practice is a hallmark of counselling psychology (Van Scoyoc, 2005)*,* then it follows that both initial training (by whatever route) and CPD logically should *revolve around* this activity. It is worth noting, however, that like all else in life, there is a cost to such emphasis on the individual and on subjectivity: see the excellent analysis of the possible costs of such individualism to a cohesive society in Thatcher and Manktelow (2007).

TRAINING AND CPD IN A WIDER CONTEXT: WHAT IS IT FOR?

Licensing the practitioner

I have so far examined what counselling psychologists are required to do in order to be licensed to practise. Licensing is an overt effort to assure some kind of quality for the public and a badge conferred on the therapist recognizing the validity of the training undergone by such a professional. But could such a social act be promising too much? Perhaps licensing as a form of social assurance carries with it an undue guarantee that the practitioner has a uniform and prescribed level of competence across the board? It is possible also that licensing is a manifestation of institutional hubris? The uniform expertise implicit in the licensing procedure is brought to question by a steady trickle of complaints against certified practitioners.

Initial training may more accurately be seen as a readiness of the practitioner to place themselves on the 'start-line'. Some trainees may indeed reach great distinction, and others may drop out either from exhaustion or because of distraction. Later in practice, the story of looping-back from a competent state to an incompetent state continues (Howell and Fleishman, 1982). It may be that a more flexible view of what training and development can provide is more apposite. There is a cogent argument that therapists of any kind are first of all people (Wosket, 1999; Frankl, 2004). Training is therefore about knowledge of the human condition and is simply a form of focus on that experience.

Wider life experiences, and the breath of the world at work on the therapist as a person, has a stronger and more efficacious effect than formal training (House, 2003). This assertion is supported by my own research (Martin, 2005) in a study of experienced practitioners who found themselves in some kind of 'crisis' which placed them once again at the beginning of a new journey. In each of the 17 stories I collected, the learning of the therapist was not usually occasioned by traditional learning but by a life-event which came out of the blue. Two women lost someone they loved unexpectedly; two other women were helpless in the face of their sons who were addicted to heroin. Another therapist's sister was murdered, two had complaints filed against them as professionals. The point in each of these cases was (a) their training to some degree helped them to process and incorporate these experiences to the benefit of their clients, but (b) that each had to make a new beginning, to learn anew what it was to be themselves beside the pain of others, called their 'clients' or 'patients'.

The kind of experience outlined above asks important questions of so-called 'competence' models of learning. Counselling psychologists are engaged in a model of learning which claims competence, and so do many other professions who espouse a form of linear learning. If it is actually the case that we learn about life in spirals, rather on the 'snakes and ladders' principle, there are implications for all training and development. It may be that rather than going through a series of tests and then claiming competence on the basis of success in those tests, we should turn our attention to the more portable skill of interrogating our developing experience. Thus training would not be focused on skills and knowledge we have now got 'under the belt', but rather on our current ability to process our experience in a way that enables therapy to take place, and increases our knowledge of ourselves. Thus a series of more or less formalized conversations with disinterested peers about personal process might be a more effective way of developing and monitoring professionals than the recording activities which is the present basis of accreditation and of CPD.

Licensing to a profession

As it is, the trained individual is eligible for professional status. Professional status is, however, in danger of being reified. Undue respect for the notion of professional status as opposed to *what professionalism means in practice* results in what Giddens calls the 'sequestration of experience' in his exposé and analysis of modernity (Giddens, 1991: 144–180). Giddens appears to mean that our unique experience is in some senses 'seized' and constrained by a concept embedded in an institution. Thus an energetic and creative person with an ideal to make the world a better place may progressively be constrained into a different construction of their life and purpose by an umbrella concept such as professionalism. The individual yields his or her own version of reality to what is referred to below as a 'shared discourse'. In some sense the original experience has been 'seized', processed and can thence only express itself through the medium of the institution.

In structural-functionalist terms (an aspect of modernism), professionalism is exemplified by such institutions as the Church, Medicine and Law. Membership of each of these requires a long training in order to learn a body of specialist and esoteric knowledge (Friedson, 1994) and expertise (Schön, 1983); entry is assessed by the institution itself, and results in the right to autonomous practice. A high level of ethical awareness and practice is then required of the professional. Thus, according to Morrell (2004), a 'folk' concept of the professional (Becker, 1970) becomes part of a shared discourse, and a source of power (Foucault, 1977). Counselling psychologists, and indeed all applied psychologists, are not exempted from these constricting and distorting possibilities. It is for us to find more fluid definitions of professionalism in a society which is always on the move.

Morrell's (2004) fecund analysis of professional work in the public sector is applied to NHS nurses, but his thinking is applicable to a wide range of caring activities. He says that the very way in which we conceptualize professionalism is problematic, and limits our understanding of the phenomenon. Morrell claims that there are no necessary or sufficient criteria to define a professional, yet there are 'undeniable status markers' between existing professions. He attributes this legacy of misunderstanding to '*naïve functionalism*' (2004: 4; italics in the original). This he characterizes as a focus on work content in which process the concept of professionalism is so anodyne that it is devoid of meaning.

Instead, Morrell sees professionalism as a verb rather than as a noun. He makes the case for a fluid, interactional and dynamic understanding of professionalism. The systems approach examines, instead, interactions between professions and organizations. These interactions consist in 'social closure, exclusion and mobility; discourse and identity; cultural capital; power, patriarchy and class' (2004: 5). He attempts to evince a more dynamic meaning by examining the interactions in key areas such as knowledge, organization and power as they impact on professionalism. This argument calls attention to the limitations of knowledge, the complex web of relations within an organization, and questions the supposed role of the professional as an agent of social good. This sociological analysis has many merits, although it is possibly less reassuring than the old functionalist arguments.

Morrell posits that profit and loss is attached to each stance that may be taken in the professionalization debate. He notes, for instance, inequality of gender in the nursing profession. He suggests that increased claims to expertise by the professional (and usually female) nurse enhance the power of this socially disadvantaged gender group, but at a cost:

> … increase technical autonomy for nurses are likely to be significant in terms of raising status via a gradual reconstruction of the role, though this may undermine a coherent professional identity and ignore other elements of the nurse's work, namely the provision of care. (2004: 20)

This cost/benefit ratio has a direct parallel in counselling psychology. A gain in technical expertise may well be a loss in core identity. For instance, an increase in the technical skills of testing may enhance status but may lead in turn to a loss of core identity, in terms of valuing the subjective realm. In psychology, as in life, the ubiquitous phenomenon of 'unintended consequences' is likely to be the winner in a situation governed by opportunity rather than conviction (Merton, 1936). It is for counselling psychologists to decide what our core identity is before it is lost to sheer pragmatism.

The notion that adequate training and development exists to service 'professionalism' as it is currently conceived has been questioned in this section. The following section returns to interrogating the learning syllabus and what we do for CPD, in an attempt to tease out the issues which are in danger of reification, in the absence of constructive questioning.

QUESTIONING THE SYLLABUS

So what of the counselling psychology syllabus as it now stands? Does it do what it sets out to do? Its key aims relating to producing '... competent, reflective, ethically sound, resourceful and informed practitioners of counselling psychology able to work in therapeutic and non-therapeutic contexts' (BPS, 2007a) would be hard to fault. They ask a lot of the trainee but it is important to question whether they are indeed achievable without a coherent container. Is the now mandatory doctorate appropriate for such a task?

The syllabus, reflexivity and the clinical doctorate

The Doctorate is fairly new as a requirement, but has effectively restricted counselling psychology training to the arcane and often highly prescriptive demands of academia. The prime model of the doctorate is still the PhD. This is a higher degree that is founded rightly on academic excellence, originality and as an apprenticeship to research. The Quality Assurance Agency for Higher Education (QAA) is a little coy about how the mix of theoretical excellence and work-based skills works out in practice:

> So-called 'professional' doctorates are doctorates that focus on embedding research in a reflective manner into another professional practice. They must meet the same core standards as 'traditional' doctorates in order to ensure the same high level of quality. (QAA, 2007)

The March 2008 document is hardly any more definitive, with the descriptor for this degree still in question. The more important issue of balance is even vaguer:

> Some respondents suggested that, while the descriptor remains appropriate for PhD candidates/graduates, it could be improved by expanding the attributes so that they are more inclusive of professional doctorates. (QAA, 2008: 2)

Dent (2002) makes a passionate case for the use of the doctorate in management settings chiefly on the basis of the need for high intellectual skills married with practical skills in industry. But is this solution necessarily applicable to the gentle art of counselling psychology?

The mapping exercise (Aldridge and Pollard, 2005: 47) conducted by BACP and UKCP recognized the concern that 'training will become excessively academic'. This is also true for counselling psychology programmes. A practitioner doctorate is caught in regulations designed for academic rather than clinical excellence. Lester (2004: 6) makes just that case in a plea for a more sophisticated interpretation of what is a practitioner doctorate:

> Parallel conceptions are beginning to appear in other doctoral programmes, for instance … [the use of the] … idea of the 'executive scholar', characterised by familiarity with advanced knowledge, analytical skill, an easy facility in the use of research and academic literature, rigour and care in judging and deciding, and a reflective, informed self. (Morley and Priest, 2001: 6)

It is uncommon for training courses to have agreed and sustained placement opportunities for counselling psychology trainees, as is the norm for clinical trainings. Although most institutions offer help with placements, the provision of training settings can be at best ad hoc. This area of the syllabus, namely to become '… competent, reflective, ethically sound, resourceful and informed practitioners of counselling psychology able to work in therapeutic and non-therapeutic contexts' (BPS, 2007a) is often the most important to trainees. Often the locations in which reflexivity can flourish are uncertain, or poorly attuned to the trainee's needs. This generates anxiety both in terms of a sense of competence and in terms of the viability of the trainee for employment.

Programmes designed to encourage reflective practice are still often forced into a mould which constrains, and which may well be an insufficient support for the trainee in year-long clinical placements. Anecdotal evidence suggests that Doctoral trainees experience great pressure, especially as the majority are not normally funded (the cost of a Doctoral programme at the time of writing at one major university provider was £20,000, admittedly including 90 hours of mandatory therapy in this case; see also Kanellakis and Kinder, 2006). This is hardly the learning environment in which reflectiveness, sensitivity to the client or patient, and academic excellence can easily thrive.

The doctorate as such is perhaps an unwieldy instrument, asked to provide the kind of depth and width of training set out in the syllabus at the beginning of this section. As noted in previous sections of this chapter, modularization of the taught part of the programme in universities can further distance the relationship and philosophy which links the so-called components of such a programme.

The syllabus, reflexivity and counselling psychology research in general

Older post-MSc courses have long included an important element of research in the syllabus. Doctoral programmes are well-placed to improve on this. Much of the final year is devoted to research in most programmes, with an increased interest in a thorough grounding in research methodology in the earlier years. This commitment offers respect and impetus to the need to create and examine theory that is counselling psychology-based.

There are grounds for encouragement in this area. Counselling psychologists doing research have needed to rely for both background and participants on *related fields* such as counselling and psychotherapy. Now (in 2008) there are 934 fully accredited counselling psychologists, as well as 728 trainees and another 650 general members. Soon it will be possible to draw on a participant cohort whose perspective is counselling psychology. *Counselling Psychology Review* in 2006 acquired status in being cited by PsychInfo (the APA database of abstract). From 2007 the editorial panel has included international counselling psychologists: this resource is vital not only to the life of the Division but also as a repository for its research output. There is now a better chance that the distinctive voice of the reflexive practitioner will be heard.

The syllabus, reflexivity and qualitative research

The need to find ways of addressing, understanding and creating dialogue about subjectivity based on the phenomenological paradigm needs some protection. The generic training envisaged in *New Ways of Working* (BPS, 2007c) could result in a concentration on the highly favoured randomized control trial (RCT). Such managerial institutions as The National Institute for Health and Clinical Excellence (NICE) has as one of its remits to 'Support the commissioning of evidence-based care for patients' (NICE, 2008a). It tends to favour more positivist approaches (see, for instance, the table in the document NICE, 2008b, where major prestige and account is awarded entirely to RCTs). It is hard to find a way of encouraging reflexivity in such methodologies, especially where they dominate to the exclusion of others. McLeod (2002), however, makes a case for the originality of qualitative research within the corpus of psychological research. He notes that:

> Some branches of qualitative research … aim to be reflexive, with priority given to the role of the researcher in the creation of meaning, or may strive to be participative, with the goal of involving and empowering research informants as 'co-researchers'. (2002: 75)

There is still a growing body of qualitative research available that is being taken into account in public policy (Etherington and Barnes, 2006; Morrow, 2007). In February 2004, *Counselling Psychology Review* produced an edition entirely devoted to case studies. Another example of an adventurous approach is found in a fine exposition of the problems encountered by a trainee counselling psychologist in dealing with the ethical problems thrown up by a qualitative approach with young and vulnerable participants. The authors of this article conclude:

> Counselling psychologists are in a very strong position to eschew more traditional methods that can undermine an individual's 'voice' or 'power' effectively, integrating theoretical knowledge and clinical practice skills into their research investigations. (Bowen and John, 2001: 23)

QUESTIONING CONTINUING PROFESSIONAL DEVELOPMENT

Continuing professional development varies widely across the so-called health and social care organizations (DoH, 2003). Khele (2007), quoting her own work (Khele, 2006), lists the functions of CPD. She says it:

- contributes to an individual's continuing effectiveness as a practitioner
- reassures the public that professionals are maintaining their competence
- keeps practitioners up to date with skills and developments within their field
- ideally should ensure the application of what has been learned
- is a contribution to lifelong learning. (2007: 41)

Yet this list begs several important questions. It is not clear that the training that is being continued is based on the most useful premises. It is not clear that a competence once established is necessarily contributed to by CPD. Rather, we seem to rely on a somewhat generalized impression that CPD is 'a good thing'. Skills for Health (2007: 9) investigate the effect of CPD in medical contexts. They agree with the Royal College of Nursing's position statement on nursing education (2002) which, while approving of high quality training, includes the caveat 'there is little evidence available on the *impact of CPD on patient outcomes*' (no page reference given; emphasis in original). There is a need for greater precision and clarity.

Khele (2007) refers to the research undertaken by the Professional Association Research Network (PARN), which recommends that organizations should aim for clarity, consistency, suitability and self-reflection when considering CPD policy (Friedman et al., 2001). Perhaps something like the opposite is actually the case? CPD, although selectively monitored by BPS, depends very much on the lively interest of the individual practitioner. Supervision may well have an important role to play here. Therapists tend to rely on this mechanism to monitor, control and support. It is, to some degree, still unusual for professions to build in support in this way, although it has always been a feature of social work. It is worth questioning whether such an institution itself needs deconstruction. Perhaps as it stands it can give rise to complacency. The work of such organizations as the British Association of Supervisors and Research, and such opinion leaders as Carroll (2004) and Wheeler (1999), seek to retain the life of this important sub-institution, yet I cannot detect radical movement within this vital aspect of counselling psychology practice. Supervision is a process that is capable of rising beyond its 'formative, normative and restorative' functions (Proctor, 1989) to become a fecund source of change in both the practitioner and in the practitioner's institutions. It may be time for counselling psychology to examine the purpose and role of this mechanism in the light of what counselling psychologists per se are all about.

Given that a framework is there for the practitioner to deliver himself or herself, the motivation may still be needed to enact a vigorous CPD programme. The BPS framework does include the provision for planning, but in practice this activity may depend on chance. Experience suggests that the individual counselling psychologists embarking on CPD activities in terms of short courses, for instance, chooses on the basis of what courses become available, which are better advertised, and who else is going. Similarly, other forms of CPD such as teaching, becoming a co-ordinator of training, or membership of professional groups such as committees, has no central organization so may be haphazard. Again, personal development may well be a function of personal crisis rather than a foreseen exercise (see Martin, 2005, but see also Gordon, 2004; Mackrill, 2007). If these observations are accurate, then either what is needed is a more regulated and prescribed framework, or preferably the facilitation of an *ethos* that encourages, stimulates and motivates. Frameworks are often poor at encouraging such 'bushfire', but they do serve often to prevent standards from falling unacceptably low. We are on a journey with CPD. We have only got to the first station stop. There is a long way to go and many junctions to be negotiated.

It may be that the ethos needs to change. A possible prerequisite of an explosion of energy is a more democratic and participative atmosphere in the Division and in the Society (BPS). Counselling psychologists in the major institutions such as BPS, trainers in the training institutions and competitive colleagues in the field are subject to the same pressures towards authoritarianism and managerialism as are our colleagues elsewhere (Bates, 2003). Counselling psychology is developing perhaps like another institution also inspired initially by a kind of idealism: the evolution of the sect to a church as an institution described by Weber (described by Dillon, 2003: 124ff) has many interesting parallels. Johnson (1963, 1971) developed Weber's typology and distinguished between a sect which rejects a given social environment and a church which accepts it. With the sect comes inspiration, energy and vision. With the institution can come reification and tradition-soaked procedure, and eventually decline. If in counselling psychology we are to keep a radical edge, we need to avoid the deadening effects of prescribed institutional growth and decline. I suggest that CPD needs to expand, increase in vitality, and leap-frog us into a continuous relationship with the prevailing zeitgeist. We need to get over form, and get back to energy and dialogue. Inevitably such a maelstrom would involve a degree of chaos, but if we are to avoid the kind of deadness that characterizes many movements in their second or third phase, we will need to take the plunge.

WAYS FORWARD?

The way forward for training and development in Great Britain and Northern Ireland depends on whether training follows already identified needs or *leads* in finding needs. Europe is a potent force for all of us. Initiatives from Europe may further bureaucratize counselling psychology, or it may return it into a wider stream of Northern European philosophy and experience. The psychotherapeutic tradition has always been heavily influenced by continental Europe, whereas British counselling training and CPD has traditionally looked towards the US. The US influence may now be less ascendant across the whole range of counselling and psychotherapy, with consequent changes in emphasis in the way in which we train and practice (Aron, 2007). Extended links with Ireland, at present in hand between The Psychological Society of Ireland and the BPS in terms of mutual recognition of training perhaps augur the future.[*]

The piloted introduction of EuroPsy aims to 'set a common benchmark for academic and professional competence in all the countries where it is issued' (BPS, 2007d). It is designed to respond to the adoption throughout the EU of Directive 2005/36/EC (EC, 2005) on the mutual recognition of professional qualifications, and to facilitate the mobility of qualified professionals across Europe. It is likely that when this qualification gains currency, many initial training courses and much CPD will be directed

---

[*] See also the European Association of Counselling Psychologists (www.counsellingpsychology.eu) and the *European Journal of Psychotherapy and Counselling* (Routledge).

towards this qualification. (At the time of writing it is open only to very restricted categories.) Indeed, the entry requirements of the BPS Register of Psychologists Specialising in Psychotherapy are based on the European model, not requiring any specific therapeutic model, but emphasizing inquiry. It is an obvious CPD route for counselling psychologists.

United States Counselling Psychology is making concerted efforts to internationalize counselling psychology. Savickas (2007: 183) conducts a fascinating summary of the various national definitions of counselling psychology (ranging from 'emphasis on health, well-being, and problem-solving' in South Africa to 'fostering and improving human functioning' in Canada). The findings conclude, however that 'multiform activities cause vagueness', and encourage the search for indigenous 'models, methods and materials' (2007: 184). Savickas quoting Arulmani (2007), says that '… counseling psychology must not be tied to the apron-strings of the West' and goes on to opine that:

> To flourish internationally, counseling psychology cannot be viewed primarily as a Western specialty rooted in logical positivism … counselling psychologists can lead the way in helping world workers and the global community adapt to postmodern information. (2007: 186–187)

It might be said that it is not only positivism that obstructs postmodernist thought, but also the values and sometimes static constructs of modernist humanism. (It is fairly common, for instance, that person-centred counselling is taught for use in diverse cultures (Schmid, 2008); perhaps another form of cultural imperialism?) In UK at the moment there is a high influx of Greek trainees. Most of us training have little idea of where and how the skills and the contexts that we teach have any real application to this ancient culture. This must change.

Whether or not Europe is the tide that sweeps training and CPD in its direction, there is a need to retain both distinctiveness and catholicity within the education and development of counselling psychologists. Cooper and McLeod make the case for a 'pluralistic framework for counselling and psychotherapy' (2007). Their paper is specifically geared towards research implications of pluralism. They define pluralism, quoting Rescher (1993: 79), as 'the doctrine that any substantial question admits a variety of plausible but mutually conflicting responses'. Rescher (1933) is more interested in 'dissensus' rather than 'consensus' Cooper and McLeod say. It is the plea of this chapter that we do not look at our needs for professionalism, for training, for continuing development as a logical deduction from some original template. We need, instead, to find our way forward through the mêlée of competing interests, through the deconstruction of so-called immutable truths and towards a quest for an authentic voice for this situation, at this time and with these people. For the rest we are better to be agnostic.

REFERENCES

Aldridge, S. and Pollard, J. (2005) *Interim Report to the Department of Health on Initial Mapping Project for Psychotherapy and Counselling.* London: DOH

APA (2008) 'What is psychology', *Psychology Matters.* Available at www.psychologymatters.org/psycdefinition.html, accessed June 2008.

Argyris, C. and Schön, D. (1978) *Organizational Learning: A Theory of Action Perspective.* Reading, MA: Addison-Wesley.

Aron, L. (2007) 'Relational psychotherapy in Europe', *European Journal of Psychotherapy and Counselling,* 9 (1): 91–104.

Arulmani, G. (2007) 'Counselling psychology in India: At the confluence of two traditions', *Applied Psychology; An International Review,* 56 (1): 69–82.

Bates, Y. (2003) 'Akhenaten's folly: Imposed beliefs in counselling and psychotherapy communities', in Y. Bates and R. House (eds), *Ethically Challenged Professions ... Enabling Innovation and Diversity in Psychotherapy and Counselling.* Ross-On-Wye: PCCS. pp. 186–193.

Becker, H. (1970) *Sociological Work.* Chicago, IL: Aldine.

Bowen, A.C.L. and John, A.M.H. (2001) 'Ethical issues encountered in qualitative research: Reflections on interviewing adolescent in-patients engaging in self-injurious behaviours', *Counselling Psychology Review,* 16 (2): 19–23.

BPS (2005) *Criteria for the Accreditation of Doctoral Training Programmes in Counselling Psychology.* Leicester: BPS.

BPS (2006) *Regulations and Syllabus for the Qualification in Counselling Psychology.* Leicester: BPS.

BPS (2007a) *Qualification in Counselling Psychology Candidate Handbook.* Leicester: BPS.

BPS (2007b) *Study Guidance of Independent Route Candidates.* Leicester: BPS.

BPS (2007c). *Summary Report: New Ways of Working for Applied Psychologists in Health and Social Care – Models of Training.* Leicester: BPS.

BPS (2007d) *EuroPsy – the European Diploma in Psychology.* Leicester: BPS.

BPS (2008) CPD homepage. Available at www.bps.org.uk/professional-development/cpd/cpd-index.cfm, accessed June 2008.

Brecher, B. (2005) 'Complicity and modularisation: How universities were made safe for the market', *Critical Quarterly,* 47 (1–2): 72.

Carroll, M. (2004) *Counselling Supervision: Theory, Skills and Practice.* London: Sage.

Cooper, M. and McLeod, J. (2007) 'A pluralistic framework for counselling and psychotherapy: Implications for research', *Counselling & Psychotherapy Research,* 7 (3).

Dallos, R. and Cullen, C. (1990) 'Clinical psychology', in I. Roth (ed.), *Introduction to Psychology,* Vol. 2. Hove: Lawrence Erlbaum Associates/The Open University. pp. 723–770.

Dent, E.B. (2002) 'Developing scholarly practitioners: Doctoral management education in the 21st century', in R. DeFillippi and C. Wankel (eds), *Rethinking Management Education.* Greenwich: Information Age Publishing.

Dienes, Z. (2008) *Understanding Psychology as a Science.* Basingstoke: Palgrave.

Dillon, M. (2003) *Handbook of the Sociology of Religion.* Cambridge: Cambridge University Press.

DoH (2003) *Demonstrating Competence through Continuing Professional Development (CPD). Final Report August 2003.* London: DoH. Allied Health Profession Project.

Dryden, W. (ed.) (1989) *Handbook of Counselling in Britain.* London: Routledge.

EC (2005) 'On the recognition of professional qualifications, L 255/22', *Official Journal of the European Union*, Available at http://eur-lex.europa.eu/LexUriServ/LexUriServ.do?uri=OJ:L:2005:255:0022: 0142:EN:PDF, accessed 26 May 2008.

Etherington, K. and Barnes, E. (2006) *Southmead Project: Processes and Practices. An exploration of drug misuse, treatment and aftercare and the processes involved.* Bristol: University of Bristol.

Foucault, M. (1977) *The Archaeology of Knowledge.* London: Tavistock.

Frankl, V.E. (2004) *Man's Search for Meaning.* London: Rider.

Friedman, A., Davis, K. and Phillips, M. (2001) *Continuing Professional Development in the UK: Attitudes and Experiences of Practitioners.* Bristol: PARN.

Friedson, E. (1994) *Professionalism Reborn: Theory, Prophecy and Policy.* Cambridge: Polity Press.

Galbraith, V.E. and Hart, N.M. (2007) 'Personal development groups in counselling psychology training: The case for further research', *Counselling Psychology Review*, 22 (4): 49–56.

Giddens, A. (1991) *Modernity and Self-identity: Self and Society in the Late Modern Age.* Cambridge: Polity Press.

Gordon, C. (2004) 'Counsellors' use of reflective space', *Counselling and Psychotherapy Research*, 4 (2): 40–44.

Grencavage, L.M. and Norcross, J.C. (1990) 'Where are the commonalities among the therapeutic common factors?', *Professional Psychology: Research and Practice*, 21: 372–378.

Harris, I.B. (1989) 'Critique of Schön's views on teacher education: Contributions and issues', *Journal of Curriculum and Supervision*, 5 (1): 13–18.

Horvath, A.O. and Greenberg, L.S. (1994) *The Working Alliance: Theory, Research and Practice.* New York: Wiley.

House, R. (2003) *Therapy Beyond Modernity: Deconstructing and Transcending Profession-centred Therapy.* London: Karnac.

Howell, W.C. and Fleishman, E.A. (1982) *Human Performance and Productivity. Vol 2: Information Processing and Decision Making.* Hillsdale, NJ: Erlbaum.

Johnson, B. (1963) 'On church and sect', *American Sociological Review*, 28: 539–549.

Johnson, B. (1971) 'Church and sect revisited', *Journal for the Scientific Study of Religion*, 10: 124–137.

Jones, R. and Jenkins, F. (2006) *Developing the Allied Health Professional.* Oxford: Radcliffe.

Kanellakis, P. and Kinder, A. (2006) 'Is the independence of counselling psychology training worth the cost?', *Counselling Psychology Review*, 21 (2): 49–51.

Khele, S. (2006) *Continuing Professional Development (CPD) and Supervision in Professional Bodies.* Lutterworth: BACP.

Khele, S. (2007) 'Continuing professional development (CPD) and supervision in professional bodies', *Therapy Today*, 18 (7): 41–42.

Lester, S. (2004) 'Conceptualising the practitioner doctorate', *Studies in Higher Education*, 29 (5): 750–777.

Mackrill, T. (2007) 'Qualified therapists' experience of personal therapy', *Counselling and Psychotherapy Research*, 7 (4): 211–219.

Martin, P. (2005) *The Effects of Current Life-events on the Work of Therapists.* Unpublished thesis, Graduate School of Education, Bristol.

Martin, P. (2006) 'Different, dynamic and determined – the powerful force of counselling psychology in the helping professions', *Counselling Psychology Review*, 21 (4): 42–44.

McLeod, J. (2002) 'Qualitative research methods in counselling psychology', in R. Woolfe, W. Dryden and S. Strawbridge (eds), *Handbook of Counselling Psychology.* London: Sage. pp. 75–92.

Mearns, D. (2007) 'Personal therapy – a structural or functional perspective?', *Therapy Today,* 18 (7).

Merton, R.K. (1936) 'The unanticipated consequences of purposive social action', *American Sociological Review*, 1 (6): 894–904.

Monk, P. (2003) 'First response: Information, innovation and the quest for knowledge', *Counselling Psychology Review*, 18 (3): 14–20.

Morley, C. and Priest, J. (2001) 'Developing a professional doctorate in business administration: Reflection and the "Executive Scholar"', in B. Green, T.W. Maxwell and P. Shanahan (eds), *Doctoral Education and Professional Practice: The Next Generation?* Armidale: Kardoorair Press.

Morrell, K. (2004) 'Analysing professional work in the public sector: The case of NHS nurses', Loughborough University Business School Research Series. Available at www.kevinmorrell.org.uk/ K_Morrell%20CV%20Mar%202009.pdf, accessed 28 April 2008.

Morrow, S.L. (2007) 'Qualitative research in counseling psychology', *The Counseling Psychologist*, 35 (2): 209–235.

Neimeyer, G.J. and Keilin, W.G. (2007) 'Tracking trends: A longitudinal look at internship placements in counselling psychology in the United States', *Counselling Psychology Quarterly*, 20 (2): 123–134.

NICE (2008a) 'National Institute for Health and Clinical Excellence: Commissioning guides – supporting clinical service redesign'. Available at www.nice.org.uk/usingguidance/commissioningguides/ commissioning_guides_8211_supporting_clinical_service_redesign.jsp, accessed May 2008.

NICE (2008b) 'The guidelines manual – Chapter 7: Reviewing and grading the evidence'. Available at www.nice.org.uk/niceMedia/pdf/GuidelinesManualChapter7.pdf, accessed 21 May 2008.

NOS (2006) *National Occupational Standards Factsheet.* Available at www.skillsforjustice.com/ websitefiles/FACTSHEET_NOS_Factsheet__Updated_May_2006.pdf, accessed July 2008.

Proctor, B. (1989) 'Supervision: A co-operative exercise in accountability', in M. Marken and M. Payne (eds), *Enabling and Ensuring*. Leicester: National Youth Bureau.

QAA (2007) 'Discussion paper about doctoral programmes'. Available at www.qaa.ac.uk/academicin frastructure/doctoralProg/ConsultationPaper.pdf, accessed 23 May 2008.

QAA (2008) 'Discussion paper about doctoral programmes: Summary of preliminary analysis'. Available at www.qaa.ac.uk/academicinfrastructure/doctoralProg/progressMarch08.asp, accessed 23 May 2008.

Rescher, N. (1993) *Pluralism: Against the Demand for Consensus.* Oxford: Oxford University Press.

Richardson, V. (ed.) (1990) *The Evolution of Reflective Teaching and Teacher education: Encouraging Reflective Practice in Education. An analysis of issues and Programs.* New York: Teachers College Press.

Royal College of Nursing (2002) 'Quality education for quality care', in Skills for Health (2007), *A Literature Review of the Relationship between Quality Health Care Education and Quality of Care.* Perivale: The Mackinnon Partnership.

Russell, T. and Munby, H. (eds) (1991) 'Reframing: The role of experience in developing teachers' professional knowledge', *The Reflective Turn: Case Studies in and on Educational Practice.* New York: Teachers Press, Columbia University.

Savickas, M.L. (2007) 'Internationalisation of counseling psychology: Constructing cross-national consensus and collaboration', *Applied Psychology: An International Review*, 56 (1): 182–188.

Schmid, P.F. (2008) *Person-Centred Psychotherapy.* Available at www.pfs-online.at/papers/ paper-pct.htm, accessed April 2008.

Schön, D. (1983) *The Reflective Practitioner – How Professionals Think in Action.* New York: Basic Books.

Shapiro, M.B. (1985) 'A reassessment of clinical psychology as an applied science', *The British Journal of Clinical Psychology*, 24 (1): 1–13.

Skills for Health (2007) *A Literature Review of the Relationship between Quality Health Care Education and Quality of Care.* Perivale: The Mackinnon Partnership.

Sugarman, L. (2004) *Counselling and the Life Course.* London: Sage.

Thatcher, M. and Manktelow, K. (2007) 'The cost of individualism', *Counselling Psychology Review,* 22 (4): 31–41.

Usher, R. (1996) 'A critique of the neglected epistemological assumptions of educational research', in D. Scott and R. Usher (eds), *Understanding Educational Research.* London: Routledge.

Usher, R., Bryant, I. and Johnston, R. (1997) *Adult Education and the Postmodern Challenge.* London: Routledge.

Van Scoyoc, S. (2005) 'The future of our profession: Time to remember our history', *Counselling Psychology Review,* 20 (2): 49–51.

Walsh, Y., Frankland, A. and Cross, M. (2004) 'Qualifying and working as a counselling psychologist in the United Kingdom', *Counselling Psychology Quarterly,* 17 (3): 317–328.

Wampold, B.E. (2001) *The Great Psychotherapy Debate – Models, Methods, and Findings.* Mahwah, NJ: Lawrence Erlbaum.

Wheeler, S. (1999) 'Can counselling be a profession? A historical perspective for understanding counselling in the new millennium', *Counselling,* 10 (5): 381.

Wosket, V. (1999) *The Therapeutic Use of Self.* London and New York: Routledge.

29

PERSONAL DEVELOPMENT

Rosemary Rizq

Curiously, we don't expect personal development to feature explicitly in the training of doctors, lawyers, politicians or teachers: professions that, arguably, like our own, are implicated in the business of power, influence and suggestion. But unlike these professions, psychotherapists have always been peculiarly reserved about their interest in and capacity for exploiting the psychological impact of one person on another. Perhaps this should not surprise us. The notion that personality might somehow be involved in influencing other people brings us perilously close once again to those early, rather disreputable practices of mesmerism and hypnosis from which psychotherapy historically has always sought to distance itself: 'here, in fact, lies the whole secret of magnetism and all delusions of a similar kind' wrote Mackay of Anton Mesmer. '… induce belief and blind confidence and you can do any thing' (1841: 317). And the fact that one rather dubious person could 'induce belief and blind confidence' in another – often, in those days, with rather alarming and inappropriate results – was what eventually sponsored Freud's plans for a more scientific psychology and resulted in modern-day psychotherapy.

In this sense, we might think of exhortations to pay heed to the 'self of the therapist' as a code for examining the far more enigmatic and frankly equivocal role of the therapist's character or personality. Professional influence can be for good or ill and perhaps an insistence on 'personal development' could be seen as the psychotherapeutic profession's attempt, not unreasonably, to ensure that the therapist's character is such that he or she will not adversely influence, exploit or take advantage of his or her client. The requirement of 'personal development' within counselling psychology training then could be seen as an attempt to highlight and help those whose characters or personalities potentially render them unfit or unsafe for practice. Of course, trying to pinpoint those who are deemed unsuited to clinical work serves a dual purpose: it preserves the hope that there are safe, reliable practitioners in the world on whom we can trust and depend; and it sustains the conviction that we belong to a profession that knows the difference. These are obviously not unimportant beliefs for clinical practitioners and trainers to maintain, despite the fact that they beg a number of rather uncomfortable questions: What constitutes 'personal development' and do the various personal development activities sponsored by training institutions actually lead to improved clinical outcomes for clients? Do we know what produces effective clinical outcomes for our clients in the first place? Do we know what aspects of the therapist's character and personality relate to clinical outcome in the client? And in any case, can we be sure that training itself improves clinical effectiveness?

That counselling psychology, as a profession, is willing to ask and explore such thorny questions is, I think, characteristic of its dual alliance both with a 'scientist-practitioner' paradigm, emphasizing the importance of an empirical basis for theory and practice, and a 'reflective-practitioner' paradigm, emphasizing the role of reflection and the use of the self of the therapist in clinical work. Indeed, Donati and Watts (2002) have claimed on this basis that counselling psychology is uniquely situated to address the role of personal development within training. In this chapter, then, I will try to address some of the foregoing questions as well as exploring and critiquing some of the research literature on various forms of personal development activities within counselling psychology and psychotherapeutic training. Readers may note that there is an emphasis on personal therapy in my review, reflecting its priority within the training of counselling psychologists.

WHAT IS PERSONAL DEVELOPMENT?

The practice of counselling psychology requires 'a high level of self-awareness and competence in relating the skills and knowledge of personal and interpersonal dynamics in the therapeutic context' (BPS, 2009). This emphasis on self-awareness in training and on the use of the self of the therapist in clinical work underpins the current place of personal development work in the training of counselling psychologists and, indeed, many other psychotherapeutic practitioners. However, it seems that 'personal development' is one of those rather loose phrases that everybody in the profession uses but nobody can clearly define. Current debates and disputes about the precise meaning of the term (Donati and Watts, 2002, 2005; Hall et al., 1999; Williams and Irving, 1996) not only attest to the potentially contentious nature of this aspect of training, but highlight the fact that personal development is often seen as the most significant aspect of counselling training whilst simultaneously being the least recognized and well-characterized (Johns, 1996).

Part of this confusion perhaps relates to the very close relationship personal development has with professional development in training: the acquisition of theory, research, skills and knowledge abuts closely with more personal dimensions such as the counsellor's personal qualities, attributes, authenticity, and his or her capacity for interpersonal engagement (Elton-Wilson, 1994). Indeed, Skovholt and Ronnestad (1996), along with Wilkins (1997), have argued that personal and professional development are mutually inter-dependent.

Ambiguities of definition inevitably lead to a degree of confusion and uncertainty about establishing relevant professional aims and outcomes for personal development activities during training. Irving and Williams, in making a fine-grained distinction between 'personal growth' and 'personal development', bemoan the lack of clarity in the current use of these terms, asserting that:

> Statements as to the need for and value of 'growth' or 'development' in the absence of a theoretical frame – as in much of the professional literature – are vacuous assertions. Certainly, the observed lack of clarity in distinguishing between personal development and personal growth in counsellor training and professional practice, and the imposition of criteria for personal growth upon personal development work, result in a confusion of aims and therefore in the use of inappropriate methods. (1999: 524)

Despite continuing claims that a clear definition of personal development is lacking, and that personal development is a poorly specified and articulated area of counselling psychology training (Donati and Watts, 2005; Galbraith and Hart, 2007), various types of personal development work have nonetheless played a central role within counselling, psychotherapy and counselling psychology training institutions. For instance, virtually all of the 80 member organizations of the United Kingdom Council for Psychotherapy (UKCP) have extensive personal therapy training requirements, one notable exception being members of the behavioural and cognitive psychology section. The British Association for Counselling and Psychotherapy (BACP) now requires evidence of self-development activities for those seeking individual accreditation, asking candidates for a rationale for the choice of activity, and to demonstrate how it contributes to their clinical practice.

Within the British Psychological Society (BPS), however, it is only the Division of Counselling Psychology that continues to stipulate a mandatory period of personal therapy for trainees undertaking either an accredited training course or the Society's Qualification in Counselling Psychology via the Independent Route. The BPS's regulations and syllabus for the Division of Counselling Psychology state that:

> Trainees will be actively and systematically engaged in personal development work so that greater understanding of personal issues is developed through:
>
> - An understanding of therapy from the perspective of the client.
> - An understanding through therapy of their own life experience.
> - An ability for critical self-reflection on the use of self in therapeutic processes. (2006)

A mandatory training therapy, of course, does not exclude other personal development activities during counselling psychology training. Training institutions will vary in what additional activities they offer; this may include personal development, experiential groups or keeping reflective learning journals. Indeed, Wilkins (1997), in commenting on his own experience of personal development, points out that individual therapy, group therapy and co-counselling all made valuable contributions to his clinical work with clients. However, as personal therapy is mandated in all counselling psychology training courses, and arguably carries the most extensive research literature, perhaps it is appropriate now to turn our attention to the arguments for and against its inclusion within the counselling psychology training syllabus.

PERSONAL THERAPY: FOR AND AGAINST

Historically, there have been a number of rationales given for the inclusion of a mandatory training therapy. The traditional view, originating with Freud (1937/57), was that a personal analysis was the main route to establishing a professional identity. Fromm-Reichmann, too, claims trenchantly that:

> because of the inter-relatedness between the psychiatrist's and the patient's interpersonal processes, and because of the interpersonal character of the psychotherapeutic process itself, any attempt to intensive psychotherapy is fraught with danger, hence unacceptable, where not preceded by the future psychiatrist's personal analysis. (1950: 42)

Psychoanalysis and other forms of dynamic therapy, then, have insisted that personal analysis is essential for safe clinical practice. However, Farrell (1996) suggests that it provides an opportunity for therapists of any theoretical orientation to understand the position of the client and to reduce the likelihood of 'blind spots' and unethical behaviour. Norcross et al. argue that the goal of the psychotherapist's personal treatment is ultimately to 'alter the nature of subsequent therapeutic work in ways that enhance its effectiveness' (1988a: 36).

Similarly, work by Williams et al. (1999) suggests that personal therapy models clinical methods, offers 'in vivo' experience of interpersonal dynamics and promotes self-awareness and personal development. Norcross et al. (1988a) identify six ways in which the therapist's therapy is said to benefit clinical work, including: improving the emotional and mental functioning of the therapist; providing the therapist-patient with a more complete understanding of personal dynamics; alleviating the emotional stresses and burdens of professional work; providing a socialization experience; placing the therapist in the client's role; and offering an opportunity to observe clinical methods 'first hand'. From the perspective of public confidence in the profession, Mace (2001) argues that patients' groups overwhelmingly prefer psychotherapists to have had personal therapy themselves.

By custom, precedent and general agreement, then, it seems that personal therapy has traditionally been regarded as an indispensable part of psychotherapeutic training. However, the issue is certainly not without controversy, as Masson's (1992) denunciation of personal therapy as indoctrination highlights. In 2002, the BACP dropped its mandatory personal therapy requirement for therapists seeking individual accreditation, claiming that such a demand was unsustainable on both intellectual and ethical grounds. BACP maintain that personal development in training:

- can take different forms
- cannot be mandated by a professional association to be in a particular modality or of a particular length apart from when to act otherwise would be incongruent with a core theoretical model
- should demonstrably contribute to the development and/or personal benefit of the therapist. (BACP, 2002)

Atkins, on behalf of BACP, points out the risks of insisting on personal therapy without good reason:

> The wisdom of mandatory therapy for those who are 'well' is questionable. There can be more perceived risks than benefits in mandatory personal therapy in training, including the existence of dual relationship (for example, therapist/assessor) or difficulties with confidentiality. (2006: 408).

Nor is there a personal therapy training requirement within the behavioural and cognitive section of UKCP. The cognitive-behavioural model traditionally emphasizes the use of specific therapeutic techniques to promote psychological change rather than the use of the relationship between client and therapist. This primarily pragmatic and didactic view has rather down-played the role of the cognitive-behavioural therapist's self-awareness, and, as a result, the training of cognitive-behavioural therapists has given little emphasis to trainees' personal development.

However, Corrie (2002), in reviewing developments in the cognitive model, specifically draws attention to the increasing interest in the use of the therapeutic relationship within CBT and raises the question of whether and how personal therapy might become more relevant for CBT practitioners. Bennett-Levy et al. (2003) have pioneered an approach to reflective practice within CBT called 'self-practice and self-reflection', or 'SP/SR', which involves trainees practising cognitive therapy techniques on themselves before reflecting on the subsequent thoughts and feelings that these evoke. In a review of mainly European training studies on self-reflection and self-practice in CBT training, Laireiter and Willutzki (2003) conclude that these may be important and highly valued aspects of CBT training that should be more widely incorporated into training courses. To date, however, there is little sign that personal therapy is likely to become a requirement for CBT therapists training in the UK.

Within counselling psychology too, Williams et al. (1999) suggest there are a number of concerns about insisting on a compulsory period of personal therapy for all counselling psychology trainees. Such an obligation does not allow for choice, which is generally thought to be the sine qua non of productive therapy; trainees are therefore placed under considerable pressure to enter, and remain in, therapy even if the work does not go well, or if they fail to establish a reasonable working relationship with the therapist. Clearly, there is a potential for emotional damage in such cases. Where difficult emotional material surfaces during therapy, trainees may be unable to focus adequately on course requirements and their academic and clinical work may suffer. Indeed, given that counselling psychology training is not only an emotionally and intellectually challenging activity, but is ever-more *financially* demanding, some individuals may simply find the cost of personal therapy prohibitive and decide against embarking on a training course.

In the teeth of these criticisms, which I think have undeniable face validity, it would seem that counselling psychology urgently needs to provide a clear rationale and evidence for the benefits of personal therapy. Whilst there are certainly moving and persuasive testaments to the personal and professional gains to be made from intensive personal therapy (Geller, 2005) in keeping with counselling psychology's endorsement of the scientist-practitioner paradigm, I would like to review a selection of the extensive research literature in this area, which, as we shall see, yields rather more equivocal findings.

PERSONAL THERAPY: SURVEY RESEARCH

There is no doubt that psychotherapists practise what they preach. In a sample of nearly 5000 psychotherapists from over 20 different countries, approximately 80 per cent of psychotherapists reported themselves as either currently in, or to have been in, personal therapy (Orlinsky et al., 1999); 90 per cent of analytic-dynamic therapists and 58 per cent of cognitive-behaviour therapists in Western countries reported either to be in, or to have been in, personal therapy, and 88 per cent of survey respondents rated their experiences of personal therapy as 'positive'. Macran and Shapiro's (1998) review of the personal therapy literature also supports the view that most therapists feel positively about their personal therapy, reporting it as a valuable professional experience. Whilst diverse reasons are given for entering therapy (Norcross et al., 1988a), Macaskill and Macaskill (1992) found that most respondents in their survey cited personal growth or resolving underlying personal problems as their main aims.

What do these surveys tell us about the benefits of personal therapy? Grimmer and Tribe (2001), citing a number of different surveys, point to self-reported benefits such as improved self-esteem, improvement in work function, symptomatic improvement and improvements in social and sex life, as well as characterological changes. Other authors report: increased awareness of the client–therapist personal relationship; awareness of transference-countertransference issues; and increased patience, tolerance and empathy (Macaskill and Macaskill, 1992; Norcross et al., 1988a).

However, Buckley et al. (1981), along with Macaskill (1988), have also highlighted a number of negative evaluations of personal therapy, including damage to marriages, destructive acting-out, and feeling that the therapist had become the most important person in the trainee's life. Other negative evaluations included depression and becoming 'too reflective'. As noted earlier, combining personal therapy and psychotherapeutic training may be experienced as significantly emotionally taxing by trainees (McEwan and Duncan, 1993), and several researchers have pointed out the difficulties experienced by the trainee therapist in treating others at the same time as undergoing personal therapy, possibly due to the emotional conflicts evoked in their therapy (Greenberg and Staller, 1981).

To date, though, there have been only two published surveys of UK counselling psychologist's views of personal therapy. Williams et al.'s (1999) survey of UK chartered counselling psychologists found that they were overwhelmingly in favour of personal therapy, and that many wanted an even more stringent mandatory training requirement. The study identified three clear areas of benefit from personal therapy: dealing with personal issues, dealing with training difficulties and, most of all, learning about therapy. Of interest was the finding that only 15 per cent of the sample were in favour of locating personal therapy at the beginning of training: this leads Williams et al. to suggest that therapy for the inexperienced trainee may be anti-therapeutic for clients and that 'first-time therapy in the early stages of training may not be the best route' (1999: 551). Rothery's (1992) earlier small survey of Irish clinical and counselling psychologists' attitudes to personal development work, including personal therapy, similarly found that all counselling psychology trainees saw personal growth work as essential in contrast to only half of the clinical psychology trainees/clinicians, opting for personal therapy as their route of choice to personal development in training, along with group process work.

It is clear then, from both US and UK surveys that, in general, therapists benefit both professionally and personally from undergoing a personal therapy during training. However, whilst surveys give us a broad overall picture of large numbers of therapists, confounding factors such as low response rates, biased samples, and the fact that those who have invested considerable time, energy and money in a lengthy personal therapy will inevitably be more likely to endorse its indispensability within training mean that results should be treated with caution. More importantly, survey reports bear little relation to therapists' actual *behaviour* in clinical practice or 'real-life' situations. For this reason, outcome studies examining the impact of the therapist's personal therapy on clinical outcome may be more useful.

OUTCOME AND EXPERIMENTAL STUDIES

Past reviews of the literature examining the effects of the therapist's personal therapy on clinical practice offer little endorsement for its impact on client outcomes. Herron concludes in his review that 'the effects of personal therapy appear complex and varied for therapists in training, with some therapists functioning effectively without personal therapy' (1988: 177).

Macran and Shapiro's more recent (1998) review of nine published studies, including those reviewed by Macaskill (1988) and Greenberg and Staller (1981), similarly concludes that neither receipt of personal therapy, nor length of time in personal therapy, positively relates to a wide range of client outcome measures. Indeed, an early, widely-quoted and controversial small-sample study by Garfield and Bergin (1971) found that the clients of trainee therapists receiving personal therapy were likely to do *less* well than those clients of trainees who were not undergoing personal therapy. By contrast, some experimental studies, albeit using analogue situations, demonstrate the contribution of personal therapy in increased therapist empathy ratings (Strupp, 1973) and countertransference awareness (McDevitt, 1987).

Additional studies have also explored within-session experiences of the client and therapist and its relationship to personal therapy. These 'process-perspective' studies provide some support for the idea that personal therapy enables the therapist to provide a warm, empathic, genuine therapeutic bond (Wogan and Norcross, 1985), non-specific factors considered to be essential in promoting a positive psychotherapeutic outcome (Lambert and Bergin, 1994; Orlinsky et al., 1994). Of note, however, is a study by Wheeler (1991) which, albeit suffering from a heavy attrition rate, found that length of time in personal therapy correlated negatively with therapist predictions of the therapeutic alliance. This somewhat unexpected finding is partially explained by Wheeler's suggestion that personal therapy may give the therapist the confidence to allow for the development and expression of negative transference within the therapeutic relationship.

Overall, however, these kinds of results can give proponents of mandatory training therapy little satisfaction. But a more recent study by Sandell et al. (2002, 2006) based on data derived from the Stockholm Outcome of Psychotherapy and Psychoanalysis Project (STOPPP) found a more complex relationship between length of training therapy and clinical outcomes. The authors found that length of the therapist's training therapy was negatively related to patient change in psychotherapy, but positively related to change within psychoanalysis. By way of possible explanation, the authors suggest that those who have undertaken a lengthy personal analysis are likely to identify with their psychoanalyst's approach and may inappropriately attempt to apply psychoanalytic standards of neutrality and abstinence to brief psychotherapy work with clients, resulting in suboptimal clinical outcomes. By implication, this is less likely to occur with those whose personal therapy was shorter and those who may be less closely identified with their therapist's way of working.

CRITIQUE

Traditional quantitative research, then, appears to offer little by way of a clear endorsement for the role of personal therapy in training and its putative benefits for clinical work. Whilst most of the research sampled above suffers from a number of methodological limitations, including the possibility that trainees who have undertaken a personal therapy may be given, or may choose to work with, more challenging clients, the central issue is the extent to which personal therapy may be sought by trainees because of psychological distress. Therapists with significant psychological problems may simply be less effective with clients, even after personal therapy, than those who have had no therapy at all because they did not need it. Indeed, Beutler et al. (1994) argue that a failure to distinguish amongst the possible diverse reasons for undertaking personal therapy render its average effects uninterpretable.

Another difficulty is that of theoretical orientation. The frequent use of personal therapy by psychoanalytically trained therapists – who also appear to provide the most frequently used type of personal therapy – means that it is impossible to compare experienced psychoanalytic practitioners with or without personal therapy. Since relatively few therapists choose cognitive or behavioural therapy for themselves (Norcross et al., 1988b; Norcross, 1990), there is also a particular need to explore how therapists of other theoretical orientations perceive the impact of different types of personal therapy on their clinical practice (for notable exceptions, see Laireiter and Willutzki, 2003, and McNamara, 1986). This issue is of particular relevance to counselling psychology, which explicitly endorses a theoretically pluralistic view of training and practice; it is here that an understanding of the differential impact of a range of personal therapy orientations on client work is most urgently needed.

QUALITATIVE RESEARCH

There are considerable methodological and conceptual problems, then, in establishing a linear relationship between a therapist's receipt of personal therapy and better client outcomes. However, a number of researchers have pointed to the limitations of the above types of research, with Wiseman and Shefler arguing that 'the quantification of experience on Likert scales seems far too impoverished to describe the experience of personal therapy' (2001: 131). The shift in interest from 'whether' to 'how' personal therapy influences client work is mirrored in the more recent personal therapy research that focuses on process rather than outcome, on subjective understanding of individual therapists' experiences rather than objective measures, on qualitative rather than quantitative methodologies.

Macran et al.'s (1999) UK study used interpretative phenomenological analysis to explore therapists' experiences of their own therapy. Interviewing seven experienced therapists of differing therapeutic orientations, they aimed to elicit detailed descriptive accounts of personal therapy and of its influence on client work. Amongst 12 common themes, organized into three overall domains, it was the last domain 'listening with the third ear' that was found to be associated with the 'most subtle' effects of personal therapy. This included helping participants to understand their clients more deeply, via verbal and non-verbal communications.

In a similar study, Wiseman and Shefler (2001) looked at the impact of personal therapy on the personal and professional development of experienced, psychoanalytically-oriented therapists. Using a methodology based on the consensual qualitative research (CRQ) strategy (Hill et al., 1997), the authors found that personal therapy is perceived not only as essential within training, but also as 'essential to the therapist's ongoing process of individuation and in the development of the ability to use the self to achieve moment-to-moment authentic relatedness with one's clients' (2001: 129).

A qualitative study of British counselling psychologists' experiences of personal therapy has been carried out by Grimmer and Tribe (2001). This study used grounded theory analysis to explore 14 recently qualified and trainee counselling psychologists' opinions as to the impact of a mandatory personal therapy on their professional development. Four core categories of experience emerged: reflection on being in the role of the client; socialization experiences; support of the emerging professional; and interactions between personal and professional development. Grimmer and Tribe conclude that while personal therapy leads to a range of outcomes for therapists, results vary widely for each participant, and that it was not possible to assess the extent to which personal therapy led to actual changes in behaviour within therapy.

Qualitative research has been much-criticized for failing to supply the necessary theoretical framework which might guide future exploration and research (cf. Chamberlain, 2000). It is certainly true that the previously mentioned studies, whilst providing interesting perspectives on how individual therapists feel personal therapy has impacted on their personal and professional lives, neither synthesizes the data into a coherent framework, nor links it to any of the relevant social or psychological literature. Rizq and Target (2008a, 2008b) have attempted to address this lacuna in the literature by drawing on attachment-related research to contextualize results from an interpretative phenomenological analysis of nine experienced counselling psychologists' descriptions of the meaning and significance of personal therapy. Results showed that participants valued personal therapy primarily as a means of developing the ability to reflect on the self: being seen by a therapist appeared to form the foundation for participants' capacity to tolerate aspects of themselves; this in turn was felt to be the basis of an identification with clients and the capacity to distinguish between self and client issues, leading to more effective empathic clinical work. The authors draw on Fonagy and Target's (1996) model of mentalization to amplify and understand participants' accounts, and situate themes emerging from their narratives within a developmental framework that takes account of what participants describe of their early attachment experience and its implications for self-reflexivity.

Overall, we can see that research into the benefits of personal therapy for therapists has followed a similar path to psychotherapy research in general: moving away from the global question of 'Does therapy work?' to the more specific issue of 'What kinds of therapy work for which kinds of therapist/clients?' The more recent qualitative research studies offer some pointers for possible future research: What effect does compulsory training therapy have on the trainee's experience of it? What distinguishes an authentic from an inauthentic experience of personal therapy? What aspects of personal therapy are trainees most likely to reproduce in their own clinical work? What effect does receiving personal therapy in one theoretical orientation have on clinical practice in another? What developmental factors facilitate or hinder the trainee's capacity to benefit from personal therapy in training? This last issue, of course, brings us to the issue of alternative personal development activities that may be provided during counselling psychology training, and it is to these that we now turn.

PERSONAL DEVELOPMENT GROUPS

Over half a century ago, t-group, sensitivity training, process groups and encounter groups were all popular practices within psychotherapy training, aimed at fostering individuals' self-awareness, interpersonal sensitivity and understanding of group processes. As with personal therapy, such groups are now widely regarded as a significant element of counsellor training (Johns, 1996), and constitute an additional personal development activity included by some counselling psychology training institutions. Counselling psychology trainees may take part in varying types of experiential groups, depending on the core theoretical model and interests of the training institution; participation may continue throughout their training, or may be limited to a pre-determined period of time. Where such groups take place (and, unlike personal therapy, there is no mandate for training courses to provide experiential groupwork), these groups are generally unassessed apart from trainee attendance.

But what exactly is a personal development group? First of all, we should clearly distinguish it from its first cousin, group analysis, which serves a specific purpose in training participants in group therapy. By contrast, Galbraith and Hart define personal development groups rather loosely as:

the specific, dedicated and facilitated group work that takes place within counselling and counselling psychology training courses, whereby the aim is often perceived to be an opportunity for trainees to experience being a group member in a group-therapy context as well as the group operating as a vehicle for self-development and growth. (2007: 50)

The personal development group, then, appears to be a somewhat generic term referring to a range of rather diverse theoretical and organizational approaches to interpersonal learning, growth and development. Hall et al. (1999) outline several characteristics of small group training. These include: membership of an average of 12 participants; the presence of a group leader, facilitator or consultant, whose role is to focus the group's attention on interpersonal or group dynamics; volunteer members with varying levels of experience of group-work; boundaries of time and space are usually set explicitly by the group leader, but any other 'rules' in the group are commonly agreed by negotiation.

Whatever the makeup of the personal development group, Gilbert and Shmukler suggest there are some common potential benefits to be gained:

In a well-functioning counselling group, members have the opportunity to change and update their schemata and rigid categories for processing reality. They can build more effective and rewarding relations with others and may also address issues of the meaning and relevance of their lives in the larger socio-political context in which they share common concerns with members of the human race. (1996: 443)

RESEARCH ON PERSONAL DEVELOPMENT GROUPS

But how can we evaluate whether or not practice improves as a result of participation in such groups? If we turn to the research to adjudicate we can see that much of the literature derives from the 1960s and 1970s when groups first started to become standard in counselling training. Lieberman et al.'s (1973) review of outcomes from a variety of encounter groups found mainly positive results for the majority of participants, although this much-criticized review also reported a high number of what has been commonly identified in the literature as group 'casualties' (see below). By contrast, reviews of small group training by Hartman (1979) report fewer damaging effects and that participants developed a positive view of themselves, with enhanced feelings of self-efficacy and control.

Irving and Williams' (1999) study of groupwork and preferred learning styles found that differences in perceptions of groupwork were correlated with self-reports of preferred learning style, distinguishing between 'activists', 'reflectors', 'theorists' and 'pragmatists'. Results indicated that pragmatists, who like to see a clear link between what they are learning and how to apply it, were most likely to see groupwork as important and to enjoy the experience. They were also less likely to be aware of others' feelings of threat or discomfort. By contrast, 'activists' and 'reflectors' found the experience of groupwork unhelpful and, significantly, all learning style groups were unclear about the purpose and aims of groupwork. Once again, we are back to the lack of clarity in the definition, aims and purpose of such activities – a contention supported by Donati's (2002) survey of trainee counselling psychologists which identified a considerable disparity in their views about the definition, facilitation and assessment of personal development work during training. Indeed, it is clear that the BPS, along with BACP, provide surprisingly few guidelines on personal development training in general.

Hall et al.'s (1999) study surveyed counsellors who had participated in one of two small-group training groups as part of their course. Results showed participants reported positive outcomes from both a Rogerian small group and a Group Dynamics group. Hall et al. point out that those skills that trainees typically find hardest to acquire, such as challenging, handling silence and giving and receiving feedback, were identified by participants as learned during their personal development group training. Despite a low response rate, the authors make the point that personal development groups were regarded as memorable by participants, even over a period of 20 years. A 'sleeper' effect was noted with gains in professional tolerance, educational value and counselling skills perceived over time.

Some trainees display a clear ambivalence for group work, as Irving and Williams (1999) found. Perhaps this is not surprising, given the earlier-mentioned potential for 'casualties' in groupwork: 'Not only do some individuals fail to benefit from these experiences', warn Irving and Williams, 'some may be damaged by it' (1999: 139). The rather emotive term 'casualty' is broadly defined by Hall et al. (1999) to refer to 'long-term psychological distress which causes people to engage in maladaptive and defensive behaviours' (1999: 109).

An early naturalistic study by Yalom and Lieberman (1971) identified seven types of group leader over a range of group types. 'Aggressive-stimulator' leaders were found to have produced almost all the casualties, by what Aveline sombrely describes as a 'toxic combination' (2005: 160) of an authoritarian, highly confrontational personality style and an insistence on participants' immediate emotional disclosure, emotional expression and attitude change. Such research strongly implies that participation in personal development groups is not for the faint-hearted, and dramatically highlights the central place of the facilitator in determining the safety and effectiveness of the group. Certainly, the training institution bears a heavy responsibility for choosing a suitably skilled and personally mature individual to lead the group. But clearly, it is not just the personality style of group leaders that results in trainee ambivalence. Galbraith and Hart (2007) point out, along with Johns (1996), the dilemma for training courses of whether course team members should act as group facilitators or whether external members of staff should be brought in for the purpose: trainees may feel understandably cautious about sharing personal material with core team members. Whilst Johns (1996) is a clear proponent of including core team members in personal development groups, Galbraith and Hart (2007) point out that trainees may be unwilling to share personal issues and problems with core team members for fear of being seen – and assessed – as emotionally vulnerable and unsuitable for counselling psychology training. This is likely to limit full and engaged participation in the group, and, by extension, to limit trainees' capacity to gain from such groups. In addition, of course, group facilitators vary in their skills and interests, and it should not be assumed that counselling psychology trainers are all able and willing to run personal development groups, nor that they have the capacity to deal with the complexities of group dynamics and transference that can, and often do, arise.

The difficulties of ensuring a safe, constructive experience within groupwork have been discussed by Spencer (2006), and such difficulties in many ways parallel the problem of establishing whether trainees are benefiting from individual therapy. Indeed, given such difficulties, it seems well-nigh impossible to assess the extent to which trainee participation impacts on clinical efficacy. Galbraith and Hart's (2007) review of the personal development groups' literature highlights the paucity of outcome research on personal development groups, in particular that crucial link between trainees' experiences of groupwork and their clinical practice. One of the main methodological difficulties in assessing this is that different types of groups offer very different types of experience. Different forms of groupwork will not only have different types of facilitator and aim for very different kinds of outcome, but any identified outcomes themselves are likely to be heavily dependent on the individual training course's main theoretical model.

The issue is further muddied by the ambiguous role of self-awareness in the self-report data that forms the basis for many studies examining the impact of groupwork. Connor's study examining the role of self-awareness in relation to trainees' ability to practice has found that: 'the effect of heightened self-awareness does not necessarily imply an increase in perceived ability. In this research increased self awareness often led to a decrease in perceived abilities' (1986: 299).

This raises the complex issue of the role and limits of self-awareness in contributing positively to clinical outcome. Is it possible to be too self-aware? Beyond a certain point, does self-awareness actually render us less clinically effective? Or does self-awareness merely heighten a sense of what one does not know, which subsequently informs and biases self-report data? As in personal therapy, there seems to be not only a need to explore and research, in imaginative and flexible ways, the association between therapist groupwork and clinical outcome (Payne, 1999); there is also a related need to determine the objectives of groupwork and to define its parameters within a particular training programme and its core theoretical position.

REFLECTIVE LEARNING JOURNALS

Another personal development training tool in use by many counselling and counselling psychology training institutions is the reflective learning journal (Bolton, 2001; Moon, 1999). Reflective learning journals, variously described as professional journals, course diaries, learning or personal logs, are used 'to explore and reflect upon complex concepts, professional knowledge, ethical considerations in psychotherapeutic practice and clinical expertise' (Sutton et al., 2007: 388). Based on Schon's (1983) work, they are thought to provide trainees an opportunity for 'reflection-on-action' and a space to explore their changing impressions, feelings, difficulties and issues in both personal and professional domains. Johns argues that learning journals carry the potential to be:

> a safety valve, a crucial mechanism for making learning concrete and specific, a 'transitional object' security blanket to which deepest thoughts, feelings and fears can be safely expressed, the place for reality testing or an arena, reinforced by exploration with others, for establishing identity, accepting and having dialogue amongst sub-personalities and setting objectives for self-as-counsellor growth. (1996: 94)

These journals are rarely assessed in their entirety; trainees are usually required to submit a résumé and discussion of the journal's contents for evaluation. But is there any evidence for the benefits of this type of activity? Research literature on the use of personal learning journals within counselling is sparse and focuses mainly on their use within nursing and teacher training. No studies on the use of reflective learning journals in counselling psychology training were identified at the time of writing. However, Moon's (1999) classic review of learning journals points to evidence of improved learning and reflection on practice over a number of professional fields. Sutton et al. (2007) also cite a number of studies exploring the role of reflective learning journals, including those by Lane (1996) in the context of nursing practice and Howard (1997) in the context of general practice, which support the view that such activities indeed improve learning and reflective practice.

But how useful do trainees find these learning journals? Sutton et al.'s (2007) unusual qualitative study examined the role of learning journals within a post-graduate cognitive-behavioural therapy training course. Using focus groups to interview trainees, the study established several perceived benefits including carthartic experiences, improved reflection and self-knowledge via the discovery and exploration of feelings and beliefs and increased empathy with clients. In common with the outcomes discussed earlier in personal development groups, there was a 'sleeper' effect where participants who chose to re-read their journals reported a further cycle of reflection. This resulted in what Sutton et al. term 'deeper' levels of learning that were particularly evident in the more experienced trainees.

The study, however, highlighted the previously noted complaint that neither the purpose nor the expected requirements of the learning journal were made sufficiently explicit to trainees, and it was clear that most trainees were uncertain about how such a subjective piece of work could possibly be evaluated and marked. Perhaps more importantly, the study raised a number of ethical concerns. Some trainees' entries revealed that the demands of the course and of completing the reflective journal itself evoked feelings of depression and anxiety, feelings that appeared to be related to trainees' perceptions of lack of support and guidance from the course in developing their reflective writing skills. This raises the considerably more contentious issue of how training teams propose to address any potential evidence of trainee psychological distress, unethical clinical practice or abuse of clients that might come to light within a reflective journal. More commonly, and in line with the other personal development activities reviewed here, it is difficult, if not impossible, for training courses and trainers to ensure the integrity of the journal, as trainees are likely to edit their entries before submitting any part of the journal for assessment.

On the basis of this study, Sutton et al. make a number of recommendations about reflective learning journals for psychotherapy training institutions:

- Students should be given a clear and explicit rationale for the purpose of learning journals.
- Marking and assessment criteria should be made explicit, and methods other than formal marking should be considered within the curriculum – for example, markers might indicate the emotional impact they experienced reading the journal, or offer comments inviting further reflection.
- Where possible, feedback should be from staff not directly involved in the everyday running of the programme.
- Support networks for trainees should be in place.
- Trainees should be given a possible structure for the learning journal.
- Links between the journal and other personal development activities should be encouraged.
- The learning journal should be explicitly discussed at the start of the training programme, and be clearly detailed in all course and module handbooks.
- Trainees should be encouraged to re-read their journals at regular intervals. (2007: 401)

PERSONAL DEVELOPMENT: CONCLUSIONS AND FUTURE DIRECTIONS

Personal development comprises, of course, far more than personal therapy, personal development groups and reflective learning journals. It can include a myriad of activities: reading, reflecting, co-counselling, experiential work and life experiences of various kinds. None of these activities are exclusive to the training period, and counselling psychologists are expected to continue their personal development over the course of their professional lifetimes.

Any discussion of the benefits of personal development within counselling psychology training must be placed against the wider backdrop of whether counselling training itself is successful in producing effective practitioners. Whilst this topic is covered by another chapter in this *Handbook*, suffice it to say that this is a highly controversial and methodologically challenging area of research. A review of the meta-analytic literature by Lambert and Ogles (2004), comparing the clinical outcomes of professional and para-professional therapists, rather worryingly concludes that professional training does not make much difference to clinical efficacy (though see Stein and Lambert, 1995). Beutler et al. (2004), too, are extremely cautious in their conclusions about the impact of psychotherapy training in general, suggesting in their review that: 'These findings tend to cast doubt on the validity of the suggestions that specific training in psychotherapy, even when unconfounded with general experience, may be related to therapeutic success or skill' (2004: 239).

The apparently equivocal efficacy of professional training itself, though, needs to be set against the yet wider context of the current state of psychotherapy outcome research in general. The very issue of which personal development activities sponsor a more effective *therapist* begs the question of what constitutes an effective *therapy*. It is interesting that, despite an increasingly forceful political and economic agenda within the NHS (Layard, 2004), the field has yet to overturn Luborsky et al.'s (1975) original 'dodo bird' verdict demonstrating that all psychotherapies are similarly effective. Perhaps for this reason there is increasing interest in the contribution of the therapist to psychotherapy outcome, with recognition that variations, for example, in skilfulness (Okiishi et al., 2003) and attachment status (Dozier et al., 1994), may account for significant individual differences in therapists' clinical outcomes. Aveline makes the heartfelt claim that 'personal characteristics are not the only factor in effectiveness, contributing only 10–20 per cent of the variance, *but what a vital portion*' (2005: 162; my italics). Therapist factors, then, are likely to take centre-stage in psychotherapy research, as increasingly sophisticated research designs identify client–therapist matching on a number of different variables as significant in predicting clinical outcome variance.

We have returned full circle, then, to the fascinating issue of the impact of the therapist himself or herself with which I started this chapter. The extent to which personal development activities of various kinds can impact on the 'self' of the therapist, thereby positively influencing clinical outcome, remains the goal of exploration and research in this complex, diverse and often controversial area of training. However, the above literature perhaps attests to the awesome difficulties in defining, specifying and evaluating the impact of personal development within training. I strongly suspect this is an area that the profession as a whole is in two minds about. Indeed, Rizq and Target's (2008a) study of experienced counselling psychologists' views on personal therapy found that these seasoned practitioners and trainers were generally highly ambivalent about specifying any outcomes or goals for personal therapy, apparently feeling that this was somehow a 'special' area of training, exempt from the encroaching demands of an increasingly regulated and audited profession. Nevertheless, these demands are already a reality, despite those who deplore the culture of managerialism and professionalization within current therapeutic training (House, 2007). Whilst counselling psychology is likely to see many changes over the next few years, particularly in the context of proposed statutory regulation by the Health Professions Council, personal development is likely to remain a central feature of training. If we are to keep it there, the profession will need to find meaningful and creative ways of identifying, defining and researching its use in training, its impact on trainee self-awareness and its effects on clinical outcome.

REFERENCES

Atkins, P. (2006) 'Personal therapy in the training of therapists', *European Journal of Psychotherapy and Counselling*, 8 (4): 407–410.

Aveline, M. (2005) 'The person of the therapist', *Psychotherapy Research*, 15 (3): 155–164.

Bennett-Levy, J., Lee, N., Travers, K., Pohlman, S. and Hamernik, E. (2003) 'Cognitive therapy from the inside: Enhancing therapist's skills through practising what we preach', *Behaviour and Cognitive Psychotherapy,* 31 (2): 143–158.

Beutler, L.E., Machado, P. and Neufeld, S. (1994) 'Therapist variables', in A.A. Bergin and S.L. Garfield (eds), *Handbook of Psychotherapy and Behaviour Change*. New York: Wiley.

Beutler, L.E., Malik, M., Alimohamed, S., Harwood, T.M., Talebi, H., Noble, S., and Wong, E. (2004) 'Therapist variables', in M. Lambert (ed.), *Handbook of Psychotherapy and Behaviour Change*, 5th edn. New York: Wiley. pp. 227–306.

Bolton, G. (2001) *Reflective Practice: Writing and Professional Development*. London: Sage.

British Association for Counselling and Psychotheraphy (2002) *Accreditation of Training Courses*, 4th edn. Rugby: BACP.

British Psychological Society (2001) *Guidelines for Continuing Professional Development for Counselling Psychologists*. Leicester: BPS.

British Psychological Society (2006) *Division of Counselling Psychology: Professional Practice Guidelines*. Leicester: BPS.

British Psychological Society (2009) available at: www.bps.org.uk/careers/what-do-psychologists-do/areas/counselling.cfm, accessed 30 June 2009.

Buckley, P., Karasu, T. and Charles, E. (1981) 'Psychotherapists view their personal therapy', *Psychotherapy: Theory, Research and Practice*, 18: 299–305.

Chamberlain, K. (2000) 'Methodolatry and qualitative health research', *Journal of Health Psychology*, 5 (3): 285–296.

Connor, M. (1986) 'Training in counselling: The development, implementation and evalution of "listening and responding": an approach to teaching counselling skills to nurses'. PhD thesis, University of Keele.

Corrie, S. (2002) 'The role of the therapeutic relationship in promoting psychological change: A cognitive-behavioural perspective', *Counselling Psychology Review*, 17 (2): 23–31.

Donati, M. (2002) 'Personal development in counselling psychology training: A critical investigation of the views and experiences of trainers and trainees'. Unpublished PhD thesis, City University, London.

Donati, M. and Watts, M. (2002) 'Personal development in counselling psychology training: The case for further research', *Counselling Psychology Review*, 15 (1): 12–22.

Donati, M. and Watts, M. (2005) 'Personal development in counsellor training: Towards a clarification of inter-related concepts', *British Journal of Guidance and Counselling*, 33 (4): 475–484.

Dozier, M., Cue, K. and Barnett, L. (1994) 'Clinicians as caregivers: Role of attachment organisation in treatment', *Journal of Consulting and Clinical Psychology*, 62 (4): 793–800.

Elton-Wilson, J. (1994) 'Is there a difference between personal and professional development for a practising psychologist?', *Journal of Educational and Child Psychology*, 11 (3): 70–79.

Farrell, W. (1996) 'Training and professional development in the context of counselling psychology', in R. Woolfe and W. Dryden (eds), *Handbook of Counselling Psychology*. London: Sage.

Fonagy, P. and Target, M. (1996) 'Playing with reality: 1. Theory of mind and the normal development of psychic reality', *International Journal of Psychoanalysis*, 77: 217–233.

Freud, S. (1937/57) 'Analysis terminable and interminable', in J. Strachey (ed.), *Complete Psychological Works of Sigmund Freud*. London: Hogarth.

Fromm-Reichmann, F. (1950) *Principles of Intensive Psychotherapy*. Chicago, IL: University of Chicago Press.

Galbraith, V. and Hart, N. (2007) 'Personal development groups in counselling psychology training: The case for further research', *Counselling Psychology Review*, 22 (4): 49–57.

Garfield, S. and Bergin, A. (1971) 'Personal therapy, outcome and some therapist variables', *Psychotherapy: Theory, Research and Practice*, 8: 251–253.

Geller, J. (2005) 'My experiences as a patient in five psychoanalytic psychotherapies', in J. Geller, J. Norcross and D. Orlinsky (eds), *The Psychotherapist's Own Psychotherapy: Patient and Clinician Perspectives*. Oxford: Oxford University Press.

Gilbert, M. and Shmukler, D. (1996) 'Psychological therapy in groups', in R. Woolfe, W. Dryden and S. Strawbridge (eds), *Handbook of Counselling Psychology*, 2nd edn. London: Sage.

Greenberg, R. and Staller, J. (1981) 'Personal therapy for therapists', *American Journal of Psychiatry*, 138: 1467–1471.

Grimmer, A. and Tribe, R. (2001) 'Counselling psychologists' perceptions of the impact of mandatory personal therapy on professional development – an exploratory study', *Counselling Psychology Quarterly*, 14 (4): 287–301.

Hall, E., Hall, C., Harris, G., Hay, D., Biddulph, M. and Duffy, T. (1999) 'An evaluation of the long-term outcomes of small-group work for counsellor development', *British Journal of Guidance and Counselling*, 27 (1): 99–112.

Hartman, J. (1979) 'Small group methods of personal change', *Annual Review of Psychology*, 30: 453–476.

Herron, W. (1988) 'The value of personal therapy for psychotherapists', *Psychological Reports*, 62: 175–184.

Hill, D., Thompson, G. and Williams, E. (1997) 'A guide to conducting consensual qualitative research', *The Counseling Psychologist*, 25: 517–572.

House, R. (2007) 'Training and education for therapeutic practitionership: "Trans-modern" perspectives', *Counselling Psychology Quarterly*, 21 (1): 1–10.

Howard, J. (1997) 'The emotional diary: A framework for reflective practice', *Education for General Practice*, 8: 288–291.

Irving, J. and Williams, D. (1999) 'Personal growth and personal development: Concepts clarified', *British Journal of Guidance and Counselling*, 27 (4): 517–26.

Johns, H. (1996) *Personal Development in Counsellor Training*. London: Cassell.

Laireiter, A.-R. and Willutzki, U. (2003) 'Self-reflection and self-practice in training of cognitive behaviour therapy: An overview', *Clinical Psychology and Psychotherapy*, 10: 19–30.

Lambert, M. and Bergin, A. (1994) 'The effectiveness of psychotherapy', in A. Bergin and S. Garfield (eds), *Handbook of Psychotherapy and Behaviour Change*, 4th edn. New York: Wiley. pp. 143–189.

Lambert, M. and Ogles, B. (2004) 'The efficacy and effectiveness of psychotherapy', in A. Bergin and S. Garfield (eds), *Handbook of Psychotherapy and Behaviour Change*, 5th edn. New York: Wiley. pp. 139–193.

Lane, A. (1996) 'Developing healthcare educators: The application of a conceptual model', *Journal of Nursing Staff Development*, 12 (5): 252–259.

Layard, R. (2004) *Mental Health: Britain's Biggest Social Problem*. Available at www.strategy.gov.uk/downloads/files/mh_layard.pdf, accessed 9 February 2009.

Lieberman, M., Yalom, I. and Miles, M. (1973) *Encounter Groups: First Facts*. New York: Basic Books.

Luborsky, L., Singer, B. and Luborsky, E. (1975) 'Comparative studies of psychotherapies. Is it true that "everyone has won and all must have prizes?"', *Archives of General Psychiatry*, 32: 995–1008.

Macaskill, N. (1988) 'Personal therapy in the training of the psychotherapist: Is it effective?', *British Journal of Psychotherapy*, 4: 199–226.

Macaskill, N. and Macaskill, A. (1992) 'Psychotherapists-in-training evaluate their personal therapy: Results of a UK survey', *British Journal of Psychotherapy*, 9 (2): 133–138.

Mace, C. (2001) 'Personal therapy in psychiatric training', *Psychiatric Bulletin*, 25: 3–4.

Mackay, C. (1841) *Memoirs of Extraordinary Popular Delusions and the Madness of Crowds*. London: Office of the National Illustrated Library.

Macran, M. and Shapiro, S. (1998) 'The role of personal therapy for therapists – a review', *British Journal of Medical Psychology*, 54: 203–212.

Macran, S., Stiles, W. and Smith, J. (1999) 'How does personal therapy affect therapists' practice?', *Journal of Counseling Psychology*, 46 (4): 419–431.

Masson, J. (1992) *Against Therapy*. London: Fontana.

McDevitt, J. (1987) 'Therapists' personal therapy and professional self awareness', *Psychotherapy*, 24 (4): 693–703.

McEwan, J. and Duncan, P. (1993) 'Personal therapy in the training of psychologists', *Canadian Psychology*, 34 (2): 186–197.

McNamara, J.R. (1986) 'Personal therapy in the training of behaviour therapists', *Psychotherapy*, 23: 370–374.

Moon, J. (1999) *Learning Journals: A Handbook for Academics, Students and Professional Development*. London: Kogan Page.

Norcross, J. (1990) 'Personal therapy for therapists: One solution', *Psychotherapy in Private Practice*, 8: 45–59.

Norcross, J., Strasser-Kirtland, D. and Missar, C. (1988a) 'The processes and outcomes of psychotherapists' personal treatment experiences', *Psychotherapy*, 25: 36–43.

Norcross, J., Strausser, D. and Faltus, F. (1988b) 'The therapist's therapist', *American Journal of Psychotherapy*, 42: 53–66.

Okiishi, J., Lambert, M., Nielsen, S. and Ogles, B. (2003) 'Waiting for supershrink: An empirical analysis of therapist effects', *Clinical Psychology and Psychotherapy*, 10 (6): 361–373.

Orlinsky, D., Grawe, K. and Parks, B. (1994) 'Process and outcome in psychotherapy', in A. Bergin and S. Garfield (eds), *Handbook of Psychotherapy and Behaviour Change*. New York: Wiley. pp. 270–37.

Orlinsky, D., Ambuhl, H., Ronnestad, M., Davis, J., Gerin, P., Davis, M., Willutzi, U., Botermans, J.-F., Dazord, A., Cierpka, M., Aapro, N., Buchheim, P.K., Bae, S., Davidson, D., Frus-Jorgensen, E., Joo, E., Kalmoykove, E., Meyerberg, J., Northcut, T., Parkes, B., Scherb, E., Schroder, T., Shefler, G., Stwine, D., Stuart, S., Tarragona, M., Vasco, A., Wiseman, H. and The SPR Collaborative Research Network (1999) 'Development of psychotherapists: Concepts, questions and methods of a collaborative international study', *Psychotherapy Research*, 9: 127–153.

Payne, H. (1999) 'Personal development groups in the training of counsellors and therapists: A review of the research', *European Journal of Psychotherapy, Counselling and Health*, 2 (1): 55–68.

Rizq, R. and Target, M. (2008a) '"The power of being seen": An interpretative phenomenological analysis of how experienced counselling psychologists describe the meaning and significance of personal therapy in clinical practice', *British Journal of Guidance and Counselling*, 36 (2): 131–152.

Rizq, R. and Target, M. (2008b) 'Not a little Mickey Mouse thing: How experienced counselling psychologists describe the significance of personal therapy in clinical practice and training. Some results from an interpretative phenomenological analysis', *Counselling Psychology Quarterly*, 21 (1): 1–20.

Rothery, N. (1992) 'Personal growth work in the training of counselling and clinical psychologists in Ireland', *The Irish Journal of Psychology*, 13 (2): 168–175.

Sandell, R., Carlsson, J., Schubert, J., Broberg, J., Lazar, A. and Blomberg, J. (2002) 'Varieties of therapeutic experience and their associations with patient outcome', *European Psychotherapy*, 3: 17–35.

Sandell, R., Carlsson, J., Schubert, J., Grant, J., Lazar, A. and Broberg, J. (2006) 'Therapists' therapies: The relation between training therapy and patient change in long-term psychotherapy and psychoanalysis', *Psychotherapy Research*, 16 (3): 306–316.

Schon, D. (1983) *The Reflective Practitioner.* New York: Basic Books.

Skovholt, T. and Ronnestad, M. (1996) *The Evolving Professional Self: Stages and Themes in Therapist and Counsellor Development.* London: Wiley.

Spencer, L. (2006) 'Tutors' stories of personal development training – attempting to maximize the learning potential', *Counselling and Psychotherapy Research*, 6 (2): 108–114.

Stein, D.M. and Lambert, M.J. (1995) 'Graduate training in psychotherapy: Are therapy outcomes enhanced?', *Journal of Consulting and Clinical Psychology*, 63 (2): 182–196.

Strupp, H. (1973) 'The therapist's performance: A comparison of two professional groups', in H. Strupp (ed.), *Psychotherapy: Clinical Research and Theoretical Issues.* New York: Aronson.

Sutton, L., Townend, M. and Wright, J. (2007) 'The experiences of reflective learning journals by cognitive behavioural psychotherapy students', *Reflective Practice*, 8 (3): 387–404.

Wheeler, S. (1991) 'Personal therapy: An essential aspect of counsellor training, or a distraction from focussing on the client?', *International Journal for the Advancement of Counselling*, 14 (3): 193–202.

Wilkins, P. (1997) *Personal and Professional Development for Counsellors.* London: Sage.

Williams, D. and Irving, J. (1996) 'Personal growth: Rogerian paradoxes', *British Journal of Guidance and Counselling*, 24 (2): 165–72.

Williams, F., Coyle, A. and Lyons, E. (1999) 'How counselling psychologists view their personal therapy', *British Journal of Medical Psychology*, 72: 545–555.

Wiseman, H. and Shefler, G. (2001) 'Experienced psychoanalytically oriented therapists' narrative accounts of their personal therapy: Impacts on professional and personal development', *Psychotherapy*, 38: 129–141.

Wogan, M. and Norcross, J. (1985) 'Dimensions of therapeutic skills and techniques: Empirical identification, therapist correlates and predictive utility', *Psychotherapy*, 22: 63–74.

Yalom, I. and Lieberman, M. (1971) 'A study of encounter group casualties', *Archives of General Psychiatry*, XXV: 16–29.

30

SUPERVISION

Ray Woolfe and Margaret Tholstrup

Supervision in the UK is a mandatory requirement for all counselling psychologists at all stages of their careers as well as for counsellors and psychotherapists covering the whole range of psychological therapies. The *Guidelines for Supervision* produced by the Division of Counselling Psychology describe it as 'a requirement for every counselling psychologist and covers all aspects of their practice throughout their professional life. This ... applies equally to all counselling psychologists regardless of their level of qualification or seniority' (BPS, DCoP, 2006: 5). In a similar vein, the *Ethical Framework for Good Practice in Counselling and Psychotherapy* published by the British Association for Counselling and Psychotherapy minces no words when it refers to the 'general obligation for all counsellors, psychotherapists, supervisors and trainers to receive supervision/consultancy support independently of any managerial relationships' (BACP, 2009). This reflects the importance attached to it within the world of therapy as the basis for ethical and effective practice and this is manifested in the publication of a collection of papers on supervision produced by the Division (BPS, DCoP, 2008), a copy of which was sent to every member. A number of papers in that edition are referred to in this chapter. In their introduction to that document, Shillito-Clarke and Tholstrup (2008) express the hope that the ideas will be both thought provoking and act as a stimulant to discussion.

Our intention is that these sentiments will also be true of this chapter, but there is something in particular that we would like to explore in the chapter. Given the importance attached to it, it is not surprising that supervision is seen as a good thing. It is as if this is self-evidently true and that to question it is akin to heresy. However, perhaps the matter is not quite as straightforward as this. Perhaps supervision contains within itself the seeds of conflict. Perhaps the needs of various stakeholders can sometimes clash with each other. Perhaps supervision can be threatening or boring or irrelevant. To frame supervision in this manner is not to dismiss its value but rather to challenge the taken-for-granted assumptions made about it which perceive it as next to godliness. In this formulation, the intention is to frame it as an arena of conflict, or potential conflict, in which, at the very least, there is potential for debate about who benefits and in what circumstances.

While the Division of Counselling Psychology was the first within the British Psychological Society to insist on supervision for its members, in recent years its value has come to be more widely recognized within the Society. However, this British requirement is not necessarily repeated worldwide. In the USA, for example, it is largely confined to trainees. The term 'supervision' itself has a rather authoritarian or hierarchical feel to it, and while it can be argued that this is not inappropriate when applied to trainees, perhaps the process of supervision for trained practitioners might be more collegially designated as consultancy or consultative support. However, for the moment we are stuck with this term and what supervision is, what it entails and how it is carried out are described in the *Guidelines for Supervision* (DCoP, 2006) and are summarized later in this chapter. For the moment, suffice it to say that the emphasis is on the importance of regular supervision and it being a separate activity to line management.

While this chapter will explore the dynamics of supervision, it will also address the evidence about the efficacy of supervision and some of the conflicts and difficulties faced both by those who offer supervision and those who receive it: supervisees. There will also be consideration of the organizational context which frames supervision for many practitioners.

In thinking about the justification for supervision, it is perhaps important to emphasize that which is obvious and yet can easily be overlooked, namely the immensely private and interpersonal nature of the therapeutic relationship and the feelings which this can throw up for both parties. Supervision offers a vehicle for self-care in the context of a form of work which is emotionally involving and stressful and has the potential for isolation and abuse. Supervision is a sounding board which protects and assists client and therapist.

THE HISTORY OF SUPERVISION

Supervision is not just a characteristic of therapy. It has a distinguished pedigree within the field of social case work. However, there is a long history within therapy, and this can be traced back to the early days of psychoanalysis. Early Freudian groups acknowledged the need for supervision when they met, initially in Freud's home, to discuss each other's clinical work. There were a number of debates about the subject, with followers of Freud in Vienna arguing that the roles of teacher and therapist should be separated, while an alternative approach developed in Budapest, known as the Hungarian School, in which the trainee's analyst also acted as his or her supervisor. In other words, super-vision was carried out within the context of the trainee's therapy. However, this approach did not become mainstream, and understood through the prism of contem-porary insights can be seen to clash with the ethical prohibition on dual relationships. While this point has now become something of an article of faith, the reality on the ground can generate complexities. For example, many psychologists working in NHS settings are faced with the difficulty that their designated supervisor is also their line manager.

Of course, before the modern development of formal courses in counselling psycho-logy and cognate disciplines, the only way in which the academic or teaching function could be performed was as integral to and carried out within supervision. However, in the modern format, the teaching function for trainees is largely confined to the university/institute, while the supervision of their clinical practice is normally performed within the placement.

As it developed, the psychodynamic approach to supervision came to match the form of the therapeutic practice. So, for example, the emphasis on countertransference and projective identification in therapy was reflected in the supervision in that the super-visee was understood to be unconsciously playing out the relationship with the client in his or her relationship with the supervisor. What the supervisor experienced with the supervisee paralleled what the supervisee was experiencing with the client. An uncon-scious communication had taken place. The term 'parallel process' is now widely used in talking about the practice of supervision (see Mattinson, 1977; Morrisey and Tribe, 2001). Another familiar and related concept is that of the 'internal supervisor' popular-ized by Casement (1985). He saw this as the supervisee's capacity to reflect within the session on the meaning of the patient's communication in relation to the therapist.

In a similar fashion, the 1950s, spread of American approaches to counselling as expressed in the work of humanistic psychologists such as Rogers and Maslow, cognitive theorists such as Ellis and a variety of mixed practices such as Gestalt (Perls) and Transactional Analysis (Berne) was matched by the adoption of the equivalent humanistic or cognitive method respectively within the supervisory relationship. While skills training featured prominently in the former, empathic listening skill and the presence of the Rogerian core conditions, particularly congruence, was emphasized in the latter. The practice of matching the process of supervision to the therapeutic modality is also prominent in relatively contemporary approaches and, for example, Waskett (2006) employs the term 'treasure hunting' to describe how solution-focused supervision matches the emphasis in the therapy on searching for the client's strengths rather than deficiencies.

In effect, therefore, models of supervision were based on models of therapeutic practice. However, with the expansion of counselling training courses, the importance of supervision as an activity related to but separate from counselling began to be emphasized, and there gradually emerged a body of literature exploring a variety of models rooted specifically in the practice of supervision itself. We might describe these as supervision-specific theories. These included developmental models based upon the view that supervisory skills need to be adapted to suit the stage of professional development reached by the supervisee. Stages were defined in terms of levels of competence (see Stoltenberg et al., 1998; Holloway, 1987). Webb (2000) suggests that, developmental theories of supervision acknowledge that the trainee has to learn how to become a supervisee. Brightman (1984) argues that, within the psychodynamic tradition, training supervision is best understood as a holding environment during a time of narcissistic vulnerability when the supervisee's self-esteem may be very low.

Holloway (1995) is also associated with a systems model based upon the roles, responsibilities, tasks and functions of the supervisor. In the UK, Page and Wosket (1994) developed a cyclical model based upon a flexible series of stages incorporating an outward journey moving from contracting to finding a focus, to the supervisory space and then a return journey leading back into the clinical work. Carroll (1996) described a linear model connecting goals, functions and tasks and describes the roles performed by the supervisor. However, the model which has gained particular popularity in this country has been that of Hawkins and Shohet (1989), whose process model conceptualizes supervision as a series of six separate foci located within two interlocking matrices respectively of client–counsellor and supervisor–counsellor. They encourage the supervisor to think about whether the focus of a session is on one or the other.

SUPERVISION AND LEARNING

Supervision is an aspect of reflective practice, the model of the reflective practitioner being an integral part of the identity of the counselling psychologist. This concept emphasizes the importance of learning through experience. In Kolb's well-known model (Kolb, 1976, 1984), this has four stages. A concrete experience (that is, working with a client) is followed by observation and reflection out of which emerges abstract concepts and generalizations leading to active experimentation. The process is iterative as it is continually repeated. A useful discussion of the model as applied to therapy can be found in Sugarman (1985). Carroll (2008) suggests that this type of experiential learning cycle represents the theory of learning underlying supervision. The supervisee develops 'propositional/declarative' learning as reflective learning becomes embedded in and supported by theoretical thinking and understanding. This leads potentially to what he terms 'transformational learning and change'.

WHAT IS SUPERVISION?

The Divisional *Guidelines* (BPS, DCoP, 2006) define supervision as the following:

- An activity
- A process
- A relationship
- A practice.

The account of each item which follows is based on the description in the *Guidelines*. It is essentially a précis and you are advised to examine the document if you have not already done so.

Supervision is an *activity* (2006: 4) in the sense that practitioners discuss their work so that it can be reflected upon by one or more professionals. It is conducted in a 'boundaried' space that can allow for 'uncensored reflection' so that work done can be evaluated and future possibilities explored. It is also an ethical activity that recognizes the critical importance of support for all participants in the process extending beyond formal codes and guidelines. At a later point in the publication, the ethical principles are defined under the headings of 'General respect', 'Privacy and confidentiality', 'Informed consent' and 'Self-determination'. As an activity, it differs from therapy and from line management.

Supervision is a *process* of 'ongoing, collaborative, experiential and transformative learning' (2006: 4) using evidence from research and practice. This is reflected upon and applied to future practice. Willingness of both parties to engage on an 'intersubjective' basis is highly valued.

Supervision is a *relationship* of 'mutual trust, respect and integrity which models best practice and sensitivity to the learning needs of the supervisee' (2006: 4).

Supervision is a *practice* based on 'shared and explicit models of supervision' (2006: 4) bounded by a mutually negotiated contract defining roles and responsibilities and the limits of confidentiality.

The *Guidelines* identify the aim of supervision as being to promote best practice in the interest of the client. The focus on the client is emphasized as it is in the more behavioural list of objectives which is provided. On the face of it, this seems sensible and it is tempting, therefore, to regard supervision in a taken-for-granted sort of way as a self-evidently worthwhile and equal encounter that takes place in a one-to-one relationship between consenting adults and which is inherently unproblematic. We shall have more to say about this in the next section.

A more rounded, though similarly rather taken-for-granted view of supervision is provided by Lane and Corrie, who summarize the benefits as offering protection to clients, allowing practitioners a reflective space in which to identify their strengths and weaknesses, to facilitate learning from peers and to keep up to date with professional developments (2006: 19). Additional benefits might include the following:

- alerting practitioners to ethical and professional issues in their work and promoting ethical watchfulness
- providing a forum to consider and hold the tensions that emerge from the needs of the various stakeholders in the supervisee's work
- allowing practitioners to measure the impact of their work on their lives
- receiving feedback from the supervisor
- facilitating the client's welfare and protecting the client's interests
- creating a forum of accountability for those to whom the practitioner is responsible: the client, the organization, the profession
- updating workers to the best in innovation, insights and research in their chosen areas of work. (See Carroll, 2007)

What is being described here are essentially what are usually referred to in the literature as the 'functions of supervision'. These have been termed by Kadushin (1968, 1985) as 'educative, supportive and managerial' and then by Proctor (1986) as 'formative, restorative and normative'. The formative function involves the supervisor's responsibility for monitoring the work of the trainee to ensure that it serves the interests of the client. The restorative function is concerned with the professional development of the counsellor, supporting therapists in their work. Carroll (1996) refers to this as the 'containment' side of supervision. Finally, the normative function introduces the ethical dimension in the form of quality control in which the supervisor helps the counsellor to ensure that the needs of clients are being met within the framework of appropriate ethical and professional practice.

All these attempts to define supervision tend to leave a feeling of it as a rather dry and uninspiring activity, so perhaps it is helpful to emphasize the excitement and challenge of supervision as something that moves us out of our comfort zones and alerts us to new vistas and opportunities. Case study 30.1 is illustrative; based upon the experience of one of the authors of this chapter, it demonstrates the complexity of the subject and some of the dilemmas faced by supervisors.

CASE STUDY 30.1

Janet was a counselling psychologist with about five years' experience. She had qualified via a well-regarded university course. The initial experience of her was of a pleasant, intelligent woman who seemed open to sharing her work and who said that she wanted to be challenged in the supervision. However, as the work progressed, it became apparent that Janet's pleasantness, while attractive was also a defence in that she found it difficult to see her task with clients as other than to be nice to them.

(Continued)

(Continued)

The effect was that her work lacked edge. But while Janet had accurately revealed her need to be challenged in supervision, attempts to challenge this feature of her practice appeared to have no impact upon her. She responded to the comments made by the supervisor by taking copious notes and agreeing with the supervisor's understandings and saying how much she valued the supervision. However, in her practice nothing changed. It seemed that nothing was really being taken in, and the supervisor became more and more frustrated.

The problem was taken by the supervisor to the supervisor of the supervision, who commented that perhaps Janet needed to idealize the supervisor and that this was present in her need for clients to like and admire her. The two were able to talk about this together and as a consequence Janet began to be more real, both with the supervisor and her clients. Their relationship improved, the supervisor's feeling of frustration lifted and Janet became much more confident and assertive in her work with her clients. Eventually she was able to share with the supervisor a number of transference issues which affected how she used supervision and the need to address these issues outside supervision in therapy or some other form of personal development activity.

TYPES OF SUPERVISION

What all writers on supervision emphasize is the importance of a clear contract, and in the words of Hawkins and Shohet, 'to decide what managerial, educative and supportive responsibilities the supervisor is carrying' (1989: 44). They suggest four main categories, namely tutorial, training, managerial and consultancy. The question then to be asked is what are the tasks or responsibilities inherent within each type. We would suggest that creating a learning relationship and monitoring ethical and professional issues are consistently important across each type.

Tutorial supervision

Tutorial supervision is carried out within the educational context by members of staff of the training institution rather than in the placement. The main task is teaching, helping trainees link practice in their placement settings with the theoretical orientation of the course. It is usually carried out in groups from the same cohort.

Training supervision

In the context of training supervision, there is normally a relationship between the educational institution and the placement organization. This can be a cause of difficulty, and Izzard (2003) offers some observations about the conflicts and difficulties which can occur as well as emphasizing the need for a clear contract between the two organizations. Universities traditionally evaluate students on the basis of written work, which is fine for academic subjects but more problematic for subjects such as counselling psychology where academic prowess may not be matched by clinical competence. Case study 30.2 illustrates some of the dilemmas which this may cause.

CASE STUDY 30.2

Peter was a student on a post-graduate degree course in counselling psychology. His academic work was excellent, but the supervisor in his clinical placement reported that his work with clients was inappropriate to the modality which he was claiming to employ, was highly directive and theoretical and in which his own perceptions were constantly being foisted onto his clients. His clinical supervisor was of the opinion that his future as a clinician was problematic, but this created a dilemma for his course supervisor who argued that as he had passed his written work he could not be failed on the basis of an outside supervisor who had no formal role within the university. This exposed a number of unresolved underlying issues about the contract between the university department and the placement agency.

Within placement settings, trainees are in a kind of apprenticeship role and the emphasis is upon the educative function. The supervisor has some responsibility for the work being done with clients and therefore has a managerial or normative role. In this situation, trainees may be uncertain about their competence and be afraid of making mistakes and possibly reluctant to acknowledge this fact within supervision.

There is inevitably a power imbalance which has a potential for abuse (see Kaberry, 2000). In her small-scale qualitative study, she found that blurring of boundaries frequently featured in cases where power was being abused. She quotes one case in which 'the supervisor was the manager and offered counselling and socialising as well. The supervisee was also invited to help the supervisor as a trainer in workshops held by the agency' (2000: 45). While this example may seem extreme, perhaps it is not as unusual as it might appear at first sight. Imagine a qualified counselling psychologist who is assigned a supervisor who is not only their line manager but is also of a different theoretical orientation. They do not discuss boundary issues between the two roles and the supervisee feels increasingly uneasy about sharing some aspects of her work with her supervisor. Because of the power differential it may be difficult for the supervisee to find the courage to request a different supervisor.

Monitoring administrative aspects of the work such as availability of rooms, completion of written records and ensuring confidentiality of client records are foreground features (Tholstrup, 1999). In addition, the trainees' own emotional issues may be activated by the nature of the clinical work, but the boundary between supervision and therapy needs to be maintained.

Consultancy supervision

Consultancy supervision occurs among qualified and experienced professionals whose need is to consult collegially with similarly experienced colleagues about clinical work rather than to learn about theory or have their competency evaluated. These latter tasks may also occur, but usually as the result of an overt contract with the supervisor rather than as an intrinsic part of the supervision itself. Hawkins and Shohet (1989) suggest that the responsibility for the work with clients remains with the supervisee, and the term 'consultant' implies that the supervisor is something other than trainer or manager.

Managerial supervision

In a managerial supervision situation, where the practice supervisor is also the line manager, the imbalance of power again becomes prominent and the power balance in the relationship changes from supervisor–supervisee to manager–subordinate. This dynamic alters the supervisory tasks. Quality of the learning and teaching relationships are affected, as both become the absorbing of accepted wisdom instead of exploring and reflecting upon aspects of the learning experience. Evaluating and managing ethical and professional boundaries can become complicated to discuss as the supervisor has the task of straddling the roles of supporting the supervisee in their learning, ensuring the well-being of the client and meeting the needs of the organization. Of course, if the supervisee is an experienced practitioner, the balance of these three functions may alter.

Supervision of supervision and research supervision

In addition to these four types of supervision, we can add two further types. The first is the increasing emphasis on the importance of supervision of supervision. Wheeler and King (2000) found in a survey of 70 counselling supervisors that all except six claimed to have supervision for supervision. In response to a question about issues raised in supervision, four categories were prominent: boundaries, competence of supervisees, training and ethics. Although called supervision of supervision, 'consultancy' would be a more accurate descriptor because of the level of experience of the participants.

Research supervision is a non-clinical application of the practice of supervision, but which nevertheless involves a contract. This allows for a learning relationship to be established which involves monitoring the professional and ethical as well as the academic and administrative aspects of the research.

FORMATS FOR SUPERVISION

There are a number of different formats for supervision of which the main ones are one-to-one, facilitated group, and peer (in pairs or group).

One-to-one supervision is probably the most common form of supervision. In many cases, as for those working in independent practice, the choice of a supervisor is left to the supervisee. In other contexts where the counselling psychologist works for an organization such as the NHS, the selection of a supervisor is generally made for them. The format offers the individual the maximum amount of time and has the advantage of replicating the one-to-one relationship of the therapeutic dyad. Disadvantages may include absence of perspectives, opinions or support from others and an enhanced risk of a dependent or collusive relationship developing.

Facilitated group supervision is the norm in many therapy placements and organizations. Proctor (1986) suggests that there are three broad types of group-facilitated supervision. One she describes as authoritarian, in which the supervisor supervises each member of the group as if in an individual supervision. The others listen but are not expected to participate unless asked. The second is participative, in which the supervisor encourages contributions from others in respect of the case being discussed. The third approach is consultative, in which the supervisor mentors participants in supervising each other. The advantages of group supervision include the possibility of receiving feedback from others besides the supervisor, and a more democratic environment as the supervisor is not regarded as the only expert in the room. The dilution of supervisory power means less opportunity for collusion or dependency. Disadvantages include less time for each member to bring case material, while group dynamics may result in individuals feeling lost or overwhelmed. There may also be competition between members of the group.

Peer supervision is democratic as well as cheaper. However, there are a number of risks, including insecure boundaries, unequal time and responsibility and social chat intruding into or even taking over sessions. Cummings (2002) describes an example of text-based computer-mediated communication in counsellor supervision.

In addition to these common forms of supervision, in some circumstances, perhaps particularly in systemic family therapy, there may be a possibility of live supervision. In this the work is observed via a one-way mirror. This can be very powerful in drawing attention to issues missed by the therapist.

An experienced counselling psychologist might be able to avail himself or herself of a combination of these modalities. For example, we might imagine an individual who works in a primary care setting for two days a week and satisfies the need for supervision by meeting fortnightly for group supervision with a senior psychologist. However, the person also has an independent practice in which he or she works with EAP clients. For this work individual supervision is purchased. Finally, the person themself supervises a group in a counselling agency for which they attend a monthly supervision of supervision consultancy group.

CONFLICTS AND TENSIONS: WHO BENEFITS FROM SUPERVSION?

We need to ask whether the view of supervision as an arena in which the needs of all parties can be met without friction is perhaps over-simplistic. Is it possible that the various objectives of supervision might potentially be in conflict with each other? Indeed, Davy refers to supervision as 'a contested locus in which several potential opposing beliefs and interests are at play' (2002: 230). So, for example, the goal of ensuring that the client's best interests and well-being remain a primary concern might clash with the aim of facilitating the professional development of the supervisee. This conflict can be acute, particularly if the latter is a trainee which by its nature involves allowing the learner to make mistakes.

We have already referred to the situation many counselling psychologists working in the NHS find themselves, in which clinical case supervision is provided by the line manager. For one person to carry out both functions implies the need for careful contracting and maintenance of transparency. Gale and Alilovic (2008) offer a discussion about how to combine these two roles effectively. They point to the complexity of the interface between the two sets of activities. Not the least important of these is the contemporary emphasis on clinical governance, which means that the work of the therapist should be consistent with the best interests of the wider public. This suggests that the supervisor has an important monitoring function, and the question then arises of whether supervision can realistically be provided completely independently of a managerial involvement.

In some contexts, supervisors and supervision formats are assigned rather than chosen. This may result in personality clashes which interfere with the work and the supervisee's learning, as they may feel neither safe nor supported. At a very basic human level, supervision opens up the possibility of shame and humiliation for the supervisee as their work is exposed to the gaze of another person. Perhaps this is reflected in a qualitative piece of research by Valance of counsellor perceptions and experiences; she found that there was 'counsellor censorship of clients and the total absence of some clients in supervision' (2004: 571). Milton (2008) refers to his own less positive experiences of supervision; suffering envious attacks from one supervisor and being bored by another. Stafford refers to 'working with seven different supervisors, I encountered negative power imbalances, untold difficulties with family transferences, plus corollary gender issues about working with men' (2008: 39). The reference to gender is taken up by Henderson (2008), who suggests that perhaps there are differences in the way in which male and female supervisors think about supervision and the way cross-gender relationships influence the process.

Peyton (2004) offers a number of examples of bullying within supervision. These included such things as downright sarcasm as well as telling the supervisee that he would have to get used to the way she worked even if he found it difficult. She points out that an essential characteristic of bullying is not the intention of the supervisor but the impact on the supervisee. In the example of Janet (see Case study 30.1), the supervisor was concerned that attempts to challenge her ran the risk of her beginning to feel bullied. While she herself always denied that she felt at all harassed, subsequent reflection on the case suggests that at the very least what she experienced was not helpful until underlying transference issues were explored.

Kaberry (2000: 55–57) developed a typology of abuse within supervision based upon her research. This consisted of the following profile (within each category, I have selected just a few of the abusive practices identified by the researcher):

- *The context*: in a situation where there is no choice of supervisor and where there is no mechanism for taking into account the difficulties which the supervisee may have faced in a previous relationship with the supervisor. In addition, the two may be involved in other networks.
- *Attitude*: lack of respect by the supervisor may be revealed in lack of warmth or attention; 'too much may be offered in the way of friendship or counselling'. The supervisee's previous experience may not be valued or there may be criticism of a personal nature such as having time off to have a baby.
- *Gratification of the supervisor's needs*: the supervisor may have unresolved personal issues and may be defensive if challenged. The supervisor may have a need to be admired and may have difficulty in holding the boundaries by, for example, offering therapy or friendship.
- *Lack of awareness*: for example, lack of understanding of group dynamics or of the parallel process or of what constitutes persecutory behaviour.
- *The role of the supervisee*: supervisees may well feel persecutory anxiety, which the author suggests 'can be a normal and healthy protective mechanism'. However, the supervisor has to be alert to this rising to unacceptable levels and to be aware of how even the mildest or most gentle feedback can be perceived in this way.

Kaberry sums up this typology by suggesting that 'no matter what the behaviour of the person in the less powerful role, the more powerful person is responsible for not abusing that power' (2000: 57).

A different kind of challenge occurs when the practitioner is placed with a supervisor with a different theoretical orientation. While an experienced therapist can learn from this experience, a trainee might feel confused or feel compromised about how to conceptualize clients and the work with them. In some cases, a counselling psychologist might be supervised by an individual who may not even be a psychologist, much less a counselling psychologist, and might adhere to a different ethical code. This situation is likely to become more common with the advent of multidisciplinary teams in the NHS. Within the primary care sector of the NHS, the emphasis is on brief, short-term work with a search for relatively new approaches such as solution focused therapy and eye movement desensitization and reprocessing (EMDR), and it may be difficult to find supervisors who are themselves trained in these modalities.

ORGANIZATIONAL AND CONTEXTUAL DIMENSIONS

The fact that many practitioners work within an organizational context adds an additional dimension. There can be great pressure, particularly within the NHS, to reduce waiting lists by limiting the amount of sessions allowed to see clients. This may not be in the individual client's best interests, but the alternative may be to reduce the amount of time available for supervision, which may not be in the practitioner's best interests. Trusts are often dominated by medical ideologies and practices and supervision may well be perceived as an unnecessary luxury. Of course, particularly for the trainee, there is a power differential with the supervisor who, in the organizational context, may be influential in the provision of a placement or even in providing job security. Pilgrim (1997) refers to supervision as a form of 'surveillance'. Davy (2002) points out that as with counselling, much work has focused on dyadic or triadic interactions and in the process has diverted attention from or ignored the socio-cultural, political and organizational contexts in which these interactions take place.

For the independent practitioner, supervision may involve a fairly straightforward task of reaching a contract with an external consultant and/or peer group. However, where an organization is involved, a whole series of complexities come to the surface. These have considerable impact upon the practice of supervision (see Towler 2008; Gonzalez-Doupe, 2008). The dynamics may be very different when an organization delivers only counselling services in contrast to one where, for example, the counselling provision is for employees of the organization. In the latter setting, the supervisor is faced with the challenge of negotiating between all the different participants and stakeholders. Does the supervisee have some input into who supervises them; in which format;

is the supervisor solely responsible for clinical work or expected to report back in some form of managerial capacity?

In one case we came across, a business organization had set up counselling provision for its staff only to find that the therapists they had hired expected casework supervision as part of their contract. An in-house person was employed for this purpose but did not understand the importance of client confidentiality and reported back to the organization on who used the service. Attendance dropped off, morale within the service was low until an outside supervisor was employed. However, managers in HRD were unhappy as they felt that this arrangement was outside their control. The moral of the story is that supervisors need to be sensitive to the culture and ethos of the organization. Remaining alert to the possibility of parallel process between the organization and the counselling provision is part of the supervisor's task, and identifying, naming and working with these dynamics adds to the complexity of supervision.

Each organization providing counselling has different beliefs and understandings about what supervision is and what it should include. Towler argues that the literature of counselling supervision does not fully acknowledge the implications of how the context influences the process of supervision and refers to how supervisors and supervisees have to 'wrestle with relational boundaries' (2008: 39). He refers to the organization as the 'invisible client' (2008: 38). The culture of the organization is highlighted by Gonzalez-Doupez (2008), who explores the particular issues which arise in supervision in organizations concerned with crisis management such as the police, fire service, prisons or hospices. She points to some of what she calls the 'tension points' between supervision work and crisis work. These include conflicts such as those between 'taking time' (emphasized in supervision) versus 'reducing time' (emphasized in crisis work) and emphasizing 'reflection' in problem solving (supervision) as opposed to 'responding' (crisis services). Another conflict is described as 'sharing with others' as opposed to 'self-reliance' (2008: 50–51).

The reference to services whose focus is on dealing with crises reminds us that organizational contexts vary from agencies whose specific objective is to offer counselling services to organizations in health, education and work settings which have different purposes. Some organizations offer in-house counselling services to their employees. Others use Employee Assistance Programmes (EAPs), which act as agencies for companies that contract to provide counselling services for them on their behalf. Copeland (2000) points out that organizational culture needs to be understood in order to make sense of the issues that supervisees bring. She adds that the counsellor and the supervisee need to work with and not against the organization. In another paper Copeland (2002) explores the organizational impact upon the professional dilemmas experienced by counselling supervisors. She found that both in-house and external supervisors were exposed to dilemmas focused around issues of responsibility, confidentiality, boundaries, professionalism, relationships, contracts and ethical practice. These issues can become particularly acute when EAPs are involved and no less than five parties become stakeholders in the counselling process, namely client, counsellor (supervisee), supervisor, EAP and company employing EAP.

Imagine a health setting such as a hospital in which a nurse with some counselling training is expected to spend half her time in each role. This is likely to lead to boundary confusion possibly involving a clash of different ethical codes. It is not difficult to envisage the inherent conflict between counselling agencies which tend to have a learning and development culture and an organization or department within an organization which may have much more of a bureaucratic culture with an emphasis on such things as financial efficiency, competition and even creating a culture of insecurity as a motivator.

The relationship between supervision and management in organizations is taken up by Gale and Alilovic (2008), who ask the reader to consider some basic assumptions about the separation of the two roles. They point out that while the BPS distinguishes between line management and supervision, there is limited discussion of the 'interface' between the two (2008: 62). In particular they suggest that the supervision function which creates the most complexity is that of clinical governance; that is, that the activity should be monitored so as to serve the best interests of the wider public. They list a range of cognate health professions in which supervision is carried out by those ultimately accountable for the work. In reaching a view on this topic they emphasize the importance of context and suggest 'unbundling' what supervision is considered to be in the context of the service provided by the organization. They offer a range of examples of the balance between supervision which might legitimately be seen to lie within the management domain and areas of supervision which might be more appropriately dealt with outside this frame. Hawkins and Shohet refer to the need for organizations to work 'towards a learning culture' (1989: 131) in which supervision can be most effective. They suggest that the response of many organizations to dealing with increased pressures is piecemeal, involving panicky responses such as sending managers on short supervision-skills courses.

RESEARCH ON THE IMPACT OF SUPERVISION

In 2002, Davy commented that 'there is little evidence concerning the effectiveness and outcomes of clinical supervision' (2002: 228). In 2009, we are fortunate in being able to draw upon the results of an exhaustive, more recent research study commissioned by the BACP (Wheeler and Richards, 2007) on the impact of supervision on counsellors and psychotherapists, their practices and their clients. A literature search elicited over 8000 studies, of which only 33 were deemed sufficiently rigorous to be included in the review (the final sample was 25). To be included, studies had to examine some level of impact and not just be about the supervisee's satisfaction with the supervision. Most of the studies concerned the impact of supervision on trainees and not upon experienced practitioners.

The findings are almost inevitably complex. The researchers concede that supervision 'does seem to offer opportunities for supervisees to improve practice and gain in confidence and raises the likelihood that client outcome is improved as an indirect result of supervision. However, the link to improved outcome is tentative … and there are no studies in this review to support improvement in client outcomes' (Wheeler and Richards, 2007: 35).

The methodological rigour applied by the researchers which tended to favour quantitative at the expense of more subjective qualitative studies means that the number of studies on which these findings are based is small; in a number of cases as few as one. Nevertheless, they offer a challenge to the conventional wisdom and in the words of the authors suggest that there is no more than 'limited evidence that supervision has a beneficial effect on the supervisee, the client and the outcome of therapy' (Wheeler and Richards, 2007: 3). In a rather tongue-in-cheek fashion, the authors suggest that based upon the existing evidence, supervision would be unlikely to be approved and included in NICE Guidelines (35).

These findings run counter to the rather idealized view of supervision as presented in the literature, in which supervision is largely presented rather uncritically as a good thing. Davy expresses this rather well in a neat turn of phrase when he says that 'there is curiously little evidence, but much emotional rhetoric, supporting the value or clarifying the purposes of supervision' (2002: 221). Not surprisingly, Wheeler and Richards conclude that there is a need for more randomized controlled trials of supervision and highlight the lack of British research in this field. This point is echoed by Rickets and Donohoe, who suggest that 'the effect of supervision itself has not been the focus of a significant amount of research within cognitive behavioural psychotherapy' (2000: 126).

However, in considering the results of this research, we need to remember the debate described in Chapter 3 of this book about what constitutes evidence. The notion of effect has a deceptive simplicity which obscures the complexity of the supervision process. It is now well recognized that the key variable in the therapeutic process, transcending all the theoretical orientations, is the quality of the relationship between client and therapist, and this view is heavily represented in the supervision literature. Valance (2004), in a study of counsellor perceptions of the impact of supervision on clients, found that supervision impacts client work both helpfully and unhelpfully, and suggests the need for more qualitative studies of both client and counsellor experiences. However, in carrying out such a piece of research, West and Clark noted that 'our participants' unprompted recall of what actually happens in a supervision session may not be strictly accurate' (2004: 23). This topic is addressed by West (2003), who draws on research in supervision to highlight a number of areas identified as problematic. These include power and control, spirituality, touch, ethical issues and secrecy. He notes that when supervisees are asked about their experience of supervision, one-third say that it is excellent, another third describe it as good enough, while the remaining third describe it as problematic.

CONCLUSION

Where does the examination of supervision in this chapter take us? Is supervision a necessary and unquestionably desirable element in the training and ongoing development of counselling psychologists or is the matter more complex? If we accept the first position, where does this lead in practice? For example, does the injunction against dual roles mean that there are no circumstances in which this is acceptable? Must every clinician at whatever stage of their career be bound by the same rules about ratios of practice to supervision? Are we prepared to accept that variables such as the financial cost to the therapist or the economics of the organization or the need for clinical governance or time pressures can simply be dismissed in the face of an ideological missionary statement?

Spinelli (1994) has commented that the therapy profession has a propensity to create escalating in-house demands for its own services. The growing insistence on supervision of supervision leads down an interesting path, for at what point do we ask who supervises the supervisors of supervision and so on? Where does it all stop? The evidence that supervision is effective, particularly in the area of client outcomes, is thin on the ground. To assert that supervision is valuable is not the same as identifying what this value is. The practice is inherently hierarchical and contains within it the seeds of conflict between what Cornforth and Claiborne refer to as 'the contradiction between hierarchical expertise and collaborative reciprocity' (2008: 156). It could be argued that it functions as much to give legitimation to the therapy profession as to offer a form of quality control or to satisfy the needs of its practitioners. This conflict becomes most apparent in the way in which BACP and BPS, when dealing with formal complaints, often use supervision as a penalty for misconduct when continued membership of the organization is made dependent on a satisfactory supervisor's report.

On the other hand, the experience of thousands of therapists of all kinds is that supervision has been found to be valuable. It can offer insight and protect both client and therapist. The challenge is to identify more clearly what benefits it does offer and in what circumstances. In the final resort it would not be helpful to throw out the baby with the bathwater.

REFERENCES

Brightman, B. (1984) 'Narcissistic issues in the training experience of the psychotherapist', *International Journal of Psychoanalytic Psychotherapy*, 10: 293–317.

British Association for Counselling and Psychotherapy (2009) *Ethical Framework for Good Practice in Counselling and Psychotherapy*. Rugby: BACP.

British Psychological Society, DCoP (2006) *Guidelines for Supervision*. Leicester: BPS.

British Psychological Society, DCoP (2008) *Occasional Papers in Supervision*. Leicester: BPS.

Carroll, M. (1996) *Counselling Supervision: Theory, Skills and Practice*. London: Cassell.

Carroll, M. (2007) 'One more time: What is supervision?', *Psychotherapy in Australia*, 13 (3): 34–40.

Carrroll, M. (2008) 'Supervision, creativity and transformational learning', in BPS, DCoP, *Occasional Papers in Supervision*. Leicester: BPS.

Casement, P. (1985) *On Learning From the Patient*. London: Tavistock.

Cornforth, S. and Claiborne, L.B. (2008) *British Journal of Guidance and Counselling*, 36 (2): 155–163.

Copeland, S. (2000) 'New challenges for supervision in organisational contexts', in B. Lawton and C. Feltham (eds), *Taking Supervision Forward: Enquiries and Trends in Counselling and Psychotherapy*. London: Sage.

Copeland, S. (2002) 'Professional and ethical dilemmas experienced by counselling supervisors: The impact of organisational context', *Counselling and Psychotherapy Research*, 2 (4): 231–237.

Cummings, P. (2002) 'Cybervision: Virtual peer group counselling supervision – hindrance or help', *Counselling and Psychotherapy Research*, 2 (4): 223–229.

Davy, J. (2002) 'Discursive reflections on a research agenda for clinical supervsion', *Psychology and Psychotherapy, Theory, Research and Practice*, 75: 221–238.

Gale, N. and Alilovic, K. (2008) 'Relationships between supervision and management: Challenges and rewards in practice', in BPS, DCoP, *Occasional Papers in Supervision*. Leicester: BPS.

Gonzalez-Doupe, P.A. (2008) 'Group supervision in crisis management organisations', in BPS, DCoP, *Occasional Papers in Supervision*. Leicester: BPS.

Hawkins, P. and Shohet, R. (1989) *Supervision in the Helping Professions*. Buckingham: Open University Press.

Henderson, P. (2008) untitled article, *Therapy*, 19 (9): 40.

Holloway, E.L. (1987) 'Developmental models of supervision: Is it development?', *Professional Psychology*, 18 (3): 189–208.

Holloway, E.L. (1995) *Clinical Supervision: A Systems Approach*. Thousand Oaks, CA: Sage.

Izzard, S. (2003) 'Who is holding the baby?', *Counselling and Psychotherapy Journal*, 14 (5): 38–39.

Kaberry, S. (2000) 'Abuse in supervision', in B. Lawton and C. Feltham (eds), *Taking Supervision Forward: Enquiries and Trends in Counselling and Psychotherapy*. London: Sage.

Kadushin, A. (1968) 'Games people play in supervision', *Social Work*, 13 (July): 23–32.

Kadushin, A. (1985) *Supervision in Social Work*, 2nd edn. New York: Columbia University Press.

Kolb, D.A. (1976) *Learning Style Inventory: Technical Manual*. Boston, MA: McBer.

Kolb, D.A. (1984) *Experiential Learning*. Englewood Cliffs, NJ: Prentice-Hall.

Lane, D. and Corrie, S. (2006) 'Counselling psychology: Its influence and future', *Counselling Psychology Review*, 21 (1): 12–24.

Mattinson, J. (1977) *The Reflection Process in Casework Supervision London: Institute of Marital Studies*. London: Tavistock Institute of Human Relations.

Milton, M. (2008) 'Expectations of supervision? Everything to everyone … or nothing to no-one?', in BPS, DCoP, *Occasional Papers in Supervision*. Leicester: BPS.

Morrisey, J. and Tribe, R. (2001) 'Parallel process in supervision', *Counselling Psychology Quarterly*, 14: 103–110.

Page, S. and Wosket, V. (1994) *Supervising the Counsellor: A Systems Approach*. London: Routledge.

Peyton, P.R. (2004) 'Bullying in supervision', *Counselling and Psychotherapy Journal*, 15 (6): 36–37.

Pilgrim, D. (1997) *Psychotherapy and Society*. London: Sage.

Proctor, B. (1986) 'Supervision: A co-operative exercise in accountability', in M. Marken and M. Payne (eds), *Enabling and Ensuring: Supervision in Practice*. Leicester: National Youth Bureau.

Rickets, T. and Donohoe, G. (2000) 'Clinical supervision in cognitive behavioural psychotherapy', in B. Lawton and C. Feltham (eds), *Taking Supervision Forward: Enquiries and Trends in Counselling and Psychotherapy*. London: Sage.

Shillito-Clarke, C. and Tholstrup, M. (2008) 'Introduction', in BPS, DCoP, *Occasional Papers in Supervision*. Leicester: BPS.

Spinelli, E. (1994) *Demystifying Therapy*. London: Constable.

Stafford, D. (2008) 'Supervsion: The grown-up relationship', *Therapy*, 19 (9): 38–39.

Stoltenberg, C., McNeill, B. and Delworth, U. (1998) *IDM Supervsion: An Integrated Developmental Model for Supervising Counsellors and Therapists*. San Francisco, CA: Jossey-Bass.

Sugarman, S. (1985) 'Kolb's model of experiential learning: Touchstone for trainers, students, counsellors and clients', *Journal of Counseling and Development*, 64: 264–268.

Tholstrup, M. (1999) 'Supervsion in educational settings', in M. Carroll and E.L. Holloway (eds), *Counselling Supervsion in Context*. London: Sage.

Towler, J. (2008) 'The influence of the invisible client: A crucial perspective for understanding counselling supervision in organisational contexts', in BPS, DCoP, *Occasional Papers in Supervision*. Leicester: BPS.

Valance, K. (2004) 'Exploring counsellor perceptions of the impact of counselling supervision on clients', *British Journal of Guidance and Counselling*, 32 (4): 559–574.

Webb, A. (2000) 'What makes it difficult for the supervisor to speak', in B. Lawton and C. Feltham (eds), *Taking Supervision Forward*. London: Sage.

West, W. (2003) 'The culture of psychotherapy supervision', *Counselling and Psychotherapy Research*, 3 (2): 123–127.

West, W. and Clark, V. (2004) 'Learnings from a qualitative study into counselling supervision: Listening to supervisor and supervisee', *Counselling and Psychotherapy Research*, 4 (2): 20–26.

Wheeler, S. and King, D. (2000) 'Do counselling supervisors want or need to have their supervision supervised? An exploratory study', *British Journal of Guidance and Counselling*, 28 (2): 279–290.

Wheeler, S. and Richards, K. (2007) *The Impact of Clinical Supervision on Counsellors and Therapists, their Practice and their Clients: A Systemic Review of the Literature*. Lutterworth: BACP.

Waskett, C. (2006) 'The SF journey: Solution focussed supervision is like being a taxi driver', *Journal of the Faculty of Healthcare Counselling and Psychotherapy*, 6 (1): 9–11.

PART VII

FUTURE OPPORTUNITIES AND CHALLENGES

Whether or not counselling psychologists incorporate psychological testing and measurement into their own practice, in a climate of demand for more standardized assessment and evaluation, it is important that they become familiar with and reflect upon the issues involved. Chapter 31 considers the use of some common tests and thus provides the foundations for debate. Similarly, counselling psychologists often work in collaboration with medical practitioners and many clients are prescribed medication that can affect their responses to psychotherapy. Some familiarity with psychopharmacological approaches to 'treatment' is, therefore, necessary and Chapter 32 furnishes an introduction to this boundary area between disciplines.

As we have seen throughout the book, advances in theory and research, not only from within counselling/psychotherapy and general psychology, but also from other disciplines, impact on the future direction of counselling psychology. For example, ideas initially drawn from social and literary theory have contributed significantly to the emergence of the narrative approaches considered earlier. Increasingly, links are being made between the relatively new field of neuroscience and developmental psychology and these are also beginning to exert an influence on therapeutic practice. The penultimate chapter explores some of this work and the new insights and approaches to practice it suggests.

Equally, the future will be shaped in part by changing contexts of practice. Whilst Part V has explored some of the changes in contexts within which counselling psychologists work, the final chapter considers some of the other likely future challenges and in particular the changing landscape of professionalization and statutory regulation.

31

THE COLLABORATIVE USE OF PSYCHOMETRIC ASSESSMENT

Susan van Scoyoc

The traditional model of psychometric testing administration and diagnostic categorization carried out by an 'expert' on a passive respondent was subjected to challenge during the 1990s by a model in which the counselling psychologist was seen as working *in collaboration* with the client. Counselling psychologists emphasized a change in thinking from carrying out tests *on* a client to carrying out tests *with* a client, sharing the information and obtaining the client's assistance in interpreting results and reaching a conclusion.

The BPS reflected this change in thinking throughout psychology with the statement: 'Previous test guides issued by The British Psychological Society (BPS) have tended to focus on technical issues underlying tests themselves. While these are essential to the effective use of psychological tests, they represent only one aspect of good practice in testing.' It goes on to state, 'In effect, testing is a social contract in which all parties should seek a common shared understanding of the process' (BPS, 1995: 14).

Fischer (2000) in the USA wrote:

Collaborative, individualized assessment is an approach to psychological assessment in which the assessor and the client work together to develop productive understandings. Collaboration is a means of individualizing the assessment – its process, resulting suggestions, and written accounts. In this approach, life events are regarded as primary data. Test scores, categories, and related research are used as bridges into a particular life and as tools for then exploring that life (2000: 2)

Such a collaborative approach using psychometric assessments and structured interviews has been shown to improve the therapeutic alliance (Hilsenroth et al., 2004) and to facilitate commitment to treatment from individuals with borderline personality disorder (Ben-Porath, 2004). It has also been shown to improve outcomes with suicidal clients (Jobes et al., 2005).

This is reflected in my personal emphasis when carrying out assessment emphasizing collaboration with the client, using the results of carefully selected psychometric assessments, and other documentary material available but combined with clinical interview. The resulting formulation and conclusions are then discussed in detail with the client. It is possible to reach a formal diagnosis when required, but it is more useful therapeutically to develop a detailed evidence-based formulation with which to work with the client as a result of collaboration with the client. Psychometric assessment results can be used as starting points for discussion, establishing which traits or symptoms cause the client difficulties in their life and considering therapeutic methods to explore and possibly target these for change where appropriate. The progress of therapy and outcomes may be monitored with updated psychometric assessment results, which are again shared with the client. This monitoring and assessing of therapy outcomes echoes early outcome research carried out by Rogers when pioneering the effectiveness of person-centred therapy (Rogers and Russell, 2002).

HISTORY OF PSYCHOMETRICS

The development of modern psychometrics parallels that of the history of classification systems. Galton attempted to measure intelligence using sensory discrimination and reaction times and Cattell carried out research at Cambridge Univeristy, but it was in France, during the explosion of the new age of science and industrialization in that country, that the first reliable psychometric tests were used to measure the ability of school pupils in 1904. The Binet intelligence tests were developed in order to separate the 'mentally retarded' from 'normal' children, and these tests and their derivatives were used widely throughout Europe and the USA for the following 60 years. The use of psychometric assessments has expanded from these beginnings in education settings to include areas of employment, child and adult mental health, relationships, parenting and forensic settings. This success and subsequent growth in application is partly a result of the rather circular relationship tests have with the systems of classification. With each newly created classification within the *Diagnostic and Statistical Manual* series (DSM) a new psychometric test to detect its presence and measure its severity in an individual tends to follow, thus in turn confirming the category's existence (APA, 2000).

Today there continues to be discomfort with the use of psychometric assessments as a means of categorizing people rather than in facilitating understanding. This discomfort is reinforced where some service provider protocols insist on clients accessing a service being 'tested' at each visit, so disrupting the therapeutic process at each session. The drive for measuring therapeutic progress mistakenly becomes more important than supporting the development of a positive therapeutic relationship. There may also be a tendency for psychologists who are unsure of their views to rely on the 'scientific' status of psychometric results to justify their opinion on diagnosis, prognosis and issues of risk rather than consider all the information available and make an informed, professional judgement.

THINGS TO CONSIDER

If psychometric tests measure psychological constructs, are we simply creating constructs to measure and thus confirm the existence of the constructs?

Are the publishers of psychometric tests the psychology equivalent of the medical world's pharmaceutical industry?

PSYCHOMETRIC ASSESSMENT

The basis of any psychometric assessment is the measure of individual difference. Each individual is viewed as unique and from this comes the conclusion that each individual has a combination of abilities and traits which, if described accurately, would describe this uniqueness. The focus of psychometric assessment for a counselling psychologist is to assist in the comprehensive understanding of an individual and to use this additional understanding as an aid to therapy, education or rehabilitation. The most common measurement of individual differences are in the areas of mood, ability and personality.

STRUCTURED INTERVIEWS

Interviews are a traditional method of assessment within psychology and psychotherapy. Semi-structured interviews are an attempt to increase agreement on diagnosis and thus prognosis. Thus during development, they are subject to the same demands of reliability and validity as other psychometric assessments. These structured diagnostic interviews developed in parallel to the development of classification (categorization) systems. The structured clinical interview seeks to ask patients a series of questions that allow the matching of the responses to the items required to fulfil the criteria for a classification of a disorder. The use of semi-structured and structured interviews has repeatedly been shown to improve the reliability of data collection and inter-rater reliability regarding diagnosis (Falloon et al., 2005; Rogers, 2003; Miller, 2001). However, this seems inevitable in that the sequence of questions is designed to seek responses that match or otherwise the items within the requirements for DSM.

Commonly used structured interviews are:

- Structured Clinical Interviews for DSM Disorders (SCID) (First et al., 1996, 1997)
- Clinician Administered PTSD Scale for DSM-IV (CAPS) (Turner and Lee, 1998)
- Hare Psychopathology Checklist – Revised (PCL-R) (Hare, 2003)

The Hare PCL-R (Hare, 2003) is a structured interview used particularly in forensic settings to assess risk of both harm to others and recidivism. There has been some debate about its wide acceptance as a contributor to decision making regarding individuals about to be or already convicted of a crime. It has been suggested that its main usefulness is to reduce the sense of anxiety about making difficult decisions for forensic and parole board members.

PSYCHOMETRIC ASSESSMENT

Psychometric assessments take further this attempt at a structured form of assessing an individual, often with a view to assist with formal classification and diagnosis. Psychometric tests are seen as the 'scientific', non-subjective component of the full psychological assessment. They are assumed by many professionals in the occupational, medical and legal fields to tell the 'truth' about the person who has been assessed. Such assessments have now entered our every-day life, even if we are not in psychological or legal need, for example, in employment selection.

The word *psychometric* means 'mind measure'. A psychometric test is developed to measure a psychological construct using standardized methods. *Reliability* is concerned with how consistent or repeatable test results are over time or when administered by different test administrators in different contexts. *Validity* is concerned with whether the test measures what it claims to measure, while *standardization* is concerned with test administrators carrying out the steps of administration and scoring using a standard, uniform approach.

It is the claim of reliability, validity and standardization that differentiates a psychometric test from a questionnaire of the type often seen in magazines. Psychometric assessments are usually based upon an explicit model of normal distribution. This is usually represented by a graph, popularly known as the 'bell curve', using z-scores.

IQ is normally distributed with a mean of 100 and a standard deviation of 15. T-scores, used frequently in behavioural and personality measures, are normally distributed with a mean of 50 and a standard deviation of 10. Unusual or 'abnormal' results are ±2 standard deviations from the mean (therefore statistically significant from the norm). This means that IQ scores below 70 or above 130, and T-scores below

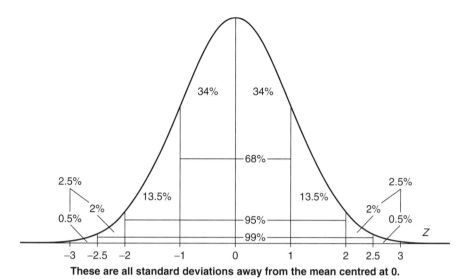

These are all standard deviations away from the mean centred at 0.

FIGURE 31.1   THE NORMAL DISTRIBUTION CURVE SHOWING STANDARD DEVIATION AND PERCENTAGES OF POPULATION AWAY FROM THE MEAN (BASED UPON ILLOWSKY AND DEAN, 2008)

30 or above 70, are 2 SD from the mean, cover only 5 per cent or less of the population and are therefore indicative of 'different' ways of being from most other people in the comparison group. These statistical properties are important in both the development of the tests and in their use (see Figure 31.1).

Standard error of measurement and confidence intervals should be an important consideration when considering any test results. The standard error of measurement recognizes that there is error in the result obtained due to variations in the performance of someone taking the test on a particular day or other influences. We, therefore, avoid the common pitfall of stating, for example, that Mr Smith has a test score of 105. Instead, we state that we can be 95 per cent confident (the confidence interval) that Mr Smith's true score falls between 101 and 109.

MEASURES OF ABILITY

These are measures of *maximum performance* as they measure how well an individual can do things or how much they know compared with others in their age group or category. The test-taker is encouraged to do their best, that is, give their maximum performance. The Stanford–Binet scale is used by some researchers and educational psychologists, but the most widely used intelligence scales are the three Wechsler scales, with each used for a different age group: the Wechsler Adult Scale of Intelligence (WAIS), the Wechsler Intelligence Scale for Children (WISC) and the Wechsler PreSchool and Primary Scale of Intelligence (WPPSI). In the UK, the British Ability Scales are also used, as well as the Raven's Progressive Matrices.

Measures of ability include those for reading, writing and mathematical ability or memory. Most of these assessment results (that is, the test-taker's position when compared with the normal distribution for those of a comparable age) are viewed as remaining relatively static in an individual over time. Therefore, if they reveal a decline in abilities within an individual, this might suggest the presence of injury or disease. For example, a brief cognitive assessment of a person with a suspected history of alcohol abuse using both the Wechsler Abbreviated Scale for Intelligence[UK] (WASI) and the Wechsler Test for Adult Reading[UK] (WTAR) for reading ability might reveal an above-average reading ability but a low average vocabulary subscale and an extremely low to borderline range of results for matrix reasoning and block design. This pattern of results is often observed in individuals with a history of long-term abuse of alcohol and suggests the presence of organic brain damage. Plans for therapeutic input based on the client's ability to think and act upon concrete concepts may be more likely to be successful than a therapeutic approach that relies upon abstract thinking. Feeding back the results to the client can be a challenge, as this is often the first time that the client has been told that he or she has, through their drinking, done permanent damage to themselves and their abilities. Thus the counselling psychologist's training in therapeutic skills is essential, offering the client a 'complete package' of testing and therapy.

Of course, there has been much debate over the appropriate use of measures of ability and the idea of a general intelligence (intelligence *g*) first proposed by Spearman (1904). Terman (1919), in his introduction to the manual for the first Stanford-Binet intelligence assessment, stated:

> It is safe to predict that in the near future intelligence tests will bring tens of thousands of … high grade defectives under the surveillance and protection of society. This will ultimately result in the curtailing of the reproduction of feeble-mindedness and in the elimination of enormous amounts of crime, pauperism and industrial inefficiency. (1919; cited in Van Scoyoc, 2004)

This illustrates clearly how the measure of ability can be misused to support eugenics or efforts to manipulate society with this form of social Darwinism. An assessment of intelligence at the age of 11 in the UK (the 11+) was believed to be reliable enough to determine what level and type of education should be offered and what later employment an individual was destined to achieve. None of these assessments of ability considered a person's cultural, social or economic influences. The lack of understanding, even within the psychology profession, of the limited properties of psychometric assessments has often resulted in an abuse of their results.

TABLE 31.1   *WAIS-III SUBSCALES*

WAIS-III subscales for IQ scores		WAIS-III subscales for index scores			
Verbal	**Performance**	**Verbal comprehension**	**Perceptual organization**	**Working memory**	**Processing speed**
Vocabulary	Picture completion	Vocabulary	Picture completion	Arithmetic	Digit symbol – coding
Similarities	Digit symbol – coding	Similarities	Block design	Digit span	Symbol search
Arithmetic	Block design	Information	Matrix reasoning	Letter-number sequencing	
Digit span	Matrix reasoning				
Information	Picture arrangement				
Comprehension					

As can be observed in Table 31.1 the intelligence assessments most widely used do not aim to provide a single figure of ability but rather attempt to give information about a range of scales and subscales. However, the widespread acceptance of both the concept of a general level of intelligence and that a single number (without any consideration of the confidence interval and standard error of measurement) may reflect an individual's absolute ability has resulted in some difficulties. When used for diagnosis in the National Health Service, the intelligence assessment result may be used to determine whether an individual is permitted to access a service, such as a learning disabilities support service or special educational needs in schools. However, in these settings there is an understanding that the IQ result is not the only factor to be considered, but also a person's ability to independently care for themselves or adapt to social demands. Unfortunately, this interpretation of the IQ result as being only one factor to consider often is not as widely understood as it should be.

Nowhere is this misguided reliance on a particular score more apparent than in the criminal justice system. The Police and Criminal Justice Act (1984) recognizes that people who have a *mental handicap* (the term used within the Act) should have a responsible adult with them when interviewed. The usual interpretation of mental handicap is someone who has a Full Scale IQ (FSIQ) of 69 or less. A range of scores or confidence intervals are not something usually considered. For example, someone who has a FSIQ of 71 (with a 95 per cent confidence interval that the true score will fall between 68 and 76) will not be protected by the law, whereas someone with a FSIQ of 69 (with a 95 per cent confidence interval that the true score will fall between 66 and 74) will be protected by the law. In the latter case, this will require a responsible adult to be present to have the interview (or confession) accepted at a hearing. No consideration of language, culture, social, economic or other variables is generally given. Neither is consideration given to newer theories, such as the multi-intelligence theory, which challenge the concept of a general unifying intelligence *g*.

Gardner (1983) has proposed a multi-intelligence theory where there is no single unified intelligence but rather a set of independent multiple intelligences which are relatively distinct from each other. Seven multiple intelligences were originally proposed consisting of:

1. Linguistic
2. Logical–mathematical
3. Spatial
4. Musical
5. Bodily-kinaesthetic
6. Interpersonal
7. Intrapersonal.

Gardner (1999) has since proposed further possible intelligences:

8. Naturalistic
9. Spiritual
10. Existential.

Gardner's theory and other debates have centred around how much meaning an IQ score has in 'real life'. For example, it is being suggested by Goleman (1995) that 'emotional intelligence', or EQ, is a better indicator of success in life and the workplace than IQ.

In my own practice this is highlighted with the assessment and psychological report for the court on two sisters arrested and charged with drug smuggling. They both claimed that the boyfriend of one of the sisters had merely offered them a holiday overseas and then arranged their transportation. They claimed not to have any knowledge of the drugs found hidden in their baggage. One of the sisters was found to have an IQ of 64, whilst the other sister was found to have an IQ of 75. One was sent to trial and the other was not. The BPS publication *Learning Disability: Definition and Contexts* (2000) gives useful guidance on these matters.

MEASURES OF PERSONALITY

People appear to have long held a desire to categorize each other in order to attempt to understand and predict their behaviours. Methods have ranged from bodily humors causing specific temperaments (Galen, AD 130–200) to phrenology or head shape, popular in the eighteenth to nineteenth centuries and used in some countries to determine racial membership. Categorization features nowadays, particularly in the popular acceptance of the 'Big Five' personality traits.

These 'Big Five' are five broad descriptors of personality arrived at by factor analysis. The five-factor model was first described by Thurstone in his 1933 address to the American Psychological Association. However, he chose to develop other areas of interest to himself and did not research the language used to describe personality further. The model was largely overlooked until the work of Goldberg and others through the 1970s onwards as described by McCrae and Costa (1999). Goldberg and colleagues suggest the five factors integrate with a circumplex structure (Hofstee et al., 1992), whilst McCrae and Costa (1996) suggest the hierarchical model OCEAN, where the five personality dimensions are: openness to experience, conscientiousness, extroversion, agreeableness and neuroticism.

Personality types are presumed to be relatively constant over time, with many predispositions inherited (with some recognition of change taking place within the developing personality of young adults). The factors were seen as largely stable from young adulthood onwards, although recent research has indicated that the most change takes place between the ages of 20 and 40 and that change continues into older age (Roberts and Mroczek 2008). Personality researchers have also demonstrated a link between personality and life success (Roberts et al., 2007).

In Costa and McCrae's model, the most widely used five-factor model theory of personality assessment for clinical purposes, people are viewed as falling within a continuum on each dimension with most between the two extremes, using the principles of normal distribution. These personality measures, usually obtained from answers to self-report questionnaires and typically consisting of 2 to 400 questions, examine the way an individual reacts to other people and situations, how they tackle life problems, how emotionally responsive they are and how they cope with stress, all in comparison with other people (their position on the normal distribution curve).

A popular personality measure with both researchers and clinicians based upon the five-factor theory of personality is the Neo Personality Inventory – Revised (NEO PI-R[UK] version available), developed by Costa and McCrae (1992) for use in both research and clinical settings (see Table 31.2).

It is often in the close examination of the inter-relatedness of subscales that the richest information may be gathered. In my work with women who have suffered from relationships involving domestic violence, I often observe a combination of high subscales score on warmth, depression, dutifulness, compliance, tender-mindedness and vulnerability and low levels of impulsiveness, gregariousness, excitement seeking and achievement-striving. Exploration of these factors with the women can assist in their understanding of why some risk situations are created repeatedly as well as explain to a jury, along with the formulation from a traditional psychological assessment, why certain events were more likely to occur.

Another assessment, the Personality Assessment Inventory (PAI) (Morey, 1991), explores personality, psychopathology and has validity scales measuring the test-taker's

TABLE 31.2   THE NEO-PERSONALITY INVENTORY – REVISED (NEO PI-R[UK] VERSION AVAILABLE) DEVELOPED BY COSTA AND MCCRAE (1992)

NEO PI-R

Factors

Neuroticism	Extraversion	Openness to experience	Agreeableness	Conscientiousness
Facets				
Anxiety	Warmth	Fantasy	Trust	Competence
Angry hostility	Gregariousness	Aesthetics	Straightforwardness	Order
Depression	Assertiveness	Feelings	Altruism	Dutifulness
Self-consciousness	Activity	Actions	Compliance	Achievement-striving
Impulsiveness	Excitement-seeking	Ideas	Modesty	Self-discipline
Vulnerability	Positive emotion	Values	Tender-mindedness	Deliberation

tendency to be inconsistent in their answers or their tendency to present an overly positive or negative picture of themselves. This is being increasingly used in the forensic fields, particularly as it is seen as having a sound scientific foundation with high validity and reliability (see Table 31.3).

TABLE 31.3   THE PERSONALITY ASSESSMENT INVENTORY (PAI)

PAI scales and subscales			
Validity scales	**Clinical scales**	**Treatment scales**	**Interpersonal scales**
Inconsistency	Somatization	Aggression	Warmth
Infrequency	Anxiety	Suicide	Dominance
Positive information management	Anxiety-related disorders	Stress	
Negative information management	Depression	Non-support	
	Mania	Resistance to treatment	
	Paranoia		
	Schizophrenia		
	Borderline		
	Antisocial		
	Alcohol problems		
	Drug problems		

Source: Morey, 1991

The PAI is particularly useful in forensic settings where individuals suspected or convicted of particular crimes may choose to deliberately present themselves in a positive light and understate their negative aspects or difficulties they are experiencing. Other specialized measures such as the Test of Memory Malingering (TOMM) are also used in some assessments carried out for legal purposes where deliberate exaggeration or creation of symptoms may be advantageous for the person being assessed.

Particularly popular amongst counsellors and some occupational settings for individual workplace development is the Myers Briggs Type Indicator (MBTI). The MBTI was developed based upon Jungian archetypes using non-judgemental language to talk about serious issues in both work and personal settings. Unlike many other personality assessment measures, the MBTI is not designed as a clinical inventory but rather focuses on the 'normal' where all 16 possible types are considered valuable. Individuals who take the MBTI are given forced choice questions, so they have to choose their preference of one type of responding over another. These type preferences are: extraversion (E) or introversion (I); sensing (S) or intuition (N); thinking (T) or feeling (F); judgement (J) or perceiving (P). An individual who has completed the MBTI is given a four-letter code to summarize their results, such as ISTJ, ENFP.

One of the earliest but still most widely used personality measures is the Minnesota Multiphasic Personality Inventory (MMPI), originally published in 1942 in an attempt to offer a scientifically based personality measure. The construction of the MMPI has faced much criticism, and the description of how 13 homosexual soldiers were used to originally create the feminine scales on the masculinity-femininity (MF) scale is damning (Lewin, 1984). Recent revisions include the MMPI-2 RC Restructured Clinical Scales (2003) and the MMPI-2-RF (2008), claiming to produce scores on a theoretically-grounded hierarchically structured set of scales. Although these revisions have generally been viewed as positive, there has been much debate as to whether these revisions are indeed as scientifically or empirically based as they should be (Rogers and Sewell, 2006).

MEASURES OF AFFECT

These are usually used to aid diagnosis and to measure outcomes, but are increasingly being used to explore the client's present feelings in depth when combined with the more traditional talking assessment. Commonly used tests of affect are the Beck Inventories, including the Beck Depression Inventory (BDI) and Beck Anxiety Inventory (BAI), the Hospital Anxiety and Depression Scale (HADS) and the General Health Questionnaire (GHQ). These self-report measures are completed by the patient and scored by the counselling psychologist. A typical test will ask the test-taker to think about how they have been feeling (the person's *state*) over the past two weeks (the two-week period matches the requirements for a formal diagnosis within DSM for depression), and then underline the answer which most applies to them.

The typical test of affect contains somewhere between 12 and 30 such questions. How an individual is feeling may change substantially over short or long periods of time, so the results of such tests should not be used to predict how someone might feel in the future or assume how they felt in the past.

The use of psychometric tests is an easy method of gathering statistical information for evaluation of an individual's progress during therapy or as an outcome measure, particularly used by budget managers. One such measure widely used throughout the NHS and other therapy organizations in the UK is Clinical Outcomes Routine Evaluation – Outcome Measures (CORE-OM), developed by Barkham et al. (1998). Information on this is freely available from www.coreims.co.uk. The rationale for its use is to provide a bridge between research and clinical practice; allow for the easy collection of information without reference to any particular model of therapy; aid assessment; enhance case management; provide inter-service comparison; and enhance purchasing, planning and development (Evans, 2003). Outcomes are measured using a client self-report outcome measure and a clinician-completed assessment form. However, it does seem to the writer that there is little standardization of administration of CORE (or other equivalent simple measures) in actual practice. Indeed, there are a few services that send CORE through the post for individuals on the waiting list to complete at home and then return by post before attendance at their first appointment. This ethically questionable practice provides no immediate response to, or scrutiny of, indications of suicidal thoughts or plans. In addition, it has questionable reliability or validity as there is no guarantee that the future client is the one who completes the questionnaire, nor that they do so without consulting others. Perhaps the official rationale is that these psychometric assessments are viewed as so simple to administer that there is no need for special training regarding ethics, standardization, reliability or validity. The result is that there are wide discrepancies in when and how they are administered.

CHOOSING APPROPRIATE TESTS

THINGS TO CONSIDER WHEN ASKED TO CARRY OUT A PSYCHOLOGICAL ASSESSMENT

- Will diagnosing a disorder or carrying out the psychometric assessment benefit the client?
- Will diagnosing a disorder or obtaining the psychometric assessment results harm the client?
- Where is the request for diagnosis or psychometric assessment coming from, and will it benefit the referring organization more than the client?

- Who else might have access to these assessment results? Have you thought about Data Protection Act requirements? How long will they be kept and where? Will they enter into a 'lifetime record' such as NHS records?

It is essential that counselling psychologists engaging in the use of any psychometric assessment ensure that the test chosen is appropriate for use with this particular client and that language, social, cultural, educational and any other influences are considered carefully. Information on various psychometric tests can be obtained from www.psychtesting.org.uk, the BPS-run Psychological Testing Centre, and from the Mental Measurement Yearbook http://buros.unl.edu/buros/jsp/search.jsp. Once a test has been provisionally selected from examination of this information, as well as recommendation from colleagues and scrutiny of research papers it is essential to examine the test manual. This is necessary in order to fully understand the purpose of the test, its reliability and validity as well as the population used to obtain the 'norms' on which your testee will be compared with in order to obtain the results. It may be at this point a decision is made that no psychometric assessment will be carried out on the grounds of fairness and appropriateness.

FAIRNESS AND APPROPRIATENESS

Issues of *fairness and appropriateness* are of major importance in all psychometric testing. Any psychometric assessment should be seen to be valid, that is, the measurement of X is carried out by a test designed and commonly used for X. However, issues of fairness and appropriateness are more than issues of validity and reliability. It is important that information gathered through the use of psychometric assessment is not used for an inappropriate purpose or unfairly. The test itself should be fair to the test-taker, that is, the questions or task presented for completion should take into account their culture, ethnicity, religion, social, economic, gender and educational experience. However, the psychometric industry has been slow to develop culturally and socially aware psychometric assessments. Literal translations of psychometric test materials ignore both language interpretation and cultural differences, so although this has frequently been carried out to cover different populations, it cannot yet be viewed as reliable or valid and, most importantly, to be fair or appropriate in use.

The reasoning behind the decision to request or administer a psychometric assessment should be considered carefully. Is this in the best interests of the client and how will the results affect decisions about the client? For example, an adult has been receiving support from the learning disabilities team for some years with daily living. A request for a new intelligence assessment may be for benign purposes, but may also be because the service suspect they can remove the adult from their case load if the result indicates an IQ score above their cut-off range. It is therefore essential that these issues are considered before, during and after any psychometric assessment, and especially when providing any formulation or written report impacting on access to services.

Recent work has recognized the difficulties of using standardized psychometric measures with individuals with learning disabilities. McKenzie et al. (2004) found that the WAIS III was being adapted by individual practitioners to make it more understandable to their clients, but as a consequence standardized procedures were being ignored. This deviating from standard instructions may be common practice when psychologists find their client struggling to comprehend the instructions for any test. Marshall and Willoughby-Booth (2007) suggest a simplified version of the clinical outcomes in routine evaluation–outcome measure (CORE-OM) for use with those with learning disability, reinforcing the notion that psychologists are having to adapt assessments themselves at present. This raises the question whether the standardized, scientific assessment is truly as standardized as it is assumed to be. The interaction of the tester and testee, the verbal and non-verbal feedback that are given and the natural tendency of the tester to develop a 'personal style' will all change the 'standardized administration'. Further anecdotal evidence of these personal changes has been found during the teaching of a workshop on administering Wechsler tests. One person described how a line had been drawn onto the final page of the stimulus book for Block Design in their NHS department, and only on attending the workshop did they realize the significance of giving this extra information to the testees.

Concerns over the fair and appropriate use of psychometric tests must also encompass the fair and appropriate use of the results obtained. No test result should be used in isolation to make decisions about the individual test-taker, and yet this is seen increasingly in the employment arena where applicants for a specific role are 'screened' using psychometric assessments and only if they fit the 'profile' sought will they be interviewed. It is essential for counselling psychologists to meet with and assess an individual in the more traditional therapeutic style in order to corroborate or dispute the psychometric assessment findings and thus to maintain standards of good practice.

A study carried out in the USA by Grant et al. (2004) using a variety of psychometric measures found that 15 per cent of the adult population (approximately 31 million people) 'suffer from at least one type of personality disorder'. This highlights a common problem that counselling psychologists should continue to question. Our knowledge of the fundamentals of psychometric assessments and normal distribution curves means that to have a recognizable 'disorder' we usually require symptoms or characteristics to be 2± standard deviations from the mean. But how can 15 per cent of the adult population suffer from a personality disorder? This challenges us to be cautious and remember the issues around the social construction of madness (see Chapter 2 of this book).

TEST USE TRAINING REQUIREMENTS

In the UK until relatively recently it has been particularly difficult to obtain appropriate training in the use of psychometric tests. Most psychologists who are using psychometric tests within clinical settings have learned through the 'apprenticeship model'. This means that they have: (1) observed a test being administered and interpreted by a colleague; (2) administered and interpreted a test under observation by a colleague; and (3) administered and interpreted a test alone with the results and interpretation being again checked by the colleague. To date there has been no formally required training in the use of psychometric tests for either counselling or clinical psychologists working in clinical settings. This contrasts with the Level A and B psychometric trainings available to occupational psychologists, and more recently Level A for educational psychologists.

Unfortunately, this lack of formal training or proof of competence has resulted in much confusion and resulted in some NHS departments suggesting that counselling psychologists are not 'qualified' to administer or interpret psychometric tests. The Psychological Testing Centre (PTC) run by the BPS regards all test use as based on competence rather than the route of training (that is, clinical, health, occupational routes).

Perhaps much of the misunderstanding has arisen out of the test publishers' refusal, until recently, to sell Wechsler assessment materials to counselling psychologists. During my own discussions on behalf of PTC with the UK publisher, I learned that there had not been any intention to communicate that counselling psychologists could not use the tests. The sale of Wechsler materials was restricted to clinical and educational psychologists by Wechsler in the terms of his will. However, counselling psychology did not exist in the UK at this time, and indeed it is my experience that in the USA Wechsler materials are sold to counselling psychologists routinely. Again, as it should be, the concern is that the psychometric assessment materials are used by those who can administer and interpret them competently. It has been with this intention – to raise the standard of test administration and interpretation – that the Division of Counselling Psychology has offered clinically focused masterclasses in psychometric assessments.

It is anticipated that recognition of competence in psychometric test use in Health and Social Care settings will be launched shortly by the BPS and PTC. The working party involved with these developments has recommended, as of August 2008, that Level 1 and 2 certificates are developed, where Level 1 requires operating under supervision and Level 2 recognizes the ability to operate independently within a defined domain or set of domains. As with many other competence-based certificates, there will be a period of grand-parenting when those practitioners using testing materials will be able to qualify for the certificates through evidence of past training and experience.

COLLABORATIVE TEST USE AND COUNSELLING PSYCHOLOGISTS

When teaching experienced clinicians about the collaborative use of psychometric assessments, I find many already integrating the scientific, standardized test application and interpretation with a collaborative, explorative sharing with their clients. This collaborative approach allows us to remain true to the underlying philosophy of counselling psychology and not become mere technicians applying psychometric tools. Whilst Rogers concerned himself with how the use of tests may raise the expectation of psychologists being the 'expert' and thus someone with solutions, he also acknowledged that 'tests are of value when used constructively by the client in making decisions or taking positive actions' (1942: 251). It is my view that counselling psychologists, with careful consideration of the issues, can use psychometric assessments so that they are a useful contribution to our understanding of, and of help to, our clients. It is important to recognize the individuality of the person being assessed and to remember that the science of psychology and psychometric tests is not absolute. It is in the combination of the science of psychometrics and the art of therapeutic assessment that a fully rounded formulation and level of understanding can be obtained.

CASE STUDY 31.1: COLLABORATIVE WORKING WITH 'JEFF'

Jeff is a 45-year-old man who was referred to our service by his GP for 'depression'. At our first meetings he described how he had married five years previously to a woman who had two teenage sons. They now lived together and the relationship between Jeff and his wife was becoming strained. Before this Jeff had lived at home with his mother. His father had died when Jeff was a teenager, and two years ago his mother had died. Jeff worked for a local accountancy firm and had started with them upon leaving school at the age of 18.

We began our therapeutic sessions without thought of using psychometric assessments. Jeff knew he was not happy and that the struggle in his life was his relationships with others. We explored his early relationships and his present life.

A turning point in the therapy came when Jeff's employer asked if there was any way they could help Jeff in his workplace. Jeff revealed that he had been struggling with learning how to use the newly introduced computer system for his work and had attended two group presentations for staff and still could not 'get it'. I was worried that his employers were looking to somehow dismiss Jeff after 27 years of service because of new systems rather than a sudden change in Jeff. Jeff and I discussed all of our concerns and the possible advantages of carrying out some basic cognitive assessments,

---

including an examination of learning styles. Jeff decided he wanted to undertake the psychometric assessments.

Jeff and I carried out the WASI and also a learning styles questionnaire based upon Gardner's theory of multiple intelligence. The results indicated that Jeff had average verbal abilities but superior (well above 130) performance abilities. His learning and thinking tended to be mainly visual and kinaesthetic rather than verbal, which explained why his attending two verbal presentations of the new computer-based tools had not particularly helped him understand the changes.

The knowledge the psychometric assessments gave Jeff allowed him to go to his employer and explain that he needed new materials and procedures to be presented to him in a visual, practice-based style rather than the verbal group presentations usually used. His employer agreed to this and training was offered one-to-one which Jeff found very useful. Interestingly, Jeff also told his work colleagues about his 'gifted' scores for performance IQ. This lead to a reframing by his work colleagues of their view of Jeff, who went from office oddity to office gifted eccentric, able to help others with anything visual or practically based.

This reframing also occurred at home in his personal life. His wife continued to struggle with Jeff's inability to communicate well verbally (as she apparently did), but accepted this now rather than believe Jeff was being deliberately uncommunicative. She did recognize that he more than made up for this in his abilities to organize practical things around the house or for holidays. Of course, we continued with the therapeutic focus upon his relationships with others, but it was interesting to both of us to see the shift within his relationships that took place because of the collaborative use of psychometric assessment.

INDEX OF PSYCHOMETRIC MEASURES

BAI	Beck Anxiety Inventory
BDI	Beck Depression Inventory
CAPS	Clinician Administered PTSD Scale for DSM-IV
CORE-OM	Clinical Outcomes Routine Evaluation – Outcome Measures
GHQ	General Health Questionnaire
HADS	Hospital Anxiety and Depression Scale
Hare PCL-R	Hare Psychopathology Checklist – Revised
MBTI	Myers Briggs Type Indicator
MMPI	Minnesota Multiphasic Personality Inventory
NEO PI-R	Neo Personality Inventory – Revised
PAI	Personality Assessment Inventory
SCID	Structured Clinical Interviews for DSM Disorders
TOMM	Test of Memory Malingering

WAIS   Wechsler Adult Scale of Intelligence
WASI   Wechsler Abbreviated Scale for Intelligence
WISC   Wechsler Intelligence Scale for Children
WPPSI   Wechsler PreSchool and Primary Scale of Intelligence
WTAR   Wechsler Test for Adult Reading

REFERENCES

APA (2000) *Diagnostic and Statistical Manual of Mental Disorders*. Washington, DC: American Psytriactric Association.

Barkham, M., Evans, C., Margison, F., McGrath, G., Mellor-Clark, J., Milne, D. and Connell, J. (1998) 'The rationale for developing and implementing core outcome batteries for routine use in service settings and psychotherapy outcome research', *Journal of Mental Health*, 7: 35–47.

Ben-Porath, D.D. (2004) 'Stategies for securing commitment to treatment from individuals diagnosed with borderline personality disorder', *Journal of Contemporary Psychology*, 34 (3): 247.

British Psychological Society (1995) *Psychological Testing: Allser's Guide*. Leicester: BPS.

British Psychological Society (2000) *Learning Disability: Definitions and Contexts*. Leicester: BPS.

Costa, P.T., Jr. and McCrae, R.R. (1992) 'Normal personality assessment in clinical practice: The NEO Personality Inventory', *Psychological Assessment*, 4: 5–13.

Evans, C. (2003) *Psychometric and Methodological Aspects of the CORE (Clinical Outcomes in Routine Evaluation) System*. Available at www.psyctc.org/stats/COREtools/Stokmarknes2003-Chris_Evans.doc, accessed 25 May 2008.

Falloon, I.R., Mizuno, M., Murakami, M., Roncone, R., Unoka, Z., Harangozo, J., Pullman, J., Gedye, R., Held, T., Hager, B., Erickson, D., Burnett, K.; Optimal Treatment Project Collaborators (2005) 'Structured assessment of current mental state in clinical practice: An international study of the reliability and validity of the Current Psychiatric State interview', CPS-50, *Acta Psychiatrica Scandinavia*, 111 (1): 44–50.

First, M.B., Gibbon, M., Spitzer, R.L., Williams, J.B.W., Benjamin, L.S. (1997) *Structured Clinical Interview for DSM-IV Axis II Personality Disorders (SCID-II)*. Washington, DC: American Psychiatric Press.

First, M.B., Spitzer, R.L., Gibbon, M. and Williams, J.B.W. (1996) *Structured Clinical Interview for DSM-IV Axis I Disorders, Clinician Version (SCID-CV)*. Washington, DC: American Psychiatric Press.

Fischer, C.T. (2000) 'Collaborative, individualized assessment', *Journal of Personality Assessment*, 74 (1): 2–14.

Gardner, H. (1983) *Frames of Mind: The Theory of Multiple Intelligences*. New York: Basic Books.

Gardner, H. (1999) *Intelligence Reframed: Multiple Intelligences for the 21st Century*. New York: Basic Books.

Goleman, D. (1995) *Emotional Intelligence: Why It Can Matter More Than IQ*. New York: Bantam.

Grant, B.F., Hasin, D.S., Stinson, F.S., Dawson, D.A., Chous, S.P., Ruan, W.J. and Pickering, R.P. (2004) 'Prevalence correlates, and disability of personality disorders in the United States: Results from the national epidemiologic survey on alcohol and related conditions', *Journal of Clinical Psychiatry*, 65 (7): 948–958.

Hare, R.D. (2003) *The Hare Psychopathology Checklist-Revised (PCL-R)*, 2nd edn. Toronto: Multihealth Systems.

Hilsenroth, M.J., Peters, E.J. and Ackerman, S.J. (2004) 'The development of therapeutic alliance during psychological assessment: patient and therapist perspectives across treatment', *Journal of Personality Assessment*, 83 (3): 332–344.

Hofstee, W.K.B., de Raad, B. and Goldberg, L.R. (1992) 'Integration of the Big Five and circumplex approaches to trait structure', *Journal of Personality and Social Psychology*, 63, 146–163.

Illowsky, B. and Dean, S. (2008) *Connexions Website*. Available at http://cnx.org/content/m16979, accessed 14 October 2008.

Jobes, D.A., Wong, S.A., Conrad, A.K., Drozd, J.F. and Neal-Walden, T. (2005) 'The collaborative assessment and management of suicidality versus treatment as usual: a retrospective study with suicidal out patients', *Suicide and Life-Threatening Behaviour*, 35 (5): 483–496.

Lewin, M. (1984) 'Psychology measures femininity and masculinity: From "13 gay men" to the instrumental-expressive distinction', in M. Lewin (ed.), *In the Shadow of the Past: Psychology Portrays the Sexes*. New York: Columbia University Press.

Marshall, K. and Willoughby-Booth, S. (2007) 'Modifying the clinical outcomes in routine evaluation measure for use with people who have a learning disability', *British Journal of Learning Disabilities*, 35 (2): 107–112.

McCrae, R.R. and Costa, P.T. (1996) 'Toward a new generation of personality theories: Theoretical contexts for the five-factor model', in J.S. Wiggins (ed.), *The Five-Factor Model of Personality: Theoretical Perspectives*. New York: Guilford. pp. 51–87.

McCrae, R.R. and Costa, P.T. (1999) 'A five-factor theory of personality', in L.A. Pervin and O.P. John (eds), *Handbook of Personality: Theory and Research*. New York: Guilford. pp. 139–153.

McKenzie, K., Murray, G.C. and Wright, J. (2004) 'Adaptations and accommodations: The use of the WAIS III with people with a learning disability', *Clinical Psychology Forum*, 43: 23–26.

Miller, P.R. (2001) 'Inpatient diagnostic assessments: 2. Interrater reliability and outcomes of structured vs. unstructured interviews', *Psychiatry Research*, 105 (3): 265–71.

Morey, L.C. (1991) *The Personality Assessment Inventory Professional Manual*. Lutz. FL: Psychological Assessment Resources.

Roberts, B.W. and Mroczek, D. (2008) 'Personality trait change in adulthood', *Current Directions in Psychological Science*, 17: 31–35.

Roberts, B.W., Kuncel, N., Shiner, R.N., Caspi, A. and Goldberg, L.R. (2007) 'The power of personality: The comparative validity of personality traits, socio-economic status, and cognitive ability for predicting important life outcomes', *Perspectives in Psychological Science*, 2: 313–345.

Rogers, C.R. (1942) *Counseling and Psychotherapy: Newer Concepts in Practice*. Boston, MA: Houghton Mifflin Company.

Rogers, C.R. and Russell, D.E. (2002) *Carl Rogers: The Quiet Revolutionary, An Oral History*. Roseville, CA: Penmarin Books.

Rogers, R. (2003) 'Standardizing DSM-IV diagnoses: The clinical applications of structured interviews', *Journal of Personality Assessment*, 81 (3): 220–225.

Rogers, R. and Sewell, K.W. (2006) 'MMPI-2 at the crossroads: Aging technology or radical retrofitting?', *Journal of Personality Assessment*, 87 (2): 175–178.

Spearman, C. (1904) '"General intelligence" objectively determined and measured', *American Journal of Psychology*, 15: 201–293.

Terman, L.M. (1919) *Measurement of Intelligence*. London: Harrap. Cited in J. Rust and S. Golombok (1989) *Modern Psychometrics: The Science of Psychological Assessment*. London: Routledge.

Turner, S. and Lee, D. (1998) *Measures in Post Traumatic Stress Disorder: A Practitioner's Guide*. London: NFER-Nelson.

Van Scoyoc, S. (2004) 'Counselling psychology and psychological testing: Professional Issues', *Counselling Psychology Review*, 19 (4): 5–7.

32

THE INTERFACE BETWEEN PSYCHOPHARMACOLOGICAL AND PSYCHOTHERAPEUTIC APPROACHES

Diane Hammersley

TWO PARADIGMS

In many settings in which psychotherapy is offered, medical treatments often sit alongside psychological interventions. There is widespread tacit acceptance of this, although psychologists sometimes express concern about whether these two approaches are compatible, complementary, or inevitable and beyond question. Perhaps it is more worrying when there is no concern or it appears difficult or dangerous to express those concerns. It is, however, part of a counselling psychologist's approach to maintain a critical stance in relation to evidence, and to question thoroughly what is in a client's best interest from a position which takes into account different and sometimes competing realities. It is equally important, but less often stated, that the psychologist offering therapy needs to consider what is in their own best interests, that is, not to allow themselves and their interventions to be undermined.

This chapter outlines some of the assumptions, constructs and implications of these two paradigms and how they may interact with each other. This is set within the social and political context of the influence medicine has within the NHS and wider society, and how the concept of mental illness has evolved as a way of explaining and categorizing psychological distress. There is a brief outline of psychopharmacological drugs, their uses and the guidelines for their prescription, and a discussion of how they may affect the individual's thinking, feelings and behaviour. The implications for therapy and the therapeutic process are explored through the psychodynamic literature and original research, with a conclusion which returns to the ethical responsibility to consider the evidence base.

THE MEDICAL MODEL

The medical model as a way of explaining problems or psychopathology has a number of assumptions around a faulty mental mechanism characterized as a disease (Freeth, 2007). This tends to offer explanations of biochemical imbalance as the faulty mechanism, and such an assumption fits comfortably with concepts of illness, diagnosis, expert interventions and medication as a means of alleviating symptoms and hence cure. It also has assumptions around the relationship between the doctor and the patient where the helping doctor is seen as expert and knowledgeable and the patient accepting the explanations as facts and complying with the treatment. As Freeth points out, these assumptions are taken for granted in the NHS, and the NICE guidelines (2007) for mental disorders use the same language for psychological therapies as for medical treatments. Treatments are thought to be disorder-specific and can be evaluated by results which can be measured in randomized controlled trials.

Freeth then goes on to describe therapy as a developmental process, outlining assumptions about the conditions within which the client can explore their subjective realities and meanings. Sanders argues strongly that counselling and psychotherapy must separate themselves from the medical model of mental distress, which he claims 'does not work, and in practice is iatrogenic' (2007: 35). He makes the point that 'illness is a metaphor for distress' (2007: 36) and not a fact, and such a metaphor is in need of revision, although it is still taken for granted by the general public and the majority of practitioners in psychology, psychotherapy and counselling. A similar critique of the dominance of the biological explanation to the exclusion of the psychological and social is offered by Read, who illustrates the point that psychiatry is dominated by the drug companies who influence their conferences, journals and research agendas through gifts he calls 'kickbacks and bribes' (2005: 596).

While psychologists may argue against the medical model, there is widespread agreement that it is the dominant model in the NHS and is likely to remain so within the 'psychological therapies', and practitioners must find a way to bridge the divide. In an attempt to find a highway between the worlds of therapy and psychiatry, Pointon (2006) interviewed two psychiatrists with therapeutic training. They agree that therapists need to have a basic template of psychiatric diagnosis, and need to be able to spot symptoms which indicate when to refer on people who need more specialist help. They think it is crucial therapists understand about the drugs doctors are prescribing and need to be confident in communicating with doctors and learn to speak their language. If only similar recommendations could be outlined for what doctors need to be able to do to bridge the gap from their side! Maybe they need to have a basic template of psychological processes, and need to recognize when a psychological problem is beyond their competence and they need to refer on for more specialist help. Perhaps one might add to the list an understanding of the drugs they prescribe.

Resnick (2003), who works with attention deficit disorder, argues that psychologists should be allowed to prescribe medication on the grounds that medication is effective for some patients and can then be combined with other psychological programmes. Given that psychologists would be trained in both models, he and colleagues argue that prescribing rights would also confer the authority to discontinue medications that have been inappropriately prescribed by others sometimes because they lack sufficient training in understanding psychiatric problems. Johnstone (2003a) argues that there is no such thing as a pharmaceutical 'treatment' for any form of mental distress, because the biological basis of any form of mental distress has not been established. The assumption that a change in brain chemistry is the cause of mental distress remains untested and unproven. In a separate article on the use of electroconvulsive therapy, Johnstone (2003b) makes the point that while all psychological states have their physiological correlates, this does not imply causality, and until we have established causality we cannot make claims about cure.

THE SOCIAL AND POLITICAL CONTEXT

As we have seen above, when therapy is offered within the context of the NHS, the political reality is that psychological problems are usually framed by the medical model, and organizational policies about what can be offered at a particular service level have been determined in advance and are generalized rather than allowing people to be treated as a single case. Time-limited therapy is the norm, and assumptions are made about which treatments are possible in the short term, which are cost-effective and readily available. What is measurable and predictable is usually preferred by managers, accountants and politicians who might regard open-ended therapy which is not structured as a bottomless pit that will soak up valuable resources. There may be some truth in that, as there may be a grain of truth in the claim that what the NHS offers is a sticking plaster until the patient comes through the door again. 'Customer satisfaction surveys' speak for themselves, but as reliable evidence for effectiveness they have their limitations.

Within this context, prescribing medication seems predictable at least as far as cost is concerned, and has been categorized as being for specific conditions, for specific time-frames, with specific populations, with specific symptom control. In addition, medicine has an established reputation that therapy has not yet attained. Referral processes both in the NHS, in medical insurance provision and more recently in occupational health settings have tended to rely on medical practitioners to act as gatekeepers, just as have government benefit agencies. This has given medical diagnosis and opinions enormous power to define problems and prescribe solutions. In legal contexts there has been a tradition of relying on medical opinion because of the medical profession's high level of regard in the eyes of the public.

As well as the influence of the NHS with its emphasis on cost efficiency and the social power of the medical profession in influencing prescribing and therapy provision, there has been a growing awareness of the influence of the marketing strategies of pharmaceutical companies. Quite apart from their control of clinical drug trials, evidence that only studies which show the effectiveness of drugs are published and together with the suppression of adverse studies, the companies have been very effective in influencing a climate of opinion through their direct marketing to the public in the USA. Lacasse and Leo (2005) show that a suggestion in advertising to consumers in the USA that SSRI antidepressants may correct a serotonin deficiency which causes depression, has gradually been translated into a 'fact' and picked up by the medical profession, much of whose post-qualifying training is sponsored by pharmaceutical companies. It did not take long to cross the Atlantic Ocean and become established as a 'fact' in the UK, in spite of consumer-directed advertising of medication not being permitted in the UK.

THE CONCEPT OF MENTAL ILLNESS

The medical model relies upon diagnosis; that is, the ability to define and describe illness or disease in the organic body and psychopathology of the mind. Reference is usually made to the *Diagnostic and Statistical Manual* (DSM) of the USA (American Psychiatric Association, 1980). Kutchins and Kirk (1997) make the point that there are two major problems with the DSM, namely validity and reliability. You can have agreement amongst experts without validity, since that does not establish the truth, as those who promoted theories of a flat earth have shown us. While some psychiatrists would agree that some disorders may not be valid, many believe that there is agreement that schizophrenia and depression are examples of mental illness. However, there is a large body of literature which questions the validity of even these categories (Bentall, 2003; Boyle, 1990).

There are also problems about getting agreement between experts as to what constitutes mental illness. Kutchins and Kirk refer to a study (Williams et al., 1992) in which seven studies were conducted in the USA and Germany to test whether pairs of experienced and specially trained clinicians could interview patients and make accurate diagnoses. They interviewed 600 patients in a supervised research setting so that this should have produced the best possible level of reliability. The study showed that the pairs of clinicians frequently disagreed, even though the standard of agreement was very generous, in that diagnosing a personality disorder even if a different disorder, counted as agreement. This shows that mental health clinicians are as likely to agree or disagree that a person has a disorder and as likely to agree or disagree about which of over 300 DSM disorders it is.

The widespread belief that DSM diagnoses are scientific and accurate contributes to the myth that pharmacological treatments are also scientific and specific, but this is much more questionable than many people believe. One example of this is the widespread myth that depression is caused by serotonin deficiency: 'In fact, there is no scientifically established ideal chemical balance of serotonin let alone an identifiable pathological imbalance' (Lacasse and Leo, 2005). They point out that backward reasoning that allows assumptions about the cause of disease based upon the response to treatment is illogical, in the same way that we cannot infer that headaches are caused by aspirin deficiency because aspirin is an effective treatment for headache.

Recent studies (Kirsch, 2005) call into question the efficacy of SSRIs when evidence of the clinical trials showed that placebo duplicated about 80 per cent of the response and 57 per cent of these trials failed to show a statistically significant difference between SSRIs and placebo. These high rates of placebo response are not found in the treatment of well-studied imbalances, such as insulin deficiency, which casts doubts on the serotonin hypothesis.

Another problem is that some treatments for depression do not target serotonin levels and no major difference has been shown between SSRIs and tricyclic antidepressants (TCAs). St John's Wort and placebo have out-performed SSRIs in some studies, and exercise was found to be as effective as an SSRI in one trial. In addition, SSRIs are approved for the treatment of eight separate psychiatric diagnoses, such as social anxiety disorder and obsessive compulsive disorder, but serotonin deficiency is not claimed to be the cause of these disorders.

In conclusion, Lacasse and Leo state that there is no rigorous corroboration of the serotonin hypothesis and a significant body of contradictory evidence. Further, there is no peer-reviewed article which directly supports serotonin deficiency in any mental disorder, nor does the DSM list serotonin as a cause of any mental disorder. Nevertheless, popular public and medical opinion still promotes serotonin deficiency as a 'cause' of depression, and drugs are widely prescribed to correct it.

BELIEFS AND EXPECTATIONS

The medical model and a psychological model which result from different paradigms do not really fit well together, although in practice they are often combined. Different paradigms have different sets of assumptions, but often the prescriber, the patient and the therapist have different expectations and beliefs about the part that medication or therapy might play in helping people resolve psychological distress. Where medication and therapy are both offered to the patient, conflicting messages may be implicitly given. It is important to recognize that frequently within the NHS, the first consultation will have been with a prescriber, although in other settings this may not have taken place and the psychologist may be conducting the first consultation.

Examples of implicit messages:

- Prescribing:

  - You have an illness/deficiency which can be cured/corrected by medication.
  - You are not coping, therefore you need something from outside to help you cope.
  - Drugs will control your symptoms, so that you can sort yourself out.
  - You should not be upset or distressed; a drug will make you feel better.

- Therapy:

  - You are not ill but have upset feelings which can be understood.
  - You have the resources within you to sort out your life.
  - Your symptoms are not the real problem, but they may point you to what is.
  - Facing up to issues may be painful, but it helps to resolve them.

A further set of expectations which a client may hold when first seeking therapy may be around combining these two approaches. It may not have occurred to the client that medication might affect therapy in any way, that there may be unwanted side-effects, that the medication might not be making any difference, that feeling worse may not be evidence of getting worse but may be due to medication, that all drugs are the same, that all therapy is the same and so forth. Given the powerful position that medical practitioners hold, it may be difficult for clients to realize that the decision about whether to take medication or not is usually theirs and not the role of the doctor or the therapist. If the doctor is sympathetic and caring, as most probably are, it could seem churlish or ungrateful not to accept the help offered or to question it overtly. Just because a doctor offers drugs does not mean he or she is recommending them.

Finally, therapy might seem rather vague or imprecise and the therapist may not be able to state clearly what will happen, how soon the client will feel better, and how it works. Beliefs about medication being a scientific treatment and therapy being a bit 'alternative' might undermine a client's willingness to engage in what appears to be 'only talking'. While it may be wise to consider whether the doctor had enough time in the first consultation to discuss the implications of medication in order for the client to make an informed decision, it may be wise to consider what messages about therapy might have been conveyed either overtly or covertly. As alternatives or in combination, the choice of medication and/or therapy is not a clear-cut issue and the relationship between them is at best uneasy.

CASE STUDY: IAN – PART 1

Ian had been prescribed an antidepressant 14 years ago when he was signed off work following a 'breakdown'. He had continued with the drug because he had been told that it would stop the 'illness' coming back. Somehow this was less shameful than admitting he could not cope with life and wanted to be taken care of for a while. There had never been any suggestion that he needed any therapy, or that a traumatic bereavement, breaking his leg and having to take weeks off work had anything to do with feeling depressed.

PHARMACOLOGICAL APPROACHES

Having a clear idea of what drugs are prescribed, and for what, is the starting point for psychologists who want to begin to build a bridge between pharmacology and psychotherapy. Put simply, psychotropic drugs alter moods and are either 'uppers' or 'downers'; that is, they are stimulants or sedatives. The second point is to understand that psychotropic drugs belong to a number of groups of similar drugs, so that knowing which group a drug is included in immediately conveys quite a lot of information about the drug. A third point to bridge-building is to realize that drugs are known by their generic name by prescribers and pharmacists and in the literature, although they also have brand names which relate to the name given to them by the manufacturer. The one major point of reference is the *British National Formulary* (BNF) (British Medical Association, 2008), which gives both generic and brand names and such information as the group, what it is prescribed for (indications), what it should not be prescribed for (contraindications), side-effects, dosage and advice.

Antipsychotics (sedatives)

Examples:	chlorpromazine, clozapine, thioridazine, haloperidol, sulpiride, risperidone.
Uses:	schizophrenia, psychotic episodes, hallucinations, in low dose for anxiety.
Unwanted effects:	sedation, dry mouth, blurred vision, constipation, sexual dysfunction, menstrual disturbances, dizziness, tremor, slowness, apathy, emotional withdrawal, agitation, restlessness, depression, palpitations, rashes.
Guidelines:	Short-term use: severely disturbed patients in hospital and for severe anxiety.

Long-term use: low doses for anxiety, schizophrenia and other psychoses. They should be withdrawn gradually.

Lithium (sedative)

Uses: manic depressive psychoses, bi-polar disorder, stabilizing mood swings.
Unwanted effects: tremor, thirst, excessive urination, weight gain, nausea, diarrhoea, emotional flatness.
Guidelines: It is used long-term to prevent mood swings in manic-depressive illness. It is seldom withdrawn, but when it is done, it should be reduced gradually.

Antidepressants

Examples: (tricyclic, sedative) imipramine, amitriptyline, (SSRI, stimulant) fluoxetine, paroxetine.
Uses: depression, anxiety, phobias, obsessional disorders, insomnia associated with depression, eating disorders.
Unwanted effects: sedation, dry mouth, blurred vision, constipation, sexual dysfunction, dizziness, nausea, palpitations, sweating, tremor, loss of or increase in appetite and weight gain, worsening depression, suicidal thoughts, rashes, confusion, dependence.
Guidelines: They are usually prescribed for three months to a year and often longer. The dose is increased gradually until the desired antidepressant effect is obtained, and to allow for tolerance to side-effects to develop. This usually takes from two to four weeks. They should be withdrawn gradually and there is a recognized withdrawal syndrome.

Benzodiazepines (sedatives)

Examples: diazepam, lorazepam, temazepam, nitrazepam. (Similar drugs: buspirone, zopiclone.)
Uses: anxiety, insomnia, panic attacks, muscle relaxation, stress.
Unwanted effects: nausea, constipation, headache, tinnitus, dizziness, sexual dysfunction, tiredness, drowsiness, lethargy, poor concentration, impaired memory, anxiety, depression, agoraphobia, panic attacks, aggressive outbursts, dependence.

Guidelines: Anxiety – they are 'indicated for the short-term relief (two to four weeks only) of anxiety that is severe, disabling or subjecting the individual to unacceptable distress' (BNF, section 4.1).

Insomnia: – they 'should be used to treat insomnia only when it is severe, disabling or subjecting the individual to extreme distress' (BNF, section 4.1). They should be withdrawn gradually.

Others

Methyphenidate Hydochloride (Ritalin) (stimulant)
Use: Attention-deficit hyperactivity disorder in children.

HOW DRUGS AFFECT THINKING, FEELINGS AND BEHAVIOUR

Thinking

Drugs can affect people cognitively at each stage of perception, processing, consolidation and recall. For example, people given sedatives after bereavement may not be able to recall the events around the death and the funeral. Clients may find difficulty concentrating, or linking ideas both within a therapy session and at other times. They may also flit between ideas without really being able to reflect or go deeper. Sometimes, especially with antipsychotic drugs, clients may have difficulty retaining work done in therapy until the next session.

Feelings

When clients are sedated, they may appear to be emotionally withdrawn or uninvolved. They may also be unable to re-experience feelings related to past events, describing events in a rather flat tone. Sometimes therapists may become aware that feelings of anger are suppressed or denied. Most drugs sometimes produce paradoxical effects so that the opposite effect is obtained. For example, sedatives may make people excited and stimulants may make people depressed.

Behaviour

People may be passive both in their lives and in therapy, seeming to be unwilling to make changes. In one sense they might be seen to have handed over part of themselves for someone else to care for or fix. This might be observed both within the family dynamics or in the relationship with health professionals. They may disengage from work, relationships and social activities. Conversely, people may express obsessive ideas and demonstrate compulsive and repetitive actions. Sometimes they can be paradoxically irritable, aggressive or disinhibited.

Associated issues

Drugs are often part of the problem in inhibited, protracted or unresolved grief, depression and agoraphobia. There is a close trilogy of issues between substance abuse, sexual abuse and eating disorders. One does not necessarily lead to another, but where two are present, it is likely that the client or someone close to them has the third, so it is important to be alert to the possibility when conducting an assessment for therapy.

IMPLICATIONS FOR THERAPEUTIC PRACTICE

The meaning of symptoms

Symptoms mean more to the psychologist than merely a definition of the problem, such as anxiety or depression, since they point to what the problem is about. Much therapy is essentially about defining and working through the problems which underlie symptoms. So they are not only the means of access to the underlying problem but also indicators of the resolution of the problem. Sometimes in the early stages of therapeutic work, people experience new symptoms or an increase of existing ones. This can be interpreted in two ways. It may be seen as evidence of an uncovering of what is the underlying problem, or it can be seen as 'getting worse'. When people have the expectation that symptoms should be eliminated as evidence of progress or 'getting better', this may undermine the therapy. Clients who have accepted medication may not expect an increase of symptoms unless this is discussed early on in the process of contracting. It follows that suppression of symptoms with drugs may prevent monitoring of progress.

Motivation

A second but related factor which needs to be considered is the question of the client's motivation in seeking therapy. Hayward et al. (1989), who investigated the combination of benzodiazepines and cognitive behavioural therapy, suggest that drugs may reduce the motivation for psychological approaches by giving the illusion of improvement and interfere with the development of tolerance to stress. They warn that state-dependent learning may be difficult to generalize, that is what is learned while taking drugs is not applied when people have stopped the drugs. Furthermore, people may attribute their improvement to the drugs rather than their own efforts, and clients may forget what they have learned in sessions.

CASE STUDY: IAN – PART 2

Ian had come for therapy to deal with relationship difficulties where he and his partner kept having rows over trivial matters and he finished up devastated for days. He had not discussed the drugs in depth because he did not think they were part of the problem and he was only taking 'a low dose'. By chance he went away on a business trip and forgot to take the drugs with him and after three days felt nauseous, shaky and dizzy. He rang me and was shocked when I suggested he was having a withdrawal reaction and should restart the drugs immediately which should correct it. Were the drugs connected to the rows and relationship difficulties in any way, I wondered?

Kahn (1993) suggests that most research assumes that psychotherapy and drugs work additively on different aspects of illness: psychotherapy for social functioning and medication for abnormal mood and thought content. This is probably a widely held view and would explain how medication and psychotherapy are so frequently combined. However, it assumes that thinking and mood are abnormal and not related to the rest of psychological functioning or what is happening in a person's life.

Kahn refers to the Boston–New Haven Collaborative Study of Depression which produced four negative hypotheses. First, they propose that drugs are a negative placebo, increasing dependency and prolonging psychopathology. Second, they point out that drug relief of symptoms could reduce motivation for therapy. Third, they suggest that drugs could eliminate one symptom but create others by substitution if underlying conflicts remain intact. And fourth, that drugs decrease self-esteem by suggesting that people are not interesting enough, or suited to, or capable of insight-oriented work.

The therapeutic relationship

Whatever the therapeutic approach, the client first needs to experience the relationship with the therapist as fully as possible. Second, the re-experiencing of past events and working through them or noticing the emotional effects of changing cognitive distortions might be crucial to therapeutic work. Rosin and Köhler (1991), in exploring psychodynamic aspects of psychopharmacology, suggest that drugs reduce the intensity and alter the quality of the observation of inner and outer experience. This seems to be highly significant to therapists whose clients may be taking drugs, and suggests that therapeutic work cannot be really finished until the client is abstinent. Only then can the client judge whether they have really engaged in the therapeutic relationship and been able to reflect on the understandings gained and experience changes in their emotions.

When medication is useful

However, drugs are sometimes necessary or helpful in a person's life, and combining medication and psychotherapy may involve using drugs sensitively and intermittently to support extreme distress and symptoms, reducing drugs when possible to allow therapy. Ostow (1993) recognizes the two treatment approaches and defines them essentially as psychoses needing medication and neuroses needing psychotherapy. He then describes two situations where he advocates combining treatments. The first is in treating depression with antidepressants and following soon with psychotherapy, and the second for the control of excessive affect in borderline, manic or attention deficit disorder patients. He further notes that medicated patients display rigidity in analysis, that the process is affected, there is nominal compliance, superficial insight and limited behaviour change in combined treatment patients. He suggests that medication seems to affect the depth at which therapy operates. This may mean that the goals of therapy may have to be limited by what is realistic and possible.

ADVANTAGES AND DISADVANTAGES OF COMBINING APPROACHES

Antipsychotics

Long-term medication may be essential for clients with a diagnosis of schizophrenia. Therefore the depth of therapy is likely to be limited. The client can still benefit from therapy related to managing their lives and coping with the illness/condition.

Antipsychotics are not useful in the treatment of anxiety because they interfere with the process of therapy and have side-effects which mimic the symptoms of anxiety.

Lithium

Long-term medication may be essential to control the manic-depressive mood swings in a person with a diagnosis of bi-polar disorder. The client can benefit from therapy related to managing their lives and coping with the illness/condition. Clients may be able to work at greater depth.

Antidepressants

In severely depressed clients who are dysfunctional, antidepressants may lift the mood sufficiently to allow the therapy to start and the client to engage in the relationship. Severe depression makes people inaccessible to therapy.

Clients on antidepressants can engage in therapy, but the depth of work may be limited. Since these drugs have no effect in some cases, therapy may not be affected. Clients cannot be sure the therapeutic work is completed until the drugs are withdrawn.

Benzodiazepines

When clients are dependent, benzodiazepines must be continued until they have made the decision to withdraw. Gradual withdrawal should be integrated with the therapy (Hammersley, 1995). Clients taking benzodiazepines cannot fully engage in therapy. Therapy can be directed towards motivating the client to come off drugs, but the underlying issues cannot be fully dealt with until after the client is abstinent.

Examples of advantages of medication combined with therapy

- Medication is useful or necessary in order to control extreme psychotic symptoms.
- Antidepressants may sometimes improve therapeutic access when clients are very depressed.
- Continuing the prescribing is essential in order to prevent a withdrawal syndrome when clients are dependent on their drugs. Drug withdrawal should be very gradual, at the client's own pace.
- Medication may be necessary to control fits in epilepsy.
- Benzodiazepines are used to prevent convulsions in alcohol withdrawal.
- Methadone and subutex are used to stabilize mood and reduce harm for clients who are addicted to opiates.

Examples of disadvantages of medication combined with therapy

- Removal of symptoms may give false hope or false evidence of change.
- Antipsychotics, benzodiazepines and antidepressants may limit therapeutic access, interfere with cognitive and affective processing and increase distance in the therapeutic relationship.
- All medication may have unwanted or unrecognized side-effects.
- Some medication promotes physical and psychological dependence.
- Medication may increase psychological defences of denial, avoidance and splitting.
- Continuing medication may reinforce the assumptions of the medical model.
- There is a risk that the prescriber may act independently, thus undermining the therapy.

HOW MEDICATION AFFECTS THE PROCESS OF THERAPY

Accessibility

In a qualitative research study exploring how a variety of therapists viewed the therapeutic process with their clients who were taking drugs (Hammersley, 2002), all the participants had noticed an effect of some kind. Many of them identified problems around therapeutic accessibility, either internal accessibility of material for the client or external accessibility in the relationship between the client and the therapist. In the first case they identified interference of thinking processes or emotional depth. Given that many psychotropic drugs, and in particular the benzodiazepines, have been thought to interfere with grieving (Committee on Safety of Medicine, 1988), I selected this topic to explore with participants what they had noticed about internal accessibility. There were four outcome propositions, namely that benzodiazepines suppress emotional processing; loss of memory affects narrative competence; grieving is inhibited, prolonged or unresolved; and that it is only after withdrawing from their medication that clients realized what life experience they had lost while taking drugs.

Examples:

'I had a client who was her mother's carer and when her mother died she'd lost her identity in life. She was given benzodiazepines and then years later she still hadn't gone through the grieving process. It's like they're in a coma … like they're asleep.'

'It seems to not exactly block people's feelings … they actually don't have the feelings so much. They contain them and then they don't need to talk about them.'

'And they could feel sadness, but it was not a good grief; it was more like sadness. Not deep as grief in those circumstances should have been.'

Engagement

Therapists referred to clients not really 'letting them in' or 'getting stuck', or clients not turning up or not returning to therapy. Some felt that clients did not want any challenge to their view of their internal world, and poor motivation was mentioned. Others mentioned a reduced potential for insight, and a slower and harder process. For those therapists who used the relationship between them and the client, they noticed that clients seemed to depend on the drugs rather than the therapist and eventually themselves.

Examples:

'I feel you cannot counsel someone non-directively and if you try you get stuck. In fact, you may not even get to being stuck.'

'There is a reduced motivation to do psychological work because they invest the drug with the power to make them better.'

'Therapy is less effective. There is a feeling of not going forward together, the feeling of marching on the spot.'

'I think the thing that stands out for me is they were depending on it, and how it can feel safer than depending on the therapist or the therapy.'

Reinforced defences

Respondents mentioned drugs increasing a client's defences which might at first seem useful to them in managing their lives, but which can prove to be a hurdle in therapeutic work. Denial, avoidance, resistance, splitting, anger, disowning and disconnecting, intellectualization, rationalizations were all mentioned.

Examples:

'They're just not in touch with their suffering. It's a kind of denial.'

'Everything is "you this, you that" and I have endeavoured to get him to personalize statements, but there is just this enormous resistance.'

'People say, "I don't know what I'm doing here" and "There are a lot of people and I know you have a long waiting list" and "Am I wasting your time?" I would interpret that as a defence mechanism, resistance.'

Adjustments to therapy

Therapists commented that the focus of therapy had to be on the drugs first and that might mean giving advice and guidance to the client and being more directive than they otherwise might be. Myths about drugs needed to be confronted, clients might need guidance over drug withdrawal rates, or they need to be forewarned about withdrawal syndromes and withdrawing at a much slower pace than they had first thought. There is often an issue over who is in control of the process, with clients having the same expectation of the therapist that they have of their doctor being in control. Sometimes clients are more demanding or more challenging of the boundaries and there may be more conflict.

Examples:

'Coming off becomes the focus of the work to start with, so that is different because they are bringing a very concrete problem into therapy.'

'I think it's probably harder for people who work in a person-centred or psychodynamic way, because it's to do with being directive. The counsellor has to set the agenda when they believe that the client should set the agenda.'

'There's more potential in these circumstances for therapy to be sabotaged. I don't think doctors were knowingly trying to sabotage the kind of relationship you have with the client, but it wasn't very helpful and you have to deal with it very diplomatically.'

'I think there was a danger of me colluding with them, partly because of my fear of rejection, and therefore I lower or raise my threshold to challenge. In other words, I would challenge less often or allow escape on a challenge, which I don't think I would allow with other clients.'

In another study of the experiences of psychotherapists conducted in Sweden, Schubert (2007) used two opinion surveys to ask respondents who were either psychotherapists or trainees about different aspects of psychotherapy combined with antidepressant medication. For very depressed patients, antidepressants were seen as an aid to functioning before therapy could be started. Surprisingly, some respondents thought medication made some less-depressed clients more accessible and better motivated, but others thought it impaired the patients' motivation. Medication was seen to obstruct the psychotherapy process as well as making it difficult to evaluate progress, particularly if patients were still taking medication when therapy ended. Using only surveys limited a deeper exploration of some of these issues.

ASSESSMENT OF THE CLIENT TAKING DRUGS

It is important to include questions about medication in any assessment session so that the implications can be discussed with the client before therapy starts. This assessment will allow for the diagnosis to be discussed in relation to the client's past and present life, a reformulation of the presenting issues if this is appropriate, and may provide the client with an opportunity to seek further information about the drugs and how they might impact on therapy. If the client needs antipsychotic drugs to maintain stability and a better quality of life, then the depth of therapy can be adjusted accordingly.

If benzodiazepines have been taken for more than a few weeks, then physical dependence is a real possibility and the client should be made aware of the withdrawal syndrome and a discussion about gradual withdrawal during the course of therapy can take place. If the client is taking antidepressants, a discussion may provide an opportunity to review whether they have been helpful or not and whether to continue them during therapy. Of course, it is possible that a client may decide to continue taking medication and decline therapy once the implications have been explored.

Examples of questions to discuss with the client:

1. Name and dose of any drugs being taken.
2. How long have these drugs been taken?
3. How are the drugs being taken? Regularly or intermittently?
4. Has the client taken any drugs in the past?
5. What problems was the client having when the drugs were first prescribed?
6. Did the drugs help then? If so, how?
7. What did the doctor say about how the drugs should be used and for how long?
8. What does the client think the drugs do or are for?
9. Are the drugs still helping? If so, how?
10. Does the client still have the problem that they were prescribed for, or do they have different problems?
11. Has the client sought any other help where drugs might have been prescribed?
12. Has the client ever reduced or stopped taking their drugs? What happened?
13. What effects does the client notice the drugs have? Physical? Psychological?
14. Do the drugs affect the client's thinking, concentration or memory?
15. Do the drugs affect the client's ability to feel emotions or express them?
16. Do the drugs affect the client's behaviour or relationships with others?
17. What are the advantages of taking the drugs?
18. What are the disadvantages of taking the drugs?
19. Has the client informed the prescriber that they are seeking therapy? What did he/she say?
20. Has the client discussed their drug use with the prescriber recently? What did he/she say?

Motivation and readiness

Readiness for change is an important issue in working with clients who use illegal drugs (Prochaska and DiClemente, 1984) and can usefully be imported into work with clients using prescribed ones. Addressing drug issues in a complete way with the client gives the message that they are an important component in the client's treatment or process and the psychologist is interested in them. Many clients are surprised at first, perhaps thinking that drugs are in a separate medical domain and have nothing to do with therapy. If that assumption is present, it is important to question it; it may reflect an assumption made by the prescriber. Of course, that may have been an assumption made by the therapist, too.

As a result of a thorough discussion, some clients may decide to stay on the drugs they are taking and not embark on any therapy either now or in the future. Mostly people who decline therapy may leave the door open in case their circumstances or views change. The assessment may reveal that this is not the right time, or people may need to do some other things in their life first. Some clients will decide to do some brief preliminary work, and perhaps return at a later date. This is a much better outcome than fudging the decision or agreeing to therapy and then dropping out.

Another outcome may be that the client decides to continue with their drugs and engage in therapy, either in the long-term or the short-term. If the two are to be combined for some reason, either of the client's choosing or out of therapeutic necessity, then the goals and strategies or the therapeutic approach may need to be varied. If the client decides to start therapy and discontinue drugs after therapy has been established, then the pace and mode of withdrawal needs to be discussed. This is not the moment to refer the client back to the doctor to sort it out, because drug withdrawal needs to be an individual process which is integrated within therapy.

PSYCHODYNAMIC PERSPECTIVES

The client–therapist relationship

The first dynamic to explore is the complex relationship between the client, the therapist and the drug. Whenever a person is either taking psychotropic medication or participating in therapy, there is usually only one relationship to consider, but when the two are being engaged in at the same time a person has a relationship with both the therapist and the drug. There are important psychodynamic implications in this which have to do with issues of power, dependence, ingratiation and seduction, and these are often overlooked. Kaufman (1994) describes therapists who continue to treat someone in psychotherapy, when they are actively dependent on drugs, as over-involved and over-enabling, because of the lack of confrontation. Although this comes from a psychodynamic model, whatever the approach used by the therapist, ignoring the drug use would need to be questioned.

It is important to remember that in almost all drug treatment settings, abstinence is usually a goal to be achieved before entering psychotherapy to explore the underlying issues. This is often assumed to be because drugs affect cognitive processing and affect resolution. However, Ghodse (1995), from a viewpoint of the addiction literature, reminds us that the client must use the relationship with the therapist to identify and alter intra-psychic processes using techniques of insight, restructuring of belief systems and cognitive reframing and that drugs impair awareness, concentration and memory. He sees the supportive relationship between patients and therapists becoming a substitute for drug dependency, just as drug dependency may be a substitute for aspects of important relationships. Psychotropic drugs and psychotherapy therefore both have important psychodynamic and object-relations functions.

Kohut (1977), from an object relations perspective, explored the connection further by suggesting that a person uses a drug to cure the central defect in his or her self, and it becomes a substitute for the self-object which failed him or her. In psychotherapy, the client's transferences to their drugs (that is, the unconscious hopes, desires and fears) are replaced by transference to the therapist, and that transference, unlike the one to the drug, is used to promote growth. The meaning of client's transferences to their drugs may be contained in the metaphors which clients use to describe them (Montague, 1988). Words such as 'pacifier, consoler, comforter' or 'crutch, band-aid, support', 'life-line, security' clearly indicate how people transfer their hopes and expectations onto drugs.

However, drugs do not calm people, rather they sedate them; do not promote autonomy, rather they undermine it; do not make people secure, rather they increase their insecurity. The role of the drug is to act as a transitional object, which Winnicott saw as representing the 'maternal imago or part object breast and the mother's supportive tension-regulating functions' (1971: 527). Paradoxically, drugs replicate the symbiotic relationship that a person had with their mother's breast, but unlike the dependence on a therapist, do not 'repair' the damaged object relationship and so do not promote healing. Levy (1993) reminds therapists that whenever drugs are used during therapy, their meaning and usefulness must be constantly scrutinized to prevent the unconscious avoidance of the task.

The patient–doctor relationship

Hausner (1993), like Levy, assumes the therapist is also the prescriber, and identifies three dynamics in the patient's transference to the drug, the soothing effect, the placebo effect, and compliance. He goes on to explore the doctor/therapist's counter-transferences, such as identifying with the patient's anxiety and feeling soothed when prescribing, fear of loss of control if the patient is disturbed, regressed or distressed, or emotionally disengaging from the patient, among others. He comments that substituting medication for oneself may mean that the source of well-being and security may become invested in the medication itself, with the potential to undermine the therapeutic relationship.

Nevins (1993) explores what he sees as the psychological meaning of medication but focuses also on the medical counter-transference as three types. His first is that the symptom is an invading enemy to be fought off in a battle, a hypothesis which is unquestioningly accepted literally. An example of this is the unquestioning acceptance of the serotonin deficiency myth, or that chemicals make brain connections work better. The second form of counter-transference is of manipulation of the existing emotional system, such as the hypothesis that depression has occurred due to some blocking mechanism which must be removed. The third type of intervention conveys to the patient that biological mechanisms provide the exclusive explanation of symptoms and treatments, and if the doctor does not know what is wrong, how could the patient possibly know either.

Goldhamer (1993) says that the patient may have fantasies of being poisoned, manipulated, coerced or seduced by the omnipotent parent-doctor, while on the other side is a desire for a magical cure. In this dynamic the patient wants to be loved and understood, and the medication is a gift signalling concern and understanding of the patient's suffering. The gift may provoke ambivalent feelings of being dismissed, and the pills are an alternative to being listened to. Goldhamer identifies the need for the doctor to be active so that when the doctor cannot make a diagnosis of a physical condition, he still feels he must do something and so prescribes.

The doctor–therapist relationship

The third range of psychodynamic influences is less frequently considered as having an impact on the interface between psychotherapy and psychopharmacology, and that is the dynamic interplay between the doctor and the therapist. However well the therapist may have set the boundaries to prevent external contamination of the therapeutic relationship, what often goes unnoticed is that most clients taking medication will be returning to their prescriber during the course of therapy for a repeat prescription. At one level, if the prescriber was also the referrer, it may seem courteous to enquire how therapy is progressing and to apply outcomes of symptom reduction or 'progress through feeling better' to the evaluation of therapy that is implicit in such a question.

In this situation, it is important to discover early on whether such a referral was a 'referral up' to a higher authority or a 'referral down' to a lesser one. This process of referral often carries within it unconscious issues of power and control, and whose task it is to determine the outcome as successful or not. A medical practitioner who has referred 'up' will be more likely to limit himself to prescribing and to defer to the therapist who is a specialist in psychotherapy. One who has referred 'down' will be much more likely to comment, change the prescribing or refer elsewhere without reference to the therapist. They should be given short shrift, but some therapists may adopt a dependent position and defer to the doctor who has no knowledge of the process and would not dream of interfering in any medical specialism!

When two practitioners are sharing the treatment, as is the case with a prescribing medical practitioner and a counselling psychologist, there is potential for competition to see who the patient will prefer. This may lead to dynamics of seduction, where both may seek to impress the patient, or ingratiation where they may compete to gratify the patient. There is also potential for dynamics, such as splitting where the doctor is thought to be treating the symptoms while the therapist is focused only with life issues. Patients may themselves be drawn into such splitting, for example, by consulting the doctor about sleep difficulties for which the doctor prescribes a sedative without either being aware of the implications for the therapy. This is made worse when the therapist is excluded from the process, or worse still when the therapist does not consider it to be any of their business!

Further underlying dynamics of envy may be present where the psychologist envies the doctor's power to diagnose and prescribe, which may lead to mimicking of medical language and behaviour. The opposite may also occur where the doctor envies the therapist's time with the patient and the ensuing relationship, which may lead to attempts on the part of doctors to counsel the patients themselves. The alternative scenario may occur in medical settings where the dominance of the medical paradigm may mean that the therapist feels unable to challenge the doctor's authority and becomes compliant.

CASE STUDY: IAN – PART 3

After the withdrawal experience, Ian decided to gradually withdraw from the antidepressants and I agreed that he would do it at his own pace. I advised him how to do it safely by making a small reduction to minimize withdrawal symptoms and wait until he had recovered fully before he made another. His experience of an abrupt withdrawal was seen as useful because it helped him to see he was physically as well as psychologically dependent on the drug. However, when he went to get his repeat prescription, he was told that the doctors were now going to see him every month to monitor how he was, not trusting that the psychologist knew what she was doing because she had not put a withdrawal schedule in place.

PROFESSIONAL AND ETHICAL RESPONSIBILITY

Recognizing the problems which may appear as cracks in the interface between the medical paradigm and the psychological paradigm is an important professional and ethical responsibility. Those cracks may at times only be hairline cracks but at other times they may become vast crevasses, and any friction between these two paradigms will not be soothed by the oil of complacency. With other professionals with whom clinical responsibility for patients is shared, counselling psychologists have an ethical responsibility to ensure that any treatment benefits the client and minimizes harm and risks to safety. This is where the evidence base is important. Given that a meta-analysis of the clinical trial data shows that adults given SSRI antidepressants are five times more likely to commit suicide than those given placebo (Healy, 2003), and that the response to SSRIs is largely a placebo effect not a drug effect (Kirsch, 2005), it is irresponsible not to use that knowledge in the consultation and supervision which leads to ethical decision making. That knowledge, if it is integrated with clinical experience, needs to be shared with medical practitioners rather than leaving them to guess at it or flounder on their own.

Respect for the client means that they too need to be informed about the sometimes complex issues around medication and therapy that will allow them to achieve self-determination and make a choice. Leaving it up to the client without engaging in the debate and the decision is not respecting the client's autonomy. Reliance on codes of conduct which are 'rules', procedures such as referring to psychiatrists when people are considered to be at risk, following guidelines such as NICE recommendations are often more a defence against complaints and litigation than a commitment to ethical practice. It is inevitable that at times when two paradigms are close together, there will be some friction. What is needed is greater honesty and openness on all sides about our search for understanding of psychological distress and the limitations of both approaches.

REFERENCES

American Psychiatric Association (1980) *Diagnostic and Statistical Manual of Mental Disorders,* 3rd edn. Washington, DC: APA.

Bentall, R.P. (2003) *Madness Explained: Psychosis and Human Nature.* London: Penguin.

Boyle, M. (1990) *Schizophrenia: A Scientific Delusion? London:* Routledge.

British Medical Association and The Royal Pharmaceutical Society (2008) *British National Formulary.* London: The Pharmaceutical Press.

Committee on Safety of Medicines (1988) 'Benzodiazepines, dependence and withdrawal symptoms', *Current Problems,* 21: 1–2.

Freeth, R. (2007) 'Working within the medical model', *Therapy Today,* November: 31–34, BACP.

Ghodse, H. (1995) *Drugs and Addictive Behaviour,* 2nd edn. Oxford: Blackwell Science.

Goldhamer, P.M. (1993) 'The challenge of integration', in M. Schachter (ed.), *Psychotherapy and Medication.* Northvale, NJ: Aronson.

Hammersley, D.E. (1995) *Counselling People on Prescribed Drugs.* London: Sage.

Hammersley, D.E. (2002) 'An exploration of how therapists view therapeutic process in relation to clients who are taking benzodiazepines'. Unpublished PhD thesis, Regent's College & City University, London.

Hausner, R. (1993) 'Medication and transitional phenomena', in M. Schachter (ed.), *Psychotherapy and Medication.* Northvale, NJ: Aronson.

Hayward, P., Wardle, J. and Higgitt, A. (1989) 'Benzodiazepine research: Current findings and practical consequences', *British Journal of Clinical Psychology,* 28: 307–327.

Healy, D. (2003) 'Lines of evidence on the risks of suicide with selective serotonin reuptake inhibitors', *Psychotherapy and Psychosomatics,* 72 (2): 71–79.

Johnstone, L. (2003a) 'Back to basics', *The Psychologist*, 16 (4): 186–187.

Johnstone, L. (2003b) 'A shocking treatment', *The Psychologist*, 16 (5): 236–239.

Kahn, D.A. (1993) 'Medication consultation and split treatment during psychotherapy', in M. Schachter (ed.), *Psychotherapy and Medication*. Northvale, NJ: Aronson.

Kaufman, K. (1994) *Psychotherapy of Addictive Persons*. New York: Guilford Press.

Kirsch, I. (2005) 'Medication and suggestion in the treatment of depression', *Contemporary Hypnosis*, 22 (2): 59–66.

Kohut, H. (1977) *The Analysis of the Self*. Madison, CT: International Universities Press.

Kutchins, H. and Kirk, S. (1997) *Making Us Crazy: DSM – The Psychiatric Bible and the Creation of Mental Disorders*. London: Constable.

Lacasse, J.R. and Leo, J. (2005) 'Serotonin and depression: A disconnect between the advertisements and the scientific literature', *PLoS Medicine*, 2 (12): e392 DOI: 10.1371/journal.pmed.0020392. Available at www.tinyurl.com/8vywy, accessed 4 January 2007.

Levy, S.T. (1993) 'Countertransference aspects in the treatment of schizophrenia', in M. Schachter (ed.), *Psychotherapy and Medication*. Northvale, NJ: Aronson.

Montague, M. (1988) 'The metaphorical nature of drugs and drug taking', *Journal of Drug Issues*, 26: 417–424.

Nevins, D.B. (1993) 'Psychoanalytic perspectives on medication for mental illness', in M. Schachter (ed.), *Psychotherapy and Medication*. Northvale, NJ: Aronson.

NICE (2007) *Depression: Management of Depression in Primary and Secondary Care*. CG 23. Available at www.nice.org.uk

Ostow, M. (1993) 'On beginning with patients who require medication', in M. Schachter (ed.), *Psychotherapy and Medication*. Northvale, NJ: Aronson.

Pointon, C. (2006) 'Gulfs and bridges', *Therapy Today*, May: 16–18.

Prochaska, J.O. and DiClemente, C.C. (1984) *The Transtheoretical Approach: Crossing Traditional Boundaries of Therapy*. Homewood, IL: Dow-Jones-Irwin.

Read, J. (2005) 'The bio-bio-bio model of madness', *The Psychologist*, 18 (10): 596–597.

Resnick, R. (2003) 'To prescribe or not to prescribe – is that the question?', *The Psychologist*, 16 (4): 184–186.

Rosin, U. and Köhler, G.K. (1991) 'Psychodynamic aspects of psychopharmacology in functional somatic complaints', *Psychotherapy and Psychodynamics*, 56 (3): 129–134.

Sanders, P. (2007) 'Decoupling psychological therapies from the medical model', *Therapy Today*, November: 35–38.

Schubert, J. (2007) 'Psychotherapy and antidepressant medication: Scope, procedure and interaction. A survey of psychotherapists' experience', *European Journal of Psychotherapy and Counselling*, 9 (2): 191–207.

Williams, J.B.W., Gibbon, M., First, M.B., Spitzer, R.L., Davies, M., Borus, J., Howes, M.J., Kane, J., Pope, H.G. Jr, Rounsaville, B. and Wittchen, H.-U. (1992) 'The structured clinical interview for DSM-III-R (SCID): II multisite test-retest reliability', *Archives of General Psychiatry*, 49 (8): 630–636.

Winnicott, D.W. (1971) *Playing and Reality*. London: Routledge.

33

ATTACHMENT AND ITS RELATIONSHIP TO MIND, BRAIN, TRAUMA AND THE THERAPEUTIC ENDEAVOUR

Mary Brownescombe Heller

During the last two decades or so, there has been increasing research interest in the neurophysiology and neuropsychology of the brain, as it relates to the processes involved in the development of attachment bonds between mother and infant. This has included the processes that take place in the brain when the individual experiences traumatic events – whether as a child or an adult. Although some controversies continue regarding the neuronal circuitry and localization of brain processes, many of these neuroscientific findings on the nature of attachment in relation to the brain are highly relevant to an understanding of what happens in counselling and psychotherapy within and between the minds of therapist and client, as well as the processes that take place in their two interacting brains.

MIND AND BRAIN – HOW ARE THEY TO BE DISTINGUISHED?

The puzzle of what is mind and what is brain and the relationship between them is one that has not only exercised the neuroscientists, but has been a subject for philosophers through the ages. The problem has been conceptualized in the form of two related questions: 'How does the mind emerge from the brain?' and 'How does consciousness emerge from the brain?' (Solms and Turnbull, 2002: 46). The brain is easier to describe in that it is an organ of the body composed largely of nerve cell assemblies, chemical neurotransmitters and molecules. But what is meant by 'mind' and how does it emerge from and relate to something as mundane as a collection of nervous tissue? As Steven Rose points out:

> Mind is a process, not a thing – a process enabled by the brain, but not reducible to it [...] brains enable us to have minds, but thinking – minding – is a property of the person for which our minds are essential. (2007: 37)

Solms and Turnbull (2002) and Rose (2006) have presented thoughtful accounts of the history and current understanding of the mind–brain problem for those who wish to pursue this complex subject further. In summary, though, what is seen to characterize the mind is our capacity for looking inwards for introspection and self-awareness, whilst having an appreciation of the separate minds of others. This 'theory of mind' (Baron-Cohen, 1995) includes the ability to perceive ourselves not only from our own perspective but from the viewpoint of others, whilst remaining grounded in our own bodily selves; to reflect on ourselves, to be able to represent ourselves and our personal experiences, our feelings and intentions internally – in our minds – and to be able to represent and think about the mental states of others. This complex process has been referred to as 'reflective self-functioning' (RSF) or 'mentalization' (Fonagy, 1995).

ATTACHMENT THEORY: A BRIEF HISTORY

Mary Ainsworth can be considered the mother of attachment theory and John Bowlby the father. The Strange Situation Test, developed by Ainsworth, observed under laboratory conditions how very young children responded to brief absences by their mothers. The main focus was on how babies *reunite* with their mothers following a short separation; since it was this coming together again that was seen to throw most light on the attachment relationship. This work led to the distinctions between 'secure', 'avoidant', 'ambivalent' and (somewhat later) 'disorganized' patterns of attachment – and the ways that such attachment styles, observed in these young children, were directly related to the nature of their everyday social, behavioural and affect-related interactions with their mothers or main caretakers (Ainsworth et al., 1978; Main and Solomon, 1990; Main, 1999).

A great deal of research has been undertaken using the Strange Situation Test, with findings being remarkably consistent in terms of attachment patterns and styles. Steele et al. (2002), for example, found that babies rated as insecurely attached to their mothers at 12 months of age had similar attachment classifications when rated in adolescence. Strathern (2007) found that mothers with 'avoidant' styles of attachment, as classified on the Adult Attachment Interview (Crittenden, 2004; George et al., 1996), showed different patterns of brain activation in response to infant distress, in comparison to mothers rated as having 'secure' attachment styles. Bowlby stressed that for optimal child development, parental care-giving should be sufficiently consistent, sensitive to the child's needs, affectionate, comforting and age-appropriate. This, he argued, provided the baby and growing child not only with a 'secure base' from which to explore and learn about his or her environment, but also with attachment figures on whom to rely, and an internal, secure confidence about his or her own worth. These early attachment relationships were seen to form the prototype for later, adult relationships.

Many of Bowlby's ideas on the role of the environment in the development of psychopathology were based on the work he undertook with 'juvenile delinquents' at the London Child Guidance Clinic (Bowlby, 1944; Holmes, 1993). Bowlby considered that the child's capacity for attachment, in combination with the mother's (or primary caretaker's) ability to form secure attachment bonds with her infant, were powerful motivational drives and primary for the survival of the species. The nature of these attachment bonds were seen to powerfully influence the child's behaviour and developing personality. Attachment bonds, mediated through a variety of behaviours, served to establish and maintain optimal proximity (Bowlby, 1988; Crittenden, 1997; Fonagy, 2001; Heard and Lake, 1997). Relating and proximity-seeking in infancy and early childhood was viewed as a primary developmental goal, unrelated to such physiological needs as hunger. Bowlby argued that the infant's and young child's instinctual need to attach to a caregiver was so powerful it overrode even harsh or neglectful behaviour in the caretaker. Nevertheless, the type of attachment formed to such a caretaker would be likely to be anxious, avoidant or disorganized, rather than secure (Bowlby, 1969, 1979; Buchheim and Kachele, 2003; Mace and Margison, 1997; Steele, 2003; Swain et al., 2007).

Bowlby described the development of what he termed 'internal working models' (1980), which were adaptively structured through the ways in which the child experienced his early attachment relationships. These served as organizing blueprints or templates for future action – a kind of unconscious learning from experience. The major developmental attainment of the 'internal working model', based on the child's attachment experiences, was that of being able to create a processing system in relation to the self and other people 'in terms of a set of stable and generalised intentional attributes, such as desires, emotions, intentions and beliefs inferred from recurring invariant patterns in the history of previous interactions' (Fonagy et al., 2003: 416). The formation of this stable, yet flexible, representational system enabled the child to think about and predict what was likely to happen when he behaved in certain ways rather than others, and, as a consequence, to adjust his behaviour in socially rewarding and self-enhancing ways within the environment in which he lived.

THE DEVELOPMENT OF SECURE AND INSECURE ATTACHMENT

As Sue Gerhardt states in her introduction to *Why Love Matters*, 'the human baby is the most socially influenced creature on earth' (2005: Introduction); thus the child's early attachment experiences form the building blocks of his emotional, social and representational world (Steele, 2003). The to-and-fro responsiveness that takes place between mother and infant has been termed 'attunement' and promotes a 'secure base' and secure attachment bonds (Stern, 1985; Heard and Lake, 1997). These provide both emotional resilience and a 'psychological immune system' against trauma-induced psychopathology in both children and adults (Fonagy et al., 2003; Holmes, 2001; Huopainen, 2002). Secure attachment facilitates 'experience dependent' growth and the formation of close, satisfying relationships; a history of secure and loving attachments supports the effective self-regulation of affects and impulses, enhances cognitive attainment and promotes the development of reflective functioning. This enables the growing child to become capable of making flexible assessments of situations based on previous experiences and then to choose responses that are appropriate, without being stereotypically tied to them. In this way learning can be taken forward to use adaptively in other future situations (Bowlby, 1988; Fonagy, 2001; Schore, 2001).

If care-giving is inconsistent, abusive, dysfunctional, withdrawn too early for too long, or emotionally unresponsive (perhaps due to mother's depression), then the child's attachment behaviours, including the ability to form adult need-satisfying relationships, can become highly disrupted. A young child, experiencing a prolonged absence from his attachment figure, goes through a cycle of what Bowlby described as 'Protest → Despair → Detachment'. At the 'Detachment' stage strategic defences are formed: first, as an organized system for the exclusion of disturbing thoughts; second, to keep a separation between distressing affect and those situations or individuals initially arousing such affect (Bowlby, 1980; Robertson and Robertson, 1989). If the attachment environment in which the child lives is not conducive to the formation of stable internal working models and the development of a 'secure base', then 'disorganized' attachment and psychopathology may be the result (Bowlby, 1944, 1953, 1979).

In situations where there is an early significant loss, or some kind of traumatic incident, the ways in which such situations are contained and handled by the parents or caretakers are of particular importance. If the child can be helped to deal with the reality of the loss or trauma in a loving and age-appropriate way, then this enables the child to develop greater resilience. The experience can be gained that such events, though distressing and painful, can be thought about, put into narrative form and managed successfully in the future. If this is not the case and the environment is deficient in good-enough attachment experiences, or is one involving serious neglect, or the parents avoid, dismiss or even ridicule the child's distress (perhaps because of unresolved painful experiences of their own), then the traumatic event may become lodged in the child's mind as something unknowable and unthinkable – a transgenerational transmission of trauma. Such experiences, particularly if repeated, can result in declining cognitive performance and personality disturbances. The capacity for empathy, reflective self-functioning and mentalization may be reduced and the development of flexible affect-regulating neuronal structures impeded (Blum, 2003; Fonagy et al., 2003; Strathearn, 2007).

Nevertheless, Bowlby, Ainsworth and other attachment theorists stress that early attachment experiences do not *determine* the individual's life as an adult. Human beings are adaptable, can learn from both their good and their bad life experiences, and their 'internal working models' have considerable plasticity. Nor do good and secure early attachment experiences *necessarily* protect the individual from future adverse or traumatizing situations in adulthood. Genetic endowment, economic hardship, poor housing, social isolation and educational disadvantage all have their part to play in the parent's ability to provide adequate child-rearing, and the child's ability to find the internal resilience necessary to cope with adverse events and traumatic incidents (Schoon and Bartley, 2008).

NEUROSCIENTIFIC FINDINGS AND ATTACHMENT

Infant stimuli activate basal forebrain regions [in parental attachment figures], which regulate brain circuits that handle specific nurturing and caregiving responses and activate the brain's more general circuitry for handling emotions, motivation, attention and empathy – all of which are crucial for effective parenting. (Swain et al., 2007: 262)

Recent developments in the field of neuroscience provide additional scientific underpinning for Bowlby and Ainsworth's work on the psychobiological and socio-emotional aspects of attachment and attachment failures. Neurological and neuropsychological research is beginning to discover which brain areas are important in parenting, as well as confirming that the attachment relationship plays a major part in the organization of the baby's developing brain. Neurobiological research, including functional neuro-imaging techniques (fMRI), demonstrates that from early infancy, representations of our experiences and the feelings that we have about people and events are laid down in brain structures which then influence, at both cortical and sub-cortical levels, how we perceive the world and our place in it (Damasio, 1994; Schore, 2001, 2003; Solms and Turnbull, 2002; Strathearn, 2007; Swain et al., 2007).

As Schore (2003) points out, the baby's brain is 'experience dependent'. Early attachment experiences organize the maturation of the baby's labile neuronal brain structures at cortical and sub-cortical levels; in so doing they shape, structure and regulate the emotional and social dynamics of the mind and the developing personality. The form and content of these neuronal structures provide a 'blueprint' to organize parental behaviour once the baby becomes an adult.

Neurobiological and neuro-imaging studies suggest that the neuropeptide hormone *oxytocin*, which helps reduce stress and anxiety, is released during breast-feeding. This provides reward-based signals which motivate maternal care and assist in the promotion of maternal 'attunement'. Nevertheless, these signals can be disrupted if the mother herself has a history of disrupted or adverse attachments (Strathearn, 2007). In female cocaine users, the release of oxytocin is significantly reduced, leading researchers to suggest that cocaine-exposed mothers, even when not actively using drugs, may be less able to respond to their infants' cues and may find their interaction with their babies less rewarding. Since such mothers may well have had adverse attachment experiences of their own, which predisposed them to substance abuse, the causative factors are clearly complex (Johns et al., 2005; Light et al., 2004; Swain et al., 2007).

Strathearn (2007) has proposed that differing patterns of attachment styles in human mothers, in response to cues from their infants, can be distinguished by different patterns of brain activation. His findings suggest that mothers with 'dismissing' attachment patterns show a deficiency in their levels of oxytocin production, whereas those with 'pre-occupied' patterns of attachment show abnormally low levels of *dopamine* production – also found to be an essential component in promoting attachment. In a further study (2008), Strathearn and colleagues demonstrated that 'secure' mothers show significantly enhanced activation of those brain regions involving reward-based dopamine, in response to the emotions expressed by their babies, than do 'insecure' and 'avoidant' mothers (as classified on Crittenden's 2004 version of the AAI). These research studies could well have far-reaching consequences for the understanding and differential help for those mothers with adverse attachment experiences who may be at risk of neglecting or harming their babies.

The right hemisphere is dominant in the first year of life and has a particular role in the production and regulation of emotional and social processes (Schore, 2001, 2003). As language develops, the left hemisphere becomes prominent in cognitive processing, including the ability to construct our own narrative history, to reflect on ourselves and to describe in words the feelings that we experience (for some left-handed people this hemispheric dominance is reversed). There is, nevertheless, a complex inter-relationship between the two hemispheres, with certain functions being able to be undertaken by either hemisphere in the event of damage to specific regions, and localization is never fully confined to particular areas or hemispheres, since the brain acts as a multiple interactive system (Rose, 2006).

The right hemisphere also has an important survival function, in that it is uniquely equipped with a 'body-state map' with which to initiate very rapid responses. In situations where the individual's survival is at stake, or is *perceived* to be at stake, right-hemisphere survival templates are activated so rapidly that they bypass the conscious reflective monitoring and logico-deductive thought processing of the left hemisphere (Damasio, 1994). These affect-laden action sets (fight, flight or freezing) function as an appropriate means of avoiding danger when faced with a current and reality-based life-threatening situation. However, when the response is based on experiences that are deeply embedded in an attachment history which has involved unprocessed anxiety, pain, distress and danger, its activation may well not be relevant to the current situation. Such a response can lead to an increase in the danger and risk situation, rather than to its reduction (Crittenden, 1997; Garland, 1998).

'Mirror' neurons are located primarily in the pre-frontal cortex of the brain and, to a lesser extent, in the temporal and parietal cortices. These neurons, which are activated whenever the subject is performing some form of motor task or experiencing some painful stimulus, show broadly similar activity when the subject is watching someone else performing that same task or experiencing pain. It is as if these neuronal circuits are carrying out a kind of internal empathic mirroring of what the other person is doing or feeling (Imeri, 2007; Singer et al., 2004). It has been suggested (Gallese, 2007) that autistic-spectrum children and adults may have a dysfunction of their mirror neuron system, which underlies their specific difficulties in empathically 'tuning-in' to the implicit socio-emotional communications of other people.

Research, using brain imaging techniques, has indicated that individuals with secure attachment patterns show activation in the 'mirroring' areas of the brain when given empathy-eliciting tasks, whereas individuals with disorganized attachment patterns show significantly less activation – suggesting that their capacity for empathy is impaired (Buchheim et al., 2006). Clearly the capacity for empathy is important in parental behaviour if it is to promote secure attachment in the infant. Ranote and colleagues (2004) found that the mirroring areas and other parts of mothers' brains involved in attachment showed significant activation when shown video clips of their own babies, in comparison to unknown infants. Other studies note that in mothers found to be at risk of maltreating their infants, hearing an audiotape of a crying baby can elicit high levels of neuro-physiological activity, suggesting that such parents have difficulty in modulating their emotional arousal; with the result that the crying then becomes a risk factor for harming their baby (Soltis, 2004; Swain et al., 2007).

These neuro-scientific findings on mirror neurons and the discovery of brain circuits for empathy give evidence-based support for the ways in which affect-based phenomena can be communicated, and then hopefully contained and thought about, in the therapeutic relationship.

TRAUMA: ITS EFFECTS ON MIND AND BRAIN

Trauma is to do with that which cannot be taken in and assimilated. Since trauma cannot be digested and metabolized, it ruptures the containing skin of the mind, leading to a catastrophic collapse of psychic structure. Trauma implies a break with the continuities of life, a threat to survival, a terrifying meeting with death. This can lead to the emergence of primitive defences to ward off unbearable, unthinkable anxieties (Garland, 1998). The ability to cope with traumatic events is in part to do with the nature of the event itself, but will vary between individuals, depending on personality, attachment history and other previous experiences (Blum, 2003; Bremner, 2002; Damasio, 1999; Holmes, 2001; Saporta, 2003). Severe trauma can, nevertheless, have the effect of overwhelming and disrupting both the psychological immune system and the brain's neuronal processing, leading to a disruption in the core sense of self. In Janoff-Bulman's vivid description (1992), all previous assumptions about the world lie in pieces.

From his work with traumatized soldiers in the Great War of 1914–1918, Freud described the psychologically wounding effects of trauma as a breaching of the 'protective shield' (Freud, 1920). He suggested that a psychic 'crust' formed over early childhood traumas, insulating the individual from the unbearably painful nature of the experience. He noted that the traumatic event itself might be cognitively remembered, but the affect attached to the experience might remain inaccessible to conscious memory. Conversely, the traumatizing event might be 'forgotten', while the affect attached to it remained dynamically operational. A traumatic situation that is experienced in adult life can activate these 'forgotten' conflicts and crises, along with unresolved earlier traumas, such that these earlier traumatic events become subsumed within the current event, resulting in an exacerbation or amplification of its impact (Blum, 2003). A study that I undertook (Heller, 2001), employing the Adult Attachment Interview (Crittenden, 2004) to explore the attachment histories of 22 individuals with chronic PTSD, found just such an effect, as I shall describe later in this chapter.

Traumatic experiences that take place during infancy and childhood are thought to produce a 'chronic stress response that can affect the child's neurobiological, emotional, behavioural, cognitive and interpersonal development. [...] This process may have adverse effects on childhood brain development contributing to Post-traumatic stress disorder (PTSD), cognitive-learning problems and co-morbid mental illness' (De Bellis et al., 2005: 153).

Stress releases chemicals, such as the glucocorticoids, small amounts of which promote greater efficiency in the functioning of the neural circuitry. Traumatically experienced events, however, interfere with neural functioning in relation to the information and affect processing centres of the brain. Trauma-induced neurological changes produce feelings of disbelief and helplessness which have been associated with a wide range of psychological and physical health disorders, referred to by Bremner (2002) as the 'trauma-spectrum disorders'. When an event is experienced which is so stressful that it overwhelms the brain's capacity to process it, the mind cannot properly represent the experience, organize it on a symbolic level and store it in an explicit memory system for future reference (Saporta, 2003). Such an experience appears to have undergone a disruption and fragmentation at the memory encoding stage. The event cannot be verbally stored in memory; its magnitude cannot be borne because it is experienced as *unbearable* by the mind and as *unregisterable* by the brain (Mollon, 1998). Wilfred Bion (1962) graphically described the state of an infant whose anxieties have not been contained by the maternal function of 'reverie'. Such a child is beset by what Bion called 'catastrophic chaos', 'unthinkable anxiety' and 'nameless dread'. In essence, this is to do with terrifying doubts about the possibility of survival in a world full of attackers.

When an event occurs which is experienced as traumatic, the brain and mind can become subject to a psychophysiological *dissociative* mechanism which comes into play in the process of encoding the event (Fonagy, 1999; LeDoux, 2002; Saporta, 2003; Schooler and Eich, 2000; Van der Kolk, 2002; Vasterling et al., 2005). This creates a mental structure that serves as an 'early warning system' against a recurrence of the conscious experience of the trauma (Bromberg, 2003). Dissociative defences appear to be most pronounced in children (Chu, 1998). This is scarcely surprising since the capacity to dissociate offers a survivally effective shield against being flooded by unmanageable feelings at a time when the child is developmentally vulnerable and may not have the resources to psychologically manage the traumatic event. Nevertheless, such a child's brain becomes at risk of developing later mental health problems, such as PTSD or BPD (Fonagy et al., 2003). In writing about the trauma of childhood sexual abuse, Diamant (2001) states that the therapeutic process of constructing narrative memories regarding the abuse event can be problematic because these dissociative phenomena have impeded encoding into past memory systems.

The dissociative mechanism in severe trauma appears to be based on a blocking mechanism of the neural pathways that link the medial pre-frontal cortex, the neo-cortical verbal and representational information processing circuitry and the memory processing and categorizing centres of the hippocampus and amygdala (Shin et al., 2005). The brain chemicals involved in such blocking need further research, but appear to involve an excessive production of certain stress hormones, including the stimulant noradrenaline, along with a reduction of other stress hormones, such as cortisol – which regulates blood-pressure, amongst other life-preserving functions (Bremner, 2002; LeDoux, 1996). Research into the function of mirror neurons and their location within the neo-cortex of the brain would suggest that the dissociation that can take place in severe trauma also interferes with the individual's capacity to engage in 'empathic mirroring', since this requires an ability to 'step into the other's shoes' and 'feel for them' whilst retaining the secure knowledge of a separate identity.

Very early traumatic experiences are primarily encoded in the emotional and implicit-procedural memory circuitry of the right hemisphere. Because such experiences are stored in preverbal, emotional and non-symbolic form, they are unavailable for conscious, reflective thought, verbal narratives and conscious working-through. Nevertheless, they continue to make their influence felt in social, emotional and cognitive aspects of life through childhood and into adulthood (Imeri, 2007). These traumatic experiences can be repeatedly re-lived by being 'acted out' in a variety of action-based behaviours. They can also be projected into others, appear in the form of dreams, or be communicated via the body. As Freud put it:

> We may say that the patient does not remember anything of what he has forgotten and repressed, but acts it out. He reproduces it not as a memory but as an action; he repeats it, without, of course, knowing that he is repeating it, [...] he cannot escape from this compulsion to repeat; and in the end, we understand that this is his way of remembering. (1914: 150)

PSYCHOTHERAPY WITH TRAUMATIZED INDIVIDUALS

What is of crucial importance for those of us engaged in therapeutic work is the extent to which it is possible to enable appropriate and positive change to take place in the minds of the distressed people we see, particularly those who have experienced early attachment traumas. As Blum (2003) points out, psychopharmacological agents may be helpful in reducing the anxieties, sleep disturbances, hypervigilance and depressions found in individuals who have experienced severe traumas, but drug treatments should never be viewed as substitutes for therapeutic work, if real and lasting change is to take place. Having the opportunity to tell one's story has the potential to restore a sense of continuity and wholeness, leading to a more integrated and robust sense of self (Holmes, 2001; Imeri, 2007; Keane et al., 2007; Richman, 2006).

In his Memorial Lecture, Schore underlined the finding that 'an affect-focused, developmentally orientated treatment can alter internal structures within the patient's brain/mind/body systems' (2001: 303). Recent neuroscientific research demonstrates that therapy is capable of altering the functional activity of the brain which specific changes in the neural circuitry are correlated with therapeutic outcome, and that such changes are particularly found in the pre-frontal lobes – the major centres for information processing (Bakker et al., 2001; Blum, 2003; Kumari, 2006; Saporta, 2003; Slipp, 2000; Solms and Turnbull, 2002, 2003; Strathearn, 2007; Swain et al., 2007).

In order to give words to trauma, the therapeutic setting needs to be one which provides as much security and interpersonal safety as is possible, whilst at the same time providing enough sensitively handled challenge. Feelings of guilt, shame, terror and helplessness play an inevitable part of the working-through of traumatic experiences, especially those which involve early developmental trauma (Bromberg, 2003). The therapist needs to be acutely sensitive to their emergence, otherwise an impasse can occur, leading to therapeutic 'stuckness'. If the emerging feelings are insensitively handled, then a *repetition* of the trauma within the therapeutic setting may take place, rather than its appropriate *working through* (Brewin, 2005). The pain of empathically sharing the emotional experience can be hard to bear for the therapist as well as the client. What is therapeutically important is that if the therapist has been insensitive or enacted some aspect of the client's history, this can be acknowledged, without blame, otherwise the client's feelings of guilt, shame and underlying despair may become exacerbated. If the therapist can find the courage to recognize when they have behaved in ways that reproduce aspects of the client's history of attachment relationships, this can promote new understanding and a new reality for both participants.

POST-TRAUMATIC STRESS DISORDER

The symptoms of post-traumatic stress disorder (PTSD) have been well documented (for example, APA, 1994; Friedman et al., 2007). Briefly, they include intrusive and upsetting recollections of the event; involuntary flashbacks to the event; hypervigilance and startle-responses to anything that might resemble the event; alongside attempts to actively avoid, or emotionally numb, any internal thoughts or external situations that act as reminders of the event. In *chronic* PTSD, these trauma experiences remain *in situ*, sometimes for many years, being continually repeated and re-lived. The individual with chronic PTSD is unable to assimilate and process the traumatizing experience so that it can be consigned to a past memory system. The consequence is a mind which retains an ever-active dread of what is about to happen, rather then a memory of a distressing, frightening event which happened in the past but which can be thought about, given a narrative and have learning extracted from it – learning which can be relevant for certain specific present and future situations (Horowitz, 1993; Van der Kolk, 2002; Zohar et al., 1998). As a member of my research group said to me, 'I feel as if I am in a terrible nightmare that I can't wake up from' (Heller, 2001).

In terms of brain mechanisms, it appears that the hormonal neurotransmitter *serotonin* has a major role in regulating what Bromberg (2003) has referred to as an 'early warning system' and Van der Kolk and Fisler (1995) describe as a 'smoke detector'. Neuroimagining studies of the brain which have investigated PTSD suggest that the amygdala, which is involved in the conditioned fear response, may become hyper-responsive in individuals with this condition (Shin et al., 2005). When developmentally early trauma is experienced, serotonin production is affected. This can lead to difficulties in moderating affect and emotional arousal, thus producing a tendency to hypersensitivity to what might normally be considered as mildly arousing or anxiety-producing situations (Bromberg, 2003; Van der Kolk and Fisler, 1995). It follows that individuals who have experienced a severe early trauma which has undermined their neuro-physiological capacity to moderate the effects of a potentially traumatizing situation are, as a consequence, more likely to be at risk of developing PTSD as adults. They are, in effect, 'an accident waiting to happen' (Heller, 2001, 2009).

AN EXAMPLE FROM MY RESEARCH

My research study explored the relationship between childhood attachment disturbances (as classified on Crittenden's 2004 version of the AAI) and chronic PTSD in a group of 12 men and 10 women referred to an NHS clinic (Heller, 2001). They were aged between 30 and 56 years, came from all social groups and were all physically and mentally well before the onset of the PTSD. The AAI scripts revealed that almost all the group had experienced significant losses and/or traumas in their childhood, with these childhood events being generally regarded as having little or no significance in their current life. As one participant remarked, 'I must have developed PTSD because nothing bad has ever happened to me before, so I didn't know how to deal with something like this.' Yet at the age of five, this participant had experienced the near death of her father in a terrible mining accident. He was left severely disabled, unable to work again and the family became destitute.

What I found in the research group was that the nature of the losses and traumas in their childhood frequently bore a striking resemblance to the material event in adulthood that had precipitated the PTSD. For example, the teacher whose PTSD began after a child in his class died during a PE lesson he was taking. In his AAI he told me that as a 6-year-old, he had watched his much loved granddad and father-substitute die in front of him while they were out walking together. Such similarities led me to propose that the *real* trauma was the earlier one, which had never been integrated but had remained actively alive in a timeless, dissociated state; the 'material event' took up and amplified all the unexpressed affect attached to the earlier trauma and acted as its proxy. The *chronicity* of PTSD in the research group appeared to be linked semantically with these early, unresolved and apparently 'forgotten' losses and traumas. The 'forgetting' had been successful in that the group had remained mentally and physically well as adults, but was always precarious and broke down under the impact of the semantically equivalent 'material event'.

Not only did these findings support neuroscientific data which suggests that preexisting attachment disturbances create vulnerability for the development of PTSD in adulthood, but three distinct and statistically different subgroups emerged within the PTSD group as a whole. The first cluster comprised a group of individuals with 'preoccupied' attachment strategies, who expressed considerable anger about the traumatic incident that had precipitated their PTSD and who ruminated on thoughts of retaliation or revenge. The second cluster consisted of individuals of mixed 'avoidant' and 'passive-aggressive' attachment strategies. The third cluster were compulsively avoidant, clinically depressed and minimized the effects of their traumatizing experiences. Given the significant differences in these three PTSD clusters, a 'one-size-fits-all' PTSD treatment approach seemed unlikely to be helpful and could be anti-therapeutic.

For example, Greg, who was in the 'High A' PTSD cluster, had been shifting crates on the dockside when a sling-load of steel bars, being lowered by a crane, swung around and knocked him to the ground. He lay petrified, seeing the sling-load of steel slowly descend towards him. It was brought to a halt just inches short of where he lay. For eight years Greg had experienced nightmares and almost daily 'flashbacks' of a near delusional type. Anti-depressant and anxiolytic medication had not helped, nor had several sessions of cognitive behavioural therapy. As the years continued with no improvement, Greg had made several suicide attempts and when I met him (he was by then in his early 50s), he was attending a day centre several days a week and was in a dejected and hopeless state.

In his AAI he told me:

> I'll open the door to the living room … and it's like I'm there … the whole thing happening again. Steel has a taste, you know. And I can see, taste, smell, hear, feel … that sling-load of steel as it comes towards me. Your heart starts racing and you're physically sick. It's there … and you can't get away from it.

This description notes, in first-person speech, the here-and-now experience that confronts him every time he opens the door to his living room. All his five senses are involved in this terrifying image which continuously repeats itself. A sudden change of person occurs as he sees the steel coming towards him – his use of 'you' distances the terror; it is 'you' that can't get away and no longer him. This is a typical speech pattern of the 'avoidant' individual. Greg had lost a number of close relatives as a child, but there was no evidence of his having come to terms with any of these losses. His childhood was emotionally deprived and bleak, with a repeated theme of having accidents – suggesting that he was an 'accident prone' child. He produced a vivid memory of his father being brought back from work after a serious accident; with blood all over his clothing.

Greg was offered a year of once-weekly therapy which focused on the safe expression of affect; enabling him to acknowledge and express the shame, guilt, anger and humiliation that he felt about what had happened to him. During this time he was able to reduce his avoidant pattern and make contact with the workmates he had not seen since the accident eight years before. After his therapy had ended, he was offered a job as caretaker for a block of residential flats. He wrote to his therapist about the offer:

> Thanks to you I am going to take this offer, something I would never have thought about a year ago when we first met. […] I hope it is going to be some time before I see you again. This is no slight at all on you, as I am indebted to you for all you have done for me. Thank you.

His therapist did not take it as a slight on her; she understood that Greg was telling her he now had a 'theory of mind' in which he could reflect on his past experiences, rather than have them continually repeat themselves in the present.

CONCLUDING COMMENTS

Maternal care at the early stage of human life is of particular importance in the development of the baby's brain and mind. The capacity to empathize, to engage in reflective functioning and to develop a coherent 'theory of mind' all appear to depend on the ability of the mother to bond well with her infant and to provide him or her with a secure base. As Winnicott pointed out in his remarkable paper 'Hate in the countertransference' (1947), there are many reasons for a mother to hate her baby. In disrupted, disturbed attachment the balance of love and hate, at both a psychic and a brain level, becomes tipped in the direction of hate. This can have disastrous and tragic consequences – both for the baby and for that baby when she or he becomes a parent. Such hate needs to be counterbalanced and overcome by the rewards inherent in the attachment process at brain, mind and dynamic levels. As Winnicott (1960) so helpfully put it, what is required of mothers – and parents in general – is simply to be 'good enough'. I think we could say that this applies to psychotherapists as well.

Neurobiological research not only indicates the extraordinarily complex nature of the neuronal circuitry and neuroendocrine systems underlying attachment, but provides information that can inform clinical practice. Attachment theory and its associated findings in the neurosciences are providing a much greater understanding of *why* 'good enough' parental caregiving is important in raising human infants, and also of the neurological underpinnings to do with *where* this importance is reflected in the brain. These findings help towards optimizing developmental outcomes and preventing further abuses by parents who have themselves suffered problematic attachment experiences. The concepts acquired through brain imaging techniques provide an 'understanding of the neurobiology of attachment that can help formulate and address the pervasive problem of child abuse and neglect' (Strathearn, 2007: 122).

Under conditions of attachment trauma involving significant unresolved loss, emotional and physical abuse and other traumatizing incidents, attachment strategies are likely to become highly avoidant, overly enmeshed, coercive and/or disorganized (Crittenden, 1997; Fonagy et al., 1996; George and West, 1999). Protocols such as the Adult Attachment Interview can provide insights to do with the transgenerational transmission of attachment failures and traumas, thus pointing the way to their early detection, prevention and the specific forms of therapeutic treatment that are likely to be required. In providing the psychotherapeutic means to understand and repair the damage done by traumatic failures, abuses and losses in attachment, these findings provide empirical validation for the importance of 'containment' as envisaged by Bion (1962), 'primary maternal preoccupation', as proposed by Winnicott (1956), and the 'secure base' described by Bowlby (1988).

As Slade notes, increases in the understanding of the neural bases for the observed differences in attachment organization have begun to validate many of the basic premises of the organization and development of attachment. She concludes 'A continuing and rich dialogue between clinicians and neuroscientists will only enrich the way both think about and make meaning of human experience' (Slade, 2007: 139).

REFERENCES

Ainsworth, M.D., Blehar, M.C., Waters, E. and Wall, S. (1978) *Patterns of Attachment: A Psychological Study of the Strange Situation.* Hillsdale, NJ: Erlbaum.

American Psychiatric Association (1994) *Diagnostic and Statistical Manual of Mental Disorders,* 4th edn. Washington, DC: American Psychiatric Press.

Bakker, A., Van Balkom, A.J. and Van Dyck, R. (2001) 'Comparing psychotherapy and pharmacotherapy', *American Journal of Psychiatry,* 158: 1164–1166.

Baron-Cohen, S. (1995) *Mindblindness: An Essay on Autism and Theory of Mind.* Cambridge, MA: MIT Press.

Bion, W. (1962) 'A theory of thinking', *International Journal of Psycho-Analysis,* 43: 306–310.

Blum, H.P. (2003) 'Psychic trauma and traumatic object loss', *Journal of the American Psychoanalytic Association,* 51: 415–431.

Bowlby, J. (1944) *44 Juvenile Thieves.* Harmondsworth: Penguin.

Bowlby, J. (1953) *Child Care and the Growth of Love.* Harmondsworth: Penguin.

Bowlby, J. (1969) *Attachment and Loss*, Vol. 1: Attachment. London: Hogarth Press and the Institute of Psychoanalysis.

Bowlby, J. (1979) *The Making and Breaking of Affectional Bonds.* London: Tavistock.

Bowlby, J. (1980) *Attachment and Loss*, Vol. 3. New York: Basic Books.

Bowlby, J. (1988) *A Secure Base.* London: Routledge.

Bremner, J.D. (2002) *Does Stress Damage the Brain? Understanding Trauma-Related Disorders from a Mind-Body Perspective.* New York: Norton.

Brewin, C.R. (2005) 'Encoding and retrieval of traumatic memories', in J.J. Vasterling and C.R. Brewin (eds), *Neuropsychology of PTSD: Biological, Cognitive and Clinical Perspectives.* New York and London: Guilford Press.

Bromberg, P.M. (2003) 'Something wicked this way comes: Trauma, dissociation, and conflict: The space where psychoanalysis, cognitive science, and neuroscience overlap', *Psychoanalytic Psychology*, 20: 558–574.

Buchheim, A. and Kachele, H. (2003) 'Adult attachment interview and psychoanalytic perspective: A single case study, *Psychoanalytic Enquiry*, 23: 81–101.

Buchheim, A., George, C., Kachele, H., Erk, S. and Watter, H. (2006) 'Measuring adult attachment representation in an fMRI environment: concepts and assessment', *Psychopathology*, 39: 136–143.

Chu, J. (1998) *Rebuilding Shattered Lives: The Responsible Treatment of Complex Post-traumatic and Dissociative Disorders.* New York: Wiley.

Crittenden, P.M. (1997) 'Towards an integrative theory of trauma: A dynamic maturational approach', in D. Cicchetti and S. Toth (eds), *The Rochester Symposium on Developmental Psychopathology, Vol. 10. Risk, Trauma, and Mental Processes.* Rochester, NY: University of Rochester Press. pp. 34–84.

Crittenden, P.M. (2004) '"Adult attachment interview": A Dynamic-Maturational Approach to Analysing the Adult Attachment Interview'. Unpublished manuscript.

Damasio, A. (1994) *Descartes' Error.* New York: Grosset/Putnam.

Damasio, A. (1999) *The Feeling of What Happens: Body and Emotion in the Making of Consciousness.* New York: Harcourt Brace.

De Bellis, M.D., Hooper, S.R. and Sapia, J.L. (2005) 'Early trauma exposure and the brain', in J.J. Vasterling and C.R. Brewin (eds), *Neuropsychology of PTSD: Biological, Cognitive and Clinical Perspectives.* New York and London: Guilford Press.

Diamant, I. (2001) 'On not being able to know others' minds: The debate on recovered memories of abuse from a relational perspective', *British Journal of Psychotherapy*, 17 (3): 344–352.

Fonagy, P. (1995) 'Playing with reality: The development of psychic reality and its malfunction in borderline personalities', *International Journal of Psychoanalysis*, 76: 39–44.

Fonagy, P. (1999) 'Guest editorial: Memory and therapeutic action', *International Journal of Psychoanalysis*, 80: 215–223.

Fonagy, P. (2001) *Attachment Theory and Psychoanalysis.* New York: Other Press.

Fonagy, P., Leigh, T., Steele, M., Steele, H., Kennedy, R., Mattoon, G., Target, M. and Gerber, M. (1996) 'The relation of attachment status, psychiatric classification and response to psychotherapy', *Journal of Consulting and Clinical Psychology*, 64: 22–31.

Fonagy, P., Target, M., Gergely, G., Allen, J.G. and Bateman, A.W. (2003) 'The developmental roots of borderline personality disorder in early attachment relationships: A theory and some evidence', *Psychoanalytic Enquiry*, 23: 412–459.

Freud, S. (1914) 'Remembering, repeating and working through further recommendations on the technique of psychoanalysis', *Standard Edition*, 12: 47–56. London: Hogarth.

Freud, S. (1920) 'Beyond the pleasure principle', *Standard Edition*, 18. London: Hogarth.

Friedman, M.J., Keane, T.M. and Resick, P.A. (eds) (2007) *Handbook of PTSD Science and Practice*. New York: Guilford Press.

Gallese, V. (2007) 'Empathy, embodied simulation and mirroring mechanisms', *Neuropsychoanalysis*, 9 (2): 146–151.

Garland, C. (ed.) (1998) *Understanding Trauma: A Psycho-Analytical Approach*. Duckworth: Tavistock Clinic Series.

George, C., Kaplan, N. and Main, M. (1996) *The Adult Attachment Interview*, 3rd edn. Unpublished protocols, University of California, Berkeley.

George, C. and West, M. (1999) 'Developmental versus social personality models of adult attachment and mental ill health', *British Journal of Medical Psychology*, 72: 285–303.

Gerhardt, S. (2005) *Why Love Matters: How Affection Shapes a Baby's Brain*. London and New York: Brunner-Routledge.

Heard, D. and Lake, B. (1997) *The Challenge of Attachment for Caregiving*. London and New York: Routledge.

Heller, M.B. (2001) 'The dynamic relationship between childhood experiences of loss and trauma and chronic post-traumatic stress disorder in adults'. Unpublished doctoral thesis in clinical psychology, University of Teesside, Cleveland.

Heller, M.B. (2009) 'It was an accident waiting to happen', in M.B. Heller and S. Pollet (eds), *The Work of Psychoanalysts in the Public Health Sector*. London: Routledge.

Holmes, J. (1993) *John Bowlby and Attachment Theory*. London and New York: Routledge.

Holmes, J. (2001) *The Search for the Secure Base: Attachment Theory and Psychotherapy*. Hove and Philadelphia, PA: Brunner-Routledge.

Horowitz, M.J. (1993) 'The effects of psychic trauma on mind: Structure and processing of meaning', in J. Barron, N. Eagle and D. Wolitski (eds), *Interface of Psychoanalysis and Psychiatry*. Washington, DC: American Psychological Association. pp. 489–500.

Huopainen, H. (2002) 'Freud's view of hysteria in light of modern trauma research', *Scandinavian Psychoanalytic Review*, 25: 92–107.

Imeri, L. (2007) 'Review of *Psicoanalisi e Neuroscienze* [Psychoanalysis and Neuroscience]', *International Journal of Psychoanalysis*, 88 (6): 1573–1577.

Janoff-Bulman, R. (1992) *Shattered Assumptions: Towards a New Psychology of Trauma*. New York: Free Press.

Johns, J.M., Elliott, D.L., Hofler, V.E., Joyner, P.W., McMurray, M.S., Jarrett, T.M., Haslup, A.M., Middleton, C.L., Elliott, J.C. and Walker, C.H. (2005) 'Cocaine treatment and prenatal environment interact to disrupt intergenerational maternal behaviour in rats', *Behavioural Neuroscience*, 119: 1605–1618.

Keane, T.M., Brief, D.J., Pratt, E.M. and Miller, M.W. (2007) 'Assessment of PTSD and its comorbidities in adults', in M. Friedman, T. Keane and P. Resick (eds), *Handbook of PTSD Science and Practice*. New York: Guilford Press.

Kumari, V. (2006) 'Do psychotherapies produce neurobiological effects?', *Acta Neuropsychiatrica*, 18: 61–70.

LeDoux, J.E. (1996) *The Emotional Brain*. New York: Touchstone.

LeDoux, J.E. (2002) *The Synaptic Self*. New York: Viking.

Light, K.C., Grewen, K.M., Amico, J.A., Boccia, M., Brownley, K.A. and Johns, J.M (2004) 'Deficits in plasma oxytocin responses and increased negative affect, stress and blood pressure in mothers with cocaine exposure during pregnancy', *Addictive Behaviours*, 29 (8): 1541–1564.

Mace, C. and Margison, F. (1997) 'Attachment and psychotherapy: An overview', *British Journal of Medical Psychology*, 70: 209–215.

Main, M. (1999) 'Mary D. Salter Ainsworth: Tribute and portrait', *Psychoanalytic Inquiry*, 19 (5): 682–736.

Main, M. and Solomon, J. (1990) 'Procedures for identifying infants as disorganised/disoriented during Ainsworth Strange Situation', in M. Greenberg, D. Ciccetti and E. Cummings (eds), *Attachment in the Pre-School Years: Theory, Research and Intervention*. Chicago, IL: University of Chicago Press. pp. 121–160.

Mollon, P. (1998) *Remembering Trauma: A Psychotherapist's Guide to Memory and Illusion*. Chichester, New York, Toronto: Wiley.

Ranote, S., Elliott, R., Abel, K.M., Mitobell, R., Deakiu, J.F.W. and Applebg, L. (2004) 'The neural basis of maternal responsiveness to infants: An fMRI study', *NeuroReport,* 15: 1825–1829.

Richman, S. (2006) 'Finding one's voice: Transforming trauma into autobiographical narrative', *Contemporary Psychoanalysis*, 42: 639–665.

Robertson, J. and Robertson, J. (1989) *Separation and the Very Young*. London: Free Association Books.

Rose, S. (2006) *The 21st-Century Brain*. London: Vintage.

Rose, S. (2007) 'Making sense of neuroscience', *Therapy Today*, 18 (8): 37.

Saporta, J. (2003) 'Synthesizing psychoanalytic and biological approaches to trauma: Some theoretical proposals', *Neuro-Psychoanalysis,* 5: 97–110.

Schooler, J. and Eich, E. (2000) 'Memory for emotional events', in E. Tulving and F. Craik (eds), *The Oxford Handbook of Memory*. Oxford: Oxford University Press.

Schoon, I. and Bartley, M. (2008) 'The role of human capability and resilience', *The Psychologist*, 21 (1).

Schore, A.N. (2001) 'Minds in the making: Attachment, the self-organising brain, and developmentally orientated psychoanalytic psychotherapy', *British Journal of Psychotherapy*, 17 (3).

Schore, A.N. (2003) 'The human unconscious: The development of the right brain and its role in early emotional life', in V. Green (ed.), *Emotional Development in Psychoanalysis, Attachment Theory and Neuroscience*. Hove and New York: Brunner-Routledge.

Shin, L.M., Rauch, S.L. and Pitman, R.K. (2005) 'Structural and functional anatomy of PTSD: Findings from neuroimaging research', in J.J. Vasterling and C.R. Brewin (eds), *Neuropsychology of PTSD: Biological, Cognitive and Clinical Perspectives*. New York and London: Guilford Press.

Singer, T., Seymour, B., O'Doherty, J., Kaube, H., Dolou, R.J. and Frith, C.D. (2004) 'Empathy for pain involves the affective but not sensory components of pain', *Science*, 303: 1157–1162.

Slade, A. (2007) 'Commentary on Chapter Four', in L.C. Mayes, P. Fonagy and M. Target (eds), *Developmental Science and Psychoanalysis*. London: Karnac.

Slipp, S. (2000) 'Introduction to neuroscience and psychoanalysis', *Journal of the American Academy of Psychoanalysis and Dynamic Psychiatry,* 28: 191–202.

Solms, M. and Turnbull, O. (2002) *The Brain and the Inner World: An Introduction to the Neuroscience of Subjective Experience*. London and New York: Karnac.

Solms, M. and Turnbull, O. (2003) 'Memory, amnesia and intuition: A neuro-psychanalytic perspective', in V. Green (ed.), *Emotional Development in Psychoanalysis, Attachment Theory and Neuroscience*. Hove and New York: Brunner-Routledge.

Soltis, J. (2004) 'The signal functions of early infant crying', *Behavioural and Brain Sciences*, 27: 443–490.

Steele, M. (2003) 'Attachment, actual experience and mental representation', in V. Green (ed.), *Emotional Development in Psychoanalysis, Attachment Theory and Neuroscience*. Hove and New York: Brunner-Routledge.

Steele, M., Steele, H. and Johansson, M. (2002) 'Maternal predictors of children's social cognition: An attachment perspective', *Journal of Child Psychology and Psychiatry*, 43 (7): 189–198.

Stern, D. (1985) *The Interpersonal World of the Infant*. New York, Basic Books.

Strathearn, L. (2007) 'Exploring the neurobiology of attachment', in L.C. Mayes, P. Fonagy and M. Target (eds), *Developmental Science and Psychoanalysis*. London: Karnac.

Strathearn, L., Fonagy, P. and Montague, P.R. (2008) Poster presentation to the Human Brain Mapping Meeting in Melbourne, Australia, July 2008 (personal communication).

Swain, J.E., Lorberbaum, J.P., Kose, S. and Strathearn, L. (2007) 'Brain basis of early parent–infant interactions: Psychology, physiology, and *in vivo* functional neuroimaging studies', *Journal of Child Psychology and Psychiatry*, 48 (3/4): 262–287.

Van der Kolk, B.A. (2002) 'Posttraumatic therapy in the age of neuroscience', *Psychoanalytic Dialogues*, 12: 381–392.

Van der Kolk, B.A. and Fisler, R. (1995) 'Dissociation and the fragmentary nature of traumatic memories: Overview and exploratory study', *Journal of Traumatic Stress*, 8: 505–525.

Van der Kolk, B.A., McFarlane, A. and Weisaeth, L. (eds) (1996) *Traumatic Stress: The Effects of Overwhelming Experience on Mind, Body and Society*. London: Guilford Press.

Vasterling, J.J. and Brewin, C.R. (eds) (2005) *Neuropsychology of PTSD: Biological, Cognitive and Clinical Perspectives*. New York and London: Guilford Press.

Winnicott, D.W. (1947) 'Hate in the countertransference', in D.W. Winnicott (ed.), *Through Paediatrics to Psycho-Analysis*. London: Hogarth.

Winnicott, D.W. (1956) 'Primary maternal preoccupation', in D.W. Winnicott (ed.), *Through Paediatrics to Psycho-Analysis*. London: Hogarth.

Winnicott, D.W. (1960) 'The theory of the parent–infant relationship', *International Journal of Psychoanalysis*, 41: 585–595.

Zohar, J., Sasson, Y., Amital, D., Iancu, I. and Zinger, Y. (1998) 'Current diagnostioc issues and epidemiological insights in PTSD', *CNS Spectrums (Supplement Monograph)*, 3: 12–14.

34

THE FUTURE OF COUNSELLING PSYCHOLOGY

Ralph Goldstein

This is a particularly poignant time (Spring, 2008) in which to attempt prophecy, since the Health Professions Council (HPC) is poised to become the body responsible for registering applied psychologists and thus take over some of the functions developed on our behalf by our own colleagues meeting as the British Psychological Society (BPS). The Division of Counselling Psychology took its professional place in this family only in 1994, and a special edition of *Counselling Psychology Review* (Woolfe, 2006) marked this coming of some kind of age. In attempting to contextualize this development as a good counselling psychologist should, Woolfe, writing in this Special Edition, brilliantly sustained a metaphor of growing up in a fractious family. Counselling psychology began early to 'flex its muscles' and to be a rival to 'big sister clinical psychology' and the 'elder brother CBT who was a bit of a bully'. However, at the end of the story, 'the infant had grown into a responsible adult'.

Currently, I suggest, *the developmental question is just what kind of adult world are we entering and how are we equipped to deal with it?*

This question requires that we consider the context in which counselling psychology currently finds itself; there are indeed clouds gathering around both the child and its family of origin. The nature of these difficulties, even threats, will be explored and then there will be an attempt to find an adult place in the sun.

If we want to discern the adult future of counselling psychology we will first have to come to an agreement about the *identity* of counselling psychology and its dimensions. Since the professions of psychology and psychotherapy are notoriously fractious, having inherited both good and not so good things from the ancestors, such agreement might prove difficult. Indeed, the word 'fractious', which my writing tool has just helpfully flagged for me, refers to the notion of resisting authority. Nevertheless, I will attempt to offer some (considered) views of counselling psychology and its context, then propose that 'authority', in the form of governmental reforms, may decide to dispense with our distinctive services. Finally, I will propose some hypotheses about how we might like counselling psychology to develop. Will the fractious generation, who rioted in favour of general liberties in 1968, be joined by the newer generations and once more constructively resist authority beyond 2008?

PROFESSIONAL IDENTITY: DEFINED BY TECHNICAL COMPETENCE

The notion of *identity* is a rich and important one in both psychology and sociology as well as in the consulting room. How do the Divisions of the BPS contribute to the professional identity of their members? We might wonder whether our identity descends from any *authoritative* source, or simply from a self-proclaimed training syllabus leading to chartered, or registered, status? One might offer the following postulate:

> *If our professional identity stems primarily from a syllabus that can be redefined according to almost any arbitrary whim or fashion, then we have no distinctive ground from which to venture forth and profess our calling.*

An academic syllabus can be readily, even radically, altered by new research or new ideas – for ideas read fashion or other (political and economic) exigency. Let me invite you to think how quickly (neo-)behaviourism yielded to the cognitive revolution, as it was called, and then to recall how the acronym 'CBT' resisted alteration, even when rather little therapy now contains any elements which may be properly called *behavioural*. The acronym is also resistant to the widespread professional knowledge that there are many kinds of cognitive therapies of which CBT would be a special, albeit ancestral, case.

This resistance is a serious developmental block, for it impinges on our collective ability to think clearly; to properly recognize the unfortunately loose connection between academic cognitive psychology and the psychological practice of various cognitive therapies. One pernicious consequence is to leave an uncultivated ground which may be colonized by those who would make technical manuals for the treatment of certain conditions. If the provinces of clinical, health and counselling psychology may in significant part be reduced to technical manoeuvres, then the professional future will be mainly limited to teaching and researching techniques and checking on their efficacy. This is not the future most of us had in mind when we joined the Division.

And this technical future is *already* being defined outside the arenas of research and practice, although still with borrowings from the academy. I am refering to bodies such as Skills for Health, who have been commissioned to develop the competencies needed to train mental health workers for various grades of 'low' and 'high intensity' work.

This brief summary ought to be sufficient to make the case for seeking our identity in something beyond technical skill, for whilst technical skill is a wonderful thing in any area of human endeavour, skill alone cannot constitute an identity – and yet occupational standards are an attempt to achieve just such an end.

PSYCHOLOGY AS A SCIENCE AND AS A PRACTICE

One favoured candidate for a descriptive identity amongst clinical psychologists has been that of 'scientist-practitioner', whilst counselling psychologists have favoured 'reflective-practitioner'. Just to add confusion, more recent statements by clinical psychologists (syllabus and regulations for training in clinical psychology, BPS, 2002) indicate that they are claiming allegiance to both identities now. Actually, both descriptions are now over-played; the advent of the National Institute for Clinical Excellence (NICE) implies that all providers of treatments, whether psychological, surgical or pharmacological, must practise in the light of scientific evidence. The more recent requirement to undertake continuous professional development based on planning means that we all must reflect on our practice and at least some of our shortcomings.

Nevertheless, the stance of scientist-practitioner implies a philosophy based on empiricism, which provides the important possibility of describing the extent of benefits as well as harm inherent in any therapeutic endeavour. The stance of reflective-practitioner allows another philosophical position to enter the stage, which was integral to the founding of counselling psychology as a Division in the first place.[1] The humanistic values of reflection and relationship were amongst the Division's midwives and once this door was open, the somewhat different but cognate philosophical position of the intersubjective tradition could enter. The new syllabus and regulations for training in counselling psychology (2003) is the only syllabus amongst all the Society's Divisions to begin with a philosophical statement, designed to address the basis of this sub-discipline within the family of applicable psychologies.

The explicit purposes of this philosophically inclined statement were twofold: to state the values which counselling psychologists espoused; and to *identify*, or locate, the discipline academically. It has always been a surprise to me that such a statement needed defending not so much for its precise content, but for its very existence, for without it we are left *merely* with a syllabus. If we recall that academic psychology in this country

---

[1] Readers of the Special Edition of *Counselling Psychology Review* (Woolfe, 2006) will know that there were many important *pragmatic* moves additionally necessary to the foundation of the Division!

grew, with sociology, from philosophy departments, then it seems all the more remarkable to omit an identifying philosophical statement from any major psychological endeavour. How often are we consulted by persons who feel uprooted and alienated from some identifying system of values and expectations? And this sense of uprootedness is accompanied by often severe *emotional* difficulties – emotions are what make people seek us out, not cognitions. It would appear to be fundamental to any success we may have that we ourselves are rooted in something of deep value.

However, emotions are messy and clinical and counselling psychologists – and let us not forget psychotherapists and psychoanalysts – tend rather curiously to share the same interests with governments; namely, to contain, or even improve upon, the messiness of life. The interests of governments are more collective, whilst those of psychologists are more concerned with the individual, the dyad and the small group. This leads to an interesting professional separation between those psychologists who are concerned primarily with persons who are currently in a mess, and those who are more concerned with the technical means of addressing messiness. I do not mean to propose a stark binary distinction, but the tendency of the first group is to analyse the *material conditions* shaping a person's life, such as power, poverty, class, and then finding a psychological means of getting alongside that individual, whilst the tendency of the second group is to think of a treatment modality and its empirical support for addressing a certain kind of mess, which may be described in terms of a diagnosis. Let us refer to the first group as 'reflectors' and the second group as 'scientists'.

It is, of course, possible for a single psychologist to bridge both modes, but that requires a capacity for multiple identities – which we all have, but do not always like to bring to work. For example, the reflectors would have to think about their own roles and responsibilities, whilst applying knowledge and skill, whereas the scientists find scope in the skilled exercise of techniques, whilst reflecting on their greater or lesser reliability, validity and value to the client groups. In so far as counselling psychologists *identify with* the latter group, they can be part of the wider family of psychologists united against outsiders who tend to disdain empiricism.

IDENTIFYING SUB-GROUPS

The trouble is this. The group who analyse the material conditions of their patients – meaning the ones who suffer – are a minority and also find themselves more firmly in opposition to many initiatives by government, and not just initiatives concerning cost-cutting. The scientists may feel equally discomfitted, but are more likely to find a means of working with government. To my mind, this has shown itself most clearly in the markedly different strategies adopted by the two (overlapping!) groupings in response to statutory registration and to changes in the Health Service. For confirmatory evidence, one may compare the material which has been posted on the BPS website concerning statutory registration with that summarized in a special issue of the *Journal of Critical*

Psychology, Counselling and Psychotherapy edited by Newnes and Goldstein (2005). The Society's position has always been in support of statutory registration per se, but not by means of the HPC, whereas for the most part the papers in *Critical Psychology* are vehemently against statutory registration because of the violence it may do to our values and its irrelevance to preventing the kind of abuses registration is claimed to reduce.

I point to two government initiatives to illustrate the existence of two different tendencies within the family of psychology. Clinical psychologists have been prominent, but not alone, in lending their expertise to the Improving Access to Psychological Therapies initiative. The UKCP also wanted involvement in the sense that this body of psychotherapists wishes to insist that a wider range of therapies is accepted as part of the equitable provision to those in need. Some counselling psychologists, including this one, are somewhat aghast at the entire undertaking, agreeing with the suggestion of Smail (a clinical psychologist by training) who wrote in conclusion: 'I am suggesting that, through becoming unthinkingly over-extended, it [psychotherapy] is in danger of being ethically misused or abused' (1987).

The second initiative is Agenda for Change in the NHS. It was probably impossible to effectively oppose this old-fashioned job-analysis scheme, but as I have argued elsewhere (Goldstein, 2007), this scheme is a major part of the grand, unified plan to allow the emerging dominance of more technical and hence cheaper treatments, and to support a radical revision of training. Clinical psychologists of a scientific persuasion are perfectly well aware of a professional threat to their very existence, never mind identity, and have responded with training plans of their own, designed to find an accomodation with the Department of Health and its agenda, whilst preserving some major work to be undertaken by psychological scientists. Such plans have indeed been formulated, although there have not yet been any moves to use them in formulating a new post-graduate training syllabus. These ideas have become known by the names of their authors: this is the Kinderman-Wang plan (see Kinderman, 2005).

My first prophecy is that the next step will be to find a strategy for aligning this training plan with the training requirements of HPC – the so-called threshold for entry, which at the time of writing looks likely to be at Master's level rather than the level of professional doctorate, which is the standard the Society, our tribal guardian, wishes to maintain. Once again, one might postulate that:

> *There is a clear and present danger: our professional identity will indeed be defined by training standards and the associated syllabus.*

BEYOND SYLLABUS AND TRAINING: A TRUER IDENTITY

There was a tendency to favour the notion of giving psychology away in the sense that publicly funded research belongs ultimately with those who sponsored the costs.

Psychologists were historically always willing to provide teaching outside academia and to pass on knowledge and techniques. In the present context, giving away some of the techniques of CBT will serve as an example. But there is a difference between the Society's centennial motto of 'Bringing psychology to society' and giving away packages of techniques, even if a fee is involved. We are treating psychology as so many have treated various Eastern philosophies; appealing systems which apparently can arbitrarily be reduced to small but attractive packages and then commodified. It is at this point we have to ask ourselves some hard ethical questions, turning on the way reductionism of the crudest kind can support commodification. In other words, we should oppose the current zeitgeist which holds that we may break down the application of any knowledge into packages of *competencies*, which may then be used to solve any pressing problem cheaply. This is a modern version of Taylorism taken out of the factory and applied to mental health. Nobody has yet explained how such an approach may truly help the person alienated by work or social relations.

This failure of explanation perhaps invites consideration of a different approach to doing psychology, which will be briefly addressed below in the section 'Returning to values'.

HOW MIGHT COUNSELLING PSYCHOLOGY PROGRESS?

First, I should emphasize that I am not arguing against the notion of insisting on competencies per se. How could one reasonably argue against judging a programme of training by its outputs any more than we would wish to argue against a programme of psychotherapy being judged by some shared understanding of successful therapy? What I am arguing against as strenuously as I may, whilst remaining polite, is the deliberate use of a helpful idea such as the development of competency frameworks as a means to achieve the aims outlined in the previous paragraph. One important way for us to put our side of the argument is not only to argue against something, but to set out our own stall for all to see. We need to identify ourselves to our public and describe what kind of counselling psychology we wish to promote. This is a different and more positive sense of 'Bringing psychology to society'.

The future should present a *praxis*[2] which is person- and community-oriented, which means that while we pay close attention to the needs of persons we never forget their embeddedness in a social, political and economic community. (I have not mentioned transcendent values, but that is not to imply that I do not believe their importance, only that if we attend to the needs of persons adequately we will be keeping in mind spiritual values also.)

It has been pointed out recently (Thatcher and Manktelow, 2007) that we have tended to ignore action in the community, and this is an omission that we should seek to rectify, but together with the other considerations described here, we can see only too clearly that

---

[2] Definition: translating an idea into action; 'a hard theory to put into practice' (WordNet).

as a profession we are rather more than the mere voyeurs we are sometimes accused of being. We are, in fact, a meddlesome lot who even in our silences are far from neutral *in our impact on people*. In jointly creating a space to meditate upon the context in which lives – all our lives – are lived, we must take great ethical care with every one of our utterances. We are not socially and politically neutral, because we constantly point to the impact of external events on internal experiences. I contend that:

> *This is an elaborated and inductive psychology true to its history and steadfast in its purposes, for psychology has always been concerned with the effects of the internal representations of external events.*

In this modern psychology there is both intellectual stimulus and encouragement to develop theories of inter-subjectivity in the fields of social and developmental psychology and to encourage the further development of these concepts within inter-subjective and relational psychotherapies. There is a renewed opportunity for the mutual nourishment of psychology and psychotherapy between each other. This mutual dialogue is no longer restricted to the cognitive arena, nor does it privilege – or reify – a cognitively-based discourse above all other aspects of psychology.

Such a psychology embraces emotions and embeds such studies in evolutionary biology and neurophysiology – see, for example, the work of Gilbert on the evolutionary background to emotions (1995, 2004) and Gray on anxiety, neurophysiology and consciousness (work summarized in 1995).

REVISITING CLINICAL SCIENCE VIA PSYCHOTHERAPY

The Register of Psychologists Specialising in Psychotherapy (revised *Report*, Goldstein et al., 2005) was always committed to the notion of a two-way street between psychology and psychotherapy and in this way sets up a view of how psychologists specializing in psychotherapy develop a *post-qualifying* identity. The *Register* is based on a set of six related principles (q.v.), but the first principle is sufficient for the present discussion. This states:

Principle 1: Psychologists as Psychotherapists:

Main Aim 1

To be familiar with, and able to draw on, knowledge and approaches in psychology, which have particular relevance for psychotherapeutic understanding and practice.

Main Aim 2

To be able to think psychologically about approaches and issues in psychotherapy, which have significant implications for psychology, and use this knowledge and understanding to elaborate aspects of psychological therapy and/or practice. (Goldstein et al., 2005: 7)

These statements are especially relevant to the notion of pursuing a clinical science, which is committed, ethical and likely to lead to improved interventions with various groups of clients. The notion is well expressed by Westen et al.:

> One way of selecting treatment strategies more systematically is to use clinical practice as a natural laboratory. Thus, as investigators, we might take advantage of the wide variation that exists in what clinicians do in practice and use correlational analyses to identify intervention strategies associated with positive outcome, initially and at multiple-years follow-up. Instead of requiring individual investigators to predict, on the basis of their best guesses and theoretical preferences, which treatments are most likely to work, this approach allows us to extend scientific method to the context of discovery. Once we have identified potentially useful interventions (and moderators) correlationally, we can then set our experimental sights on the interventions that appear most likely to pay off as well as on experimentally derived interventions that have received support in the laboratory. (2004: 657)

This approach to establishing empirically supported therapies begins with unselected samples in the community and then turns to experimental designs, in the community, in the laboratory/specialist research centre, or both. There is nothing new here; studies of animal behaviour were hugely enriched by the methods of ethology at least as long ago as the 1960s, and developmental psychology was also enriched by these same methods of naturalistic observation. The point, it seems, is that meaningful research which generalizes with good validity requires an inversion of the classical randomized control methodology, which well-trained psychologists have known perfectly well since the 1960s.

The principles of the *Register* serve both to draw us back to our psychological roots and to point a way forward; the way forward requires us to recognize the empirical and theoretical state of the psychotherapies in some realistic fashion. This means a recognition that there are many ways to work with people and that the common factors (for example, the therapeutic alliance) are empirically supported in a way that different schools or brands are not – and will not be until more fitting methods of research are widely adopted.

RETURNING TO VALUES

There are a number of movements within psychology which reflect different value systems; one is *positive* psychology (for example, Seligman, 2002), another is *critical* psychology (for example, Prilleltensky, 1999) and another is coaching psychology. Positive psychology explicitly undermines the idea that we should always focus on deficits, on unhappiness and misery, rather than on increasing the sum of human happiness. This viewpoint is generally consistent with the ideas behind coaching psychology, which is also concerned to maximize human potential and action. In this sense, critical psychology stands apart, for we are invited to engage with a wider social context than that present in a consulting room or a coaching arena. An example concerning schizophrenia is outlined below, but first we should note that any discussion of *values* is in fact embedded in a wider social context, so that we should reflect on the uses to which our labours may be directed by those with greater power. I have in mind the notion that effective psychotherapy may be promoted, and paid for, in order to patch people up and return them to the self-same sources of stress which required our ministrations in the first place.

There are many ways in which counselling psychologists can develop from the point of attaining chartered status; towards increasing competence in psychotherapy recognized by membership of the *Register*; towards clinical science by disseminating research; and towards a wider set of skills, such as group and organizational development, and community-based efforts. The latter are particularly difficult to realize; somehow new developments have to be funded ahead of demonstrating benefits, and current structures are much too directed towards targets to make new initiatives feasible. New developments in the NHS seem to be increasingly handed down from authoritative sources in or near government, which then control the funding directly by 'ring-fencing' the monies. (There is an interesting study to be done in examining the proceses whereby new initiatives are, nevertheless, developed in the current climate.)

Continuous professional development (CPD), one of the major projects of recent years within the Society, might also provide an interesting limitation, or disincentive, to community-based working unless imagnatively developed. Currently, individual psychologists are asked to reflect on their (professional) developmental needs and to plan, and report, accordingly. There is nothing inherently against working collaboratively and reporting personal progress, but thinking based on group activities is certainly not the first idea encouraged by this individualistic model. Of course, many publications are produced by several authors and this might be a useful model, or precedent, for major projects in a community-based setting, such as attempts at minimizing the impact of schizophrenia by energetically intervening at the first onset of psychosis (see the IRIS programme at www.iris-initiative.org.uk). The essence of the IRIS approach is rehabilitation centred on *an assertive outreach team* and funded in the manner outlined in the previous paragraph. The emphasis of the programme is early intervention with those people suffering their first episode of schizophrenic illness, and then working with families and the wider context to minimize both the personal and social impact of such illnesses.

Thus, good clinical science is a matter of careful thought about what needs to be achieved followed by reflection on what is possible within the bounds of ethical research, properly supported. The appropriate lessons, not necessarily the ones favoured by fund-holders, then need to be well implemented, which may be much more difficult to achieve than the original research.

What I am suggesting is no revolutionary enterprise, but a reanimation of the values expressed in the founding mission of the Royal Institution, which was 'diffusing the knowledge … of useful mechanical inventions and improvements; and for teaching, by courses of philosophical lectures and experiments, the application of science to the common purposes of life'. It is the application of philosophy to the common purposes of life which are central to my argument.

CONCLUSION

If psychology is indeed something we wish to bring to society, because of its intrinsic rather than commercial worth, then we will find that worth in its philosophical values and purposes. So the stance of a counselling psychologist, of a psychotherapist and of a psychoanalyst is a matter of an ethical position, which demands something of its practitioners well beyond competence. We must *profess* – in the original religious sense – these values in all that we do and we must put these values before the public, before they realize they have been mistreated by (health) technologies and then ask us why we did not do more to help.

REFERENCES

British Psychological Society (2002) *Criteria for the Accreditation of Postgraduate Training Programmes in Clinical Psychology. Leicester: BPS*

British Psychological Society (2003) *Criteria for the Accreditation of Postgraduate Training Programmes in Counselling Psychology.* Leicester: BPS

Gilbert, P. (1995) 'Biopsychosocial approaches and evolutionary theory as aids to integration in clinical psychology and psychotherapy', *Clinical Psychology and Psychotherapy*, 2 (3): 135–156.

Gilbert, P. (ed.) (2004) *Evolutionary Theory and Cognitive Therapy.* New York: Springer.

Goldstein, R. (2007) 'Introducing an "efficient" workforce into the NHS', *Counselling Psychology Review*, 22 (3).

Goldstein, R., Newell, A., Mair, M. and Watts, M. (2005) *The Register of Psychologists Specialising in Psychotherapy: Principles and Procedures.* Leicester: British Psychological Society.

Gray, J.A. (1995) 'The contents of consciousness: A neuropsychological conjecture', *Behavioral and Brain Sciences*, 18 (4): 659–722

IRIS Initiative in the UK (2008) 'Integrating physical and mental health services to reduce the duration of untreated mental illness'. Available at: www.iris-initiative.org. uk, accessed March 2008.

Kinderman, P. (2005) 'The applied psychology revolution', *The Psychologist*, 18 (12): 744–746.

Newnes, C. and Goldstein, R. (2005) *Journal of Critical Psychology, Counselling and Psychotherapy: A special issue on Registration*, 5 (4).

Prilleltensky, I. (1999) 'Critical psychology foundations for the promotion of mental health', *Annual Review of Critical Psychology*, 1: 100–118.

Royal Institution of Great Britain. Available at: www.rigb.org (May 2008).

Seligman, M.E.P. (2002) 'Positive psychology, positive prevention, and positive therapy', in C.R. Snyder and S.J. Lopez (eds), *Handbook of Positive Psychology.* New York: Oxford University Press. pp. 3–9.

Smail, D. (1987) 'Psychotherapy and "change": Some ethical considerations', in S. Fairbairn and G. Fairbairn (eds), *Psychology, Ethics and Change.* London: Routledge & Kegan Paul.

Thatcher, M. and Manktelow, K. (2007) 'The cost of individulaism', *Counselling Psychology Review*, 22: 4.

Westen, D., Novotny, C.M. and Thompson-Brenner, H. (2004) 'The empirical status of empirically supported psychotherapies: Assumptions, findings, and reporting in controlled clinical trials', *Psychological Bulletin*, 130: 631–663.

Woolfe, R. (2006) 'A journey from infancy to adulthood: The story of counselling psychology', *Counselling Psychology Review. Special Edition: The First 10 Years*, 21 (1): 4–7.

INDEX